A Compan
Latin American Philosophy

MW00532592

Blackwell Companions to Philosophy

This outstanding student reference series offers a comprehensive and authoritative survey of philosophy as a whole. Written by today's leading philosophers, each volume provides lucid and engaging coverage of the key figures, terms, topics, and problems of the field. Taken together, the volumes provide the ideal basis for course use, representing an unparalleled work of reference for students and specialists alike.

A Companion to Latin American Philosophy

Edited by
Susana Nuccetelli, Ofelia Schutte,
and Otávio Bueno

WILEY-BLACKWELL

A John Wiley & Sons, Ltd., Publication

Blackwell Publishing was acquired by John Wiley & Sons in February 2007. Blackwell's publishing program has been merged with Wiley's global Scientific, Technical, and Medical business to form Wiley-Blackwell.

Registered Office
John Wiley & Sons, Ltd, The Atrium, Southern Gate, Chichester, West Sussex, PO19 8SQ, UK

Editorial Offices
350 Main Street, Malden, MA 02148-5020, USA
9600 Garsington Road, Oxford, OX4 2DQ, UK
The Atrium, Southern Gate, Chichester, West Sussex, PO19 8SQ, UK

For details of our global editorial offices, for customer services, and for information about how to apply for permission to reuse the copyright material in this book please see our website at www.wiley.com/wiley-blackwell.

Library of Congress Cataloging-in-Publication Data

A companion to Latin American philosophy / edited by Susana Nuccetelli, Ofelia Schutte, and Otávio Bueno.
    p.   cm. – (Blackwell companions to philosophy)
  Includes bibliographical references and index.
  ISBN 978-1-4051-7979-9 (hardcover : alk. paper) - ISBN 978-1-118-59261-8 (pbk. : alk. paper)
1. Philosophy, Latin American.   2. Philosophy–Latin America.   I. Nuccetelli, Susana.
II. Schutte, Ofelia.   III. Bueno, Otávio.
  B1001.C65 2010
  199'.8–dc22
                                        2009015236

A catalogue record for this book is available from the British Library.

Cover image: Constructive by Joaquin Torres-Garcia (1874–1949). Private Collection / Photo © Christie's Images / The Bridgeman Art Library.
Cover design by Workhaus.

Set in 10/12.5pt Photina by SPi Publisher Services, Pondicherry, India
Printed in Malaysia by Ho Printing (M) Sdn Bhd

1   2013

Contents

About the Editors

Susana Nuccetelli is Professor of Philosophy at St. Cloud State University, Minnesota. Her articles on Latin American philosophy, ethics, epistemology, and philosophy of language have appeared in *Analysis*, the *American Philosophical Quarterly*, *Metaphilosophy*, *Inquiry*, and other journals. She is co-editor of *Ethical Naturalism: Current Debates* (2012), *Themes from G. E. Moore: New Essays in Epistemology and Ethics* (2007), *Philosophy of Language: The Central Topics* (2008), and *Latin American Philosophy* (2004); editor of *New Essays on Semantic Externalism and Self-Knowledge* (2003); and single author of *Latin American Thought: Philosophical Problems and Arguments* (2002).

Ofelia Schutte is Professor of Philosophy Emerita at the University of South Florida, Tampa. She is the author of *Cultural Identity and Social Liberation in Latin American Thought* (1993), *Beyond Nihilism: Nietzsche without Masks* (1984), and numerous articles on feminist theory, Latin American thought, and continental philosophy. A former Fulbright Senior Research Fellow to Mexico, her work has appeared in *Hypatia: A Journal of Feminist Philosophy*, *Journal of Social Philosophy*, *Philosophy Today*, and *The Philosophical Forum*, among other journals and edited collections.

Otávio Bueno is Professor of Philosophy and Chair of the Philosophy Department at the University of Miami, Florida. His work in philosophy of science, philosophy of mathematics and philosophy of logic has been published in *Noûs*, *Mind*, *Philosophy of Science*, *Synthese*, *Journal of Philosophical Logic*, *British Journal for the Philosophy of Science*, *Erkenntnis*, *Studies in History and Philosophy of Science*, and *Analysis*, among other journals and collections. He is editor-in-chief of *Synthese*.

Contributors

Jesús H. Aguilar is Assistant Professor of Philosophy at the Rochester Institute of Technology.

Arturo Arias is Professor of Latin American Literature and Culture at the University of Texas, Austin.

Horacio Arló-Costa is Associate Professor of Philosophy at Carnegie Mellon University.

Lawrence Blum is Distinguished Professor of Liberal Arts and Education, and Professor of Philosophy at the University of Massachusetts, Boston.

Otávio Bueno is Professor of Philosophy at the University of Miami.

Mario Bunge is Frothingham Professor of Logic and Metaphysics at McGill University, Canada.

Bernardo J. Canteñs is Associate Professor of Philosophy at Moravian College.

Meri L. Clark is Assistant Professor in the Department of History and Political Science at Western New England College.

William F. Cooper is Emeritus Professor of Philosophy at Baylor University.

Alberto Cordero is Professor of Philosophy at the City University of New York (Graduate Center and Queens College).

Eleonora Cresto is Assistant Researcher at the CONICET (National Council of Scientific and Technical Research) Argentina.

Newton C. A. da Costa is Professor of Philosophy at the Federal University of Santa Catarina, Brazil.

Nythamar de Oliveira is Associate Professor of Philosophy at the Pontifical Catholic University, Porto Alegre, Brazil.

Claus Dierksmeier is Associate Professor of Philosophy at Stonehill College.

María Luisa Femenías is Professor of Philosophy at the Universidad Nacional de la Plata, Argentina.

Eduardo Fermé is Associate Professor at the Mathematics and Engineering Department at the University of Madeira, Portugal.

David Ignatius Gandolfo is Assistant Professor of Philosophy at Furman University.

Manuel Garrido was Professor of Logic and chair of the Department of Logic and Philosophy of Science at the Universidad Complutense de Madrid until his retirement in 1991.

Gregory D. Gilson is Assistant Professor at the Department of History and Philosophy at the University of Texas-Pan American.

María Cristina González is Professor of Philosophy at the Universidad de Buenos Aires and at the Universidad Nacional de Rosario, Argentina.

Jorge J. E. Gracia is Distinguished Professor and Samuel P. Capen Chair in Philosophy at the University of Buffalo.

Guillermo Hurtado is chair and researcher at the Instituto de Investigaciones Filosóficas of the Universidad Nacional Autónoma de México.

A. Pablo Iannone is Professor of Philosophy at Central Connecticut State University.

Alex Levine is Associate Professor of Philosophy at the University of South Florida.

Renzo Llorente is Associate Professor of Philosophy at Saint Louis University, Madrid Campus.

James Maffie is Associate Professor of Philosophy at Colorado State University.

Iván Márquez is Associate Professor of Philosophy at Bentley University.

Oscar R. Martí is Associate Professor of Chicano Studies at California State University, Northridge.

Pablo Navarro is Professor of Philosophy of Law at the Universidad Nacional del Sur, Bahía Blanca, and Blas Pascal University, Argentina.

Adriana Novoa is Assistant Professor of Humanities and American Studies at the University of South Florida.

Susana Nuccetelli is Professor of Philosophy at St. Cloud State University.

Gustavo Ortiz-Millán is research-professor of philosophy at Instituto de Investigaciones Filosóficas, Universidad Nacional Autónoma de México.

Gregory Fernando Pappas is Associate Professor of Philosophy at Texas A & M University.

Diana I. Pérez is Professor of Metaphysics at the Universidad Nacional de Buenos Aires, Argentina.

Luis Fernando Restrepo is Professor of Spanish and Latin American Studies at the University of Arkansas, Fayetteville.

Eduardo Rivera-López is Associate Professor of Law and Philosophy at Universidad Torcuato Di Tella, Argentina.

Ofelia Schutte is Professor of Philosophy at the University of South Florida.

Liza Skidelsky is Senior Lecturer of Metaphysics at Facultad de Filosofía y Letras, Universidad Nacional de Buenos Aires, and Associate Researcher at the National Council of Scientific and Technical Research (CONICET), Argentina.

Ilan Stavans is Lewis Sebring Professor in Latin American and Latino Culture at Amherst College.

Roderick Stewart is Professor of Philosophy at Austin College.

Nora Stigol is Associate Professor of Philosophy at the Universidad Nacional de La Plata.

Gregory Velazco y Trianosky is Professor of Philosophy at California State University, Northridge.

Acknowledgments

The three of us would like to acknowledge here the help of our editors at Wiley-Blackwell, Jeff Dean and Tiffany Mok – from whom we received judicious guidance and patient attention throughout the process of compiling this volume. We would also like to thank Dean Michael Halleran and Senior Associate Dean Perri Roberts from the University of Miami College of Arts and Sciences for their support for the preparation of the index for this volume. Finally, we would like to thank the copyright holder of a selection by Miguel León-Portilla reproduced in chapter 1 (*Fifteen Poets of the Aztec World*, 1992, pp. 80, 83. Copyright © 1992 by the University of Oklahoma Press, Norman. Reproduced by the publisher's permission).

Susana Nuccetelli is grateful to a number of people who have been helpful to her in her work on this collection. Above all, Gary Seay deserves thanks for his encouragement and advice throughout the project, without which she would not have been a co-editor of the project at all. She is also indebted to Stefan Baumrin, Jorge Gracia, and Ernest Sosa – all of whom offered insightful advice that resulted in a project much better than it would otherwise have been. Ilan Stavans should also be mentioned for his early advice on strategies for publication, as should Travis Sulander, Jordan Busse, and Reese Petersen for their skillful assistance at crucial points in the project.

Ofelia Schutte wishes to thank Roger Ariew, chair of the Philosophy Department, and her colleagues at the University of South Florida, Tampa, for their support of research and teaching in Latin American philosophy. She especially thanks her graduate students for their interest in the Latin American philosophy graduate seminar. She extends her deep appreciation to her friend, Carmen Diana Deere, who served as Director of the Center for Latin American Studies at the University of Florida, Gainesville, during the period this manuscript was researched and assembled, for her interest in the project, and for facilitating her use of the outstanding Latin American Collection at UF's Smathers Library. Finally, she thanks Richard Phillips, Head Librarian at the UF Latin American Collection, and the entire staff of the Collection, for their generous and enduring assistance.

Otávio Bueno wishes to thank all of his teachers at the University of São Paulo from whom he learned what philosophy is and how it is done in Latin America, with special thanks to José Chiappin, Newton da Costa, Andrea Loparic, Pablo Mariconda, Oswaldo Porchat Pereira, and Caetano Plastino. He also wants to thank all of his colleagues at the University of Miami for creating such a stimulating place to do philosophy, and for making Miami the special home it is. Finally, he wants to thank his wife, Patrícia Maragliano, for her unconditional support over so many years, for the joys she brings to life, and to Julia and Olivia for making sure that we all spend enough time under the sun.

Introduction

SUSANA NUCCETELLI, OFELIA SCHUTTE, AND OTÁVIO BUENO

Although there is increasing intellectual curiosity about Latin American philosophy, in the English-speaking world there is no easy access to comprehensive, yet up-to-date, materials on its developments – whether topical, historical, or disciplinary. We believe that the volume that we have put together will remedy this problem by making available to English-speaking readers, for the first time, a comprehensive collection of previously unpublished writings by leading experts in the field exploring such developments. Some of its chapters are designed to offer in-depth overviews representing current Latin American perspectives on topics such as globalization, human rights, women's rights, language, race, and ethnic identity. Others aim at providing accurate discussions of either topics in the history of the discipline that are of interest today, or metaphilosophical questions about the sub-disciplines of philosophy that have flourished in Latin America. Each chapter has been newly commissioned on the basis of expertise in the philosophical tradition most appropriate to its content, independently of whether the scholar is working in one or another Latin American country, or elsewhere. The final product is a coherent volume addressing the central issues and arguments of Latin American philosophy, while preserving its diversity of voices and approaches.

The book is divided in four parts. Although there is unavoidable overlapping among the chapters that make these up, each part contains precisely those chapters that we have judged more relevant to its subject: namely, the history of Latin American philosophy and its movements (Part I), philosophical topics of special interest in the discipline now (Part II), recent developments in the sub-disciplines of philosophy in Latin America (Part III), and biographical information about some of Latin American philosophy's great figures. For each of these parts, we envisioned chapters that would not only be illustrative of major lines of work but also qualify for being state-of-the-art, rigorous yet accessible to those unfamiliar with the discipline.

A close look at the volume would reveal that some chapters bear on philosophy *in* Latin America, others on a philosophy that is *distinctively* Latin American. But arguably, these two (not at all uncommon) construals are in fact compatible. And even when the expression 'Latin American philosophy' is ambiguous in at least these two ways, for most cases that semantic shortcoming can be eliminated by appealing to context. We expect that attentive readers will do so to avoid equivocation of the sort that often plagues debates about what, exactly, is Latin American philosophy. Readers interested in a distinctive Latin American philosophy are more likely to find that construal in Part II, some of whose chapters reflect on it explicitly. Those curious about philosophy in Latin America could more easily detect this construal in the chapters of Parts I and III.

As editors of this *Companion*, we have adopted a pluralistic view of the discipline also in some other ways. For example, besides philosophy itself, disciplines such as literature, history, politics, and the social sciences in Latin America are represented in the collection whenever there is evidence of their contribution to philosophical topics within the scope of this collection. In addition, we commissioned chapters written from a number of philosophical traditions such as continental philosophy, analytic philosophy, feminist theory, and liberation philosophy.

These remarks, together with the table of contents, make clear our criteria for organizing the chapters: historical in Part I (in chronological sequence), topical in Part II, metaphilosophical in Part III, and biographical in Part IV. In designing Part I, we faced one of the most pressing questions concerning the history of Latin American philosophy: When did it begin? Some have it that it was not until the so-called *fundadores* (founders) of the early twentieth century, often credited with initiating a 'normal' period of academic philosophy in the subcontinent. Others hold that philosophy began with the boom of nineteenth-century Latin American positivism. But such cuts, if not biased, seem at best arbitrary. After all, there is evidence pointing to scholastic philosophy devoted to topics raised during the Conquest and three centuries of colonial ruling that followed – which qualifies, at least topically, for being Latin American. Moreover, the Maya and other pre-Columbian peoples left well-preserved texts that attest their philosophical concerns – which can also be found in the writings of early travelers and missionaries. Thus, we decided to include discussions of these periods in Part I. The reader of these chapters, however, will find that historical issues there go beyond mere exegesis or history of ideas to enter into philosophical argumentation. In doing so, we expect that they will contribute to a deeper understanding not only of the history of the discipline but also of debates at the center of recent scholarship on topics such as whether the philosophical concerns of pre-Columbian cultures or the writings by Spanish philosophers about the morality of the Conquest could be considered part of Latin American philosophy at all.

Part II offers a set of diverse contributions to topics of current interest in Latin American philosophy. Some topics such as identity, colonization, and *mestizaje* have had a long trajectory of recognition in philosophical discussions, while others such as the nature of ethnic group terms, the impact of postmodern thought, and the thoughts of Latina/o philosophers on race and ethnicity have a more recent trajectory. In all cases these chapters provide current approaches to the analysis, interpretation, or critical evaluation of the selected topics. While they help to define certain logical or philosophical features of the topics in question, the arguments offered should be taken as open ended in terms of their potential for opening up further discussion and debate.

Colonization is most often studied and debated in historical, cultural, economic, or political terms. Less often, as our topics chapter does here, is it considered in terms of the emergence of new linguistic practices. What role did the Spanish language play in the context of colonization, it may be asked. What insights may the socio-linguistic features of such contemporary phenomena as Spanglish offer as a way of understanding the processes of colonization in the sixteenth century? The argument presented holds that there is still much to be known and assessed regarding indigenous speakers' resistance to the official imposition of Spanish as the language of empire in the Americas.

With regard to identity, a major topic throughout the twentieth century and up to our own times has been what constitutes the identity of Latin American philosophy. The historiographical approach included here explains the central role the concept of identity has played in constituting the very notion of a Latin American philosophy. In addition to the traditional categories used in classifying how the identity of Latin American philosophy should be construed – that is, whether it should be regarded from a universalist, culturalist, or critical position, the more recent concept of Latin American philosophy as the philosophy of an ethnos is presented. In this view, what belongs to an ethnos should be understood in historical, not essentialist, terms and as subject to changing conditions.

One interesting feature of contemporary approaches to issues occupying a longstanding tradition in Latin American scholarship and philosophy is the incorporation of new perspectives resulting from recent debates in metaphysics and epistemology, for example, the critique of essentialism with regard to the positing of historical, cultural, ethnoracial, sexual, and other forms of identification and identity. Although the critique of essentialism is often associated with postmodern approaches to the concept of identity, its influence has ranged well beyond postmodernism as shown in the featured topics of identity and *mestizaje* in Part II. What is clear is that some of the old designators of identity such as the concept of *mestizaje* are subject to re-signification, partly due to the introduction of women writers who no longer theorize this concept from a masculine position, but also due to the experiences of Latinos whose experience contrasts significantly from that of many Latin Americans south of the border. As the entry in this section shows, the sense of dislocation experienced by many U.S. Latinos/as with regard to any single racial identity undermines the essentialist nature of older concepts of *mestizaje*.

Among the more recent topics of debate in Latin American philosophy we find the conversation between North American philosophers and Hispanic/Latino philosophers on the latter's contrasting approaches to race and ethnicity, given that the topics of race and ethnicity have also drawn much recent attention among non-Hispanic philosophers in the United States. Here we include one view, regretfully limited (due to the size constraints of the volume) specifically to the analysis of three important contemporary Latino/a philosophers. In particular, attention is given to the questions of how to construe the meaning of race or ethnicity in view of claiming reparations for past (and present) discrimination, how to define the constitutive features of an ethnic group, and how to conceptualize the lived experiences of racialization in a racist society in such a way as to resist and transform the cultural and socioeconomic values undergirding racism.

Another central recent topic of philosophical debate addresses three sets of related questions: whether ethnic-group terms should be considered names or predicates; how and why the analyses by proponents of either view differ in defining the semantic properties of such terms; and the nature of some normative issues involved in the selection and use of ethnic-group terms. Yet another covers the introduction and development by a group of Brazilian logicians of a new kind of logic called 'paraconsistent logic.'

This particular kind of logic has received international attention for its innovative outlook in dealing with various logical impasses pertaining to the topic of inconsistency as conceived by traditional logic. Its range of application encompasses problem-solving in philosophy, technology, physics, and mathematics.

The impact of social, economic, and political conditions in Latin America as the latter interact with socio-political philosophy and cultural theory has had a long trajectory of discussion in Latin American philosophy. The topics covered in Part II on this broad theme, however, are broadly contemporary. Among them is the question over the relevance in today's world of a praxis of liberation (understood in the light of liberation theories introduced in Latin America since the late 1960s). We also cover an analysis of three influential theoretical movements especially prominent in the 1990s – subaltern studies, post-Occidentalism, and cultural criticism – associated with postmodern and postcolonial theory. These movements, whose influence is still operative today, problematize the links and intersections among philosophy, politics, and culture, including the politics of the production of knowledge about Latin America. Yet another central topic, globalization, demands a careful philosophical analysis, a sample of which we offer while also realizing the complexity of this topic and the multiple approaches that mark its analysis in today's world. The perspective offered here proposes a multifaceted pragmatic approach – one substantively tied to democratic action and qualified by a degree of skepticism regarding the capacity of laws, institutions, and social agents to implement effective reforms.

Part III addresses some disciplinary developments in Latin American philosophy. The chapters in this part cover a wide range of issues where either a distinctive Latin American approach has been developed in a given sub-discipline of philosophy, or relevant work in such sub-discipline has been done in Latin America. Our goal in selecting which sub-disciplines to include has been guided by the attempt to cover developments that were particularly significant, although given the size constraint of the volume the selection clearly cannot be comprehensive. The result is a wide-ranging group of disciplinary developments ranging from how Latin American philosophy can be characterized through developments in traditional areas of philosophy (such as ethics and political philosophy, legal philosophy, philosophy of science, and epistemology) to issues in feminist philosophy, cultural studies, and the connections between philosophy and literature.

The picture that emerges from this work is one in which central philosophical topics are addressed, but often with a different, distinctive twist. Let us offer some illustrations. Since the beginning, the very nature of philosophy has been the source of philosophical investigation and controversy (consider, for example, longstanding discussions about the nature and possibility of metaphysics). It may come as no surprise then that, as mentioned above, since the beginning, the very nature of Latin American philosophy has been the source of philosophical investigation and controversy as well. What may be unexpected, however, is that in examining the latter issue, certain moves in philosophy of language become so prominent, as one disambiguates the question of the existence of Latin American philosophy.

In philosophy of science outside Latin America, two different traditions have emerged. On the one hand, formal approaches have been developed by exploring the resources provided by developments in logic and the foundations of mathematics.

These approaches offer a clear formal framework to examine philosophical issues about science, but they tend to be highly idealized and pay very little or no attention to actual scientific practice. On the other hand, informal approaches, which tend to be very sensitive to the complexities of scientific practice, have also been devised. But they tend not to offer a formal framework to understand scientific reasoning, and have very little or no unity. Now, in Latin American philosophy of science, a combination of these two approaches has been articulated, integrating the expressive resources of a formal approach with the sensitivity to the details of scientific practice. A more unified approach has then emerged.

A similar sensitivity to practice is also found in certain approaches to philosophy of law in Latin America. In this case, rather than scientific practice, legal practice is the relevant focus. As opposed to traditional forms of legal positivism, some Latin American philosophers of law have argued that when legal officials, such as judges, justify decisions regarding legal rights their reasoning is often informed by moral considerations. Thus, the traditional conception of legal justification that emphasizes that this justification is established in court by invoking only legal norms and facts is rejected. Moral norms have a crucial role in legal justification, and on this anti-positivist conception, they inform the actual decision processes of legal officials.

When we consider the contributions to feminist philosophy in Latin America, we also find its distinctive character. Sensitivity to women's concrete lives and their vulnerability to discrimination and oppression have been important features of feminist philosophy inside and outside Latin America. But in the case of Latin American women, both the debates on the relationship between theory and practice and the special complexities of race and ethnicity (e.g., the so-called mulata and Black population, and the original peoples) have transformed feminist theory in significant ways. The facts that some Latin American women have identified themselves as part of marginalized ethno-racial groups and that this identification has motivated them in their search for social justice become significant features that inform Latin American feminist philosophy, with its sensitivity to the historical and cultural specificities in which the understanding of race and ethnicity occurs in Latin America.

These are merely a few illustrations of ways in which disciplinary developments in Latin American philosophy have a distinctive character. As will become clear to readers, several additional cases are examined in this part of the volume.

But let us now turn to Part IV, which contains two chapters that we believe will be of interest to those unfamiliar with the figures of Latin American philosophy. An entirely biographical chapter may help reduce unfamiliarity with the lives and work of philosophers (broadly construed as to include early philosophical thinkers), while a chapter on the philosophical development of a prominent Latin American philosopher of science (Mario Bunge) may help reduce unfamiliarity about the reception of an important philosophical tradition in the subcontinent.

Needless to say, the selection criteria adopted for the biographical entries are far from being optimal. But as usual, considerations of space and consistency conflicted with more permissive standards that could have allowed us to include biographies of many others who no doubt deserve a place in the discipline. Our criteria for inclusion in the biographical chapter are these: for all figures, having done notable work on some of the major issues, movements, and/or disciplines that make up Latin American philosophy (in either of the above construals); second, for authors prior to 1900, being either philosophers or nonphilosopher essayists on philosophical topics; and third, for authors after 1900, being *academic* philosophers born prior to 1950 who either work in Latin America or write on Latin-American-related philosophical topics.

We hope that the volume contributes to the further development of Latin American philosophy among all those interested in this field.

Part I

Historical Perspectives

1

Pre-Columbian Philosophies

JAMES MAFFIE

The indigenous peoples of what is now called "Latin America" enjoy long and rich traditions of philosophical inquiry dating back centuries before being characterized by their European "discoverers" as "primitives" incapable of or unmotivated to think philosophically. Pre-Columbian societies contained individuals who reflected critically and systematically upon the nature of reality, human existence, knowledge, right conduct, and goodness; individuals who puzzled over questions like "How should humans act?," "What can humans know?," and "What can humans hope for?" This chapter focuses upon the philosophies of Andean and Aztec societies, the two most prominent indigenous philosophies flourishing during the period of contact (i.e., of mutual encounter, interaction, exchange, and conflict between Europeans and indigenous peoples) in the sixteenth century.

Our understanding of Andean and Aztec philosophies is limited by the fact that we lack pre-contact primary sources written in their respective indigenous languages. Reconstructing pre-Columbian philosophies therefore involves triangulating from a variety of alternative sources. First, we have the ethnohistories of early indigenous, *mestizo*, and Spanish chroniclers. For Andean philosophy, these include the writings of Spaniards such as Pedro Cieza de Léon (1967), Juan de Betanzos (1996), and Bernabé Cobo (1990), and of indigenous Andeans such as Felipe Guaman Poma de Ayala (1936) and Juan de Santa Cruz Pachacuti Yamqui Salcamaygua (1873). For Aztec philosophy, these include the writings of Spanish missionaries such as Bernardino de Sahagún (1953–82), Diego Durán (1971, 1994), and Alonso de Molina (2001). Second, we have Andean *quipus* or knotted-strings that were used for recording information, and Aztec pictorial histories, ritual calendars, maps, and tribute records. Third, in both cases we have archaeological evidence such as architecture, statues, pottery, jewelry, tools, and human remains. Finally, we have contemporary ethnographies of relevant surviving indigenous peoples, e.g.: Classen (1993), Isbell (1978), Seibold (1992), and Urton (1981) in the case of Andean philosophy; Sandstrom (1991) and Knab (2004), in the case of Aztec.

Contact-Period Indigenous Andean Philosophy

Inca philosophers inherited a vibrant tradition of philosophical reflection from a long line of predecessors in the Andean region. The Inca empire (ca. 1400–1532) – called *tahuantinsuyu* ("the four parts together or unified") in Quechua, the lingua franca of the Incas – was merely the last and best known in a series of pre-Columbian Andean cultures including Chavín and Paracas (900–200 BCE), Nazca and Moche (ca. 200 BCE–550 CE), Huari and Tiahuanaco (ca. 550–1000) and Chimú (ca. 1000–1400). There was no single, pan-Andean philosophy shared by all Andean peoples prior to the conquest, and therefore we must distinguish Inca from non-Inca Andean philosophies. "Non-Inca philosophy" refers broadly to the many provincial philosophical views of local *ayllus* – a Quechua word for a social unit bound together by kinship, lineage, ritual, territorial, political, and economic ties – and ethnic groups in the Andean region. "Inca philosophy" refers specifically to the philosophical views espoused by Inca *amautas* (singular, *amauta*), i.e., "sages," "poet-philosophers," "priests," or "thinkers." Inca philosophy drew upon a wealth of non-Inca Andean philosophical themes while at the same adapting these to Inca imperial purposes and circumstances.

Their many specific differences notwithstanding, Inca and non-Inca philosophies nevertheless shared in common several fundamental metaphysical themes regarding the nature of reality, human beings, and the interrelationships between human and nonhuman realms. These, in turn, set the stage for a shared vision of wisdom and ethics. I attribute these to Andean philosophy broadly construed and explore them below.

First, Andean philosophy claims that the cosmos along with all its contents is vivified or animated by a single life force (Cobo, 1990; Pachacuti Yamqui Salcamaygua, 1873). In colonial-era documents, this life force is sometimes called *camaquen* or *camac*, other times, *upani* and *amaya*. Human beings, plants, mountains, water, wind, light, mummified human remains, textiles, and stone structures are infused with this force. It appears to be coextensive with existence as such. It is dynamic, flowing, and constantly circulating throughout the regions and inhabitants of the cosmos. Water, light, rainbows, and the human life–death cycle serve as conduits for its circulation and recycling.

This force also assumes the guise of interdependent, mutually arising, complementary dual forces: e.g., night/day, sun/moon, celestial/terrestrial, above/below, cultivated/uncultivated, insider/outsider, and life/death. Life and death, for example, are cyclically interrelated as well as mutually arising and mutually interdependent. The desiccated remains of the dead serve as seeds for new life. Andean dualities oppose one another but never exclude or contradict one another. Andeans conceived rainbows as double-headed serpents that physically embodied this complementary dualism. They regarded double-faced textiles, woven so as to display a single design on both sides but with colors reversed, as visually expressing the concept of a single reality assuming two guises or forms. Dualism also plays an important role in Quechua mathematics' understanding of odd and even numbers as well as pairs of numbers. These dual forces are also gendered. Day, sun, celestial, above, and cultivated are male; night, moon, below, and uncultivated are female. Domestic, social, political, and economic relations are rooted in this metaphysics and accordingly conceived in dualistic, gendered terms. Invaders are male; original inhabitants, female. Tilling the soil is male; sowing seeds, female.

Andean dualities contribute jointly to a single, orderly whole. Indeed, the cosmos consists of the continuing alternation of these dualities. This process is governed by *ayni*, i.e., by relationships of reciprocity and mutual exchange. When dualities reciprocate equally and as a result coexist in equilibrium, the cosmos enjoys a *pacha* – i.e., "world/time/space/state-of-being," "age," or "sun" – of relative existential and spatio-temporal order and stability. The equilibrium of the present pacha makes possible human existence. Pachacuti Yamqui Salcamaygua (1873) writes of a diagram kept in the Coricancha, the principal temple in Cuzco, the capital city of the Inca empire. He claims that the diagram graphically expressed the foregoing conception of the cosmos as organized by gendered, mutually reciprocating, polar dualities. His hand-drawn reproduction of the original depicts a series of paired, complementary polarities, including sky and earth, sun and moon, summer and winter, and man and woman. The various elements of the diagram are brought together by a cross of stars and a large oval representing the Inca's creator deity, *Viracocha*, or perhaps the Milky Way.

Reciprocity between dualities eventually breaks down, however, and disequilibrium ensues. Each cosmic age undergoes cataclysmic disintegration and *pachacuti*, i.e., a "turning around, alternating or overturning" (*cuti*) of "world/time/space/state-of-being" (pacha). This is a time of disorder, instability, and transition; a time betwixt and between ages. And yet a new cosmic age begins as an inevitable consequence of this "turning around." Each ending cyclically unfolds into a new beginning. According to Guaman Poma de Ayala (1936), the cosmos had undergone four such ages prior to the Incas, who lived during the fifth. The fifth had "turned around" upon the Spanish invasion, initiating the current, sixth age.

The Andean cosmos is "open" in the sense that it allows the causal participation of human beings in its continuing equilibrium. Through their actions humans affect – positively or negatively – the balance of the cosmos. What humans do makes a difference to the equilibrium and hence continuing existence of the current cosmic age. Moreover, human participation is absolutely necessary. Human life occurs within and is defined by an intricate and fragile matrix of reciprocity relations (ayni) with other elements of the cosmos (e.g., water and earth). These relations bring with them a host of obligations to reciprocate. Humans contribute positively to cosmic equilibrium when they perform the requisite, obligation-fulfilling reciprocal actions. They disrupt cosmic equilibrium by failing to perform these actions. The continuing equilibrium of the cosmos depends upon humans' fulfilling their reciprocity obligations. In sum, human reciprocal activity is an *integral* part of as well as *integrating* force in the cosmos.

The foregoing metaphysical picture sets the stage for what we might call an "ethics of reciprocity." Human beings are *in* the world and *of* the world. As such, they are obliged to perform reciprocating actions that maintain the equilibrium and continuing existence of the cosmos and humankind. They are obliged to organize all aspects of their lives according to the norm of reciprocity. Such obligations are simultaneously moral, prudential, and religious. Wisdom consists of knowing how, when, and where to act so as to maintain reciprocity between humans and cosmos. The wise person knows how to guide humans through the dualities, cycles, and reciprocal relationships defining human existence so that humans may enjoy relatively stable, harmonious, and thriving lives. Such know-how requires constant revising based upon the interpretation of a variety of phenomena, including eclipses, droughts, crop successes or failures, dreams, visions, and the condition of slaughtered camelid lungs and entrails.

Finally, humans have at their disposal two calendars: daytime and nighttime. These are embodied in the unfolding of various cosmic cycles. As such, the two calendars function as practical action-guides or maps for human activity directed at maintaining reciprocity, equilibrium, and the continuing existence of the current cosmic age (Cobo, 1990; Guaman Poma de Ayala, 1936; Pachacuti Yamqui Salcamaygua, 1873).

Contact-Era Aztec or Nahua Philosophy

Mesoamerica is standardly defined as a broad, historical cultural tradition consisting of a dynamic, complex intermixing of various local and regional indigenous cultures. Geographically, Mesoamerica covers the southern two-thirds of Mexico, all of Guatemala, El Salvador, Belize, and the western portions of Nicaragua, Honduras, and Costa Rica. The origins of Mesoamerica are standardly associated with Olmec culture (ca. 1150–300 BCE), which was followed by (to name only a few) the cultures of Monte Albán (ca. 250 BCE–700 CE), Teotihuacán (ca. 150 BCE–750 CE), the Classic Maya (ca. 250–900 CE), the Toltecs (ca. 900–1200), Chichén Itzá (ca. 900–1200) (often referred to as Post-Classic Maya), and the Aztecs (ca. 1350–1521). Each was ethnically, linguistically, politically, culturally, and/or regionally distinct. Earlier cultures influenced later ones, as successive generations of descendants from earlier cultures interacted through migration and trade with the members of later ones. Contemporaneous cultures influenced one another through trade and migration. The members (in the case of the Aztecs) or descendants (in the case of the rest) of these cultures all faced invasion and military defeat by the Spanish beginning in the sixteenth century. So, for example, even though Classic and Post-Classic Maya cultures had by this time long since ceased flourishing, Spanish invaders nevertheless encountered Mayan language speakers following beliefs and practices derived from their ancestral cultures.

The Aztecs were one among many Nahuatl-speaking peoples who migrated in successive waves from outside of Mesoamerica (in what is now northwestern Mexico–southwestern United States) to the central highlands of Mexico during the thirteenth and fourteenth centuries. Nahuatl is member of the Uto-Aztecan linguistic family along with Hopi, Ute, and Huichol. Contact-era Nahuatl-speakers included (among others) the Mexica (dubbed "Aztecs" by European and North American scholars), Texcocans, Tlacopans, Tlaxcaltecs, and Chalcans. In light of their common language and culture, scholars refer to Nahuatl-speakers as "Nahua" and to their culture as "Nahua culture." This chapter follows this practice. Nahua culture flourished in the fifteenth and sixteenth centuries prior to 1521, the official date of the fall of Tenochtitlan, the Aztec capital city (Carrasco, 2001).

Contact-era Nahua philosophy draws jointly from its Uto-Aztecan cultural roots *and* from its adopted Mesoamerican cultural inheritance. It views the earth as an extremely perilous place for human beings (Sahagún, 1953–82). Humans lose their balance easily while walking upon the earth and as a consequence suffer pain, hunger, thirst, sorrow, disease, and madness. Nahua *tlamatinime* (*tlamatini*, singular), i.e., "knowers of things," "poet-philosophers," or "sages," conceived the raison d'être of philosophy as providing practicable answers to what they saw as the central question of human existence: "How can humans walk in balance and so flourish upon the earth?" This existential situation-cum-question defines the *problematic* framing Nahua philosophy. Nahua philosophers conceived ethically, epistemologically, and aesthetically good (*cualli*) conduct, attitudes, objects, and states of affairs in terms of humans

12

maintaining their balance and flourishing upon the earth (Burkhart, 1989; Durán, 1971, 1994; León-Portilla, 1963; López Austin, 1988, 1997; Maffie, 2007; Sahagún, 1953–82).

This problematic is rooted in Nahua metaphysics. The starting point of Nahua metaphysics is the claim that there exists a *single*, dynamic, vivifying, eternally self-generating and self-regenerating sacred power or force. The Nahua referred to this power as "*teotl*." Teotl is always active, actualized, and actualizing energy-in-motion. The cosmos and all its constituents are constituted by, as well as ultimately identical with, the sacred force of teotl. Teotl permeates, configures, and vivifies the entire cosmos and its contents (Durán, 1971, 1994; Sahagún, 1953–82).

Process, motion, transformation, destruction, and creation define teotl, hence reality per se, and hence the cosmos and all its contents. Teotl is properly understood as *neither* being *nor* non-being but as *becoming*. Teotl neither *is* nor *is not*; teotl *becomes*. As a consequence, reality per se and hence the cosmos and its inhabitants are unstable, evanescent, and transitory. Reality is devoid of static states of being, order, and permanent structure. Teotl creates (and re-creates) the cosmos – along with all its inhabitants – out of itself. They are teotl's immanent self-presentation – not its creation ex nihilo. They neither exist apart from nor outside of teotl (Maffie, 2007; Sahagún, 1953–82).

Nahua metaphysics may be viewed as a form of pantheism. Everything is bound together by an all-inclusive and interrelated sacred unity: teotl. Everything does not merely exist inside teotl, and teotl does not merely exist inside everything (as panentheism claims). Rather, everything is identical with teotl. Although vivifying, teotl is nonpersonal, non-agentive, and non-intentional. It is not a deity possessing power in the manner of a ruler or king.

Nahua metaphysics is further shaped by several additional intuitions. First, that which is real is that which becomes, changes, and transmutes – contra most Western metaphysics which claims that that which is real is that which is immutable, stable, and static. Reality is characterized by Becoming – not by Being or "is-ness" as such. To exist is to become, move, transform, and change. Second, that which is real is that which makes things happen. Being real consists of the power to create, destroy, transform, act upon, or affect change in things. To be is to be (causally) effective. Nahua metaphysics is committed to the mutual equivalence of existence, power, energy, motion, becoming, causing, and transforming (both of self and others). Third, reality is irreducibly ambiguous – contra most Western philosophers' claims that reality (as opposed to appearances) is unambiguous. Fourth, nature follows function: what something *is* follows from what it *does*. In sum, according to Nahua metaphysics processes rather than perduring objects or substances are ontologically fundamental. Activity, motion, flux, time, change, and transformation are the principal notions for understanding things.

Nahua philosophy also conceives teotl in terms of the autochthonous Nahua notion of *nepantla*. Nepantla plays a central role in Nahua metaphysics' descriptive account of the nature of reality and of the human condition, and a central role in Nahua value theory's (i.e., ethics, epistemology, and aesthetics) conceptions of good conduct, good cognizing, good art, and the good life for human beings.

Durán (1994) glosses "nepantla" as "betwixt and between" (*en medios*), "neither one nor the other," and "neither fish nor fowl" (*neutros*). Molina (2001) glosses "nepantla" as an adverb, meaning "in the middle of something" (*en el medio, o en medio, o por medio*).

13

Nepantla primarily modifies activities, processes, doings, and becomings. It tells us how, when, or where an agent(s) or thing(s) acts, behaves, or does something; or how, when, or where a process occurs. Nepantla-processes take place "in the middle of," "betwixt and between," or "in the balance between" two or more things. They place people or things in *nepantlatli*, i.e., in the middle of, or betwixt and between, two endpoints. Nepantla-processes are also middling in the sense of actively middling their *relata*. Nepantla also conveys a sense of abundant reciprocity or mutuality; one that derives from being "middled." Nepantla-processes occupy, use, and apply the middle as well as create a middled product. They are "nepantla-middling" or "nepantla-balancing." The Nahua regarded weaving, sexual commingling, the joining, shaking, or mixing together of things, and reciprocal greeting, pardoning, and befriending as nepantla-middling and -balancing processes (Burkhart, 1989; López Austin, 1997; Maffie, 2007; Molina, 2001; Sahagún, 1953–82).

Nepantla-processes are simultaneously destructive *and* creative and hence essentially transformative. Consider weaving. On the one hand, weaving creates something new – a fabric that is neither warp nor weft yet at the same time both warp and weft held in reciprocal tension with one another. On the other hand, weaving destroys the prior identities of individual warp and weft fibers. The transformation from fibers to fabric is simultaneously creative and destructive. The creation of something new is predicated upon and emerges from the destruction of something prior.

Nepantla-processes suspend things within a dynamic, unstable, and destabilizing *ontological zone* between conventional categories: a zone in which things become ill-defined, ambiguous, and anomalous; a zone in which things disappear into the interstices between conventional categories; and finally, a zone from which emerges a novel *tertium quid*. Things previously categorized as "fish" and "fowl" are subjected to a transformative process that destroys their erstwhile independent, well-defined status as "fish" vs. "fowl" while also creating a tertium quid that is neither fish nor fowl. "Fish" and "fowl" are destroyed in the course becoming something that is neither fish nor fowl yet simultaneously both fish and fowl: something ill-defined, unsettled, and unstable; something that "cuts across" the conventional categories of fish and fowl. Nepantla-processes place their participants within an ambiguous ontological zone that transcends "either/or" and "this" vs. "that." The Nahuas regarded the crossroads (*onepanco*) as a paradigmatic example of nepantla. The crossroads is the "center" or "middle" of two intersecting roads. This intersecting creates a new space, one betwixt and between two roads; a marginal, anomalous, unstable, and ill-defined place; a place that is ultimately "no place" at all. The crossroads is ontologically ambiguous: it is neither this road nor that road yet simultaneously both roads at once. In sum, nepantla-processes place people and things within a "borderland," i.e., a dynamic zone of mutual interaction, reciprocal influence, unstable and diffuse identity, and transformation (Maffie, 2007).

Nahua metaphysics conceives teotl as a nepantla-process. Teotl oscillates middlingly betwixt and between being and non-being. Teotl is at bottom ontologically ambiguous since it is neither being nor non-being yet simultaneously both being and non-being. That is, it is becoming. Similarly, teotl is neither ordered (determined or governed top-down by laws or principles) nor disordered (chaotic) but rather *unordered*. It captures an ontological tertium quid: unorderliness. Since they are identical with teotl, reality, cosmos, and human existence are likewise defined in terms of nepantla, i.e., by transformative dialectical reciprocity and abundant mutuality. It follows that they, too, are dynamic, processive, constantly changing, irreducibly ambiguous, and inescapably caught betwixt and between order and disorder, and being and non-being.

Although essentially processive and devoid of Being as well as permanent order, structure, and substances, teotl's ceaseless becoming and self-presenting are nevertheless characterized by an overarching pattern or rhythm. This rhythm is expressed simultaneously in two, ultimately equivalent ways: as the agonistic, dialectical reciprocity of complementary dualities, and as the two calendars. According to the former, teotl presents itself as the ceaseless, cyclical alternation or tug-of-war between coexisting, mutually interdependent and arising, complementary dualities or polarities. These include being/not-being, order/disorder, life/death, light/darkness, male/female, and drought/humidity. Life and death, for example, are mutually arising and interdependent, complementary aspects of one and the same cyclical process. Life contains the seed of death; death, the seed of life. Without death, there is no life; without life, there is no death (Durán, 1994; Sahagún, 1953–82). The dialectic of life and death is also one of abundant mutuality and reciprocity. The same applies to order and disorder, male and female, light and darkness, etc. Although each moment in a cycle consists of the dominance of one or the other paired opposite, in the long run the cycle manifests an overarching dynamic balance. Short-term imbalances are woven into long-term balance. What produces and explains this overarching balance and rhythm of complementary dualities? Teotl as nepantla-process.

The cyclical alternation and momentary dominance of each of these complementary opposites produces the diversity of the cosmos across time and place as well as the momentary arrangement of the cosmos at any given moment. The genesis of the cosmos falls into five successive ages or "suns," each representing the temporary dominance of a different aspect of teotl. The present era, the "Age of the Fifth Sun," is the one in which human beings live. Like its four predecessors, however, the Fifth Sun will eventually succumb to catastrophic imbalance, the earth will be destroyed by earthquakes, and humankind will vanish (Durán, 1971, 1994; Sahagún, 1953–82).

Nahua dualism differs profoundly from the Zoroastrian- and Manichean-style dualisms that characterize so much of Western thinking. These standardly claim that order, goodness, life, or light, on the one hand, and disorder, evil, death, or darkness, on the other, are mutually contradictory, incompatible, and exclusive. They view history as consisting of the either/or struggle of these contradictories. At the end of history, one or the other of these contradictories will or ought to defeat and eliminate the other. Nahua dualism claims that order and disorder, life and death, etc., alternate endlessly and interdependently without resolution. It rejects as foolish the ideas that life is inherently good and that death is inherently evil as well as the idea that life will or ought to triumph over death. It rejects as equally foolish the quest for eternal life. Lastly, and especially noteworthy, "good" and "evil" do not show up on the Nahuas' list of complementary dualities. Reality and hence human existence are not defined in terms of a conflict between good and evil.

The overarching rhythm of teotl's nepantla-balancing also presents itself as the spiraling cycle of time-place captured by the two calendars – the *tonalpohualli* or 260-day count, and the *xiuhmolpilli* or 360+5-day count – that characterize the Age of the Fifth Sun. Calendrical counts frame human existence. A person's birth date according to the

15

tonalpohualli determines her *tonalli*: a general cosmic force that suffuses the earth's surface and determines a person's innate character predispositions. Each day carries its own tonalli, and each tonalli carries its own causal influence upon the earth. The Nahua used the tonalpohualli to ascertain the specific tonalli reigning on any particular day (Durán, 1971, 1994; Sahagún, 1953–82).

In the final analysis, teotl is essentially an undifferentiated, unordered, unstable, and seamless processive totality. As a nepantla-process, teotl falls betwixt and between being/non-being, order/disorder, life/death, etc. It is simultaneously neither alive nor dead yet both alive and dead, neither orderly nor disorderly yet both orderly and disorderly, etc. Teotl cuts across conventional categories and is therefore ambiguous and ill-defined relative to such categories. It is neither this nor that, yet both; neither something nor nothing, yet both. Moreover, given that time-place (as defined, mapped, and counted by the two calendars) is yet another self-presentation of teotl, teotl is also ultimately untimed and unplaced. It is neither here nor there, yet both; neither now nor then, yet both.

Nahua philosophers understood teotl's self-presenting and self-transforming in two additional, closely interrelated ways. First, they conceived it as a shamanic process. The cosmos is teotl's *nahual* ("disguise" or "mask"). The Nahuatl word "nahual" derives from "*nahualli*" signifying a form-changing shaman. The becoming of the cosmos consists of teotl's shamanic self-masking or self-transforming. Second, they conceived it as an artistic process, one consisting of teotl's creating and re-creating itself *into* and *as* the cosmos. The cosmos is teotl's *in xochitl in cuicatl* or "flower and song." "Flower and song" refers specifically to the performing of song-poems. It also refers more broadly to transformative, artistic activity per se (e.g., goldsmithing, featherworking, and painting-writing). Nahua tlamatinime commonly characterized earthly existence as consisting of pictures painted-written by teotl on teotl's sacred *amoxtli* (a native papyrus-like paper). The tlamatini Aquiauhtzin characterizes the earth as "the house of paintings" (trans. by León-Portilla, 1992, p. 282). Xayacamach writes, "Your home is here, in the midst of the paintings" (trans. by León-Portilla, 1992, p. 228). Like the images on amoxtli painted-written by human artists, teotl's images are fragile and evanescent. Nezahualcoyotl, sings:

> With flowers You paint,
> O Giver of Life!
> With songs You give color,
> with songs you give life on the earth.
> Later you will destroy eagles and tigers:
> we live only in Your painting
> here, on the earth.
> With black ink you will blot out
> all that was friendship,
> brotherhood, nobility.
> You give shading
> to those who will live on the earth.
> We live only in Your book of paintings,
> here on the earth.
> (trans. by León-Portilla, 1992, p. 83)

16

Because they regarded everything earthly as teotl's disguise or mask, Nahua tlamatinime claimed that everything earthly is dreamlike. Tochihuitzin Coyolchiuhqui sings,
"We only rise from sleep, we come only to dream, it is *ahnelli* [unrooted, inauthentic,
untrue], it is *ahnelli* that we come on earth to live" (trans. by León-Portilla, 1992,
p. 153, brackets mine) Nezahualcoyotl sings:

> I, Nezahualcoyotl, ask this:
> Is it *nelli* [well-rooted, authentic, true] one really lives on the earth?
> Not forever on earth, only a little while here.
> Though it be jade it falls apart,
> though it be gold it wears away,
> though it be quetzal plumage it is torn asunder.
> Not forever on this earth, only a little while here.
> (trans. by León-Portilla, 1992, p. 80, brackets mine)

Nahua philosophers conceived the dreamlike illusoriness of earthly existence in epistemological – not ontological – terms. They spoke of the dreamlikeness of earthly life
in order to make the epistemological point that the ordinary, pre-reflective epistemic
condition of humans is to be deceived by teotl's disguise and hence to misunderstand
teotl – not the Platonic-style metaphysical point that earthly existence is ontologically
substandard and not fully real. Earthly existence provides the occasion for human mis-
perception, misjudgment, and misunderstanding. The dreamlikeness of earthly existence
is a function of our human perspective – not an ontological dualism of appearances
and reality inherent in the make-up of reality.

The human existential condition is no exception to the above metaphysical picture.
Human existence is defined by nepantla, i.e., by the ceaseless alternating of life and
death, order and disorder, being and non-being, male and female, etc. Succinctly put,
human beings are *in* nepantla as well as *of* nepantla. Human life occurs on *tlalticpac*,
the earth's surface. The word "tlalticpac" literally means "on the point or summit of
the earth," suggesting a narrow, jagged place surrounded on all sides by unrelenting
dangers (Burkhart, 1989). The Nahuatl proverb recorded by Sahagún, "*Tlaalahui,
tlapetzcahui in tlalticpac*," "It is slippery, it is slick on the earth," was said of a person
who had lived an upright life but then lost her balance and fell into wrongdoing, as
if slipping in slick mud (Sahagún, 1953–82, vol. 6, p. 228, trans. by Burkhart, 1989,
p. v). Humans lose their balance all too easily on the slippery earth, and as a consequence suffer pain, sorrow, hunger, thirst, death, and mental and physical disease
as well as domestic, social, political, and environmental strife and discord. With this
in mind, the *huehuetlatolli* ("words of the elders," "words of the ancients") recorded by
Sahagún include the following speech from a mother to her daughter:

> On earth we live, we travel along a mountain peak. Over here there is an abyss, over there
> is another abyss. If thou goest over here, or if thou goest over there, thou wilt fall in. Only
> in the middle doth one go, or doth one live. (Sahagún, 1953–82, vol. 6, p. 101)

Human life takes place *in* nepantla, i.e., in the middling, oscillating tension betwixt and
between life and death, being and non-being, male and female, etc. That is, human

17

existence takes place "in the crossroads." As a result, human existence is inescapably unstable, ambiguous, fragile, treacherous, evanescent, and perilous.

Human existence is *of* nepantla in the sense that the very activity of living consists of nepantla-balancing the forces of order and disorder, life and death, male and female, etc. Living is a nepantla-process involving constant change, transition, becoming, and transformation (Durán, 1971, 1994; Maffie, 2007; Sahagún, 1953–82).

In light of these circumstances, Nahua philosophers asked, "How can humans maintain their balance, minimize misfortune, and live flourishing lives upon the slippery earth?" (Sahagún, 1953–82, vol. 6). They conceived the raison d'être of philosophical inquiry to be the providing of practicable answers to this question. They accordingly defined wise behavior, attitudes, and states of affairs in terms of promoting balance, minimizing misfortune, and maximizing flourishing upon the earth.

Nahua philosophers turned to their metaphysics for guidance concerning how humans ought to behave wisely, knowledgeably, and appropriately. Given its centrality in Nahua metaphysics, they turned to teotl as nepantla-process. They regarded teotl as nepantla-process as the ideal normative model *for* human behavior since they regarded teotl as nepantla-process as the ideal model *of* nepantla behavior. They accordingly enjoined people to live their lives in a teotl-like, nepantla-balancing way, and based their prescriptive claims regarding how human beings *ought* to conduct their lives upon teotl's example. Nepantla thus figures prominently in Nahua normative conceptions of the good life for human beings, good conduct, good cognition, and good art. Nepantla plays a central role in Nahua ethical, epistemological, and aesthetic prescriptions concerning how humans ought to behave, think, feel, judge, speak, and eat; work, farm, and trade; treat their nonhuman surroundings; and play music, paint-write, and weave. Nahua tlamatinime thus apparently reasoned that since reality and the human existential condition are inescapably middling, humans must therefore behave middlingly. In short, in a cosmos defined *by* nepantla, one must live a life *of* nepantla.

The inescapably painful and unstable nature of human existence did not, however, prompt Nahua philosophers to reject earthly life in favor of some transcendent, other-worldly life. There simply is no such life to be had for humans. The earth's surface is the only time-place where the three vital forces comprising human beings – *tonalli* ("inner heat," "vitality," "potency," and "innate personality") concentrated in the head, *teyolia* ("that which gives life to someone," "that which moves someone") concentrated in the heart, and *ihiyotl* ("breath," "wind," "respiration") concentrated in the liver – are fully integrated, and hence the only time-place where humans enjoy the potential for well-being (López Austin, 1988; Molina, 2001; Sahagún, 1953–82). The Nahua thus resolved to live as best they could here on *tlalticpac*.

Nahua wisdom is accordingly this-worldly. It deems as intrinsically valuable (i.e., worth pursuing, doing, or having for its own sake) living a flourishing, genuinely human life on earth. After likening the human condition to walking down a narrow, jagged path along a mountain peak, the mother quoted above advises her daughter, "*zan tlanepantla in uiloa, in nemoa*," "only through the middle can one go, or live." The mother invokes *tlanepantla*, "in (or through) the middle." A Nahua adage recorded by Sahagún states, "*Tlacoqualli in monequi*," "the middle good is necessary" (Sahagún, 1953–82, vol. 6, p. 231, trans. by Burkhart, 1989, p. 134). Those striving to walk in balance upon the earth must pursue a nepantla or middling way of life. One's life must be a skillfully executed nepantla-process. One must avoid doing too much and too little of any activity: e.g., eating, working, sleeping, or bathing. When one slips and eats too much, for example, one must restore balance by eating too little. In this manner, one weaves the unavoidable, short-term imbalances of daily existence into a life of long-term balance.

Nahua wisdom aimed at teaching humans how, like skilled mountain climbers, to maintain their balance upon the narrow, jagged summit of the earth. Alternatively, it aimed at teaching humans how, like accomplished weavers, to weave together the various forces and tensions in the cosmos and in their lives into a well-balanced fabric. In order to live wisely, live artfully, and thus live a flourishing, genuinely human life in a cosmos characterized by nepantla, one's living must actualize nepantla-balancing. One's living must be a well-crafted nepantla-process. And from what better teacher to learn how to do this than from teotl itself? When ultimate reality is characterized by constant change, motion, and becoming, one needs to learn how to change, move, and become in balance. One cannot find stability in transcendent Being. One cannot find balance by clinging to a "rock of ages," for even rocks and ages come and go. Living wisely consists of embracing and mastering nepantla – not trying to avoid, minimize or escape nepantla.

Nahua philosophy conceived *tlamatiliztli* ("wisdom" or "knowledge") pragmatically in terms of human balancing and flourishing (Sahagún, 1953–82). Tlamatiliztli is active, creative, practical, concrete, situational, and performative – not passive, abstract, theoretical, representational, or contemplative. It consists of knowing *how* to act mid-dlingly, *how* to maintain one's balance, and *how* to flourish as one walks upon the jagged path of life. Wisdom does not consist of knowing *that* certain facts are the case, or of apprehending abstract principles, laws, or conceptual truths. Nahua epistemology does not embrace semantic goals such as truth for truth's sake, correct description, or accurate representation. The aim of cognition is walking in balance upon the slippery earth, and epistemologically good (cualli) cognition is that which promotes this aim.

Flourishing upon the earth requires not only that humans know how to accommodate themselves to the various spiraling cycles constituting the Age of the Fifth Sun, but also that they know how to contribute to the overall balance of these cycles and in so doing contribute to the continuation of the Age of the Fifth Sun. How human beings act makes a difference to the balance and continuing existence of the present cosmic age. Human activity is both an integral as well as integrating element of the Fifth Sun. Human existence is implicated within a complex web of reciprocity relationships between humans and cosmos, and these entail a host of corresponding reciprocity obligations. Humans contribute to the equilibrium of the Fifth Sun when they successfully perform these obligation-fulfilling actions. They disrupt equilibrium when they fail to do so. The continuing equilibrium and existence of the Fifth Sun thus depends upon human beings' fulfilling their obligations (Durán, 1971, 1994; Sahagún, 1953–82).

Neltiliztli ("truth") is an indispensable feature of wisdom and knowledge. Nahua philosophy conceives truth in terms of authenticity, genuineness, and well-rootedness *in* and non-referential disclosing *of* teotl – not in terms of correspondence, aboutness, or representation (contra most Western philosophy). It characterizes persons, actions, and things equally and without equivocation in terms of truth (and falsity). That which is well rooted in teotl – be it a person, song-poem, ritual action, painted-written text,

19

or sculpture – is true, genuine, well balanced, and non-referentially disclosing and unconcealing of teotl; that which is unrooted is false, non-genuine, inauthentic, imbalanced,
and concealing of teotl.

Humans cognize knowingly if and only if their cognizing is well rooted (*nelli*) in teotl,
and their cognizing is well rooted in teotl if and only if teotl burgeons and flowers within
their heart. This, in turn, occurs if and only if humans possess a *yolteotl* or "*teotlized
heart*" (León-Portilla, 1963, p. 143; Sahagún, 1953–82, vol. 3, p. 69), i.e., a heart that
attains nepantla-balancing. A teotlized heart moves middlingly, well balancedly, and
thus in harmony with the oscillating moving of teotl. Such a heart is charged with teotl's
sacred energy and enjoys sacred presence. The person possessing a "teotlized heart" is
said to have "teotl in his heart" and to be "wise in the things of teotl." Teotl discloses
itself *to* and *through* a well-rooted, well-balanced heart. As the generative presentation
of teotl, human knowing constitutes one of the ways that teotl genuinely discloses itself
on earth. Humans cognize unknowingly (dully, foolishly, or confusedly), by contrast,
when their cognizing is poorly rooted if not unrooted (*ahnelli*) in teotl. Such cognizing
is false, inauthentic, non-genuine and non-disclosing. Teotl fails to burgeon and flower
within such a heart (Sahagún, 1953–82, vols. 3, 6, 10). Unknowing, not-good (*ahmo
cualli*) cognizing constitutes a form of cognitive dementia, disease, and imbalance. It is
one of the ways that teotl masks itself on earth.

Nahua tlamatinime drew three consequences from the fact that teotl is ultimately
unordered, unstable, betwixt-and-between, and neither-this-nor-that. First, knowing
teotl requires a non-binary – i.e., non-either/or – mode of experience. Humans experience teotl knowingly via a mystical-style union of their hearts and teotl. Teotl burgeons
and flowers within their hearts. This enables humans to bypass conventional binary
categories and in so doing experience teotl without distortion by such categories.
When this occurs, one's thinking is no longer befogged by the "breath on the mirror"
(as the Maya text, the *Popol Vuh* [Tedlock, 1985, p. 167], puts it) constituted by
perceiving and conceiving teotl through conventional binary categories. Second,
expressing one's understanding of teotl requires a non-binary mode of expression, viz.
"flower and song" (León-Portilla, 1963, p. 75). Artistic activity generally, but especially
singing poetry – rather than advancing of discursive arguments – is the truest, most
authentic way of expressing one's understanding of teotl. Philosophers are perforce
poet-singers and artists who unconceal teotl through metaphorical speech and artistic
image. Finally, because teotl is unordered, betwixt-and-between, etc., human beings
are unable to fully comprehend teotl.

Nahua philosophers conceived language primarily as a practical instrument for
guiding behavior and making things happen in the world – not as an instrument
for representing facts or reporting propositional truths. The spoken word is causally
efficacious, and when used wisely, affects change in the course of human *and* nonhuman events with an eye toward human and cosmic balance.

Nahua ethics evaluates the goodness of human conduct, attitudes, and states of affairs
from the standpoint of creating, maintaining, and restoring balance and flourishing.
It characterizes ethically good (cualli) conduct as "*in quallotl in yecyotl*," i.e., "fitting
for" and "assimilable by" humans. Ethically good conduct balances people and helps
them become more authentically human. Not-good (ahmo cualli) conduct throws
people out of balance, causing them to impoverish their lives and to become defective

"lump[s] of flesh with two eyes" (Sahagún, 1953–82, vol. 10, p. 3). To the degree humans live balanced lives, they perfect their humanness and flourish; to the degree they do not, they destroy their humanness and suffer miserable beastly lives (Burkhart, 1989; López Austin, 1988; Sahagún, 1953–82, vols. 6, 10).

The Nahuas used "flower and song" to refer broadly to artistic activity and its products. They did not, however, have a modern concept of art in the sense of "art for art's sake." The Nahuas had no notion of a distinctly aesthetic – as opposed to moral or epistemological – point of view from which to judge the goodness of human artistry. They defined aesthetic goodness in terms of human flourishing. Aesthetically good (cualli) "flower and song" improves both its creator and audience metaphysically, morally, and epistemologically, and is an essential ingredient of a flourishing life. Aesthetics is thus shot through with moral and epistemological purpose. That which is aesthetically good – be it a song-poem, woven fabric, or person – is morally and epistemologically good (and vice versa). It is well rooted, well balanced, true, genuine, and non-referentially unconcealing of teotl. That which is aesthetically not-good (ahmo cualli) is unrooted, undisclosing, inauthentic, and false.

Conclusion

Pre-Columbian Aztec and Andean philosophies conceived of ways of *being-human-in-the-world* that stress the fact that humans are both in the world and of the world as well as the need for humans to live in balance with the world. In this respect they differ from those conceptions of being-human-in-the-world advanced by leading secular and religious Western philosophies. The latter typically view humans as in the world but not of the world, and regard nature as something to be exploited for human self-aggrandizement. However, as Western philosophies prove increasingly unsustainable in the face of catastrophic environmental collapse, thinking people of the West would do well to critically reexamine their philosophical preconceptions as well as engage in dialogue with pre-Columbian philosophies. After all, as once noted (Hickman and Alexander, 1998, p. 21), for John Dewey Western European philosophy is only a "provincial episode."

Related chapters: 2 The Rights of the American Indians; 3 Colonial Thought; 16 Language and Colonization; 24 Latin American Philosophy.

References

Andean Philosophy

Betanzos, J. de. (1996). *Narrative of the Incas*. (R. Hamilton & D. Buchanan, Eds). Austin: University of Texas Press.

Cieza de Léon, P. de. (1967). *El señorío de los Incas; 2a. parte de la croníca del Perú*. Lima: Instituto de Estudios Peruanos.

Classen, C. (1993). *Inca cosmology and the human body*. Salt Lake City: University of Utah Press.

21

Cobo, B. (1990). *Inca religion and customs*. (R. Hamilton, Ed. & Trans.). Austin: University of Texas Press.

Guaman Poma de Ayala, F. (1936). *Nueva corónica y buen gobierno*. Paris: Travaux et Mémoires de l'Institut d'Ethnologie 23.

Isbell, B. J. (1978). *To defend ourselves: ecology and ritual action in an Andean village*. Austin: University of Texas Press.

Pachacuti Yamqui Salcamaygua, J. de S. C. (1873). *Narratives of the rites and laws of the Yncas*. (C. R. Markham, Ed. & Trans.). London: The Hakluyt Society.

Seibold, K. E. (1992). Textiles and cosmology in Choquechancha, Cuzco, Peru. In R. V. H. Dover, K. E. Seibold, & J. H. McDowell (Eds). *Andean cosmologies through time: persistence and emergence* (pp. 166–201). Bloomington: Indiana University Press.

Urton, G. (1981). *At the crossroads of the earth and sky: an Andean cosmology*. Austin: University of Texas Press.

Aztec Philosophy

Burkhart, L. M. (1989). *The slippery earth: Nahua–Christian dialogue in sixteenth-century Mexico*. Tucson: University of Arizona Press.

Carrasco, D. (Ed.). (2001). *The Oxford encyclopedia of Mesoamerican cultures: the civilizations of Mexico and Central America* (3 vols.). Oxford: Oxford University Press.

Durán, D. (1971). *Book of the gods and rites and the ancient calendar*. (F. Horcasitas & D. Heyden, Eds & Trans.). Norman: University of Oklahoma Press.

Durán, D. (1994). *The history of the Indies of New Spain*. (D. Heyden, Trans.). Norman: University of Oklahoma Press.

Knab, T. J. (2004). *The dialogue between earth and sky: dreams, souls, curing and the modern Aztec underworld*. Tucson: University of Arizona Press.

León-Portilla, M. (1963). *Aztec thought and culture: a study of the ancient Nahuatl mind*. (J. E. Davis, Trans.). Norman: University of Oklahoma Press.

León-Portilla, M. (1992). *Fifteen poets of the Aztec world*. Norman: University of Oklahoma Press.

López Austin, A. (1988). *The human body and ideology: concepts of the ancient Nahuas* (2 vols.). (T. Ortiz de Montellano & B. R. Ortiz de Montellano, Trans.). Salt Lake City: University of Utah Press.

López Austin, A. (1997). *Tamoanchan, Tlalocan: places of mist*. B. R. Ortiz de Montellano & T. Ortiz de Montellano (Trans.). Niwot: University Press of Colorado.

Maffie, J. (2007). The centrality of *nepantla* in conquest-era Nahua philosophy. *The Nahua Newsletter*, 44, 11–31.

Molina, A. de. (2001). *Vocabulario en lengua Castellana y Mexicana y Mexicana y Castellana*. 4th ed. México, D.F.: Porrúa.

Sahagún, B. de. (1953–82). *Florentine Codex: general history of the things of New Spain* (12 vols.). (A. J. O. Anderson & C. Dibble, Eds & Trans.). Santa Fe, NM: School of American Research and University of Utah.

Sandstrom, A. R. (1991). *Corn is our blood: culture and ethnic identity in a contemporary Aztec Indian village*. Norman: University of Oklahoma Press.

Tedlock, D. (1985). *Popol Vuh: the definitive edition of the Mayan book of the dawn of life and the glories of gods and kings*. New York: Simon & Schuster.

Conclusion

Hickman, L. A., & Alexander, T. M. (Eds). (1998). *The essential Dewey* (2 vols.). Bloomington: Indiana University Press.

2

The Rights of the American Indians

BERNARDO J. CANTEÑS

In the sixteenth century, philosophical and theological thought flourished in Spain, pro-ducing treatises and disputations, in scholastic style, that rivaled those produced at the height of medieval scholasticism (1250–1350). For this reason, this era of Spain's his-tory is referred to as "the second scholasticism." Universities were a major contributor to Spain's second scholasticism, particularly the University of Salamanca. There a group of theologian-philosophers were engaged in the new sociopolitical realities fac-ing Spain in the New World, from a Thomistic philosophical perspective, the dominant paradigm in sixteenth-century Catholic thought. A result of these systematic studies was the development of new treatises on political morality, human rights, and inter-national jurisprudence based on natural law (*ius naturae*) and the law of nations (*ius gentium*). These theologian-philosophers are referred to as "the School of Salamanca." After the unification of Spain and Portugal in 1580 by Phillip II of Spain (Phillip I of Portugal), many Jesuits were sent to the University of Coimbra. There they continued the work begun by the School of Salamanca. These Jesuits are known as "the Conimbricenses." The School of Salamanca and "the Conimbricenses" produced the first elucidation of the foundations of modern International Law, which was later system-atized by Hugo Grotius (1583–1645), John Selden (1584–1654), and Samuel Pufendorf (1632–94).

Some of the most prominent Spanish and Portuguese philosopher-theologians belonging to the School of Salamanca and the School of Coimbra include the follow-ing: Martín de Azpilcueta (1491–1586), Francisco de Vitoria, O.P. (1492–1546), Domingo de Soto, O.P. (1494–1560), Alfonso de Castro (1495–1558), Melchior Cano, O.P. (1509–60), Bartolomé de Medina, O.P. (1527–80), Pedro de Fonseca, S.J. (1528–99), Domingo Bañez, O.P. (1528–1604), Francisco de Toledo, S.J. (1532–96), Benito Pereiro, S.J. (1535–1610), Luis de Molina, S.J. (1535–1600), Francisco Suárez, S.J. (1548–1617), Gregorio de Valencia, S.J. (1549–1602), Gabriel Vázquez, S.J. (1549–1604), and Juan Martînez de Ripalda, S.J. (1594–1648). These thinkers broached a broad range of topics in philosophy, religion, theology, law, economics, and sociopolitical morality that were relevant to the fabric of contemporary Catholic Europe, Spanish society, and the New World.

Spain's political, economic, and intellectual flourishing was intertwined with its discovery of the New World and its conquest of the American Indians beginning in

1492. The Spanish conquest and colonialism raised two central moral questions for Spanish authority: (1) What, if anything, morally justified the Spaniards to go to war with the Indians? and (2) What rights, if any, did the Indians have as humans and as members of autonomous communities or nation-states? The Spanish monarch, Charles I (Charles V of Germany), was the Holy Roman Emperor (1516–56) and his connection with the Roman Catholic Church strongly motivated him to have the most knowledgeable moral theologians and the most learned philosophers investigate the complex political affairs that occupied Spain in the Americas. Spanish authorities, therefore, were continuously seeking the opinion and advice of Spanish and Portuguese moral theologians. The Dominican friars Francisco de Vitoria, O.P. (1485–1546) and Bartolomé de las Casas, O.P. (1484–1566) were two of the first Spanish political theorists who developed a systematic view of these moral and sociopolitical questions, and, as a result, the first to elaborate a legal foundation for their resolution. Their source was the moral and political philosophy of Augustine, and Thomas Aquinas's *Treatise on Law* and his conception of natural law in his *Summa Theologiae*. Their efforts to resolve these international, sociopolitical, and legal issues constitute the basis for attributing to the School of Salamanca its important role in the history and development of modern International Law and human rights.

Their method was strictly scholastic and thus their writings illustrate distinctive scholastic characteristics. The scholastic method first presents the thesis or the central issue, usually as a question. For instance, in *On the American Indians* Vitoria begins with the question: "Whether sinners can be true masters?" The scholastic method then considers objections to the thesis; in other words, it develops arguments that support the view the author wishes to reject. Third, the author then presents counterarguments, refuting the opposing view, and solutions to difficulties and objections. This dialectical, scholastic methodology takes on the form of rigorous disputation. Another characteristic of the scholastic method is its use of authoritative texts. Vitoria's and las Casas's works are permeated with authoritative references to scripture, Greek philosophers, and medieval theologians. The number and sophistication of the arguments elaborated by both Vitoria and las Casas is also a customary feature of the scholastic method.

Vitoria and las Casas were primarily theologians, and they considered legal questions concerning the rights of the Indians to fall within their province of study. While lawyers treated questions of human law (*lex humana*) or positive law, which constituted the laws enacted by humans for the purpose of maintaining order on a daily basis in society, theologians were responsible for issues concerning Divine Law. Since human laws are promulgated for the purpose of establishing order in a local community, the jurisdictional power and scope of human law is limited to the community in question and thus cannot be enforced universally or on other communities. According to Vitoria and las Casas, the world is ruled by the providence of God or by Divine Reason. Divine Law, then, refers to God's providence in the world, which is both eternal and universal, having jurisdictional power and scope over all of time and the entire world.

Vitoria and las Casas held the Thomistic view that natural law is rational creatures' participation, through their use of reason, in God's Eternal Law; therefore, they considered natural law to fall in between human law and Divine Law. Aquinas maintained that God's Law was imprinted in human nature so that the proper use of reason could reveal the natural end, and thus the moral good, for human beings. Therefore, natural law is derived from human reason and, since it participates in Divine Law, it has universal jurisdiction. In addition, because natural law participates in Divine Law, it also pertains to a theologian's province of study.

Vitoria argued further that the law of nations, which establishes the universal principles of government among independent, sovereign nations in the world, is closer to natural law than to human law, because it "has the sanction of the whole world," and thus cannot be ignored by any nation. As a consequence of its close association with natural law and its universality, the law of nations was considered to fall within the domain of theological study. In addition, according to Vitoria and las Casas, natural, human rights (*iura*) are a consequence of God's Eternal Law and therefore fall within the scope of the discipline of theology. Following Aquinas's conception of natural law, Vitoria and las Casas held that human nature was essentially *rational* and endowed with inalienable rights to life, freedom, and security.

Vitoria

Vitoria was born in 1485 in Burgos, Spain. In 1506, he entered the Order of Preachers and became a Dominican friar at the monastery of San Pablo, Burgos. In 1509, he went to College de Saint-Jacques at Paris to complete his studies. He stayed in Paris as an instructor until 1523, at which time he moved back to Spain to become Professor of Theology and Director of Studies at the College of San Gregorio in Valladolid. In 1526, Vitoria was elected to the Prime Chair of Theology at the University of Salamanca, and he stayed there for twenty years until his death in 1546. Vitoria never published anything during his lifetime, and his works have come down to us from his students' lecture notes at Salamanca. These works were of two kinds: (1) commentaries and lectures on Aquinas's *Summa Theologiae* and (2) *relectiones* or re-readings, which consisted of investigations of particular contemporary social, moral, political, or economic problems. Some of his most important and significant *relectiones* were *On Civil Power*, *On The American Indians*, and *On the Law of War*.

In *On Civil Power*, Vitoria defends an Aristotelian view of public secular power, arguing that the development of cities is part of the natural evolution of human beings, who are essentially social beings. Human partnerships and communities are a necessary and useful instrument for human safety, survival, and progress. He considers, then, the primitive origin of cities and commonwealths to be the product of natural law and not human invention. Moreover, public power and governments are a necessary force for the stable development of any city and commonwealth; therefore, public power or government, no matter its particular manifestation (monarchy, aristocracy, or democracy), is also justified as a direct evolution of natural law. According to Vitoria, then, secular power is justified by the strongest of all possible arguments: it is a useful, natural, and necessary end for rational beings. Vitoria's view of civil power and the rights of commonwealths had important consequences for the legal status and rights of American Indian cities and governments, since it gave them a prima facie right to exist and conduct their own affairs without the intervention of the Spanish government.

In *On the American Indians*, Vitoria addresses the specific concerns of the rights of the American Indians in three questions: (1) What right have the Spaniards to rule the

Indians? (2) What powers does the Spanish monarchy have over the Indians on civil and temporal matters? and (3) What power does the Spanish monarchy or the Church have over the Indians in religious matters? With respect to the first question, Vitoria maintained that the American Indians possessed true dominion over their public and private affairs before the Spaniards arrived and, moreover, that no Spanish right to rule over the Indians can be justified. A view that has been incorrectly attributed to Vitoria is that the condition of being sinners or unbelievers can deny the Indians their natural right over their land, possessions, bodies, and freedom. These rights, Vitoria argued, are natural and grounded in God's natural law rather than God's Grace; therefore, if a secular ruler is a heretic or a sinner, his inalienable natural rights cannot be denied, and he cannot be deposed in virtue of this alone. In addition, while Vitoria concedes that irrational beings or madmen cannot have legal rights of possession, he denies, despite his many ethnocentric biases, the empirical claim that the Indians are irrational or madmen. He argues that their societal order, customs, and traditions provide sufficient evidence to undermine these claims.

In response to the second question, Vitoria reasons that the Spanish emperor cannot justify his power over the Indians on civil and temporal matters. He examines seven possible justifications, and he demonstrates that none succeed in undermining the Indians' natural rights of self-government, property, and freedom. The first argument claims that since the Spanish emperor is the master of the whole world, the American Indians are his servants and subject to his rule. Vitoria counters by rejecting the claim that the emperor is master of the whole world. Nevertheless, even if the emperor's power were so extensive so as to reign over the entire world, this would only provide him with *jurisdictional* powers and not *property* powers. Jurisdictional powers are concerned with legislative and governmental powers while property powers are concerned with either the control of property (*possessio*) or the ownership of property (*dominium*). Therefore, even if the argument could be made that the laws and legal decisions of the Spanish emperor could legitimately affect the Indians (i.e., via jurisdictional power), this would not grant him authority over the Indians' properties. Thus, the Spanish emperor would still lack the right to do as he pleases with the lands and possessions of the Indians. The second argument states that since the emperor is acting on behalf of the Supreme Pontiff, he has the legitimate power to take possession of the Indians' territories. Vitoria rebuts this argument by claiming that the pope's authority is only over spiritual matters and not civil matters. Therefore, if the Indians refuse to recognize the pope's dominion, war cannot be declared against them nor can their possessions be seized. The third argument is based on the right of discovery. According to the law of nations, territories that have no owner and are unoccupied can be legitimately claimed as property by the power that discovers and occupies them. Vitoria discards this argument as support for the Spanish emperor's ownership over the Indian territories in America, since the land at issue was legitimately owned and occupied by the Indians when the Spaniards arrived.

The fourth argument in support of the emperor's power rests on the American Indians' lack of faith in Christ. Vitoria contends that while there might be religious and spiritual consequences related to one's personal salvation for those who are presented with the Christian faith under proper conditions and reject it, no secular authority has the right to inflict upon these unbelievers temporal punishments. Therefore, the Indians' rejection of the Christian faith does not deprive them of their natural rights to property, freedom, and security. The fifth justification is based on the sins of the American Indians. Vitoria refutes this claim as well, arguing that one's sins do not provide reason to have one's lands or possessions confiscated. If it did, he argued, kingdoms in Europe would be exchanged on a daily basis, and this is absurd. In addition, as in the above argument, the Spanish emperor and the Church have no right to inflict punishment on non-Christians who sin, because it is not within their legal jurisdiction to do so. The sixth argument in support of the Spanish emperor's power over the Indians states that the Indians' voluntary submission to the emperor's rule legitimizes it and sanctions the emperor's right over the Indians' possessions and lands. Vitoria argues that a decision to submit oneself to another's rule must meet several conditions. For instance, an agent or nation must recognize and have full knowledge of the circumstances surrounding their submission (e.g., the rights they are renouncing and conditions under which they are doing so); moreover, the decision must not be made under duress or fear. According to Vitoria, even if these conditions are met, since the Indians have their own rulers, they cannot change rulers without following the appropriate and customary procedures. In addition, a ruler cannot submit the will of his subjects to another ruler without the approval of the subjects. The seventh alleged justification for the emperor's power over the Indians is the prophetic view that God has condemned the Indians and willed their destruction at the hands of the Spaniards as punishment for their unchristian lives. Vitoria refused to engage arguments based on unsubstantiated prophesy. Nevertheless, he points out that even if the destruction of the Indians were part of Divine providence, the acts of those responsible for the destruction are not excusable and thus are considered mortal sins. In conclusion, Vitoria argues persuasively that the Spanish monarch cannot justify his powers over the Indians on civil and temporal matters.

Law of nations and the justification of war

In response to the third question, Vitoria discusses the rights of nations to go to war (and in special cases to rule over other nations) based on three types of justifications, depending on whether these involve (1) self-defense, (2) defense of a nation's legitimate rights as sanctioned by the law of nations, or (3) defense of the legitimate rights of others. In the case of (1), he thinks that a nation has the right "to meet force with force." Therefore, if the Spaniards are attacked, they have a right to defend themselves and as a consequence enter into war with the Indians. Second, Vitoria argues that if a nation's safety and peace are threatened by another nation and the only alternative available is the use of force, it can defend itself by conquering and subjecting the other nation to its rule. In both of these cases, Vitoria qualifies the use of force by adding that the force used ought to be measured and should not exceed what is considered proportional to the force required for self-defense in the particular circumstances.

The justification for (1) is connected with that for (2), since Vitoria characterizes a nation's self-defense broadly to include a nation's defense of its power to exercise its basic rights. He argues that Spain or any country has certain basic rights that are universal and justified by the law of nations. First, a nation has a right to travel in and through another country's territory if it causes no harm in doing so. The right of travel in a foreign land is justified by the law of nations' basic precept that all nations should treat strangers in their territories humanely and hospitably, unless there are reasons not to do so. Second, a nation has a basic right to carry on trade with other nations as long as they do no harm to the homeland. He considers human laws that intervene or obstruct free trade among nations to be prima facie unreasonable and a violation of a nation's basic rights. Third, there are territories that, because of their public and common nature, should be considered as common property, and their use should not be denied to foreigners. For instance, if the Spaniards have a right to travel in a foreign land, then they must also have a right to use certain territories such as roads and rivers in that land. Fourth, children born of parents who are not citizens of the birthplace gain the rights of the natives of that nation in virtue of being born there. According to the law of nations a citizen is a person born in a community; therefore, she should enjoy all of the privileges and share in all the burdens of citizenry. Fifth, if the Spaniards are denied any of these rights, as governed by the law of nations, they have the right to fight to protect them. Moreover, as a last resort, when all other possible diplomatic avenues have been attempted and have failed, the Spanish emperor has the option of using force to defend Spanish rights. And sixth, Spaniards have the right to preach the gospel and if this right is denied by the Indians, the Spanish emperor has a just cause for war.

In the case of (3) above, Vitoria claims that the Spanish emperor is justified to go to war and rule over the Indians if such rule is required for the protection of Indian converts from the persecution of their princes. A second justification might arise if the ruler of the Indians is a tyrant and his cruelty to his subjects is excessively brutal and oppressive. In order to protect the innocent, even if they are not converts, Spanish authorities can intervene and depose an Indian ruler and set up a new ruler. A third justification for a just war is based on defending the will of the masses. For instance, Vitoria argues that if there is a free election in which the majority of the Indians elect the Spanish emperor as their ruler, then the Spanish emperor can rule over the Indians legitimately. A majority vote has the power of natural law, thus it can be the basis for a legitimate title to power. A fourth justification for just war is based on the defense of an allied nation that has been unjustly attacked. If one nation enters into a just war based on self-defense with another nation, and it calls upon an allied nation to help it in its war effort, the allied nation can enter into a just war against the common enemy. Thus Spain may also enter into a just war if it does so in defense of an Indian community that has been unjustly attacked by another Indian community. Finally, if a community or nation lacks the capacity to govern itself, then the Spanish emperor is justified to rule over it and its possessions. Vitoria does not believe that this is the case with the Indian communities; in fact, he defends the view that the Indians have demonstrated a capacity for self-government. Nevertheless, Victoria claims that even if it were the case, the Spanish emperor would have to rule *for* the benefit and good of the Indians and not for the profit of the Spaniards.

The discovery of America introduced international political issues that were without precedent, setting the stage for the construction of international laws concerning universal human rights and just war theory. Vitoria adeptly formulated such doctrines within a Thomistic philosophic framework and scholastic methodology. Moreover, his search for just resolutions to the complex, international political issues of the time was not thwarted by the powers and interests of the Catholic Church or the Spanish monarchy. His contribution set the foundation for not only a Spanish school of international law but also for the future development of modern international law.

Las Casas

Las Casas was born in Seville in 1484. He traveled to Hispaniola in 1502, only ten years after the arrival of Christopher Columbus in the New World. During his first several years in the Americas, he participated in the conquest and was part of an *encomienda* system which he inherited from his father. The *encomienda* was a labor system put into place in 1493 that resembled a medieval feudal system, where the *encomendores* were given control of the land and Indians they conquered, in return for providing order and evangelization. Las Casas's attitude changed slowly as he became more conscious of the abuses of the *encomienda* system and of the Spanish conquistadores. In 1512 he became the first Catholic priest to be ordained in the Americas, and he entered the Order of Preachers in 1522. He was named bishop of Chiapas, Mexico in 1544, and in 1547 he returned to Spain and remained there until his death in 1566.

Las Casas worked tirelessly to protect the rights of the American Indians against the abuses of the Spanish colonialists. His efforts earned him the name "The Apostle of the Indians." Between 1502 and 1547 he crossed the Atlantic five times, with the purpose of gathering support in Europe for Indian rights and fostering change that would protect the American Indians. While his efforts were not always as effective as they might have been, they did influence the highest authorities in Europe and in the Roman Catholic Church to make changes directed at curbing the cruelties and abuses of the Spanish. For instance, las Casas's work induced Pope Paul III's papal bull *Sublimus Dei* in 1537, which declared the Indians to be rational beings with rights to life and liberty, thus prohibiting their enslavement. His work also prompted Charles V, King of Spain and Holy Roman Emperor, to enact the *New Laws* of 1542 which ended, at least in theory, the *encomienda* system.

Unlike Vitoria, las Casas was present in the New World and had firsthand knowledge of the events and abuses of the Spanish colonists. Moreover, he wrote, as a historian, *Apologetic History of the Indies* (1527) and *A Short Account of the Destruction of the Indians* (1542), serving as a witness to the injustices and abuses committed by the Spaniards against the Indians. These historical accounts were also written with the purpose of providing evidence in support of the view that the Indians had a sophisticated culture, traditions, and complex forms of societal organization, thus demonstrating that they were rational beings. Las Casas, therefore, provided important empirical evidence that complemented Vitoria's formal, theoretical arguments. As a Dominican friar, las Casas devoted his life and all his energies to protecting the Indians against the Spanish colonists and conquistadores. He defended the Indians as fellow human beings and as legitimate, sovereign communities of nations with authentic traditions and cultures that should be respected. He sought to protect the Indians' natural inalienable rights, derived from natural law, to live autonomously, freely, and peacefully. This effort and the general debate over the rights of the Spanish monarchy vis-à-vis the American Indians came to a culmination in 1550–1 at the famous debate between las Casas and Juan Ginés de Sepúlveda (1490–1573) at the Council of Valladolid.

Sepúlveda was one of Charles V's chaplains and royal historian, thus he occupied a privileged and influential position. He wrote *The Second Democrates: On the Just Causes of War* in which he defended Spain's conquest of the Indians (*The First Democrates* attempted to justify the sack of Rome in 1527 by Charles V) and the Spanish conquistadores' right to rule the Indians, seize their lands and possessions, and enslave them. Charles V requested Melchior Cano, O.P. and Bartolomé de Carranza, O.P., two of University of Salamanca's most respected theologians, to review the book in order to determine its consistency with Christian doctrine. Their assessment was that Sepúlvelda's *The Second Democrates* lacked the logical rigor to demonstrate its conclusions and, as a consequence, should not receive the royal license necessary for its publication. Sepúlveda objected and brought the issue to the Council of the Indies. He requested the opportunity to defend his views. As a result of this contention, the Council organized the Valladolid debate in 1550 between Sepúlveda and las Casas in which Melchior Cano, O.P., Bartolomé de Carranza, O.P., and Domingo de Soto, O.P. (among others) were appointed as jurists to the council. While Sepúlveda and las Casas never actually met face to face, their ideas clashed, and became symbolic of the tension and controversy between the rival positions of this sociopolitical debate which resounded throughout Spain.

Sepúlveda presented four main arguments in defense of the Spanish conquest, based on Aristotelian philosophy, the authority of Catholic theologians such as Augustine and Thomas Aquinas, and Scripture. The first argument, based on Aristotle, was that the Indians were a barbaric people who lacked sufficient intelligence for self-government (Hanke, 1959). They were *natural slaves* who, on the authority of natural law, ought to surrender all power and authority to the Spanish emperor. According to Sepúlveda, the submission of the Indians to Spanish authority was in accordance with the natural order of things in which the less superior is ruled by the more superior. He argued that if the Indians refused to submit, Spain was justified to use force and even go to war to ensure their submission. The second argument was based on the Indians' sins against Divine Law and natural law. He maintained that Spanish authority is justified to punish and correct the Indians' acts of idolatry and their acts of human sacrifice. Moreover, such sins are of such a grave nature that they justify the Spanish emperor to go to war with the Indians in order to prevent them. The third argument justified (or even obligated) the Spanish emperor to go to war with the Indians in order to protect innocent Indians who were being oppressed and abused by their native rulers. The Spanish emperor ought to prevent such abuses even if he has to conquer and rule the Indians to do so. The fourth argument was based on religious duty. The Spanish emperor is morally obligated, as a Catholic servant and main representative of the Roman Catholic Church, to spread the gospel to all unbelievers. Unbelievers needed to be not only invited to share in Christian faith but compelled to do so. Even the use of violence can be justified if it is necessary for the dissemination of Christian belief and faith, which is the only true salvation of all people. Sepúlveda appealed to the authority of Scripture and the success of Constantine's authoritative rule over pagans for the spreading and flourishing of Christianity through coercion. In addition to concluding that the Spanish conquest was just, Sepúlveda argued that the Spanish empire ought to receive legitimate title to all of the properties, possessions, and territories acquired as a result of the conquest. He went so far as to argue that even individual Spanish soldiers should be permitted to retain any land or property resulting from the conquest, while reject-ing the idea that the Spanish government or soldiers were required by natural law to make restitution for properties acquired by just war.

Las Casas's response lasted several days, and he painstakingly countered each of Sepúlveda's four arguments. Against the first argument, las Casas held that there are four distinct kinds of barbarians. The first kind are people who are cruel and brutish; their lives are guided by passions, such as anger and hate, rather than by reason. The second kind are people who have no language; they may be wise and prudent and still be called barbarians because they lack language. The third kind are people who are barbarians in the strict and proper meaning of the word; they are people who are savages, cruel, and who lack the cognitive capacity to cultivate or participate in friend-ship or any other kind of social structure or organization. These are the barbarians that Aristotle refers to as "slaves by nature." According to las Casas, the Indians do not fall into this category of barbarianism. Moreover, he reasoned that God loves all men, and it is His will to save all of mankind. Since the true barbarian lacks rationality (or at least the degree of rationality necessary for salvation), he cannot seek or love God; there-fore, it is reasonable to believe that God would have created few barbarians in the strict and proper sense. The fourth kind of barbarian are people who do not acknowledge Christ. If we reflect on these distinctions, it is evident that Sepúlveda's first argument, based on the premise that the Indians are barbarians, fails because it lumps together all four distinct kinds of barbarians and thus commits the fallacy of equivocation. In conclusion, Sepúlveda's justification for Spain's going to war with the Indians based on the claim that the Indians are "barbarians" and thus are natural slaves is unsuccessful.

The second argument rests on the Indians' crimes against natural law and Divine Law. Las Casas shows that neither the Church nor Christian rulers have jurisdiction in civil matters over non-Christian subjects who have never embraced the Christian faith. Unlike the case of heretics, who live as subjects to Christian rulers in Christian kingdoms, in virtue of their birth, dwelling, and most importantly, professed commit-ment to abide by Church doctrine and beliefs, the Indians have not been exposed to the Christian faith and have not made any sort of commitment to the truths it pro-claims. Las Casas's argument for the limitation of jurisdiction of the Church and the Spanish emperor is developed in Chapter 6 of *The Defense of the Indies*. There he argues that no monarch or institution can have more jurisdictional power than Christ, and the power of Christ over people who have never heard or accepted the Christian faith is only power in potentiality and not in actuality. These unbelievers are subject to His power potentially because either they will come to accept Christ in their lifetime or they will be subject to God's power in the afterlife. In short, "pagans who have never received the faith are not voluntary and actual subjects of Christ but potential subjects" (las Casas, 1992B, p. 57). Therefore, the Church or the Spanish monarch has no legit-imate power or right to punish non-Christians no matter how atrocious an act against Christian beliefs they commit (more on the different kinds of unbelievers later).

Las Casas concurs, in part, with Sepúlveda's third argument that Spanish author-ities have a moral obligation to protect innocent Indians who are being sacrificed, oppressed, or abused by their rulers. However, las Casas qualifies his view by adding that not all methods adopted for the prevention of such abuses can be morally justified.

31

The case of the Indians presents a moral dilemma in which one has to choose between two evils: (1) go to war with the Indians to stop the injustices committed by their rulers, or (2) allow the injustices to continue. On his view, in cases of moral dilemmas where two options are inherently evil, one ought to choose the lesser evil. In the particular case of the Spanish in the Americas, they should refrain from going to war with the Indians and tolerate the injustices taking place within the Indian communities, since the latter is the lesser evil. His support for this conclusion is based on the precept that "the death of the innocent is better or less evil than the complete destruction of entire kingdoms, cities and strongholds" (las Casas, 1992B, p. 191). This does not mean that other non-violent methods cannot be used in an effort to persuade Indian rulers to give up their oppressive and abusive practices.

On the other hand, for Sepúlveda the Indians' practices of human sacrifice, cannibalism, and idolatry demonstrate that they are not fully rational and thus could not be persuaded through argumentation of any kind. Las Casas, in defense of the rational nature of the Indians, invoked the probable error doctrine. The probable error doctrine explains how Indians could derive conclusions of "probable error," such as cannibalism, without sacrificing their rational nature. He argued that Indians maintained these practices upon the authority of their leaders and wise men, and since these men are believed to have, on most occasions, true beliefs, it explains why a rational person might view such practices as morally permissible. Las Casas, of course, considered the Indians to be in grave error in holding such beliefs.

Finally, las Casas addresses Sepúlveda's fourth argument that Spanish authority is justified (and maybe even morally obligated) to compel the Indians to accept the Christian faith, because the Spanish emperor, as a chief representative of Christianity, has the duty to spread the Gospel of Christ. Moreover, since the salvation of souls is at stake, the degree of compulsion justified is not limited to non-violent methods; forceful coercion and even forced submission through conquest are justified to spread the Gospel of Christ – while to Las Casas that is a gross misinterpretation of the spirit of Christianity. In fact, he believes that Sepúlveda's argument contradicts the very nature of the Gospel of Christ, which is based on the charity and love of our neighbors. In short, las Casas holds Sepúlveda's argument to be "astonishingly" fallacious and thus raises suspicion about his intentions. Las Casas asserts, "Surely Selpúlveda speaks wickedly and commits many errors to the destruction of his soul, especially on three points" (las Casas, 1992B, p. 268).

The first point is Selpúveda's failure to distinguish between the four relevantly distinct types of unbelievers. The first type are unbelievers who belong to other religions, such as Judaism or Islam, and who live peacefully under Christian rule. The second type is the apostate or heretic, who at one point in his life made a commitment to Christianity and later betrayed this commitment. The third type are the unbelievers who belong to a different religion and persecute Christians by war, such as the Turks or Moors. The fourth type are idolatrous unbelievers who live in very remote provinces and have never encountered Christianity, such as the American Indians.

The lack of appropriate distinctions between the different kinds of unbelievers leads Sepúlveda to conflate unbelievers who fall within the legitimate jurisdiction of Christian rulers and the Church with those who do not fall within such jurisdiction; that is, while Christian rulers may have jurisdiction to punish unbelievers who are heretics and live within Christian territories, they do not have jurisdiction over unbelievers who are not heretics or apostates and who live in remote territories. This error ushers Selpúlveda's argument into the grossly mistaken conclusion that the Spanish emperor has a right to punish or compel by force the American Indians with the purpose of spreading the Gospel. According to las Casas, Sepúlveda's error is similar to the one he commits in the second argument above, namely, attributing powers to the Spanish emperor over incorrect jurisdictions, and thus not accounting for the emperor's legal limitation of powers.

The third mistake Selpúveda makes, according to las Casas, is his incorrect interpretation of the parable of the "Great Feast" in Luke 14 (15–25). The story is about a man who gives a great feast and when none of his invited guests show up, he tells his servant to invite all the poor to the feast. Since there is still room the man asks his servant to go out to the country and *make* [emphasis added] others come so that his house is full. Sepúlveda uses this parable as evidence that God encourages his disciples to compel unbelievers to accept the Gospel, even by force if necessary. Las Casas contends that Sepúlveda's interpretation of this parable cannot be supported by any of the Church doctors, and, more importantly, contradicts the Christian spirit of benevolence and charity. He argues that it makes no sense "that the gospel (which is the good and joyful news) and the forgiveness of sins should be proclaimed with arms and bombardments, by subjecting a nation with armed militia and pursuing it with the force of war. What do joyful tidings have to do with wounds, captivities, massacres, conflagrations, the destruction of cities, and the common evils of war?" (las Casas, 1992B, p. 270).

There was no collective consensus or formal decision as to the winner of the Valladolid debate (Hanke, p. 74). Even today the jurors' decisions remain unknown. In fact, the Council of the Indies found it difficult to obtain a verdict from some of the jurors. Nevertheless, even without a clear verdict, the debate did have several important consequences. First, it resulted in las Casas's most important work, *In Defense of the Indians*, which was written during 1548–50. Second, the fact that there was no immediate impact on the realities of Latin America and that the victory remained indecisive motivated las Casas to continue his mission to protect the rights of Latin American Indians, which he did for fifteen more years, until his death in 1566.

Finally, las Casas's works appear to have contributed to the infamous Black Legend (*La Leyenda Negra*), which was an exaggerated and biased interpretation of the Spaniards as cruel, fanatical people and the Indians as innocent, childlike people, whom the former exploited and oppressed to the extent of genocide. One popular version of why the Black Legend came about is based on a conspiracy theory headed by Spain's political enemies, who desired to see Spanish imperialism weaken. Spain's political foes took advantage of las Casas's stories of Spanish abuses and cruelty toward the Indians, as recounted in his *A Short Account of the Destruction of the Indians*, and exaggerated them to portray a dark, exploitative, oppressive, and totally negative picture of Spain. In part, the creation of this purely negative and exaggerated image of Spanish colonialism was intended to undermine Spain's power by revealing the grossly immoral and unchristian foundation upon which such power rested. Interestingly, however, twentieth-century scholars point out that only in Spain was there an effective movement that gave way to real political action in defense and protection of the human rights of the American Indians.

Related chapters: 1 Pre-Columbian Philosophies; 3 Colonial Thought; 13 Liberation Philosophy; 16 Language and Colonization; 21 Liberation in Theology, Philosophy, and Pedagogy.

References

Casas, Fray Bartolomé de las. (1992B). *In defense of the Indies*. (Stanford Poole, C.M., Trans.). DeKalb: Northern Illinois University Press (Original work published 1552–3).

Hanke, Lewis. (1959). *Aristotle and the American Indian*. Chicago: Henry Regnery Company.

Vitoria, Francisco de. (1991A). *On civil power*. (Anthony Pagden and Jeremy Lawrance, Eds). *Francisco De Vitoria political writings* (pp. 1–44). Cambridge: Cambridge University Press (First published in 1557).

Vitoria, Francisco de. (1991B). *On the American Indians*. (Anthony Pagden and Jeremy Lawrance, Eds). *Francisco De Vitoria political writings* (pp. 231–92). Cambridge: Cambridge University Press (Original work published 1557).

Further Reading

Brown, Chris. (1999). Universal human rights: a critique. In T. Dunne & N. J. Wheeler (Eds). *Human rights in global politics* (pp. 103–27). Cambridge: Cambridge University Press.

Bull, Hedley, & Watson, Adam. (Eds). (1985). *The expansion of international society*. Oxford: Oxford University Press.

Casas, Fray Bartolomé de las. (1992). *Obras completas*. (Ramón Hernándes, O.P. & Lorenzo Galmés, O.P., Eds). Madrid: Alianza Editorial.

Casas, Fray Bartolomé de las. (1992). *The only way*. Helen Rand Parish (Ed.). (Trans. Francis Patrick Sullivan, S.J.). New York: Paulist Press (Original work published 1537).

Casas, Fray Bartolomé de las. (1974). *The devastation of the Indies: a brief account*. (Herma Briffault, Trans., with introduction by Bill M. Donovan). Baltimore: Johns Hopkins University Press (Original work published 1542).

Casas, Fray Bartolomé de las. (1999). *Brevisima relación de la destrucción de Las Indias: primera edición crítica*. (Isacio Pérez Fernández, O.P., Ed.). Madrid, España: Punto Print, S.L. (Original work published 1542).

Casas, Fray Bartolomé de las. (1999). *Brevisima relación de la destrucción de Africa: preludio de la destrucción de Indias. Primera defensa de los guanches negros contra su esclavización*. Isacio Pérez Fernández, O.P. (Ed.). Salamanca: Editorial San Esteban.

Casas, Fray Bartolomé de las. (1974). *Los indios de México y Nueva España: antología*. (Edmundo O'Gorman, Ed.). Mexico: Editorial Porrua.

Huxley, G. L. (1980). Aristotle, las Casas and the American Indians. *Proceedings of the Royal Irish Academy*, 80, 57–68.

Marks, Greg. C. (1992). Indigenous peoples in International Law: the significance of Francisco de Vitoria and Bartolomé de las Casas. *The Australian Yearbook of International Law*, 13, 1–51.

Menéndez Pidal, Ramón. (1963). *El padre las Casas: su doble personalidad*. Madrid: Espasa-Calpe.

Pagden, Anthony. (1981). The "School of Salamanca" and the "Affairs of the Indies." *History of Universities*, 1, 71–112.

Pagden, Anthony. (1987). *The fall of natural man: the American Indian and the origins of comparative ethnology*. Cambridge: Cambridge University Press.

Pagden, Anthony. (1990). Dispossessing the barbarian: the language of Spanish Thomism and the debate over the property rights of the American Indians. In A. Pagden (Ed.). *The languages of political theory in early-modern Europe* (pp. 79–98). Cambridge: Cambridge University Press.

Pagden, Anthony. (1990). *Spanish imperialism and the political imagination.* New Haven and London: Yale University Press.

Pagden, Anthony. (1993). *European encounters with the New World: from Renaissance to Romanticism.* New Haven: Yale University Press.

Pagden, Anthony. (1995). *Lords of all the world: ideologies of empire in Spain, Britain, and France c.1500–c.1800.* New Haven: Yale University Press.

Sterba, James P. (1996). Understanding evil: American slavery, the Holocaust, and the conquest of the American Indians. *Ethics,* 106, 424–48.

3

Colonial Thought

LUIS FERNANDO RESTREPO

The history of philosophy in the Indies, as the American continent and the Caribbean were known under Iberian rule (roughly 1492–1810), can be approached in at least two ways. One is a restricted, disciplinary perspective that focuses on the institutional history of philosophy. The second is a much broader perspective of the intellectual history of the continent that allows us to consider the reflections that emerged out of the colonial experience itself. Addressed by colonial and church officials, writers, historians, theologians, and scientists, the most pressing intellectual issues of the period were not limited to the traditional, academic history of philosophy.

Here we will begin with a brief presentation of the history of philosophy in the Indies, a promising but understudied field with a considerable corpus of works. Our main concentration, however, will be on a selection of colonial, native, and Creole (American born of European descent) thinkers, following the broader approach to the intellectual history of the period, a path that has been taken by philosophers, historians, literary critics, and other scholars such as Silvio Zavala (1947), Octavio Paz (1961), Edmundo O'Gorman (1961), Leopoldo Zea (1963), Enrique Dussel (1995), Walter Mignolo (1995), Susana Nuccetelli (2002), and others. In our second section, we will examine some epistemological and ethical questions that originated from the colonial experience, with close attention to authors such as Gonzalo Fernández de Oviedo and Jose de Acosta. Fray Bartolome de las Casas's important contributions to the debate about the legality and morality of the conquest of America are addressed in a separate chapter in this volume. In our third section, we will examine three post-conquest indigenous texts that seek to provide and affirm a comprehensive view of a native knowledge being suppressed by colonial officials: the Mayan *Popol Vuh*, the Aztec *Florentine Codex*, and the Andean chronicle of Felipe Guamán Poma. Fourth, we will discuss two seventeenth-century Creole thinkers, Sor Juana Inés de la Cruz and Carlos de Sigüenza y Góngora. Finally, we will discuss the works of Francisco Javier Clavijero and José Celestino Mutis in the context of the Spanish American experience of the Enlightenment.

I. The Institutional History of Colonial Philosophy

With universities founded in Mexico, Lima, and Santo Domingo by the mid-sixteenth century, and later in every other major colonial city such as Córdoba, Havana, and

Santa Fe de Bogotá, the study and teaching of philosophy in the Indies has a rich institutional history. The Jesuits, for example, established an impressive network of schools (*colegios*) and universities that educated a significant section of the region's elite until its expulsion in 1767. As conceived by the founder of the order, St. Ignacio de Loyola, the Jesuit higher education curriculum or *ratio studiorum* included three years of grammar, rhetoric, logic, physics, metaphysics, moral philosophy, and mathematics followed by four years of specialization in theology, law, or medicine, with two additional years for a doctorate in theology. Texts such as Aristotle's *Politics* and his *Poetics* were regularly taught at the *colegios* and universities throughout Latin America. At the University of Mexico, for instance, courses on St. Thomas Aquinas, John Duns Scotus, and Francisco Suárez were regularly offered.

The academic philosophical tradition in the Indies initially followed Iberian scholasticism and humanism, and later incorporated many modern thinkers such as Bacon, Descartes, Newton, Galileo, and others. However, it was never a unified school of thought. Instead, there were marked differences among the philosophical traditions of the Augustinians, Dominicans, Jesuits, and other religious orders.

Scholars from nearly thirty universities of the Indies produced a considerable corpus of primary documents including *cursus* (classroom treaties on logic, physics, metaphysics, ethics, and theology) and a wide array of texts on science, mathematics, law, politics, and other topics. This is reflected by titles such as *Relectio de dominio infidelium* and *Physica speculatio* (1555) by Alonso de Veracruz from Mexico, *Commentarii ac questiones in universam Aristotelis ac Subtilissimi Doctoris Ihoannis Duns Scoti Logicam* (1609) by the Franciscan Gerónimo Valera from Peru, *De usu et abusu doctrinae Divi Thomae* (1704) by Juan Martínez de Ripalda from New Granada, and *Philosophia naturalis* (1754) by the Mexican Diego José Abad.

Colonial Latin America's contributions to and critical reception of the metropolitan (continental) philosophical traditions are a debated topic. In his *History of Philosophy in Colonial Mexico*, Mauricio Beuchot argues that scholasticism has been viewed as an ideological weapon for colonial control by thinkers such as Agustin Rivera, Samuel Ramos, and Leopoldo Zea. For others, scholasticism also served to fight for justice, human rights, and independence by figures such as Fray Bartolomé de las Casas and Fray Servando Teresa de Mier (Beuchot, 1998, p. 18). These diverging views suggest that a more balanced approach is needed to better understand the complex role of scholastic philosophy in colonial society.

There is a growing interest in the academic history of colonial philosophy. One recent collection that provides a continental overview of the period is *La filosofía en la América colonial* (1996) edited by German Marquínez Argote and Mauricio Beuchot. The collection documents the philosophical traditions in Mexico, Central America, the Caribbean, New Granada (Present-day Colombia), Venezuela, Ecuador, Peru, Argentina, Chile, and Brazil. The study of this tradition is becoming more feasible as editions of primary works appear, such as the 2002 CD-ROM edition of twenty-four philosophical works of colonial Colombia by Manuel Dominguez Miranda.

The development of modern thought in colonial Latin America is also a topic that has been addressed by the histories of science, such as Juan José Saldaña's *Science in Latin America* (2006).

II. The Conquest of America: Some Epistemological and Ethical Questions

The violent experience of the Iberian conquest of America, the encounter of vast lands and numerous indigenous populations unknown to Europeans, and the subsequent development of a heterogeneous colonial society raised fundamental epistemological and ethical issues that challenged Europeans' understanding of the world. The global reach of the geographical exploration of both the Portuguese and the Spanish empires and the encounter of civilizations such as the Maya and the Aztecs with sophisticated time-reckoning systems that could account for past events far beyond that of ancient and biblical cultures shook European's notions of time and space. From this perspective, 1492 was a traumatic experience for European consciousness, a rupture in Western thought that inaugurated the modern age, as it was unquestionably a catastrophic event for the indigenous peoples of the Americas and subsequently the enslaved Africans forcibly brought to this continent.

Thus, some of the most pressing questions of the time were why was the "New" World not mentioned in the scriptures nor by the great philosophers of antiquity? What was known about and what could be said of a continent that Europeans believed to be with no written history and no authorities to consult? Was the conquest of America just and legitimate? Who were the Indians? What did they know about the world and its origins? Approaching critically the colonial period, we may also consider other fundamental questions that were not asked at the time, such as what did indigenous thinkers have to say about Western culture and thought. And also, how native thinkers as well as those of Afro descent understood the colonization.

Gonzalo Fernández de Oviedo and the colonial order of things

Raised in the Spanish court and familiar with the Italian Renaissance culture, official chronicler Gonzalo Fernández de Oviedo (1478–1557) sought to produce a comprehensive picture of the Indies in his *Historia general y natural de las Indias* (1535). A colonist himself and long-time resident of Hispaniola (present-day Dominican Republic), Oviedo provided an impressive corpus of detailed firsthand descriptions of the Indies and transcribed a considerable collection of firsthand accounts about the conquest expeditions.

In the *Historia*, two recurrent perceptions of the Indies are their novelty and incommensurability. Oviedo stressed that Indies were "far from everything ever written, ab initio until our times" (Oviedo, 1959, I: p. 8; my translation). As a result, he stated that to produce the natural history of a whole continent, "from scratch," was a daunting task of epic proportions:

> Who could understand the vast multitude of languages and customs of the peoples of the Indies? Such great variety of wild and docile animals? Such uncountable multitude of trees, full of all sorts of fruits [. . .]? (Oviedo, 1959, I: p. 8; my translation.)

To accomplish this enormous task, Oviedo followed Pliny's organizing scheme for his *Natural historia* (first century AD), incorporating detailed information about the geography, minerals, plants, animals, customs of the indigenous peoples, and adding accounts of the conquest expeditions (Oviedo, 1959, I: 11). The expedition accounts offered a humanist perspective of the conquest, judging the conquerors for their vices and virtues. At work in Oviedo's *Historia* is the production of a considerable corpus of empirical knowledge about the natural world, as illustrated by the vivid description of American plants such as the pineapple. Rough on the outside, the American fruit pleasantly appeals to the senses in its sight, smell, and taste (Oviedo, 1959, I: 239–40). The insufficiency of European languages, knowledge, and reference frameworks is stressed throughout his descriptions of the Indies. The Garlics (*ajes*) of the Hispaniola island, for instance, are similar to those of Spain but have different skin and color (Oviedo, 1959, I: p. 233). American fauna does not seem to fit into the classification scheme inherited from antiquity. Following Pliny's grouping of the animals (land, water, flying, insects) Oviedo placed the iguana in the water animals. In the second edition of the *Historia* (1547), he hesitantly stated that "Now I decided to put it in this book with the land animals" (Oviedo, 1959, II: p. 32). Oviedo's comparisons with the Old World (by analogy) and a growing taxonomy derived from native languages are rather eclectic and unsystematic compared to the taxonomies developed later during the Enlightenment by natural scientists Carl Linnaeus, Cuvier, Bernard Germain Étienne de La Ville, conde de Lacépède, and others. As Pliny, Oviedo's observations are guided by wonder and curiosity more than a systematic classification of the internal structures of the flora and fauna of the New World that we will find in eighteenth-century Latin American thinkers such as Francisco Javier Clavijero and José Celestino Mutis.

At any rate, the emerging empirical knowledge we find in Oviedo's *Historia* and other books about the New World began eroding the authority of antiquity and the scriptures regarding the natural world and the Torrid Zone in particular. For this reason the Crown and the Church enforced tight control over the new knowledge being produced. In this respect, a key issue is how the new knowledge was framed within the accepted paradigms. For example, Oviedo presented the wonders of the New World as a revelation of God's master plan: "the wonderful and innumerable works that God, our Lord, reveals to us, to praise him even more" (Oviedo, 1959, I: p. 1; my translation).

Thus, the *Historia* is a modern text that, appropriating an ordering scheme of antiquity, managed to offer a humanist perspective of the New World that was also Christian and imperial. It is not surprising that the *Historia* would be used in the famous sixteenth-century debate about the wars of conquest. Opposing las Casas's defense of the Indians, Juan Ginés de Sepúlveda cited Oviedo as an authoritative and expert opinion supporting the conquest and the view that the Indians were barbarians.

The New World in a Christian framework: Fray José de Acosta's Historia natural y moral de las Indias

Born in Spain, José de Acosta (1540–1600) traveled to the Indies in 1572 and spent fifteen years in Peru and two in Mexico. He taught theology in Lima and learned Quechua while visiting the Andean regions of Cuzco, Arequipa, Cuquisaca, La Paz, and Potosi in present-day Peru and Bolivia. In 1588, Acosta presented to Phillip II his book *De procuranda indorum salute*, a comprehensive treatise on how to convert the Indians to the faith. For Acosta, fluency in the native languages and an in-depth knowledge of indigenous culture was required for evangelization. His model was spread by the Jesuits throughout Latin America.

Quite conscious that knowledge about the New World posed unavoidable questions for Christian orthodoxy, Acosta rigorously examined the main misconceptions the ancients had about the shape of the world, the Torrid Zone, and the antipodes in his *Natural and Moral History of the Indies* (1590). Acosta devoted several chapters to discussing these topics in the scriptures, Aristotle, Pliny, Plato, St. Augustine, and others. For example, in the chapter titled "Of Aristotle's Opinion of the New World and What it Was that Caused him to Deny it" Acosta refutes ancient perception of the Torrid Zone. Ancient authorities are safely questioned from an orthodox religious point of view. For Acosta, Aristotle's error is understandably human, and it illustrates "how weak and inadequate is the philosophy of the wise men of our world in divine matters, for even in human affairs, where they think they know so much, they are sometimes mistaken" (Acosta, 1996, I: pp. 36–7).

After discussing the geography, natural resources, and animals of the Indies, in the last chapters of the *Natural and Moral History* Acosta presents the history of the Aztecs, the Incas, and other indigenous groups in a providential framework. For Acosta, Spanish colonialism was beneficial for the indigenous people, a claim that was questioned by the native Peruvian intellectual Felipe Guamán Poma, as we will see ahead. In the metropolis, Acosta's systematic examination of Western thought did not go unnoticed. His *Historia* was soon translated into Italian, Latin, Dutch, French, and English.

Tomás de Mercado and the moral conditions of the colonial market

The moral issues raised by the emerging colonial markets were addressed by Dominican philosopher Tomás de Mercado in his *Suma de tratos y contratos* (1571). Born in Seville, Mercado moved to Mexico, where he was ordained in the Order of Preachers and appointed lecturer of arts at the Convent of Santo Domingo from 1558 to 1562. Later he studied in Salamanca and subsequently taught philosophy, moral theology, and law in Seville. The *Suma de tratos* is considered a classic in economic theory examining topics later addressed by political economists such as Adam Smith, David Ricardo, and others (Beuchot, 1998, p. 68). Mercado based his arguments in Aristotle, Plato, St. Augustine, St. Thomas, and the scriptures. However, it is a hybrid text that addresses both moral and practical issues regarding commercial exchanges. Conceived from a Christian point of view, the *Suma* addressed moral issues related to the market, including usury, restitution, and slavery. For Mercado, natural law, derived from reason, should guide commercial transactions: "Trading with justice is to apply equality and fairness in contracts. Natural law, born of our reason, dictates that we should not wrong anyone" (Mercado, 1975, p. 112; my translation).

The concept of value determined by social conditions is clearly articulated in Mercado's text, thus highlighting the social dimensions of the economy. Citing Aristotle's *Ethics*, Mercado argues that goods are valued because they are useful and needed, a value that may vary from place to place, since not all societies need nor have the same things. In pre Hispanic America, only the Aztecs and the Incas valued gold, but just as a jewel and adornment (*joya y gala*) (Mercado, 1975, p. 158).

In Mercado, we also find the modern notion of civil society, where commercial transactions are seen as social relations determined freely by the individuals themselves as private citizens separate from the state. In chapter 3 of the first book, for example, Mercado distinguishes between legal justice and a universal notion of justice (Mercado, 1975, pp. 113–19).

Additionally, in the second book of the *Suma de tratos*, Mercado devotes one chapter to the Portuguese slave trade in Cape Verde (chapter 20). According to Mercado, it is licit to capture or sell blacks or any other people for reasons such as war, public crimes, as well as the parents' rights to sell their children out of necessity. If the Africans are tricked or forced into slavery in other unjust ways, Mercado advocated for liberation and restitution (Mercado, 1975, p. 280). In the legality of slavery, Mercado coincided with Salamanca scholar Francisco de Vitoria. For Vitoria, the Portuguese could buy those enslaved by Africans themselves, without imputing their conscience. At any rate, for Vitoria and Mercado, the slaves, as any other human being, had to be treated justly (Zavala, 1947, p. 104).

Alonso de Sandoval and African slavery

A more substantial philosophical inquiry about slavery was written in the seventeenth century by the Jesuit Alonso Sandoval (Seville 1576–Cartagena de Indias 1652), bishop of Lima and later of Cartagena de Indias. In *De instauranda Aethiopum salute* (1626), Sandoval examined critically ancient and biblical knowledge about Africa and the world in general. The treatise sought to provide information about African cultures for evangelization purposes, in particular addressing the needs for preaching to those brought to the Indies as slaves. Sandoval cites Acosta and it is clear that both *De procuranda* and the *Natural and Moral History* provide the general framework for writing the *De instauranda*. Sandoval initially described Africans as lawless barbarians, in the Aristotelian sense: "All these nations live in the jungle as savages, without agriculture, without order in their republics, without laws and any human bond, living in caverns and holes in the ground, sustaining themselves with roots, wild fruits, and the flesh and blood of wild beasts" (Sandoval, 1956, p. 14).

However, for Sandoval not all African slaves were inferior beings. He stated that some were capable of understanding the mysteries of the Catholic faith: "Not all are incapable or without reason" (Sandoval, 1956, p. 198; my translation). Thus, he argued that they could and should be evangelized. Furthermore, he suggested that it was the owners' responsibility to care for the physical and spiritual wellbeing of their slaves (Sandoval, 1956, p. 193). Clearly, Sandoval came far from questioning slavery as an institution. The rigor of the scholastic tradition was used to justify the colonial order, albeit advocating for a much more humanitarian treatment of slaves. Much was at stake, since the Jesuit order was one of the largest property owners in colonial Latin America, whose lands were cultivated by considerable numbers of African slaves.

The issue of slavery also was discussed by many other colonial thinkers. Las Casas, for instance, in the *History of the Indies* had suggested the importation of African slaves to replace Indian labor in the Indies. He later reconsidered his position and condemned slavery (Zavala, 1947, p. 104). In 1682, Capuchin friar Francisco José de Jaca wrote *Relación sobre la libertad de los negros*, in which he strongly criticized slavery: "Nature created us free and no one as a slave." Thus, "Slavery is against rational nature" (cited in Marquínez Argote & Beuchot, 1996, pp. 147–8; my translation). For the most part, slavery would remain basically unquestioned in colonial Latin America, even by eighteenth- and nineteenth-century intellectuals who proclaimed the French declaration of the Rights of Men.

III.   Post Conquest Indigenous Perspectives

The European Middle Ages coincides with the time of the classic Maya civilization, when large city states such as Copán and a sophisticated culture flourished in what are present-day Mexico, Guatemala, Honduras, and Belize. The Maya and later the Aztecs and the Incas developed substantial intellectual traditions, cultivated in a variety of media, including pictograms, textiles, pottery, oral poetry, and songs. For example, the renowned scholar in Aztec culture, Miguel León-Portilla, has drawn attention to the rich corpus of pre-Hispanic texts reflecting on the world and human existence. They include accounts of the ages of the world or "suns"; descriptions of the earth and the spheres of the cosmos or "cemanahuac"; as well as doctrines about the god of duality, "Ometéotl," and the concept of enclosure and unity or "Tloque Nahuaque." An established tradition of native thinkers known as "Tlamatinime" or "those who know something" has left us a number of concepts such as "flower and song," "face and heart," "dream and root" that may be considered a developing philosophy (León-Portilla, 1966, p. 5). A well-known tlamantinime is Nezahualcóyotl, a fifteenth-century poet from Texcoco. Nazahualcóyotl's poems reflecting about the transient human existence are clearly classic American texts: "Not forever on earth; / only for a short time here" (León-Portilla, 1966, p. 33).

Considered idolatries by Spanish missionaries, most of the pre-Hispanic intellectual legacy was systematically destroyed and only a fraction of that knowledge survived. For example, in his *History of Yucatan*, sixteenth-century Franciscan historian Diego de Landa (1524–79) reported burning hundreds of ancient Maya texts. Only four ancient Maya hieroglyphic texts have survived until today. As a result, our inquiry into native thought traditions is limited to the existing traces of an incomplete corpus.

There are several existing post conquest texts such as the *Cantares Mexicanos*, the Mayan *Books of Chilam Balam* and the *Popol Vuh*, among others, that have been used to reconstruct pre-Hispanic thought. However, their vision of a pre-conquest past cannot be read uncritically, since they are the product of the violent colonial experience. The fact is that post conquest texts are at the crossroads of two colliding intellectual traditions. Thus, more than a vision of the past, post conquest texts offer us a native perspective of the conquest and of Western culture.

The Popol Vuh *and Maya knowledge under Spanish eyes*

The *Popol Vuh* or Council Book is the foundational Maya book narrating events from creation to historical events of the mid-sixteenth century in the town of Quiche, Guatemala. The surviving manuscript is a copy made in 1701 by Dominican priest Francisco Ximénez. The anonymous sixteenth-century native writers announce that they will write the Ancient Word about the origin of everything: "We shall write about this now amid the preaching of God, in Christendom now. We shall bring it out because there is no longer a place to see it" (Tedlock, 1996, p. 63). This clear reference to the conquest and Christian thought expresses a conscious affirmation of Maya knowledge, which was being suppressed under colonial rule. Acknowledging the repressive colonial context, the autochthonous intellectual tradition is surreptitiously affirmed by the anonymous writers: "There is the original book and ancient writing, but the one who reads and assesses it has a hidden identity" (Tedlock, 1996, p. 63). Although lost, the hieroglyphic *Popol Vuh* dates from the classic Maya period (AD 300–600). It was transcribed into alphabetic script in ca. 1550 by three Maya lords who most likely were taught to write alphabetically by Spanish missionaries. In this context, the secret retelling of the *Popol Vuh* may be read as an act of resistance to Christian thought and the Spanish colonization.

Drawing from a rich oral narrative tradition, the *Popol Vuh* offers a number of entertaining stories about creation, mythic heroes, and the first humans that unfold apparently quite easily and straightforwardly. However, its highly symbolic narrative condenses numerous aspects of the Maya worldview, presenting a multilayered native knowledge (botanical, astronomical, geographical, historical, etc.), that requires sophisticated competence in Maya culture. For example, character names such as One Hunahpú, One Death, One Monkey, allude to the different Maya time-reckoning schemes such as the 260-day divinatory calendar or the Venus calendar (Tedlock, 1996, pp. 205–9). The ball game of One and Seven Hunahpú, for instance, "corresponds to the appearance of Venus as the morning star on the day that bears their name" (Tedlock, 1996, p. 207). The *Popol Vuh* can also be read as a moral treatise, where arrogant figures such as Seven Macaw and cruel beings such as the wood people are destroyed. Furthermore, the text offers a political commentary on the unjust colonial relations, where the idealized images of benevolent and just pre-Columbian Maya lords are an implicit critique of the abuses suffered under the Spanish. Maya lords were truly valued and respected, and did not take vassals by force (Tedlock, 1996, p. 186).

An asymmetric intercultural dialogue: Fray Bernardino de Sahagún and the native informants of the Florentine Codex

Composed of pictograms and Nahuatl text, the *Florentine Codex* provides one of the most comprehensive descriptions of Aztec culture. It was produced by the native informants of the Franciscan friar Bernardino de Sahagún (1500–90) for his *General History of the Things of New Spain* (1577). The *Florentine Codex* is the product of the multilingual intercultural dialogue that occurred at the school for the natives that the Franciscans founded in Tlatelolco, Mexico, based on the *Calmecac*, the pre-Columbian school for the Aztec elite. The Tlatelolco students learned Spanish, Latin, and the Aztec pictographic tradition. The result of this collaboration is twelve books providing detailed information on Aztec religion, daily life, medical and botanical knowledge, native arts, philosophy, and history. However, the intellectual project was supervised and controlled by the Franciscans, who considered that knowledge of Aztec culture was necessary for the evangelization of the natives. More important, as Walter Mignolo has pointed out, the organization of the twelve books of the *Florentine Codex* is most likely based on Western sources such as Pliny and Bartholomaeus Anglicus, and discards the native scheme for the organization of knowledge (Mignolo, 1995, p. 194). For historian Serge Gruzinski, in contrast, initiatives such as the *Florentine Codex* bring together diverse intellectual traditions in a highly innovative process where new, hybrid cultural forms of expressions are created. At any rate, the detailed information about native beliefs and customs included in the *Florentine Codex* and the intercultural dialogue that the school fostered seemed to be too controversial for the times. As a result, the *Florentine Codex* was censored along with Sahagún's *General History*.

Felipe Guamán Poma's Andean perspective of the world

Felipe Guamán Poma de Ayala (ca. 1530–ca. 1616) was a native Andean intellectual who wrote a long letter addressed to Philip III in 1615 providing detailed information about the Andean world and denouncing colonial abuses by Spaniards, priests, and government officials. Written around 1615–16 in Spanish with Quechua commentaries and accompanied by a collection of illustrations, the *First New Chronicle and Good Government* was not published until the twentieth century. The *New Chronicle* seeks to bring together the Christian creation story (part 1), the Spanish conquest (part 2), and the ages of the Indians (part 3). According to Guamán Poma, he based his chronicle on a variety of sources including "*quipus* and reports in many languages, together with Castilian–Quechua, Inca, Aymara, Puquina Colla, Canche, Cana, Charca, Chinchaysuyu, Andesuyu, Collasuyu, Condesuyu, all the speech of the Indians" (Poma de Ayala, 2006, p. 7). As a clear refutation of colonial views about the Indians, Guamán Poma argued that Andean people were not barbarians, but a civilization with clear and reasonable laws and forms of government. He gives a detailed description of the ordinances given by Topa Inca Yupanqui and his royal council (Poma de Ayala, 2006, pp. 57–68). In his defense of Andean civilization, Guamán Poma follows las Casas's *Treatise of Twelve Doubts* (1564), which advocated the restoration of Inca sovereignty.

Guamán Poma de Ayala's critical view of colonialism is most significant when examined in contrast to the perspective provided by Acosta. Guamán Poma questions the moral inferiority of the Incas asserted by Acosta and the progress brought by the Spanish conquest, since Andean people are presented as dutifully worshiping their gods and following the Ten Commandments (Poma de Ayala, 2006, p. 28). As Rolena Adorno has argued, the illustrations of the *New Chronicle* place corrupt colonial officials off the center of the painting, suggesting a world out of balance and justice, conceptualized by the Andean notion of "the world upside down" (Adorno, 1986, pp. 80–119). In addition, as critic Walter Mignolo has highlighted, Guamán Poma's illustrations of the world, in particular two drawings titled "mapamundi" and "pontificial mundo," offer an Andean perspective that challenges the colonial image of the world being produced by the imperial mapping project known as the *Relaciones geográficas*. The *Relaciones* were a set of questionnaires inquiring about every aspect of each province in the Indies, including its history, natural resources, population, and native customs, commissioned by Philip II around 1570 (Mignolo, 1995, p. 308).

We selected the above three post conquest native texts primarily because, in certain way, they contested the barbarian image of the Indians and affirmed native intellectual traditions under a repressive colonial order, an asymmetrical context they expressly or tacitly address. These texts are part of a larger archive that could include figures such as Inca Garcilaso de la Vega, Joan de Santa Cruz Pachacuti Yamqui, Fernando de Alva Itlilxóchitl, Fernando Alvarado Tezozomoc, and others. It is an intellectual tradition neglected by a philosophical curriculum concentrated on continental philosophy and intellectual thinkers writing in European languages (Latin, Spanish, Portuguese, French, or English). Such a curriculum is not sufficient for a continent with more than 400 indigenous languages and significant collections of pre-Hispanic and colonial indigenous documents and artifacts such as the Andean *quipus* or the Mesoamerican codices containing the millenarian intellectual traditions of the Americas.

IV.   Creole Perspectives: Two Seventeenth-Century Intellectuals

Based on the Iberian notion of purity of blood, colonial society established a social hierarchy that placed Spaniards and those of Spanish descent at the top, with Indians, Africans, and mixed-blood people occupying the lower ranks. Access to higher education was limited to whites, who had to document their family's "good" origin to enter schools and universities. By the seventeenth century, a growing number of educated Creoles (American-born whites) began articulating new perspectives about the Indies and the colonial experience. Distant from the metropolis and its prestigious learning centers and facing issues particularly related to the colonial experience in America, the Creole thinkers ambivalently sought to affirm their place in an asymmetrical intellectual field divided by the Atlantic. The Creoles' awareness of such conditions determining access to, and the production of, knowledge resulted in the development of a proto nationalist intellectual tradition that has been studied recently by various scholars included in the edition prepared by José Antonio Mazzotti (2000) among others. In this section, we will look at two seventeenth-century Creole thinkers, Sor Juana Inés de la Cruz and Carlos de Sigüenza y Góngora.

Sor Juan Inés de la Cruz and women intellectuals in colonial Latin America

Formal education for women in colonial Latin America was imparted only in female convents and only at basic levels. Under supervision of church officials and male confessors, women were encouraged to study and write. As a result, there is a considerable corpus of texts of women religious intellectuals including Francisca Josefa del Castillo, Gerónima de Nava, Ursula Suárez, and many others, as Electa Arenal and Stacy Schlau have shown in *Untold Sisters: Hispanic Nuns in Their Own Works* (1989).

One of the colonial women writers that more clearly articulated the asymmetrical conditions for women's intellectual work in colonial society is Juana Ramírez de Asbaje or Sor Juana Inés de la Cruz (Mexico 1651–95). A prolific and recognized poet and playwright, Sor Juana got involved in a dispute with church officials on women's right to knowledge that left us a remarkable proto feminist text known as "The Answer to Sor Filotea." Known for her vast knowledge in literature, music, history, astrology, and other fields, and for possessing one of the largest libraries in colonial Latin America, Sor Juana also wrote several poems addressing philosophical topics. We will

45

begin discussing the "Answer," and then we will pay close attention to "First Dream," a long, philosophical poem about the limits of human knowledge.

With an established reputation as a literary author and intellectual figure, Sor Juana participated in the Mexican intellectual debates of the time. In 1690, Sor Juana ventured into a theological discussion, a realm historically reserved for men. For this reason, she was publicly reprimanded by the Bishop of Puebla, Manuel Fernández de Santa Cruz. Without her approval, the Bishop published Sor Juana's "Letter Worthy of Athena," an essay against a well-known sermon, written some forty years earlier by the Portuguese Jesuit Antonio Vieira. Sor Juana challenged Vieira's view that Christ's greater gift to humanity (*finezas*) was the love for others. For Sor Juana, Christ's greatest gift to humanity was freedom. However, the real issue for the Church officials seemed to be a woman's incursion into theology. Thus, under the pen name of Sor Filotea, the Bishop admonished Sor Juana to abandon such improper intellectual pursuits for a religious woman who should be dedicated to the service of God.

Sor Juana did not back down. Strategically organized following classical rhetoric conventions, her nearly thirty-five page defense makes the case for women's right to knowledge. According to Sor Juana, God would not have given women intelligence if he did not want them to have access to knowledge. Her defense takes her to challenge canonical readings of the scriptures. Based on Bible scholar doctor Arce, Sor Juana adds her own commentary to Paul the Apostle's dictum *mulieres in Ecclesiis taceant, non enim permittitur eis loqui* [Let women keep silence in the churches, for it is not permitted them to speak] (Cruz, 1994, p. 80). Arce considered that women should not lecture publicly but could and should be encouraged to study and write privately. Sor Juana adds:

> Clearly of course, [Arce] does not mean by this that all women should do so, but only those whom God may have seen fit to endow with a special virtue and prudence, and who are very mature and erudite and possess the necessary talents and requirements for such a sacred occupation. And so just is this distinction that not only women, who are held to be so incompetent, but also men, who simply because they are men think themselves wise, are to be prohibited from the interpretation of the Sacred Word, save when they are the most learned, virtuous or amenable intellect and inclined to the good. (Cruz, 1994, p. 81)

In this way, Sor Juana leveled the gender imbalances in the realm of knowledge. Intellectual capacity and competence were the primary conditions for the production of valid knowledge. And wittingly, Sor Juana remarked that all topics were worthy of academic pursuit to reveal the secrets of nature, observing the patterns of how a children's top spins or how sugar reacts to water when cooking: "Had Aristotle cooked, he would have written a great deal more" (Cruz, 1994, p. 75).

Also remarkable in Sor Juana's defense is her own inscription into a women's intellectual tradition. In the "Answer" Sor Juana cited forty-two exemplary women from different historical eras, including Debora, Esther, Hannah, the Sibyls, Minerva, Zenobia, Hypatia, St. Catherine of Alexandria, St. Gertrude, Queen Isabel, and St. Theresa de Avila. Considering the genealogies of the region's intellectual traditions, it is not surprising that Sor Juana herself has become an iconic intellectual for many generations of Latin American writers and thinkers such as Rosario Castellanos, Octavio Paz, Elena Poniatowska, and Margo Glanz.

46

Sor Juana's poetry has rich philosophical reflections. In the "Answer," she mentions her "First Dream," a poem examining the conditions for human knowledge, inspired in Hermetics, which combined astrology, alchemy, mechanics, optics, music, cabala, and other esoteric sciences to reveal the secrets of the universe. Sor Juana draws in particular from the work of Jesuit Athanasius Kircher (1602–80).

"First Dream" represents the search for truth. Released from bodily restraints, the soul attempts to gain full understanding of the cosmos. Blinded by the light, the fragile human soul fails to achieve the all-encompassing platonic or mystic vision. Next, following Aristotelian categorization, the soul seeks to understand the world starting from the simplest natural phenomena up. This path fails too, since the soul is unable to fully understand how even a simple flower blooms. The poem ends with the awakening of the body, suggesting that the senses are the basis for empirical knowledge of the world. As a baroque poem with many esoteric references, "First Dream" offers an elaborate reflection on knowledge. Critic Jean Franco suggests that through mythic references, Sor Juana reflects on the ethical implications of the search for truth. Nictimene and other night figures in the poem represent the appropriation of the knowledge/labor of others. Nictimene, according to classical mythology, was turned into an owl for committing incest. In Sor Juana's poem, Nictimene steals oil from the votive lamps dedicated to Minerva, goddess of wisdom. In contrast, the poem mentions other mythical figures associated with the light such as Arethusa, Venus, and Phaeton. These luminous figures offer other alternatives in the search for knowledge, not without its dangers, such as Phaeton's ambitious attempt to drive the sun's chariot or Venus's vanity. From this perspective, Arethusa's journey to Pluto's underworld to redeem Persephone represents a more ethical search for knowledge. As Franco has noted, there is also a critique of the masculine search for knowledge, stressed at the end of the poem, which strategically ends with a gendered, feminine subject of knowledge that was undetermined throughout the text until the last line: "And I awake" ("y yo despiert*a*") (In Spanish, the "a" of "despierta" corresponds to a female poetic voice).

Carlos de Sigüenza y Góngora and the ambivalences of creole proto-nationalisms

A contemporary of Sor Juana, Carlos de Sigüenza y Góngora (Mexico 1645–1700) was a prolific scholar and literary writer whose broad intellectual interests also include geography, astronomy, mathematics, and Aztec history. He was ordained as a Jesuit in 1662 but expelled from the order in 1667 for multiple night escapades. Sigüenza later studied theology at the University of Mexico, where he was appointed Chair of Astrology and Mathematics in 1672. We will concentrate on two aspects of his intellectual work. We will examine how, as many other Creole intellectuals, Sigüenza articulated a proto nationalist discourse that ambivalently appropriated indigenous knowledge, idealizing Columbian society, but showing disdain for contemporary Indians. Next, we will discuss his participation in a polemic with Mexican and European scholars about a comet that appeared in Mexico in 1680. In this dispute, Sigüenza would demonstrate his familiarity with modern scientific methods.

Sigüenza's proto-nationalist discourse is one of the early expressions of an Indian identity of the Latin American regions, a trait in Latin American thought that would

47

reach its highest point in the early twentieth-century *indigenismo* movement, which is associated with the Mexican Revolution and figures such as the Mexican muralist Diego Rivera, Nobel laureate Miguel Angel Asturias from Guatemala, and the Peruvian Jose Carlos Mariátegui.

The proto-nationalist inscription of the landscape is evident in Sigüenza's bucolic poems "Primavera Indiana" (1664) dedicated to the Virgin of Guadalupe, and "Parayso Occidental" (1683). However, it is in his *Teatro de virtudes políticas que constituyen a un príncipe* where we find more evident the problematic Creole appropriation of Aztec history. The *Teatro de virtudes* provides the script and design for a temporary arch of triumph destined to celebrate the arrival of Viceroy Conde de Paredes to Mexico in 1680. As the humanist princely manuals of the Renaissance, the *Teatro* provided advice to the incoming viceroy with idealized portraits of virtuous pre-Hispanic Aztec rulers such as Montezuma and Cuauhtémoc, who are paired with Tito, Cato, and other great rulers of antiquity. This idealized vision of a pre-Hispanic past contrasts with the contemptuous image of the Indians that Sigüenza expressed a decade later in his *Alboroto y motín de los indios de México*, about an urban riot due to a short supply of food to Mexico City.

Sigüenza's modern scientific views are present in his texts about the comet seen in 1680. Refuting popular belief that the comet was an evil omen, in 1681 Sigüenza published *Manifiesto filosófico contra los cometas despojados del imperio que tenían sobre los tímidos*. Martin de la Torre, a Flemish resident in Campeche, Mexico, answered to Sigüenza in his *Manifiesto cristiano en favor de los cometas*. Sigüenza in turn answered with a text, now lost, entitled *Belerofonte matemático contra la quimera astrológica de Don Martín de la Torre*. Having recently arrived in Mexico from Germany, Father Eusebio Francisco Kino (or Kuhn), a Jesuit scholar, joined the polemic, siding with de la Torre with a text titled *Exposición astronómica*. Sigüenza's final contribution was his *Libra astronómica y philosophica*, which was not published until 1690. In *Libra*, Sigüenza offers a well-documented text demonstrating his familiarity with the most recent thinkers such as Descartes, Gassendi, Galileo, and Kepler (Beuchot, 1998, p. 117). According to Beuchot, the value of Sigüenza's critique is that he bases his claims by means of experimentation, logical argumentation, and a rigorous application of the scientific method. Knowledge is not based on authorities but reached by experience (Beuchot, 1998, p. 119). Thus, Sigüenza represents a significant rupture with the predominant scholastic tradition. In the final analysis, Sigüenza's interest in the pre-Columbian past and modern thought expresses a predicament faced by many Latin American intellectuals who have sought to reconcile the region's search for an identity rooted in its indigenous traditions and their role of as importers and brokers of modern thought.

V.   The American Experience of the Enlightenment

Although the eighteenth century has received less critical attention than the sixteenth, it is a century of profound social and political transformations and significant cultural activity in colonial Latin America. The Enlightened ideas of progress, wealth, liberty, equality, fraternity were tested on the ground by colonial intellectuals who had to face the marked social inequalities and racial discrimination of the colonial society at home and increased pressures for reform from the metropolis. In the context of a European economic expansion, scientific inquiry and commercial interests coincide to provide a new look at the natural resources of the Indies.

Under the Bourbons, the Spanish Crown sought to implement a series of economic and political reforms seeking to increase agricultural production and transatlantic trade as well as exerting greater control of the colonial administration. Seeking a better assessment of the colonies' natural resources, population, and infrastructure, the Crown financed several scientific expeditions and commissions such as Charles Marie de la Condamine's expedition to Quito in 1737. Accompanying la Condamine were two Spanish officials, Jorge Juan (1713–73) and Antonio de Ulloa (1716–95), who wrote *Noticias secretas de América* (1749), a confidential report on the state of the colonies based on their travels. Similar initiatives such as the Royal Botanical Expedition to New Granada (1783–1808) and the visit of Alexander von Humboldt (1769–1859) to the Indies (1799–1804) made a significant impact on the academic culture of the region, promoting a renovated curriculum based on the experimental and exact sciences, and challenging the traditional scholastic education. In such contexts, it is important to consider the impact of the expulsion of the Jesuit order in 1767, whose *colegios* and universities were the leading educational institutions of the region. The expulsion of the Jesuits left a significant vacuum in the intellectual field of the region. But the establishment of Royal Universities and libraries (with the confiscated collections of the Jesuits) created the conditions for a new intellectual culture that included literary salons and academies such as the Sociedades de Amigos del País where elite culture met to discuss a variety of topics including politics, the economy, and literature. In these associations, a strong opposition to colonial rule was developed, and it would eventually lead to the national independence movements.

The eighteenth-century scientific expeditions have also been considered a second conquest of America. In *Imperial Eyes* (1992) Mary Louise Pratt argues that the natural sciences of the Englishmen provided a new framework to map the natural resources of the world that go hand in hand with the emerging industrial capitalism. For example, the classificatory system established by Carl Linnaeus in his *Systema naturae* (1735) made possible an unprecedented inventory of the economic potential of American flora and fauna. Thus, eighteenth-century expeditions express European scientific and commercial interests of global reach, representing a new planetary consciousness (Pratt, 1992, p. 15).

Francisco Javier Clavijero and the New World dispute

Francisco Javier Clavijero (Mexico 1732–Bologne 1787) was among the Creole Jesuits that made significant contributions related to Latin America from exile. Like the Chilean Juan Ignacio Molina (1740–87) who wrote the *Compendio della storia geografica, naturale e civile del regno de Chile* (Bologne 1776) and the *Historia del Reino de Quito en la America Meridional* (1789) written by Juan de Velasco (1727–92), Clavijero also wrote in Italian a history of the lost homeland, the *History of Mexico* (Cesena, 1780–1). These American intellectuals engaged in a well-known dispute, studied by Antonello Gerbi and more recently by Jorge Cañizares-Esguerra (2002), with French scientists George-Louis Leclerc (Buffon) and Cornelius de Pauw, and the Scottish historian William

Robertson. These European intellectuals made some striking derogatory comments about American nature and its population, based on climatic determinism, hearsay, and sheer ignorance. For example, American plants and animals were supposedly smaller and weaker than their European counterparts because of the excessive humidity of the region and the alleged short age of the continent. Regarding its native cultures, the French intellectuals, based on la Condamine's travel account, suggested that indigenous people of America were incapable of abstract thought. "The languages of America, says M. de Paw, are so limited, and so scarce in words, that it is impossible to express any metaphysical idea in them. In no one of those languages can they count above the number of three" (Clavijero, 1979, I: p. 394). Proficient in Nahuatl and familiar with numerous Aztec codices, Clavijero wittingly pointed out the conceptual intricacies of Aztec thought, their sophisticated calendars, and numerical system. In his *History of Mexico*, Clavijero provided a table with Nahuatl concepts for counting from 1 to 48,000,000 and a list of Nahuatl concepts such as unity, trinity, eternity, time, soul, mind, knowledge, thought, reason, doubt, truth, love, virtue, prudence, justice, patience, humility, etc. (Clavijero, 1979, I: pp. 395–9).

In his *Physica particularis* (ca. 1765) Clavijero presents the modern conception of the cosmos, assessing the magnitude and shape of the Earth, and the Ptolemaic and Copernican views of the universe. He examines celestial objects and phenomena such as the stars, the moon, comets, and eclipses. In the last part of the text he examines the human body, its internal systems, the senses, and faculties. As Beuchot has noted, his *Suma* tries to reconcile his scholastic methodology with modern thought (Beuchot, 1998, p. 159).

José Celestino Mutis and the Royal Botanical Expedition to New Granada

One of the most comprehensive early modern scientific expeditions was the Royal Botanical Expedition to New Granada (1783–1808). Under the direction of José Celestino Mutis (Cadiz, Spain 1732–1808), the Botanical Expedition produced a plant collection of more than 20,000 species, 5,000 detailed paintings, an observatory, and several documents regarding the population, climate, and natural resources of the region. Trained in medicine, Mutis arrived in New Granada in 1760. He was appointed chair of mathematics at the Colegio del Rosario in Bogotá, where he participated in a well-known public dispute with Thomist scholars on the Copernican perspective of the universe (Marquínez Argote & Beuchot, 1996, p. 161). In his *Elementos de filosofía natural* (1764) Mutis advocates for modern science. Based on a scientific method and reason, the natural sciences could provide insights into the work of the Creator as well as useful, practical knowledge (Marquínez Argote & Beuchot, 1996, p. 161). Members of the Botanical Expedition participated in the Independence campaign and became targets of Spanish persecution. All the collections of the Expedition were confiscated and some of its members were executed, including zoologist Jorge Tadeo Lozano and botanist Francisco José de Caldas.

The two thinkers presented in this section, Clavijero and Mutis, illustrate that the Spanish American experience of the Enlightenment articulated a critical reassessment and negotiation of traditional (scholastic) and modern thought. This process was neither an acritical adoption of Enlightened thought and science nor a blank abandonment of the humanist, scholastic tradition. Furthermore, Creole scholars confronted metropolitan thinkers and scientists and adapted modern thought to address local concerns.

Another important issue to consider is that the arrival of Enlightened thought in the Indies coincided with the expansion of a European economy entering the industrial age, needing raw materials and new markets for its manufactured goods. In this context, the scientific expeditions of the period were far from objective and disinterested intellectual endeavors. They were well-orchestrated efforts of a new political economy of the emerging European powers of the moment (French and British imperialisms) which, based on the natural sciences, were able to produce an unprecedented inventory of the planet's natural resources.

Colophon

The authors and issues discussed here make it evident that Latin America can offer multiple reflections on the colonial experience of modernity. The three centuries of Iberian rule were a traumatic experience that has been revisited often by Latin American intellectuals of all times, who have turned to the colonial period to understand the historical processes that have shaped contemporary Latin American society. Faced with the marked social inequalities that persist in the region, Latin American intellectuals today are questioning if colonialism has ever ended at all.

Related chapters: 1 Pre-Columbian Philosophies; 2 The Rights of the American Indians; 16 Language and Colonization; 22 Philosophy, Postcoloniality, and Postmodernity; 24 Latin American Philosophy.

References

Acosta, J. (1996). *De procuranda indorum salute* (2 vols.). (G. S. McIntosh, Trans.) Scotland: Tayport.

Acosta, J. (2002). *Natural and moral history of the Indies.* (F. Lopez Morillas, Trans.). Durham: Duke University Press.

Adorno, R. (1986). *Guamán Poma. Writing and resistance in colonial Peru.* Austin: Texas University Press.

Arenal, E., & Schlau, S. (1989). *Untold sisters: Hispanic nuns in their own works.* Albuquerque: University of New Mexico Press.

Beuchot, M. (1998). *The history of philosophy in colonial Mexico.* Washington, DC: Catholic University of America.

Cañizares-Esguerra, J. (2002). *How to write a history of the New World.* Stanford: Stanford University Press.

Clavijero, F. (1979). *The history of Mexico.* (C. Cullen, Trans.). New York: Garland.

Cruz, S. J. (1994). *The answer/la respuesta.* (E. Arenal & A. Powell, Eds). New York: The Feminist Press at the City University of New York.

Dussel, E. (1995). *The invention of the Americas.* (M. Barber, Trans.). New York: Continuum.

Fernández de Oviedo y Valdés, G. (1959). *Historia general y natural de las Indias* (5 vols.). (Juan Pérez de Tudela Bueso, Ed.). Madrid: Biblioteca de Autores Españoles.

León-Portilla, M. (1966). Pre-Hispanic thought. In *Major trends in Mexican philosophy* (pp. 2–56). Notre Dame, IN: University of Notre Dame Press.

Marquínez Argote, G., & Beuchot, M. (1996). *La filosofía en la América colonial.* Bogotá: Arte y Folio.

Mazzotti, J. A. (Ed.). (2000). *Agencias criollas.* Pittsburgh: Instituto de Literatura Iberoamericana.

Mercado, T. (1975). *Suma de tratos y contratos.* (R. Sierra Bravo, Ed.). Madrid: Editora Nacional.

Mignolo, W. (1995). *The darker side of the Renaissance.* Ann Arbor: University of Michigan Press.

Nuccetelli, S. (2002). *Latin American thought: philosophical problems and arguments.* Boulder, CO: Westview Press.

O'Gorman, E. (1961). *The invention of America.* Bloomington: Indiana University Press.

Paz, O. (1961). *The labyrinth of solitude.* New York: Grove Press.

Poma de Ayala, G. (2006). *The first new chronicle and good government.* (D. Frye, Trans.). Indianapolis, IN: Hacket.

Pratt, M. L. (1992). *Imperial eyes: travel writing and transculturation.* New York: Routledge.

Sahagún, F. (1955). *Florentine code: general history of the things of New Spain.* (A. Anderson & C. Dibble, Trans.). Santa Fe, NM: School of American Research.

Saldaña, J. J. (Ed.). (2006). *Science in Latin America: a history.* Austin: University of Texas Press.

Sandoval, A. (1956). *De instauranda Aethiopum salute.* Bogotá: Biblioteca Presidencia de la República.

Sigüenza y Góngora, C. (1984). *Seis obras.* (I. Leonard, Ed.). Caracas: Ayacucho.

Tedlock, D. (Trans.). (1996). *Popol Vuh. The Mayan book of the dawn of life.* New York: Touchstone.

Zavala, S. (1947). *La filosofía política de la Conquista de América.* México: Fondo de Cultura Económica.

Zea, L. (1963). *The Latin American mind.* Norman: University of Oklahoma Press.

4

The Emergence and Transformation of Positivism

MERI L. CLARK

Nineteenth-century Latin American positivists argued that the intellectual elite and ruling classes should help their societies to evolve. Social evolution needed stimuli to produce change and quicken improvement. State education was a common answer of the positivists. Many analyzed their colonial and national histories to show that revolutions appeared to induce change, but had thwarted real progress. Latin American positivists believed that political transformations did not modify society immediately, if at all. If the positivist aspiration was to engineer a better society, then abrupt revolutionary change was a necessary but insufficient condition to do so. Social reform was a slower process, motivated by revolution but not fully achieved by it. This long-term social restructuring, as nineteenth-century positivists understood it, was integral to what they considered the "modernization" of Latin America. Questions lingered as they grappled with the character of Latin American republics. Did Latin Americans require such vigorous systems of order to achieve progress that dictatorships secured the only path toward industrialization, modernity, and autonomy? Were Latin Americans inherently unsuited to live in "modern," industrialized societies? Was the evolutionary goal of human society really to extend social welfare and ensure justice?

The different contexts of such questions, and their varied answers, will be explored below in the emergence and development of positivism in Argentina, Mexico, Chile, and Colombia. First, the essay identifies the strains of nineteenth-century European positivism that influenced the main ideas of Latin American positivists. Second, the essay compares the development of positivist philosophy in Argentina, Mexico, Chile, and Colombia. The common threads of Latin American positivism were that it emerged from liberal idealism, it transformed into strong state conservatism, and it often helped to justify authoritarianism.

European Positivism through a Latin American Lens

For nineteenth-century positivists, human society could be perfected through the acquisition of knowledge based on scientific study. Positivists rejected religion and metaphysics as pre-scientific thought and maintained that human thought would surpass these. The word "positive" connotes knowledge based on the observable world.

53

Positivism understood knowledge as that which was produced through a systematic scientific study of phenomena; laws were supposed to derive from this study. Positivists cautioned against theology and metaphysics because these tried to move beyond the observed world to reveal first causes and final ends. Positive philosophy could point to general principles underlying scientific observations, but it did not allow metaphysical speculation. Positivists did not draw a distinction between the physical and social sciences: they took them to share the same basic scientific method.

Positivism influenced many fields, including history, sociology, and psychology. The French socialist Claude Henri Saint-Simon (1760–1825) argued that political designs must be rooted in the historical and social sciences. Saint-Simon's work inspired Auguste Comte (1798–1857), who developed the influential model of "positive philosophy." Comte argued that human thought had developed from theological and metaphysical stages toward a final, positive stage in which facts were collected and correlated. He applied the scientific method to society to discover its laws of operation and to diagnose flaws that impeded progress. In this, Comte claimed he had pioneered sociology as the positive study of social structures and development.

British intellectuals like John Stuart Mill (1806–73) cultivated empiricism and positivism in progressive programs of economic, political, and social reform. Later, Herbert Spencer (1820–1903) and his "synthetic philosophy" influenced Latin American education, with varied results in the state and private sectors. Spencer assumed an evolutionary principle that every animal is disposed to make itself into what it will, unless it is maladaptive to its environment. Spencer denied that evolution was a matter of chance. He argued that species and societies adapt in relationship to environments and toward a state of equilibrium. He believed in an attainable, perfected human society and that, in the progress toward that perfection, immorality and evil would disappear. These ideas raised profound concerns for Latin Americans, especially regarding theology. As positivist thought spread in Latin America, conflicts intensified between positivists and their critics – theologians and conservatives – about the role of religious instruction, the nature of faith, and the place of the Catholic Church in national development.

Latin American positivism emerged after a period of competition between scholasticism and Enlightenment philosophies, which led to a break with Spain that the Spanish American elite deemed necessary – if not entirely viable. Soon after independence was consolidated across Latin America in the 1820s, many elites argued that social disorder and political chaos dispensed with the possibility of direct representative governments. European-descended elites worried that enslaved and free peoples of color threatened to overturn their tenuous authority. Positivism developed during this long period of turmoil in concert with elite views that social hierarchy formed the backbone of political and economic progress.

Comtean positivism appealed to Latin American elites facing political turbulence and social disorder during national consolidation. Auguste Comte's "positive philosophy," developed in his *Cours de philosophie positive* (1830–42) and *Système de politique positive* (1851–4) among other works, traveled across the Atlantic after the 1850s. Comte's positivism also represented anti-clericalism and anti-conservative politics to many of his followers and interpreters. These ideas and politics became popular from the 1850s onward, especially in France and Latin America. Brazil adopted positivism in the First Republic (1889–1930); the country's motto became "Order and Progress."

Latin American positivism transformed along the peculiar lines of Latin American social and political development during the civil wars between conservatives and liberals in the second half of the 1800s. Positivism expressed itself most clearly in the appeal for progress and reform through education. Positivism was an elite project, but by the late 1800s it permeated the public sphere through the media, education, policing, and state medical care. This was the result of efforts by nineteenth-century positivists who studied "progress" and the evolution of knowledge, society, and law in order to reform them. By mid-century, many Latin American elites agreed that economic liberalism – free markets with limited or no state intervention – promised the brightest future for Latin America. Ironically, many Latin American states coupled laissez faire economics with strong governments that pursued distinctly conservative social reform projects that were informed by positivist ideas. Hence positivism is most often remembered as a state project of the conservative oligarchs and authoritarian rulers of the late nineteenth century, like Porfirio Díaz (1830–1915) of Mexico or Rafael Núñez (1825–94) of Colombia. These conservative rulers used positivist thought to justify projects that would industrialize, centralize power, and erase identities (regional, ethnic, or racial) that impeded Latin American "evolution."

Nineteenth-century positivism was generally optimistic about the possibility that the scientific method would improve human society. In Latin America, positivism emerged from utilitarianism and utopian socialism. In societies rising from the ashes of war, amalgams of positivism and Catholicism developed in Latin American governments and universities. Elites wanted to establish national sovereignty, defend "civilization," and "correct" multiracialism. In the early national period, elites tried different solutions to the puzzles of autonomy. They wanted governments truly independent of Spain and Portugal after 300 years of those empires' political dominion over the Americas. They wanted autonomous economies after centuries of mercantilism. But with disdainful pessimism, many wondered how the indigenous, African, and racially mixed majorities of the Americas would ever govern themselves. Few elites promoted liberal egalitarianism to enfranchise these majorities. Most advanced a liberal economic program (free markets) without democratic pretensions.

American-born elites of Spanish descent (Creoles) struggled to establish their own intellectual, political, social, and economic prestige, but they often fought on European philosophical and political terms. Nineteenth-century thinkers hewed to European models but worked in differently charged political and religious contexts. Some worked in government and law, others in markets and the military, and still others in newspapers and the Catholic Church. Across Latin America from independence to the century's end, these thinkers (the majority of them men) tackled a common project: to improve society and strengthen the nation. Their experiments varied in kind and in relative success.

After an initial hearty embrace, several governments (for example, Colombia) denounced utilitarianism and even banned teaching utilitarian philosophy in academies and universities – specifically, that of Jeremy Bentham (1748–1832). Before the 1820s, most Spanish-American elites knew Bentham's writings only in translation into French. However, these translations were also interpretations that had reduced the complexity of Bentham's original language and had even omitted some of his more radical proposals. After Napoleon's invasion of Spain in 1808, Bentham began to contact elites across Spanish America, eventually proposing to independence leaders that he write the constitutions and legal codes for their future republics. One of Bentham's intentions was to apply the basic principle of utilitarianism – happiness is pleasure and the absence of pain – to reform what he perceived as the cruelest system of old European regimes and their colonial counterparts: the prison.

During the independence wars, liberal elites saw Bentham as a defender of the right to protest tyranny, decry cruelty, and to do so in a free press. At first, revolutionary leaders like Simón Bolívar (1783–1830), the Venezuelan who became the president of Great Colombia (which split into the separate states of Colombia, Venezuela, and Ecuador in 1830), and his vice-president Francisco de Paula Santander (1792–1840) endorsed Bentham's philosophy and welcomed his thoughts on shaping a new republic, independent of the Spanish empire. However, early Latin American leaders did not necessarily advocate the enlistment of specific Benthamite ideas in state policy (Harris, 1998, p. 131). In Argentina, for example, Bernardino Rivadavia (1780–1845) considered several proposals from Bentham about organizing the government (a republic, not a constitutional monarchy), the economy (promote free markets by dropping custom duties), education (limit Church power), and the penal code (a panopticon prison). Rivadavia, like Bolívar in Colombia, instituted many reforms as a state minister and president (1826–7). However, these reforms fit into larger projects of nationalization, centralization, and industrialization that did not stem directly from Bentham's utilitarian philosophy or recommendations. Bolívar, Rivadavia, and others may have used an alliance with Bentham to lend intellectual credibility to the emancipated states of Latin America without having investigated or advocated any of Bentham's schemes (Harris, 1998, pp. 137–9). Bentham was an important icon of liberalism, but Latin American leaders faced so many complicated challenges to their rule that Bentham was jettisoned when gauged politically and economically expedient. Rivadavia, for one, had stopped all correspondence with Bentham by 1825 (Harris, 1998, p. 146).

Utilitarianism and positivism faced the political crossfire in the early national period. The mid-nineteenth century saw bloody battles rage between liberals and conservatives over the political and constitutional character of Latin American states. Early political liberals tended to respect the rights of individuals before states, whereas conservatives privileged the rights of states over individuals. This question became extremely complicated as governments experimented with reforms that dispossessed certain constituencies to promote others, such as a shift in economic support from old landed elites toward new commercial sectors in Colombia, Argentina, and Mexico. In Mexico, landed elites retrenched their economic and political power through longstanding alliances to the Catholic Church, successfully fighting government redistribution of Church property. Across Latin America, the early national schism between liberals and conservatives grew wider because of battles over Catholic Church power: liberals wanted to reduce or eliminate Church power and conservatives wanted to maintain the Church as a partner and authority.

Latin American Positivism

Nineteenth-century Latin American positivism (hereafter, simply "positivism") encompassed a wide range of thought, and many positivists disagreed quite vehemently with each other. Positivism has been poorly defined, in part, because of the eclectic nature of the thinkers who aligned themselves with the philosophy or who were posthumously aligned with it. A distinct shift occurred in intellectual life as the wars against Spain ended and most of the newly independent Latin American nations lurched repeatedly into civil war.

From the 1830s to the 1870s, Latin American intellectuals were usually men who wore many hats in government, academia, the arts, sciences, and commerce. This new generation of intellectuals and bureaucrats, born as citizens of nations not as colonial subjects of a monarchy, turned to European philosophy for aid as their predecessors had. They dwelt on similar anxieties as their colonial forebears, but found that the Enlightenment did not offer satisfactory inspiration and solutions. Like the Spanish Americas, Europe was in flux in the aftermath of the Napoleonic wars. Yet, as never before, elites recognized the need to create their own solutions for problems particular to Latin America. Intellectuals still looked to European philosophy, but they also tried and tested their own ideas.

Positivist philosophy provided ample experimental ground for nineteenth-century Latin Americans. Positivists hold that there are primary causes for extant human society, but these are natural not supernatural causes. Positivism is a deterministic philosophy because it maintains that natural causes produce every observable phenomenon. The purpose of scientific – "positive" – thought is to uncover these natural causes in order to correct the phenomena they produce and promote human progress.

Interesting variants of positivism emerged in Latin America. Orthodox positivists accepted all of Comte's views on society, religion, and science, as did his closest adherent, Pierre Laffitte (1823–1903). Nineteenth-century Brazilians welcomed Comtean philosophy so enthusiastically that they established a church for the "religion of humanity." More influential in Latin America was Comte's student Emile Littré (1801–81), who promoted positivism as a method of attaining and organizing knowledge but who eventually rejected Comte's "religion of humanity" as specious mysticism. On the other hand, empiricist John Stuart Mill refuted Comte's denial of individual freedom, but accepted his philosophy of history.

Comte lived during the upheaval of the French Revolution and Napoleonic Wars, leading him to declare that the primary goal of social reorganization should be to promote progress and ensure order. One of his theses in the sixth book of *Cours de philosophie positive* became central to Latin American positivism:

> The ancients used to suppose order and progress to be irreconcilable; but both are indispensable conditions in a state of modern civilization, and their combination is at once the grand difficulty and the main resource of every genuine political system. No real order can be established, and still less can it last, if it is not fully compatible with progress, and no great progress can be accomplished if it does not tend to the consolidation of order. (Lenzer, 1975, p. 197)

Order and progress became keywords for nineteenth-century Latin American elites. Comte emphasized that the "scientific spirit" and the "spontaneous ability" of "positive politics" would support order and progress. His proposal to achieve this – chiefly, his religion of humanity – did not take off in Spanish America, although in Brazil it did.

57

However, the framework of Comte's evolutionary theory of society and politics caught on across the Americas. Even though most governments found the actual project of reforming society unwieldy or unworkable, many still made the attempt.

Positivists took up Comte's ambitious thesis in different forms, as they also adapted British utilitarian philosophy to their needs. Early national leaders adopted utilitarianism to solve constitutional and legal problems of the new republics. They did not agree on a single constitutional path. Only a few imagined democracies that represented directly the will of the people. Many wanted to temper a strong executive with a legislative or a federated system. Differences in political philosophy broke into war in Argentina, Colombia, and Mexico: centralists fought federalists, liberals fought conservatives, and secularists fought pro-clericalists.

Beyond constitutional battles, Latin Americans struggled over the Catholic Church as an institution and intellectual authority. Elites called for economic progress, political cohesion, and social order, but how were financially precarious governments of uncertain legitimacy to achieve that? The Catholic Church controlled the production and dissemination of knowledge in the colonies for centuries. How were these governments to deal with its intellectual authority and, more importantly, with the material wealth that backed it? Mexico and Colombia tried to appropriate the Church's wealth and authority, but then faced angry reactions from devout Catholics who resented the attack on Church power, the closure of convents, and the removal of priests as teachers. In societies in which Catholicism dominated all other religions, most states pursued diplomatic relations with the Church to ensure that the Vatican recognized their independence.

Catholicism imbued nineteenth-century political and intellectual life. Hence the perplexity, and often outrage, that greeted early positivists who professed atheism. For some positivists in the first phase of its emergence in Latin America, such as José Victorino Lastarria (1817–88) of Chile or Gabino Barreda (1820–81) of Mexico, liberalism applied to economics, politics, and religion alike. In pursuit of the best application of the scientific method to perfecting humanity, these positivists rejected "superstitious" Catholicism for declaring faith a premise of knowledge. Other positivists, such as Mariano Ospina Rodríguez (1805–85) of Colombia, held Catholicism at the core of knowledge and human progress. The feat for these positivists was to reconcile the scientific method to Catholic creed. Positivism allowed a wide scope of interpretation.

Positivists believed that society was in the midst of an evolutionary process and would improve with help from the ruling class, variously defined as the intellectual or government elite or some combination. That process needed stimuli to change and quicken improvement. State education and pro-immigration policies were common proposals. Positivists also critiqued revolution and dictatorship, producing historical analyses of indigenous, colonial, and national societies. They argued that political transformations like revolutions did not modify society. They aspired to engineer better societies in the long term. Abrupt change was a necessary but insufficient condition to do so. Social reform was slow – evolutionary, in positivist terms. Revolutions might stimulate change, but could never achieve full reform. Instead, careful restructuring would "modernize" Latin America. The different social, racial, political, and religious characteristics of their nations posed difficult questions for positivists seeking order, stability, and homogeneity. Their disparate answers in Argentina, Mexico, Chile, and Colombia will be explored below.

Latin American Positivism Compared

Social context is crucial to understanding the varied purposes of positivists. National and local politics and culture shaped positivism through higher education, intellectual networks, and government policy-making. For example, nineteenth-century Argentine liberal idealism wilted under political and intellectual repression by the dictatorial, federalist government of Juan Manuel de Rosas (1793–1877) from 1829 to 1832 and 1835 to 1852. Rosas exiled many important liberal thinkers, including Juan Bautista Alberdi (1810–84) and Domingo Faustino Sarmiento (1811–88). Alberdi and Sarmiento joined an international coalition of exiles that pressured the Rosas regime into collapse. Both liberals, they struggled to achieve the best form of liberalism in its second generation in Argentina. Put together, these two defined the major characteristics of laws and politics in Argentina in the second half of the century.

Alberdi and Sarmiento were early autochthonous positivists. Alberdi articulated crucial political philosophy for his young nation. Returned from exile, in 1852 Alberdi published his most important political treatise, *Bases and Starting Points for the Political Organization of the Argentine Republic* (Alberdi, 2003), which influenced the assembly that drew up the Liberal constitution of 1853. Alberdi argued that Argentina needed strong state institutions before it could truly apply liberal philosophy and reform society through laws.

Sarmiento thought education would erase the troublesome, dilatory qualities of native peoples of Argentina and introduce traits from more "advanced" European nations. He thought Latin Americans were unsuited to liberalism, having lived under Spanish rule for so long. In 1845, this thesis became his most famous book, *Facundo: Civilization and Barbarism* (Sarmiento, 2003). In *Facundo*, industrialization and urbanization oppose the culture of *gauchos* (cowboys) – "civilization" should stamp out "barbarism." Sarmiento spent his life promoting education as a primary means of "progress," but he also wanted foreign capital and immigrants to foster "civilization."

Many positivists believed that state-directed education and immigration would ameliorate the social and racial "degeneration" inherited from the colonial era. As president (1868–74) and education minister (1875, 1881–82), Sarmiento cultivated international relationships and domestic policy that promoted European migration to Argentina. As happened in the United States, Brazil, and Uruguay, large demographic shifts generated unexpected social and political consequences. For example, immigrants hastened the rise of socialism and anarchism among Argentine intellectuals and working classes.

José Ingenieros (1877–1925) embodied the dramatic demographic and intellectual shift in Argentina. Born in Italy, Ingenieros studied medicine and psychology in Argentina, becoming a prominent example of a positivist who voiced socialist concerns. He worked in the Argentinean academy, and became the psychiatric director for the police and director of the Institute of Criminology in Buenos Aires. He published prolifically and was read widely in Europe. Ingenieros worked during the apogee of positivism, when it symbolized modernity, progress, and action. Positivism dominated Argentinean universities at the close of the nineteenth century. Generally, Argentine positivists defended science and anti-clericalism, believed in human perfectibility, and disparaged metaphysics. Ingenieros pushed positivism into historical analysis of

Argentinean thought in *The Evolution of Argentine Ideas* (1918–20). He argued that Argentinean ideas (and politics and society) developed in an evolutionary process in which liberty battled despotism from the first phase of "revolution" that led to "restoration" and closed with an absolutist phase of "organization." The question for Ingenieros, and for Justo Sierra, the positivist historian of Mexico, was whether revolutions created a crisis great enough to provoke a profound break with despotism.

In Mexico, positivism flourished in a different political and economic context than Argentina. From mid-century, Argentine elites directed the fate of domestic policies from immigration to education in a way that was relatively unencumbered by foreign interests besides those they chose. In contrast, Mexicans dealt constantly with civil wars and imperial threats from the Hapsburgs (1864–67) and the United States. In that context, positivism in Mexico commanded more sustained attention from national policy-makers and more deeply affected the state, economy, and society of the country compared to other Latin American nations. Mexican positivism developed, in part, as a survival mechanism in the face of constant threats. After civil wars had torn apart Mexico for years, President Benito Juárez (1806–72) instituted reforms that separated church and state, codified civil marriages, and nationalized Church property. The French war on Mexico interrupted his presidency in 1863 when Juárez ceded the government to Maximilian of Hapsburg. After Maximilian's execution in 1867, Juárez continued his presidency and liberal reforms. He employed Comtean and Spencerian doctrines to direct education reform, appointing Gabino Barreda (1820–81) as minister of education in 1867. Barreda studied with Comte but did not adhere to his dogma, such as the "religion of humanity." He emphasized logic over faith. Barreda wanted the government to teach that political and moral obligations bound Mexicans to each other and to the state. For him, education shaped individual character to promote social improvement. Barreda mandated free public schools, obligatory for children over five, based on the scientific method. This generation of positivist-influenced school children would become the men who led a different set of reforms under Mexican President Porfirio Díaz (1830–1915), whose long dictatorship was called the "Porfiriato" (1877–80, 1884–1911).

During the Porfiriato, the older conception of positivism as a liberal, anti-clerical, and progressive philosophy changed considerably. Porfirio Díaz's rule was marked by the centralization of political power through patronage, repression of dissent, and rapid industrialization built on extensive foreign investment. Positivists working in the state and private sectors helped generate an economic bonanza led by the export sector.

In the 1890s, Justo Sierra (1848–1912), an important positivist, liberal intellectual, proposed far-reaching reforms to the Mexican government. Sierra belonged to a group called the *científicos* (scientists) because they claimed to study "scientifically" political and social problems to craft their reform proposals. At first, the *científicos* presented themselves as critics of the Porfiriato. Sierra and others wanted the government to allow the permanent tenure of judges, freedom of the press, and effective suffrage. These democratic ideas clearly opposed Díaz's centralized power.

This view had changed by the time Sierra analyzed Mexican history in *The Political Evolution of the Mexican People* (1900–2). While he rejected dictatorship, Sierra justified Mexico's historical course from Spanish conquest, political revolution against Spain, Juárez' Reform, French Intervention, and, finally, to the Porfiriato. From his standpoint at fin de siècle, Sierra argued that these were necessary phases in the evolution of genuine Mexican society and identity. Revolutions were anathema to positivists like Sierra. They imagined themselves as the vanguard of reform that would help the government to compel gradual social change, encourage material progress, and realize true independence. "Scientific" education would provide Mexicans with tools to secure material prosperity through industrialization. Once the economic imbalances that produced poverty were removed, and once all Mexicans were equipped intellectually to work in a unified and modern society, only then would Mexico surpass the dictatorial phase and become truly free.

Sierra emphasized slow and orderly progress toward this positivist outcome. He sacrificed liberalism because he argued that Mexicans were not evolved enough to handle the freedoms that liberals espoused. Ironically for this critic of dictatorship, his notion fit well with Díaz's concept of state authority. Soon after the publication of Sierra's history, Díaz appointed him the Secretary of Public Education of Mexico (1905–11). Díaz absorbed many positivists from the *científicos* clique into government administration.

Wealth produced during the Porfiriato did not spread to the majority of Mexicans; only elites and some urban sectors enjoyed the benefits of "modernization." Sierra did not acknowledge, or did not recognize, that discontent with that inequality was gathering force as he wrote *Political Evolution*. Even if he had, Sierra still might have hoped to stem the revolutionary tide through education that promoted moral and economic development. But resentment and dissent culminated in the Revolution of 1910 that saw Díaz flee into exile and, after a decade of civil war, extensive nationalization. The revolution rejected all that the positivist Porfiriato had wrought: deep inequality, failed national education, a foreign-run economy, opportunism, and authoritarianism.

In Chile, positivism emerged in a less repressive context than in early nineteenth-century Argentina and developed in a less turbulent context than late nineteenth-century Mexico. Positivists shaped Chilean education and economy late in the century. The historian José Victorino Lastarria (1817–88) was the earliest proponent of Comtean positivism in Chile, although he claimed to have developed his own positivist theories before reading Comte's *Cours* in 1867. For Lastarria, the spur to action as a positivist came in 1873 when the government yielded to conservatives and allowed Catholic schools to operate without state regulation (Woll, 1976). In protest, Lastarria founded the Academy of Fine Arts, dedicated to promoting scientific education in all disciplines. Vehemently anti-clerical, he called for massive reforms to replace the theology that dominated state practice. Lastarria's positivist writing shaped the interests of his student, Valentín Letelier (1852–1919). Letelier advanced the positivist social sciences in Chile to a much greater degree than did Lastarria.

Letelier proposed that historical analysis should be founded on scientific principles in order to understand the social laws that limited individual will and action. Letelier faced tremendous opposition from Chilean conservatives and the Catholic Church for his "irreligious" portrayal of history in *La evolución de la historia* (1901). He argued that no proof existed for biblical events and geologists had shown that the earth was more than one million years old, so religious history could not be accepted as fact (Woll, 1976). In his view, individuals were products of society and were thus subject to the laws of society, not to divine or human will. Letelier used statistics like marriage and death rates to demonstrate how society should be analyzed scientifically so that the government could decide better policies. One important positivist principle was that society should change gradually. Letelier wanted to show that individuals, no matter how strong and determined, could not change the operation of social laws alone. Thus the state had to make laws to prevent individual errors (such as crime) and reduce the possibility of contradicting social laws. Positivist governments should, Letelier argued, prevent the conditions that caused social diseases like poverty or rebellion.

Colombian positivism bore many of the political and social markings discussed in the other cases, but did not follow a single pattern. Civil wars caused Colombian positivism to lurch between strength and weakness. Liberals and conservatives battled repeatedly to write and defend different constitutions; conservatives triumphed by the 1880s. Political philosophy there, like most of Latin America at the end of the century, stressed institutional before individual development, order before liberty, and markets before mores. Most Latin American positivists grounded philosophical interest in tangible concerns and looked to governments to solve problems. This pragmatic, state-centered gaze distinguishes Latin American positivism from its philosophical siblings globally.

At the end of the century, Colombia turned toward a strong, conservative state under President Rafael Núñez (1880–2, 1884–94). "Regeneration" refers to this conservative era, deriving from Núñez' dictum: "Fundamental administrative regeneration or catastrophe." It marked the zenith of conservative positivism and it fit nicely with the Brazilian motto after 1889: "Order and Progress."

The Regeneration built upon decades of war between Colombian conservatives and liberals. José María Samper Agudelo (1828–88) presents an important example of a Colombian intellectual whose changing politics over the course of the century reflected, in part, the shifting sands of national politics and philosophy. Samper was a journalist, poet, playwright, novelist, essayist, businessman, and politician.

Samper's 1861 "Essay about the Political Revolutions and the Social Condition of the Colombian Republics" is a significant indicator in the shift in his thought from liberal to moderate conservative. Samper voiced the pessimism of positivists like Sarmiento in Argentina or Sierra in Mexico. He thought *caudillismo* – the personalist rule of strongmen called *caudillos*, self-styled as "dictators on horseback" – undermined the achievement of true democracy. Samper criticized the conservative government of Colombia for "governing too much" (Samper, 1980, p. 270). He lamented the surfeit of laws and regulations without a generalized understanding of rights and duties. He faulted historical evolution: colonialism had molded Latin Americans into dismal, monomaniacal law-abiders with no sense of larger political or social purpose (Samper, 1980, p. 268).

While Samper was born in the young republic of Colombia and moved from liberal to conservative positivism over his lifetime, the consummate conservative Mariano Ospina Rodríguez (1805–85) never wavered from a conservative viewpoint. Ospina shaped Colombian law in several government offices and, as a writer, espoused a distinctly conservative positivist philosophy. Ospina argued that only a scientific education would create a homogenous civil society that worked toward progress. Later in life, Samper and his onetime foe agreed that the government should first support efficient, practical, and universal education. Samper and Ospina agreed on schools but disagreed about pedagogy and control.

In Mariano Ospina's view, faith did not contradict science. While Ospina believed that Catholicism was the foundation of a successful, progressive society, Samper did not always equate "civilization" to Catholicism. Even later in life, when Samper had reevaluated his earlier liberalism and rejected some of his youthful ideals, he presented a mixed view of the place of religion in a scientifically organized society.

Education was the most important battleground in the war against irreligion for Ospina. Ospina did not exclude religion from scientific education, but embraced it. He denounced "impious" skeptics and atheists. He wanted to train Catholic clergy in Colombia to become "a Clergy whose science places them on the highest rung of the ladder of civilization," and who could then battle against the "disciplined phalanx of free thinkers" who threatened "Catholicism and, with it, Christian civilization" (Ospina, 1990, pp. 460–1). He criticized the Church and fellow Catholics for their laxity and apathy in the face of threats to religion. Ospina called for an invigorated and pedagogically active Church, one that taught young people to combat heresy and immorality.

As nineteenth-century intellectuals, neither Samper nor Ospina questioned the racism prevalent in their day. They did not consider racist categorizations and hierarchies to be social problems. Indeed, racial theories were central to many positivists' prescriptions for social and political reform. For example, their Mexican contemporary Justo Sierra argued that the "energetic" character of the Spanish enabled Mexicans to be "noble" and "ruthless" in the "struggle to rise" but that Spanish colonialism had stopped Spanish Americans from evolving (Sierra, 1969, p. 131). Like Sierra, Samper did not criticize race-based nationalism. Samper distinguished between "Saxon" and "Latin" characters and accomplishments. He faulted the "Hispanic character" for permitting tyrants to rule in the name of democracy. He identified "ethnic and physical" factors as the root problem with establishing and maintaining democratic republics in Latin America (Samper, 1980, p. 270).

What were these troublesome factors that beleaguered democracies, favored despotism, and promoted the abuse of power? According to Samper, the "jealous, suspicious, and petulant spirit of the political parties of Hispano-Colombia" stemmed from the "social defects" inherent in Latin American societies. He blamed the "petulant and vain Spanish character" for the "notable weakness" of Spain and its American heirs. Samper reproached *mulatos* for even worse temper and conceit, which he attributed to their "mixture with the Spanish and their spirit of imitation" (Samper, 1980, p. 271). The term *mulato* often referred to a descendant of enslaved Africans, but it also indicated a general category including peoples of mixed African, European, and indigenous descent.

Like Alberdi and Sarmiento in Argentina, Samper worried about the distances that separated Latin Americans. Vast, difficult terrain kept Latin Americans from understanding the broader society to which they belonged. Social obligation could temper selfishness, but only if Latin Americans lived in society. Distance promoted an overdeveloped sense of independence that operated as self-interest. In Samper's account, Latin America's "mixed and youthful" society resembled an immature adolescent. Self-absorbed Latin Americans lacked "the spirit of equality, the idea of liberty, and the habit of concurring with a collective enterprise with one's vote, word, or arm, that inspires each citizen to believe in their skill, their capacity, and the need that their fellow citizens have to count on them" (Samper, 1980, p. 271). If they did not communicate better, then Latin Americans would retain divisive regional identities that worked against larger social aims.

63

Samper did illustrate optimism in arguing that racial and geographic "defects" could "one day transform into qualities" (Samper, 1980, p. 271). Sierra similarly analyzed Mexican social and political "evolution" (Sierra, 1969). Their hope in future reform tempered pessimism about the past. For these positivists, inevitable historical forces had shaped society (i.e., Spanish colonization and racial mixing), but those forces could be transformed through a combination of spontaneous actions (i.e., revolution against Spain) and persistent reforms (i.e., public education) that would eventually alter the character of Latin Americans. Thus positivist philosophy offered a practical and forward-looking analysis of history that "scientifically" explained (or constructed) the contemporary world and showed how to avoid a similar fate in the future.

Positivists proposed reforms of contemporary society that depended on state intervention. For instance, Samper recommended several "logical government actions": expand the public school, library, and museum system. Like Alberdi and Sarmiento, he encouraged "European immigration and that from other regions chosen with prudent and liberal criteria in order to strengthen society in its struggle against its most formidable nature and to enlighten, purify, and equilibrate the races and *castas* through the infusion of an active blood that carries the great force of civilization" (Samper, 1980, p. 275). He wanted immigrants to colonize *tierras baldías* (empty lands). But these lands were not always empty of people. Indigenous peoples understood communal property ownership in *tierras baldías*; others held unregistered, contested, or ambiguous land titles. State agencies could, and did, ignore these problems when proposing immigrant colonization projects. Like many positivists, Samper hoped immigrants would bring all regions into better communication and push "wild tribes into civil life" (Samper, 1980, p. 275).

Following the liberal-versus-conservative struggles of this long century, Colombia turned toward the model of a strong state and social order imposed from above, as had Mexico, Brazil, and Argentina. Colombian president Núñez favored centralization, protectionism, and military strength. He thought decades of federalism under Liberals had upset the social order and weakened national politics; the best answer was a strong state, scientific education, and material progress. Colombian thinkers like Samper and Ospina helped to inflect Núñez's rule with positivist concerns.

The Legacy of Nineteenth-Century Positivism in Latin America

Núñez's command to "regenerate" – remake the state and society or face disaster – announced the urgency of positivist reformers in the last quarter of the century. Positivists' metaphors invoked science, medicine, and "Darwinian" evolutionary theory, as shaped primarily by Herbert Spencer. Justo Sierra's historical diagnosis of Mexican politics used such metaphors about the "social organism" (Sierra, 1969). Sierra, Núñez, and other positivists considered how to "cure," or simply eliminate, ailing members of the social organism. Positivists like Ingenieros wrote of their worries about social "diseases" like poverty, alcohol abuse, prostitution, and hoped to help the state to identify the weakest members of society who were prone to such illnesses. Positivists argued that the state, through laws, ought to prevent problems before they emerged. They proposed different remedies for social ills, including mandatory education in reform schools or imprisonment in houses of correction. Positivists did not want to risk human social progress by allowing individual freedom to run amok.

Many Latin American elites aspired to civilization along European lines – imitating everything from technology to fashion – and yet they fretted about losing their original culture and corrupting their genuine national identities. Hence the positivists' dilemma: what *was* the essence of a society so obviously mixed in terms of races, languages, and cultures? Latin American elites were of two minds about Europe: they favored certain influences while deriding others, for instance, contrasting the "civilized" British to the "selfish" Spanish. Many early liberal Latin Americans did not want to trade an old master for a new one. Early conservatives often favored European aid and intervention, as in the case of Rivadavia's approval of British loans to Argentina in the early nineteenth century. After mid-century, foreign investment grew in Argentina and across Latin America, reflecting a political shift toward consensus on free markets.

Not all elites advocated the erasure of indigenous and African society in the Americas. Many would have found such removal impossible to imagine, let alone accomplish, given the majority in countries like Mexico, Brazil, Venezuela, Bolivia, Peru, the Dominican Republic, and Guatemala. Demographics would not stop later racial theorists and eugenicists from trying to engineer a society "purified" of African and indigenous people.

One contrast between nineteenth- and twentieth-century positivism lay in the methods they advocated for such engineering. Some late nineteenth-century positivists backed the racist and quasi-evolutionary "science" that the "weakest" members of society would inevitably disappear because they would not be able to support themselves physically or intellectually during a phase of accelerated industrialization and social change. For these positivists, "weak" groups were usually indigenous, black, or racially mixed. By the twentieth century, a stark difference was the state capacity to annihilate specific categories of people deemed "deficient," "diseased," or otherwise problematic.

Nineteenth-century states across the Americas attacked, deracinated, forcibly restrained, and annihilated indigenous populations. For decades, the Argentine government drove the Araucanian people from their territory on the vast grasslands (*pampas*). This campaign to "subdue Indians" and "conquer" frontier territories paralleled contemporary efforts by the United States government. As president (1868–74), Sarmiento pushed "civilization" to the frontier, pushing Araucanians there too. The expulsion policy gathered force under General Julio Roca (1843–1914), culminating in his vicious "pacification" campaign from 1878 to 1879, or the "Campaign of the Desert" (in Spanish, *desierto* referred to the pampas as deserted lands; they were not deserts). Roca's genocidal attacks on Araucanians secured the large southern frontier for the state and secured the presidency for Roca (1880–6). These brutal and methodical campaigns relied on the state's use of armed cavalries; in the twentieth century, the exterminating capacity of the state took on even more horrific scope.

In the mid-nineteenth century, Latin American liberals had triumphed in several civil wars, yielding federated constitutions and increasingly secularized public education systems. Later national conflicts saw conservatives win, begetting centralist constitutions, strong executives, and schools that reincorporated the tenets and texts of the Catholic Church. By the end of the nineteenth century, Latin American intellectual and political culture tilted dramatically toward conservatism, supplanting classical polit-ical liberalism. Conservatives and liberals came to agree that free markets promised the only secure, prosperous future, and centralized government prevailed.

One unmistakable trend emerged by the end of the 1800s: positivism reigned over the experimental and social sciences. Positivist thought influenced presidents, histor-ians, doctors, sociologists, psychologists, criminologists, and novelists. Positivists heeded the call of governments to promote development and suppress – or, better yet, inhibit – disorder. "Positivism" had come to signify modern, European, scientific, prestigious, and progressive in Latin American academic and policy circles.

Nineteenth-century positivism left a mixed legacy. Positivists had sculpted everything from medical training and historiography to criminology and penal codes. In reaction, many early twentieth-century intellectuals fought the social-racial hierarchies that pos-itivists recommended or imposed through state policies. Others defied the positivist premise that the only valid knowledge was that acquired through the scientific method. Instead they sought truth in spiritualism, one that diverged as much from traditional Catholic religiosity as the scientific method.

Related chapters: 5 Early Critics of Positivism; 6 The Anti-Positivist Movement in Mexico; 7 Darwinism; 8 Krausism; 9 'Normal' Philosophy.

References

Alberdi, J. B. (2003). *Bases y puntos de partida para la organización política de la República Argentina*. Córdoba: El Cid Editor (Original work published 1852).

Harris, J. (1998). Bernardino Rivadavia and Benthamite "discipleship." *Latin American Research Review*, 33:1, 129–49.

Ingenieros, J. (1961). *La evolución de las ideas argentinas*. Buenos Aires: Editorial Futuro (Original work published 1918–20, re-edited 1937).

Lenzer, G. (Ed.). (1975). *Auguste Comte and positivism: the essential writings*. New York: Harper & Row.

Ospina Rodríguez, M. (1990). El catolicismo en Colombia. In D. Wise de Gouzy (Ed.). *Antología del pensamiento de Mariano Ospina Rodríguez* (Vol. I, pp. 456–62). Bogotá: Banco de la República (Original work published 1872).

Samper, J. M. (1980). Ensayo sobre las revoluciones políticas y la condición social de las repu-blicas colombianas. In L. Zea (Ed.). *Pensamiento positivista latinoamericano* (Vol. I, pp. 267–76). Caracas: Biblioteca Ayacucho (Original work published 1861).

Sarmiento, D. F. (2003). *Facundo: Civilization and barbarism; the first complete English translation*. (K. Ross, Trans.). Berkeley: University of California Press (Original work published 1845).

Sierra, J. (1969). *The political evolution of the Mexican people*. (C. Ramsdell, Trans.). Austin: University of Texas Press (Original work published 1900–2).

Woll, A. L. (1976). Positivism and history in nineteenth-century Chile: José Victorino Lastarria and Valentín Letelier. *Journal of the History of Ideas*, 37:3, 493–506.

Further Reading

Katra, W. H. (1996). *The Argentine generation of 1837: Echeverría, Alberdi, Sarmiento and Mitre.* Madison: Fairleigh Dickinson University Press.

Park, J. W. (1985). *Rafael Núñez and the politics of Colombian regionalism, 1863–1886.* Baton Rouge: Louisiana State University Press.

Woodward, R. L., Jr. (Ed.). (1971). *Positivism in Latin America, 1850–1900: are order and progress reconcilable?* Lexington: D. C. Heath and Co.

5

Early Critics of Positivism

OSCAR R. MARTÍ

Toward the end of the nineteenth century two literary figures, José Martí (Cuban, 1853–95) and José Enrique Rodó (Uruguayan, 1872–1917), felt misgivings about some of the main assumptions of positivism and a deep mistrust of its social implications. Positivism is a European doctrine with autochthonous roots that in Latin America had become, by the end of the century, almost an official doctrine. Martí and Rodó believed that positivism considered only the material elements of the world and treated ethics as but a justification for the pursuit of economic gains. Left out were art and poetry, the imagination and ideals, compassion and humanity. Echoing some of these criticisms, philosopher Carlos Vaz Ferreira (Uruguayan, 1872–1958) and scientist José Ingenieros (Argentine, 1877–1925) undertook a revision of the doctrine that led to a reevaluation of the metaphysics it censured and of the ethics it advocated.

European Positivism

Positivism was first conceptualized by Auguste Comte (1798–1857), redefined by John Stuart Mill (1806–73), and reformulated by Herbert Spencer (1820–1903). Common to all was the belief that positive knowledge is strictly derivable from observable events (phenomena), and independent of the imagination; and that it would constitute the foundation of philosophy and the physical and social sciences. Propositions that cannot be derived from experience, such as metaphysical claims about the ultimate nature of reality or the existence of God, etc., are to be excised from philosophy as meaningless. They also held in common the goal of science: to predict and control nature. "Science aims at prediction; and prediction at action" (Comte, 1975, p. 88). Finally, they agreed that the methods of science were well suited to explain and predict individual and social actions, and consequently to improve political, social, economic, and moral conditions.

Comte, Mill, and Spencer disagreed on how philosophy could lead to social action, and on the kind of action needed. In the *Cours de philosophie positive* (Course on positive philosophy, 1830–42), Comte argued that positive science is organized hierarchically from the most abstract – astronomy and physics, to the most concrete – biology and sociology (Comte, 1975, p. 97). Historically, the most abstract sciences developed first, preparing the groundwork for the more concrete ones – a process accounted for by the Law of the Three Stages: science and society progress through three discrete stages, the mythical, the metaphysical, and the positive. The sciences first accept anthropomorphic explanations about nature in terms of gods or deities; they then advance to explanations in terms of causes or forces; and eventually settle into statistical correlations among phenomena as the only possible explanation, thus increasing the accuracy of predictions. Similarly, societies or cultures progress from the autocratic or militaristic stages, through the ecclesiastical or legislative stages, to reach the positive stage, in which technologically advanced societies are run by an elite of trained philosopher-sociologists whose task it is to adduce the operant social laws and employ them for the common good.

Mill generally agrees with Comte about the structure and ends of science, but in *Auguste Comte and Positivism* (1865) he expresses reservations about the means used to achieve those ends and about the kind of society that would emerge from their application. Mill argued that instead of justifying actions in terms of some specific end, such as the instauration of an industrial society, utility should be the criterion – the best actions are those that yield the greatest pleasure and the least pain for humanity. When faced with social problems, a scientist's task is to examine the facts, list the alternatives and their consequences, and formulate the means to achieve them – the choices of which to adopt being left to legislators and the electorate.

Spencer also agreed with Comte about the nature and function of science and philosophy but, in *Reasons for Dissenting from the Philosophy of M. Comte* (1864) and in *First Principles* (1862), took pains to distance himself from Comte's social conclusions. Instead, he argued that all natural processes are subject to the laws of evolution: the gradual change from the simple to the complex, from the homogeneous to the heterogeneous. In nature, organisms are constantly being challenged by the environment and by other organisms. To survive, they must adapt by undergoing suitable internal or external alterations and by passing these new traits to the species. If these changes result in fitter individuals, the species survives; else, it perishes. To avoid begging the question – that the fittest survive because they are fit – Spencer interpreted "fittest" as more complex, stronger, more aggressive, or more cunning individuals. This gladiatorial struggle for survival is a slow process, but always leading to an increase in organism complexity. Societies, like individual organisms, must also conform to the laws of evolution. In competing with other societies for limited resources, societies must increase in complexity and heterogeneity, thus increasing the chances of producing a winning combination. Since the allocation of social resources is the purview of political economy, policies that allow for an unfettered social competition and unobstructed growth, such as laissez-faire, will increase a society's chances of survival.

Latin American Positivism

In Latin America, positivism was originally cultivated to encourage the growth of science, and in the hands of liberals like Gabino Barreda (Mexican, 1818–81), as a weapon for breaking the intellectual stranglehold of a conservative colonial mentality and for refuting the claims of scholasticism and of Church dogma. Comte's positivism appeared first, around mid-century. In Brazil and Chile, it took a definite religious turn; in Mexico, Uruguay, and Argentina it played an important role in educational and economic policies. What was its appeal? First, an alliance with the sciences was meant to give philosophy rigor and a justification, provide it with renewed prestige, and set problems and direction for future discussion. Alternative philosophic viewpoints such as eclecticism or scholasticism, no matter how popular or well entrenched, lacked such strong backing, and offered only beliefs justified by tradition, by abstractions, or by might. Second, positivism offered clear, concrete solutions for solving social problems – for instance, a well-articulated program of general education, the development of science, stimulating industrial growth, fostering national unity by means not of religion but of rational principles. Alternative political views offered only promises based on failed solutions or on the exercise of coercion. Finally, it predicted that in a not too distant future, with the advent of a scientific-industrial society satisfying the material needs of a nation, the right social changes would occur, just as they had in France or Britain. Alternative doctrines offered only otherworldly rewards, the status quo, or a return to colonial dependence on a bankrupt Spain.

Toward the last quarter of the century, Spencer's positivism had replaced in Latin America much of Comte's vision of philosophy. Social evolutionists like Justo Sierra (Mexican, 1848–1912) went further by adding to the doctrine's social promises explanations of and justifications for the social disparity, political backwardness, and widespread poverty in Latin American societies. If these states of affairs were seen at first as marks of backwardness – shameful and in need of change – writers like Domingo Faustino Sarmiento (Argentine, 1811–88) portrayed them as natural phases of the evolutionary development of young societies. In the struggle for survival, these elements would be replaced by the healthier, stronger, more intelligent and aggressive individuals and social wholes that would eventually constitute the backbone of the nation. Anticipating Spencer by ten years, Sarmiento had pointed out, in *Facundo: civilización y barbarie* (Facundo: civilization and barbarism, 1845), the importance of ethnic and geographic factors in the formation of political character. Sarmiento argued that humanity evolves gradually from a bucolic, barbarian state to a complex urban culture – a path Argentina was to travel on the road to civilization. In *Conflicto y armonías en las razas de América* (Conflict and harmony among the races of America, 1883), he finds kinship with Spencerian evolutionist arguments in favor of a radical racism: Latin America's backwardness was due to racial inferiority, to the mixture of Indian, African, and Mediterranean blood. Since improving the racial mixture would engender progress, Sarmiento argued for an unrestricted immigration of northern Europeans to Argentina.

Martí

If positivism had proven to be an intellectually useful tool against scholasticism, many Latin American intellectuals saw some of its assumptions as unsatisfactory and many of its implications as unacceptable. One of the earliest intellectuals to make this appraisal was José Martí. A poet, a writer, and a politician, Martí's output encompasses an enormous range of topics – poetry, literary theory, history, economics, and politics

– all scattered through newspaper and magazine articles, pamphlets and broadsides, plays and children's stories, political speeches and social commentaries, reports, and poems. Though he did not write about philosophy in general or about positivism in particular, he cast doubts over many aspects of the latter, especially in his analysis of Latin America's social problems and in his criticism of racism.

Positivism, social or evolutionary, asserts that the progress of a people can be read in the history of their advancement toward a complex industrial society. This is put forth as the consequence of a cosmic law of progress or evolution. To many, this trajectory shows that Latin American societies are evolutionarily backward, as is evidenced by their social and political circumstances (Sarmiento, 1960, pp. 6–16). Martí took issue with some assumptions and implications of this claim. In "Nuestra América" ("Our America," 1891), he argued against the racism of Spencerians like Sarmiento because they accepted as evidence only immediate material conditions yet ignored historical and cultural factors (Martí, 2002, pp. 289–90). Backwardness in Latin America was a result not of natural development but of political and economic policies imposed by Spain to keep the continent under its control for over 250 years, and in the past century, of the efforts of industrial nations to keep it economically dependent (Martí, 2002, pp. 289–90). Evolutionary theory, if anything, is a rationalization by wealthier nations for allotting a lesser treatment of the poorer ones. As an observer of the First Pan American Conference of 1889 and as Uruguay's delegate to the 1891 International Monetary Conference, Martí noted that the political structures of the more powerful nations, such as the U.S. House of Representatives, pressured the poorer Latin American nations for more favorable trading concessions. "The nation that buys, commands. The nation that sells, serves" (Martí, 2002, p. 307).

Positivists proposed modern industrial nations as models for social development. In "The Truth about the United States" (1894), Martí pointed out that as the North American political model was not suitable to the Latin American temper, as some of its gains, such as strength, unity, and prosperity, had been acquired at the expense of its underclass – the poor, the emancipated black slaves, its indigenous population. Latin America could not and should not adopt the American model because it stimulates the "violence, discords, immoralities, and disorders of which the Hispanoamerican peoples are accused" (Martí, 2002, pp. 332–33).

Martí the writer offers us astute observations about life, culture, and politics in the United States and in Latin America. But intermixed with the descriptive narrative are evaluations that invoke values and moral standards shared by the reader and the writer and meant to persuade, convince, or condemn. This is Martí, the moral idealist. Whether he describes a celebration, a dance, or a marathon, he touches on some standard of conduct or some value present or absent in his subject matter and recognizable by the reader as wrongs to be righted, sins to be atoned, errors to be corrected, ideals to be lived for. Martí's ideals are moral and political virtues, such as justice, respect for the individual, republicanism, universal enfranchisement, social harmony, and governing through political consensus – to be found in noble actions and assumed as conditions for the possibility of political life rather than justified or examined as abstract philosophical concepts. They are understood and accepted by all, so they do not stand in need of justification; but they are not followed by many, so they stand in need of persuasion.

Rodó

Like Martí, Rodó is a writer and an intellectual. Though his writings discuss ethical and aesthetic problems, he did not offer a philosophical system or a unifying conception of the world, nor did he consider himself a philosopher. His relations with positivism are mixed. In a way, he is sympathetic to it: he conceives philosophy, along Spencerian lines, as a synthesis of the most general conclusions of science; he agrees with the importance of science for culture and civilization; and he also allows for the truth of evolutionism. As late as 1899, he acknowledges the doctrine's influence: "I belong with all my soul to that great reaction that gives character and meaning to the evolution of thought during the last stages of this century, to the reaction that, departing from literary naturalism and philosophic positivism will lead them, without detracting from their fertility, to dissolve themselves in the highest conceptions" (Rodó, 1967, p. 191. Hereafter my translations). Yet, he sees positivism as flawed. Why?

As a philosophy that seeks to explain behavior and be a guide for conduct, positivism lacks a sense of ideals. For Rodó, ideals are neither elements of a metaphysical theory that makes of reality an idea nor just social virtues. They are, instead, intrinsically valuable goals and moral principles. They have emerged from two great traditions, the Greek and the Christian. The first offers Truth, Goodness, and Beauty; the second Faith, Love, and Charity. One aspires to the pursuit of knowledge, the other to human compassion. Yet, positivists have proven unable to account for both, turning one into pedantry and the other into sentimentalism. Morality presupposes some forms of human conduct that are considered superior to others and idealized as norms. Positivists, again, managed to equate conduct with human behavior and in the confusion lost sight of ideals.

These failures of positivism are due to its espousal of utilitarianism: "in the sphere of life and in the discernment of its activities, we must return to ideas – as norms and as objects of human purposes – many of the privileges of their sovereignty that were snatched away by the overflowing tide of utility" (Rodó, 1967, p. 521). Rodó reads utilitarianism as a doctrine that identifies the good with the useful and demands that human activities be oriented toward an immediate finality of interests (Rodó, 1967, pp. 222–3). Thus, utilitarianism fails to distinguish the beautiful and the noble from the useful, neglects art for its sake, and takes culture to be simply a matter of social polish. Wedded to positivism, it becomes a narrow, exclusivist ethical criterion that considers only material interests, lacks ideals, proposes a debased conception of human purposes and destiny, and ignores whatever is not practical or useful (Rodó, 1967, p. 519).

Utilitarianism also fails as an ethical standard for Latin America. Rodó details this incompatibility in his best-known work, *Ariel* (1900) – a conversation between Prospero, a teacher, and his disciples about values, ideals, culture, and art. Rodó's inspiration was the philosophical drama *Calibán* (1878), by Ernest Renan (French, 1823–92), who had taken Shakespeare's characters in *The Tempest* to set up a discussion about the political conflict between an intellectual aristocracy (Prospero), democracy (Caliban), and religion (Ariel). Rodó's *Ariel*, however, is a book about culture, moral ideals, and intellectual faults. In it, Prospero is made to represent wisdom and the intellect, Caliban sensualism and the lower passions, and Ariel a desire for higher values. The book's goal is to show the inadequacy of utilitarianism as an ethical model for Latin

Americans, to reassess the continent's conditions, specifically the relations with the United States, to achieve a better understanding of the Hispanic past, and to offer an optimistic assessment of its future.

In *Ariel*, Rodó equates the United States with the utilitarian spirit of Caliban. The North American nation is admirable: "though I do not love them, I admire them" (Rodó, 1967, pp. 232–8). It is highly industrialized; it has institutionalized democracy and preserved individual liberties, but the price paid for these accomplishments is too high: art, literature, refinement in manners, good taste – what was called "higher culture" – are lost. Worse, even the love of truth for its own sake has been abandoned, leaving utility as the only motive for scientific investigation. The American spirit embodies a positivism without worthy ideals. Its most profound philosophy is expressed by Ben Franklin, and writers like Emerson and Poe are anomalies.

Martí and Rodó are among the earliest intellectuals to warn Latin America of the dangers inherent in an unqualified emulation of the more industrialized nations. Martí feared U.S. political and economic ambitions while admiring its pluralistic and democratic ideals. Rodó criticized the vulgarization and the materialism of democracy while enjoining us to seek nobler ideals. Unlike Martí, Rodó sees democracy as pulling toward mediocrity and materialism not because it is intrinsically mediocre or materialist, but because a utilitarian education encourages such a state. His alternative is a spiritual elite that can extricate the nation from the absolutism of numbers, not as Renan's omnipotent oligarchy of the wise, or as Plato's aristocracy of the *Republic*, but as an elite at the service of all.

Vaz Ferreira

A contemporary of Rodó, Carlos Vaz Ferreira also undertook a reevaluation of positivism and of the ethics it implied. The result was a rethinking of the goals and methods of philosophy – one that anticipated the critical reasoning movement by half a century. For Vaz Ferreira, the philosopher's task is to free the discipline from dogmatism and closed systems. This position is evident in his philosophical approach. He presents his views in the form of aphorisms, fragments, general discussions that purposely avoid overarching theses or systems. The accent is on a careful reading of the text, in looking at pros and cons or possible nuances, in pointing out where mistakes have been made or could occur, and in suggesting where the arguments could be improved – always careful not to force beliefs or take sides. The philosopher cannot do or say any more "because we do not know any more; to promise anything else one would have to be a genius or an ignoramus" (Vaz Ferreira, 1957–63b, vol. 25, p. 200). Unlike Socrates who feigns ignorance in order to replace unexamined beliefs with clearer ones as a condition for solving philosophical problems, Vaz Ferreira aims only to bring out the confusions that result when important distinctions are ignored – to clarify rather than solve.

What about solving philosophical problems? Vaz Ferreira points out that a perusal of the history of philosophy suggests that the solutions approach has been largely unsuccessful, and that philosophers are still working on the problems first raised by Plato. For any progress to occur in philosophy the original formulation must be discarded.

73

The proper procedure is to state the problem, make all the relevant distinctions and clarifications, reformulate it in contemporary terms, point out the implications, look for faulty logic or improperly made distinctions, and make more clarifications until all possible ramifications have been explored. Once this is accomplished, others can offer solutions, with an awareness of the possibilities and difficulties. Clearly, this philosophic approach is eminently suitable not just for dealing with traditional philosophical problems but for examining social or legal issues, or for any topic in which conceptual analysis is imperative, be it about issues of democracy, women's rights, land or university reforms. Granted that distinctions and clarifications do tend to pile up, and one can lose sight of the original problem and end in casuistry or sophistry, but at least this approach would give one a sense of just how difficult philosophical problems really are.

Casuistry can be circumvented by making constant appeals to experience, thus avoiding distortions or misrepresentations. By experience, Vaz Ferreira means not written records or collected data but what he calls *psiqueos* (psychifications) – the concrete, living, and fluid awareness that is part of thinking and sensing before it is distorted by language, abstractions, generalizations, or theories. But even here, Vaz Ferreira is guarded, for the power of experience is limited. Often, when experience shows something contrary to opinions or beliefs, people refuse to make the connection, perceive it as unrelated, or confuse its import. And this is never more evident than in the social and political arenas. "By reasoning, humanity learns very little," and he adds ironically "but from experience it learns nothing" (Vaz Ferreira, 1962a, p. 123). Still, he feels that empiricism is the most reasonable position; one should just be aware of its limits.

Vaz Ferreira's philosophical approach can best be appreciated in his critical reading of positivism. In a 1952 essay, "Sobre la enseñanza de la filosofía" ("On teaching philosophy"), he recaps his assessment of the doctrine by making a number of distinctions and clarifications:

> If by 'positivism' it is understood to accept as certain only these facts that have been verified, if by 'positivism' it would be understood to grade beliefs, having as certain only the certain, as doubtful the doubtful, as probable or possible the probable or possible, if by 'positivism' it is understood, once more, knowing how to distinguish, to discern what we know well from what we do not know well, if 'positivism' means the feeling of admiration and love for pure science without, in its name, making exceptions, then positivism is a good and commendable position. But 'positivism' has also been understood to be the systematic limitation of human knowledge to science alone, a prohibition against leaving its confines, forbidding the human spirit to speculate about, meditate on, or *psychify* affectively about those problems alien to what is measurable, to what is acceptable by the senses. So understood, positivism is a doctrine or tendency intrinsically inferior and with unfortunate consequences. (Vaz Ferreira, 1957–63b, vol. 22, pp. 164–5)

Vaz Ferreira has two major objections to positivism: that it seeks the elimination of metaphysics from philosophy, and that it accords too prominent a role to naturalistic ethical systems. He agrees with positivists about eliminating classical metaphysics from philosophy as meaningless and as something to outgrow. However, he makes a distinction between bad metaphysics and good metaphysics – between bad metaphysics as figments of the imagination and good metaphysics without which our quest for knowledge will be severely curtailed. What does he mean by good metaphysics?

Science collects and classifies facts, and explains them by means of empirical laws. It aims at prediction, discovery, and invention. Scientific concepts, if theoretical, are non-hierarchical and non-transcendent symbols – they are instruments. But, as scientists delve into the nature and possible uses of these concepts, they have to transcend empirical limitations and move into the realm of scientific imagination and speculation, that is, into good metaphysics. And science is but solidified metaphysics. Vaz Ferreira clarifies the difference between science and metaphysics with a metaphor: Everyday science is like the surface of the sea. It involves measurement, regulation or adjustment, building and harvesting. But as scientists move from these clear, sharp problems of the surface, they plunge into the deeper regions of the ocean where there are no clear or exact concepts, only hypotheses, guesses, and hunches about what there is (Vaz Ferreira, 1962b, p. 125). This is the region of metaphysical thought, where scientists must descend if they want to extend their knowledge or find inspiration for investigations.

From this perspective, the main difference between scientific concepts and good metaphysical concepts is the degree of clarity – not degrees of generality or of a difference in essences, but in degrees of connection to experience. There is no sharp demarcation between science and good metaphysics, and when scientists have to speculate about their fields, they are doing good metaphysics. Given the nature and extent of human knowledge, speculation is inevitable. And if science is to advance by investigating its fundamental concepts, metaphysics is inevitable. Further, unless scientists can do good philosophy, they will be condemned to do bad metaphysics (Vaz Ferreira, 1962a, pp. 81–2).

The source of metaphysics is, for Vaz Ferreira, thought, but living thought in its pre-verbal plasticity, at its most spontaneous, unclear, and amorphous. It includes doubts, hesitation, and contradiction – the kind of thinking peculiar to philosophers or scientists when they give free rein to their imagination and wonder about reality. A rich ferment (hence a "fermentario") allows us to depart from immediate experiences and explore the possible. Unfortunately, when we formulate those living thoughts in language by applying logical and grammatical constraints, we fall into old patterns and routines, the cause of errors and intellectual stagnation. The philosopher's task is to capture living thought, fresh, without regard to logical rules or verbal schema.

If efforts to create closed systems caused positivism to misconstrue the nature of science and overlook the function and value of metaphysics, the same attitude led to a distortion of the nature and function of morality. Ethics or morality, for Vaz Ferreira, is living and fluid. It cannot be expressed by dogmatic injunctions or captured in systems. Moral judgments deal with practical rather than theoretical situations. They are a matter of conscience and of feelings, of intellect and emotion, of ideals and of what we experience when faced with concrete choices. One must moralize with feelings, not with words.

For Vaz Ferreira, the aim of morality has always been practical: the clarification of moral problems. The philosopher's task is not to create abstract moral theories but to help the reader better understand their own – that is, to rescue a living morality from those moral systems that force the vitality of life into sterile categories and

75

schematisms. His ethical method is designed to clarify specific moral problems or ideals and avoid the pitfalls and fallacies that prevent understanding them clearly (Vaz Ferreira, 1962c, pp. 17, 62–3). His most important book on ethics is *Moral para intelectuales* (Morals for intellectuals, 1909), a guide for professionals – lawyers doctors teachers, etc. – who though trained in a given field, seldom examine the moral problems these fields entail and who pay lip service to a theoretical morality that has very little to do with actual conduct, with what should be done (Vaz Ferreira, 1962c pp. 569–60). In practice, what often obscures a problem is a bad or fallacious argument. For instance, presenting only one side of an issue – its faults or advantages – and ignoring alternative views. This attitude can lead to prejudices and serious moral errors Moral decisions should always be made after exploring as many sides of the problem as are possible. Only then can one reach a fair decision (Vaz Ferreira, 1962b, p. 273)

Vaz Ferreira also opposes systematization in ethics. Too much systematization falsifies or restricts decisions, for systems tend to lead to exclusivist points of view Systematizations also polarize the spirit, ignore the plasticity characteristic of life, and prevent a person from making intellectual and moral progress. For instance, explaining moral problems in terms of some determined system of value with which one feels comfortable is a result of one's inclination toward oversimplifying things (Vaz Ferreira 1962c, pp. 190–1; 1962b, pp. 148–9). The answer is to think with thoughts rather than with words, and to feel with instincts rather than through injunctions or moral rules (Vaz Ferreira, 1962c, p. 200).

Taking a broad view of the moral phenomenon, he points out the multiplicity of ethical systems and of definitions of "right," "good," or "ideals," all claiming to be true. Given that there are many possible approaches to understand ethical problems, Vaz Ferreira allows for the existence of a plurality of moral foundations, all legitimate, and all equally suited to human affairs (Vaz Ferreira, 1962c, pp. 148–9). In the realm of facts we seek to avoid contradictions, but in the realm of values, ideals always clash. This is their nature, and even when we try to be consistent, we can never be assured that whatever ideal we choose will never clash with those already accepted. This is a reminder that one should maintain a guarded and skeptical attitude toward all moral problems.

Yet, to avoid systematic moral skepticism, or even worse, ethical relativism, Vaz Ferreira posits a moral sense (Vaz Ferreira, 1962c, pp. 181–2). By following their moral intuitions, people can recognize what is right or wrong, good or bad. "Keep in mind that a person's ideal should be to feel – not just by means of reason, but through a kind of sense – that which is good and true. We should make our souls be like a sensitive instrument that feels and reveals the good and the true, like a delicate receiver" (Vaz Ferreira, 1962c, p. 200).

The need for positing a moral sense is due to the nature of moral judgments; they cannot be stated without exceptions because they are normative rather than factual. If factual problems admit of definite solutions, normative problems are questions of pros and cons, advantages and disadvantages, weighing and deciding, of choosing between possible outcomes, all related, all dependent on what the agent perceive, feels, senses. They do not admit of ideally perfect solutions because of the presence of feelings, experiences, intuitions – all making conflicting demands on the individual (Vaz Ferreira, 1962a, pp. 131–2; 1962c, pp. 191–2).

Ingenieros

If Vaz Ferreira was a philosopher influenced by science, Ingenieros was a scientist deeply influenced by philosophy. Like Vaz Ferreira, he saw value in positivism, but objected to its dogmatism and its dismissal of metaphysics. And though his assertion of the evolutionary nature of ethics places him closer to positivism than Vaz Ferreira, he also advocated an idealism that is fundamentally at odds with that evolutionism – an inconsistency he never resolved.

Ingenieros's positivist stand is evidenced by his empiricism: "Knowledge of Reality, always relative and necessarily limited, is a natural result of Experience. It is relative to the imperfect structure of our instruments of experience (natural or artificial: the senses or the various technologies); it is limited to that part of Reality that can modify the equilibrium of those instruments" (Ingenieros, 1919, pp. 96–7). Changes that occur in the world can be explained adequately in terms of Spencerian evolutionary laws that predicate a movement from the simple to the complex (Ingenieros, 1960, pp. 36–7). These changes occur at the levels of function and structure, and are such that each stage can be explained in terms of the preceding one – and more radically, that each event determines the next.

Because of this determinism, Ingenieros favors genetic explanations. If one understands the development of a concept, a position, a school – if one knows its genealogy – one can then discern its most important features and foresee future outcomes (Ingenieros, 1960, p. 32). Like social theories, contemporary philosophical doctrines cannot be understood apart from their historical, political, social, or religious contexts. But when one looks at the history of philosophy, one finds an appalling lack of clarity and no progress. Constantly arguing about concepts, philosophers have made no headway nor offered any solutions to the problems they set out to solve. Ingenieros sees two reasons for the aridity, backwardness, and dogmatism of the discipline. One reason is the hypocrisy of its practitioners: Politically conservative philosophers have used and abused philosophy to justify rather than to change the prevailing ideas of their time (Ingenieros, 1960, pp. 16–17). These philosophers subscribe to a double truth: they speak of universal, eternal and immutable verities but then proceed to assert specific political dictates, particular moral dogmas, or theological superstitions. The other reason is the abuse of philosophical jargon. Philosophical language is unnecessarily complicated by vague and ambiguous concepts (Ingenieros, 1960, pp. 85–9). Philosophers not only coin their own concepts, but also reinterpret the meanings of those previously formulated. What is needed, he proposes, anticipating much of twentieth-century philosophy, is the development of a clear and precise philosophical language, like the language of science.

There are merits in Ingenieros's and Vaz Ferreira's demand for clarity in philosophy. For Vaz Ferreira, this is an integral aspect of the philosophic endeavor, a dialectic which ends only if one ceases to philosophize. Ingenieros is less radical: distinguishing genuine from manufactured problems would be a major step toward their solution (Ingenieros, 1960, pp. 109–10). Anticipating logical positivism, Ingenieros believes that the difference between genuine and pseudo-problems lies precisely in that the former are formulable in a clear language and the latter are not (Ingenieros, 1960, p. 87). Classical metaphysics has muddled philosophical discourse with its use of meaningless jargon. Purging it from philosophy would be a step toward progress. Yet, unlike positivists logical or classical, Ingenieros grants meaningfulness to some metaphysical propositions.

For Ingenieros, to eliminate metaphysics from science is neither necessary nor legitimate, since it is "convenient in every system to distinguish what is observed from what is imagined, the certain from the probable, the probable from the credible, experience from hypothesis – in a word, what is already science from what is still metaphysics" (Ingenieros, 1919, p. 107). Here he echoes Vaz Ferreira's dictum in *Conocimiento y acción* (Knowledge and Action, 1908), "knowledge of metaphysics is essential in order to be a true positivist in science" (Vaz Ferreira, 1957–63a, p. 85).

If Vaz Ferreira the philosopher makes a psychological distinction between good metaphysics and bad metaphysics, Ingenieros the psychologist makes a philosophical distinction between a priori and a posteriori metaphysics: a priori or classical metaphysics deals with transcendental or supernatural realities (Ingenieros, 1960, pp. 61–3). Since it entertains a reality that is neither generated nor verified by experience, a priori metaphysics is useless for dealing with empirical problems, and since it subordinates truth to conventional morality and to theology, it is hypocritical. On both counts, it should be cast off from philosophy. The second kind, a posteriori metaphysics, emerges when investigating what lies beyond the present reach of experience. Taking the most fundamental laws of science as points of departure, the scientist makes conjectures about what remains to be known and tests them experientially. These conjectures are legitimate metaphysical hypotheses about what is unknown (Ingenieros, 1960, pp. 115–16). Like Vaz Ferreira's conception of a good metaphysics, this kind of dependent metaphysics is the main source of scientific inspiration.

It is by means of a posteriori metaphysics that knowledge is extended beyond its present limits – but always subject to empirical control. "The known was always the base for explaining the unknown; wherever actual experiences are not sufficient to formulate a law, the imagination can anticipate them by filling the gaps with a hypothesis that refers to *possible experiences*" (Ingenieros, 1919, p. 98). This does not amount, Ingenieros warns us, to enunciating dogmas or eternal truths, but to a search for the plausible or likely, yet always grounded in experience. When a hypothesis is experiential, its legitimacy depends on experimental methods and on verification; when it is inexperiential, i.e., metaphysical, its legitimacy depends on logical methods that guarantee its coherence and consistency with experience – logical methods that help the scientist rule out those hypotheses that are intrinsically independent of experience. "It is evident to me," he observed, "that the degree of legitimacy of an inexperiential hypothesis could be determined in accord with the probability calculus" (Ingenieros, 1960, p. 72).

More complex is Ingenieros's approach to ethics. Here, the influence of Spencer's evolutionism is evident. Experience determines how we think and act, including our norms. Morality is a result of our social experience: a system of reciprocal relations agreed to by members of a group so as to insure the best survival changes. And these relations (call them "morality," "customs," even "religion") are ultimately the result of biological and evolutionary processes. Even good and evil are not the dictates of a supernatural agency but statements about what is socially sanctioned or condemned, and have their biological sources in pleasure and pain (Ingenieros, 1913, pp. 20–2).

As with philosophical discourse, Ingenieros argues, vested interests intent on preventing progress and holding on to power have obscured the true nature of morality. Conservative philosophers have infected the field with dogmas and obfuscations. Religion is a glaring example. It was created by the ruling classes to avoid progress and to keep the lower classes from revolting. And just as eliminating dogmatism from science fosters scientific progress, eliminating it from morality will accelerate the moral progress of mankind.

To rescue morality from conservative clutches, Ingenieros proposes, in *Hacia una moral sin dogmas* (Towards a morality without dogmas, 1917), a replacement of moral dogmas with ideals (Ingenieros, 1972, pp. 12–13). Ideals are not mysterious entities, divine revelations, mystical intuitions, or a priori rules. They are social norms evolution selects from experience in order to help individuals and societies adapt better. As generalizations from the data of experience – and always responsive to it – ideals are both complex sets of beliefs about the future and hypotheses of conduct. Like predictions, they can be true or false, correct or incorrect, depending on future outcomes (Ingenieros, 1973, p. 12). Since the ultimate nature of ideals is purely biological, they are determined by the natural laws that govern evolutionary and psychological processes (Ingenieros, 1960, pp. 95–102; 1973, pp. 11–13). Ingenieros calls them archetype hypotheses of perfection or perfectible hypotheses, functioning like the metaphysical hypotheses of science.

If Ingenieros were to maintain this evolutionary approach, his view would be consistent. Morality is an outcome of evolution, contributing to the struggle for survival by preserving a social structure whose function is to protect from common dangers. Ideals, as components of this morality, provide an advantage in the struggle for survival by being instruments of foresight. However, these ideals also possess a characteristic Ingenieros had already attributed to them in *El hombre mediocre* (The mediocre man, 1913): the power to lead an individual or a society to a better life – that is, to choose rather than adapt – thus they are instruments of human perfectibility. He assigns this role to ideals when he criticizes the mediocre man as imitative, conservative, only adapting to circumstances, and preserving stability regardless of its social cost. Naturally a creature of habit, the mediocre man would be the greatest single obstacle to evolution (Ingenieros, 1973, pp. 39–40). Why? Because evolution hinges on variation, and the species that stagnates perishes. Ideals that thwart variation, such as equality, would be disastrous for any species. If a species like mankind would be forced into equality, no evolution would occur and humanity would soon become extinct. It stands to reason that the future rests with the unequal, the superior, and the original individual. Virtue, for Ingenieros, is going against the herd, taking the lead, creating values, and establishing new ideals.

This view is inconsistent with Ingenieros's commitment to biological evolutionism: humans must adapt to survive; since the mediocre individual is best at adapting, it would make sense to argue that it is with him that the future rests. Some mediocre people might refuse to change; but if truly mediocre, truly followers, they would put up no objections and do what they were told to do, especially by a changing environment. Instead, it would be the outstanding individuals who – because they are always trying to innovate and change – would have the greatest difficulties adapting to nature. If this is the case, then it is the superior individual who is doomed to perish because of an inability to adapt to new situations. It is difficult to envision a working society of rebels, of superior individuals, so heterogeneous as to bar mediocre people, an army of generals and no soldiers. Social cohesion would be, at best, weak – a definite hindrance in the struggle for survival. The ideal social order, Ingenieros should have argued, must consist of a small elite of superior individuals and a large following of mediocre ones. This arrangement would probably achieve Ingenieros's ethical goals of adaptation and survival more efficiently, but it would have been at odds with his idealism.

A premature death prevented Ingenieros from resolved the conflicting roles he had assigned to ideals. The motives for this double assignment, however, are clear: On the one hand, he wanted to present a unified picture of humans as biological entities that evolve along fixed lines. On the other, he was committed to an anarchist vision of humans as politically autonomous entities working together, under no governmental coercion, toward a mutually beneficent goal. In both cases the goal was identified with the idea of progress. It should be noted that in spite of these inconsistencies, Ingenieros's idealism proved to be very influential among political reformists during the first three decades of the century.

This kind of idealism is very different from Martí's. Ingenieros advocates an elitism which Martí, the consensus seeker, would have found intolerable. And if Ingenieros conceives of future adaptations to the environment as necessarily modifying the ideals to live by, for Martí ideals retain their force even in the face of adversity. Is Ingenieros then advocating a Rodó-like idealism? There are important similarities between them. Both are critics of the status quo: both see ideals as created by outstanding individuals, not by the masses; for both culture and ideals must oppose the establishment to achieve the desired social order – a framework which, for Rodó, is based on beauty, and for Ingenieros, on intellectual freedom and social justice. And both want to replace the prevalent political qualifications – wealth and social position – with moral and intellectual ones, with culture and talent. However, they justify their ideals differently: Rodó stresses the normative and axiological nature of ideals, and Ingenieros points to their functional and hypothetical character and traces them to biological and evolutionary roots (Rodó, 1967, p. 56). Rodó acknowledges an evolutionary foundation of ideals, but desires to resist the encroachment of science on art and the imagination while Ingenieros sees scientific ideals as improving art and the imagination. For Ingenieros, "reality can never equal the dream in a perpetual pursuit of the illusion" (Ingenieros, 1973, p. 17).

Related chapters: 4 The Emergence and Transformation of Positivism; 6 The Anti-Positivist Movement in Mexico; 7 Darwinism; 8 Krausism; 9 'Normal' Philosophy.

References

Comte, A. (1975). *Auguste Comte and positivism. The essential writings.* (G. Lenzer, Ed.). New York: Harper Torchbooks.

Ingenieros, J. (1913). *Sociología argentina.* Madrid: Daniel Jorro.

Ingenieros, J. (1919). *Principios de psicología.* Buenos Aires: L. J. Rosso (Original work published 1911).

Ingenieros, J. (1960). *Proposiciones relativas al porvenir de la filosofía*. Buenos Aires: Editorial Losada (Original work published 1918).

Ingenieros, J. (1972). *Hacia una moral sin dogmas*. Buenos Aires: Editorial Losada (Original work published 1917).

Ingenieros, J. (1973). *El hombre mediocre*. Buenos Aires: Editorial Losada (Original work published 1913).

Martí, J. (2002). *Selected Writings*. (E. Allen, Trans.). New York: Penguin Classics.

Mill, J. S. (1976). *Auguste Comte and positivism*. Ann Arbor, Michigan: Ann Arbor Paperbacks (Original work published 1865).

Rodó, J. E. (1967). *Obras completas*. Madrid: Aguilar.

Sarmiento, D. F. (1883). *Conflictos y armonías de las razas en América*. Buenos Aires: S. Ostwald. Editores.

Sarmiento, D. F. (1960). *Facundo: civilización y barbarie*. México: Porrúa (Original work published 1845).

Spencer, H. (1937). *First principles*. London: Watts and Co. (Original work published 1862).

Spencer, H. (1968). *Reason for dissenting from the philosophy of M. Comte and other essays*. Berkeley: The Glendessary Press (Original work published 1864).

Vaz Ferreira, C. (1957–63a). *Conocimiento y acción*. Vol. 8: *Obras completas* (25 vols.). Montevideo: Cámara de Representantes (Original work published 1908).

Vaz Ferreira, C. (1957–63b). Sobre la enseñanza de la filosofía. (Vol. 22, pp. 158–78). *Obras completas* (25 vols.). Montevideo: Cámara de Representantes (Original work published 1952).

Vaz Ferreira, C. (1962a). *Fermentario*. Buenos Aires: Editorial Losada (Original work published 1938).

Vaz Ferreira, C. (1962b). *Lógica viva*. Buenos Aires: Editorial Losada (Original work published 1910).

Vaz Ferreira, C. (1962c). *Moral para intelectuales*. Buenos Aires: Editorial Losada (Original work published 1909).

Further Reading

Ardao, A. (1956). *La filosofía en el Uruguay en el siglo XX*. México, D.F.: Fondo de Cultura Económica.

Martí, O. (1989). Sarmiento y el positivismo. *Cuadernos Americanos*, 3, 142–54.

Martí, O. (1998). Jose Martí and the heroic image. In J. Belnap & R. Fernández (Eds). *José Martí's Our America: from national to hemispheric cultural studies* (pp. 317–38). Durham: Duke University Press.

Sierra, J. (1969). *The political evolution of the Mexican people*. Austin: University of Texas Press (Original work published 1900–2).

Vaz Ferreira, C. (1953). *Sobre los problemas sociales*. Montevideo: Ministerio de Instrucción Pública (Original work published 1922).

Vaz Ferreira, C. (1957–63c). *Curso expositivo de filosofía*. Vol. 25: *Obras completas* (25 vols.). Montevideo: Cámara de Representantes (Original work published 1908).

6

The Anti-Positivist Movement in Mexico

GUILLERMO HURTADO

The anti-positivist movement in Latin America was a cultural phenomenon of continental dimensions whose participants included distinguished thinkers such as Alejandro Korn and Coriolano Alberini in Argentina, Raimundo de Farías Brito in Brazil, Enrique Molina in Chile, José Vasconcelos and Antonio Caso in Mexico, Alejandro Deústua and Francisco García Calderón in Peru, and José Enrique Rodó and Carlos Vaz Ferreira in Uruguay. A complete history of Latin American anti-positivism would surely unearth important similarities in the ideas and ideals defended by the philosophers who participated in this movement: for example, in the writings of almost all of them the influence of Kant, Schopenhauer, James, Croce, Boutroux, and Bergson is evident. The coincidences are such that we could speak of an *intellectual climate* shared by a whole generation of Latin American thinkers. Perhaps the document that best expresses this climate is *Ariel*, written by José Enrique Rodó, and read by all the Latin American intellectuals of the early twentieth century. The anti-positivist movement in Mexico does, however, show certain philosophical and extra-philosophical characteristics that justify studying it separately. One such characteristic, perhaps the most important – as I shall try to show in this chapter – is the significant way in which this intellectual movement was linked to the ideological process of the Mexican Revolution.

1. The Origins of the Ateneo de la Juventud

In Mexico, the anti-positivist movement was characterized by its generational nature. In late 1909, a group of young people, who rejected the positivism of their teachers, founded the Ateneo de la Juventud, a learned society aimed at propagating classical and modern culture. Among the members of the Ateneo were some of the most important Latin American intellectuals of the century: Antonio Caso, Alfonso Reyes, José Vasconcelos, Diego Rivera, Julio Torri, and Pedro Henríquez Ureña, to mention only a few of the best known. One can say without the slightest fear of exaggeration that it is impossible to understand the Mexican culture of the twentieth century without taking into account the intellectual and artistic work of the Ateneo de la Juventud. Most of the texts by the members of the Ateneo that are relevant for this study can be found in the volume *Conferencias del Ateneo de la Juventud*, compiled by Juan Hernández Luna in 1962 and enlarged by Fernando Curiel in 2000.

The reaction of young Mexicans against positivism – and against all that it meant in generational, political, cultural, and vital terms – began some years earlier with a group formed around the magazine *Savia Moderna*. Several of the future members of the Ateneo group (the "Ateneístas" as I shall refer to them), such as Henríquez Ureña, Caso, and Reyes, participated in this earlier group, whose most outstanding members were Alfonso Cravioto, Rafael López, Roberto Argüelles Bringas, Luís Castillo Ledón, and Ricardo Gómez Robelo. We cannot understand the Ateneo de la Juventud without taking into account its precursor in that group of young intellectuals that came together in the first months of 1906.

In his memoirs (*Memorias*), written – somewhat precociously – in 1909, Pedro Henríquez Ureña relates how, despite all his philosophical and literary readings, he was still a positivist at the beginning of 1907. What made him begin to change were the reviews of his book *Ensayos críticos*, written by Andrés González Blanco and Ricardo Gómez Robelo, who criticized him for being excessively optimistic and positivistic. Henríquez Ureña continued to discuss these matters with Gómez Robelo and with Rubén Valenti, until one evening in mid-1907, he and Antonio Caso were finally convinced by Valenti that positivism was beyond redemption. The authors on whom Valenti based his position were Boutroux, Bergson, and James, and, as Henríquez Ureña tells us (2000e, pp. 126–6), the following day, he and Caso went running to the bookshops in search of works by these writers; one can surmise, therefore, that they had not up to that point read any of them. We can then conclude that, while it was Caso and Vasconcelos who launched the most lasting criticism of positivism between 1908 and 1910, it was Gómez Robelo and Valenti who began – several years earlier – the dissemination among the younger intellectuals of the new ideas contrary to this doctrine.

García Morales (1992, pp. 133–46) has referred to the influence that may have been exercised among the Ateneístas by the writings of the young Peruvian critic Francisco García Calderón. From Paris, where he resided, García Calderón used to send texts in which he not only disseminated knowledge of the new French philosophy – in particular, that of Boutroux, whose pupil he was – but also presented a panorama of the philosophy of the Latin American countries. He placed particular emphasis on how positivism, which had been adopted in almost all of these countries, was being repudiated by the new generation and displaced by the idealist, spiritualist, and anti-intellectualist philosophy coming from France. In an article translated and annotated by Henríquez Ureña, and published in the *Revista Moderna* in late 1908, García Calderón stated – rather anticipating the facts – that in Mexico Bergson had dethroned Spencer.

The magazine *Savia Moderna* ceased publication in July 1906, and the Ateneo de la Juventud was formed in October 1909. By that date the group's readings had already broadened, and their rejection of positivism had intensified. Besides their interest in Hellenic culture – particularly the work of Plato, whose dialogues they read aloud – the Ateneístas studied Kant, Lessing, Schopenhauer, Nietzsche, Boutroux, Bergson, James, Croce, Winckelmann, Ruskin, and Wilde, just to mention the main ones.

In the summer of 1909, Antonio Caso delivered at the Escuela Nacional Preparatoria a celebrated series of seven lectures in which he set forth a historical panorama of positivism and offered a critique of that doctrine. It is interesting to note that the inauguration was attended by Porfirio Parra, at that time director of the Escuela Preparatoria and Mexico's most respected positivist philosopher. Caso's lectures are not conserved in full manuscript or published form, although a review of them exists written by the Dominican Pedro Henríquez Ureña, which was published in two parts in the July and August issues of the *Revista Moderna*. In the first part, Henríquez Ureña tells us that the first three lectures were not up to expectations, with regard to either the historical or the critical aspects. Henríquez Ureña affirms that while in Europe the positivism of Comte was a corpse and Spencer's evolutionism was in its death-throes, in Mexico, these philosophies together with that of Mill – for which he expressed greater respect – had continued to hold sway over education since the reform of Barreda, and thus it was important that they should receive their due criticism. Henríquez Ureña's review is interesting, not because it was the product of any original philosophical thought, but because it gives us an idea of the philosophical readings on which the rejection of positivism was based. In the second installment of the review, Henríquez Ureña concedes Caso greater merit and, above all, devotes more space to relating the contents of Caso's last four lectures that dealt with Mill, Spencer, and Taine.

In a later letter written to Reyes, Henríquez Ureña recalls Caso's lectures and expresses the opinion that the philosopher was "afraid of launching a head-on attack against the tradition of the School (I think it is fair to present the situation thus) and did not speak at great enough length about new ideas, nor did he censure Comtism strongly enough" (Martínez, 1986, p. 225). According to García Morales, the parenthesis encapsulates the insinuation that Caso was not only afraid of the tradition of the School, but of the power of the *científicos* (the positivist intellectuals who served as the regime's ideologues) and this was the reason why he did not launch a full-scale attack on positivism.

This reading seems to me to be rather off the mark. Since we do not have the text of the lectures, we can do no more than hypothesize upon what Caso himself said later regarding the above-mentioned event, the testimonies of third parties, and the brief synopses of the lectures published in the school's Bulletin (*Boletín de la Escuela Nacional Preparatoria*). Based on the considerations above, I believe that Caso's lectures should be understood as an event connected with the homage to Barreda of the previous year. Caso's purpose in his lectures was to offer an *historical* vision of positivism with the aim of clarifying how much of this doctrine was salvageable and how much needed to be superseded. This was the position of both Porfirio Parra and Justo Sierra, the intellectual leader of the *científicos* and, at the time, Minister of Education. It is thus absurd to suppose that Caso was pulling his punches in order not to offend the regime. Parra's attendance at the inaugural lecture can even be read as an act of public support for Caso, which gives us the idea that not even Parra was out to defend positivism as orthodoxy. It is likely that it was Parra himself who invited Caso to give the lectures so that the students would both be aware of the central tenets of positivism and have a basis for adopting or rejecting such ideas. In any case, Henríquez Ureña (2000a, p. 325) himself recognized that in the last lecture, Caso openly defended the cultivation of metaphysics, which had been frowned on for decades in the Escuela Nacional Preparatoria. This suffices to show the central place that Caso's lectures occupied in the critique of positivism. In his "Panegírico de Barreda" of 1908, Sierra had already cast doubt on the positivist doctrine, but Caso, in his 1909 lectures, went further and actually

84

defended metaphysics. This position was endorsed in a series of articles published later in the same year in the *Revista Moderna*, in which Caso made very clear his defense of religious thought and metaphysics against the positivist critique.

As we have seen, the readings of the Ateneístas were extremely varied. Nevertheless, the principal influence was that of the new French philosophy, and very much to the foreground that of Henri Bergson. Spiritualism appears in France from the mid-nineteenth century as a reaction to the scientistic or materialist conception of the universe and human beings. Among the precursors of this intellectual current, Maine de Biran, Jules Lequier, and Charles Renouvier are often mentioned. It is, however, Emile Boutroux who posits the main objections to the Comtean idea that the laws of nature, including those of sociology, are invariable. The best-known work of Boutroux is perhaps *De la contingence des lois de la nature*, of 1874. Other important works on related subjects are *De l'idée de loi naturelle dans la science et la philosophie*, of 1895 (Caso did a translation of this book which was published in Mexico in 1917), and *Science et religion dans la philosophie contemporaine* of 1908. Whatever the case, in 1910 the leading exponent of French spiritualism – and one of the great figures of the philosophy of his time – was Bergson. By that time he had already published three books in which he offered a profound critique of the doctrines of Comte and Spencer: *Essai sur les données immédiates de la conscience*, published in 1889, in which he rejects the positivist conceptions of time and freedom, *Matière et mémoire*, of 1896, and *L'évolution créatrice* of 1907, in which he criticizes Spencerian evolutionism.

This is not the place to carry out a detailed examination of Bergson's objections to positivism, but I shall indicate three ideas that can be extracted from them that are particularly relevant to our subject. The first is that, for the positivists, human reason may have certain knowledge of a mechanical, material world governed by fixed laws. Bergson, by contrast, considers that science or even reason do not reveal to us all there is; this does not mean that he regards neither science nor reason as having anything to tell us. The universe, for Bergson, is not governed absolutely by a fixed totality of immutable laws. The fact is that, besides matter, there is spirit; and thus there is a space in the universe for spontaneity, for creativity, in other words, for freedom.

This brings us to the second idea. Freedom occupies a very important place in the philosophical systems of Comte, Spencer, and Mill; however, the conception of freedom held by the positivists, particularly Mill, is negative, in the sense that Isaiah Berlin (1969) gave to the term: in other words, to be free, according to the positivists, means the absence of external restrictions upon the carrying out of a chosen course of behavior. Bergson, in contrast, defends a positive conception of freedom, again in Berlin's sense of the term: to be free is to have the internal faculty to do what one chooses to do. The freedom sought by the Mexican positivists was that which could be won within the existing order (for instance, this was an idea defended by Gabino Barreda in "De la educación moral"). The freedom sought by subsequent revolutionaries included destroying that order, if necessary, so as to construct a new and better one.

The third idea that Bergson developed later in his book *Les deux sources de la morale et de la religion* – and which in Mexico had been developed previously and independently by Caso and by Vasconcelos – is as follows: Spencerian evolutionism is false because it is not true that human beings are governed only by natural laws. Thus morality cannot – as Barreda claimed – be based on science. It is not science that tells us how we ought to live. Since free will is possible, it is also possible for human beings to be motivated by other things than selfish interests (in other words, what might in general terms be classified as exclusively instrumental motivations). Human beings are free and may go beyond their selfish interests, thus are capable of disinterest and charity; they relate to the world not only by means of reason, but also through intuition, imagination and feeling.

2. The Lectures at the Ateneo de la Juventud

The Ateneo de la Juventud organized a series of lectures in celebration of the Centenary of Mexican Independence during the months of August and September 1910. It is rather striking that none of the lectures dealt with the subject of Independence. There was, on the part of the Ateneístas, no "officialist" type of speech praising the heroes or commemorating the famous events of Independence or of Mexican history. All the lectures were academic in inspiration and dealt with Mexican or Ibero-American writers or thinkers of the recent or remote past. It could be said that the Ateneo celebrated the independence of Mexico by giving a sample of its own intellectual independence.

Of the lectures delivered in the Ateneo in September 1910, three – those by Caso, Henríquez Ureña, and Vasconcelos – were of a philosophical nature. I shall deal here mainly with the latter, which I regard as the richest and most important of all. But first I shall say something about the other two, since they confirm the general agreement in philosophical outlook that existed in the Ateneo in late 1910, particularly as concerns the predominant influence of Boutroux and Bergson.

Caso's inaugural lecture dealt with the moral philosophy of the Puerto Rican thinker Eugenio M. de Hostos, but it can also be read as a response to Barreda's work "Sobre la educación moral." Hostos, like Barreda, stated that the laws of morality formed part of the natural order. Hostos thought that the human reason was the faculty that enabled us to know not only truth but also the good; therefore the cultivation of intelligence ought to be an aim of education. Against this, Caso maintained that the human soul is more than reason: it is heroism, it is love. But Hostos was also wrong in seeking to build morality upon scientific bases. Caso (2000, p. 38) says:

> Science cannot provide us with more than relative results, never rules necessary for action; and only on the bases of necessary principles can rational beings like men be obligated. By ignoring the essence proper to scientific speculation, requiring of it data for the elaboration of moral theories, Hostos ignored the contingent value of cosmic laws. (Hereafter, translations of quotes are mine.)

The premise that the results of science are contingent and relative was based on Boutroux, but Caso adds to the argument the idea that moral norms must have a necessary character, a thesis that he would later set aside in the moral system sketched in *La existencia como economía, desinterés y caridad*. According to that thesis, moral actions do not spring from the rational observation of universal norms, but from the feeling of charity toward others.

The second lecture with a philosophical content was that by Henríquez Ureña on the work of José Enrique Rodó. After making a brief summary of the intellectual career of this Uruguayan thinker, Henríquez Ureña reviews *Los motivos de Proteo*, published

86

in 1909. According to Henríquez Ureña, the originality of Rodó's book lies in its having "linked the cosmological principle of creative evolution with the ideal of a norm of action for life" (2000b, p. 62). In this, Rodó had gone further than Boutroux and Bergson, on whose work he based his rejection of positivist determinism. For Rodó, it is our duty to watch over, look after, and guide our own constant transformation, and that is the aim of education – not merely the education imparted in schools, but above all that which one has to seek out for oneself.

The last of the addresses was given by José Vasconcelos and was entitled "Gabino Barreda y las ideas contemporáneas." It is no coincidence that this lecture, which symbolically closed the cycle mounted by the Ateneo at such a significant moment, should have dealt with Gabino Barreda. Like Sierra in his celebrated "Panegírico de Barreda" of 1908, Vasconcelos settles scores against the work and the legacy of Barreda. But he does so from the perspective of his own generation, that of the Ateneo, and by doing so, not only distinguishes himself from what Sierra had done in 1908, but implicitly settles accounts with the work and legacy of Sierra. What Vasconcelos does in his Centenary address is to repudiate the bases of Spencerian evolutionism with which the group of establishment intellectuals known as the "científicos" justified the dictatorship of Porfirio Díaz as a necessary evil. The real opponents implicated by this superb speech of Vasconcelos were not only Barreda and Comte, but Spencer, and thus, Sierra – and finally, the whole system of ideas that were used to legitimate the exercise of power by the científicos and Porfirio Díaz himself. We cannot read this lecture without taking into account the political environment of the time. Throughout 1909 Vasconcelos participated actively and centrally in the movement led by Francisco I. Madero against Díaz's reelection, directed the newspaper El Antirreleccionista, and invented the watchword "Sufragio efectivo, no reelección" (effective suffrage, no re-election). Although toward the end of 1909 he distanced himself from the Maderista party due to differences regarding the way the movement was being run, his opposition to the dictatorship continued to be total and radical. This is indispensable information for understanding the meaning of this critique of positivism. As we know, Caso had previously made a public critique of positivism as an official pedagogical doctrine, but it seems to me that Vasconcelos' criticism of positivism embraces a political aim that is absent in that of Caso. If Henríquez Ureña had said that, in Caso's 1909 lectures, he had heard once again the voice of metaphysics within the walls of the old positivist school, I seem to hear in Vasconcelos' 1910 lecture not only the voice of metaphysics but also – between the lines, but quite clearly – the voice of the Revolution. Let us not forget that Vasconcelos was, by then, someone who had already made a definitive break with the nineteenth-century evolutionist taboo against the idea of revolution.

In the first pages of his text, Vasconcelos sums up the positivist theses regarding knowledge, cosmology, values, and the relation between the mind and the body. The positivist position – as he expounds it – is that knowledge is based on the exercise of the senses, the observation of facts, and the noting of constant relations. The world is presented to us in the form of a series of phenomena that vary from the simple to the complex and from the particular to the general. As for morality, Barreda had taken from Comte three values: solidarity, altruism, and the cult of ancestors. Vasconcelos believed that the former was the most fruitful in Barreda's Mexico. Finally, positivism defended the subordination of the mental to the organic, of the psychic to the biological. These were,

GUILLERMO HURTADO

said Vasconcelos, the ideas by means of which Barreda tried to orient the national spirit along the route of modern thought. Thanks to these, Mexicans were trained to adopt the science and technology that were required for material and economic progress; likewise, they endowed their minds with the discipline needed to understand and adopt new ideas. But then Vasconcelos (2000a, p. 100) says:

> Nevertheless, between the ideas of those times and those of today there is an abyss. What is that modern element – in what does it consist – that makes us now feel different as human beings, despite the fact that not quite a half-century has run since the propagation of those teachings? How is it – if only yesterday Spencer was the official philosopher among us – that we now find ourselves at such an enormous distance from the man who systematized evolutionism?

Note the fact that in this quotation, and without previous warning, almost as if it were a mere slip, Vasconcelos indicates Spencer and not Comte, as the official philosopher. This is important, because here one notes that his criticism is not only directed at Barreda's Comtean positivism, but also at the Spencerian positivism of the generation of his own teachers: Justo Sierra, Ezequiel A. Chávez, and Porfirio Parra. Vasconcelos begins his answer to the questions he raised in the passage quoted above by stating unequivocally that it was not at school that he discovered the new teachings. He says:

> I believe our generation has the right to affirm that it owes almost all its advance to its own efforts; it was not at school that we were enabled to cultivate the highest reaches of our spirit. It was not there – where moral positivism is still taught – where we could receive the luminous inspirations, the rumor of deep music, the mystery with a voice, that fills contemporary feelings with a renewed and profuse vitality. (Vasconcelos: 2000a, p. 100)

Harsh words these! Especially for having been spoken within the very scholarly precinct that Vasconcelos was criticizing. His generation, as he described it, was a self-taught generation, one characterized by rupture with the intellectual past, and which had found its way out of the climate of spiritual prostration thanks to the philosophy of Schopenhauer and the music of Wagner.

In the central part of his lecture, which is the section of greatest philosophical density, Vasconcelos offers a summary of those ideas about knowledge, cosmology, values, and the mind–body problem that he regards as "contemporary." The tenor of these ideas is clearly Bergsonian, but one notes in them the first steps of an original philosophical thought. Vasconcelos recalls the idea defended by Bergson in *L'évolution créatrice* that matter is a falling movement while life is an ascending one. Thus, the vital impulse cannot be material. And this spirit recognized by the newest philosophy and science is an act of total liberty. Freedom to do and, above all, to be: to be oneself. Thus, he tells us, the moral ideal of the times is sincerity toward ourselves. In this part of his text, Vasconcelos makes certain reflections that anticipate those later made by Antonio Caso in his essay *La existencia como economía, desinterés y caridad*. Vasconcelos wonders how it is possible for a disinterested act to take place in the universe, how the natural circle of the economy of effort, the egoism of animal acts, is broken, how are altruism and charity possible. All these are questions that Caso was later to ask in the most important of his works and which was to be the axis not only of his future reflections

88

but of the intellectual and moral influence that he exercised through his teaching on some of the most outstanding individuals of the generations following the Mexican Revolution. However, while Vasconcelos poses the same questions, he does not answer them, since he still views them as mysterious. He says:

> Be that as it may, our age is living as if it were imagining an action in the universe whose laws were different to the phenomenal ones; and men, once they begin to meditate, find within themselves the rising, within their own consciousnesses, of that indestructible power capable of abnegation, and thus more powerful than all the rest in the universe [. . .]. The generous act, in the midst of the meanness of the universe, is the strangest contradiction of the facts, and yet it has not been sufficiently meditated upon. (Vasconcelos, 2000a, p. 106)

These ideas are not only very different from those of the positivists, but they were to have an important role in the ideology of the Revolution. The interesting thing is that, as Vasconcelos says, they were ideas adopted by his age-group, his generation. Thus they were shared by Madero and by other young people of thought and action who joined together to struggle for the wellbeing of the rest.

On completing his setting forth of contemporary ideas, Vasconcelos posed the question of how one can know – among so many philosophical systems that were on offer – which systems were the most solid and which merely the effects of uncontrolled metaphysical speculation. Vasconcelos puts forward three meta-theoretical criteria for determining whether a new philosophical system should be accepted: the first is that the system in question should not be in contradiction of scientific laws; the second that it should not defy the laws of logic; and the third that the moral consequences of the system be taken as a measure of its vitality. On the basis of these three criteria, Vasconcelos affirms, without offering much in the way of argument, that Mexican youth can adopt with confidence the new French philosophy, but should reject without major deliberation North American pragmatism.

> With the due prudence counseled by the norms I have just examined, we have sought to welcome the new ideas. The positivism of Comte and Spencer could never satisfy our aspirations: nowadays, since it is in disagreement with the data of science itself, it has become devoid of vitality and reason, it seems that we are relieving ourselves of a weight on our consciousness and that life has broadened. The renovating longing that fills us has begun to discharge its indeterminate potency in unconfined spaces, where everything seems posible. (Vasconcelos, 2000a, p. 109)

Vasconcelos' philosophy is a dynamic philosophy of freedom and moral heroism. This type of thought not only makes conceivable, but also justifies, radical changes in the established social order. At the end of his essay, Vasconcelos accepts that there is no way of knowing whether, rather than achieving triumph, everything will fall into the abyss; but the possibility of defeat, he tells us, must not prevent the sacrifice of comfortable individual advantage in the struggle for a better future for all. Vasconcelos proclaims this in the final lines of the essay:

> And in the strange pain of hope, a glimpse of the future, rapid and tragic, shows what is still inapprehensible and distant: we feel the pointlessness of what is individual to us and

we sacrifice it in longing for the future, with that emotion of catastrophe that accompanies all grandeur. (Vasconcelos, 2000a, 110)

3. The Ateneo de la Juventud and the Mexican Revolution

All kinds of opinions have been offered regarding the connection between the *Ateneo* and the Revolution. From the 1970s a number of authors began to argue that there was no relation at all between the two phenomena or that, if there was, it was insignificant; the Ateneo was, despite its critique of positivism, a cultural phenomenon of the Porfirist bourgeoisie (see, e.g., Córdova, 1973; Raat, 1975; Villegas, 1972). Others, on the other hand, have persisted in viewing the Ateneo as an intellectual precursor of the Revolution, or at least a parallel movement – in other words, one that pointed in the same direction and was guided by similar ideals, and which thus was able to connect with it and even exercise some kind of influence, however minor, on its evolution. This was the position defended by the Ateneístas themselves and by most of those who studied this period until the appearance of the revisionism of the 1970s (see, e.g., Vasconcelos, 2000b, 2000c; Henríquez Ureña, 2000c, 2000d; Reyes, 2000; Lombardo, 2000; Zea, 1974; Rojas Garcidueñas, 1979; Curiel, 1998; Hernández Luna, 2000). I am convinced that the second group is closer to the truth, but before offering my reasons, I should like to clarify a few points.

The first thing I wish to observe is that if one looks for a *general* answer to the question of the relation between the Ateneo and the Revolution, one is doomed to failure. Each member of the Ateneo had different, and changing, relations with the Revolution, so that it is impossible to provide any general account of the relation. For instance, while until 1910 the principles of the Ateneístas coincided in their theoretical rejection of the positivist doctrine, there was no agreement between them regarding the political consequences that such a rejection might have, if in effect they thought it would have any. Antonio Caso, as we know, was a fervent anti-positivist, but although he privately confessed his dissatisfaction with the current situation of Mexico, this did not lead him to abandon his active support for the reelection of Díaz with Ramón Corral as Vice-President. José Vasconcelos, in contrast, connected his anti-positivism with anti-reelectionism; we may recall that he had been an active supporter of Madero since 1909. Alfonso Reyes, on the other hand, was in the difficult situation of being a son of the General Bernardo Reyes (who held important posts in Porfirio Díaz's governments) and younger brother of Rodolfo Reyes (who was a well-known opponent of Díaz), and this obliged him to be discreet in his opinions and sympathies (which, it is obvious, did not coincide with those of either Sierra or Caso); perhaps for this reason he preferred to state that he had little "enthusiasm for epic and political matters" (see Martínez, 1986, p. 169). Henríquez Ureña, for his part, due to his situation as a foreigner, but also to his character, was a critical observer of all the events; he did not take sides, although it is quite clear that he bore little sympathy for Caso's pro-establishment position.

However, even if we accept that in 1910 the Ateneístas held a variety of opinions regarding the imminent Revolution, that should not prevent us from considering the political dimension of their ideas in opposition to positivism, whatever their degree of awareness or agreement with revolutionary aims.

It has also been suggested that the lectures at the Ateneo de la Juventud were endorsed by Justo Sierra and Ezequiel A. Chávez, as witnessed by their presence at the inauguration of the cycle of lectures and by the fact that the event was staged as an official celebration of the centenary of Mexican Independence. This *official* character of the Ateneo lectures could be seen as a sort of "pat on the back" by the regime's cultural authorities to the Ateneo; and it could also be said that by participating in the Centenary festivities the Ateneo was *aligning* itself with those same cultural authorities of the regime that had organized the Centenary with clearly political purposes. If this reading is correct, it can also be stated that Sierra and the remaining members of the establishment intelligentsia did not see in the defiant note of intellectual liberty on the part of the Ateneístas anything to worry about. On the contrary, one might suppose that Sierra and his entourage viewed with sympathy the movement of intellectual renovation promoted by the young Ateneístas and that they even saw in their so explicit rejection of Barredian positivism a means for promoting the Ministry's cultural policy, for example the creation of a new Faculty to be known as the Escuela de Altos Estudios.

This reading of the events has a grain of truth in it, but remains at the superficial level. There is no reason to reproach the Ateneístas for having supported Sierra on this and other occasions. It was the best thing they could have done in the circumstances. Sierra's work had represented an enormous cultural and educational achievement for the country. Between the spirit that moved Sierra and that which inspired the Ateneo there were obvious affinities and important coincidences. The Ateneístas never rejected Justo Sierra as a tutelary figure. Nonetheless, if Sierra and the other members of the group of the *científicos* were not concerned at the political repercussions of the Ateneo lectures, they should have been. The philosophy of the Ateneo was breaking with the positivist dogma that held that the sciences provided the ultimate explanation of a material and mechanical universe, and that society ought to evolve in a gradual manner in accordance with individualistic and practical principles. For the Ateneo, reality included the spirit and hence the possibility of full liberty, even the freedom to change the established social and moral order, sacrificing individual interests for the sake of the common good. In the context of 1910, the thought of the Ateneo was indeed subversive.

Having said the above, there are still historians who find it difficult to understand the relation between the philosophical defense of the spirit made by Vasconcelos and Caso, and the outbreak of the Mexican Revolution – as if this relation were somehow anachronistic or incongruous. The nature of the relation between the "intellectual revolution" at the Ateneo – as Vasconcelos called it from 1911 onward – and the social revolution of Mexico was sufficiently explained by Vasconcelos, Caso, Reyes, and Henríquez Ureña and by certain authors of later generations such as Lombardo Toledano. There is nothing more to add on this point unless one has the peculiar suspicion that all the above-mentioned authors were participating in a kind of conspiracy to deform the facts. This incomprehension has also clouded the comparison of the philosophical spiritualism of the Ateneístas with the esoteric spiritism of Francisco Madero. It is evident that there are many differences between spiritualism and spiritism – it is hardly necessary to enumerate them here – but the coincidences are sufficient to take them very seriously into consideration. Both doctrines reject positivist materialism and this enables them to accept free will and, in particular, the capacity of human beings to transform themselves in order to attain not only individual moral perfection, but that of those who surround them – in the final account that of humanity as a whole – even at the cost of personal benefit. The latter is one of the central ideas of *La sucesión presidencial*, since in the *Dedicatoria* of that book Madero claimed to be writing particularly for those patriots who saw the connection between the notions of freedom and abnegation. As is well known, Madero entered into contact with spiritist ideas during his stay in Paris between 1887 and 1892. It is possible that there Madero might also have read or heard something about the new ideas that were rejecting materialist positivism – let us recall that the *Essai sur les données immédiates de la conscience* was published in 1889. This would help us to explain the peculiar harmony that existed between Madero and the Ateneístas. But perhaps there was something else: let us remember that, in his 1910 lecture – two years after the publication of *La sucesión presidencial* – Vasconcelos connected in a very similar way the concepts of liberty and abnegation. Is this a coincidence or a case of influence by Madero on Vasconcelos? And if, as I mentioned above, the use of the notion of charity in Caso recalls that which Vasconcelos made of the notion of abnegation, could we trace a possible indirect influence of Madero's thinking on that of Caso?

In an attempt to answer these questions we could hardly fail to consider the section on public education in *La sucesión presidencial*, which, as is well known, Madero had just written at San Pedro, Coahuila, in October 1908. In that section, Madero launched a critique of the Porfirio Díaz regime's poor results in education, for which blame was due to the "inept persons" with whom he had surrounded himself. While Madero made no explicit reference to Justo Sierra, it is obvious that he had him in mind, and this, among other reasons, explains the fact that, among the demands of the revolutionaries in the peace negotiations of 1911, was a demand for a change in the Education Ministry. Madero stated that he would not comment on "the type" of teaching offered in the official institutions, since that had already been the object of criticism by Francisco Vázquez Gómez, but that he would say something about the type of person graduating from those schools. What Madero tells us is that a youth educated in those schools has all the knowledge necessary to build his personal future, but lacks principles and ideals, is selfish and skeptical and unwilling to sacrifice himself for his country. Young people have naturally an enthusiasm for the great and the beautiful; what happens, according to Madero, is that

> in the official schools [. . .] those noble and optimistic sentiments are being undermined, while their hearts are sown with desolate skepticism, cold incredulity, the love of the positive, of what they feel, what they see; and when they reach maturity, this is the only thing they consider to be real; the words fatherland, liberty, abnegation are regarded as concepts proper to the metaphysics that they are accustomed to treat with a measure of contempt. (Madero, 1985, p. 196)

In what reflections or readings did Madero base this very hard critique of the official positivism? Let us remember that he was himself not educated in public sector schools and when he wrote those lines he had not yet had any contact with the Ateneístas. From the reference he makes to Francisco Vázquez Gómez it can be surmised that he was aware of the polemic the latter had unleashed in the early months of 1908, when he published a pamphlet in which he attacked the official positivist education, and probably it was this source that led him to hold this opinion. In any case, Madero's claims are very close to those of the Ateneístas. We could say that on this point there is a co-incidence between the thought of Madero and that of the Ateneístas, although until that moment there was no direct relation between them. The important thing is to have established that anti-positivism formed part of the original agenda of Madero's revolution and that, for the same reason, the anti-positivism of the Ateneístas was in tune with the Revolution that was then in gestation. But more important still was the very similar way in which Madero and the Ateneísta philosophers, i.e., Vasconcelos and Caso, understood the concepts of *liberty* and *abnegation* and the way in which they linked both concepts within their moral *Weltanschauung*. This coincidence between the thought of the national hero and that of the philosophers of the Ateneo is a fundamental fact of Mexican intellectual history.

Related chapters: 4 The Emergence and Transformation of Positivism; 5 Early Critics of Positivism; 7 Darwinism; 8 Krausism; 9 'Normal' Philosophy.

References

Barreda, G. (1941). De la educación moral. In *Estudios* (pp. 105–18). Mexico City: Biblioteca del estudiante universitario, UNAM.

Berlin, I. (1969). Two concepts of liberty. In *Four essays on liberty* (pp. 118–72). Oxford, Oxford University Press.

Caso, A. (1972). La existencia como economía, desinterés y caridad. In *Obras completas*, Vol. III. Mexico City: UNAM.

Caso, A. (2000). La filosofía moral de Don Eugenio M. Hostos. In Caso et al. (Eds). *Conferencias del Ateneo de la Juventud* (pp. 29–40). Mexico City: UNAM.

Córdova, A. (1973). *La ideología de la Revolución Mexicana*. Mexico City: Editorial Era.

García Calderón, F. (1908). Las corrientes filosóficas en América Latina. *Revista Moderna*, November, pp. 34–47.

Curiel, F. (1998). *La revuelta: interpretación del Ateneo de la Juventud*. Mexico City: UNAM.

García Morales, A. (1992). *El Ateneo de México*. Sevilla: Publicaciones de la Escuela de Estudios Hispano-Americanos de Sevilla.

Henríquez Ureña, P. (2000a). El positivismo independiente. In Caso et al. (Eds). *Conferencias del Ateneo de la Juventud* (pp. 317–25). Mexico City: UNAM.

Henríquez Ureña, P. (2000b). La obra de José Enrique Rodó. In Caso et al. (Eds). *Conferencias del Ateneo de la Juventud* (pp. 57–68). Mexico City: UNAM.

Henríquez Ureña, P. (2000c). La revolución y la cultura en México. In Caso et al. (Eds). *Conferencias del Ateneo de la Juventud* (pp. 145–52). Mexico City: UNAM.

Henríquez Ureña, P. (2000d). La cultura de las humanidades. In Caso et al. (Eds). *Conferencias del Ateneo de la Juventud* (pp. 153–62). Mexico City: UNAM.

Henríquez Ureña, P. (2000e). *Memorias, diario, notas de viaje*. Mexico City: Fondo de Cultura Económica.

Hernández Luna, J. (2000). Introducción. In Caso et al. (Eds). *Conferencias del Ateneo de la Juventud* (pp. 7–23). Mexico City: UNAM.

Lombardo Toledano, V. (2000). El sentido humanista de la Revolución Mexicana. In Caso et al. (Eds). *Conferencias del Ateneo de la Juventud* (pp. 163–80). Mexico City: UNAM.

Madero, F. I. (1985). *La sucesión presidencial en 1910*. Mexico City: Editorial Offset.

Martínez, J. L. (Ed.). (1986). *Alfonso Reyes/Pedro Henríquez Ureña. Correspondencia 1907–1914*. Mexico City: Fondo de Cultura Económica.

Raat, W. (1975). *El positivismo durante el porfiriato*. Mexico City: Sep Setentas.

Reyes, A. (2000). Pasado inmediato. In Caso et al. (Eds). *Conferencias del Ateneo de la Juventud* (pp. 181–209). Mexico City: UNAM.

Rojas Garcidueñas, J. (1979). *El Ateneo de la Juventud y la revolución*. Mexico City: Biblioteca del Instituto nacional de estudios históricos sobre la Revolución Mexicana.

Sierra, J. (1991). Panegírico de Barreda. In *Obras completas*, Vol. V (pp. 387–96). Mexico City: UNAM.

Vasconcelos, J. (2000a). Gabino Barreda y las ideas contemporáneas. In Caso et al. (Eds). *Conferencias del Ateneo de la Juventud* (pp. 95–110). Mexico City: UNAM.

Vasconcelos, J. (2000b). "El movimiento intelectual contemporánea de México." In Caso et al. (Eds). *Conferencias del Ateneo de la Juventud* (pp. 113–30). Mexico City: UNAM.

Vasconcelos, J. (2000c). La juventud intelectual mexicana y el actual momento histórico de nuestro país. In Caso et al. (Eds). *Conferencias del Ateneo de la Juventud* (pp. 131–4). Mexico City: UNAM.

Villegas, A. (1972). *Positivismo y porfirismo*. Mexico City: SEP.

Zea, L. (1974). *Positivism in Mexico*. Austin: University of Texas Press.

Further Reading

Beller, W. et al. (1985). *El positivismo mexicano*. Mexico City: UAM-Xochimilco.

Caso, A. (1973). Perennidad del pensamiento religioso y especulativo. In *Obras completas*, Vol. II (pp. 3–24). Mexico City, UNAM.

7

Darwinism

ADRIANA NOVOA AND ALEX LEVINE

Most studies of late nineteenth-century philosophy in Latin America have focused on positivism as the dominant influence. As Glick, Puig, and Ruiz Samper have noted, one trouble with this approach is that most of the scholars responsible for it "had little interest in science and did not regard it as falling under the purview of 'philosophy.'" Indeed, they argue, in the countries with a Comtean tradition, "the Comtian phase was followed by an equally – if not more – tenacious Spencerian phase," which resulted in the "ineluctable introduction of the Darwinian paradigm – first in social thought, then in biological" (Glick et al., 2001, p. x).

In this chapter we will try to show how the introduction of Darwinian evolutionary theory transformed metaphysics and, in particular, the philosophical understanding of the temporality of being. In the interests of brevity, we will focus on one significant aspect of the impact of Darwinism on Latin America. We will consider how universal temporality was called into question after the publication of *Origin of Species* in 1859. The coexistence of continuity with discontinuity in nature implied that the operation of a single set of forces might not have the same consequences for all populations. The hope that progress and civilization would eventually result in the unification of the diverse populations of most Latin American countries became less plausible under a theory that not only proposed constant transformation, but also the concurrent presence of different evolutionary timelines. We trace these developments in the work of three central figures of Latin American thought: José Martí, José Enrique Rodó, and Euclides da Cunha. All three of these men were extraordinarily versatile thinkers, and each has been the subject of voluminous secondary literature. But the first two, unlike some other influential figures – such as, famously, José Ingenieros of Argentina – were no Darwinians. Still, we have chosen to discuss them *because* of this last fact, and not despite it. As for da Cunha, though he accepted the basic canons of the new evolutionary theory, he remained ambivalent about its application. All three struggled, each in his own way, to come to terms with the Darwinian legacy, and each found his thinking profoundly shaped by this struggle; they offer us three different, unique perspectives on the impact of Darwinism. The magnitude of the new evolutionism can only be understood if we consider the wide range of discussion it triggered in consequence of its profound philosophical impact.

Continuity and Discontinuity in Darwinism

Though the details varied from country to country, Darwin's influence was felt throughout Latin America. Of nearly universal impact were the dual Darwinian conceptions of *continuity* and *disruption* in nature. *Continuity*, in this sense, consists both in the unlimited variability of organisms and their traits, and in the continuous, gradual evolution to which such variation gives rise under natural selection. But this evolutionary process, unlike that described by Lamarck earlier in the nineteenth century, inevitably leads to extinction: a *disruption* in the continuity of a lineage. Darwinian continuity implies the mutability of species, and the nearly limitless potential for their transformation by means of natural or artificial selection. But the ever-present possibility of *regression* or *atavism* means that the threat of extinction always remains.

Species mutability as a consequence of variation and selective retention also means that populations and lineages have a tendency to *diverge*; the prediction that a given population might evolve toward increasing uniformity and unity thus becomes prima facie implausible. The world marched not toward final unity, but toward increasing complexity, heterogeneity, and separation between individuals. A shared past – the common ancestor – could still be taken as given, even reconstructed through genealogy, but not a shared future.

Darwin's evolutionary theory, like Boltzmann's thermodynamics, marked a departure from the Newtonian conception of absolute time that had dominated the Enlightenment. Geological time, evolutionary time, was *not* universal, in the sense that it might well transform certain lineages completely, while leaving others unchanged. It is thus no surprise to find so many of the racist narratives inspired by evolution pointing to the stubborn immutability of the Indian, his failure to evolve, by contrast with the racial perfection of the Anglo-Saxon, honed in the struggle for existence.

The philosophical framework within which such claims were articulated and defended during the late nineteenth century coalesced around what this period called *materialism*, a blend of evolutionary and positivist notions characterized by its rejection of dualist and idealist metaphysics, and by its ascription of all change to purely mechanistic natural laws. Previous generations of Latin American intellectuals had had their understanding of science shaped by romanticism, and by Alexander von Humboldt's vision of harmony in nature. The new materialism, of which Darwinism was an important current, had a diametrically opposed perspective. The natural world was a realm not of harmony, but of struggle and competition. Evolution occurred as a consequence of struggle; but such evolution was a matter of survival, not progress. Certain types survived and flourished; others, better suited to the conditions of a prior epoch and unable to adapt, stagnated or foundered.

The thinkers canvassed in this chapter all demonstrate a clear understanding of the contradictions in which the latest discoveries of civilized science had immersed them. On the one hand, species types (and, by extension, racial and national types) were mutable and transient; but on the other, some remained stuck, weighed down by the unshakable burden of their history. How could a heterogeneous population subject to evolutionary pressure toward increasing diversity ever achieve unity?

Darwinism in Latin America

By the end of the 1870s Darwinism was broadly represented among the intellectual classes of Latin America. As an indicator of the extent to which the discussion of Darwin's ideas had taken hold, we point to the 1877 publication in the *Revista de Cuba* of an article announcing the forthcoming publication of the Spanish translation, by Enrique Godinez, of *Origin of Species*. The unidentified author claims to have seen Godinez's manuscript, which he compares to the several French editions already in print. The same volume of the *Revista de Cuba* also contains an article by Julián Gassié on the work of German naturalist Ernst Haeckel, of interest not only because it displays a high level of interest in biological evolution, but because of its clear and explicit attempt to apply the new theory to local conditions. Born in Havana in 1850, Gassié was a lawyer and philologist, one of the founders of the Anthropological Society of Cuba. As a political activist, he served as co-founder of the Liberal Party. He died in 1878, less than a year after the article on Haeckel appeared.

Gassié's generation came to maturity in the midst of the reception of Darwinism, and was deeply affected by it. He mentions the "profound revolution" under way in the biological sciences, discusses its impact in other areas of scientific research, and concludes that it has become "impossible for us to remain indifferent to such a remarkable event" (Gassié, 1877, p. 257. All translations in this chapter are ours, except where otherwise indicated). The publication of *Origin* in Spanish, he claims, has finally "placed the majority of our audience in a position to appreciate the value and achievements of the new doctrine." Originally of interest only to a minority of English and German savants, since 1868, with the publication of Haeckel's *Natürliche Schöpfungsgeschichte* (Natural history of creation) Darwinism has increasingly become the focus of revolutionary thought, such that by 1877 it boasts "hundreds of partisans on both continents" (Gassié, 1877, p. 256).

Gassié's analysis of two books of Haeckel recently translated into French, *Histoire de la création d'êtres organisés d'après les lois naturelles* (History of the creation of organized beings in accordance with natural laws; originally *Natürliche Schöpfungsgeschichte*, 1868) and *Anthropogénie ou histoire de l'évolution humaine* (Anthropogenesis, or the history of human evolution; originally *Anthropogenie*, 1874), reveals much about his understanding of Haeckel's philosophical context. Germany's receptivity to Haeckel's Darwinism owes much, Gassié claims, to Goethe, a precursor to Darwin. It is also indebted to

> the genial qualities of the [German] race, and to the preparation of its spirits by way of the well-known Hegelian principle of *process* (the metaphysical conception corresponding to the scientific doctrine of evolution), which greatly facilitated [Darwinism's] diffusion. What's more, thanks to the capacity for generalization and breadth of spirit that have made the Germans, like the Aryans of India, the synthetic race *par excellence*, the German savants have applied the principles of Darwin's system to linguistics, psychology, history, morality, medicine, and nearly every branch of the human sciences. (Gassié, 1877, p. 257)

Darwinism per se, with its implicit materialism and its emphasis on struggle, may have been too inconsistent with past ideas – but as corrected by Haeckel, supplemented by a metaphysical account of progress and reconciled with German idealism, it becomes much more congenial with pre-Darwinian ideology. Not surprisingly, Gassié's self-conscious adoption of Haeckel as the standard-bearer for evolutionary theory has its parallels throughout Latin America. As for Darwin himself, his works "are written in a style, and employ a method at odds with our intellectual habits. Their approach is not always the most suited to assimilating the principles that sustain [the theory] and the consequences that follow from it." Haeckel's works, by contrast, "bring a solid German foundation to a purely French form, as neat and concise as might be wished" (Gassié, 1877, p. 259). In place of Darwin's impoverished metaphysics, Haeckel "explains evolution itself by means of *monism*," a new conception of reality "toward which the development of all contemporary sciences appears to be headed, providing a philosophical foundation for the theory and gaining the assent of thoughtful minds" (Gassié, 1877, p. 260).

Whereas Darwin lacks Haeckel's "generalizing intelligence," the German naturalist combines intelligence, imagination, and intuition, allowing him to "comprehend nature in its unity, without losing sight of it in the details of merely empirical research." Darwin offers no philosophical system in which his ideas might be reconciled with those of the past, nor is he interested in formulating the kind of synthesis that might serve as the underpinning of a well-defined philosophical movement. Gassié agrees with Haeckel that "empirical naturalists who don't take the trouble to arrange their observations philosophically, or who lack any general insight, do very little toward the advancement of science." The main worth of their "painstakingly collected details consists in the general results some more comprehensive intellect will extract from them later" (Gassié, 1877, p. 262).

Gassié's article is representative of a broad-based tendency on the part of Spanish American thinkers of his generation to look to Haeckel for a philosophical correction of Darwin. This tendency amounts to a return to the "cosmological" explanations of natural unity and harmony that were so important to romanticism, and to Humboldt in particular. Some members of the intellectual elites of Latin America also embraced Haeckel, rather than Darwin, because the English naturalist had failed to link his conception of science with a concept of nation.

Spanish American Anti-Materialism

José Martí

José Martí (1853–95) was a prominent critic of the state of philosophy in the wake of Darwin. A leading Cuban intellectual and revolutionary who also spent a great deal of time in foreign intellectual circles, Martí was well informed on contemporary scientific debates. He wrote several pieces on Darwinism, reserving his fiercest attacks for the strict materialism closely associated with it.

Martí's views on Darwinian evolutionary theory are clearly expressed in a July, 1882, article in *La Opinión Nacional* of Caracas, entitled "Darwin ha muerto" ("Darwin is dead"; he had died on April 19, 1882). He calls it an "exaggerated theory," though one based on "loyally observed" facts (Martí, 1975, vol. 15, p. 372). The new science may be true, but it is not the whole truth. Darwin himself was "a strong man who could never forgive others for being content in their weakness"; a fortunate man who "never learned the science of forgiveness that comes with a long life, or a sad one" (Martí, 1975, vol. 15, p. 375). The article concludes by extolling the power of Darwin's observations of nature, while lamenting his failure to comprehend the totality: "He saw well, despite the blinders; for though they blocked his sight of the whole of being, still he saw the half" (Martí, 1975, vol. 15, p. 380). Remarkable though his observations were, his thought never rose to the level of genuine philosophical insight.

Such insight, Martí believed, was urgently needed. Though not the whole truth, Darwinism could not simply be ignored; it had provoked a philosophical crisis that demanded a solution. In a draft for an article never published and possibly intended for a literary magazine, he reflects on the memoirs of the French politician and writer Adolphe Thiers, who had died in 1877. In this book Thiers had considered his country's politics following its devastating defeat in the 1870 war with Prussia. Martí ponders the account of this conflict, identified at the time as an example of the decline of the Latin race and the ascent of the Anglo-Saxon, in the context of the philosophical ideas that dominated European culture.

> Philosophers today are preoccupied with two great projects: the study of the Earth, and the study of life: Lyell with the former, Darwin with the latter. They have cast down the proud and erroneous intuitions of Cuvier and Linnaeus. The world is not a series of acts, separated by catastrophes, but a single immense act, wrought by an incessant labor of union. It improves with age, but naturally and regularly. A man is not some proud central being, an individual member of the one species around which turn Earth and sky, animals and stars. He is the head of a great zoological order, implacable in its similarities, rigorous in its comparisons, invincible in its taxonomic rules.
>
> The theory of catastrophes, Cuvier's hollow conception, and the anthropocentric theory, the presumptuous conception of the systematic spiritualist school, have both died. (Martí, 1975, vol. 15, p. 195)

If Darwinism had killed anthropocentrism, it had not replaced it. More was needed. Martí clearly understood the problems that the so-called materialism of his day, with its blend of positivism and Darwinism, entailed for nations still under construction. In an 1888 article in *La Nación* of Buenos Aires, he comments approvingly on a paper by physician Edward C. Mann, delivered at a recent anthropologists' conference in New York. The furor over Darwinism's novelty having worn off, "one may no longer be a Darwinist to the left of Haeckel, as scientific parlance would have it." Instead the intellectual must be content to remain "an honored partisan of what nature teaches in the simultaneous, unified development of human corporeality and incorporeality – in other words, to the right of Schaafhausen" (Martí, 1975, vol. 11, p. 479). Hermann Schaafhausen (1816–93) had published the first description of a Neanderthal skull in 1857. Martí is alluding to the ongoing polemic concerning the relationship between the Neanderthals and modern humans. A considered view of Darwinian evolution, Mann argues and Martí agrees, takes the struggle for existence as merely a *mechanism* for evolutionary change, and not the *purpose* of such change.

As evidenced by his unpublished notes, Martí often returned to his attempt to come to grips with Darwinism, either by finding a place for it within some broader philosophical schema, or by overcoming the defects of the rigid materialism he took it to imply. Of particular interest is one of his undated philosophical fragments (Martí, 1975, vol. 19, pp. 366–7) in which, as we discuss below, he compares Darwinism with the Eleatic school of pre-Socratic philosophy. In this text Martí explores the subject–object distinction, which he appears to view as an artifact of philosophical missteps, and an obstacle to be overcome.

> The great Hegel established the relationship between them [Subject and Object], and Krause, greater still, set out to study them in the Subject, in the Object, and in the individual subjective manner in which Relation [between one and the other] takes the examining subject to the examined object – It was a great pleasure to me to find this intermediate philosophy in Krause . . . which I had thought to call the Philosophy of Relation. (Martí, 1975, vol. 19, p. 367)

The path to Martí's discovery of Karl Krause is complex. As Miguel Jorrín has shown, it had deep roots in Cuban spiritualism, a tradition running from Father José Agustín Caballero through to Enrique José Varona, with which Martí was well versed, and which prepared him for his encounter with Krause's work as a student in Spain. Krause's philosophical approach was a "religion of humanity with a new vision of man as the synthesis of the universe" (Jorrín, 1960, p. 91). For both Martí and many of his Latin American contemporaries, romanticism in general was another source of the broadly perceived need to reconcile the opposing principles of subject and object, and of spirit and matter.

Darwinism and positivism, the two main contributors to the materialist current Martí rejected, not only failed to produce the desired reconciliation, they only heightened the opposition. We agree with Jorge Mañach that idealism served to "heal the wound that scientific materialism had inflicted on the Cuban spiritualist vocation" (Mañach, 1960, p. 455). This offending scientific materialism may be traced to Darwin's work. But for Martí, neither the new evolutionary theory nor materialism were unique, nor particularly original; their shortcomings were ancient. The aforementioned philosophical fragment continues with a list of "relations" between ancient and modern philosophical approaches:

> Aristotle and Bacon
> Descartes and Plato –
> Metaphysicians and spiritualists
> Physicists and materialists.
> Elea and Darwin
> Philosophical naturalism – Empedocles and Heraclitus. (Martí, 1975, vol. 19, p. 367)

Martí's association of Darwin with the Eleatic school of Parmenides and Zeno is suggestive, though he leaves the precise basis for the comparison unstated. The Parmenides poem can be read as articulating a paradox of unity: the One collapses, and a combinatorial explosion of being follows, just as, on the hypothesis of common descent, the original unity and simplicity of life gives rise to increasing degrees and modes of diversity and complexity. Martí was not alone in drawing connections between Darwin and the pre-Socratics. Nietzsche also saw a connection between Darwinism and "the Heraclitean doctrine of absolute becoming," a doctrine he viewed Hegel as having rediscovered before Darwin, such that "without Hegel, there could be no Darwin" (Nietzsche, 2001, p. 218). "In this," he concluded in one of his notebooks "we are as far from Kant as we are from Plato and Leibniz: even in the spiritual domain, we believe only in becoming. We are historical through and through." This was precisely "the great revolution of Lamarck and Hegel – Darwin is only an afterthought. The Heraclitean and Empedoclean way of thinking has been revived" (Nietzsche, 1967–80, vol. 11, p. 34, our translation). While Nietzsche views Darwin as an "afterthought" to Hegel's rediscovery of the primacy of becoming, Martí's assessment is perhaps less complementary. Still, if Darwin's views are objectionable, they are, he thinks, hardly new, as he insists in an article published in *La América* of New York in 1884, "Darwin y el Talmud."

> A patient student of ancient books [Ernest Renan] has found numerous proofs in the Talmud that the Hebrew authors were perspicacious observers of Nature. He has recently published a collection of writings from the sacred book of the Jews, demonstrating that, even in those distant times, they had ideas similar to those that now pass as new, and are attributed to Darwin. (Martí, 1975, vol. 15, p. 401)

Neither Darwinism nor positivism was really new. In fact, according to Martí, Ralph Waldo Emerson had anticipated Darwin. Martí wrote extensively about Emerson, but of greatest significance, for purposes of this chapter, is the way in which he contrasted the Emersonian with the Darwinian view of nature. On Martí's reading, Emerson had recognized biological evolution. But unlike Darwin, he had seen a philosophical dimension to this process. Positivists had tried to fill the void in Darwinism by incorporating elements of Herbert Spencer's system, especially his analogy between the biological and the social. By contrast, Martí preferred the Emersonian analogy between human beings and the cosmos. His obituary for Emerson, published in May, 1882, in the Caracas newspaper *El Observador*, praises Emerson for making idealism "human." In opposition to the materialism of post-Darwinian intellectual culture, Emerson's idealism was no mere "vague desire for death," but rather the "conviction of an afterlife" attained by the practice of virtue in this one (Martí, 1975, vol. 13, p. 29). Such transcendence, in his view, was essential to any future for the nations of the Americas. To remain mired in the prevailing currents of materialism was to

> run the risk of rendering one's mind incapable of comprehending and penetrating the ensemble. In this way, from the study of a single point of the universal analogy, like the incomplete dedication of a truth published by the Universe, the Darwinian theory arose . . . No one who has seen the followers of this fashion in action would believe, with the Darwinian rabble, that men came from the apes; rather, we are becoming apes. (Martí, 1975, vol. 22, pp. 200–1)

José Enrique Rodó

Like Martí, José Enrique Rodó (1871–1917) set about formulating a response to the threats of materialism, utilitarianism, and U.S. imperialism. He was a leading Uruguayan intellectual molded by the unsettled atmosphere created by the new evolutionism. He explained the philosophical transition endured by his generation in a 1910 piece entitled "Rumbos nuevos" (New directions), in which he recapitulates the most important problems raised by Darwinism: the problem of divergence, and the problem of realizing any ideal type. "Might not the respective virtues of two differ- ent types be reconciled on a higher plane, producing a new type, higher still?" His response is emphatic. "I believe they can. I believe it is possible not only to perform ideal constructions, but also, albeit rarely, to express spiritual structures in the reality of life" (Rodó, 1956, p. 634).

Throughout the ensuing discussion, Rodó blends Darwinian analogies with idealistic theses in a way that seems often contradictory – but as he explains, his generation had labored toward a synthesis of the religious idealism "of Renan's positivism"; of Guyau's work; of "the heroic sentiments of Carlyle; the powerful metaphysical recon- struction of Renouvier, Bergson, and Boutroux; seeds blown in by the opposing gusts of Tolstoy and Nietzsche," into which mixture it finally incorporated its "renewed contact with the inexhaustible springs of ideality in classical and Christian culture." Commenting on the eclipse of positivism, he remarks that his generation has tended "to restore *ideas* as the norm and object" of human activity. But he hastens to differ- entiate this sort of idealism from that of the generation of his "grandparents, the spir- itualists and romantics of 1830, and the revolutionaries and utopians of 1840. The two kinds of idealism are separated by the positivism of our fathers." Positivist mater- ialism, which incorporated Darwinian biology, had contributed "its powerful sense of relativity, and its due attention to terrestrial realities . . . [as well as] its respect for the particularities of time and space." Summarizing the product of this grand synthesis, Rodó dubs his generation the "neo-idealists," whose idealism is shaped by the critique of materialist utilitarianism, against which it asserts a metaphysical revival (Rodó, 1956, p. 642).

So while Rodó's synthesis displays a great deal of idealism, especially where he dis- cusses final unity and harmony, it also incorporates important Darwinian concepts, and the Darwinian emphasis on selection and genealogy. *Ariel* contains clear references to Darwin, and a deliberate appropriation of his concept of sexual selection as a mech- anism for planned evolution. The analogies by which Rodó explicates the concepts of race and transformation are also of direct Darwinian provenance. This strategy is particularly evident in *Los motivos de Proteo*, published in 1909, in which he identifies evolution with vitality. "To live is to reform oneself," he asserts at the beginning of the first section, which concludes, in a Heraclitean vein,

> We persist only in the continuity of our modifications . . . we are the wake of a ship's pas- sage, whose material entity never remains the same from one moment to the next, for without ceasing it dies, to be reborn amidst the waves – the wake, less persistent reality than traveling shape, a succession of rhythmic impulses, worked in a constantly renewed object. (Rodó, 1956, pp. 266–7)

For Rodó, as for Darwin, constant change remains consistent with continuity. In a short article entitled "El genio de la raza," he asserts, "For all that the Spanish American peoples may advance, increase, and succeed in imprinting their cultures with their own, original seal, the filial bond that ties them to [Spain] . . . must remain indestructible" (Rodó, 1956, p. 780). The genesis of a nation is a truly evolutionary process, in which something is both retained and discarded. Both continuity and discontinuity have their parts to play.

> Throughout the evolution of our civilization, the assimilating power of racial character will endure, capable of modification and adaptation to new conditions and new times, but incapable of losing its essential virtue. If in this world we hope to maintain our collective personality, a way of being that defines us and sets us apart, we must remain faithful to tradition, so long as it does not oppose the free and resolute progress of our forward march. (Rodó, 1956, p. 780)

Material constituents and physical features are transient; only through a transcendent principle, like that of racial character, can the continuity of identity be assured. Writing from Rome at the end of 1916, Rodó observes that the sentiment of Spanish American unity grows stronger among those living in Europe, and reflects that only through the cultivation of such sentiment may "the idea of our America as a common force, as an indivisible soul, as a single fatherland, take in the consciousness of our peoples" (Rodó, 1956, p. 849).

The new scientific perspective introduced by Darwin has influenced Rodó's view. For all his desire for unity and harmony, he is never caught up in the limitless romantic optimism of earlier generations. Everything has its cost, and for continuity to be maintained, something must be lost, some discontinuity must be accepted. In the only direct reference to Darwin in *Los motivos de Proteo*, in which the discoveries of the English naturalist, along with those of Humboldt and Haeckel, are taken as evidence of the epistemic value of travel, Rodó extols such journeys as a great "museum in which nothing is missing." Still, the results of such investigations must always be subjected to "new touchstones" of induction, "what Bacon called *tables of presence and absence*" (Rodó, 1956, p. 401, original emphasis).

The Latin American intellectuals who had assimilated Darwinism, coming to see the natural world as the constantly shifting battleground of the struggle for life, understood that in this world, each presence implied an absence, for where one triumphed, it was always at the cost of another. Remnants of past skirmishes, and intimations of those to come, were on display in the museum of the world, accessible to experience. The observer's task was to trace the lines of continuity in the effort to find a future both attainable and desirable.

Rodó, like other intellectuals of his generation, interprets many Darwinian concepts through the filter of Nietzsche. In *Ariel*, for example, he remarks "The new science speaks of choice [*selección*] as a necessary condition for all progress." Later in the same paragraph he continues, "the formidable Nietzsche counters the ideal of an average humanity with an apotheosis of souls, surging above the level of humanity like a living tide," before concluding, "Everywhere today there sounds the most fervent desire for a rectification of the social spirit sufficient to secure an atmosphere of dignity and justice more conducive to a life of *heroism* and thought" (Rodó, 1956, p. 185, original emphasis). Nietzsche, like Rodó, read Darwin's theory of natural selection as a social theory or a theory of culture. For Nietzsche, "'survival of the fittest' denotes a passive, if not reactive principle of life" (Pearson, 1998, p. 26). Following Nietzsche's lead, in *Ariel* Rodó thus focuses on human choice, rather than natural selection. In this respect,

Rodó's use of Nietzsche is typical of many Latin American critics of Darwinism. As Keith Ansell Pearson has pointed out, this aspect of Nietzsche's reception is a function of the fact that "at the very heart of Nietzsche's outline of his fundamental concerns in his major text, *On the Genealogy of Morality*, we find a critical engagement with the Darwinian paradigm of evolution" (Pearson, 1998, p. 6).

According to Rodó, diversity without unity is chaos, and unity without diversity is sterile. While insisting on the importance of the "ongoing renewal of vitality, the progressive motion of our ideas," he also warns against turning this process into "an enclosed mechanism, like the gearbox of a clock, confined within the circle of theoretical knowledge." Instead, it must be expressed in "sentiments and acts, enhancing the organic evolution of our moral lives" (Rodó, 1956, p. 459). In this way, the "dialectical unfolding" of moral life remains bound to the manifold of action and experience.

Knowledge brings order and unity to the diversity and potential chaos of this manifold by discovering that "characters that appear contradictory are at bottom one" (Rodó, 1956, p. 454). Amidst the chaos of a post-Darwinian world of limitless variation and multiplicity, Rodó insists on the existence of an ordering, a higher-order idea that allows the soul to discover "unity and order in life's dissonance" (Rodó, 1956, p. 454).

The Materialism of Euclides da Cunha

In Brazil, as in Spanish America, Darwinism received substantial attention in both scientific and political circles. It was peculiar, however, in that the emperor himself was an important participant in the debate surrounding the new science. Pedro II "was the only ruler and Brazilian citizen ever to be elected to one of the eight main positions open to foreigners in the French Academy of Sciences." Indeed, the study of the reaction to Darwin's theory in Brazil "reveals a triangular relationship involving Brazilian scientists (generally educated in Europe), their European colleagues (including Darwin and his great opponent Quatrefages), and the Brazilian Emperor" (Bertol Domingues & Romero Sá, 2001, p. 68). As his correspondence with Quatrefages makes plain, Pedro II was an active opponent of Darwinism.

The discussion of Darwinism proper began in the 1870s as a current in the broader debate on the evolutionary thought inherited from the French Enlightenment, and imported more recently from Spencer. Various Brazilian savants, like their counterparts elsewhere in Latin America, attempted to craft a synthesis. Sylvio Romero, trained in the Recife Law School, wrote in 1899 that "the application of Darwin's theory to history, linguistics, law, philosophy and sociology had begun more than twenty years before" (quoted by Bertol Domingues & Romero Sá, 2001, p. 80).

As is well known, positivism had a tremendous impact on nineteenth-century Brazilian thought. Its influence took hold toward the middle of the century, beginning with students at the military academy in Rio de Janeiro. As Frederic Amory has noted, it entered a new, more combative phase following the Paraguayan war, when Luis Pereira Barreto attacked the Brazilian Catholic Church "in two volumes of his *Três filosofias*, a work which, corresponding to Comte's three stages of intellectual history, presented critiques of Christian theology and Cartesian metaphysics" (Amory, 1999, p. 87).

Benjamin Constant Botelho de Magalhães, a career officer and educator, became a professor of mathematics at the military academy in 1873. He immediately began introducing Comte's ideas to his students, including many members of the country's future military elite. By the end of the century, Brazilian positivism had divided into two distinct currents, "towards science and education under the inspiration of Benjamin Constant, and towards a secular spirituality and a national mystique under the twin leadership of his successors" (Amory, 1999, p. 88). Already strong in the 1870s, the political influence of the positivists increased dramatically following the declaration of the Republic in 1889, when many of them attained high official posts and other positions of prominence.

A member of this generation, Euclides da Cunha (1866–1909) was introduced to positivism by Constant while studying mathematics at the military academy. But as Amory has shown, he came to gradually abandon Comte in favor of Darwin. As in Spanish America, the way had been prepared for Darwin by the interaction of positivism with the philosophically congenial thought of Herbert Spencer. From Spencer, following the trajectory of many of the Latin American thinkers with interests in natural philosophy, da Cunha progressed to Darwin, and by 1898 he had supplemented Darwin with Haeckel.

> Let the incontestable assertion suffice that in our [Brazilian] scientific inquiries preponderated exclusively all along the line of Germanic monism [e.g. of Ernst Haeckel] and English evolutionism. (da Cunha, quoted in Amory, 1999, p. 91)

The transition from an ideology geared toward final unity to one predicated on variation, diversity, and extinction caused a break between those who adopted the new biological language and the positivists who continued to defend the Religion of Humanity. Unlike Martí and Rodó, both of whom criticized materialism and Darwinism while supporting the revival of idealism, da Cunha embraced the materialist discourse. His case provides us with an example of the harnessing of Darwinism in the service of a triumphalist national ideology that celebrated the mutual adaptation between man and environment through conflict and selection.

Da Cunha resigned his commission in the army at the beginning of the 1890s for a career in geological and civil engineering. In this capacity, during the unstable early years of the Republic, he bore witness to the Canudo Rebellion, a popular uprising led by the charismatic Antonio Conselheiro in the harsh and impoverished northeast of the country. It was finally brought to a close in 1897, after a brutal campaign in which Conselheiro's followers were virtually exterminated. Da Cunha's understanding of Brazil was transformed by his experiences during the uprising and subsequent annihilation of the rebels. Five years later he wrote *Os Sertões* (*Rebellion in the Backlands*), considered by many to be a foundational text of Brazilian national identity. The structure of the book is a reflection of its three basic themes, each informed by Darwinian and Spencerian discourse: Land, Man, and Struggle. Its narrative is propelled by the struggle to adapt (or adapt to) the environment, and the struggle among men.

Though his orientation is different from the other figures discussed or mentioned in this chapter, da Cunha was also obliged to confront the same two problems imposed by the Darwinian legacy: the problem of variation, diversity, and divergence – an

ADRIANA NOVOA AND ALEX LEVINE

obstacle to any attempt to unify a population and a nation; and the problem of atavism
– an obstacle to change and, more specifically, progress. *Rebellion in the Backlands*, like
Martí's *Our America* and Rodó's *Ariel*, is a narrative of unification, a search for a unifying principle in response to the political, scientific, and philosophical impediments of
the day. But unlike them, it attempts a scientific understanding of Brazilian evolution.
The Darwinian character of this attempt is most apparent in da Cunha's discussion of
miscegenation.

Mestiços, to whom da Cunha refers, in one section of his book, as an "irritating parenthesis," are a symptom of a harmful development; "An intermingling of races highly
diverse is, in the majority of cases, prejudicial." According to "the evolutionist, even
when the influence of a superior race has reacted upon the offspring, the latter shows
vivid traces of the inferior one. Miscegenation carried to an extreme means retrogression" (da Cunha, 1944, p. 85). Da Cunha understands evolution as a gradual
process of interaction with an environment, a matter of long-term change through cumulative selection. An attempt to evolve independently of an environment, through
hybridization alone, thus runs contrary to the natural order. Genuine intermediate types
are a result of the struggle for life, not mere mixing.

> As in algebraic sums, the qualities of the juxtaposed elements are not increased, subtracted
> from, or destroyed by the positive and negative signs that are present. The mestizo – mulatto,
> mameluco or cafuso – rather than an intermediary type, is a degenerate one, lacking the
> physical energy of his savage ancestors and without the intellectual elevation of his
> ancestors on the other side. (da Cunha, 1944, p. 85)

The degenerate *mestiço* is thus a temporal anomaly, not adapted to any given environment. Rather than the cumulative product of the selection of many advantageous
traits, he is a mere hybrid, at times brilliant, but "unstable, restless, inconstant, flaring
one moment and the next moment extinguished, victim of the fatality of biologic laws,
weighted down to the lower plane of the less favored race." He is also impotent when
it comes "to forming any bonds of solidarity between the opposed forebears from
whom he sprang, he can reflect only their various dominant attributes in a permanent
play of antitheses" (da Cunha, 1944, p. 86).

For da Cunha, the struggle for life must play out in the proper temporal sequence.
Those who disrupt the sequence by mixing two different stages – primitive and modern
man – attempt an unwise and ultimately detrimental evolutionary saltation. In a
Spencerian vein, da Cunha presents neurasthenia and other mental disorders as
symptoms of the maladaption to the environment of those displaced in their evolutionary
sequence. Unlike the Spanish American figures discussed above, he views the *mestiço*
that results from miscegenation alone not as a hopeful symbol of union but as a disruption. He is the product of diversity, and not a source of unity.

> The fact is that in the marvelous competition of peoples, all of them evolving in a
> struggle that knows no truce, with selection capitalizing those attributes which heredity
> preserves, the mestizo is an intruder. He does not struggle; he does not represent an
> integration of forces; he is something that is dispersive and dissolvent, suddenly spring-
> ing up without characteristics of his own and wavering between the opposite influences

106

of a discordant ancestry. The tendency toward a regression to the primitive race is a mark
of his instability. (da Cunha, 1944, p. 86)

If certain groups are inferior, interbreeding is no solution to their inferiority. Evolution
occurs when an inferior group slowly improves over time.

We began this chapter by noting that Darwinism implies problematic modes of both
continuity and discontinuity. Da Cunha understands the Darwinian discontinuity quite
clearly, and he embraces it. For the *mestiços*, the "superior race" inevitably becomes
"the remote objective" toward which they tend, and in doing so they are "merely obeying their own instinct for self-preservation and defense." But the laws of evolution "are
inviolable ones," and so *mestiços* are doomed to become "inevitable casualties in an unseen
conflict that endures down the ages. In this latter case the strong race does not destroy
the weak by force of arms; it crushes it with civilization" (da Cunha, 1944, p. 87).

To expose a *mestiço* to an environment or society to which he does not belong by
inheritance transforms the struggle for life into an internal struggle, in which his organism succumbs to degeneration. As a temporal anomaly, the *mestiço* lacks organic
unity. But the case of the Canudo Rebels was different. "The abandonment in which
they were left by the rest of the country had a beneficent effect." Having been freed
"from a highly painful adaptation to a superior social state" they were prevented from
"slipping backwards through the aberrations and vices of a more advanced milieu."
The process of fusion that took place "occurred under circumstances more compatible
with the inferior elements. The pre-eminent ethic factor, while transmitting to them
civilized tendencies, did not impose civilization upon them" (da Cunha, 1944, pp. 87–8).
Da Cunha's description of the situation of the Canudo rebels evokes Darwin's discussion of isolation in *Origin of Species*. Isolation, says Darwin, "by checking immigration
and consequently competition, will give time for any new variety to be slowly improved;
and this may sometimes be of importance in the production of a new species" (Darwin,
1861, p. 98).

In his differentiation of two modes of *mestiçagem* (miscegenation), one leading to
degeneracy and dissolution, and the other to a kind of unity, da Cunha, too, appears
to have felt compelled to reconcile the continuity and discontinuity implicit in the
Darwinian legacy. A *mestiço* population may enjoy continuity, but only under primitive
environmental conditions more favorable to the inferior "least common denominator"
of the population.

While both Martí and Rodó extolled the possibility of a spiritual union, achieved through
a synthetic process that acknowledged materialist insights while returning to idealism,
in *Rebellion in the Backlands* unity is to be achieved by strictly material means. The laws
of evolution apply uniformly to all populations, and demand a particular temporal
sequence. The final union of men will occur only when all populations have completed
their evolutionary path toward civilization. Primitive man could endure and evolve
only if isolated and allowed to "transcend his primitive state" in his struggle with the
environment in the due course of time (da Cunha, 1944, p. 106). Brazil could become
a unified nation when all the diverse evolutionary stages that currently coexisted
arrived at the same final product.

It is for this reason that "the very core of our nationality, the bedrock of our race"
was in the Canudos, in the primitive population that was evolving in Brazil (da Cunha,

1944, p. 464). Unlike Martí, who negated the importance of race, or Rodó, who recognized its importance though in less materialistic terms, da Cunha closely followed the logic of evolutionary time in race formation, taking it as an inescapable natural law. Uninterested in a metaphysical account, or in transcendent principles, in his view the union of the nation could only take place according to biological principles. In fact Brazil, the nation, could only emerge as the result of an evolutionary struggle.

Related chapters: 4 The Emergence and Transformation of Positivism; 6 The Anti-Positivist Movement in Mexico; 8 Krausism; 20 *Mestizaje* and Hispanic Identity.

References

Amory, F. (1999). Euclides da Cunha and Brazilian positivism. In *Luso-Brazilian Review*, 36, 87–94.

Bertol Domingues, H. M., & Romero Sá, M. (2001). The introduction of Darwinism in Brazil. In T. F. Glick, M. A. Puig, & R. Ruiz Samper (Eds). *The reception of Darwinism in the Iberian world* (pp. 65–82). Berlin: Springer.

Da Cunha, E. (1944). *Rebellion in the backlands*. (S. Putnam, Trans.). Chicago: University of Chicago Press (Original work published 1902).

Darwin, C. (1861). *On the origin of species by means of natural selection or the preservation of favoured races in the struggle for life*. New York: D. Appleton and Company.

Gassié, J. (1877). La antropología de Heckel [sic] y el transformismo unitario en Alemania. *Revista de Cuba*, 2, 256–63.

Glick, T. F., Puig, M. A., & Ruiz Samper, R. (2001). Preface. In T. F. Glick, M. A. Puig, & R. Ruiz Samper (Eds). *The reception of Darwinism in the Iberian world* (pp. ix–xii). Berlin: Springer.

Jorrín, M. (1960). Martí y la filosofía. In M. P. González (Ed.). *Antología crítica de José Martí* (pp. 459–78). Mexico: Editorial Cultura.

Mañach, J. (1960). Fundamentación del pensamiento Martiano. In M. P. González (Ed.). *Antología crítica de José Martí* (pp. 443–57). Mexico: Editorial Cultura.

Martí, J. (1975). *Obras completas* (2nd ed., 27 vols.). Havana: Editorial de Ciencias Sociales del Instituto Cubano del Libro.

Nietzsche, F. (1967–80). *Kritische Studienausgabe*. G. Colli & M. Montinari (Eds). Berlin: de Gruyter.

Nietzsche, F. (2001). *The gay science: with a prelude in German rhymes and an appendix of songs*. (J. Nauckhoff & A. del Caro, Trans.) Cambridge: Cambridge University Press.

Pearson, K. A. (1998). Nietzsche contra Darwin. In D. W. Conway & P. S. Groff (Eds). *Nietzsche: critical assessments* (pp. 7–31). London: Routledge.

Rodó, J. (1956). *Obras completas de José Enrique Rodó*. Buenos Aires: Ediciones Zamora.

Further Reading

Bradford Burns, E. (1980). *The poverty of progress: Latin America in the nineteenth century*. Berkeley: University of California Press.

Ette, O. (1994). "Así habló Prospero": Nietzsche, Rodó y la modernidad filosófica de Ariel. *Cuadernos Hispanoamericanos*, 528, 48–62.

Fountain, A. (2003). *José Martí and U.S. writers*. Gainesville: University Press of Florida.

Gracia, J. E., Rabossi, E., Villanueva, E., & Dascal, M. (Eds). (1984). *Philosophical analysis in Latin America*. Berlin: Springer.

Guerra, L. (2005). *The myth of José Martí: conflicting nationalisms in early twentieth-century Cuba.* Chapel Hill: University of North Carolina Press.

Levine, R. M. (1992). *Vale of tears: revisiting the Canudos massacre in northeastern Brazil, 1893–1897.* Berkeley: University of California Press.

Martí, J. (2002). Our America. In E. Allen (Ed. & Trans.). *Selected writings* (pp. 288–96). New York: Penguin.

Millán-Zaibert, E., & Salles, A. L. F. (2005). *The role of history in Latin American philosophy: contemporary perspectives.* Albany: SUNY Press.

Nuccetelli, S. (2002). *Latin American thought: philosophical problems and arguments.* Boulder: Westview Press.

Rodó, J. (1988). *Ariel.* (M. Sayers Peden, Trans.). Austin: University of Texas Press (Original work published 1900).

Schutte, O. (1993). *Cultural identity and social liberation in Latin American thought.* Albany: SUNY Press.

8

Krausism

CLAUS DIERKSMEIER

The Spanish and Latin American social-democratic liberalism called Krausism is one of the most fascinating topics in the history of ideas. Based upon translations and adaptations of the works of the German philosopher, Karl Christian Friedrich Krause (1781–1832), various Krausist thinkers in the late nineteenth and early twentieth centuries anticipated both problems and solutions of contemporary philosophy in areas as diverse as women's liberation, animal rights, ecological sustainability, and global governance.

Yet for many decades Krause's theory did not play much of a role in the international academic scene. In his German homeland, Krause was studied only rarely, and his theories never made headway in the Anglo-American world. Even in Iberophone countries, where in the late nineteenth and early twentieth centuries his theories had an enormous impact, Krause was for many years all but forgotten. Driven, however, by the democratic rejuvenation of Spain, Argentina, and Uruguay in the 1980s, interest in Krausist liberalism rekindled. German and Latin American academics joined Spanish researchers in the 1990s, resulting in a small but vibrant global community of Krause scholars – spearheaded by the Instituto de Investigación sobre Liberalismo, Krausism y Masonería at the Universidad Pontificia Comillas in Madrid. In this chapter, I first provide a brief overview of some basic concepts of Krause's philosophy. Then I trace their impact on Spanish and Latin American thinkers.

The Philosophical Context in Jena around 1800

From 1798 until 1804, Karl Christian Friedrich Krause studied in Jena and began his teaching career at its renowned university. During this time he cooperated with Fichte, Schlegel, Schelling, and Hegel. Krause was extremely popular. Contemporaries felt, for example, that he surpassed Hegel in charisma and talent (Ureña, 2001), so it comes as a surprise that by the end of his short life only a few scholars took notice of him.

There are several reasons for the failure of Krause's academic career. First, Krause withdrew from the academic scene in Jena in 1804. He had witnessed how Fichte and Schelling were driven out of Jena after having been charged with *atheism* and *pantheism* respectively. As their student, Krause feared similar harassment, and chose to work out

110

his philosophy in the peaceful anonymity of nearby Rudolstadt. Second, a few years later, Krause drew attention to himself by taking some overly progressive political standpoints (Orden Jiménez, 1998a). His career was then hampered by influential German free-masons (Findel, 1886), whose policies he had criticized in a text published under the title "The Three Oldest Documents of the Brotherhood of Freemasons" (Coil & Roberts, 1996).

Trying to stand by his convictions, Krause chose a highly technical language to ward off populist attacks and to reduce the risk that his works could be willfully misunderstood. Over the years he developed an ever more intricate idiom that became increasingly difficult to decode. This contributed to the curious fact that Krause's writings were read much more in translation than in the German original.

A Metaphysics of Freedom

Krause's theory is best summarized as a *metaphysics of freedom* (Dierksmeier, 2003a) that relies on an ultimate principle of reality that Krause tries to locate in our self-consciousness. Resulting from this inward journey, Krause develops a philosophy of absolute being; however, he rejected as an "unfortunate conception" the then popular term "the Absolute," since it transforms (absolute) being linguistically into a subject (1874, p. 150; throughout the text, translations from Krause are mine).

To distinguish his position from both theism and pantheism, Krause coined the term *panentheism* (All-in-God theory), which suggests that everything exists within (absolute) being; it is not, however, identical (as typically claimed by *pantheism*) with the life it enables (1828c, p. 419). Nor does (absolute) being ("Wesen") enter or influence the phenomenal world (as typically in *theism*), either directly (as in most religions) or by "becoming its other" (as, e.g., in Hegel's system). Being, conceived *absolutely*, does not "suffer" from, or under, the various contradictions and failures of finite life; hence, there is no need for dialectics to offer an all-encompassing reconciliation (1828c, p. 392). Krause's model allows for life to develop and to supersede itself with ever-higher life-forms but nowhere does he dialectically prescribe such progress. The world is not seen teleologically, and hence life need not be interpreted along predetermined stages that a speculative philosophy alone could unveil.

This panentheistic metaphysics has a methodological purpose. Although Krause's system does offer dialectical patterns for conceiving the world we live in, his theory – in marked contrast to the general gist of early German Idealism – does not demand that the world accommodate itself to the patterns of our speculation (1828c, p. 221). Instead, Krause formulates an almost fallibilistic position *avant la lettre*. Pitting his own empirically informed "constructions" against the speculative "deductions" of Fichte and Schelling, Krause insisted that one cannot generate knowledge by conceptual effort alone (Krause, 1804, p. 85). True knowledge needs to be informed by natural and social phenomena (1828b, p. 273).

Dialectical thinking and speculation are a heuristic, not a prescriptive, function. Krause employs them in order to guide empirical observation and to formulate expectations about reality. "For as a foundation for every experiment, if it is to have any meaning and value, there must at least be the representation of a presumptive or aphoristically known idea" (1804, p. 84). The function of metaphysics is hence not to replace, but

111

to process experience (Krause, 1804, p. 83). In the constellation of the speculative philosophy then prevalent in Jena this stance is remarkable (Ende, 1973).

Krause's methodological innovations did not go unnoticed. In 1804, the renowned *Jenaische Allgemeine Literatur-Zeitung* (vol. 4, p. 89) featured a highly favorable review of Krause's first attempt at natural philosophy by Johann Jakob Wagner, who judged, "Both the essence of nature and the essence of scientific construction are developed in it with a certainty and clarity that one misses in many similar works . . ." (1804). Throughout his works, Krause held fast to these insights of his early days. In one of his main later works, he defends the heuristic use of philosophical construction as a method of philosophizing *with* concepts, while dismissing all efforts to philosophize *out of* concepts alone:

> Crassly, one has misinterpreted this position as if the philosopher who uses constructions would conceive of himself as a speculative world-maker; likewise it is a misinterpretation to view scientific construction as if the philosophical intention was to construe, deduce, or demonstrate the temporal, infinitely determined individuality of things. (1828b, p. 337)

The elevated methodological status of experience in Krause's philosophy is important for the later development of Krausism, since already in Krause it carries over to the objects of such experience: namely, history and nature. Krause has a novel view of nature that is radically opposed, for instance, to Fichte's theory of nature as the irrational Other of the mind. While Fichte sees nature in opposition to the human spirit, to its rationality and its freedom – that is, as something that always and in all forms must forcefully be brought under rational domination – Krause does not. He begins his philosophical life with the quest to understand nature in its very own freedom and absoluteness ("in ihrer inneren Freiheit und Absolutheit" (1804, p. 82); from this perspective Krause derives an unusually progressive environmental philosophy.

Analytic and Synthetic Philosophy

One of the main functions of speculative thinking lies in its contribution to moral reasoning. In many realms of life, rigorous philosophical skepticism is not practicable, according to Krause. We cannot abstain from forming opinions about how to live well, about the significance of death, freedom, and so forth (1892, pp. 51–4). Whenever we need orientation but cannot obtain it other than through ideas, it is better to employ cautious philosophical speculation open to anyone's rational critique than arbitrarily to follow our emotional predilections, cultural prejudices, or religious preferences.

What is needed is a method to bring our analytic and empirical knowledge fruitfully together with our speculative and intuitive faculties. Krause comes up with the following methodology (1828c, p. 30): Conceptual analysis stirs up antinomies that cannot be solved by analytic tools alone. Synthetic thinking responds with an attempt to reconcile the heretofore incompatible concepts through integrative ideas, which in turn are generated by introspective methods and conceptual constructions.

The analytic part of the system is constantly adapting to the different experiences and themes that every philosophizing subject deals with. Because only synthetic ideas

112

in harmony with the analytic part can legitimately organize our knowledge, changes in the analytic part drive the philosophical system to internal reform (1828c, p. 276). The analytic part of Krause's philosophy is hence not merely a transitory stage on the way to an ultimate philosophical system but serves as the actual opening where the system keeps contact with ever-changing reality (1828c, p. 16). When, for instance, based on new experiences and insights, reasonable doubt arises as to the validity of certain synthetic speculations, the analytic–synthetic investigation is taken up anew. The philosophical endeavor is hence perennial; the resulting metaphysics is of transitional permanence only and remains forever open to change (Orden Jiménez, 1998a, p. 659).

Krause aims to promote only ideas that anyone willing, and able, to join the conceptual work of philosophy could endorse because he holds that one must make *freedom* both the prime *content* of philosophy and its principal *method*. Hence his philosophy is participation-oriented throughout (employing quasi-dialogical approaches, phenomenological analyses, etc.) in order to assure the free consent of his readers and listeners (see 1828c, p. 14). Many of the astounding results which set Krause's metaphysics so distinctly apart in his time and render it so interesting in the present are due to this methodological openness (Dierksmeier, 2004a).

The *theoretical* stance for everyone's free intellectual participation in philosophical endeavors, for instance, is matched in Krause's *practical* philosophy by the idea of a universal right to participation in one's social, political, and economic environs, with special emphasis on the needs of all marginalized individuals (Dierksmeier, 2003a). Those who cannot raise their own voice must be legally represented by others. Society is by default the proxy of those who cannot realize their own rights. As early as 1803, Krause applied this principle to argue for the protection of the rights of children, the emancipation of women, the human dignity of disabled persons, and the rights of future generations (1803, pp. 95–108).

Metaphysics of Humanity

The *idea of humanity*, comprising each and every person regardless of their position in time and space, renders the highest mundane source of legitimacy of ethical and legal norms according to Krause. The historical *genesis* of legal norms is, however, very often not congruent with their systematic *validity*. Historically, one's gender, nationality, religion, and ethnicity may have helped establish one's rights. Yet conceptually, such aspects are accidental; they do not constitute adequate philosophical reasons for the rights so conveyed. "What is law is law not because it prevails but because there is legal rationale for it. If this legal rationale is changed, [or] destroyed, so is the law" (1893, p. 111).

For Krause, the source of human rights lies in the general fact that we are persons and thus particular features of one's personality must not give one legal privileges over others. That one's rights are coterminous with the rights of any and all human beings affects their content (Dierksmeier, 2004b). When the community of all persons is the principle and limit of all legal sovereignty, no one can legitimately claim rights that go against the rights of humanity (1904, p. 197). Hence we must never, according to Krause, make use of our rights in a manner that deprives others of theirs.

113

A call for the reform of legal institutions follows suit: Wherever persons influence one another there must be laws to protect their human rights (1874, p. 350). Wherever people ought to have legal protection but lack it, the idea of human rights, reflecting back onto itself, calls for institutional change: If one has a right, one also has a right to attain this right. That is, if one is granted primary legal entitlements, then this should include secondary rights to institutions to realize such rights, and entail tertiary rights to advocate for legal reform in order to create said institutions. This "empowerment-right" entitles everyone to "gain the ability to utilize his rights" (1874, pp. 260–1) and aims at making people intellectually and economically capable of realizing their human rights effectively (1890a, p. 159).

A very important difference from contemporary efforts in legal theory is that Krause strongly rejects establishing basic rights based upon a symmetrical barter between rational maximizers of self-interest (1892, p. 165). Instead he declares that we must establish human rights for everyone, even if that means imposing asymmetrical obligations. Thus, he embraces the notion of managing the rights of disabled or otherwise legally incapacitated individuals on their behalf:

> Insofar as the individual citizen can be struck by one or more unavoidable limitations in body or mind, he may be, or become, over the course of his life, incapable of rendering some of his legal obligations. He who is born without wit, without sight, the deaf-mute, the naturally debilitated, et al., belong in this group, as well as those debilitated by sickness or mechanical damage to their body, mind, or both. Now, since, as has been shown, the owning of the entitlements to rights is in no way originally established through one's reciprocal actions, but rather through everyone's rational needs, therefore such unfortunate persons cannot [. . .] be deprived of their rights by their misfortune." (1890a, p. 149)

Everyone enjoys one's own rights and is obligated to help establish and defend the rights of all other persons. Should national law not be able to cover all forms of human contact – and Krause felt it often failed to do so – then supranational legal institutions must needs be created (1874, p. 539). The moral legitimacy of any particular legal entity depends on whether and how much this entity can be seen as an appropriate institution for the realization of the rights of humanity. Krause's philosophy does not limit to particular entities (such as nation-states) the competence and legitimacy of creating valid societal norms. Since instead he acknowledges each and every legal structure intent on and capable of realizing human rights (Miller, 1884; MacCauley, 1917), Krause emphatically welcomes – much against the nationalist sentiment of his times – the transfer of national sovereignty to regional and transnational bodies and postulates global governance structures (1811, p. 60; 1814, p. 17).

Socioeconomic Philosophy

The world belongs to humanity in common (1874, p. 320) and the ultimate function of legal entitlements is to enable everyone to live in freedom (1874, p. 453). Personal liberty, however, is not identical with unrestricted arbitrary choice. True liberty means living freely under laws that anyone could reasonably endorse (1828b, p. 514), which, by and large, are laws that educate and foster the very capabilities that make us human (1811, p. 183).

Herein one clearly sees the Kantian legacy. Krause, however, goes further than Kant in the political application of this idea (Dierksmeier, 1999b). Real freedom is contingent upon conditions, some of which need to be created first. "Not only existing freedom matters, but that freedom be brought to existence, and then enhanced" (1892, p. 126). Law, for Krause, is therefore not (as in Kant) merely the negation of a negation of already established liberties but rather "that everyone receive the possibility of being externally effective, – in other words law has to establish the (positive and affirmative) conditions that everyone have his due sphere of external freedom, wherein necessarily lies the equitable limit of everyone else's freedom" (1892, p. 113). This is why the law not only has to ensure (negatively) that individual freedom is not infringed upon, but must also (positively) ensure that all individuals have access to the very freedoms to which they, as human beings, are entitled.

The interests of all persons (including the poor within our society, the destitute abroad, and future generations) count for Krause as an inherent corrective of any private right to property (1874, p. 287). Crass violations of this regulative principle justify corrective measures – even expropriations, if properly qualified (1828a, p. 175). The strong demand for social justice that permeates these postulates Krause brings also to the global level. Universal distributive fairness is, in fact, the central focus of his legal and social philosophy.

Krause predicts that the people of the earth must ultimately enter into a global legal union (for which he drew up an impressively prescient constitution) in order to render to each what they are due (1811, p. 66). Krause saw regional federations of nation-states, such as a European Union, for which he developed detailed and far-sighted plans (1814, p. 11), as an important stepping stone in this direction. Krause hoped that when people saw the material benefits that such regional unions could bring, they might become more receptive to the idea of supranational governance in general (Dicke, 1996).

At a time when most believed that the final word in the affairs between nations was endless strife, and when many eminent philosophers even went so far as to laud war as a premier gateway to civilization, Krause stood for world peace through global governance. Desiring a world of various creeds and customs that allowed for a peaceful interchange of ideas and practices, his ideas of world federalism aimed at the cooperation of diverse powers under a common legal roof, not at a hegemonial superstate or a world monoculture (1803, p. 69). A peaceful world of free personal and economic interchange could arise, Krause believed, when the cultural diversity of regional characters and customs was allowed to thrive in a system that provided legal security for everyone on the globe. The fairness of the thus-enabled cultural and commercial relations should be guaranteed by an international law centered round the idea of global distributive justice (1893, p. 108; 1828a, p. 172).

The Natural World

Krause's philosophy considers nature not just as a resource for human life that, for all sorts of prudential reasons, ought to be used in a sustainable manner. He also holds

115

that there is intrinsic value to all forms of life (1828a, p. 182). Human law, notwith-standing its anthroporelational focus, must avoid an anthropocentric bias and try to respect nonhuman interests too. In stark opposition to most of his contemporaries who defined animals as mere objects, Krause concentrates on the subjectivity of animal life. In compelling passages, he argues that animals are beings that feel and perceive them-selves and sometimes even reach a level of conscious personality. Krause ranks all life-forms according to their respective capacity to be a self because "everybody will agree that it [the law, C.D.] must be extended and expanded in regard to every being that we recognize as a self-centered, self-conscious, self-feeling, and self-willing being" (1892, p. 14). Once in place, a critical hierarchy of beings puts the burden of proof on those who want to utilize nature for their purposes. They have to show that their actions will create a greater good than they set out to destroy (1892, p. 176). This does not give animals the same rights as humans, but since some animals show rudimentary forms of personality, humans may well act as their proxies, representing their inter-ests much like the interests of senile individuals, or of disabled people. If we hold human rights to be unconditional, and do not, for instance, dismiss the value of dis-abled persons when they cannot give something back in return for our care, why not acknowledge the unconditional rights of animal life – appropriately graduated by species – too? For example, when it comes to the slaughtering of animals, Krause's posi-tion is that, because of their ontological supremacy, humans may kill lower life forms, as long as they can only thus keep themselves alive (1904, p. 300). Krause held, however, that this qualified legitimation immediately becomes a limitation as soon as people readily can find adequate food alternatives – and that, he thought, was pre-dominantly the case already in his time.

Harmonious Freedom

Krause's overall concern for marginalized and underrepresented interests shows that his is a liberalism of a different sort. In a number of (neo-)liberal ideologies, respect for others who cannot affect us in return (either positively or negatively) plays merely a secondary role (Dierksmeier, 2007). In Krause's philosophy it is primary. His regard for otherness and his intention to harmonize antagonistic interests through integra-tive ideas are not accidental, but originate from deep within Krause's system. It is due to the integrative metaphysics and participatory methodology of his philosophy that Krause puts so much emphasis on the harmonization of particular (individual and national) interests with the larger and cosmopolitan concerns of the human family (1811, p. 164). In fact, it seems quite plausible that much of the international success of Krausism can be attributed to this very tendency of Krause's "harmonic liberalism" (Gil-Cremades, 1985, p. 221).

Krause's Philosophy in Spain

In recent years, Krause's philosophy has received renewed attention. After Spain, Uru-guay, and Argentina – the former mainlands of Krausist influence – freed themselves

116

from dictatorial reign in the 1980s, research into their democratic past and their Krausist traditions got under way. It has unearthed a complex and multifaceted history of how Krausism entered Latin America. In addition to and interconnecting with certain mainstreams of influence, on which we will focus, Krausist thinking spread around the globe via numerous other routes. Important lines of reception ran, for instance, through Belgium and France, based upon the works of Heinrich Ahrens (1808–74) and Guillaume Tiberghien (1819–1901). In the following, we cannot do justice to these ramifications but shall concentrate on how Krause's philosophy came to Spain and from there to the Latin American world.

Sanz del Río's adaptation of Krause's philosophy

It has been quipped that the success of Krausism in Spain was due mainly to sharp opposition from the Catholic Church. There is some truth to this statement. Annoyed by Krause's firm stance against theocracy (1890a, p. 50; 1811, p. 64), Catholic authors charged Krause's panentheism with pantheistic or atheistic tendencies or both. Krausist writings (starting with some works of Ahrens) were quickly put on the Catholic Index of forbidden books, which in turn made these books and their authors quite popular with Spain's intellectual avant-garde. Yet, none of this could have put Krause firmly on the map, had there not been the towering figure of Julián Sanz del Río (1814–69). Thanks to a research grant he had received to bring back to Spain a modern philosophy suitable for social and legal reform, Sanz del Río had gone to Germany to study political philosophy. Germany was then the home of the vanguard of political philosophy and Spain felt the need to catch up with the rest of Western Europe. It lagged behind in terms of democratic development, having yet to transform a super-annuated structure of feudal and clerical hierarchies into a more modern, functionally organized society.

Hegel versus Krause

In Berlin, Hegel and his school ruled the academic scene. Sanz del Río, however, remained unimpressed and chose Krause as his intellectual patron. The reasons for his rejection of Hegel are telling. In a letter dated May 26, 1862 to the Krause-disciple Karl David Friedrich Röder, Sanz del Río praises Krause's measured balance of speculation with experience over Hegel's sheer logicism (Ureña, 1993, p. 123). On the same day, del Río writes along the same lines to Leonhardi, Krause's son-in-law, that Hegel was forced by his own (only synthetic) method to confine himself to speculative comments on established facts, i.e., on the past. Krause's both synthetic and analytic methodology, instead, allowed for the integration of future developments (op. cit., p. 128).

His critique conforms with Krause's impetus to integrate empirical information, as Sanz del Río very much wanted philosophy to be open to all kinds of new vistas, especially, given his mission, for untried political experiments (Orden Jiménez, 1998b, p. 94). Hegel, however, used the speculative concept to transform the historically given reality into a necessary component of the philosophical idea and system. Hegel thus cemented the given reality philosophically, lending too much emphasis to the then predominant model of government, i.e., the highly centralized and bureaucratic

117

(Prussian) nation-state, while disregarding alternative governance models. With a view to Spain's need for social transformation from below, other Krausistas chimed in with this critique, also rejecting Hegel's system as too inflexible, monolithic, and too beholden to the state (García Cué, 1985, p. 49). Krause, who emphasized the need for flexible government structures according to the principle of subsidiarity, proved much more attractive. Because of its colonial past, Spain had to deal with the remnants of empire and hence with intricate questions of *international* relations. At the same time Spain was struggling internally with semi-autonomous provinces and thus was also in dire need for *intranational* integration. So, Krause's laterally and vertically malleable federalism seemed indeed a natural choice.

Ideal de la humanidad *(the ideal of humanity)*

Setting out to promote Krause's ideas, Sanz del Río compiled translations from Krause's works into a text published under the title *Ideal de la humanidad para la vida*. The book, which is in effect a translation of Krause's work *"Urbild der Menscheit"* (1811), augmented by translations from two articles from Krause, enjoyed a major triumph in Spain. This was in part owing to the impression that what the book presented was not simply German thought in Spanish language but genuinely Spanish philosophy. A group of editors annotated (the widely transmitted second edition of) the text with a statement. It declared that the book, "although inspired by the beautiful work of Krause, is an exposition completely free from its direction, accommodated to the spirit of our people and to the most pressing needs of its culture" (Sanz del Río, 1871). Clever ruse or honest error, the mistaken impression that *Ideal de la humanidad* displayed "essential differences" and "entirely new parts," compared to its original, started the popular myth that Krausism was an intellectual movement quite distinct from its German roots, authentically grown out of Spanish soil.

One can understand how the contents of Krause's works facilitated this erroneous conception. Idealistic in its quest for social change, yet realistic in its valuation of experience, advocating peaceful reform instead of violent revolution, and taking a clear anti-theocratic stance while never lashing out against religion itself, the philosophy of Krausism seemed custom-made for nineteenth-century Spain. Its vertical cosmopolitism linked Spain's traditional Catholic universalism to the country's future need for political integration into Europe; at the same time, being laterally adaptive to all sorts of legal entities, it could also integrate most of the antagonistic forces of the contemporary Spanish society. No wonder then that the philosophy of the *Ideal de la humanidad* was quickly embraced as Spain's long-awaited contribution to political liberalism.

The Institución Libre de Enseñanza

In an effort to consolidate and spread their worldview, Spanish Krausistas, led by the charismatic legal philosopher and pedagogic innovator Francisco Giner de los Ríos, established the Institución Libre de Enseñanza (ILE). The ILE, the first private academic institution in Spain to evade control by both state and church (Garrido, 2001), aimed through its pedagogy to demonstrate the relevance of Krausist natural and social philosophy for real-life issues. Themes pertinent to the life of students were taught in an interdisciplinary fashion, with varying intensity according to the age and advancement of the respective student. From year to year, the instructors revisited these themes, gradually adding more and more knowledge or methodological finesse to the subject (Mateo, 1990). The Krausistas thus created a holistic learning experience, where in a cycle of years a student would go over a certain set of topics time and again. This "cyclical" education added to the political impact of Krausism, as it managed to link the academic learning of the young Krausistas firmly with their private and social lives (Garrido, 2001, p. 59).

Overall, the project of the ILE seems to have been a great success. The years between 1870 and 1930 witnessed an outburst of Krausist ideas in Spain's cultural life, as, to name but a few, the works of Benito Pérez Galdos (1843–1920), Leopoldo Alas (Clarín) (1852–1901), and Urbano Gonzáles Serrano (1848–1904) demonstrate. Numerous later prominent members of the Spanish and Latin American intelligentsia studied at the Institución Libre de Enseñanza, and many of them also lived communally together in the associated Residencia de Estudiantes. The Krausist identity that the Institución Libre de Enseñanza managed to inspire in its students reached deep into their private lives – according to their opponents, the Krausistas even displayed a common sense of fashion in their (allegedly predominantly black) garments. Until closed down by Franco, the ILE exerted an enormous intellectual influence in Spain.

Indirect Krausist influence

Yet there was also much Krausism outside the Institución Libre de Enseñanza. Before the ILE was up and running, and based upon mostly non-Spanish sources, we witness an important Krausist reorientation in Spain's socioeconomic thinking. The most sustained effect in this field was enjoyed by the "Treatise on Political Economy" (*Tratado de hacienda pública*, 1869) by Piernas Hurtado. The *Tratado* fleshes out Krause's social philosophy in the realm of macroeconomics toward a social-democratic liberalism; it served several generations of Spanish students as their economics textbook. Far ahead of its time, Hurtado departs from an economics of growth maximization in favor of optimization theories of welfare, and argued that quantitative standards do not suffice for the normative evaluation of the economy; instead qualitative goals, elaborated by economic philosophy, must be formulated (Malo Guillén, 1998). This was an important theoretical achievement because it gave Krausism the intellectual tools to be critical of excess capitalism without coming out in favor of socialism; the critique of social ills remains one from within the open society, based upon Krause's "harmonic" notion of freedom (Dierksmeier, 2003b).

The Krausist impact on Spanish and Latin American intellectuals is not always immediately palpable or even acknowledged by its protagonists. Indeed, intellectuals impacted by Krausism often did not consider themselves Krausistas. A point in case is Ortega y Gasset (1883–1955). His explicit references to Krause are few and far between. Yet many of the central tenets of Ortega y Gasset's philosophy remarkably reverberate the Krausist doctrine; among them, (1) his sociopolitical postulates in search of a liberalism for all classes and beyond the fray of political parties (Marichal, 1990, p. 40), (2) his program of advancing political progress through improved education (see his

Pedagogía social como programa político), and (3) his overall anti-revolutionary "reform-ismo" based upon his "pragmatismo idealista." Some scholars (see Garrido, 2001, p. 103) hence claim Ortega y Gasset for the "third generation" of Krausism (with the first generation being concentrated on Sanz del Río and second-generation Krausism gravitating around Francisco Giner de los Ríos). Their circumstantial evidence gains in significance if we consider the metaphysical foundations of Ortega y Gasset's political postulates.

Just like Krause, Ortega y Gasset criticizes Fichte for making the subject–object difference constitutional through a solipsistic approach to philosophy. Instead, Ortega y Gasset bases his philosophy on the often quoted formula: "I am myself and my circumstance, if I don't save it, I won't save myself" (Ortega y Gasset, 1983, p. 322). Against Fichte's move *beyond* the subject–object difference toward a transcendent absolute entity, Ortega delves, so to speak, *beneath* this difference. He suggests a metaphysical concept of life that unites subjects and objects on a pre-conscious level, but, on the conscious level, allows for a "perspectivismo," with diverging approaches to truth for each respective class of being. Consequently, Ortega y Gasset rejects physicalistic conceptions of the world as a time-space container for abstract things-in-themselves in merely mechanical relations. He views our world historically, as an ever-dynamic fabric, constantly remade out of the manifold strands of everyone's free decisions and their personal as well as social consequences. If we compare this with the relational conception of life as moral decision-making under social and environmental inter-connectivity in the pedagogical philosophy of Ramiro de Maeztu and Francisco Giner de los Ríos, Ortega's Krausist teachers (Marichal, 1990, p. 27; Cachu Viu, 1999, p. 176; Marías, 1960, p. 126), we see that, in fact, Ortega's "perspectivismo" is consistent with Krausist tenets. This finding has some significance, as it was precisely Ortega's concept of the relational self with its sensitivity to cultural and historical contexts that became – passed on from him to José Gaos and thence to Leopoldo Zea – central for many contemporary Latin American philosophers.

Latin American Reception

Krausism came to Latin America in the form of (mostly French and Spanish) books, through emigrating and traveling Spanish scholars, and, last but not least, through a coterie of Latin American intellectuals who studied in Spain, such as José Martí and Eugenio María de Hostos (Stoetzer, 1998b, p. 205). Through Ortega y Gasset, Martí, María de Hostos, and many others, Krausist ideas had a deep impact on the political history of Latin America in the nineteenth and twentieth centuries. A distinct Krausist influence can be attested for Mexico (Krumpel, 2001), Brazil (Paim, 1998), Columbia (Orden Jiménez, 1999), Guatemala (Stoetzer, 1998b, p. 136), Ecuador (Ossenbach-Sauter, 1983), and Peru (Himmelblau, 1979; Vetter, 1987).

In the following, we will concentrate on Argentina and Uruguay, where Krausist thinking still influences constitutional theory and presidential politics. For more information on Krausism in the other Latin American countries we highly recommend one of the few English books on the subject, Carlos Otto Stoetzer's comprehensive study *Karl Christian Friedrich Krause and His Influences in the Hispanic World* (1998b).

120

Krausist beginnings in Argentina and Uruguay

At the Río de la Plata Krausism found prominent promoters in the Uruguayan president José Batlle y Ordóñez (1856–1929) and the Argentine president Hipólito Yrigoyen (1852–1933). Both were friends with leading Krausistas, and, remarkably, both began as law professors, transitioning from there into legal philosophy and later into political office (Roig, 1969).

In Argentina, Krausism began with Wenceslao Escalante (1852–1912). Escalante's *Lecciones de filosofía del derecho* (1884) was used for many years as the Argentinean textbook on legal theory. As a politician, being in turns cabinet minister of the interior, finance, agriculture and, later, president of the National Bank, Escalante inaugurated a great number of Krausist reforms (Álvarez Guerrero, 1986). These prepared the ground for Hipólito Yrigoyen, whom Stoetzer ranks as the source of "unquestionably the most remarkable and strongest Krausean influence in the entire Ibero American continent" (Stoetzer, 1998b, p. 360). Argentina's president from 1916 to 1922, and again from 1928 to 1930, not only did Yrigoyen take Krause for his personal lodestar in politics, he also made Krausism the intellectual bedrock of Argentina's socio-liberal party, the Unión Cívica Radical (UCR). The UCR, still a strong force in Argentinean politics, acknowledges this debt to Krause explicitly and, notably, recent leaders (such as Raúl Alfonsín) are still declaring themselves publicly as Krausistas (see Romero, 1998).

A similar development occurred in Uruguay, where Krausism was popularized by the end of the nineteenth century through president José Batlle y Ordóñez and his intellectual companion Prudencio Vázquez y Vega, who taught legal philosophy based upon textbooks by Tiberghien and Ahrens. To give an impression of the impact Krausism must have had then, one should consider that in the years 1878–93 more than two thirds of all juridical dissertations in Montevideo dealt in one way or another with Krausist topics (Monreal, 1993, p. 201).

Like Yrigoyen, president Batlle felt personally indebted to Krausism. During his second presidency he wrote on the title cover of his copy of Ahrens's "Curso de derecho natural" (Course of Natural Law) (that in form and content strictly follows Krause's legal philosophy), "This exemplar of the work of Ahrens [. . .] is a gift that I value much because through this great work I have formed my judgment about the law, which has served as my guide throughout my public life." (See the facsimile in Ardao, 1951, pp. 176–7.)

Practical results were to result from this reading. In a famous speech on June 20, 1925 before the "Convención Batllista" in Montevideo, the "first" Batlle (the family has later produced more presidents) laid out a distinctly Krausist socioeconomic program that tied personal property back to the common good (Biagini, 1989, p. 222). The ensuing socio-democratic program soon became baptized as "batllismo" (Ardao, 1950; Ardao, 1951). Even today, "batllismo" stands for policies that pursue social peace through redistributive and educative policies, and continues to shape Uruguayan politics (Monreal, 1993).

Under the tutelage of José Batlle y Ordóñez and Hipólito Yrigoyen, the early constitutions of Argentina and Uruguay were shaped. Hence the curious fact that, as addressee and sovereign of these constitutions, not only the people of Uruguay and Argentina are invoked – but also, in good Krausist fashion, "humanity." In later years, calls for intergenerational justice and environmental sustainability were added in the same spirit (Hector Gros Espiell, 1966).

With humanity as ultimate political focus, both countries pursued pacifist and anti-imperialistic foreign policies. Argentina, for instance, withstood much pressure on part of the United States to enter World War I. In the aftermath of the war, Argentina criticized the Western alliance for misusing its position of power to deny their former enemies equal standing in the League of Nations. Ultimately Argentina left the League of Nations in protest with the slogan "Victory does not confer rights!" – a phrase that could have been taken directly from any contemporary Krausist compendium of legal philosophy (Stoetzer, 1998b, p. 384).

Until World War II, the ideas of Krausist "harmonism" clearly dominated domestic politics and foreign policies at the Río de la Plata (Piñeiro, 1989, p. 7). Moreover, when in 1931 Spain gave itself a new constitution that aspired to several Krausist tenets, this document, although soon rescinded by Franco, inspired subsequent constitutional reforms in Argentina and Uruguay and reinforced the overall Krausist influence (Espiell, 1966, p. 109).

Argentina and Uruguay – return to the future

The Krausist era ended in the second half of the twentieth century when the republics at the Río de la Plata fell prey to military juntas. Until the return of democracy (to Argentina in 1983, and Uruguay in 1984), Krausist philosophy was suppressed. Then, however, it underwent a quick renaissance. During their presidencies, Raúl Alfonsín in Argentina and Jorge Batlle in Uruguay (a distant relative of Batlle y Ordóñez, and son of the former, also Krausist, president Luis Batlle) brought back Krausism to the Río de la Plata with a vengeance (Stoetzer, 1998b).

Shortly after his inauguration Alfonsín published a book that ascribes to the Krausist legacy the pacifism, social harmonism, and cosmopolitanism of the Unión Cívica Radical, as well as its fervor in the protection of human dignity, its advocacy of a humanistic education and its rejection of coercive measures (Alfonsín, 1985, pp. 24, 83). Jorge Batlle on his part engaged in many public discussions, for example the debate over the role of religion in politics, with explicit references to Krause. This went so far that Uruguayan dailies, such as *Búsqueda* and *El Observador*, prodded academics to comment on whether the president had interpreted Krause correctly. Both politicians used their pulpits repeatedly to remind their audiences that with Krause's philosophy the role of politics can and must be redefined. They advocated that politics must turn from a narrowly conceived endeavor in favor of national interests, and instead embark on a humanitarian quest for peace, pacifist conflict regulations, and the rights of future generations. By these tenets, past and present Krausistas converge with broader currents of popular political sentiment in Latin America. This is also borne out by the fact that in recent years Latin American research on Krause has found its way outside the confines of academia. Journalists and political foundations, such as the Fundación Arturo Illia in Buenos Aires, are doing much to bring the subject back into the public realm.

Conclusion

Krausism in Latin America is a complex phenomenon. Krause's ideas came to Latin American countries in manifold ways, and often the lines of reception crossed and intertwined. In addition, numerous Krausist authors took liberties with the theories of Krause; they adapted them to their respective contexts and mixed them freely with other contemporary theories, creating hybrid ideologies such as the so-called "krauso-positivismo" (Jiménez García, 1997; Abellán, 1989). Naturally, an exacting study of the history of Krausism must strive to differentiate clearly between Krause's original thoughts, transformations through translation, unplanned mutations, and, lastly, deliberate alterations.

Here, however, we emphasized not the differences but the commonalities of Krause's philosophy with the works of his disciples and interpreters. For *some* features *are* constitutive of almost all Krausist positions, viz.:

1 Especially important for the entire movement is Krause's emphasis on the re-conciliation of historical and scientific experience with speculative philosophy. Continuous internal reform keeps his philosophy forever open to new problems and novel insights. This reform is brought about by the use of (dialogical, discursive, and phenomenological) methodologies that insist on the broadest possible intellectual participation. Krausist thinkers hence advocate for better universal education.

2 From improved insight Krausists expect social improvements through voluntary reform "from below" rather than through forced (intellectual or practical) change "from above." Politically, this approach translates typically into an advocacy of grad-ual, harmonic transformation over radical and abrupt change, i.e., of peaceful reform over violent revolution.

3 The commitment to peaceful change interlinks with Krause's idea of "harmonic" freedom. Tying the individual quest for liberty back to the promotion of freedom for all, the idea of a universal harmony of freedom demands to fight for all under-privileged and marginalized interests. The defense of debilitated persons and the fight for the rights of minorities are therefore not accidental features of Krausism; nor is its impressive humanitarian cosmopolitanism and environmental sensitivity.

For to follow Krause means, above all, one thing: that freedom is not only the prime end but also the premier means of all philosophical and political efforts.

Related chapters: 5 Early Critics of Positivism; 7 Darwinism ; 9 'Normal' Philosophy; 10 Ortega y Gasset's Heritage in Latin America.

References

Abellán, J. L. (1989). La dimensión krauso-positivista en Eugenio María de Hostos. *Cuadernos Americanos. Nueva Época*. Año/Year III, 4, Vol. 7/8, 58–66.
Alfonsín, R. (1985). *Qué es el radicalismo*. Buenos Aires: Sudamericana.

123

Álvarez Guerrero, O. (1986). *Política y ética social. Yrigoyen y el Krausism. Orígenes ideológicos de la UCR*. Buenos Aires: Leviathan.

Ardao, A. (1950). *Espiritualismo y positivismo en el Uruguay*. Mexico: Fondo de Cultura Economica.

Ardao, A. (1951). *Batlle y Ordóñez y el positivismo filosófico*. Montevideo.

Biagini, H. (1989). Precursores del estado benefactor. In *Orígenes de la democracia argentina. El trasfondo krausista* (pp. 207–25). Buenos Aires: Legasa.

Cachu Viu, V. (1999). La Institución Libre de Enseñanza: De la restauración a la generación de Ortega. In E. M. Ureña & P. A. Lázaro (Eds.). *La actualidad del Krausism en su contexto europeo* (pp. 171–87). Madrid: Editorial Parteluz.

Coil, H. W., & Roberts, A. E. (1996). *Coil's Masonic encyclopedia*. Richmond: Macoy Pub & Masonic Supply Co.

Dicke, K. (1996). Lieber hätt'ich von Dir den Kranz des Friedens empfangen. In K. M. Kodalle (Ed.). *Der Vernunftfrieden – Kants "Entwurf" im Widerstreit*. Kritisches Jahrbuch der Philosophie (pp. 21–36). Würzburg: Königshausen & Neumann.

Dierksmeier, C. (1999b). Kant versus Krause – sobre o comum e as diferencas no fundamento da moral e do direito. *Estudios em Homagem a Joachim M. da Silva Cunha* (pp. 87–100); reprinted in German as: Kant versus Krause – Über Gemeinsamkeiten und Differenzen in der Begründung von Moral und Recht. *Studia Iuridica*, 45, 71–82.

Dierksmeier, C. (2003a). *Der absolute Grund des Rechts. Karl Christian Friedrich Krause in Auseinandersetzung mit Fichte und Schelling*. Bad Cannstatt: Frommann-Holzboog Verlag.

Dierksmeier, C. (2003b). Die Wirtschaftsphilosophie des 'Krausism'. *Deutsche Zeitschrift für Philosophie*, 4, 571–81.

Dierksmeier, C. (2004a). Deduktion/Konstruktion versus Mechanismus/Organismus. Zu Methodologie und Inhalt der Sozialphilosophie im Deutschen Idealismus. In R. Ahlers (Ed.). *System and context: early Romantic and early Idealistic constellation / System und Kontext. Frühromantische und frühidealistische Konstellationen* (pp. 229–62). Lewiston/Queenston/Lampeter: Edwin Mellen Press.

Dierksmeier, C. (2004b). Recht und Freiheit. Karl Christian Friedrich Krauses 'Grundlage des Naturrechts' im Kontext des Jenaer Idealismus. In *International Yearbook of German Idealism / Internationales Jahrbuch für Deutschen Idealismus*, 2, 309–34.

Dierksmeier, C. (2007). Qualitative oder quantitative Freiheit? *Rechtsphilosophisch, Hefte XII*, 107–19.

Ende, H. (1973). *Der Konstruktionsbegriff im Umkreis des deutschen Idealismus*. Meisenheim/Glan: Hain.

Espiell, H. G. (1966). *Esquema de la evolución constitucional del Uruguay*. Montevideo: Fundación de Cultura Universitaria.

Findel, J. G. (1886). *History of Freemasonry: from its rise down to the present day*. Leipzig/New York.

García Cué, J. R. (1985). Krausism y Hegelismo. In: J. R. García Cué (Ed.). *Aproximaciones al estudio del Krausism andaluz*. Madrid: Tecnos.

Garrido, F. (2001). *Francisco Giner De Los Ríos. Creador de la Institución Libre De Enseñaza*. Granada: Editorial Comares.

Gil-Cremades, J. J. (1985). Die politische Dimension des Krausism in Spanien. In K. M. Kodalle (Ed.). *Karl Christian Friedrich Krause (1781–1832) – Studien zu seiner Philosophie und zum Krausism* Hamburg: Feliz Meiner Verlag.

Himmelblau, J. (1979). *Alejandro O. Deústua. Philosophy in defense of man*. Gainesville: University Press of Florida.

Jiménez García, A. (1997). *El krausopositivismo de Urbano Gonzáles Serrano*. Badajoz: Diputación Provincial.

Krause, K. C. F. (1803). *Grundlage des Naturrechts, oder philosophischer Grundriss des Ideales des Rechts. Erste Abtheilung*. Jena.

124

Krause, K. C. F. (1804). *Anleitung zur Naturphilosophie. I. Deduction der Natur, II. Anleitung zur Construction der Natur.* Jena/Leipzig: Cnobloch.

Krause, K. C. F. (1811). *Das Urbild der Menschheit. Ein Versuch. Vorzüglich für Freimaurer.* Dresden: Arnold.

Krause, K. C. F. (1814). Entwurf eines europäischen Staatenbundes als Basis des allgemeinen Friedens und als rechtliches Mittel gegen jeden Angriff wider die innere und äußere Freiheit Europas. Quoted according to the 2nd edition from 1920, H. Reichel (Ed.). Leipzig: Felix Meiner.

Krause, K. C. F. (1828a). *Abriss des Systemes der Philosophie des Rechtes oder des Naturrechts.* Göttingen: Dieterich.

Krause, K. C. F. (1828b). *Vorlesungen über Grundwahrheiten der Wissenschaft, zugleich in ihrer Beziehung zu dem Leben. Nebst einer kurzen Darstellung und Würdigung der bisherigen Systeme der Philosophie, vornehmlich der neuesten von Kant, Fichte, Schelling und Hegel, und der Lehre Jacobi's. Für Gebildete aus allen Ständen.* Göttingen: Dieterich.

Krause, K. C. F. (1828c). *Vorlesungen zum System der Philosophie.* Göttingen: Dieterich.

Krause, K. C. F. (1874). *Das System der Rechtsphilosophie – Vorlesungen für Gebildete aus allen Ständen.* K. A. D. Röder (Ed.). J. A. Brockhaus. Leipzig: Schulze.

Krause, K. C. F. (1890a). *Grundlage des Naturrechts oder philosophischer Grundriß des Ideales des Rechts. Zweite Abtheilung.* G. Mollat (Ed.). Vol. I, 2nd ed., Vol. II, 1st ed. Weimar.

Krause, K. C. F. (1892). *Vorlesungen über Naturrecht oder Philosophie des Rechts und des Staates.* R. Mucke (Ed.). n.p.

Krause, K. C. F. (1893). *Der Erdrechtsbund an sich selbst und in seinem Verhältnisse zum Ganzen und zu allen Einzeltheilen des Menschheitlebens.* G. Mollat (Ed.). Weimar: Emil Felber.

Krause, K. C. F. (1904). *Lebenlehre oder Philosophie der Geschichte zur Begründung der Lebenkunstwissenschaft.* 2nd ed. Leipzig: Dieterich.

Krumpel, K. H. (2001). Zur Aneignung und Verwandlung der Ideen Humboldts und Krauses in Lateinamerika – Gemeinsamkeiten und Unterschiede. *International Review for Humboldtian Studies*, II:2.

MacCauley, C. (1917). *Krause's League for Human Right and thereby world peace.* Tokyo: Fukuin.

Malo Guillén, J. L. (1998). *Pensamiento económico y filosofía social en la España del siglo XIX. Liberalismo, Krausism y reformas sociales.* Aragón: Universidad de Zaragoza.

Marías, J. (1960). Ortega, (I), circunstancia y vocación. *Revista de Occidente*, 126–30.

Marichal, J. (1990). *El intelectual y la política en España (1898–1936).* Madrid: Consejo Superior de Investigaciones Científicas.

Mateo, L. E. (1990). *El Krausism, La Institución Libre De Enseñanza y Valencia.* Valencia: Facultad de Filosofía y Ciencias de la Educación, Educación Comparada.

Monreal, S. (1993). *Krausism en el Uruguay. Algunos fundamentos del Estado tutor.* Montevideo: UCU.

Miller, W.G. (1884). *Lectures on the philosophy of law.* London: Griffin.

Orden Jiménez, R. V. (1998a). *El sistema de la filosofía de Krause – génesis y desarrollo del panenteísmo.* Madrid: Universidad Pontificia Comillas.

Orden Jiménez, R. V. (1998b). *Sanz Del Rió: Traductor y divulgador de Krause.* Pamplona: Universidad de Navarra.

Orden Jiménez, R. V. (1999). Krause's philosophy and its influence: new perspectives for the study of Krausism in Latin America. *Universitas-Philosophica*, 16:32, 139–79.

Ortega y Gasset, J. (1983). *Obras completas.* Vol. 1. Madrid: Alianza.

Ossenbach-Sauter, G. (1983). La presencia del Krausism en Ecuador. In Friedrich-Ebert-Stiftung. *Documentos y estudios*, 64, pp. 251–60. Madrid: Fundación Friedrich Ebert and Instituto Fe y Secularidad.

Paim, A. (1998). *Krausism Brasileiro.* Londrina: Edicoes CEFIL.

125

Piernas Hurtado, J. M. (1885). *Tratado de hacienda pública y examen de la española* (2 vols.). 2nd ed. Madrid: Lib. de Victoriano Suárez (Original work published 1869).

Piñeiro, A. G. (1989). *Radicalismo e intervención estatal. La revista Hechos e Ideas 1935–1941*. Buenos Aires: CEAL.

Roig, A. A. (1969). *Los krausistas argentinos*. Puebla: Cajica.

Romero, J. L. (1998). *Las ideas políticas en Argentina*. Buenos Aires: Fondo de Cultura Económica.

Sanz del Río, J. (1871). *Ideal de la humanidad para la vida*. C. Chr. F. Krause; con introducción y comentarios por Julián Sanz del Río. Madrid.

Stoetzer, O. C. (1998b). *Karl Christian Friedrich Krause and his influences in the Hispanic world*. Köln/Weimar/Wien: Böhlau.

Ureña, E. M. (1993). *Cincuenta cartas inéditas entre Sanz del Río y krausistas alemanes (1844–1869)*. Madrid: Universidad Pontificia Comillas.

Ureña, E. M. (2001). Philosophie und gesellschaftliche Praxis. Wirkungen der Philosophie K. C. F. Krauses in Deutschland (1831–1881). *Archiv für Geschichte der Philosophie*, 3.

Vetter, U. (1987). Alejandro O. Deústua. Der 'neue Idealismus' in Lateinamerika zu Beginn des 20. Jahrhunderts. *Deutsche Zeitschrift für Philosophie*, Ost-Berlin, 35:6, 548–52.

Wagner, J. J. (1804). Review on Krause. *Jenaer Allgemeinen Literatur Zeitung J.A.L.Z*, 4, 89–92.

Further Reading

Arpini, A. (1990). La traza del Krausism en el pensamiento ético-social de Eugenio María de Hostos. *Revista de Historia de América*, 110, 99–107. México: Instituto Panamericano de Geografía e Historia.

Dierksmeier, C. (1999a). Karl Christian Friedrich Krause und das 'gute' Recht. *Archiv für Rechts – und Sozialphilosophie (ARSP). Sonderheft: Deutscher Idealismus* [Archive for Legal and Social Philosophy. Special Edition: German Idealism], 85:1, pp. 75–94.

Kodalle, K. M. (1985). *Karl Christian Friedrich Krause (1781–1832) – Studien zu seiner Philosophie und zum Krausism*. Hamburg: Felix Meiner Verlag.

Krause, K. C. F. (1890b). *Das Eigenthümliche der Wesenlehre nebst Nachrichten zur Geschichte der Aufnahme derselben, vornehmlich von Seiten deutscher Philosophen*. P. Hohlfeld & A. Wünsche (Eds.). Weimar.

Lopez-Morrillas, J. (1981). *The Krausist movement and ideological change in Spain 1854–1874*. 2nd ed. Cambridge: Cambridge University Press.

Lorimer, J. (1987). *The Institutes of Law. A treatise on the principles of jurisprudence as determined by nature*. Aalen: Scientia Verlag (Reprint of the 1880 edition).

Lluch, E., & Argemí, L. (1999). *The German influence in Spain (1800–1860): from late cameralism to Jakob, Krause and List*. Third Annual Conference of ESHET, Book of extended summaries (pp. 259–62). Valencia: University of Barcelona.

Lluch, E., & Argemí, L. (2000). El Krausism económico sin Institución Libre. La influencia germánica en España (1800–1860). *Sistema – Revista de Ciencias Sociales*, 157, 3–18.

MacCauley, C. (1925). *Karl Christian Friedrich Krause, heroic pioneer for thought and life*. Berkeley: Gazette Press.

Orden Jíménez, R. (1996). *Las habilitaciones filosóficas de Krause*. Madrid: Publicaciones de la Universidad Pontificia.

Ortega y Gasset, J. (1910). Pedagogía social como programa politico. Lecture given to the 'El Sitio' Society in Bilbao. In J. Ortega y Gasset (1983). *Obras completas*. Vol. 1, pp. 503–21. Madrid: Alianza.

Ortí y Lara, J. M. (1864). *Krause y sus discípulos convictos del panenteísmo*. Madrid: Imprenta de Tejado.

Polo y Peyrolón, M. (1888). "Krause" and "Krausism." In I. Domenech (Ed.). *Diccionario de ciencias eclesiásticas*. Vol. 6 (pp. 246–9, 249–57). Valencia: Domenech.

Stoetzer, O. C. (1998a). Der geistige Einfluß Krauses in der jüngsten argentinischen Geschichte. In *Jahrbuch für Geschichte von Staat, Wirtschaft und Gesellschaft Lateinamerikas*, 25, 635–71.

Ureña, E. M. (1991). *K. C. F. Krause – Philosoph, Freimaurer, Weltbürger. Eine Biographie*. Stuttgart Bad-Cannstatt: Frommann-Holzboog.

9

'Normal' Philosophy

WILLIAM F. COOPER

In 1906, when he was 46 years old, Alejandro Korn began teaching the history of philosophy in the University of Buenos Aires. It was the beginning of a distinguished academic career. For the next twenty-four years, he taught, published, and led in the Reforma Universitaria (the university reform movement that started in 1918). After that, until his death in 1936, he continued to speak and publish, addressing issues of basic concern to him and pivotal to his own national heritage.

One of his primary concerns was Argentinean philosophy, a topic many looked upon with condescending humor. He insisted, however, that any group of human beings concerned about their own existence will have thought about their struggles and hopes. They will attempt to pull these thoughts together in some way that will give context to the struggles and ground for the hopes. They will in this way address their own reality and experience. Such was the case in Argentina.

Juan Bautista Alberdi, in the middle of the nineteenth century, had engaged in such a task and created the intellectual context in which Argentinean and, indeed, much of Latin American culture had worked for decades. Alberdi's insistence on pragmatically addressing the political, economic, and social issues faced by the Argentina of his day was an insistence from which he never deviated. Although Alberdi's thought borrowed much from here and there, it had a quality drawn from its Argentinean context that was evident. In the years that followed, other influences came to bear, the most important being those of Auguste Comte, Herbert Spencer, and John Stuart Mill. These influences, collectively known as positivism, came to dominate much of the nation-building activity of the latter half of the nineteenth century. Eventually, beginning with Korn in Argentina and Enrique Molina in Chile, José Vasconcelos, Antonio Caso, and others in Mexico, and throughout Latin America, the shift away from this positivism gathered steam and opened the intellectual doors to other influences. Francisco Romero referred to this setting aside of positivism as the beginning of the 'normal' development of philosophy in Latin America.

The 'normal' development needs to be described a bit more fully. One of the dimensions that emerged was a more careful and methodical study of works in philosophy published in Europe and to some degree in the United States. In some cases what resulted from this more thorough study was critical exposition and analysis of the texts being studied. With some thinkers this study became the basis for the development of a philosophical perspective with a quality of its own. During this period of 'normal' development, the study of philosophy becomes more widespread and the number of persons devoted to philosophical work increases considerably. Furthermore, as one would expect, the variety in philosophical perspectives also multiplies and the quality of the thought takes on added strength.

Are there any themes or issues that tend to permeate the philosophical landscape? Risieri Frondizi suggested in the mid-1970s that Latin American thinkers may tend to be more humanistically oriented in their philosophical work, leading to a healthy range of interests but at the same time an undesirable flexibility in the meaning of basic terms and some weakness in logical precision (Gracia, 1986, pp. 20–1). He also pointed out that social and political issues tend to be the magnets guiding philosophical work. This, in turn, has embedded in it a way of thinking that commends confronting the social and political issues from a given philosophical perspective. As a result of this emphasis many of the writings tend to emphasize one perspective rather than theoretical rigor.

Romero (1952, p. 17) suggested somewhat tentatively some forty years earlier that issues relating to mind or spirit, values, and liberty found resonance with Latin American thinkers during this 'normal' period.

With this as background, a summary of the work of several major figures will serve as a guide to this period in Latin American philosophy extending roughly from the 1940s to the 1980s.

Alejandro Korn (1860–1936)

Korn was the son of a German physician who left Germany during the disturbances of 1848 and settled in the town of San Vicente in the province of Buenos Aires. His son was born twelve years later. Alejandro was a diligent student and completed the requirements for his degree in medicine when he was twenty-two. He remained active in his profession until 1916, when he retired from the practice of medicine and from his position as director of Melchor Romero Mental Hospital, a post he held for nineteen years. As mentioned above, he began teaching the history of philosophy at the University of Buenos Aires in 1906. Three years later he was appointed to the Chair in Epistemology and Metaphysics at that same institution and to the Chair in the History of Philosophy at the University of La Plata.

Korn's written work, according to Romero, was more of a trail that spilled over from his responsibilities as a teacher, as a reformer, and above all as a person. The impact he had on the lives of those who came his way had a greater effect than did his writings. These covered a broad range of issues. He gave special attention to intellectual influences on Argentinean cultural development. His own philosophical views are presented in less than a dozen essays published over a period of seventeen years. He also published occasional essays on Pascal, Kant, Croce, Bergson, Hegel, and Augustine, among others. Other themes included ethical socialism, and the university reform.

As to his own philosophical views, Korn (1949) insisted on beginning with experience. Experience comes to us twofold, as interaction with the quantitative and measurable and as response to what we sense or feel. He thus gives to experience an objective dimension governed by space and an internal dimension governed by time. He

129

claimed that this dualism was not absolute since the two dimensions were inevitably interacting but they reflect two basic realms of our experience. Furthermore, the first realm is one in which science is at home and carries out its activities as it makes progress in understanding the surrounding world. It has its methods, hypotheses, theories, and norms which change and adapt with developments in science. Generally speaking, we are dealing with a mechanistic dimension that has a certain necessity to it.

Our response to what we sense and feel operates in a significantly different manner. This is a subjective rather than an objective realm and is guided by a variety of resources inherent in our life as human beings, our affect, desire, passion, pain, and aspiration. Our responses in this realm are polar in that as we are drawn toward one thing, we set aside something else; as we affirm one option, we deny another. Activity in this realm is thus value-laden. Nevertheless, we are free to espouse the values we choose, shape them, commit to them, change them as we engage in our daily tasks. This is in no way to deny the personal and social contexts that bear on each of us in different ways, nor to minimize the inherent struggle endemic to the human condition.

From this starting point, Korn develops a pragmatic function for reason. Since experience presents reason with more than its ordering and abstracting function can handle, any conclusions we attain through reason are relative to the circumstance. Absolutes are rational chimeras. Furthermore, as an abstracting process, reason leaves aside much that is crucial to the world as given to us.

As we navigate the realm of our responses, that is, the realm of our inner experience, we make choices guided by our values, values inherited and reshaped as well as values created by our own free will. Although there is a commonality to these values, this commonality is based on circumstance and social custom. Much as we may long for them, there are no ultimate values to be clearly defined once for all. Korn (1949) gave a good bit of attention to this valuing process and even drew up a chart identifying nine types of evaluation (economic, instinctive, erotic, vital, social, religious, ethical, logical, and aesthetic), their defining fundamental concepts, their ideals, historical values, and the philosophical systems that emerge from them. He would insist, however, that others could develop different perspectives that would yield different charts and that these should be matters for discussion.

Two other matters need addressing. One is that Korn insisted that regardless of what science might discover about us as human beings and about the world we live in, there is always a dimension that remains an enigma. This leaves us in a situation where the action we take becomes the crucial affirmation of who we are. So we must always insist on the exercise of our will in taking action, what he referred to as "creative freedom."

The second issue is that, granted the importance of our "creative freedom," it is not exercised in the dark but in what light can be shed by myth, art, or religion. In granting these three options, he does not intend to invoke an appeal to tradition or authority but to acknowledge these realms of human striving where light is shed on the dualism and contradictions we confront, allowing a glimpse as to how they are overcome and strengthening hope for the action we engage in.

Kant, Hegel, and Bergson were important influences in Korn's thought. His epistemological framework is Kantian. His understanding of social and historical processes is Hegelian. His view of the processes inherent in the mind of the subject is drawn from

130

Bergson. The backdrop, however, is positivism. He draws on these three, and others, as he works his way out of enlightened positivism (Korn, 1949, pp. 244–9).

Alejandro Octavio Deústua (1849–1945)

Alejandro Octavio Deústua had a long, distinguished career in his native Peru. Although his career was rooted in an academic setting, where he exercised both teaching and administrative functions, he also held posts in the national government. Among these was a role in strengthening and reforming Peru's educational systems. He wrote a good bit about pedagogical issues but his main intellectual interests turned toward how liberty or freedom, which lies at heart of human imagination and action, finds expression in the natural setting that constrains the freedom.

Deústua's primary concern was with the human spirit or consciousness. Drawing on K. F. C. Krause and Henri Bergson, he maintains that creative imagination is the fundamental dimension of the human spirit. This creative imagination or intuition is fundamentally free, expansive, and disinterested. The more obvious results of the work of this creative intuition are those that are shaped by the struggle with the natural setting. These give evidence of the curtailment of this freedom, expansiveness, and disinterest.

Deústua carefully delineates how this struggle occurs, giving form to several fundamental realms of human life. In each of these, the free, creative action of human intuition and imagination encounters restraints emerging from the surrounding natural environment. In response to these restraints, the creative intuition formulates norms that serve as guides to human action. But the free, expansive, disinterested work of the creative imagination, which he says is the aesthetic phenomenon, is never completely dominated by either natural or social constraints.

He describes four realms of human activity that interact with and emerge from the aesthetic phenomenon (Deústua, 1923). Indeed, each of these realms enriches the aesthetic endeavor while not supplanting its essentially free, expansive, and disinterested activity.

One of the more elemental realms is that of thought or intellect. The creativity of the human spirit – a dimension of reality that remains inaccessible to us save as it is manifested in these various realms – leads to the formulation of concepts and relationships that are logically structured in such a way as to lead to truth. In fact, logical analysis is an important human function that is essential to the development of our knowledge of the external world. Logical norms serve as basic guides in distinguishing the true from the false. In following these norms, however, important as they are for everyday life and scientific investigation, freedom is given up in order for the instrumental procedures of the intellect to be carried out effectively. There is creative activity but it is directed to logical and useful ends.

Deústua describes another elemental realm as economics. This encompasses human activity in the effort to become useful. It has to do with ordering the environment to facilitate the development of institutions that allow life to be engaged efficiently and effectively. The fundamental norm guiding this realm is usefulness.

It is important to recognize that in each of these realms, the creative imagination engages reality and formulates norms – logic in one case, usefulness in the other – to

131

serve as guides. The creative imagination, however, is not bound to these norms. It can still continue to function freely, expansively, and disinterestedly in creating or discovering norms in other realms or in functioning in a truly aesthetic fashion, which in its pure expression is normless.

Another realm of human action more closely interwoven with aesthetic domain is the moral realm. The defining dimension of the moral realm is action according to a norm, a norm regarded as good. The will freely submits to act in accord with a norm accepted as universal. This norm comes about through activity of the creative imagination. Once this norm is created or is in the process of being created, the freedom, expansiveness, and disinterestedness of creative imagination are curtailed in that one is free to act only in accord with the norm, expansiveness comes to an end in that other norms are no longer sought, and disinterestedness ceases because the norm becomes the focus of interest. Much is to be said, however, for the aesthetic embodiment of moral norms. Each can enhance the other, as goodness provides for certain dimensions of aesthetic expression and as aesthetic activity gives strength and beauty to what is good.

The aspect of human experience most closely linked to the aesthetic domain is religious practice and belief. In religion, the divine, which is other than and beyond what is human, either encounters what is human or comes through revelation in mysterious and inexplicable ways. But this encounter or revelation is most accessible through creative or intuitive imagination, namely, the highest manifestation of what it is to be human. This would mean that the highest ideal or norm to which the religious realm could aspire would be the fullness of God to which the fullness of being human could attain. Deústua claims this is the highest aesthetic expression of the religious norms.

He could still maintain, however, that the aesthetic activity of human spirit or consciousness cannot be reduced to religious, moral, logical, or useful domains, active as the spirit is in bringing them about and in continuing to add new dimensions to them. In fact, if we carefully consider the whole of the conscious spirit, we could find in it a tendency to free, creative activity able to create norms and abandon them as it expands its realm in new ways, uninterested in any specific end or purpose. The purest expression of this activity is creating beautiful works of art, no one of which captures the totality of this creative spirit.

Deústua moves beyond positivism with a more confident pace than Korn, who retained a respect for scientific investigation that kept him firmly rooted in a material reality to which we respond in a value-laden way but with no sure guide or norm yielding certainty. For Deústua, these norms are themselves the product of our creative intuition, whose freedom, expansiveness, and disinterest provide the guide for working with and implementing those norms. But Korn's approach falls into some of the same paths as those of Deústua as Korn points to myth, art, and religion as ways of overcoming the duality and concomitant relativism that characterize human experience.

Enrique Molina (1871–1964)

As was the case with Korn and Deústua, Molina was very much a part of the institutional and intellectual life of his native land. Born in 1871 in La Serena, just north of Santiago, Chile, he had a long, distinguished career as a university professor and administrator.

Like many forward-looking intellectuals of his day, Molina's early orientation was shaped by a positivist perspective. Readings in the work of Lester F. Ward, a U.S. sociologist who emphasized the role of psychological and sociological factors in structuring civilization, were especially influential. His meliorism, drawn from John Stuart Mill, and his sociocracy, in which social concerns place limits on individual interests, Molina found to be especially appealing. Other reading in William James and Henri Bergson led him to modify his own positivist orientation. The attraction of this orientation came in its promise for social change through education, a promise that held out great hope for Chileans struggling to implement improvements in the economy and institutions of their native land.

In order for social change to lead to progress, it must be undergirded by a sense of freedom, because the desired progress is not mere material betterment. This is because material betterment itself is only a means to enhance the fundamental values that guide the various dimensions of the human spirit. Unless freedom is both a social and political reality as well as an inner quality of the individual person, there is little hope for meaningful progress (Molina, 1951).

It thus becomes very important to understand consciousness or spirit in human experience, because this is the seat of the quality of freedom and understanding that guide the progress so central to human longing. The reason this is the case is because freedom is rooted in the human ability to make choices rather than to be impelled solely by necessity as defined by circumstances. This ability to choose requires rational intelligence to assist in evaluating options as well as to help work toward developing material circumstances to broaden the range of options. Thus, understanding the human spirit, that reality in which feeling, thought, and action occur serving as the hallmark of what it is to be human, stands as the ultimate challenge for human striving.

Understanding the nature of this reality, however, emerges as the most demanding of intellectual tasks, one undertaken traditionally by metaphysics. This task will embrace all human endeavor and creative work – the sciences, aesthetic values, morality and its norms, as well as religion. What makes this task possible is the human ability to choose and to work creatively with whatever is at hand. The freedom to act and to use reason, the supreme structure of the spirit, enables human beings to engage in creative progress.

Two observations are in order at this point. The first is that this emphasis on freedom bears interesting similarities to the approaches taken by Korn and Deústua. The second is that giving metaphysics a legitimate place reflects a major departure from his positivist roots.

José Gaos (1900–69) and José Ortega y Gasset (1883–1955)

Gaos was a major intellectual presence in Latin America for a period of some twenty-five to thirty years. A Spaniard who was close to Ortega y Gasset and much influenced by his emphasis on a person's circumstance, Gaos emigrated to Mexico in 1938 and became affiliated with what became known as The College of Mexico in addition to holding a professorship in the National Autonomous University of Mexico.

133

WILLIAM F. COOPER

One of his more influential efforts was a Seminar based in The College of Mexico. This was an institution created by President Lázaro Cárdenas for the express purpose of harboring the Spanish intellectuals who felt constrained to leave Spain as Franco came to power. Gaos's seminar focused on study of the thought in Spanish-speaking countries. The work produced by Gaos's study group, which included Leopoldo Zea, was published under by the Economic Culture Fund, a major Latin American publishing house. These publications did much to focus interest on intellectual currents and philosophical work in a good many countries in Latin America. The work of Leopoldo Zea, however, took a special interest in bringing to light the Mexican circumstance, which was explored by several authors, spurred on by research Zea himself initiated.

In addition to the effort to encourage such studies, Gaos published a great deal himself, developing an approach to philosophy that bears much of the influence of Ortega's early writings (Gaos, 1945). In these writings, Ortega was steering a course that lay between the emphasis by Edmund Husserl and others on the one hand, and that of Max Scheler and Nicolai Hartmann on the other. Husserl focused on the analysis of consciousness, seeking to identify that foundation on which knowledge could be said to rest most securely. Ortega felt this tended toward an unhealthy idealism, giving too much attention to consciousness or spirit and not enough to the surrounding world with which consciousness was continuously engaged. Scheler and Hartmann, although very much a part of this phenomenological tradition, focused on the order and dynamic that characterized the world as experienced. Ortega felt this was insensitive to the particular circumstances of our encounter with reality and focused too comfortably on so-called universal dimensions of culture. What Ortega sought was the more fruitful interweaving of both our experience and the surrounding world so that whatever the self is, it is always placed in a natural and cultural context or circumstance and whatever the natural and cultural context is, it is always interwoven with an active and knowing self. This was the beginning point he staked out for his personal and intellectual venture: "myself and my circumstance" always together.

Gaos readily acknowledged, in fact, he underscored this beginning point, exploring and developing it in ways that encouraged linking the Latin American circumstance to any philosophical work by Latin Americans. For him, it was important for anyone to come to grips with the surrounding circumstance, which includes one's own social and cultural heritage as well as one's historical and geographical setting. He insisted such an engagement was most fruitful when undertaken in a conversational setting, when those participating share in an open, perceptive way the perspectives and insights they discover. It is also crucial to acknowledge that this exploration and conversation are themselves temporal at root. This brings us to recognize the dynamic process we are and the dynamic process our circumstance is.

Philosophical thought confronted with such variety and change is loath to identify fixed and lasting ultimates and leans in the direction of non-systematic approaches. At the same time, fruitful and perceptive descriptions, sensitive to the aesthetic qualities of both our experience and what is encountered, carry us to recognize the social context as one to be respected and nurtured.

Gaos expands on these beginning points in stimulating ways, as became evident in his own publications and in the work of his students, although he was hesitant

134

about attempts on their part to load up a given cultural circumstance with unchanging traits.

Let us now turn to the work of perhaps his best-known student.

Leopoldo Zea (1912–2004)

A man of intellectual passion and cultural empathy, Zea sought to understand his circumstance as a person living in Latin America. Doing so, he served as a pioneer in breaking new philosophical ground. That new ground would open up ways of doing and being leading to a sense of humanity that was free, socially equal, and disinclined to diminish or subjugate others.

As indicated above, Zea was an active participant in the study group directed by Gaos which focused its research on the Latin American intellectual and cultural heritage. Initially, Zea focused his interests on Mexico but he soon broadened this to include all of Latin America. Picking up on Hegelian notions of historical development, he studied the patterns of intellectual and philosophical evolution. He saw these patterns as depicting conditions in Latin America that kept Latin Americans and non-Western cultures in a state of subservience and underdevelopment leading to serious negative implications. This state of underdevelopment deprived the affected cultures of the freedom and social equality that was their natural condition. How had this come to be?

Latin America as we know it today came about through Western expansion, first by colonizing efforts by Spain and Portugal primarily, that left the native population destitute and kept locally born Hispanics and *mestizos* as colonists, subservient to Iberian rule.

In the late eighteenth and early nineteenth centuries political developments and new intellectual and cultural perspectives led to the independence movements that broke the political ties with Spain and Portugal. Attempts to form new governments by the former colonies were frustrated by a complicated set of circumstances underlined by a singular ineffectiveness in establishing viable political alternatives. The people of Latin America, according to Zea, as heirs of Western culture, were unable to overcome the socially and politically subservient state to which they had been conditioned for four hundred years. As their history transpired through the nineteenth century, they turned to a cultural romanticism and then an adapted positivism to find emancipation from their deeply rooted colonial status. With positivism rejected, in the early twentieth century, new options began to emerge that focused on their identity as Latin Americans. But even as these options were clarified, new economic subjugation from European and North American sources stultified the liberation process.

However, a perceptive surge in the intensity of examining this state of underdevelopment emerged under the influence of Gaos and other Spanish intellectuals who emigrated from Spain following the Spanish civil war. Guided by Ortega's basic affirmation that I can understand myself only as I recognize my intimate link to "my circumstance," Gaos and his students focused on the "circumstance" of being Latin American and the bearing this had on philosophical reflection by Latin Americans.

As Zea took on this task, he was careful to delineate the primary features of his circumstance. The point of departure, common to all human beings, is the Word or Logos, that conscious, knowing, creative, free, individuating condition that brings our humanity to be and provides the fundamental forms of its expression. Accompanying dimensions of this point of departure are our social relationships and the possibility of our making choices. This broad, complex circumstance shapes our philosophical reflection by confronting us with problems that arise from our relationships to nature and to our fellow humans, not to mention ourselves. The philosophical issues we work with are those embedded in the problems arising from these relationships. Each cultural setting confronts us with a set of problems circumscribed by the particular time in our history when we engage in our philosophical reflection. This means that when I confront my circumstance, I will find myself shaped by my heritage and hemmed in by the problems of my concrete reality. Thus, my circumstance may be very much like yours, somewhat similar to yours or quite different. The originality of the thought that I formulate, of the solutions I seek to my problems, will depend on the degree to which I come to terms with the basic features of my reality.

As a Latin American the basic problem I am confronted with and confined by is that I am the product of Western culture, a culture that espouses a fundamental humanity that is the defining trait of all human beings, an essential feature of which is the freedom of each individual. However, what bears down on me is the insistence of this Western heritage that, as a Latin American, I am not quite fully human and am therefore not worthy of freedom. As a result, this Western stance structures subordinating relationships with me as a Latin American and even more so if my heritage is non-Western, such as African or Middle Eastern or Asian. (Zea is referring here to attitudes and practices by government institutions and agencies as well as businesses and prominent individuals here and there. Exceptions in these attitudes and practices are seen as validating the rule.)

So, I find myself alienated from this culture I would call my own. In this alienated state, one of the philosophical issues I pursue bears on development and underdevelopment as related to social, political, and economic areas of life. I am not interested in these in some generic or abstract sense, but concretely as they pertain to my specific circumstance. Another philosophical issue has to do with my understanding of what it is to be human. This in turn leads me into problems in philosophical anthropology, with guiding interests in the ways we understand our freedom as human beings, our social equality, and our non-subordination as political or economic groups.

Still another philosophical issue is how this circumstance of mine has come to be. This, of course, entails thinking along the lines of a philosophy of history, clarifying the dynamics that seem to shape human affairs and the influence those have, if any, on where we find ourselves. This is an important dimension to be explored, since Zea, taking over some of Hegel's ideas, sees Latin Americans as failing to face up to their own history as a dependent, colonial culture. Until this is done so as to come to terms with this part of their heritage, identifying with it, they will never be able to move beyond it to a culture of their own that is free, exercises social equality, and refuses to be subordinated or to subordinate.

This was the intellectual challenge Zea felt Latin American philosophers had to confront: how to formulate a sense of what it is to be human that does not allow one to either be subordinated or to subordinate. The traditional view of humanity as it had developed in Europe and North America and had been passed on to Latin America was that as humans we are allowed to subordinate those who, in our eyes, don't quite measure up. This view has led to major injustices and subjugation that must be challenged. It must be replaced with an understanding of humanity that gives no room to such inequality in theory or practice (Zea, 1969, pp. 134–60; Zea, 1963). This challenge was one that also resonated in the work of Samuel Ramos.

Samuel Ramos (1897–1959)

Some of the most turbulent times in Mexican history served as the context in which Samuel Ramos struggled to understand the circumstance of his own life. He responded with vigor and openness. The intellectual breadth and incisiveness of his work remains an important legacy in Latin American philosophy.

In the prologue to third edition of his *Profile of Man and Culture* in Mexico (Ramos, 1962), we find a summary of his studies of Mexican culture. The context for these studies is a broad sweep of pre-colonial and colonial developments that come to a crisis in the nineteenth century with the independence movements. Following independence, Mexican history suffers a series of disruptive events that Ramos sees as an outgrowth of the disjunction between the economic, social, and educational realities on the one hand and the political aspirations of the leaders on the other. He proposes in the third chapter, "Psychoanalysis of the Mexican," that the failure to gain ground in working toward a solution to these dysfunctions is due to an inferiority complex that characterizes some expressions of Mexican culture. In the Prologue to that third edition he acknowledges that it would be inappropriate to generalize this assessment and apply it to all Mexicans. He points out, however, that a great deal of the "Mexican soul" still stands in need of careful research and analysis.

He then sets the stage for studies of a more broadly based inquiry that would probe the founding dimensions of what it is to be human (Ramos, 1940). In pursuing this task he seeks to avoid understanding humans in terms of disembodied eternal forms or essences on the one hand or in terms of complex arrangements of merely material factors on the other. He sees in Creole culture, the culture of the middle class, the seedbed for new horizons for Mexico. He decries a turn toward an unbridled pragmatic industrialism. He turns his attention to the need to recognize that the living, material circumstances of a society and the people that make it up are the results of a specific history. He goes on to underscore the importance of a passion for truth and intellectual discipline, with scientific study having its rightful place in the development of a culture that "is a function of the spirit destined to humanize reality" (Ramos, 1962, p. 106). He quotes Max Scheler as providing this insight into the nature of culture. In *Toward a New Humanism* (Ramos, 1940), these ideas are developed more fully and from a different context. Here he describes the crisis that has afflicted Western culture, undermining its basic values. This has come about through a fundamental support for a culture that focuses on production and technology. These have a legitimate instrumental value but not as a goal in and of themselves. The taking of this means as an end has led to confusion and fragmentation in a culture that no longer addresses the basic dimensions of who we are as human beings.

To remedy this situation, Ramos proposes a turn to philosophical anthropology. This study can provide insight into the basic structure of who we are as humans and enable

137

us to move out of the crisis. Taking direction from Husserl and Heidegger, Ramos engages in a phenomenological description that follows proposals made by Ortega y Gasset. This approach is one that describes the various functions that make up our humanity as being levels arranged in a hierarchical order. Each function or level is dependent on the one below it but at the same time free to be different from it. These functions or levels are not assumptions we make but realities accessible to all and readily described.

The beginning level is vitality, encompassing all that is bound up with the living body. If one presses beyond vitality, two additional levels are encountered: soul and spirit. Soul encompasses those actions and processes related to oneself alone and spirit encompasses the norms and functions that are beyond one's own needs and that address norms and principles taken to be universal.

Ramos' shift from the phenomenological descriptions of Scheler and Hartmann to that of Ortega is an interesting development. It left him with a philosophical perspective that was not clearly developed, and one he did not choose to elaborate and modify to make it more intellectual fruitful. On the other hand, Romero, a contemporary of his to whom I now turn, chose to work from the perspectives of Scheler and Hartmann.

Francisco Romero (1891–1962)

Romero was born in Spain but immigrated to Argentina with his parents when he was very young. Early in life he chose a military career, graduated from the Military College, and became an officer in the Corps of Engineers. While a member of this Corps, he began publishing poems, book reviews, and translations as early as 1916. Within a few years, however, his publications included issues related to philosophy and by the late 1920s they were almost exclusively so. This philosophical work was an ongoing project that focused on the issue of what it is to be human and how humans interact with the reality of the world in which they live.

Romero began exploring these issues in a systematic way in an article published initially in 1935, "Philosophy of the Person." This article reflected that in his reading and thinking Romero was very much part of the philosophical community emerging in Europe at the time, and the German philosophical community in particular. Max Scheler was one of the philosophers from whom he drew a good bit of his initial orientation. Romero refers to Scheler and takes his three-tiered universe – matter, life, and spirit – as the context within which to address his basic philosophical concerns.

The key to understanding who we are is clarifying why our conduct pulls us in different directions. On the one hand we have behavior that centers on the individual, with knowing focused on appropriating the elements of the environment for the individual's own self-centered ends. Relationships to other humans are similarly self-centered. There is little concern for what or who these things or people are on their own merit. On the other hand, there is a way of approaching one's surrounding world with the intent of knowing it and its objects for what they are in themselves. And as regards other human beings, one relates to them on the basis of who they are themselves.

Behavior of the first kind is action by what Romero refers to as the individual, namely by one who is self-centered. Behavior of the second kind is action by what Romero refers to as the person, whose acts are spiritual acts, characterized by reaching out to know the surrounding objects on the basis of what they essentially are. The reaching out to people is also a relating to them for who they are rather than for what ends of one's own they may serve.

This tension between individual and person is a tension experienced by all human beings, because all human beings have within them both tendencies. What one should seek to enhance is the intellectual and moral activity of the person within us. To be sure, the individual dimension of humans is always there, but one should strive to make the personal dimension an increasingly acknowledged guide in one's life.

Romero goes on to elaborate each of these dimensions of the self in some detail, giving particular attention to the epistemological and ethical or value-oriented actions of the person. These he regards as acts of the spirit.

In a series of articles appearing over the next seven years, Romero continued to modify and refine his descriptions of what human beings are. One of the changes was the introduction of the notion of transcendence to refer to the action or processes inherent in reality. Romero maintained that a close observation of reality made clear that the more complex the level of reality, the greater the degree of intensity and variety in objects and events. The increase in complexity and in structural effectiveness is an increase in transcendence, an increase in the tendency of natural processes or living entities to bring about changes within themselves or lead to the creation of things beyond themselves. This "going beyond" inherent in all reality is what Romero refers to as transcendence. One aspect of transcending activity that is extremely important is the activity of spirit or mind, for it is here that transcendence finds its full expression, as a tendency toward a complete objectivity and a general universality along with a certain unity and freedom. In addition, the transcendimg activity of spirit always occurs in historical settings. For Romero, mind or spirit is the most prized dimension of human life, a dimension that any political culture would strive to enhance. Transcending action finds itself in tension with a centripetal tendency that Romero refers to as immanence.

Another change that occurs in Romero's thought is that he explores more fully the claim that all human experience occurs in time. In particular, this tends toward a programmatic context for human activity, that is, that human life is much more context-dependent as it pursues its goals. In addition, this leaves human life contingent with respect to knowledge about ultimate or non-human matters. Even issues well within human range must be approached non-dogmatically, with a reliable sense of human limitation.

A third change occurred later on in *Theory of Man* (Romero, 1964), as Romero shifted from describing human reality within Scheler's three-tiered universe of matter, life, and spirit to Nicolai Hartmann's four-tiered universe of inorganic matter, life, intentionality, and spirit.

This change enabled Romero to explore more fully the intentionality of human consciousness along with the unhindered transcending of the human spirit. These are the two defining dimensions of what it is to be human and provide a highly fruitful context for approaching the broad range of issues humans confront. These issues include those related to how humans know and what they do with their knowing, how they structure their relationships to other humans, and how culture and its institutions can be vital and creative. In each of the tiers or strata of natural and human realities, immanence and transcendence are guiding tendencies that structure objects, giving them identity, and at the same time enable them to change, adapt, and create.

We find in Romero's thought a serious engagement with European currents of his day. He takes these currents as a context within which to address fundamental issues that he along with his Latin American philosophical colleagues confronted. The most persistent of these issues was the need to understand who we are as human beings and how we engage our natural and cultural setting.

Concluding Remarks

Several other authors made important contributions to this 'normal' development of philosophy. Among them would be Carlos Astrada (1894–1970), a remarkably able interpreter of Heidegger's philosophical perspective. In his later years, drawn to social concerns, his thought reflected more interest in a Marxist orientation (Astrada, 1963). Risieri Frondizi (1910–83) also contributed substantially to the debate about human nature, making use of 'Gestalt' as a concept for understanding human complexity and promise (Frondizi, 1971). His works on value theory were also important.

Other philosophers of a more traditional bent also had significant publications. Octavio Nicolás Derisi (1907–2002) was the major figure in the rejuvenation of Thomistic thought in Latin America (Derisi, 1946). Agustin Basave Fernandez del Valle (b. 1923) wrote extensively about the human condition from an Augustinian perspective (Valle, 1963).

In Brazil, Miguel Reale (1910–2006) exercised considerable influence on issues related to the philosophy of law (Reale 1960). Luis Washington Vita (1921–68) had a broad range of interests that reflect influences from Husserlian phenomenology. An Ortegan sensitivity to circumstance turns toward an emphasis on the human condition as well as toward the history of the development of philosophical ideas (Vita, 1967).

Related chapters: 4 The Emergence and Transformation of Positivism; 5 Early Critics of Positivism; 6 The Anti-Positivist Movement in Mexico; 7 Darwinism; 8 Krausism; 11 Phenomenology.

References

Astrada, C. (1963). *Existencialismo y crisis de la filosofía*. Buenos Aires: Ed. Devenir.
Derisi, O. N. (1946). *Esbozo de una epistemología tomista*. Buenos Aires: Cursos de Cultura Católica.
Deústua, A. O. (1923). *Estética general*. Lima: Eduardo Rávago.
Frondizi, R. (1971). *The Nature of the Self*. Carbondale: Southern Illinois University Press.
Gaos, J. (1945). *Pensamiento de lengua española*. Mexico City: Stylo.
Gracia, J. J. E. (Ed.). (1986). *Latin American philosophy in the twentieth century*. Buffalo, NY: Promotheus.
Korn, A. (1949). *Obras completas*. Buenos Aires: Claridad.

Molina, E. (1951). *Desarrollo de Chile en la primera mitad del siglo XX*. Santiago: Editorial Universitaria.

Ramos, S. (1940). *Hacia un nuevo humanismo*. Mexico City: La Casa de España en México.

Ramos, S. (1962). *Profile of man and culture in Mexico*. Austin: University of Texas Press (Originally published 1934).

Reale, M. (1960). *Teoria do direito e do estado*. São Paulo: Livraria Martins Editora.

Romero, F. (1964). *Theory of man*. Berkeley and Los Angeles: University of California Press (Originally published 1952).

Valle, A. B. F. (1963). *Filosofía del hombre*. Mexico City: Espasa-Calpe Mexicana.

Vita, L. W. (1967). *Tríptico de ideas*. São Paulo: Editorial Grijalbo.

Zea, L. (1963). *The Latin American mind*. Norman: University of Oklahoma Press.

Zea, L. (1969). *La filosofía americana como filosofía sin más*. Mexico City: Siglo XXI.

Further Reading

Gracia, J. J. E., & Millán-Zaibert, E. (Eds). (2004). *Latin American philosophy for the 21st century: the human condition, values and the search for identity*. Amherst, NY: Prometheus.

Nuccetelli, S. (2002). *Latin American thought: Philosophical problems and arguments*. Boulder, CO: Westview Press.

Romero, F. (1952). *Sobre la filosofía en América*. Buenos Aires: Editorial Raigal.

Schutte, O. (1993). *Cultural identity and social liberation in Latin American thought*. Albany: State University of New York.

Vallenilla, E. M. (Ed.). (1979). *La filosofía en América. I y II*. Caracas: Sociedad Venezolana de Filosofía.

10

Ortega y Gasset's Heritage in Latin America

MANUEL GARRIDO

I.   Ortega's Thought and the Spanish Philosophical Emigration to Latin America

1.   *Ortega's philosophical revolution to 1936*

José Ortega y Gasset (1883–1955) is commonly considered the foremost Spanish thinker of the past century and one of the great founders of the European philosophy of life. His intellectual life was drastically split in two halves by the Spanish Civil War of 1936–9. From an external point of view, the first half was very successful – while the second was full of frustrations which affected his vision of the world. On the other hand, it is perhaps true that reasons of internal evolution determined a thought turn in the 1930s, not only in Ortega but also in his contemporaries Heidegger and Wittgenstein.

Born into the bosom of a family of the high bourgeoisie related to the press, Ortega's privileged youth was that of an adolescent Spanish Goethe. Educated at Marburg by the neo-Kantian Hermann Cohen, the young philosopher became acquainted with Husserl's phenomenology as it developed. But he asked for something more real and radical than method and, stimulated by the flourishing of Simmel's and Schelers's philosophy of life and culture, he found it in the radical reality of human life. The new biology emphasized the relation between living beings and the environment, and Ortega extrapolated this scientific fact to his philosophy. He thought that neither the classic theoretical reason of Aristotle nor the physico-mathematical reason of Descartes and modern science could give a complete account of the radical problems of human life. He planned to construct a rational theory of human life appealing to a new "reason" which he called "*vital*."

Already in *Meditations on Quixote* (1914), his first important book, Ortega had encapsulated his thought in the formula "I am I and my circumstance." This formula, which we can call the fundamental theorem of Ortega's philosophy, sought to be a theoretical picture of the vital dialogue between "man" (e.g., humans) and the world. A decade later, in *The Modern Theme* (1923), he carried out the first attempt at developing his system, called *ratiovitalism*.

In 1898, Spain, defeated by the United States, lost Cuba and the rest of its colonial empire. The Spanish intellectuals at the end of the nineteenth century and the

142

beginning of the twentieth reacted to that disaster with an obsessive will to regenerate their country culturally, socially, and politically. Ortega personally lived this "regenerationist" ideal as the imperative of connecting our life with our circumstance and our human group in order to assure the cultural "salvation" of both. In the following two decades Ortega, compulsively dedicated to this task of "saving" the Spanish circumstance, developed an overwhelming and varied program of cultural creation. One of its components was the magazine *El Espectador*, which he created with a "*unipersonal*" character in 1916, and of which there appeared eight volumes, the last one in 1934. The magazine was an enormous cathedral of literary and philosophical thought produced over almost twenty years by only one worker who was also its architect. Seven years later, in 1923, Ortega created the *Revista de Occidente*, the most excellent journal of thought and culture in the Spanish language of the past century. A companion of this magazine was the editorial house of the same name. Both were famous for their original productions and their translations.

Among the numerous articles and books published in this period by Ortega, the double essay *The Dehumanization of Art and Notes on the Novel* (1925) stands out. But he didn't allow enough time for the study of what we could call pure philosophy. Almost a decade passed between the *Meditations* and the appearance in 1923 of the brief essay *The Modern Theme*, which, after the publication in 1927 of Heidegger's splendid *Being and Time*, left Ortega unsatisfied.

An aspect of the cultural salvation of Spain, for Ortega, was its political salvation. While he was not in professional politics, which he considered lower than cultural creation, he nevertheless theorized seriously on political matters and devoted much time and more than a thousand written pages to them. We can mention in this area his critical and programmatic *Invertebrate Spain* (1921), his founding of the magazine *España* (1915), and his co-founding of the newspaper *El Sol* (1917), where he collaborated for thirteen years.

His *Revolt of the Masses* (*La rebelión de las masas*, 1930; Engl. 1932) contributed the most to Ortega's world reputation. With a focus on the dialectics between minorities and masses, it shows the clear influence of the Italians Mosca and Pareto with a pinch of Nietzsche and Heidegger. Critics from the Left have attacked the elitism and aristocratism of Ortega, who in this work defended liberalism and Western democracy emphatically. In the second part of his book, Ortega anticipated the idea of a European union. By the end of the 1920s, Ortega felt the need to meditate more deeply on his philosophy. The *Prologue* of his 1932 *Complete Works* manifests this philosophical turn, displaying a positive balance of his contribution to the culture of his country. There he warns us about a second, and more rigorous, "navigation" focused on books rather than newspapers. His work from 1932 until the Spanish Civil War is original and rigorous. It includes essays ("Goethe desde dentro," 1932, "Guillermo Dilthey y la Idea de la Vida," 1934, "History as a system," 1935) and a masterful course first given in 1933 and published later as *Man in Crisis*. A denser style and a predominantly ontological and historical point of view in Ortega's new writings replace the simplistic cultural vitalism of the previous ones. The principal result of this second "navigation" is the incorporation of the concept of *historical reason*, epitomized in the sentence, "*Man has no nature, but he has . . . history.*"

143

2. Ortega's life and thought after 1936

At the outbreak of civil war Ortega, afraid for his life, had to choose the path of self-exile. First he moved to Paris; however, not finding satisfactory shelter in Europe and foreseeing the imminent second Great War, he tried his luck in Argentina, but without success. The small and tranquil country of Portugal finally provided Ortega, who settled in Lisbon in 1942, a place of retirement where he wrote some of his most ambitious works. After the Allied victory in 1945, he decided to end his nine years of exile by returning to Spain, where he had to suffer ten years of cruel ostracism by Franco's regime. Ortega died in Madrid in 1955, with the comfort of having recovered his international fame in Europe and the United States in his final years and of having written many of his best pages during his retirement in Portugal. In the second stage of his life Ortega founded, during the Francoist 1940s in Spain, an "Institute of Humanities" where he taught two courses open to Spanish society. Its contents would be published later in two posthumous volumes: *An Interpretation of Universal History* and *Man and People*. These books amount to Ortega's second "visit" to history and society. The first was a confrontation with Toynbee, and the second Ortega's new and global approach to collective life. Some of Ortega's best posthumous writings, such as *The Origin of Philosophy* and *The Idea of Principle in Leibniz*, represent his philosophical testament. The theme of the first is the primitive origin and eventual future of philosophy. *The Idea* involves metaphilosophy, since Ortega meditated there on philosophy in general and on his personal philosophy in particular, in which he followed in Plato's, Descartes' and Leibniz's tradition of conceptual thought.

The Spanish Civil War of 1936–9 was the unhappy and violent culmination of a social, political, and cultural clash with an economic underground that lasted more than a century. The liberal-progressive forces were fighting to "Europeanize" Spain culturally, socially, and politically in order to put an end to its traditional distance from modern Europe; the conservative forces defended the Spanish tradition.

The cost of the Spanish Civil War was a million dead. To this tragedy we must add many other sad consequences: a military dictatorship that for forty years separated Spain more than ever from Europe; the exile, in most cases for life, of hundreds of thousands of Spaniards; and the geographical and political division of Spanish culture while the dictatorial regime lasted: the "national" one, residing in the Spanish territory, and the émigré republican.

From the point of view of the present essay there is a crucial role played by a culturally important subset of Spanish emigration represented by the republican Spanish professionals of philosophy who, as a result of the Civil War, were forced to emigrate to Latin America. The Spanish professional philosophers in 1936 were members of the Faculties of Philosophy of Madrid and Barcelona, then the only two in Spain. The dominant group was represented by Ortega and his disciples and followers, who came to constitute what has usually been named the "School of Madrid," whose natural leader was Ortega himself and whose core was integrated by Manuel García Morente, Ortega's colleague and contemporary, and their disciples Xavier Zubiri and José Gaos, one generation younger than their masters. Added to that core soon after were some recent graduates such as María Zambrano and Julián Marías. We may also include in this school the young Orteguian philosophers Granell, Rodríguez Huéscar, and Garagorri and the philosopher of law Recasens Siches.

A certain tradition in Spain distinguishes between Catalan and Castilian thought. The Catalonian émigré thinker Eduardo Nicol has coined the label "School of Barcelona" to denote the group of professional philosophers somehow organized in Spain in the 1930s around the Faculty of Philosophy in Barcelona. Heavily influenced, as were the Orteguians, by contemporary German philosophy, this group was less proselytizing and not as powerful but more open to other non-continental influences. Jaime Serra Hunter and Joaquín Xirau were its natural leaders, and among its members were Nicol, García Bacca, Ferrater Mora, and Juan Roura-Parella. Most of them were receptive to Ortega. Gaos, Serra Hunter, Xirau, and Nicol settled in Mexico, and García Bacca in Venezuela. Many other disciples of Ortega worked in other Latin American countries; some, such as Castro, Ferrater, and Zambrano, moved later to the United States or Europe. (More on these later.)

II. Ortega's Influence in Latin America

1. Ortega in Latin America

In the 1920s and '30s Ortega's reputation spread not only to Europe but also to the United States and, especially, throughout Latin America. His original works found just as warm a reception in the Latin American countries as they did in Spain. Nevertheless, historical circumstances determined that Ortega's personal presence in Latin America remained basically limited only to Argentina, which Ortega visited on three occasions, in 1916, 1928, and 1939, to teach courses and take part in conferences on philosophy. The first two visits were crowned by spectacular success. The interest, or perhaps better, the enthusiasm which his interventions awoke in the intellectual community, in the greater public, and even among the political author- ities of that country left him with the indescribable impression of having been "surprised and understood" by the Argentine people. And soon, naturally, Ortega conceived the idea of expanding to Argentina and eventually to other Latin American countries his project of "saving," by means of cultural criticism and political action, the proper circumstance.

Ortega's third trip to Argentina was, unfortunately, very frustrating. The Spanish Civil War had radically changed the circumstances. At the outbreak of the conflict in 1936, Ortega took refuge in Paris, but after three unsuccessful years, along with the fear of the world war and the subsequent invasion of France by Hitler, he decided to try a new stay in Argentina, which lasted three years (1939–42). Sadly, as a man of the "third Spain" (neither Francoist [*franquista*] nor militant republican), he did not find in that country, previously enamored of him, the comfort of a pro- fessorship, in contrast to many of his republican disciples exiled in America. Mean- while the publishing house Espasa Calpe, working again in Franco's Spain, put into practice abusive economic measures that left him, as an author, in a ruinous situation.

145

2. The Mexican connection

Latin American countries offered more generous hospitality than Europe to the emigrating Spaniards, but the Republic of Mexico was especially well disposed toward them. The Mexican president Lázaro Cárdenas, who had a great political vision and was faithful to the Mexican revolution's spirit, was responsible for the special hospitality offered to the Spanish "*emigrados.*"

José Gaos (1900–69) – together with Zubiri and García Bacca – was one of Ortega's main heirs of the "generation of 1927." Born in Asturias (Spain), he received a Ph.D. in 1928 from the Universidad Central de Madrid. Gaos had a serious training in phenomenology, philosophy of life, and existentialism, the newer and more notable philosophical currents of his time. Tutored by Ortega, Morente, and Zubiri, Gaos soon became the favorite disciple of Ortega. A member of the Socialist Party during the Republic, and already politically distanced from Ortega, he accepted the office of President of the University of Madrid in 1936, during the hardest political months of the republican Popular Front.

Gaos emigrated to Mexico in 1938 and acquired Mexican nationality in 1941. For more than a quarter of the century he was the dominant philosophical figure in Mexico. He taught philosophy courses and offered conferences in La Casa de España in Mexico (later El Colegio de México), in the Universidad Autónoma de México, and in other Latin American universities. Creator of a philosophical system "proper" (*propio*) to the circumstance, the decisive promoter of the Mexican and Latin American philosophical consciousness, and translator of the most outstanding figures of the history of philosophy into Spanish, from the pre-Socratics to Husserl and Heidegger, Gaos left an immense written heritage at his death in Mexico. The edition of his complete works will amount to nineteen thick volumes of which fifteen have already appeared.

Gaos's theory of "*transtierro*" (exile) illustrates the moral exemplarity of his personal behavior and also, to some extent, the historical significance, as a global phenomenon, of Spanish emigration to Latin America. He spoke of two homelands, one "of origin" and the other "of destination," the first given to us by involuntary chance, the second freely elected. Gaos decided not to return to Spain and never changed his mind. He died in 1969 of a heart attack while discussing a doctoral thesis at El Colegio de México.

In the middle of the 1930s, in *El perfil del hombre y de la cultura en México* (1934), Samuel Ramos (Mexican, 1897–1959) argued that Mexico needed to obtain philosophical emancipation by applying the ratiovitalist Orteguian project of salvation of man's own circumstance. Initially, the Mexican intellectual environment reacted by condemning Ramos to unfair ostracism. But Gaos's arrival in Mexico changed the balance of forces spectacularly. Gaos not only defended Ramos's ideas, but also pushed forward the "circumstancialism" of his teacher Ortega, extrapolating it to Mexico and other Latin American countries. In 1945 Gaos wrote: "American will be the philosophy that Americans, that is to say, men in the middle of the American circumstance, rooted in it, do on their circumstance, do on America" (p. 368).

Gaos's impact was enormous. Leopoldo Zea (1912–2004) – the favorite disciple of Gaos and probably the most original Mexican philosopher of the second half of the past century – has emphasized the ideological, political, and transforming dimension of Gaos's legacy. Zea criticized the Eurocentric view of the human being, history, and reason, anticipating the current postmodern and postcolonialist trends. The ghost of Ortega's circumstancialism (to which Gaos added a sensibility for social justice not present in Ortega) spread like wildfire through the global circumstance of the subcontinent. And Zea contributed decisively to lighting this fire with his teaching.

All his life, Gaos worried obsessively about the problem of reconciling philosophy's pretension of absolute truth with the historical fact of its plurality – the will to be really and universally valid expressed by the great metaphysical systems of the past with the fact that these systems are mutually contradictory. It is, at bottom, the conflict between Husserl's logicism and Dilthey's historicism, two crucial conflicting influences, which are already latent in Ortega and patent in Gaos. We find traces of this conflict in the early works of Gaos, but the deep development of it, the definitive "philosophy of the philosophy" of Gaos, is present in his most mature writings, which appeared throughout the 1960s, the last decade of his life. The voluminous *De la filosofía* and *Del hombre* are the culmination of Gaos's analysis of metaphysical discourse, denouncing the archaic character and the lack of scientific validity of the great metaphysical systems but recognizing, nevertheless, the importance of the venerable values that they try to transmit, and detecting their human substratum. In this reduction, or *"retroducción,"* from metaphysics' pretension of objectivity to the subjective ground of philosophical anthropology we may glimpse something of the Pascalian idea of metaphysics as the "reasons of the heart." But, according to Gaos, that does not exclude the eventual value of philosophy as the moral and cultural guide of society.

It is indisputable that Gaos was the most important receiver, promoter, and renovator of the Orteguian legacy in Mexico. But in fact an entire legion of Spanish thinkers, in many cases proceeding from the aforementioned schools, or groups, of Madrid and Barcelona, taught, worked, and conducted research in Mexico and contributed decisively to the development of that legacy. Given the short space available, I consider here only a few outstanding figures.

The philosopher of law Luis Recasens Siches (1903–77) paradigmatically represents the influence of Ortega beyond the limits of pure philosophy. Born in Guatemala but the son of Spanish parents, he studied in Barcelona, Madrid, Rome, and Berlin, and was a Professor of Law in several Spanish universities. After the Civil War, in 1937, he emigrated to Mexico, where he got a philosophy professorship at the National Autonomous University (UNAM). He cultivated and developed his preferred subject matter, the philosophy of law, evolving from the Neo-Kantian formalism of Kelsen and Stammler to Max Scheler's and Nicolai Hartmann's opening to the material sphere of values; he completed this intellectual evolution by providing an ontological foundation for the universe of norms in the Orteguian theory of vital reason. For Recasens the sphere of values gives material content to the formal laws of Right, and both find, thanks to ratiovitalism, their ontological roots in human life. His main work, *Vida humana, sociedad y derecho: función de la filosofía del derecho* (1940), was translated into English. His *Tratado general de sociología* and *Tratado general de filosofía del derecho* exposed his ideas on sociology and axiology.

The Basque Eugenio Imaz (1900–51) is known mainly for his translation of Dilthey's complete works. This translation documents the projection of Ortega's influence into Mexican institutions, because its eight thick volumes were edited in the publishing house Fondo de Cultura Económica, one of the main cultural institutions of Mexico. It was

147

prowess to put the thought of Dilthey – the most valuable jewel of the Orteguian cultural repertoire – into the hands of Spanish readers in the difficult years of 1944 and 1945, with World War II not yet ended. Imaz also wrote two books on Diltheyan thought: *Asalto a Dilthey* and *El pensamiento de Dilthey.*

Joaquín Xirau (1895–1946), born in Figueras, Gerona, was a brilliant and cosmopolitan Professor and Dean of the Facultad de Filosofía y Letras of the University of Barcelona. Immediately after the Civil War, in 1939, he emigrated to Mexico, where he became Philosophy Professor of the Facultad de Filosofía y Letras at UNAM. He died prematurely and tragically. His main philosophical influences were, among others, Husserl's phenomenology and Max Scheler's ethics of values. These influences inspired his first book *Introducción a la fenomenología* (1941) and also his most important *Amor y mundo* and *Lo fugaz y lo eterno.* It is interesting to note that those influences were received directly from Europe, not through Ortega. In fact, Xirau lived for some time in Madrid, where he knew Ortega. Nevertheless, as his son Ramón Xirau remembers, "he didn't follow him." (Poet and philosopher, Ramón emigrated as a child from Spain to Mexico and today is "investigador emérito" of the Mexican Universidad Autónoma. He exemplifies an exile's son, and his books show knowledge of Ortega's philosophy.)

Eduardo Nicol (1907–90) was among the more eminent of the philosophers exiled from Barcelona to Mexico. Born in Barcelona, he taught in the Facultad de Filosofía y Letras of the University of Barcelona before the Civil War and was secretary of the foundation for classical studies, Bernat Metge. In 1939, when the war ended, he took refuge for a short time in France and later traveled to Mexico, where he acquired Mexican nationality. Until his arrival to Mexico the only language in which he had written was Catalan. In 1941 he was already a professor in UNAM, where he co-founded the Instituto de Investigaciones Filosóficas and the journal *Dianoia.*

Nicol discussed Orteguian circumstancialism and perspectivism with Gaos. But we can't infer from his anti-historicist attitude in that debate that he was merely interested in intellectual abstractions, blind to the historical realities. Already his first book, *Psicología de las situaciones vitals*, documents the Diltheyan dimension of his thought. But it is in his main work, *Metafísica de la expression*, that we can better appreciate the great originality of Nicol's philosophy. The conception of man as an expressive being and the new view of metaphysics as first philosophy are two contributions of that book. The expressive condition of man entails, according to Nicol, the creation of symbols, language, communication, science, and also liberty and responsible action in society. In his new view of metaphysics as "filosofía primera," Nicol conjugates two opposed methodologies: phenomenology and dialectics. The first opens the doors of a new general ontology, and the second the doors of historical reality. In his *Principios de la ciencia*, Nicol developed his philosophy of science in parallel with his ontology; and in his last years he approached the problem of philosophy's actual crisis in three important books: *El porvenir de la filosofía* (1972), *La reforma de la filosofía* (1980), and *Crítica de la razón simbólica: la revolución en la filosofía* (1982).

3. The Venezuelan connection

Juan David García Bacca was, with his two generation-of-1927 partners Zubiri and Gaos, one of the three main figures of Spanish thought immediately after Ortega's death.

Born in Pamplona (Navarre) in 1901 and son of a modest Aragonese school teacher, he lost his father at an early age and entered, while still a boy, the Seminary of the Padres Claretianos, where he was ordained a priest in 1925. Promoted by his superiors, he undertook further philosophical and scientific studies in Munich, Louvain, Paris, and Freiburg, Switzerland.

After getting a Ph.D. in philosophy from the University of Barcelona, García Bacca soon began a brilliant career there as a university teacher and investigator. This career was suddenly interrupted by the Civil War, just after he had won a philosophy professorship at the University of Santiago de Compostela (Galicia). During the war he worked in Paris for the Republic. In 1938 he abandoned the Claretian Order and began a second life in America. First he traveled to Ecuador, invited by the University of Quito, where he taught for four years. He then received an invitation from the University of Mexico to talk about Heidegger, which he did for the following four years. Finally, receiving a third invitation in 1946, this time from the Central University of Venezuela, he moved to Caracas where he acquired Venezuelan citizenship, remaining there until his retirement in 1971. He died in Quito in 1992.

The young García Bacca already stood out, before 1936, in the philosophical group of Barcelona, where he introduced mathematical logic for the first time in Spain. Since the 1933–4 academic year García Bacca had taught Mathematical Logic and Philosophy of Science at the University of Barcelona; and he won also a professorship of "Lógica e Introducción a la filosofía" at the Centro de Estudios Universitarios (CEU) founded in Madrid by the Christian democrat leader Angel Herrera Oria. We owe to that young professor excellent papers and books on logical matters, published in the early 1930s, that were cutting edge in Spain. On the other hand, his studies abroad provided an enviable knowledge of the mathematical and physical sciences in general and of relativity theory, quantum mechanics, and biology in particular.

García Bacca was not a direct disciple of Ortega, but he clearly shows Orteguian influence. One of the main challenges of his thought, next to the simultaneous cultivation of philosophy and science, is to accommodate the Orteguian will of doing serious philosophy using the Spanish language in all its literary wealth. During the first two decades of his life as an exiled professor – the 1940s and '50s – García Bacca may be included in Ortega's vitalist and historicist camp, with a progressive bias toward Heidegger's ontology. But García Bacca's thought is always characterized by its great originality. A good sample of that is *Invitación a filosofar* (1940–2). García Bacca developed in this volume, against the background of Ortega's ratiovitalism and Heideggerian existential ontology, his idea of the transfinite, a concept which plays a decisive role in his philosophy. Transfiniteness is for García Bacca the condition that characterizes humankind.

The human, for García Bacca, is constitutively a rebellious and Promethean being. And if, according to Plato, this being is *un ser endemoniado* (a being possessed by demons), it happens because he is fatally condemned to collide at every moment with limits and barriers that he can certainly overcome in every moment, but with the sad consequence of colliding again and again with other new limits and frontiers as new obstacles to overcome. The human is always transcending his barriers. In this idea of the "transfinite" García Bacca combines ingredients as heterogeneous as the mathematical theory of Cantor's transfinite numbers, the Christian theology's curse of the fallen angels, the desire of self-overcoming of contemporary philosophy from Nietzsche to Ortega and Heidegger, and, very particularly, the Hegelian dialectic between the finite and the infinite.

The last phase of García Bacca's thought, from the 1960s until his death in 1992, was the deepest and most creative of his long life. We can characterize a crucial aspect, or dimension, of that phase as a Marxist, or perhaps better, "Marxian" turn. And, according to the historian of Spanish thought José Luis Abellán, we can describe this turn as an original critique of economic reason, which is developed in García Bacca's *Metafísica natural estabilizada y problemática metafísica espontánea* (1963) and *Humanismo teórico, práctico y positivo según Marx* (1965). According to Carlos Beorlegui, one of the greatest experts in the philosophy of García Bacca, these books are focused on (1) the social value and product of work, and (2) capitalism's unjust privatization of something that should be social and never privatized. In this period García Bacca decided to move for a time to Cambridge to consolidate his knowledge of economy. He wrote *Invitación a filosofar según espíritu y letra de A. Machado* (1967), thus confirming his will to engage in philosophy using Spanish in all its literary richness. But now his cultural model was not the Orteguian elitism and aristocratism, but the deep populism of the poet and thinker Antonio Machado, whose favorite motto was the traditional Castilian idiom, "*nadie es más que nadie*" (No one is more than anyone). The Machadian will, "to write for the people," is the main inspiration for this new book.

Two other dimensions of García Bacca's later thought are his meditations on technology and his anthropo-theology. In one of his last and deeper works, a conference with the title "El mito del hombre allende la técnica" (1952), Ortega offered us an optimistic view of technology and its development as a *gigantesca ortopedia* (a gigantic orthopedics) created by human fantasy in order to assure our cosmic survival. This view is clearly superior to the negative and pessimistic view of Western technology later elaborated by Heidegger. In his *Elogio de la técnica* (1968), García Bacca goes beyond Ortega. For him, technology is ultimately linked to the power to transform reality that subatomic physics has offered to humans.

When Jules Verne's scientific fictions are compared with those of Wells, we appreciate immediately the difference between the utopic character of the former and the critical or distopic of the second. In *Qué es Dios y quién es Dios* (1986), García Bacca defended, with a dose of pantheistic hubris more prone to the utopic vein of Verne than to the distopic discourse of Wells, a technological apotheosis or divinization of the human being.

Asturian Manuel Granell was an exemplar of fidelity to Ortega's thought. He studied Law in Oviedo, his native city, and later he took courses in "Filosofía y Letras" in Madrid, where the Orteguian circle left him fascinated. In 1950 he moved to America to teach philosophy at the Universidad Central of Caracas (Venezuela) until his retirement in 1977. He died in Asturias (Spain). The intellectual itinerary of Granell may be described as the attempt to realize two ambitious projects. The first, suggested by Ortega, culminated with the publication of his *Lógica* in 1949. Granell's objective here was to ground traditional and modern abstract logic in the Orteguian ontology; or, in other words, the elaboration of a logic of vital reason. Granell wrote also on Venezuelan thought and its circumstance. But the main project of his mature life was the foundation of Ethology, understood as ultimate reflection on human reality. His

La vecindad humana. Fundamentación de la Ethología (1969) and *Ethología y existencia* (*Fundamentaciones ethológicas*, 1977) develop his ideal of humanism.

4. Ortega's influence in other Latin American countries

In Argentina, the Latin American country preferentially visited by Ortega, his colleague and contemporary Manuel García Morente also taught philosophy; and many illustrious Spanish intellectuals emigrated to that country, such as the historian Sánchez Albornoz and the novelist and essayist Francisco Ayala, notably influenced by Ortega.

In the subcontinent's Southern Cone, Chile deserves special mention. This country was briefly but successfully visited by Ortega during his second stay in Argentina, and Zambrano and Ferrater resided for some years as exiles in Chilean territory. Many decades later, a young Spanish philosopher, Francisco Soler Grima (1924–82), continued Ortega's philosophical heritage in his interesting *Hacia Ortega: el mito del origen del hombre* (1965).

From the north, Puerto Rico claims our attention: its university was a singular and attractive example of Ortega's influence in Latin American institutions, because its president Jaime Benítez (1908–2001) modeled it as an Orteguian Weimar. Ortega's disciple Antonio Rodríguez Huescar lived and taught there for many years. His intellectual production couples fidelity to his teacher's thought with a strong dose of originality and conceptual rigor. His principal work *Perspectiva y verdad* (1966) develops the perspectivist theory of truth proposed by Ortega. His unfinished and posthumous *Éthos y lógos* (1996) contains new results and materials from that project.

Finally, the Basque Ignacio Ellacuría (1930–89), Jesuit, philosopher, and theologian, taught, wrote, and shaped philosophy in the Republic of El Salvador. Formed in Ecuador and in Austria (with Rahner), he planned first to reconcile scholastic thought with that of Ortega. But the influence of Xavier Zubiri made him change his mind. Zubiri had been, like Gaos, a direct pupil of Ortega, although later on he moved away from the phenomenological, vitalist, and existentialist tradition of Husserl, Ortega, and Heidegger, replacing the epistemological interest in meaning by the ontological interest in reality. In this context Ellacuría elaborated his major work, *La filosofía de la realidad histórica* (1991), one of the best and more original philosophical books published by a Spanish or Latin American thinker of the "new generation" in the past four decades. Historical reality is for Ellacuría the cosmic environment of reality and also an immediately given fact, which for ethical and political reasons implies our engagement in personal and collective action. In 1989, Ellacuría was the president of the Jesuit University of San Salvador, a country where he decided to become a citizen, and both he and some members of his team were murdered by the Salvadorian army.

5. Three Orteguian nomads

I call Américo Castro, José Ferrater Mora, and María Zambrano "Orteguian nomads," three thinkers who emigrated to Latin America – although, later on, Castro and Ferrater moved to the United States and Zambrano to Europe. The novelist and essayist Francisco Ayala may also be included in this group. Born in Brazil, Castro (1885–1972) was a philologist and historian of Spanish ancestry from Granada. Like Ortega y

Gasset, he belonged to the Spanish pro-European generation of 1914. He became Professor of Spanish language at the University of Madrid in 1915, and during the 1920s he enjoyed an international reputation as an erudite and essayist. After the outbreak of the Civil War he moved to Argentina – where he had founded in 1923 the Institute of Philology of the University of Buenos Aires – and from there to the United States, where he taught in several universities, but mainly at Princeton. There he developed a series of ideas that culminated in his *España en su historia: cristianos, moros y judíos* (1948), which constitutes, in the words of his disciple Guillermo Araya, a Copernican revolution in the interpretation of Spanish history. Américo Castro's main thesis is that the history of Spain is fundamentally structured on the basis of the secular relationship of coexistence and confrontation of three "*castas*" (breeds or races) of believers of three diverse religions, Christian, "Moorish," and Jewish, that competed in their mutual rejection and influence. Finally, the Christian "caste" prevailed and expelled the others from Spanish territory. An improved new edition of the 1948 book was *La realidad histórica de España* (1954) – reprinted with an author's foreword in 1966. Two of Castro's objectors were his teacher Menéndez Pidal and his colleague Claudio Sánchez Albornoz, who also emigrated from Spain to America and whose monumental *Spain, a Historical Enigma* (1957) is an anti-Castro *summa*. Castro's disciples in Latin America are countless.

Born in Barcelona, Ferrater (1912–91) was one of the more important Spanish thinkers of the second half of the twentieth century and the philosopher of widest scope from the generation of Spaniards that took part in the Civil War of 1936. From a very young age he was a member of the university philosophical group of Barcelona, led by the philosophers Serra Hunter and Joaquín Xirau. His first book, *Coctel de verdad*, appeared in 1935. During the Civil War he fought on the Republican side. His exile began in France, with the retreat of the troops defeated in 1939. From Paris he emigrated to Latin America. During the 1940s he lived and worked in Santiago, Cuba, and Santiago, Chile. In 1947 he moved to the United States, where he settled as a professor of Literature and Philosophy at Bryn Mawr College in Pennsylvania. In 1960 he acquired U.S. citizenship.

For the vast extent of his culture, his personality, the rich variety of his philosophical registers, and his polyglot writing in Catalan, Castilian, and English, Ferrater probably deserves to be referred to as a "universal Catalan." His second book, *Diccionario de filosofía*, the best known of the many he has written although far from being the best, was published for the first time in Mexico in 1941. Constantly improved in successive editions, this dictionary is today one of the best and most complete works of its genre in the world; its sixth edition, dated 1979, consists of four enormous volumes.

But what more truly credits Ferrater's universality is his philosophical system, the so-called integrationism. Beyond all eclecticism, all relativism, all dogmatism, all reductionism, and all rigidly systematic dialectics, Ferrater contemplates the diversity of conceptions and philosophical doctrines, often opposed in irreconcilable dualisms, such as those that oppose the spirit to matter, reason to the irrational, teleology to mechanics, or the individual to society. And he tries to integrate them in a vast net of polarities and conceptual frameworks that illuminates, contrasts, and preserves the most diverse theories and realities in their respective differences and partial truths. As claimed by Priscilla Cohn, his second wife and a philosopher herself, Ferrater was a bridge builder who related diverse things while respecting their diversity. *El sentido de la muerte* is his first systematic discussion of integrationism (1947). At that time the personalist and existentialist obsessive meditations, from Unamuno to Heidegger, on the sense of our death as human beings, held sway. In that essay, one of the most important published during the 1940s, Ferrater attempted to extrapolate in his meditation the idea of death beyond the human and organic beings, and to extend it to the environment of in-organic things, understanding such an idea of death as the "ceasing of being." Fifteen years later, in 1962, Ferrater would republish this book as *El ser y la muerte: bosquejo de una filosofía integracionista*, recasting and upgrading it in accordance with his new position.

Meanwhile Ferrater had taken good note of what he explained in *Cambio de marcha en filosofía* (1974). It was the time for analytic philosophy and he was the only Spanish man of his generation able to seriously cultivate the new way of doing philosophy. Later on, in 1979, already in the culminating moment of his maturity, Ferrater published *De la materia a la razón*, which amounts to a second integrationist project where the general ontology of being is replaced by the physics of matter. Later Ferrater published his brief work *Fundamentos de filosofía* (1985), maybe the best and easiest introduction to the whole of its thought. To his multiple essays on the most diverse topics of philosophy and the history of philosophy, we may add his literary and artistic work, including several novels and films.

Born in 1904, Zambrano is the most important Spanish woman in philosophy in the past century. She spent part of her childhood and adolescence in Segovia, where her father, a primary school teacher, was a good friend of Antonio Machado. Later she moved to Madrid where she attended the lectures of Ortega and Morente, and began to teach philosophy several years before the Civil War. It may be said of her, better than of any other republican intellectual, that she "inhabited the exile," because she hardly found a place of rest in Europe or Latin America. In 1984, Zambrano returned to post-Franco Spain, where she died in 1991, overwhelmed by official late honors. She embraced the ratiovitalism of her teacher Ortega, but originally replaced vital reason by "poetic reason" in order to explore the universe of poetry and dreams which was hardly glimpsed by Ortega. Zambrano wrote several political and autobiographical books, such as *Los intelectuales en el drama de España* and *Delirio y destino*. Her *Tumba de Antígona* reflects on a Greek myth of reincarnation and *Claros del bosque* on how to decipher what one feels.

6. A tentative synthesis

Ortega y Gasset contributed decisively to the development of the new paradigm of the "philosophy of life" in Europe during the first half of the twentieth century. In this sense his philosophy was revolutionary. In Spain and Latin America, it was revolutionary because, first, it implied the will to philosophize seriously in Spanish, and second, it had the vital goal of saving the Spanish circumstance. The success of Ortega's project up until the Spanish Civil War of 1936–9, that is, during the first half of his life, was spectacular. In this period he became one of the most famous thinkers in Europe and the world. His influence in Latin America was also enormous. In fact Ortega visited Argentina in 1916 and in 1928 to teach courses and take part in conferences there.

He conceived the plan of extrapolating his project of cultural salvation of the circumstance to Argentina and many other Latin American countries after his first visit. The Spanish Civil War not only interrupted and frustrated Ortega's personal philosophical projects, but also generated, with total disregard for Ortega's will, a division of his influence into a right and a left wing – each made up of direct and indirect followers. The right wing remained in Spanish territory and continued studying and developing, passively, Ortega's doctrines. The left wing, more original and creative, emigrated to the New World and contributed there to the development of philosophy.

Related chapters: 6 The Anti-Positivist Movement in Mexico; 8 Krausism; 9 'Normal' Philosophy; 11 Phenomenology; 13 Liberation Philosophy; 18 Identity and Philosophy.

References

Ellacuría, I. (1991). *Filosofía de la realidad histórica*. Madrid: Trotta.

García Bacca, J. D. (1940–1942). *Invitación a filosofar*. Mexico City: Fondo de Cultura Económica.

García Bacca, J. D. (1963). *Metafísica natural estabilizada y problemática metafísica espontánea*. Mexico City: Fondo de Cultura Económica.

García Bacca, J. D. (1965). *Humanismo teórico, práctico y positivo según Marx*. Mexico City: Fondo de Cultura Económica.

García Bacca, J. D. (1968). *Elogio de la técnica*. Caracas: Monte Ávila.

García Bacca, J. D. (1986). *Qué es Dios y quién es Dios*. Barcelona: Anthropos.

Gaos, J. (1945). *Pensamiento de lengua española*. Mexico City: Stylo.

Gaos, J. (1962). *De la filosofía. Curso de 1960*. Mexico City: Fondo de Cultura Económica.

Gaos, J. (1970). *Del hombre*. Mexico City: Fondo de Cultura Económica.

Granell, M. *Lógica*. (1949). Madrid: Revista de Occidente.

Granell, M. (1977). *Ethología y existencia (fundamentaciones ethológicas)*. Caracas: Equinoccio.

Imaz, E. (1945). *Asalto a Dilthey*. Mexico City: El Colegio de México.

Imaz, E. (1946a). *El pensamiento de Dilthey*. Mexico City: El Colegio de México.

Nicol, E. (1941). *Psicología de las situaciones vitales*. Mexico City: El Colegio de México.

Nicol, E. (1957). *Metafísica de la expresión*. Mexico City: Fondo de Cultura Económica.

Nicol, E. (1972). *El porvenir de la filosofía*. Mexico City: Fondo de Cultura Económica.

Nicol, E. (1980). *La reforma de la filosofía*. Mexico City: Fondo de Cultura Económica.

Nicol, E. (1982). *Crítica de la razón simbólica*. Mexico City: Fondo de Cultura Económica.

Ortega y Gasset, J. (1933). *The modern theme*. New York: W. W. Norton (Original work published 1923).

Ortega y Gasset, J. (1935). *History as a system*. New York: W. W. Norton.

Ortega y Gasset, J. (1948). *The dehumanization of art and notes on the novel*. Princeton, NJ: Princeton University Press (Original work published 1925).

Ortega y Gasset, J. (1957). *Man and people*. New York: W. W. Norton.

Ortega y Gasset, J. (1961). *Meditations on Quixote*. New York: W. W. Norton (Original work published 1914).

Ortega y Gasset, J. (1967). *The origin of philosophy*. New York: W. W. Norton.

Ortega y Gasset, J. (1971). *The idea of principle in Leibniz*. New York: W. W. Norton.

Recasens Siches, L. (1948). *Human life, society and law: fundamentals of the philosophy of the law*. Cambridge, MA: Harvard University Press.

Rodríguez Huéscar, A. (1994). *Perspectiva y verdad*. Madrid: Revista de Occidente (Original work published 1966).

Rodríguez Huéscar, A. (1996). *Éthos y lógos*. Madrid: UNED.

Soler, F. (1965). *Hacia Ortega. I. El mito del origen del hombre*. Santiago: Universidad de Santiago de Chile.

Zambrano, M. (1998). *Los intelectuales en el drama de España*. Madrid: Trotta.

Zambrano, M. (1967). *La tumba de Antígona*, Mexico City, Siglo XXI.

Zambrano, M. (1990). *Claros del bosque*. Barcelona: Seix Barral.

Further Reading

Abellán, J. L. (1966). *Filosofía española en América (1936–1966)*. Madrid: Guadarrama.

Abellán, J. L. (1998). *El exilio filosófico en América: los transterrados de 1939*. Madrid/Mexico City: Fondo de Cultura Económica.

Araya, G. (1983). *El pensamiento de Américo Castro*. Madrid: Alianza.

Beorlegui, C. (1988). *García Bacca. La audacia de un pensar*. Bilbao: Universidad de Deusto.

Beorlegui, C. (2006). *Historia del pensamiento filosófico latinoamericano*. Bilbao: Universidad de Deusto.

Bundgaard, A. (2000). *Más allá de la filosofía. Sobre el pensamiento filosófico-místico de María Zambrano*. Madrid: Trotta.

Caudet, F. (2005). *El exilio republicano de 1939*. Madrid: Cátedra.

Cohn, P. (Ed.). (1981). *Transparencies: philosophical essays in honor of José Ferrater Mora*. Atlantic Highlands, NJ: Humanities Press.

Ferrater Mora, J. (1963). *Ortega y Gasset: an outline of his philosophy*. New Haven: Yale University Press.

Garrido, M., Orringer, N., Valdés, L. M., & Valdés, M. M. (Eds.). (Forthcoming). *El legado filosófico español e hispanoamericano del siglo XX*. Madrid: Cátedra.

Gaos, J. (1957). *Sobre Ortega y Gasset y otros trabajos de historia de las ideas en España y América española*. Mexico City: Imprenta Universitaria.

Gaos, J. (1958). *Confesiones profesionales*. Mexico City: Tezontle.

González, J. (1981). *La metafísica dialéctica de Eduardo Nicol*. Mexico City: Universidad Nacional Autónoma de Mexico.

Imaz, E. (1946b). *Topía y utopia*. Mexico City: Fondo de Cultura Económica.

Imaz, E. (1951). *Luz en la caverna*. Mexico City: Fondo de Cultura Económica.

Izuzquiza, I. (1984). *El proyecto filosófico de Juan David García Bacca*. Barcelona: Anthropos.

Marías, J. (1983). *Ortega: Las trayectorias*. Madrid: Alianza Editorial.

Medin, T. (1994). *Ortega y Gasset en la cultura hispanoamericana*. Mexico City: Fondo de Cultura Económica.

Mainer, J. C. (1983). *La edad de Plata (1902–1929)*. Madrid: Cátedra.

Nicol, E. (1950). *Historicismo y existencialismo*. Mexico City: El Colegio de Mexico.

Ortega y Gasset, J. (1946–83). *Obras completas*. Madrid: Alianza Editorial/Revista de Occidente.

Ortega y Gasset, J. (1981). *El espectador*. Madrid: Biblioteca Nueva.

Ortega y Gasset, J. (1996). *Meditación de nuestro tiempo*. J. L. Molinuevo (Ed.). Madrid: Fondo de Cultura Económica.

Ortega y Gasset, J. (2004). *Obras completas*. Madrid: Santillana Ediciones Generales/Fundación José Ortega y Gasset.

Rodríguez Huéscar, A. (1994). *Semblanza de Ortega*. Barcelona: Anthropos.

Salmerón, F. (2000). *Escritos sobre José Gaos*. Mexico City: El Colegio de México.

Zambrano, M. (1939). *Filosofía y poesía*, Mexico City: Universidad de Morelia.

Zambrano, M. (1986). *El hombre y lo divino*. Mexico City: Fondo de Cultura Económica.

11

Phenomenology

NYTHAMAR DE OLIVEIRA

Introduction: From Continental Europe to Latin America

The birth and fate of phenomenology in Latin America can be better assessed in light
of the anti-positivist and culturalist trends that characterized the reception of
Continental thought at the end of the nineteenth century. Just as Neo-Kantian philosophy and the search for a third way between rationalist and empiricist schools were
so decisive for the emergence of Husserlian phenomenology at the beginning of the twentieth century, the Latin American reception of phenomenology (broadly conceived,
so as to comprise also existentialism, personalism, hermeneutics, and deconstruction)
has been frequently heralded as a new attempt to break away from colonialist, traditional conceptions of philosophizing. Nevertheless, as one revisits the existing writings
on the reception of phenomenology in Latin America, one is struck by the tremendous
contrast between a rather descriptive, often superficial appropriation of Husserl,
Heidegger, Hartmann, and Scheler among Hispanic American thinkers of the first half
of the twentieth century, and the highly original, creative profusion of works published
in the second half of the same century (Sobrevilla, 1988; Rosales, 1998; Zirión & Vargas,
2000). That certainly has to do with the platitude that there has been a tangible, consistent evolution of Latin American philosophy toward the turn of the century, but that
happens to be especially the case when one thinks of the consolidation of university systems, academic research, publications, colloquia, and symposia in such a vast
philosophical, interdisciplinary field. The very hermeneutic and deconstructionist
transformations inherent in the phenomenological movement, which can be clearly
traced in the development of phenomenological schools and immanent criticisms in
Europe, can be thus also detected in the evolution of different trends in Latin American
phenomenology. It was only with the creation of several phenomenological research
groups, institutions, and societies in the late 1980s and '90s that phenomenology was
finally consolidated as a genuine major philosophical movement in Latin America, side
by side with anti-positivism, culturalism, Marxism, and analytic philosophy.

Besides the historical and philosophical staging of phenomenology, hermeneutics,
existentialism, and deconstruction as important schools and styles of continental
philosophizing in Latin America, one could also focus on the reception and translation
of the main works by Husserl, Heidegger, Scheler, Gadamer, Sartre, Merleau-Ponty,

Ricoeur, Foucault, Levinas, and Derrida into Spanish and Portuguese, particularly in Mexico, Argentina, Brazil, Peru, Colombia, Venezuela, Chile, Cuba, and other Latin American countries. To be sure, the lasting influence exerted by Spanish philosopher Ortega y Gasset upon the Latin American versions of existentialism and circumstantialism ("I am myself and my circumstance"), especially in Argentina and Mexico, would remain unchallenged for many phenomenologists in recent decades, but there seems to be an overall tendency to dim or pulverize existentialist traits in order to highlight many other variables and functions in a much more complex, multiform hermeneutics of the social world, comprising cultural, economic, juridical, and institutional spheres.

According to Edmund Husserl (1859–1938), phenomenology is to be variously conceived as the science of the essence of consciousness, the philosophical science of consciousness qua intentionality, the reflective study of the essence of consciousness as experienced from the first-person point of view, the universal doctrine of essences (die allgemeine Wesenslehre), a rigorous science of all conceivable transcendental phenomena (especially, meaning). Phenomenology was thus conceived, in a nutshell, as a veritable interdisciplinary program to reconstruct and return to the things themselves (zu den Sachen selbst) (Husserl, 1999, pp. 9–66). Husserl's phenomenology may indeed be fairly described as an experiential invitation to seeing the things as they are to be seen, in their essential constitution as such. A static phenomenology would eventually pave the way for both genetic and generative accounts in Husserlian research, as the transcendental method shifts from the constitution of objects (i.e., as intended by *my* consciousness, *Gegenstände*) toward the Other, its intersubjective, linguistically, historically, and socially mediated relations, especially in Husserl's unfinished and posthumously published writings on the lifeworld (*Lebenswelt*) (Husserl, 1999, pp. 307–21; 363–78).

The so-called hermeneutic turn, together with a semantic turn and a linguistic turn, is fully effected by the innovative interpretation offered by Husserl's most brilliant pupil, Martin Heidegger (1889–1976), whose radical theses on fundamental ontology and the hermeneutics of facticity were celebrated as a phenomenological parricide or as a rupture that inaugurated a new era in contemporary continental philosophy. In order to retrieve the forgotten question of Being (*Sein*) and avoid its confusion with beings or entities within the world (*Seienden*), Heidegger invites us "to let that which shows itself be seen from itself," so that phenomenology opens up anew the possibility of thinking what remains to be thought and must thus be understood as "the method of scientific philosophy in general" or "ontology" (Heidegger, 1988, pp. 3–14).

The Latin American reception of phenomenology is marked by the Husserl–Heidegger problematic relationship, initially almost taken for granted as two diametrically opposed approaches to ontology and philosophical anthropology. But in the postwar period, as will be shown, a more nuanced view will inevitably emerge as hermeneutics and deconstruction undermine these facile polarizations between phenomenology and existential philosophy. In effect, according to Heidegger,

For Husserl, the phenomenological reduction is the method of leading phenomenological vision from the natural attitude of the human being whose life is involved in the world of things and persons back to the transcendental life of consciousness and its

157

noetic–noematic experiences, in which objects are constituted as correlates of conscious-ness. For us, phenomenological reduction means leading phenomenological vision back from the apprehension of a being, whatever may be the character of that apprehension, to the understanding of the Being of this being (projecting upon the way it is unconcealed). (Heidegger, 1988, p. 21)

Accordingly, only by means of a phenomenological hermeneutics can we rescue the fundamental sense of ontology, so as to avoid ontic and essentialist reductions, inso-far as *Dasein* (literally, "Being-there," "existence") is grasped as the unique, existential human mode of Being in the world (*In-der-Welt-sein*), so that human modes of Being, actions, and activities overall (*praxis*) can no longer be reduced to a mere "theoretical" presence-at-hand (*Vorhandenheit*, "extantness") or to a "poietical" readiness-to-hand (*Zuhandenheit*, "handiness"), such as the modes of Being found in nonhuman beings (Heidegger, 1988, pp. 291–4). Heidegger sought to radicalize Kant's opposition of human persons (as the sole autonomous beings capable of *praxis*) to things or nonhuman beings, without recourse to any humanist or metaphysical conception of the person. Things can be somewhat determined in their Being by means of their spatial, temporal causal-ity (e.g., the place that they occupy in space at a given moment) but this is, according to Heidegger, already assuming too much, as if human observers actually stood as subjects over against given objects in space and time. Hence the transcendental opposition between self and world must be also corrected, as it were, by rescuing the meaning of the question of Being prior to any misconception of a totality of entities (which fails to grasp the ontological meaning of the world) or of a supreme entity mis-takenly identified with Being itself (traditional theological conceptions). Heidegger proceeds thus to undertake a deconstruction of the history of ontology, especially in Aristotle, Descartes, and Kant. Heidegger's original intuition was, to put it simply, that although Aristotle had correctly identified the problem of the manifold sense of the Being of beings, both the Cartesian subject–object dichotomy and the Kantian transcendental subjectivity had misled us into representational thought, as exemplified in correspond-ence theories of truth and in the impossibility of reaching beyond sensible intuitions. Husserl knew this too well, as he sought to radicalize both Descartes' and Kant's attempts, but he also failed to deliver an account of consciousness that avoided mis-taking the meant object for its Being, in the very apprehension of the "existing" thing that is given to us. Granted, the mode of givenness of the thing in front of us (or meant in our thoughts) is precisely what is at stake for any phenomenological theory of mean-ing for both Husserl and Heidegger. However, Heidegger thought that by bracketing the world and evoking consciousness qua intentionality, Husserl was somehow taking human existence for granted and this must be dealt with in fundamental, ontological terms.

For Heidegger, only human *Dasein* properly deserves the attributes of existence, world, and praxis, so that rocks, plants, and animals can be objectified by human thought and science (*theoria*), just as tools, poems, and buildings are purposively made by humans (*poiesis*); while inorganic, natural beings are said to be worldless and living beings (especially animals) can display some worldly dimension, only human *Dasein* is strictly world-disclosing, correlated to worldliness (*Weltlichkeit*), and capable thus of creating worldly dimensions (through art, technology, and creative artifacts). Only because

158

Dasein is in the world, in its properly human mode of Being, can understanding, language, disclosure, and existence be fully meaningful at all. The hermeneutic, semantic turn in Heidegger consists precisely in radically departing from any instrumental use of language and meaning. It is, in this sense, that ontology, subjectivity, and language are said to be correlated.

Therefore, Heidegger both radicalizes and realizes the Husserlian original intent to overcome the natural attitude and the inadequacies and shortcomings of psychologism, formalism, idealism, historicism, and rationalism, on the one hand, and the dichotomies between theory and practice, subject and object, mind and body, self and world, on the other. French phenomenologists take this radical, paradigmatic critique further, as they carry out the detranscendentalizing move implicit in the Heideggerian deconstruction of modern subjectivity and seek to recast modern, hermeneutic problems of corporeity, power, alterity, technology, and meaning. Even though Heidegger was critical of Kantian transcendental subjectivity, the former's primacy of human existence, historicity, and linguisticality over other layers of meaning was perceived by some French interpreters as subtle blindspots or relapses into some form of transcendental thought. Merleau-Ponty thematized thus the originary, bodily openness to the world as inherent in *Dasein*'s modes of Being, while Foucault worked out an ontological account of power in human relations, Levinas developed a fundamental ethics of alterity (otherwise than Being), and Derrida denounced the self-deception of all attempts to make sense of meaning without recourse to a certain metaphysics of presence. Michel Foucault, Philippe Lacoue-Labarthe, Jean-Luc Nancy, and Bernard Stiegler have all explored many aspects and nuances of Heidegger's brilliant insights into technology, at once so essential to human praxis and so alienating of its essence, as *Dasein* cannot be reduced to the theoretical, manual, or instrumental handlings of nonhuman beings. In effect, the post-Heideggerian reflection on the non-technical essence of technology, in these authors as in many Latin American thinkers, has contributed to renewing the controversial, ongoing debates on the possibilities of relating technology to politics and the environment, especially in biotechnology and biopolitics, beyond the demonization and deification of technology. Like Heidegger, many phenomenologists saw the global threat of technological mass movements and mobilization in Nazi Germany, Soviet Communism, and consumerist capitalism. Hence, the interesting challenge of bringing together phenomenological and Marxist traditions, as exemplified by Sartre and French interpreters of German Idealism and the Frankfurt School, is also taken up by several Latin American thinkers, which have often been understandably classified as eclectic.

The First Generation

The emergence of phenomenology in Latin America, like the introduction and development of early philosophical trends in the subcontinent, hinges upon the very reception of phenomenology in the first and second decades by Iberian thinkers, particularly in Spain, since Portuguese phenomenologists who exerted some influence on Brazilian philosophers, such as Julio Fraga and Eduardo Soveral, did not flourish until the second half of the twentieth century. In this first subsection, it will be shown how the Spanish reception of phenomenology and existential philosophy paved the way for the Hispanic

159

American developments and later elaborations on phenomenological ideas. Many of the philosophers who contributed to consolidating the phenomenological movement in Latin America were not phenomenologists in the strict sense of the term used today, but their importance is mentioned here because of the legacies they helped to initiate.

The influential writings of Spanish existential philosopher José Ortega y Gasset (1883–1955) were particularly embraced as a new way of recasting existence, culture, and history, as they ultimately contributed to become an integrating part of Latin American self-identity and self-understanding. With the outbreak of the Spanish Civil War in 1936, Ortega y Gasset went into exile in Buenos Aires (his first visit there took place in 1916), where he taught and formed disciples, living also in France and Portugal until 1945, when he returned to Madrid. Both Husserl and Heidegger had been then introduced as the leading thinkers to help recast a Latin American, philosophical account of its own marginalization, historical, and axiological commitments vis-à-vis its colonial past.

Ortega y Gasset's compatriot disciple and close friend, José Gaos (1900–69) is generally regarded as one of the first great apostles of phenomenology in Latin America, especially in the Mexican landscape which he adopted as his new homeland in 1938. Gaos became a Mexican citizen in 1941, even though he ironically regarded himself as an exiled, "transterritorialized" alien (*transterrado*). From his early critical study on Husserl (*La crítica del psicologismo en Husserl*, 1930) to his introduction to phenomenology (*Introducción a la fenomenología*, 1960), Gaos contributed to disseminate in Latin America phenomenological ideas, theses, and methods, besides his meticulous translation of Heidegger's *Sein und Zeit* (Being and time) into Spanish and of other important phenomenological writings by Husserl and Scheler.

Another Spanish thinker in exile in Latin America, Juán David García Bacca (1901–92) lived in Ecuador and Mexico, before settling in Venezuela, where he founded the Facultad de Humanidades at the Central University in Caracas, in 1946, and published numerous writings on logic, philosophy of science, metaphysics, and the history of philosophy.

Other important representatives of the first period are Antonio Caso (1883–1946), in Mexico (*La filosofía de Husserl, El acto ideatorio, La persona humana y el estado totalitario*), and Francisco Romero (1891–1962), in Argentina (*Los problemas de la filosofía de la cultura, Filosofía de la persona, Teoría del hombre*). Along with José Vasconcelos, Caso founded the famous *Ateneo de la Juventud* and was president of Mexico's National University (UNAM), where he directed the Escuela de Altos Estudios for several decades and led a national, philosophical movement that sought to reconcile a Christian, personalist metaphysics with an ontical, lifeworldly conception of culture and social life. Samuel Ramos (1897–1959) followed the nationalist trend inaugurated by Caso and Vasconcelos in Mexico, under the influence of Ortega y Gasset, Scheler, and Hartmann, elaborating on a philosophical anthropology capable of doing justice to the Latin American colonial past and openness toward a new humanism.

Along with Alejandro Korn, Francisco Romero has been regarded as the most influential Argentine philosopher of the first half of the twentieth century, and contributed to recasting the *gaucho* myth of Martín Fierro within the framework of a philosophical anthropology that conjugated the phenomenological, basic concepts of transcendence, intentionality, and existence with Hegelian–Marxist conceptions of

160

historical self-consciousness and social transformation. Influenced by Scheler, Husserl, and Heidegger, the Argentine Carlos Astrada (1894–1970) published two major works in the phenomenology of this first generation: *El juego existencial* (1933) and *Idealismo fenomenológico y metafísica existencial* (1936).

The Peruvian Alberto Wagner de Reyna (1915–2006) introduced phenomenology and existentialism in his native country, and had important followers such as Francisco Miró Quesada (b. 1918), Augusto Salazar Bondy (1925–74), and David Sobrevilla (b. 1938). Wagner de Reyna studied under Heidegger and Romano at Freiburg, and published the first in-depth study in Spanish on the Black Forest thinker (Wagner de Reyna, 1939). Miró Quesada published an important work on Husserl, *El sentido del movimiento fenomenológico*, whose conceptions of delusion (*engaño*) and deception (*desengaño*) would also inspire Wagner de Reyna and other interlocutors' critical analyses of an endless quest for Latin American identity (Miró Quesada, 1941).

As early as 1943, in a famous article that came out in the journal *Philosophy and Phenomenological Research*, Afrânio Coutinho rightly remarked that, besides various interpretations of French positivism, there had been no original philosophical contribution in Brazil until then, a state of affairs which has arguably been challenged in the second half of the last century (Coutinho, 1943, p. 187). To be sure, some early works by Luís Washington Vita (1921–66) that came out in the 1950s offered phenomenological articulations of aesthetics, historicity, technology, and human nature, in light of his interpretation of Ortega y Gasset. Other early writings by Alceu Amoroso Lima (1893–1983) and Miguel Reale (1910–2006) touch upon phenomenological and existential problems such as the correlation between personality and social environment, but it is only with the first essays published by Gerd Bornheim (1929–2002) and the Czech-Brazilian thinker Vilém Flusser (1920–91) in the 1960s that one may properly speak of a Brazilian reception of phenomenology.

Finally, another phenomenological milestone for this first period is the ensemble of early contributions by Hispanic American philosophers whose major contributions lie elsewhere, such as the Mexican thinkers Eduardo García Máynez (1908–93) and Leopoldo Zea (1912–2004), who exerted a decisive influence upon Latin American legal studies and the hermeneutics of liberation, respectively. Many of the philosophers from the first generation still sought some form of reconciling their religious beliefs with phenomenological, existentialist concepts, including thus Catholic versions of existentialism (Karl Jaspers, Gabriel Marcel) and personalism (Emmanuel Mounier). Besides the religious component, many Latin American thinkers resorted to phenomenological concepts in order to thematize the originality and genius of Hispanic American literature and culture. Given the comprehensive, interdisciplinary, and intercultural scope of phenomenology, one possible way of narrowing down our survey is to confine it to the specifically philosophical contributions to the ongoing reception of phenomenology in Latin America.

The Second Half of the Twentieth Century

The fate of phenomenology in Latin America was to be drastically changed after the postwar period known as the Cold War, particularly after the Cuban Revolution on

January 1, 1959. In order to counter communism, there were military coups all over the subcontinent, and many of the greatest phenomenologists in Latin America were forced into exile because of military regimes that took power in Argentina (1962–3, 1966–73, 1976–83), Brazil (1964–85), Chile (1973–90), and Uruguay (1973–85). Undoubtedly the most important cultural movement in the subcontinent in the second half of the century was the so-called theologies of liberation, closely tied to many grassroots, social movements which sought to resist military authoritarianism. What later became identified with a philosophy of liberation was in effect an outcome of the theological, highly original contributions to postcolonial, cultural studies. Many continental thinkers directly (such as Sartre, Levinas, Ricoeur) or indirectly (Bloch, Marcuse, Apel, Habermas) related to phenomenology were then evoked by liberation thinkers in the 1960s, '70s, and '80s (Alves, Gutiérrez, Boff, Dussel).

The developments that took place in academic programs in philosophy, however, were completely cut off from religious circles, in reaction to neo-Thomistic currents, especially in public institutions, state and federal universities. The phenomenological legacy within a certain "philosophy of liberation" can be found, among others, in the Basque-Salvadoran liberation theologian Ignacio Ellacuría (1930–89), a former student of Karl Rahner and Xavier Zubiri, in the Argentine-Mexican philosopher Enrique Dussel (b. 1934), perhaps its best-known representative in North America, and in the Cuban thinker Raúl Fornet-Betancourt (b. 1946), an advocate of intercultural philosophy in Europe, especially in Germany.

Just as the adverse circumstances of military authoritarianism favored an ever-growing interest in Marxist analysis, the French politicized, existential versions of phenomenology and structuralism, especially following Merleau-Ponty's former students' radical group, *Socialisme ou Barbarie* (which included Castoriadis, Lefort, and Lyotard), and Sartre's socialist appeal, coincided with the proliferation of philosophical publications and research projects supported by federal and international research agencies in Latin America. In effect, Sartre's famous trip with Simone de Beauvoir to Cuba and Brazil in 1960 was a programmatic part of his left-wing existentialism – he deliberately avoided thus returning to the United States, in full accordance with his anti-imperialist, anti-racist agenda and in support of Third World decolonization. Several of the first important national programs to foster academic research were then created and demanded an intensive collaboration from intellectuals and philosophers from diverse backgrounds and orientations, including some of the most radical ones.

To be sure, during the postwar period there was a right-wing reception of Husserl and Heidegger in Latin America, just as vitalism and social Darwinism had paved the way for neoconservative trends that dominated many intellectual circles during the interwar period. It is enough to note that such an important a philosopher of law as Miguel Reale was an Integralist (a nationalist movement), and during the military dictatorship in Brazil, he maintained the same conservative orientation at the Brazilian Institute of Philosophy (*Instituto Brasileiro de Filosofia*), which he founded in 1949 and directed until his death in 2006.

Other thinkers who were also influenced by phenomenology, such as José Guilherme Merquior (1941–91), were committed to a centrist political liberalism that denounced as Marxist opportunism the criticism of authoritarian regimes in Latin America, perceived in the enthusiastic reception of Sartre's and Foucault's leftist ideas. Victor

Farías (b. 1940), a Chilean historian who studied with Heidegger at Freiburg and subsequently attained fame for publishing a polemical work on Heidegger and Nazism in 1987, went as far as attempting, in other publications, to establish a causal link between Allende's socialism and Nazi, anti-Semitic ideology in the Southern Cone. The same failure of a coherent articulation between Marxism and phenomenology seen in Europe was thus reproduced in Latin America, just as the unholy alliance of conservative thought with existentialism sought by Christian philosophers on the Continent failed to constitute any important legacy for the next generations of thinkers.

And yet, regardless of all ideological quarrels, the 1970s saw some of the first and most relevant international publications by Latin American philosophers conducting research in phenomenology. Alberto Rosales (Venezuela), Guido de Almeida (Brazil), and Guillermo Hoyos Vásquez (Colombia) all published seminal studies in the prestigious *Phaenomenologica* book series (Rosales, 1970; Almeida, 1972; Hoyos Vásquez, 1976).

The best way to make sense of later developments of Latin American phenomenology is by focusing on the major contributions of university departments and research centers that flourished in the subcontinent, especially in Argentina, Brazil, Mexico, and Peru. The Argentine Luis Juan Guerrero (1899–1957), author of a monumental treatise of aesthetics in three volumes, is one of those transitional thinkers who might help us understand the shift from an early axiological, anthropological phenomenology toward the more systematic divisions of the second half of the last century. Perhaps in Argentina, more than any other Hispanic American country, this transition is very subtle, given the rich production and solid continuity in the development of phenomenological schools and trends. Arturo Andrés Roig (1922–77), whose eclectic and controversial interpretations of Dilthey, Foucault, and Lyotard signal the importance of revisiting some of the most fundamental ideas in Husserl and Heidegger, is another philosopher that calls for an *ad fontes* return to phenomenology and hermeneutics. The rise of liberation thinking as over against the military, dictatorial repression of individual freedoms (in particular, freedom of thought and expression) served also to stimulate new possibilities in phenomenological fields often neglected or supposedly exhausted by previous generations of thinkers.

Roberto Walton (b. 1942), from the University of Buenos Aires, is the most significant representative of the phenomenological movement in Argentina and by all criteria, together with his compatriot Julia Valentina Iribarne, Rosemary Rizo-Patrón (from Peru), and Antonio Zirión (from Mexico), one of the most important Husserl scholars in Latin America today. Walton authored many important works in phenomenology journals and two major books, *El fenómeno y sus configuraciones* (1992) and *Husserl: mundo, conciencia, temporalidad* (1993) (Walton, 1992, 1993). He is on the council board of the international series *Orbis Phaenomenologicus* and of the *Husserl Studies*, and is the chair of the Argentinean chapter of the Círculo Latinoamericano de Fenomenología (CLAFEN). Walton has contributed to ongoing international research in phenomenology by exploring unpublished and recently published Husserl manuscripts, such as the so-called "C-manuscripts," which came out in German in 2006 (*Späte Texte über Zeitkonstitution (1929–1934): Die C Manuskripte, Husserliana Materialien VIII*). Walton successfully argued that, starting from a primal or quasi-world correlated with pre-intentionality, the constitution of the world advances to the full intersubjective world constituted by an intentionality of interests within communicative praxis.

163

Walton discerns thus different characterizations of the world as universal horizon, world-representation, whole, form, idea, and ground, so as to unveil the role of temporality at the roots of these traits of worldliness. Furthermore, the levels of world constitution are disclosed so as to differentiate a readymade ground from a ground that develops through the stages of egoical world, homeworld, lifeworld, and world-in-itself. Walton proceeds then to a further analysis of levels, given through the inquiry back into primality (*Urtümlichkeit*) as a retrogression that reveals the development from a pre-world to a genuine world. He succeeds in bringing out a permanent genesis rather than a past genesis, before showing the anticipations of post-Husserlian phenomenological views regarding an originary openness of the world in its worldliness, a realm that is prior to the manifestation of a world of objects, and a different order of manifestation than that of the world. Walton has thus shown how both the Heideggerian originary openness of the world in its worldliness and Merleau-Ponty's conception of nature as a core matter (*hyle*) of the world as experienced, together with the latter's horizontal notion of a "between" out of which subject and object emerge, are clearly anticipated in Husserl's inquiry back into the primality of the life-stream. Walton has ultimately shown that the genetic, generative phenomenology of Husserl's unpublished material (*Nachlass*) can not only fill in the missing links and gaps in static accounts of transcendental phenomenology leading all the way to the *Cartesian Meditations* and the *Crisis* lectures, but are particularly relevant for future research in phenomenological methodologies for social, empirical sciences (Walton, 2006, pp. 583–602).

Along with Alcira Bonilla and Roberto Walton, Julia Iribarne integrates the Section of Phenomenology and Hermeneutics at Argentina's National Academy of Sciences. Her guiding thesis that the transcendental theory of constitution requires a fundamental conception of intersubjectivity has been developed in her two-volume work *La intersubjetividad en Husserl* (Iribarne, 1987, 1988), which has also been translated into German, *Husserls Theorie der Intersubjektivität* (1994). Carlos Belvedere has worked and published in the area of social phenomenology, seeking to propose an original, lifeworldly conception of the social ethos, so as to bridge the ethical–political divide in correlated terms. He directs the Study Group on Phenomenology and Ethnomethodology at Buenos Aires. Aníbal Fornari created and directs the Círculo de Fenomenología y Hermenéutica de Santa Fé y Paraná.

In Brazil, Gerd Bornheim has been hailed as one of the most brilliant representatives of the Latin American appropriation of phenomenology and existentialism in the second half of the twentieth century. Together with Zeljko Loparic, Benedito Nunes, Emanuel Carneiro Leão, and Ernildo Stein, Bornheim was one of the first thinkers to have introduced Heidegger's philosophy in Brazil in the 1960s and '70s. His major, original contributions were an existentially based introduction to philosophizing (Bornheim, 1969) and two seminal studies on Sartre, whom he met and studied with in Paris, while in exile. José Arthur Giannotti, Bento Prado, Paulo Arantes, Gérard Lebrun, Marilena Chauí, Renato Janine Ribeiro, and Roberto Machado were among the first to introduce Brazilian students to Sartre, Merleau-Ponty, and Foucault. Other major Brazilian scholars who have been working in phenomenology and hermeneutics are Gilvan Fogel, Márcia Sá Cavalcante Schuback, Creusa Capalbo, Nelci Gonçalves, Paulo Cesar Duque-Estrada, and Marco Antonio Casanova, in Rio de Janeiro, where there are well-established research groups in the phenomenology of the social sciences, social medicine, existential psychology, and deconstruction; Jairo Silva, Carlos Alberto de Moura, Elsa Oliveira Dias, and José Carlos Michelazzo, in São Paulo, where the major Husserl and Heidegger research groups have been consolidated since the 1980s; Urbano Zilles, Nythamar de Oliveira, Robson Reis, Claudia Drucker, André Duarte, Ricardo Timm de Souza, Luiz Hebeche, and Marcelo Fabri, in southern Brazil, where the Heidegger and Levinas research groups are among the most productive and influential in Latin America; Marcelo Pelizzolli and Acylene Ferreira in the Northeastern region of Brazil. Besides their regional chapters, annual meetings and colloquia, the research groups hold a national meeting every other year, under the auspices of the Brazilian Association of Graduate Programs in Philosophy (Anpof) and supported by the National Research Council (CNPq).

Along with Zeljko Loparic, Ernildo Jacob Stein (b. 1934) is the most important former student of Heidegger's and hermeneutic phenomenology scholar in Brazil, having translated several of Heidegger's major works into Portuguese and published numerous articles and over twenty books in this field. His meticulous, creative writings offer a highly original interpretation of Heidegger's fourfold articulation of a fundamental ontology, a hermeneutics of facticity, an existential analytic of *Dasein*, and a deconstruction of ontology in terms of thinking the ontical–ontological difference in light of the Heideggerian turn (*Kehre*) from the transcendental approach to *Dasein* toward the eventful appropriation (*Ereignis*, "enowing") of the truth of Being in the later writings, so as to allow for a coherent, semantic unity of phenomenology, hermeneutics, and deconstruction. His overall grasp of Heidegger's *Gesamtausgabe* proves to be very reminiscent of a Heideggerian, perspectival anamorphosis: no particular interpretation of Heidegger can break away from the hermeneutic circle insofar as the interpreter simply cannot get away from her own finitude and implicit self-understanding (Stein, 1990, 2001).

Together with Roberto Walton, the Croatian-Brazilian philosopher Zeljko Loparic (b. 1939) recently edited the most updated, representative collection of essays from Latin American phenomenologists, comprising twelve papers from Spanish-speaking philosophers and sixteen from Portuguese-speaking thinkers (Loparic & Walton, 2005). Loparic translated into Portuguese Husserl's sixth *Logical Investigation* and has been regarded as one of the most original thinkers resorting to phenomenology in Latin America and combining it with research in psychoanalysis, transcendental semantics, and existential psychology. He has created and directed some of the most important Heidegger research groups in Brazil and is the founder and main editor of the phenomenological journal *Natureza Humana*, official vehicle of the Brazilian Society for Phenomenology. Loparic has been seeking to recast Heidegger's ethical, political thinking on technology in philosophical-anthropological terms, so as to overcome the shortcomings and contradictions of the National-Socialist affairs without succumbing to a postmodernist rhetoric or embracing postmetaphysical alternatives like Habermas's critique of technical nihilism (Loparic, 1990). Both Loparic and Stein have led many seminars and research projects in existential psychoanalysis, philosophical anthropology, and the philosophy of law, allowing for original, creative work to be developed in juridical hermeneutics and Heideggerian psychology.

In Mexico, Antonio Zirión has been a leading researcher and promoter of phenomenological studies. Based at the UNAM's Instituto de Investigaciones Filosóficas,

Zirión has been directing online such technological resources as the *Diccionario Husserl*, a powerful lexicon-dictionary guide that allows for important discussions, workshops, and publications on the translation of Husserl's texts. Zirión has also been extensively working on a meticulous account of the history of phenomenology in Mexico since the 1980s. In his most recent research, Zirión has been calling into question the mistaken assumption (especially among those who depart from its original, rational intent) that phenomenology's common denominator is to operate a "return to the things themselves" as if this meant a call for a deformalization of the Husserlian motto. Together with the so-called "principle of all principles" (namely, to rely on evidence) and the "phenomenological reduction" (to attain the absolute, intuitive givenness of things), the Husserlian call must ultimately carry out, according to Zirión, a radical return to lived subjectivity only to rehabilitate the *logos* of the phenomena and subjectivity (Zirión, 2005, pp. 661–78).

The last decade of the second half of the century saw also the emergence of several phenomenological societies and research groups, especially in Argentina, Brazil, Mexico, Peru, Venezuela, and Colombia. The Argentinian Phenomenological Circle (Círculo Argentino de Fenomenología) was thus created on October 30, 1992, consolidating several decades of phenomenological research in that country. On August 6, 1999, Nythamar de Oliveira, together with Ernildo Stein, Ricardo de Souza, Rui Josgrilberg, and Robson Reis, founded the Brazilian Society for Phenomenology (Sociedade Brasileira de Fenomenologia) at Porto Alegre, with official support from Rudolf Bernet, then Director of the Husserl Archives at Louvain. Three major international symposia were organized in 1999, 2001, and 2006 at the Pontifical Catholic University at Porto Alegre, Brazil, with the participation of phenomenologists from all over Brazil, other Latin American countries, and Europe. The Brazilian Society for Phenomenology has four regional chapters (South, São Paulo, Rio de Janeiro, and Northeast) and besides the Heidegger, Husserl, and Levinas research groups, several other thinkers (especially Merleau-Ponty, Sartre, Foucault, Ricoeur, Deleuze, Arendt, Jonas, Habermas, Honneth) and related fields (especially psychology, psychoanalysis, critical theory, and social philosophy) are covered and systematically studied.

With support from the Center for Advanced Research in Phenomenology (CARP) and the Organization of Phenomenological Organizations (OPO, the largest philosophical entity, with more than 170 associations and organizations from all over the planet), directed by Lester Embree, Rosemary Rizo-Patrón de Lerner founded, on August 16, 1999, together with Alberto Rosales, Raúl Velozo, Antonio Zirión, Guillermo Hoyos, and others in Puebla, Mexico, the Latin American Circle of Phenomenology (CLAFEN, Círculo Latinoamericano de Fenomenología). The Circle comprises researchers and representatives from all Latin American countries, especially Argentina, Mexico, Brazil, Peru, Chile, Colombia, and Venezuela. CLAFEN has thus far organized four international colloquia (Puebla, Mexico, August 1999; Bogotá, May 2002; Lima, January 2004; and Bogotá, August–September 2007) and has published two volumes with their proceedings (*Acta Fenomenológica Latinoamericana*). The thirty-second edition of the Husserl Circle Meeting was also supported by the Circle and held in 2002 in Lima, Peru – for the first time ever outside North America.

In Peru, on August 20, 2004, Rosemary Rizo-Patrón de Lerner, Pepi Patrón, Cecilia Monteagudo, and others created at the Pontifical Catholic University in Lima the

Círculo Peruano de Fenomenología (CIphER, Peruvian Circle of Phenomenology and Hermeneutics), which has organized many events. These have included international conferences with Jean Grondin, Renaud Barbaras, and Eliane Escoubar. Along with Roberto Walton and Antonio Zirión, Rosemary Rizo-Patrón has also contributed to the formulation of what might be regarded as the future of Husserlian phenomenology in Latin America. According to Rizo-Patrón, the itinerary that leads us from Husserl's early philosophy of mathematics toward the later phenomenology of the lifeworld allows for a rapprochement between the ontological significance of ideal objects and the inter-subjective sedimentation of meaning that we usually assign to genetic, generative accounts. Because of human finitude and the infinite possibilities inherent in rational abstraction, Rizo-Patrón can argue for a unitary account of intuitive representation and symbolic concepts, by revisiting the Husserlian insights into mathematical logic and the positive valuation of technical calculus (Rizo-Patrón, 2005, pp. 241–69; see also Rizo-Patrón, 1993).

As in Peru, Colombian phenomenology has also been particularly influenced by Gadamer and hermeneutical philosophy. Besides the seminal work produced by Guillermo Hoyos, Rafael Gutiérrez Girardot (1928–2005) and Germán Uribe (b. 1943) have contributed to the overall reception of hermeneutical and poststructuralist thought in Colombia, while Carlos B. Gutiérrez, a former student of Gadamer who teaches at the Universidad de los Andes, has been publishing and conducting research in the social, political implications of hermeneutics and its rapprochement with Nietzschean perspectivism.

Led by Alberto Rosales, the Venezuelan Society for Phenomenology was founded in 2006, and has been mainly represented by the works of Ezra Heymann and Gustavo Sarmiento. In Chile, Jorge Eduardo Rivera's superb translation of Heidegger's *Sein und Zeit* deserves special mention. Other notable Chilean phenomenologists are Raúl Velozo and Félix Schwartzmann. Several international phenomenological conferences were organized in Chilean universities in this century.

Conclusion

When one sets out to think of the future of twenty-first-century research in Latin American phenomenology, one cannot overemphasize the urgent need to rethink global issues, especially environmental ethics, bioethics, human rights, biotechnology, biopolitics, and many other subfields of applied ethics that demand a reasonable arti-culation of ontology and subjectivity lest they fall back into essentialism, naturalism, or relativism. If Husserlian-inspired phenomenology seemed too foundationalist in its original, static versions, we have seen how the developments of existential, hermeneut-ical, and deconstructionist strands have led us to a more complex understanding of phenomenology in Latin America, so as to comprise both genetic and generative dimen-sions that account for the historicality, linguisticality, and sociality of signification. Following the hermeneutic turn, language can no longer be reduced to an instrumental means to fulfill signification, but is correlated to both ontological and intersubjective dimensions of meaning. Phenomenology must thus articulate its different paradigmatic dimensions of ontology, intersubjectivity, and language with all the semantic and pragmatic implications of other major contributions in postmetaphysical thinking, as they have been broadly conceived in both analytic and continental traditions, comprising the philosophy of culture, philosophy of language, and philosophy of mind.

Phenomenological research in Latin America today seems to comprise both a more analytic orientation (in logic, philosophy of mathematics, and philosophy of science) and a more culturalist, fragmented orientation, which has also been combined with other cultural strands (such as literary criticism, structuralism, Marxist analysis, and Lacanian psychoanalysis). On the one hand, current works in neuroscience and cognitive science just confirm the collaborative analytic-continental interlocution in interdisciplinary research, which can be also found, to a lesser extent, in other fields relating to gender, race, and social, cultural studies. On the other hand, many Latin American phenomenologists are embracing a meta-phenomenological, deconstructionist, postmodernist or post-structuralist orientation as they seek to engage in intercultural, interdisciplinary dialogue with feminist, ecological, Afro-Latin, postcolonial, and cultural studies thinkers and activists. Both trends have been well represented in recent anthologies and collected papers of international symposia and research publications (De Oliveira & Souza, 2001, 2002, 2006; Loparic & Walton, 2005).

Currently the fate of the phenomenological odyssey in Latin American troubled waters seems to be very promising, as it has fared well between Scylla and Charybdis, beyond the scientific foundationalism of the early phase and the postmodernist trends of the contemporary landscape. For Latin American phenomenology has indeed been caught between two dangerous extremes, namely, that of a rigorous, scholarly approach which seems to inhibit innovation and creativity, and that of bold attempts to express a peculiar Latin American environmentality to the detriment of the exigencies of rigor and clarity inherent in the phenomenological and hermeneutic methods. This has been particularly the case with works in the interdisciplinary fields of a phenomenology of the social world, culture, and literature, where postmodernist and deconstructive trends are not rarely said to threaten the objectivity of academic undertakings. Interestingly enough, however, the reception of phenomenology, existentialism, hermeneutics, and deconstruction in Latin America in recent decades has succeeded in avoiding these two extremes, allowing both for an inclusivist, pluralist discursivity and a serious commitment to academic rigor and consistency.

Related chapters: 9 'Normal' Philosophy; 10 Ortega y Gasset's Heritage in Latin America; 13 Liberation Philosophy; 18 Identity and Philosophy; 21 Liberation in Theology, Philosophy, and Pedagogy; 22 Philosophy, Postcoloniality, and Postmodernity; 28 Feminist Philosophy.

References

Almeida, G. A. (1972). *Sinn und Inhalt in der Genetischen Phänomenologie E. Husserls.* The Hague: M. Nijhoff. *Phaenomenologica 47.*

Bornheim, G. (1969). *Introdução ao filosofar: o pensamento filosófico em bases existenciais.* Porto Alegre: Globo.

Coutinho, A. (1943). Some considerations on the problem of philosophy in Brazil. *Philosophy and Phenomenological Research, 4,* 186–93.

De Oliveira, N., & Souza, R. T. (Eds). (2001, 2002, 2006). *Fenomenologia hoje* (3 vols.). Porto Alegre: Edipucrs.

Heidegger, M. (1988). *The basic problems of phenomenology*. (A. Hofstadter, Trans.). Revised edition. Bloomington and Indianapolis: Indiana University Press.

Hoyos Vásquez, G. (1976). *Intentionalität als Verantwortung. Geschichsteleologie und Teleologie der Intentionalität bei Husserl*. The Hague: M. Nijhoff. *Phaenomenologica* 67.

Husserl, E. (1999). *The essential Husserl*. (D. Welton, Ed.). Bloomington: Indiana University Press.

Iribarne, J. V. (1987, 1988). *La intersubjetividad en Husserl: bosquejo de una teoría* (2 vols.). Buenos Aires: Ediciones Carlos Lohlé.

Loparic, Z. (1990). *Heidegger réu: um ensaio sobre a periculosidade da filosofia*. Campinas: Papirus.

Loparic, Z., & Walton, R. (Eds). (2005). *Phenomenology 2005. Vol. II: Selected essays from Latin America*. Bucharest: Zeta Books.

Miró Quesada, F. (1941). *El sentido del movimiento fenomenológico*. Lima: Librería e imprenta D. Miranda.

Rizo-Patrón de Lerner, R. (Ed.). (1993). *El pensamiento de Husserl en la reflexión filosófica contemporánea*. Lima: PUCP.

Rizo-Patrón de Lerner, R. (2005). *Anthropos arithmetizei*: Intuitive finitude and symbolic infinitude in Husserl's Philosophy of Arithmetic. In Z. Loparic & R. Walton (Eds). *Phenomenology 2005. Vol. II: Selected essays from Latin America* (Part 1, pp. 241–69). Bucharest: Zeta Books.

Rosales, A. (1970). *Transzendenz und Differenz. Ein Beitrag zum Problem der ontologischen Differenz beim frühen Heidegger*. [Transcendence and difference. A contribution to the problem of the ontological difference in the early Heidegger]. The Hague: M. Nijhoff. *Phaenomenologica* 33.

Rosales, A. (1998). La fenomenología en Latinoamérica. In A. T. Tymieniecka (Ed.). *Phenomenology of life and the human creative condition. Book III. Analecta Husserliana. The yearbook of phenomenological research* (pp. 345–55). Dordrecht: Kluwer Academic Publishers.

Sobrevilla, D. (1988). Phenomenology and existentialism in Latin America. In J. J. E. Gracia (Ed.). *Directory of Latin American philosophers* (pp. 85–113). Buffalo, NY: State University of New York, and Buenos Aires: CISP.

Stein, E. J. (1990). *Seis estudos sobre "Ser e Tempo"*. 2nd edn. Petrópolis: Vozes (Original work published 1988).

Stein, E. J. (2001). *Compreensão e finitude*. Ijuí: Unijuí (Original work published 1967).

Wagner de Reyna, A. (1939). *La ontología fundamental de Heidegger: su motivo y significación*. Buenos Aires: Losada.

Walton, R. (1992). *El fenómeno y sus configuraciones*. Buenos Aires: Almagesto.

Walton, R. (1993). *Husserl: mundo, conciencia, temporalidad*. Buenos Aires: Almagesto.

Walton, R. (2006). La mundaneidad en los escritos tardíos de E. Husserl sobre la constitución del tiempo. In N. De Oliveira, & R. T. Souza (Eds). *Fenomenologia Hoje* (pp. 583–602). Porto Alegre: Edipucrs.

Zirión Quijano, A. (2005). About the notion of phenomenology, one more time. In Z. Loparic & R. Walton (Eds). *Phenomenology 2005. Vol. II: Selected essays from Latin America* (Part 2, pp. 661–78). Bucharest: Zeta Books.

Zirión Quijano, A., & Vargas Guillén, G. (Eds). (2000). *Fenomenología en América Latina*. Serie Filosófica, No. 3. Bogotá: Universidad de San Buenaventura.

Further Reading

Bornheim, G. (1971). *Sartre: metafísica e existencialismo*. São Paulo: Perspectiva.

Ramos, S. (1962). *Profile of man and culture in Mexico*. (P. G. Earle, Trans.). Austin: University of Texas Press (Original work published 1934).

169

12

Marxism

RENZO LLORENTE

I

While the Latin American contribution to Marxist philosophy may appear rather modest when compared with Latin American Marxists' influence on such disciplines as sociology or political theory, there can be no doubt that Latin America has produced a number of thinkers and philosophers who have made significant, original contributions to Marxism. Indeed, the works of Latin American theorists have enriched a number of debates concerning central problems and issues of Marxism. These include the analysis of alienation, the theory of ideology, the nature of Marxist humanism, the relationship between socialism and national liberation, and the implications of Marxist thought for fields such as aesthetics and education. In addition, Latin American thinkers have brought a Marxist conceptual framework to bear on the analysis of themes and phenomena that have been almost entirely neglected within the Marxist tradition, including the sociopolitical status of indigenous peoples and the nature and scope of their agency in connection with an eventual socialist transformation of society. Latin America's Marxist thinkers have also done much to illuminate the nature of cultural and ideological domination rooted in economic dependency.

One reason that Latin America's Marxist thinkers have succeeded in making notable contributions to existing debates within Marxist philosophy, while also expanding the range of social phenomena addressed by Marxism, has to do with the relatively local and/or applied orientation that has informed much of their writing. Indeed, it is safe to say that "the union of theory and practice," a commitment that is supposed to define the very nature of Marxism as a political doctrine and philosophical perspective (and hence ought to govern all Marxist writing), has been far more characteristic of the work produced by Latin American Marxist philosophers than that of their counterparts in, say, Europe or North America. This has no doubt been due in part to the fact that some of these writers were themselves socialist or communist militants, or otherwise actively involved with practical politics in one capacity or another. Such was the case, for example, of the Peruvian José Carlos Mariátegui (1894–1930), perhaps the one indisputably outstanding Marxist thinker to have emerged from Latin America. Another factor has probably been the political volatility that plagued this region of the world during the twentieth century, along with the presence, especially in the wake of the Cuban Revolution, of insurrectionary movements that usually claimed to derive their inspiration from one variety or another of Marxism. But whatever the reasons for this particular, predominantly worldly orientation, it has clearly been one of the great virtues of Latin American Marxist philosophy, and the source of much of its vitality and originality. At the same time, however, the predominant tendency to adopt a more local and/or "applied" focus has perhaps also been the principal shortcoming of Latin American Marxism, insofar as the commitment to applying Marxism, or to addressing relatively immediate sociopolitical concerns, has been pursued to the detriment of a concern with more narrowly theoretical and conceptual concerns. Coupled, in recent years, with Latin American Marxists' near-total disregard for the impressive body of work that has come to be known as "analytical Marxism," the result has been relatively little development of Marxist theory in Latin America, at least as far as philosophy is concerned.

In the following sections I shall discuss seven topics which prove especially emblematic of Marxist philosophy in Latin America, both because they are topics that have figured prominently in the writings of the most important Latin American Marxist thinkers and because they have been treated in original ways by one or more of these thinkers. As we shall see, Latin American thinkers can rightfully claim some notable contributions to the Marxist philosophical tradition, even if by and large they have shown relatively little interest in various theoretical questions that have dominated debates in Marxist philosophy.

II

Marxism and the problem of the Indian

On numerous occasions throughout his works, Mariátegui insists that "the problem of the Indian" – that is, the destitution, marginalization, and exclusion endured by Peru's indigenous populations – is (or at least was during Mariátegui's day) Peru's primary or fundamental sociopolitical problem (see, e.g., 1994, p. 291; 1971, pp. 158, 171). His treatment of this problem in his book *Seven Interpretive Essays on Peruvian Reality* (1928), generally regarded as the single most important and original work of Latin American Marxism, effectively inaugurates the Marxist analysis of the "problem," an analysis which addresses both the causes of the problem and some possible solutions. In the chapter devoted to the Indian in his *Seven Essays* and elsewhere in his works, Mariátegui argues that the Indians' oppression derives from Peru's socioeconomic structure, and in particular from the prevailing system of land tenure, which he regards as feudal, or semi-feudal, in many respects. By demonstrating that an economic explanation of the Indians' condition is more persuasive than alternative accounts (e.g., an "ethnic" explanation), Mariátegui's account also shows both that the "problem of the Indian" is best explained in terms of Marx's analytical framework ("historical materialism") and that this framework points to the only real solution: a radical, and ultimately socialist, transformation of the relations of production. If, in addition, Mariátegui appears optimistic as regards the prospect for such a transformation, it is in large part because he assumes that a kind of communism existed in pre-Columbian

171

Peru and that the contemporary Indians preserve the spirit of this "Inca communism" (1971, p. 35) in many of their communal relations and agricultural practices. Thus, in a manner reminiscent of the late Marx, who, in what is often viewed as a revision of his philosophy of history, came to believe that Russia's rural communes might provide the basis for a socialist transformation of Russia, Mariátegui was confident that "the survival . . . of elements of practical socialism in indigenous agriculture and life" (1971, p. 33) might furnish the foundations for socialism in Peru, and perhaps even enable the country to circumvent some aspects or phases of capitalist development (1994, p. 188).

Mariátegui's approach to the "problem of the Indian" consists, at bottom, in a species of economic determinism – which is indeed how he tends to conceive of Marxism (see, e.g., 1996, pp. 58–9; and 1994, p. 1294) – even though historical materialism is more accurately categorized as, if anything, a variety of technological determinism. One short-coming of this approach is that it tends to ignore the autonomy of "the problem of the Indian," i.e., the extent to which some factors in the Indians' oppression, such as racism, may not be reducible to socioeconomic causes (although Mariátegui's works also include numerous incidental remarks on race which do seem to accord some auto-nomy to "the problem of the Indian"). What is more, besides leading, in all likelihood, to an oversimplification of the Indians' oppression, the reduction of this oppression to socioeconomic causes appears to generate an undue optimism in Mariátegui with regard to the possibility of eliminating this oppression. All the same, Mariátegui's analysis of the Indian question has proven extraordinarily influential, owing precisely to his efforts to situate the Indian's oppression within a larger context of oppression, and hence link their liberation to a broader project of human emancipation. Moreover, this endeavor marks a decisive advance in the development of a genuinely non-Eurocentric version of Marxist thought, involving as it does an application of Marxist theory to problems foreign to Europe. While the appropriation of many ideas from Henri Bergson, Friedrich Nietzsche, and Georges Sorel was in itself enough to ensure that Mariátegui would develop a distinctive version of Marxism, it was this commitment to applying Marxist theory to Peru's social problems that enabled him to produce works of indisputable originality.

Marxism and Latin American liberation

While Mariátegui was a champion of Latin American unity and was by no means interested in establishing socialism solely in Peru, his reflections on the dynamics of a more sweeping Latin American liberation scarcely go beyond some general remarks in favor of a principled anti-imperialism. A probing, perceptive analysis of the impedi-ments to Latin American liberation was, however, developed by a fellow Peruvian, the marxisant, and in many respects neo-Marxist, philosophy professor Augusto Salazar Bondy (1925–74). Employing concepts heavily indebted to Marx's writings and those of thinkers working within the Marxist tradition, Salazar Bondy maintains that the chief obstacle to Latin America's liberation is to be found in the relations of economic dependency and domination which generate an entire "culture of domina-tion." Salazar Bondy's view can in fact be understood as a philosophical extension, or correlate, of "dependency theory," a culture of domination being one expression of "underdevelopment" (which is the central concern of dependency theory). The most distinctive and most important features of such a culture include a tendency to imitation, a lack of creative vigor, an inauthenticity in its creations, disintegration and disequilibrium (1995, p. 128). The realization that Peruvian society, and that of the Latin American nations generally, is shaped by a "culture of domination" is, Salazar Bondy claims, a precondition for creating a "culture of liberation," itself a precondition for a genuine political and economic liberation. As a contribution to this realization, Salazar Bondy began work on an ambitious "anthropology of domination" (1995, pp. 281–322) shortly before his death. Though unfinished, this work offers useful conceptual analyses of various relations that typically accompany domination, such as dependence and liberation, as well as suggestions for typologies of domination (master/slave, employer/wage-earner, etc.) and for a phenomenology of domination.

One of the most noteworthy dimensions of Salazar Bondy's thought is his attempt to specify the ways in which Latin American philosophy, which should be viewed as a philosophy produced by domination (1995, p. 179), reflects the culture of domination from which it has emerged. The hallmarks of Latin American philosophy, according to Salazar Bondy, include its imitative character, its universal receptivity as regards foreign theories and doctrines, the absence of any characteristic or definitive tendency, and a failure to produce any original contributions to world thought (2004, pp. 388–9). (Similar criticisms of Latin American philosophy were expressed by the Chilean philosopher Juan Rivano (b. 1926) during his Marxist period in the mid to late 1960s; see Rivano, 1965, pp. 166–7 and pp. 170–2). If Latin American philosophy has assumed these traits or features, Salazar Bondy argues, it is because this philosophy has arisen and evolved within a culture permeated by domination. Significantly, he claims that philosophy itself should contribute to the elimination of domination and that it can in fact do so if Latin American philosophers turn their attention to the social realities of their own countries; such a reorientation will make it possible for their philosophy to become "authentic" and to generate a consciousness that both "cancels prejudice, myths, [and] idols," and "awaken[s] us to our subjection as peoples and our depression as men" (2004, p. 397; cf. Rivano, 1965, pp. 166–7 and pp. 170–2 for a somewhat similar prescription). Thus, Salazar Bondy's pessimism regarding the depth and pervasiveness of domination in Latin American countries, and the Third World as a whole, is to some extent offset by a surprising optimism concerning the potential of philosophy to dispel domination. Whether or not a Latin American philosophy duly attentive to the region's sociocultural realities can help to engender a "culture of liberation" – and can do so without lapsing into an excessive provincialism – is an open question. In any case, Salazar Bondy's interpretation of Latin American philosophy remains the most impressive attempt to date to explain the apparent shortcomings of this tradition from a broadly Marxist perspective.

Alienation

As noted, Salazar Bondy's account of domination centrally involves analyses of related concepts, such as dependence and underdevelopment. Another concept that figures prominently in his account of domination and his thought, generally, is alienation. According to Salazar Bondy, dependency and underdevelopment give rise to a "culture of domination," and this in turn produces an alienation that pervades all aspects of the lives of those affected (1995, pp. 276, 138; cf. 1973, p. 125). Salazar Bondy's conception of alienation is, then, as much national-collective as it is individual in nature, and for this reason it represents at one and the same time a natural extension of Marx's conception of alienation and a significant departure from it. It is a natural or logical extension of Marx's conception to the extent that the ultimate source of alienation for Salazar Bondy lies in the prevailing relations of production and, even more fundamentally, of exchange. Yet it also constitutes a significant departure from Marx, since Salazar Bondy's notion of alienation does not evoke the alienation experienced by individual producers under capitalism, but refers rather to the impact of certain economic relations on a collectivity. Accordingly, it is in some sense a less direct kind of alienation: far from being the result of, say, an individual's experience within capitalist production, it is a collective-existential condition affecting more or less all the inhabitants of an underdeveloped country. Indeed, with its postulation of an undifferentiated, all-encompassing alienation (as in the case of "Peruvian alienation" [1995, pp. 78–80]), Salazar Bondy's account implies that in the underdeveloped nations capitalists are no less alienated than the workers. It is likewise a departure from Marx in that the experience of alienation, on Salazar Bondy's view, is primarily cultural: Peruvians, for example, live inauthentic lives because they think and act in accordance with norms and values that are both dictated by others and unsuited to their historico-cultural and socioeconomic situation (1995, p. 79).

A more conventionally Marxist notion of alienation was defended by the Venezuelan philosopher Ludovico Silva (1937–88), one of Latin America's two most accomplished "Marxologists" (the other being the Argentine scholar José Aricó [1931–91], who was also an authority on Mariátegui and Gramsci). Silva's conception of alienation receives its most comprehensive treatment in *La alienación como sistema: La teoría de la alienación en la obra de Marx* (Alienation as a system: the theory of alienation in Marx's work). A largely exegetical study of Marx's references to alienation, Silva's book has two main aims. First, it purports to establish that alienation, for Marx, originates in a "system" comprising three elements: a highly advanced (i.e., capitalist) division of labor, the institution of private property (in the Marxist sense of ownership of the means of production), and the practice of commodity production (i.e., production aimed at creating exchange value). Silva's success in showing that alienation is, for Marx, a product of the conjunction of these three factors serves to support his claim that alienation is primarily an economic, rather than a philosophical-anthropological, category. Secondly, Silva seeks to demonstrate, by means of an exhaustive review of the whole of Marx's corpus, that the concern with alienation is a constant throughout Marx's writings, and not, as was widely believed in the 1960s and 1970s, a problem that ceased to interest Marx once he abandoned his preeminently philosophical orientation and began to undertake the social-scientific studies that would culminate in *Capital* (Silva, 1983a). Indeed, Silva goes so far as to claim that the Grundrisse "is perhaps Marx's most important text for the theory of alienation" (1983a, p. 10).

The most novel aspect of Silva's interpretation of alienation is undoubtedly his contention that Marx includes "ideological alienation" in his account of this phenomenon. Commentators usually claim that in the 1844 Manuscripts Marx delineates four different types of alienation afflicting workers under capitalism: alienation from the product of one's labor (and from natural objects, and hence nature generally); alienation from the work process; alienation from other people; and alienation from one's essential human nature. Silva identifies, in addition to these four types or relations of alienation, a fifth kind, which he calls "ideological alienation." This addition to the standard typology of alienation in Marx refers to the unconscious identification with interests that not only are not one's own interests, but actually run counter to one's own interests. Silva maintains that this distinctively "ideological" form of alienation arises as the effect of mystifying explanations in political economy, the inversion of values in religion, and the alienation of human needs that occurs when production is designed to meet the demands of the market instead of serving human needs (1984, pp. 208, 231; 1983a, pp. 63–9). The claim that this sort of alienation exists as a separate category in Marx's analyses of alienation is questionable, to be sure. But whether or not Silva is right on this score, his exploration of the problem of alienation in Marx's works compares quite favorably with the most acclaimed studies published by Marxists writing in English.

Marxist humanism

The relationship between Marxism and humanism, or rather the nature of Marxist humanism, aroused considerable debate in Europe and North America in the 1960s and 1970s. Not surprisingly, the issue of humanism has also been addressed by Latin American philosophers, inspired both by debates outside Latin America and by more local developments, such as the publication of Ernesto "Che" Guevara's influential essay on the humanist aims of the Cuban Revolution, "Socialism and Man in Cuba" (2003). For Ludovico Silva (1983b), the distinctively Marxist conception of humanism is linked to Marxists' aim of establishing societies in which human beings are free from alienation and full, or all-round, development becomes a real possibility, if not reality, for everyone. The emphasis on the condition of actual human beings, rather than abstract constructs of the human, provides the justification for calling Marxist humanism a materialist humanism, and is what fundamentally distinguishes this variety of humanism from classical humanism (1983b, pp. 229–30, 223, 191).

One of the noteworthy aspects of Silva's view is his fidelity to Marx's own, scanty comments on humanism in developing a properly Marxist variety of the doctrine. (Juan David García Bacca [1901–92], a Spanish philosopher who spent most of his professional career in Venezuela, adopts a similar approach to the topic of Marxist humanism; see García Bacca, 1985.) As Silva reminds us, Marx distinguishes three varieties of humanism in the 1844 Manuscripts: "theoretical humanism," "practical humanism," and "positive humanism." Yet these different types of humanism actually refer, according to the young Marx, to three phases of a single process of emancipation: theoretical humanism consists in a liberation from theology (with a corresponding shift of attention to human nature); practical humanism refers to the movement to combat the impediments to universal human self-realization and establish the conditions that will make the latter possible; and positive humanism is the name for a society in which human self-realization – the unalienated, full development of all – has actually been achieved. Marx himself called theoretical humanism atheism and practical humanism communism. Silva follows Marx, adding only that the final stage, positive humanism,

175

should be identified with socialism. This is a novel suggestion. Most commentators have assumed, often owing to the influence of Lenin's interpretation of Marx's *Critique of the Gotha Program*, that we should use "socialism" to refer to a first, lower stage of post-capitalist society, and "communism" to refer to the higher, more developed stage. Basing his thesis partly on *The German Ideology*, Silva inverts this schema, arguing that "communism," for Marx, refers to the array of practical activities (tactical decisions, political agitation, policy choices, etc.) that lead to the advent of a society free of alienation and conducive to the full development of all, and that "socialism" is the name for this society, i.e., the name for Marxists' ultimate goal or aspiration. In short, socialism is the theory, and communism is the practice (1983b, pp. 228–9, 198–9).

A very different approach to the question of humanism from a Marxist perspective can be found in the work of the Argentine thinker Aníbal Ponce (1898–1938). In his learned *Humanismo burgués y humanismo proletario* (Bourgeois humanism and proletarian humanism), published some three decades before the relationship between Marxism and humanism was widely debated in Europe and North America, Ponce examines two antithetical conceptions of humanism. The first conception, "bourgeois humanism," is, according to Ponce, an essentially elitist enterprise, as it assumes that culture should be the preserve of a few initiates. Indeed, as Ponce shows, Erasmus, the quintessential (bourgeois) humanist, believed that life's great questions should only be discussed by elites (Ponce, 2001, pp. 38, 69). Moreover, not only is bourgeois humanism indifferent to the fate of ordinary working people; it actually aims to perpetuate their ignorance and meekness, and endorses the use of religion as an instrument for keeping the people in check (Ponce, 2001, pp. 49, 50). Thus, when bourgeois humanism champions the "human," this category remains a completely abstract notion. Coupled with the humanists' ideal of detachment and their static conception of history, this indifference to the plight of actual human beings generates an outlook that furthers the consolidation of acquired social privileges (Ponce, 2001, pp. 84, 78).

In contrast to bourgeois humanism, "proletarian humanism" advances a very different humanist ideal, namely the complete development of individuals' personalities and access to culture for all (Ponce, 2001, pp. 38, 97). What is more, proletarian humanism emphasizes the objective preconditions for the realization of this ideal, for example, the advanced mechanization and automatization of industry (Ponce, 2001, pp. 93, 95). The foundations for establishing this kind of humanism were being laid, Ponce believed, in the Soviet Union.

Ideology

The Latin American Marxist philosopher whose reflections on ideology prove most original and insightful is Ludovico Silva. For Silva, the properly Marxist concept of ideology refers to a "system of ideas and beliefs aimed at affirming the existing order of domination and exploitation" (1983b, p. 203). Ideology necessarily arises, Silva argues, in all societies whose social structure, including its system of production, involves relations of exploitation; its purpose is to establish the necessity and inevitability of this exploitation in the minds of all members of society (1989, p. 19). Hence Silva's claim that "All ideology is justification of [a practice of] exploitation" (Silva, 1989, p. 19). On this view of ideology, the phrase "bourgeois ideology," a formulation used by Lenin, is a

redundancy in the context of capitalist societies, while the term "revolutionary ideology" (likewise of Leninist inspiration) is something of an absurdity (Silva, 1989, p. 13).

One distinctive feature of Silva's account of ideology is his claim that the principal
ideological basis for a commitment to capitalism is located in the preconscious, at least
in the case of the many who do not benefit from this particular socioeconomic
arrangement (Silva, 1984, p. 213). The combination of this thesis with the notion of
"ideological alienation" (discussed above) yields Silva's most original contribution to
the Marxist theorization of ideology, namely his conception of ideological surplus
value. Silva proposes this term for a cluster of phenomena, all of which are in some
sense analogous to the usual practices and meanings associated with "surplus value"
in Marx's economic writings. In these texts, the term "surplus value" refers to the
difference between the value (in monetary terms) produced by the worker during the
working day, on the one hand, and the value of her labor power as represented in
one day's wage, on the other. It is, in other words, the unpaid labor appropriated by
the employer under capitalism.

What, then, does Silva mean by ideological surplus value? Although Silva's various
characterizations of "ideological surplus value" are rather imprecise, the general
concept is clear enough. Roughly, the term refers to a certain psychic investment in
capitalism: the consciousness or psychic energy – a resource of sorts – that is "extracted"
from individuals in the form of an allegiance, or attachment, to capitalism. This
psychic investment in capitalism serves to strengthen the capitalist economic system
insofar as it yields the support needed to ensure the system's continuity and success
(i.e., maximal profit). Moreover, the "extraction" of such a psychological commitment
to capitalism is analogous to the extraction of surplus value at work because in this
process capitalism appropriates something that does not belong to it – namely, a part
of our psyches, in the form of an unconscious psychological allegiance to the capitalist system – and it appropriates it for its own benefit (the consolidation and perpetuation of capitalism). In short, as happens in the process of extracting surplus value in,
say, a factory, with the extraction of ideological surplus value capitalism gets something, ideological capital, for nothing. The upshot, then, is that exploitation under
capitalism also assumes the form of an exploitation of the human psyche, a specifically
ideological form of exploitation. The "ideological surplus value" obtained in the process serves to justify the production of material surplus value, and hence the institution of capitalism (Silva, 1984, pp. 183–255; 1989, p. 164).

Education

Education has been a concern to Latin America's Marxist philosophers since the early
part of the twentieth century. Perhaps the first significant, albeit indirect, treatment of
Marxism and education is to be found in the work of Argentine philosopher José
Ingenieros (1877–1925), a non-Marxist socialist. In *Los tiempos nuevos* (New times),
a book which deals in large part with the Russian Revolution, Ingenieros writes
approvingly of the educational reforms undertaken by the Bolsheviks in the first years
of the Revolution, thereby endorsing what are in fact typically Marxist educational
aspirations, such as a uniform curriculum and preparation for socially useful work
(Ingenieros, 2000, pp. 87–114).

Although Mariátegui wrote little on Soviet educational experiments, he, too, took a great interest in education, as is evident from the fact that he devoted one chapter of the *Seven Essays* to the topic, in addition to his numerous other essays on educational themes. In all of his writing on education, Mariátegui articulates a conventionally Marxist outlook as regards both the approach that he adopts in analyzing the problem of education and the nature of the reforms, or rather educational alternatives, which he advocates. As for the former, Mariátegui insists on a rigorous sociopolitical contextualization of educational institutions. The school is a product of the social order within which it exists – which is one reason that European educational aspirations usually make little sense in Latin America – and accordingly education is fundamentally a social and economic problem. As the state controls (public) education and the state is always the instrument of the ruling class, the operation of educational institutions has always been constrained by the aims and interests of the ruling class; students today are, therefore, educated in bourgeois principles. A true democratization of education will require a thoroughgoing economic and political democratization of society. Among the measures that would promote such a democratization, and lead to a more complete development of all members of society, would be a uniform curriculum and the elimination, in the organization and structure of education, of the division between manual work and intellectual work (Mariátegui, 1996, pp. 65–9; 1994, pp. 364, 368–9; 1971, p. 88).

Ponce, Mariátegui's contemporary, also brought a Marxist perspective to bear on educational questions. Unlike Mariátegui, however, Ponce's interest in educational questions took the form of a comprehensive account of the history of education, broadly construed, from pre-history to the early decades of the twentieth century. In *Educación y lucha de clases* (Education and class struggle), the volume in which he presents this account, Ponce seeks to demonstrate that since the advent of social hierarchies and class divisions education has been "the procedure through which ruling classes prepare the fundamental conditions of their own existence in the mentality and behavior of children" (2001, p. 303). As new classes have successively emerged and gained supremacy, new forms of knowledge – and hence new educational arrangements – have been introduced to serve the ruling classes' interests, as well as to ensure the perpetuation of their rule. This is the reason that education has never been designed to benefit the masses, and likewise the reason that the bourgeoisie has supported a limited education for workers, one that would prepare them for the exigencies of modern industrial production without rendering them intractable to exploitation (Ponce, 2001, p. 284). While Ponce's account adds few original theses to the Marxist interpretation of education, his extraordinary command of the historical record and abundant examples make *Educación y lucha de clases* a persuasive text, and an impressive work of Marxist scholarship.

Writing a few decades after Mariátegui and Ponce, Salazar Bondy likewise analyzed education from a largely, if inexplicitly, Marxist perspective. Salazar Bondy's principal claim is that education in the underdeveloped countries in general, and Latin American countries in particular, is thoroughly bound up with, and fundamentally disfigured by, domination, and that schools consequently end up reproducing and reinforcing a culture of domination. According to Salazar Bondy, this occurs in at least three ways. First, the institutional organization of the school involves relations or structures of domination (e.g., insofar as it preserves the traditional relationship between teacher and student). Secondly, institutionalized education serves as an "instrument of alienation," in that the values, ideas, and attitudes that it transmits do nothing to advance the "mental liberation" so urgently needed by Third World countries; in this respect, education thus constitutes an impediment to liberation from domination. Finally, the educational system directly favors domination because the benefits of formal education are distributed very unevenly (1995, 276–9). The importance of education in perpetuating domination, along with its enormous potential for helping to eradicate this scourge (Freire and Salazar Bondy, 1975), was plainly one of Salazar Bondy's chief intellectual concerns in the last years of his life, so much so that he would eventually become president of a commission on educational reform under General Velasco's military government. Unfortunately, Salazar Bondy's untimely death in 1974 prevented him from further developing his many insights concerning the possibility of a "liberating education."

Aesthetics and cultural criticism

Mariátegui in some sense inaugurated Marxist aesthetic analysis in Latin America, for he wrote innumerable short essays on literature, art, and culture, which include discussions of many of the leading cultural figures and movements of his time (see especially Mariátegui, 1994, pp. 514–727, and 1996, pp. 167–94). Moreover, he devotes the lengthiest section of the *Seven Essays* to an examination of Peruvian literature. In many of these writings he brings an unmistakably Marxist approach to bear on the topics under discussion.

Ludovico Silva likewise made a significant contribution to the development of Marxist aesthetic and cultural analysis in Latin America. In fact, his best-known work is probably *El estilo literario de Marx* (Marx's literary style [1975]), a brief yet stimulating study in which Silva, an accomplished poet as well as a professor of philosophy, analyzes Marx's characteristic metaphors, the dialectical character of his writing, and his polemical style. In addition to this text, Silva also produced a critique of the mass media (1989, pp. 123–222), focusing mainly on television as an instrument for the transmission of ideology, and specifically its role in promoting ideological alienation and a "culture of underdevelopment." Silva's critique of the media includes an examination of children's comics, in which he attempts to demonstrate that ideology actually permeates this ostensibly apolitical genre.

No doubt the most important Latin American contribution to Marxist aesthetics is found in the work of Adolfo Sánchez Vázquez (b. 1915), a Spanish exile who has spent his whole academic career, and nearly his entire adult life, in México. In *Art and Society: Essays in Marxist Aesthetics* (1973), Sánchez Vázquez explores, among other topics, Marx's views on aesthetics, various debates on art within contemporary Marxism, and Marx and Engels' conception of the tragic. The most original and provocative section of the book, however, consists of Sánchez Vázquez's attempt to interpret Marx's incidental observation that "capitalist production is hostile to certain branches of spiritual production, for example, art and poetry" (Marx, 1963, p. 285).

Why exactly does Marx claim that capitalism, as a socioeconomic system, is hostile to art? The answer to this question, according to Sánchez Vázquez, lies in Marx's conception of human nature. Marx holds that art and work are merely different manifestations of human beings' essentially creative nature, which strives to express itself in free activity. The separation, and eventual antithesis, between work and artistic activity only emerges with the advent of capitalism, for work only truly begins to lose its creative character with the consolidation of the capitalist mode of production. Under the latter, the content of work – now performed as wage labor – becomes a matter of indifference to the worker, since her work comes to consist of mechanical operations dictated by someone else. It thus ceases to be free, creative activity. To the extent that work undergoes this transformation it loses all artistic value, and thus becomes completely opposed to art.

The degradation of work under capitalism not only accounts for the origin of the opposition between art and work in capitalist societies; it also explains the hostility of capitalism to art. The reason that capitalism tends to purge work entirely of its artistic component is that this particular socioeconomic arrangement aims exclusively at the production of exchange value, which requires maximal productivity, and this in turn requires uniformization or standardization in production. Capitalism's interest in the products of artistic activity is likewise limited to these products' worth as bearers of exchange value. Accordingly, capitalism strives to eliminate the concrete, qualitatively unique characteristics of artistic works – characteristics which they necessarily bear as material objectifications of a specific spiritual activity – in order to achieve an abstract uniformity in production. Yet to subject works of art to this kind of transformation is to grossly diminish their value qua works of art, which derives from their status as free creations (i.e., unconstrained by market imperatives) that satisfy a need for self-expression. Any socioeconomic arrangement that requires this transformation will, then, be hostile to artistic creation (Sánchez Vázquez, 1973, pp. 157–216).

One of the great merits of Sánchez Vázquez's discussion of the status of art under capitalism is his defense of the claim, implicitly advanced by Marx, that all work can and should contain a creative, if not artistic, component, for this view is important in developing a (normative) socialist philosophy of work. Another merit of his account, and one that is related to this perspective on work, is his defense of Marx's view of humans as essentially creative beings, a view which implies a conception of aesthetics and aesthetic experience that is much broader than most conventional conceptions. Marxists would do well to explore the implications of these views, especially in pursuing new avenues of research in the somewhat neglected field of Marxist aesthetics.

III

As should be evident from the preceding account, Latin American thinkers have made a number of original contributions to Marxist philosophy. Impressive in their own right, the accomplishments of Latin American Marxist thinkers appear even more striking in light of the obstacles, impediments, and misfortunes which these thinkers have had to confront. To begin with, Latin American thinkers have often had to reckon with repressive political conditions that made it difficult, and even dangerous, to openly study or teach Marxist thought in Latin America. In addition to these very serious political constraints, there have also been formidable socioeconomic obstacles. Often working in universities with scarce resources for scholarly research, Latin American philosophers have frequently had to make do without many of the privileges and opportunities that most of their North American and European counterparts take for granted. No less important, perhaps, is the fact that Latin America possesses a relatively modest philosophical tradition: the institutional presence of philosophy has been fairly limited, and the number of professional philosophers relatively small. If the absence of a solid philosophical tradition and extensive community of philosophers were not impediment enough to the development of their thought, Latin America's Marxist thinkers have also had to endure a more or less wholesale neglect of their work and achievements on the part of Marxist thinkers and scholars of Marxism outside Latin America. For example, David McLellan devotes a mere three sentences to Mariátegui in his comprehensive and authoritative *Marxism after Marx* (2007), a book which includes an entire chapter on the Italian Marxist Antonio Gramsci, to whom Mariátegui is often compared. Finally, it is worth underscoring what has probably been the most decisive impediment of all, though the least obvious, to the development of Marxist philosophy in Latin America: the early deaths of many of the leading figures in this tradition. Mariátegui died at age 35; Ponce at 39; Salazar Bondy at 48; and Ludovico Silva at 51.

In any case, as noted at the outset and as should now be clear, one of the great virtues of Latin American Marxist thinkers and philosophers has been their insistence on applying Marxism to relatively local concerns, or to specific historical processes or movements. That is, many of the most important thinkers' writings have been concerned with relatively immediate social and political issues – issues which have been ignored by European and North American Marxists – which they have used Marxist thought to illuminate and analyze. For example, Mariátegui's chief work, the *Seven Interpretive Essays on Peruvian Reality*, exemplifies both such tendencies: the book involves an application of Marxism – "The 7 Essays are merely the application of a Marxist method" (1994, p. 165) – and the method or doctrine is applied, with the aid of impressive empirical documentation, to Peruvian problems and to polemics with other writers who have likewise sought to make sense of Peru. Ponce's major Marxist works, *Educación y lucha de clases* and *Humanismo burgués y humanismo proletario*, make excellent use of Marxist method in bringing it to bear on, and showing the limitations of, education in pre-socialist societies and the classical conception of humanism. Salazar Bondy uses a marxisant approach to elucidate, insightfully and convincingly, the causes of the characteristic shortcomings of Latin American philosophy, and also to shed light on the problems besetting education in the underdeveloped nations.

Yet if this tendency to adopt an "applied" orientation has been one of Latin American Marxist philosophy's great strengths, it is also the source one of the tradition's principal shortcomings, insofar as this attention to concrete developments among many of the tradition's most distinguished thinkers has involved a certain disregard for more narrowly theoretical problems and conceptual questions. (This is not true, however, of the work of Ludovico Silva and Adolfo Sánchez Vázquez.) Indeed, in a brief note written in 1929 and later used as preface to *Ideología y política* (Ideology and politics), Mariátegui underscores that the *Seven Essays* do not aim to offer "a political theorization" ("*una teorización política*") (1994, p. 165). It is not surprising, then, that Mariátegui hardly contributed any new concepts or distinctive analytical categories to Marxist

181

thought, despite his extraordinary intellectual range, impressive erudition, and formid-able gifts as a Marxist polemicist. (To be fair, Mariátegui was essentially a writer and activist, not a philosopher.) Accordingly, thinkers inspired by Mariátegui's works may find it difficult to produce a "Mariáteguian" theoretical analysis in the same way that, say, some writers use Gramsci's concepts to develop "Gramscian" analyses of social and political phenomena. At the same time, Mariátegui has inspired countless philo-sophers, intellectuals, and activists to adopt a different perspective on the problems besetting Latin America, and his political influence has been immense, in large part for this very reason.

If this tendency to focus on local and/or real-world issues explains the relative lack of development of Marxist philosophy among earlier generations of Marxist theorists in Latin America, a problem of a rather different sort explains the lack of development among more recent theorists – and especially among Latin American Marxists who are professional philosophers – over the past, say, twenty-five years. This problem is the scant interest in "analytical Marxism" among Latin American philosophers interested in Marx and Marxism. Latin American Marxists have for the most part thus denied them-selves the benefit of the most impressive body of Marx scholarship to appear in the past several decades. The absence of any engagement with analytical Marxism is not only evident in the work of Ludovico Silva (who died, however, in 1988) and Sánchez Vázquez, but also, and more inexplicably, in the work of contemporary Marxist writers such as the Ecuadoran Bolívar Echevarría, or the Brazilians José Arthur Giannotti, Leandro Konder, and Carlos Nelson Coutinho. In this regard, Salazar Bondy's early death proved to be an especially critical loss for Marxist philosophy, given that he was one of the few Latin American philosophers who both worked within a broadly Marxist theoretical framework and was strongly influenced by analytical philosophy. As Salazar Bondy's thought informed the early development of the philosophy of libera-tion, it is not unreasonable to assume that this movement, inspired primarily by the continental philosophical tradition, would also have been more amenable to influ-ences from analytical philosophy had Salazar Bondy lived to help shape its subsequent evolution.

IV

There is at present relatively little interest in Marxism among Latin American philo-sophers, just as there is currently relatively little interest in Marxism among philosophers in much of the rest of the world. The one exception is in Cuba, which has produced little in the way of original Marxist philosophy, despite the avowedly Marxist orienta-tion of the Cuban Revolution. However, Latin American philosophers' current lack of interest in Marxism will doubtless be short-lived, if only because Marx's thought retains an enduring philosophical interest over and above the political fortunes of Marxist politics. As Latin American philosophers once again begin to take an interest in Marxism, they will no doubt wish to address the theses advanced by the "analytical Marxists," and to respond to those authors who have sought to combine Marxist com-mitments with, say, the essential elements of feminism or environmental thought. But they will also surely seek to develop the legacy left by earlier generations of Latin American

Marxist thinkers, who, as I have tried to show in the preceding pages, can claim some notable contributions to Marxist philosophy. If Latin American philosophers interested in Marxism do indeed incorporate the insights and achievements of these authors and thinkers into their theorizing, and if professional philosophy on the whole continues to grow in Latin America, there is every reason to believe that Latin American philosophers will also make important contributions to Marxist philosophy in the twenty-first century.

Related chapters: 13 Liberation Philosophy; 22 Philosophy, Postcoloniality, and Postmodernity; 25 Contemporary Ethics and Political Philosophy; 30 Cultural Studies.

References

Freire, P., & Salazar Bondy, A. (1975). *¿Qué es la conscientización y cómo funciona?* Lima: Editorial Causachum.

García Bacca, J. D. (1985). *Presente, pasado y porvenir de Marx y del marxismo.* Mexico City: Fondo de Cultura Económica.

Guevara, E. (2003). *Che Guevara reader.* Deutschmann, D. (Ed.). New York: Ocean Press.

Ingenieros, J. (2000). *Los tiempos nuevos.* Buenos Aires: Editorial Losada.

Mariátegui, J. C. (1996). *The heroic and creative meaning of socialism.* (M. Pearlman, Trans.). Amherst, NY: Humanity Books.

Mariátegui, J. C. (1994). *Mariátegui total*, vol. 1. Lima: Empresa Editora Amauta.

Mariátegui, J. C. (1971). *Seven interpretive essays on Peruvian reality.* (M. Urquidi, Trans.). Austin: University of Texas Press (Original work published 1928).

Marx, K. (1963). *Theories of surplus-value*, vol. 1. (E. Burns, Trans.). Moscow: Progress Publishers.

McLellan, D. (2007). *Marxism after Marx.* New York: Palgrave Macmillan.

Ponce, A. (2001). *Humanismo burgués y humanismo proletario. Educación y lucha de clases.* Buenos Aires: Miño y Dávila Editores (Original works published in 1938 and 1937, respectively).

Rivano, J. (1965). *El punto de vista de la miseria.* Santiago: Facultad de Filosofía y Educación, Universidad de Chile.

Salazar Bondy, A. (2004). The meaning and problem of Hispanic American philosophic thought. In J. J. E. Gracia & E. Millán-Zaibert (Eds). *Latin American philosophy for the 21st century* (pp. 381–98). Amherst, NY: Prometheus.

Salazar Bondy, A. (1995). *Dominación y liberación: Escritos 1966–1974.* (H. Orvig & D. Sobrevilla, Eds). Lima: Fondo Editorial de La Facultad de Letras, Universidad Nacional Mayor de San Marcos.

Salazar Bondy, A. (1973). *Entre escila y caribdis.* Lima: Instituto Nacional de Cultura.

Sánchez Vázquez, A. (1973). *Art and society: essays in Marxist aesthetics.* (M. Riofrancos, Trans.). New York: Monthly Review Press.

Silva, L. (1989). *Teoría y práctica de la ideología.* Mexico City: Editorial Nuestro Tiempo.

Silva, L. (1984). *La plusvalía ideológica.* Caracas: Universidad Central de Venezuela, Ediciones de la Biblioteca.

Silva, L. (1983a). *La alienación como sistema: la teoría de la alienación en la obra de Marx.* Caracas: Alfadil Ediciones.

Silva, L. (1983b). *Humanismo clásico y humanismo marxista.* Caracas: Monte Ávila Editores.

Silva, L. (1975). *El estilo literario de Marx.* Mexico City: Siglo XXI Editores.

Further Reading

Aricó, J. (Ed.). (1978). *Mariátegui y los orígenes del marxismo latinoamericano*. Mexico City: Ediciones Pasado y Presente.

Fornet-Betancourt, R. (2001). *Transformación del marxismo: historia del marxismo en América Latina*. Mexico City: Plaza y Valdés Editores and Universidad Autónoma de Nuevo León.

Liss, S. B. (1984). *Marxist thought in Latin America*. Berkeley: University of California Press.

Löwy, M. (1999). *Marxism in Latin America*. Amherst, NY: Humanity Books.

Sánchez Vázquez, A. (1997). La filosofía de la praxis. In F. Quesada (Ed.). *Filosofía política I: Ideas políticas y movimientos sociales. Enciclopedia iberoamericana de filosofía*, vol. 13 (pp. 17–35). Madrid: Trotta.

Sobrevilla, D. (2005). *El marxismo de Mariátegui y su aplicación a los 7 ensayos*. Lima: Universidad de Lima, Fondo de Desarrollo Editorial.

13

Liberation Philosophy

DAVID IGNATIUS GANDOLFO

Introduction

One of the dominant themes in Latin American philosophy over the last century has been the search for identity and, within that, the question of what should constitute Latin American *philosophy*. Latin American poetry, literature, art, and theology were fast constituting an identity recognized and respected as unique and important – could philosophy do the same? (Cf. Ellacuría, 1985.) One of the results of this search for identity – both at the level of Latin American identity and within the discipline of philosophy – is Latin American liberation philosophy.

Broadly speaking, there are three possible answers to the question concerning the identity of Latin American philosophy. First, one might construe Latin American philosophy to be whatever a philosopher in Latin America is doing. This answer is unhelpful since, for example, there is nothing particularly "Latin American" about a philosopher working on Kant at UNAM in a way that is no different than a philosopher in Berlin. Second, one could hold that the only authentic philosophy from the region is reflective thought untainted by exposure to outside (read: European) influences – this would restrict Latin American philosophy to indigenous and pre-Columbian thought. This answer, while popular in another area of the world that also had a long exposure to European colonialism, viz., Africa, has never gained a foothold in Latin American philosophy due to the deep-seated belief in the region that the region's identity is precisely a *mixture* of indigenous and European cultures.

The third possible answer to the question of what constitutes Latin American philosophy has been the one deemed worthy of pursuing. This answer holds that Latin American philosophy consists of using the tools and methods of philosophy to make sense of reality in Latin America.

By the mid-twentieth century, most of Latin America was over a century into formal independence and yet found itself very much dependent upon economic, political, and social forces outside of its control. Philosophers began to reflect critically on what would constitute real independence, real progress. They became more concerned with the material, social, political, and economic conditions of the possibility of real independence and real progress. Latin American intellectuals began to conceive of the status quo, not as an absence of progress but as a presence of oppression, and the solution as a liberation from this oppression. In the region and all around the world grassroots movements for social change flourished as colonized and oppressed people began to demand and work for a different distribution of power. This was the praxis out of which philosophical considerations of liberation emerged.

Philosophical questions concerning liberation involve ontological inquiries about the nature of being human, ethical inquiries about valuation, and sociopolitical questions about what would constitute a more just, humane, and humanizing society. The result of pressing forward on these inquiries has been the original contribution to philosophy known as Latin American liberation philosophy. When the owl of Minerva surveyed the reality of the region, it found poverty, oppression, dependency, neocolonial imperialism, and a population that was increasingly impatient to liberate itself from these conditions. In the efforts of Latin American philosophers to construct their own philosophy, distinct from the philosophy of the colonial and neo-colonial regimes, they employed the tools of the discipline to see what could be said philosophically about this reality.

The standard presentation of the history of Latin American liberation philosophy places its beginnings in Argentina in the early 1970s when, inspired by efforts in theology to thematize liberation, a core group of philosophers began to thematize how philosophy could enlist itself in the struggle to achieve a fuller realization of the humanity of the people of Latin America. This group, which included Enrique Dussel (b. 1934), Juan Carlos Scannone (b. 1931), Arturo Andrés Roig (b. 1922), and Horacio Cerutti Guldberg (b. 1950), coined the name, "liberation philosophy." The 1976 military coup in Argentina scattered most of these thinkers throughout Latin America. Out of this dispersion developed quickly, throughout Latin America, liberation philosophy, a philosophical approach that is one of the most unique contributions of Latin American philosophy to philosophy in general and, as such, has become one of the more widely known aspects of Latin American philosophy. In many ways, Latin American philosophy came into its own as liberation philosophy.

This standard history of Latin American liberation philosophy must be tempered by recalling three additional factors. First, as Ofelia Schutte demonstrates, serious philosophical thinking in Latin America about liberation has a long and rich history, going back at least as far as José Carlos Mariátegui (Peru) and Carlos Vaz Ferreira (Uruguay) in the early part of the twentieth century, and involving a wide range of thinkers throughout the region (Schutte, 1993, pp. 35–73; Roig, 1981, pp. 115–21). Indeed, the presence of a thinker like Bartolomé de las Casas right at the birth of *Latin* America, critiquing the oppression of the Conquest, shows that the project of thematizing liberation from the side of the oppressed has roots going back to the very beginning of the Latin American people, to say nothing of critiques from within indigenous cultures.

Second, at the same time as the Argentine philosophers were appropriating the term, there were other thinkers, such as Ignacio Ellacuría in El Salvador, also writing explicitly on the topic. And third, due to the prolificity and success of one member of the original group, Dussel, the term "liberation philosophy" came to be associated with his particular way of thematizing liberation, with the result that some of the other philosophers working on liberation stopped using the term (cf. Roig, 1984). The result of these three factors is that the field of liberation philosophy is an even bigger part of Latin American philosophy than it initially seems to be.

186

What unites the thinkers in liberation philosophy, despite significant differences among them, is a rejection of idealism and a concern for the material conditions of life; a recognition of the importance of thematizing the historicity of philosophy and the philosopher; an appreciation for the importance of the history, experience, and thought of the marginalized (the poor, the oppressed, women, indigenous populations); a constant awareness of the incredible quantity of unjust misery present at the margins and, yet, at the same time, an appreciation for the hope and agency for liberation found there too; and a recognition of the need for thought to be grounded in practice.

In addition to the Argentine thinkers mentioned above, other major figures in the movement have included: Leopoldo Zea (Mexico, 1912–2004), Augusto Salazar Bondy (Peru, 1925–74), Ignacio Ellacuría (Spain, El Salvador, 1930–89), and Ofelia Schutte (Cuba, United States, b. 1945). Interest in liberation philosophy reached a crescendo in the 1980s, and work in this tradition has continued since then, especially in the thought of Roig, Dussel, Cerutti, and Schutte, and in work inspired by the assassination of Ellacuría. Dussel's work is treated elsewhere in this book; here we shall focus on Roig, Ellacuría, and Schutte. Roig comes from the core group in Argentina; Schutte has been instrumental in showing liberation philosophy as much broader, deeper, and older within Latin America than was once thought. Both Roig and Schutte structure their work in steady dialogue with other Latin American thinkers. Ellacuría represents an important and recent addition to the dialogue.

Arturo Andrés Roig (b. 1922)

Arturo Roig was born in Mendoza, Argentina. He did his doctoral work in philosophy there at the Universidad Nacional de Cuyo and postdoctoral work in Paris at the Sorbonne. He taught for a quarter century at UNCuyo before being forced into exile in 1975 by the military dictatorship. He spent ten years of exile in Ecuador, eventually returning to UNCuyo from which he subsequently retired. Since then, he has played a leading role in various Argentinean think-tanks, edited influential journals, and published important works in philosophy and educational reform.

Roig's initial training, research, and publications were in the field of ancient Greek philosophy, especially Plato. But he became increasingly interested in Latin American philosophy, phenomenology, existentialism, dependency theory, Hegel, and Marx. With these tools, he searched for a way for philosophy to contribute to the needs of the region. It became clear that the independence achieved in the previous century had been in name only. What the current times called for was a second, real independence (cf. Roig, 2003) – his thought became more and more focused on liberation. He was a member of the nucleus of Argentine philosophers who deliberately set out to elaborate a liberation philosophy in the early 1970s – work that provoked the ire of the military and brought about his exile.

Roig's liberation philosophy begins by building upon Hegel's argument for how philosophy began among the Greeks. There, spirit becoming conscious of itself entails a three-fold recognition: spirit's self-recognition, its recognition of itself as valuable, and the recognition that the culture in which it comes to these recognitions is itself valuable for fostering the other recognitions. The "for itself" this recognition entails is, thus, also a "for us."

> The subject that affirms itself as valuable, which according to Hegel constitutes the condition through which philosophy had its beginnings among the Greeks . . . , is thus not a singular but a plural subject, insofar as the categories of "world" and "people" properly refer to a universality that is only possible within a plurality. This is the reason why we can enunciate the anthropological a priori referred to by Hegel as a regard for ourselves as valuable and consequently as a holding the *knowing* of ourselves as valuable even when it may be this or that particular man who puts into play this point of departure. (Roig, 1981, p. 11; Schutte's translation, with minor changes, 1993, p. 128)

The "for us" entails a consciousness that the way of life that constitutes our cultural identity is valuable. Thus, it is important to know one's culture, to know its history, what outside influences there are or have been, where the seat of agency lies, and whether one's culture has been hijacked. This knowledge, then, leads to the recognition of the need to be mindful of nurturing one's culture against such imperialism.

The "for us" is also in contrast to a "for another" that is the hallmark of colonialism. Given that the being of human being presents itself only by way of human actions; given that human actions gather as history; and given further that this gathering happens locally; it follows both that humans are grouped together into different cultures and that individuals find themselves thrown into a cultural-historic space in which they have a range of options. Thus, human existence unfolds within a cultural identity and a philosophy of liberation must also be concerned with the agency of that identity.

Like other contributors to Latin American liberation philosophy, Roig is concerned with the role philosophy is to play in the context in which it finds itself in Latin America. Under conditions of dependency, philosophy must find a new way. Knowledge has a social function; within that context, Latin American philosophers must recognize that a new mission is required of their discipline because their context is different than that of philosophers in Europe or the United States. Philosophy has to be thematized in full consciousness of where it fits and what role it plays in the social system. Philosophers must ask of their discipline, whether it will be "added to those processes that move toward what is historically new or if, in the maturity of times, it will play a mere role of justification" (Roig, 2004, p. 402). That is, will Latin American philosophy be "for us," for the struggles needed to instantiate human justice in Latin America, or not? In short, will it be part of the liberation struggles, or simply serve to justify, after the fact, whatever emerges as the new status quo?

A Latin American philosophy that does not respond to the need for liberation and integration is empty of content (Roig, 2004, p. 407) – a Latin American philosophy that does not take seriously the situation of dependency and atomization that besets the region has nothing of relevance to offer to the region and does not deserve to be described as a "Latin American" philosophy. Roig reacts against a Heideggerian focus on being, and harkens back to a Hegelian/Marxian foundation in the historicity/experience of actual human beings. Yes, philosophy is concerned with being. But humans have no direct access to being itself, only access mediated through the act of being human. Investigating the act of being human entails coming to terms with our historicity and agency as makers and re-makers of our world. The recognition of our historicity provides the tools for "decoding oppressive discourse" and, thus, for undoing essentialist claims about groups, and opens the way to respecting the freedom required by groups to be able to make and re-make their world (Roig, 2004, p. 411).

The task of philosophy, in the context of the region, is to place itself on the side of the oppressed, i.e., to be sensitive to this voice of the other. According to Roig, constructing a liberation philosophy depends upon recognizing the need to highlight the historicity of human beings and the struggles they have engaged to overcome otherness – and this is found, not in academic philosophy, "but in the 'political discourse' of marginal and exploited elements . . ." (Roig, 2004, p. 412). The political discourse of the marginalized as they struggle against their poverty, oppression, and marginalization shows (a) that the people are dehumanized by conditions of marginalization; (b) that they recognize their conditions as dehumanizing, which is why they struggle against them; and (c) that they therefore have an (at least implicit) understanding of what would constitute humanized and humanizing conditions, i.e., what would constitute liberation. Liberation philosophy needs to be grounded in such insights.

The truth of reality is best seen not in the whole but in the marginalized particulars.

> Truth is not found primarily in the totality but in determined forms of particularity with the power, as an alterity outside of totalities, to create and re-create totalities. . . . This consciousness of alterity . . . reveals to us . . . [that] the place of the philosopher [is] at the side of that man who, by his condition of oppression, constitutes the very voice of alterity, and in whose inauthentic existence is found the root of all authenticity. (Roig, 1981, pp. 113–14)

In so far as the philosopher as such is engaged in the pursuit of truth, it is best seen with the consciousness of alterity. There, the details that are lost in the totality can be seen. The knowledge thus gained concerns how individual people are faring. Those who are faring the worst offer the truth of our current reality: oppression. And they offer the hope: the very recognition of their lives as dehumanized points towards the path to humanizing conditions.

From the 1970s to today, Roig's insistence that philosophy needs to place itself in the service of the needs of the people has brought him to a concern for the knowledge gained from the social sciences. In particular, he has found the insights of dependency theory to be useful, and thus far unsurpassed, in their capacity to explain the situation in which Latin America still finds itself (cf. Roig, 2003). Liberation consists in overcoming the conditions of dependency; the role of philosophy is to thematize dependency and liberation, and to explain why it is that a truly Latin American philosophy must, in the context in which Latin America finds itself, take up these tasks.

Ignacio Ellacuría (1930–89)

Ignacio Ellacuría, a naturalized citizen of El Salvador, was Basque, born in that region of Spain in 1930. He joined the Jesuits in 1947 and was quickly sent to El Salvador, where he lived and worked for the next four decades, except for periods when he was pursuing his education (doctorate in philosophy at the Universidad Complutense de Madrid). The key influences in the makeup of his mature philosophical thought were Aristotle, Hegel, Marx and, above all, the Basque philosopher Xavier Zubiri (1898–1983).

Ellacuría was assassinated – along with five other Jesuits with whom he lived and worked at the Universidad Centroamericana (UCA), their housekeeper and her daughter – in 1989 by a death squad from an elite battalion of the Salvadoran army (Gandolfo, 2008, pp. 31–2, n.4). The murders came toward the end of El Salvador's long civil war (1980–92). At the time of his death, Ellacuría was president of the UCA, chair of its philosophy department, and editor of many of its scholarly publications. In his quarter century with the UCA, he had played a principal role in molding it into a university whose full institutional power – that is, through its research, teaching, and publications – was directed toward uncovering and addressing the causes of poverty and oppression in El Salvador (Gandolfo, 2008, pp. 12–21). In addition, he spoke out frequently on these topics as a regular contributor to the country's newspapers, radio and television programs, and in his scholarly publications on philosophy and theology. These actions – viewed as subversive by the state – were the reasons behind his murder.

During his lifetime Ellacuría was known, primarily, as one of the principal contributors to Latin American liberation *theology* (Burke, 2000, pp. 204–5, 215n.5). However, he also spent the last two decades of his life elaborating a liberation *philosophy*. The latter work was left, at the time of his murder, unfinished, partially unpublished, and scattered across many different writings. In the years since his death, a number of scholars (Samour, 2002, has done the most work here) have pieced together his philosophical thought, and it is now possible to show that Ellacuría makes an important contribution to Latin American liberation philosophy. His was a focused working out of what kind of praxis the reality of poverty, oppression, and injustice demands from human beings. Through an analysis of the nature of reality and of being human, he is able to argue that liberation is both an ethical and a metaphysical imperative.

Ellacuría presents a post-Hegelian philosophy of history, coming from Zubiri's work, and refocuses it from the perspective of the marginalized of the "Third World." Within the philosophy of history, he argues that a way to measure progress toward liberation can be derived: the expansion of the praxis of socio-historical individuals throughout society and moving forward in time. When focused from the Global South, this legitimates a praxis that builds the social, political, and economic conditions for such liberation.

Ellacuría's philosophical thought starts from the materialist assumption that matter matters. Reality is material – if not exclusively, then at least in a fundamentally important way. (Ellacuría, as one might expect of a religious person, wants to preserve the possibility of a transcendent realm; here he follows Zubiri.) Prior to the advent of human beings, reality developed in a manner that can be described as automatic: according, first, to the forces of physics and, later, with the advent of life, according to both physical and biological forces. However, this automatic development of reality changes with the introduction into reality of the human force: praxis, free conscious action to change reality. Since the essence of praxis is freedom, once human beings arrive on the scene the further development of reality is no longer automatic but is (at least partially) determined by free conscious activity.

Human beings came into existence through the logic and causation of evolution as the animal with a nascent ability to respond not merely automatically (instinctually) with a pre-programmed spectrum of scripted responses but, rather, to respond after reflecting on the possible outcomes of various possible actions, and after choosing which of the real possibilities present will be actualized and brought into reality. This novel capacity constitutes the new force introduced into reality: praxis. Praxis is circumspective: it eyes up the situation, taking in the part of reality that it can influence and envisioning various possibilities, and then it decides how and toward what end to manipulate reality.

The development of reality, from the physical to the biological to the praxical, represents a progression of higher, more developed forces in that the subsequent forces build upon and go further than the prior ones, opening up new possibilities in reality. Praxis, the most developed force, becomes the primary determinant of the further development of reality because its effects far outpace those of the other forces. Its action cannot contradict physical and biological forces, for these prior forces have not gone out of existence. But mindful of the limits imposed by these prior forces, praxis is responsible for the further development of reality. Thus, human beings have to reflect on and decide the direction in which to take reality. We are the responsible part of reality.

Since the essence of praxis is freedom, and since praxis is the leading and responsible force in the further development of reality, human beings must now decide on the direction in which to take reality. Fortunately, clues as to what constitutes the right direction can be discerned in reality. The progression from the physical to the biological to the praxical evidences a dynamism in reality moving it toward the development of more complicated, far-reaching, and effective forces. The essence of the furthest force, praxis, is freedom, a realization of this dynamism. The project thus facing reality's responsible part – us – in this stage of reality's development is the full realization of freedom.

To remain true to our essence as praxical beings who are thereby the responsible part of reality, and true to the essence of reality, whose inherent dynamism aims toward the realization of freedom, we must act so as to further the development of praxis. Thus, the direction of this process of liberation is the liberation of liberty itself, a process for which the praxical being is responsible. The full realization of reality entails: praxical beings acting to bring about the realization of the reality in which all praxical beings can realize the fullness of their praxical essence. In other words, physical and biological forces brought about human beings; but the nature of human beings is such that we are now responsible for the further and fuller realization of reality, which realization is precisely the liberation of all human beings such that they can realize the fullness of their praxical essence. Thus Ellacuría is able to argue that the metaphysics of reality demands a liberatory praxis from us: liberation, because of the essence of human beings and the nature of reality, is a metaphysical imperative.

But the nature of freedom is that it is not *forced* to follow the direction indicated by its nature and the nature of reality. Free beings are free to choose. In addition to the metaphysical imperative, is there also an ethical imperative to be derived that would argue that free beings *should* choose acting to promote the freedom of *all* free beings? Why, after all, would the metaphysical imperative to liberate liberty not be satisfied in a radically individualistic libertarianism? For Ellacuría, the social nature of being human precludes this possibility. This comes out in his analysis of history.

191

Praxis, in its creative acting to realize possibilities present in the situation, has an effect on reality: its actions to realize certain of reality's possibilities create a new reality with new possibilities. The succession of these actions by praxical beings is human history: praxis accretes as history. In so far as praxis, then, is the most developed force in reality, history is the furthest reach of reality. However, "[h]istory does not float on itself" (Ellacuría, 1999, p. 492). History is a handing over, a delivery, to the next generation of a tradition, ways of being in reality. In this understanding of history as the handing over of tradition, "history is not . . . mere reception. . . . In the historical present, which is the physical, real moment of history, there is the past, but also the future . . ." (Ellacuría, 1999, p. 497). The handing over of the tradition to the next generation takes place within the milieu (physical, cultural, economic, etc.) that preceding generations have constituted. Those who hand over the tradition are in a position to do so due to their essence as free beings. The act of handing over *that which has been forged by free beings* to other *free beings* necessarily means that that which is handed over remains true to itself only by being in some way freely changed. In fact, it is impossible for that which is handed over *not* to change: "It can never be the same. It can try to do so, but in this case the same will appear in a form different than the earlier one, in a form of repetition, repetition of that which was not repetition . . ." (Ellacuría, 1999, pp. 498–9). History, as tradition, is a human artifact. In the act of handing it on to the next generation, it is necessarily changed; and the way for the next generation to remain faithful to the essence of history as a human artifact, i.e., the way to remain faithful to their own essence, is to continue moving history onward. The radical historicity of praxis entails a radical sociality: we exercise the freedom of praxis within a realm of possibilities handed over by previous generations. Within our own generation, the exercise of freedom is further influenced by the spectrum of possibilities present within one's social position. And the actions of this generation hand over to the next a changed realm of possibilities. A praxis that recognizes its fundamental historicity and sociality is a more fully realized praxis.

So, again we are faced with the question, in what direction should we move history? The fundamental task of human intelligence is to size up reality in order to identify the possibilities therein so that it can decide which of the possibilities to realize. In so far as human history is the furthest reach of reality, an understanding of reality demands an understanding of history, i.e., an understanding of the possibilities that constitute the world we live in. Failure to ground our comprehension of reality in history means that the intellect has not fulfilled its task: the task of identifying the possibilities present so that we can decide which to realize. Without the grounding in history, human understanding is stuck in an a-historical ideology. Thus, we can see a need for ideology-critique as a way to recognize the ground of truth in history. The Ellacurían approach insists that intellect must be tethered to history or it is simply spinning ideology that does not have to answer to history. Consider, for example, the various justifications put forth for the Conquest: "civilizing" the "barbarians," "Christianizing" the "heathens." When one immerses oneself in the reality of what actually happened, it becomes evident that the "barbarians" and "heathens" were not being "civilized" or "baptized" but, rather, raped, enslaved, colonized, and murdered. One sees more clearly what really happened when one considers what it looked like to those who were being oppressed. In that harsh light, the ideologies are shown for what they are: stories told by the powerful to legitimate their power (cf. Ellacuría, 1993).

For Ellacuría, the challenge to philosophy is "to come as close as possible, intellectually, to the reality of things" (Ellacuría, 1988, p. 643). This was necessary because Western philosophy "had not found an adequate way to encounter and care for reality" (Ellacuría, 1988, p. 633). This key notion of encountering and caring for reality summarizes a trilogy of ideas Ellacuría uses to explain the way human beings engage reality humanly.

So, how are we to encounter reality? In a dense paragraph in which the key terms are intricately interrelated, Ellacuría describes the three moments of the encounter:

> *realizing the weight of reality [el hacerse cargo de la realidad]*, which assumes being immersed in the reality of things (and not merely being faced with the idea of things or the meaning of things) . . .; *taking up the weight of reality [el cargar con la realidad]*, an expression which points to the fundamentally ethical character of intelligence, which has not been given to man in order to avoid his real commitments, but rather in order to take upon himself that which things really are and that which they really demand; *taking charge of the weight of reality [el encargarse de la realidad]*, an expression which points to the praxical character of intelligence, which only fulfills what it is, including its character of knowing reality and understanding its meaning, when it takes upon itself doing something real. (Ellacuría, 1975, p. 208, emphasis in original; my translation here has been aided by Burke's, 2000, p. 100)

In these three intertwined moments, we find ourselves immersed in the stuff of reality and we look around to see what is going on; we recognize a responsibility to use our intelligence to think creatively about solutions to problems we notice; and based on this, we undertake to do something. Without these three moments, intelligence has not "fulfilled what it is." The problem that praxical beings in Latin America have noticed, and that commands their creativity and action, is that the integrity of praxical beings is not being respected; that such integrity demands that we praxical beings work to create the conditions in which all praxical beings can achieve the fullness of their essence as praxical beings. Liberation is both a metaphysical and an ethical imperative.

Ofelia Schutte (b. 1945)

Ofelia Schutte was born in Cuba and migrated to the United States with her family at the age of 14 (cf. Schutte, 2003). A Nietzsche specialist by training and a leading feminist scholar, she approaches philosophy with a suspicion for grand narratives and absolutes, a concern for the marginalized and the place of gender in philosophizing and in oppression, and a suspicion of all norms that are not open to the possibility of transvaluation. She comes to liberation philosophy primarily through her work on the topic of cultural identity.

Schutte's 1993 work, *Cultural Identity and Social Liberation in Latin American Thought*, is the most comprehensive evaluation of the philosophical treatment of liberation in the region since Cerutti's *Filosofía de la liberación latinoamericana* a decade earlier. Her study is responsible for re-framing liberation philosophy as part of a longer history of Latin American liberatory thought. Cerutti (1998, p. 6) characterizes it as "the best analysis in English of the tradition which spans from Mariátegui to Latin American philosophy and theology of liberation." This book and her more recent work in

193

postcolonial theory have received a good deal of attention in the past decade (e.g., being the focus of a "Scholar's Session" at the 2001 annual meeting of the Society for Phenomenology and Existential Philosophy (SPEP) and of a 2004 issue of *Hypatia*). This kind of recent scholarly attention, in addition to honoring an individual scholar, highlights the continued relevance and importance of liberation philosophy.

Linda Martín Alcoff (1995, p. 178), in characterizing the key aspects of Schutte's liberatory thought, notes that she (a) recognizes "the importance of a critical orientation that rejects all dogmas;" (b) sees "the need for a dynamic approach to theory, without seeking closure or finality;" (c) is attentive "to internal difference as it manifests itself in concrete reality," by which is meant the need to pay attention to the diversity internal to important terms used in liberatory thought, like "the people" or "women," so that they do not take on a monolithic, homogeneous, essentialist character; and (d) repudiates all dualisms. Schutte herself sees her work as an attempt

> to understand the relationship between liberation, cultural identity, and Latin American social reality from the standpoint of a historically rooted critical philosophy. . . . I am concerned with exploring the relationships between cultural identity, sociopolitical theory, and social change. . . . The persistent question, how can one do philosophy from the standpoint of a Latin American interested in liberation from social oppression, has led me to a consideration of three interrelated topics: cultural identity, liberation theory, and feminist thought. (Schutte, 1993, p. 1)

More broadly, she states, "I have engaged philosophy to understand the roots of oppression and to seek clarity about ways in which social justice and personal fulfillment can be enhanced" (Schutte, 2004, p. 183).

Schutte's main concern is the need to insert gender analysis into the search for cultural identity in Latin America. This insertion has the effect of foreclosing easy instantiations of cultural identity that reinscribe the marginalization and oppression against which the search for cultural identity intends to struggle. The search for a Latin American cultural identity is precisely the search for the cultural, economic, and political conditions that allow *all* Latin Americans the freedom to determine for themselves the conditions of their own self-realization. Versions of Latin American cultural identity, then, that fail to consider the freedom for self-realization of *everyone* – e.g., identities centered on machismo or that deny equal standing to women or homosexuals – can be seen to be proof that the search for cultural identity is not complete, has not yet succeeded. The fact that gender cuts across all other social categories (e.g., class, race, and ethnicity) forces the consideration of these other categories to thematize liberation completely and not merely to displace oppression to another "other." The inclusion of gender is not only the inclusion of yet another, albeit important, social location of oppression; by touching all other social categories, it insures that thinking about oppression includes all members of society and does not consider its work done if oppression has only been displaced to a segment of the population deemed to be undeserving, or less deserving, of the project for self-realization. In effect, the inclusion of gender analysis coaxes liberatory thought toward thoroughness.

As part of the insertion of gender analysis, Schutte undertakes an appraisal of the liberatory thought from the region in the twentieth century, an appraisal that

complicates the received notion of liberation philosophy and points out important differences among its practitioners. Her work has a broad interdisciplinary scope: from
philosophy, she deals primarily with Mariátegui, Ramos, Vaz Ferreira, Salazar Bondy,
Zea, Roig, Miró Quesada, Cerutti Guldberg, and Dussel; in addition, she brings in key
figures in liberation theology, as well as the liberation pedagogy of Paulo Freire. This
engagement with the history of *Latin American* thought is something that few other
philosophers of liberation accomplish to the extent that Schutte does. She also brings
a direct engagement with feminist and postcolonial philosophy. Her attention to gender issues brings in the marginalized of the marginalized – women, poor women,
indigenous women – and raises the concern that the categories used to think about
liberation need to be thematized carefully so as not to reinscribe patriarchal domination. In all of these areas – feminist and postcolonial thought, the question of identity
– her thought both broadens and deepens liberation philosophy. In addition, Schutte's
attention to the philosophical history brings into the conversation previous attempts
at critical reflection on liberation and allows her to weave the concern for liberation
back into the question of cultural identity.

Rather than proposing a fully developed theory of liberation, Schutte's work is more
subtly focused on the question of cultural identity and the evolving treatments of this
topic by Latin American thinkers. As such it enables us to see the way in which the concern for identity in Latin American thought gave birth to the thematizing of liberation.
As Schutte characterizes it, the goal of liberation philosophy (and liberation theology),
is "to provide methods of critical analysis and models for practical action whose goals
are to defend the cultural, political, and economic integrity of the people of the region"
(Schutte, 1993, pp. 173–4). And while her focus has been primarily sociopolitical liberation, "my view of liberation reaches also into the personal. My view includes a psychological and existential component to the liberation process" (Schutte, 2004, p. 184).

Schutte is uncomfortable with the grand narratives of other liberation philosophers,
in particular, Enrique Dussel. The critique of Dussel's work (cf. Schutte, 1991; 1993,
pp. 178–81, 186–90, 199–205) forms an important part of the development of her
own liberatory thought. She faults Dussel for absolutizing the poor as the "untainted
source for" and "undisputed authority on" truth and justice; and for the simplistic and
totalizing dualistic understanding of good and evil in which alterity and the Other are
absolutely good while totality is absolutely bad (Schutte, 1993, p. 178). "This is translated politically into the absolute mandate to support the struggle of national liberation movements (alterity) against imperialism (totality)" (Schutte, 1993, p. 179). She
finds this to be an unhelpful approach that surrenders philosophy's primary task of
critical, reflective thought and, by so doing, opens up the possibility of a slide into un-
critical, Peronista populism. By turning alterity into a new absolute, Dussel created,
not the radical version of liberation philosophy which he sought, but rather a metaphysical, idealist, essentialist version that could be misused in the defense of new
oppression. As a check on these unintended consequences of an avowedly liberatory
theory, she holds that "it is important for liberation theory to be explicit about where
it stands on specific social issues" (Schutte, 1993, p. 202). In the intervening years since
she made this critique of Dussel, he has revised his position to avoid these pitfalls.

One of the unique aspects of the Latin American search for cultural identity is that
the search has been carried out from within a celebration of *mestizaje*, the mixing of

195

races and cultures, rather than any attempt to identify a pure race or culture that would count as the true identity. This formal endorsement and legitimation of the mestizo increases the theoretical pressure toward a consciousness of the sociohistorical character of identity. Alcoff (1995, pp. 180–1) notes that when cultural identity is thematized from the perspective of the mestizo, "a shared history must play a greater role than any discrete cultural tradition, set of practices or belief systems." Furthermore, from this perspective, identity is seen not as fixed but as "dynamically evolving." From within *mestizaje*, the way that identity is shaped by sociohistorical forces is more readily seen. It is important to note, however, that Schutte's thematization of *mestizaje* is non-essentialist; *mestizaje* is itself a product of historical thinking and action. In order to avoid the potential for essentialist misunderstandings, Schutte more recently speaks of "hybridization" (cf. Schutte, 1998).

True to her roots in Nietzsche, Schutte is sympathetic to postmodernism and post-structuralism. At the same time, she is aware of the dangers when applying this thought to a region that has not yet fully reaped the benefits of modernism.

> In the West, the postmodern deconstruction of the subject and of the discourse and logic of identity has often functioned as a critical tool against dominant normative discourses. In particular, postmodernism has helped to open up new conceptual spaces for the introduction of gender and racially diversified perspectives on cultural values in technologically advanced societies. But societies on the way to development cannot dispense so easily with concepts such as those of the subject, consciousness, or identity, for these are needed in order to establish and protect elementary legal and human rights, which cannot always be taken for granted . . . (Schutte, 1993, p. 5)

More recently, she combines an awareness that there are some radical and liberating aspects of modern thought worth preserving, with a critique of a Eurocentrism that would see these ideas as uniquely European (cf. Schutte, 1998). Ultimately, Schutte is working to achieve a delicate balance between, on the one hand, postmodernism's critique of totalizing narratives while, on the other, recognizing that modernism still has important things to offer to Latin America. It is her concern for social justice which oversees this balancing.

Conclusion

The concern for identity in Latin American thought opens up vistas that are not readily available in mainstream Western thought. The latter does not find it necessary to thematize the meaning of "Westernness" or "Europeanness." It *does*, of course, ask the question of the meaning of humanness. But the implicit assumption is that the answer to this question would be no different than an answer to the question about European identity. Latin Americans, however, ask both the question of the meaning of being human and the question of the meaning/identity of *latinidad*. This double consciousness, uncovered by Hegel and formulated from the perspective of the marginalized by DuBois, Fanon, and others, enriches Latin American thought. In the awareness that the meanings of *humanidad* and *latinidad* are not coterminous comes the recognition both that *humanidad* can be validly instantiated in a plurality of ways, and that some people are prevented from exercising the full dignity of their humanity because of oppression of the group with which they identify and are identified. Along with this comes the recognition of the sociohistorical determinations of group identity (the fact that what it means to be "Latin American" has been determined by the social and historical formations that produced the current distribution of power). The radical, atomistic individualism that wants to be the hallmark of Western culture; the disjointed, timeless emphasis on the new, the now, the moment – these are foreign to a consciousness that knows its identity has been shaped by social and historical forces. And the recognition that these forces have built structures that lock people, because of their group identity, into oppression begins the formation of a consciousness concerned with liberation, a task that is inherently more than theory because it grows out of the awareness of sociohistorical, concrete structures of oppression that must be concretely dismantled in social space and historical time – thus a task that inherently involves praxis. Latin American liberation philosophy has taken up this task, and in so doing has forged a unique contribution to philosophy.

Related chapters: 10 Ortega y Gasset's Heritage in Latin America; 11 Phenomenology; 18 Identity and Philosophy; 21 Liberation in Theology, Philosophy, and Pedagogy; 22 Philosophy, Postcoloniality, and Postmodernity; 23 Globalization and Latin American Thought; 24 Latin American Philosophy; 28 Feminist Philosophy.

References

Alcoff, L. M. (1995). Review of Ofelia Schutte, *Cultural identity and social liberation in Latin American thought*. *Hypatia* 10:2, 176–83.

Burke, K. (2000). *The ground beneath the cross: the theology of Ignacio Ellacuría*. Washington, DC: Georgetown University Press.

Cerutti Guldberg, H. (1998). "Liberation philosophy." In E. Craig (Ed.). *Routledge encyclopedia of philosophy*. London: Routledge. Retrieved May 3, 2008, from http://www.rep.routledge.com/article/ZA011.

Ellacuría, I. (1975). Hacia una fundamentación del método teológico latinoamericana. Republished in *Escritos teológicos* (4 vols., 2000–2). San Salvador: UCA Editores, vol. 1, pp. 93–122.

Ellacuría, I. (1985). Función liberadora de la filosofía. Republished in *Escritos políticos: veinte años de historia en El Salvador* (3 vols., 2nd edn, 1993). San Salvador: UCA Editores, vol. 1, pp. 93–122.

Ellacuría, I. (1988). La superación del reduccionismo idealista en Zubiri. Republished in *Escritos filosóficos* (3 vols., 1996–2001). San Salvador: UCA Editores, vol. 3, pp. 403–30.

Ellacuría, I. (1993). Uncovering a civilization of capital, discovering a civilization of work. In D. Batston (Ed.). *New visions for the Americas* (pp. 72–82). Minneapolis: Fortress Press.

Ellacuría, I. (1999). *Filosofía de la realidad histórica*. San Salvador: UCA Editores (Written in the 1970s and first published, posthumously, in 1990).

Gandolfo, D. I. (2008). A role for the privileged? Solidarity and the university in the work of Ignacio Ellacuría and Paulo Freire. *Journal for Peace and Justice Studies*, 17:1, 9–33.

Roig, A. A. (1981). *Teoría y crítica del pensamiento latinoamericano*. México: Fondo de Cultura Económica.

Roig, A. A. (1984). Cuatro tomas de posición a esta altura de los tiempos. *Nuestra América*, 11, 55–9.

Roig, A. A. (2003). Necesidad de una segunda independencia. *Cuadernos Americanos. Segunda Época*, 100:4, 11–41.

Roig, A. A. (2004). The actual function of philosophy in Latin America. In J. J. E. Gracia & E. Millán-Zaibert (Eds). *Latin American philosophy for the 21st century* (pp. 401–14). New York: Prometheus (Original work published 1975).

Samour, H. (2002). *Voluntad de liberación: el pensamiento filosófico de Ignacio Ellacuría*. San Salvador: UCA Editores.

Schutte, O. (1991). Origins and tendencies of the philosophy of liberation in Latin American thought: a critique of Dussel's ethics. *The Philosophical Forum*, 22, 270–95.

Schutte, O. (1993). *Cultural identity and social liberation in Latin American thought*. Albany: SUNY.

Schutte, O. (1998). Cultural alterity: Cross-cultural communication and feminist theory in North–South contexts. *Hypatia*, 13:2, 53–72.

Schutte, O. (2003). Philosophy and life: a singular case of their interconnection. In L. M. Alcoff (Ed.). *Singing in the fire: stories of women in philosophy* (pp. 119–34). Lanham, MD: Rowman & Littlefield.

Schutte, O. (2004). Response to Alcoff, Ferguson and Bergoffen. *Hypatia*, 19:3, 182–202.

Further Reading

Alcoff, L. M. (2004). Schutte's Nietzschean postcolonial politics. *Hypatia*, 19:3, 144–56.

Burke, K., & Lassalle-Klein, R. (Eds). (2006). *Love that produces hope: the thought of Ignacio Ellacuría*. Collegeville, MN: Liturgical Press.

Cerutti Guldberg, H. (1983). *Filosofia de la liberación latinoamericana*. Mexico City: Fondo de Cultura Económica.

Ellacuría, I. (1975). Diez años después: ¿Es posible una universidad distinta? Republished in *Escritos universitarios* (1999, pp. 49–92). San Salvador: UCA Editores.

Hassett, J., & Lacey, H. (Eds). (1991). *Towards a society that serves its people: the intellectual contribution of El Salvador's murdered Jesuits*. Washington, DC: Georgetown University Press.

Schutte, O. (1984). *Beyond nihilism: Nietzsche without masks*. Chicago: University of Chicago Press.

Whitfield, T. (1995). *Paying the price: Ignacio Ellacuría and the murdered Jesuits of El Salvador*. Philadelphia: Temple University Press.

14

Analytic Philosophy

DIANA I. PÉREZ AND GUSTAVO ORTIZ-MILLÁN

Introduction

During the twentieth century, most of the traditions that dominated the Latin American philosophical scenario were imported from Germany, France, and Spain: positivism, Krausism, phenomenology, existentialism, neo-Thomism, Marxism, vitalism, and many others. From the 1940s and 1950s on, several groups of young Latin American philosophers in Argentina, Brazil, Mexico, and Peru turned their attention to the development of mathematical logic in Europe, and they saw it as a powerful instrument that would allow them to do more rigorous analysis of a number of philosophical problems. It is interesting to notice that many of them were not professional philosophers, but lawyers interested in the analysis of legal norms and in the philosophy of law in general, or scientists interested in the foundations of knowledge. Little by little, lawyers, scientists, and philosophers alike came under the influence of analytic philosophy: they saw this new philosophy as a tool for opposing some of the theories that were in vogue at that time, improving the arguments proposed to defend their ideas, and the conceptual precision used to present their positions.

In the last few decades of the twentieth century, an increasing number of Latin American philosophers were trained in analytic philosophy. Even though the work of many of these philosophers has been just the beginning of a new tradition by importing the discussions that take place in the Anglo-American context, some have developed new theories or have adapted analytic philosophy to advance original views. Even though several Latin American philosophers have been taught in non-analytic departments, with professors from other traditions, the interest in this kind of philosophy is growing in Latin America. In a broad sense, all those who read, discuss, or produce philosophy according to the analytic tradition can be labeled "analytic philosophers," even if this tradition is not the only one to which they belong.

In this chapter, we will recount a brief history of the origins and development of Latin American analytic philosophy in the broadest sense (so broad that we are not sure that every philosopher we mention will be pleased with this label). In our presentation we will proceed geographically, even though there are strong links between philosophical communities in Latin America, and in many cases the development of analytic philosophy in certain countries cannot be explained without the general context of Latin

American analytic philosophy. We will devote more space to those countries where analytic philosophy has an older history and has been more developed: Argentina and Mexico. We will then analyze the cases of other countries where analytic philosophy is increasing its presence.

Here we will offer a historical introduction to this kind of philosophy and the work of some major figures. Our overview has two constraints: one is geographical, the other temporal. Given the former, only the work of those philosophers who have done philosophy in Latin America is considered. There are many Latin American philosophers who emigrated for political, social, economical, or personal reasons. Given the latter, some who have left very recently are excluded. Furthermore, since our focus is on the work of early analytic philosophers, the chapter does not consider analytic philosophy produced in Latin America in the past 15 years.

Argentina

The history of analytic philosophy in Argentina can be divided into four periods: 1940–56, 1956–66, 1966–83, 1983–today. These periods correspond roughly to some political facts that had enormous impact on academic philosophical life.

In the first period, from the 1940s through 1956, groups of people started reading analytic literature, and the first translations into Spanish of Moore's and Russell's works were made. People engaged in these first reading groups were not professors from philosophy departments within the universities (as we might expect), but people with a scientific background, interested in the foundations of science (mainly physicists and mathematicians), or lawyers (professors and students from law schools, interested in the foundations of law). Among others we can mention: Grupo Argentino de la Academia Internacional de Historia y Filosofía de la Ciencia, Instituto Libre de Estudios Superiores, and Círculo Filosófico de Buenos Aires. In some of these groups, Gregorio Klimovsky, Rolando García, and Mario Bunge, among many others, introduced discussions of the foundations of logic, mathematics, and physics.

In the second period, from 1956 to 1966, analytic philosophy entered the universities. Some of these physicists, mathematicians, and lawyers started teaching, mainly epistemology and logic at the Universidad de Buenos Aires (UBA) (Klimovsky and Bunge) and at the Universidad de Córdoba (Andrés Raggio and Ernesto Garzón Valdéz). The first foundational books were written: Mario Bunge's *Causalidad* (1961) and Thomas M. Simpson's *Formas lógicas, realidad y significado* (1964).

Gregorio Klimovsky is undoubtedly the main figure in the introduction of the classical issues in philosophy of science (both formal and natural) into the country. Even though he is self-taught, he had a strong background in mathematics, and he introduced this "new logic" to Argentina, as well as discussions of the foundations of mathematics (Russell's logicism) and set theory. He also introduced the authors of the Vienna Circle – such as Carnap and Hempel – and also Popper and the first Wittgenstein. He trained many generations of philosophers of science in the country: he never left it even in its darkest ages. He also had influence beyond philosophical circles because he worked on epistemological problems of psychoanalysis (there is a huge community of psychoanalysts in Buenos Aires), and he used to participate in public debates on mass media, moral issues, and the Jewish question. Mario Bunge, on the other hand, probably the best-known Argentine philosopher of science abroad, taught at the University of Buenos Aires for a brief period, and then emigrated to North America, where he worked all his life. His influence in Argentina did not last. Something similar occurred with Rolando García.

Thomas M. Simpson is the most important philosopher of language in Argentina. He published *Formas lógicas, realidad y significado* in 1964, a pleasing but deep book where he discusses the main semantic issues at the time. He presented Plato's problem about nonexistence, the different solutions to this problem (Russell's theory of descriptions, Strawson's theory of presuppositions, Frege's distinction between sense and reference, Quine's theses about ontological commitment), and examined at length the consequences of these different theories, in particular to principles of logic (especially the principle of non-contradiction), the paradox of analysis, and belief contexts. Later, in 1973, Simpson published *Semántica filosófica: problemas y discusiones*, an anthology containing the most important papers in the field at that time, rigorously translated and commentated, a collection with no parallel even in English.

Finally, in the Law Department at UBA, Carlos Cossio and after him Ambrosio Gioja, although neither an analytic philosopher, introduced the study of formal logic and Anglo-Saxon philosophical literature on the foundations of law, as part of the texts discussed in a reading group in which the first generation of Argentine analytic philosophers of law participated: Genaro Carrió, Carlos Alchourrón, Eugenio Bulygin, Ernesto Garzón Valdés, Eduardo Rabossi, and Roberto Vernengo. Later, a second generation emerged with philosophers such as Martín Farrell and Carlos Nino. The main contribution of this group is, without any doubt, *Normative Systems*, the book published by Alchourrón and Bulygin in 1971. In this book, they propose a logic for legal systems, and discuss other issues such as legal "gaps," normative completeness, the truth values of norms, and the revision of norms. (See Pablo Navarro's chapter in this volume.)

Carlos Alchourrón was the most outstanding figure in Argentinean analytic philosophy, and the one with the most significant impact on the international community. Besides his contributions to the logic of norms developed in collaboration with Bulygin, he began a collaboration with David Makinson on the logical structure of changes in legal codes, and a bit later he expanded the research to the logic of contraction and revision of theories, including Peter Gärdenfors as a coauthor. The three of them developed what is known as the "AGM paradigm" of belief revision, publishing an influential series of papers in the 1980s. His contributions had enormous weight even beyond the philosophical community, mainly with computer scientists. (See Horacio Arló-Costa and Eduardo Fermé's chapter in this volume.)

The third period, from 1966 to 1983, was a complicated and dark time in the history of Argentina. Owing to a military regime, democratic professors, including all analytic philosophers, were expelled from the university in 1966. Many of them (such as Raggio, Coffa, Bulygin, Alchourrón, Carrió, Simpson, and Rabossi) left the country for voluntary or involuntary exile in the United States or the UK, where they continued their philosophical studies, some of them for two or three years while others never returned. In this period, they promoted analytic philosophy in other Latin American countries, such as Mexico (the exchange with the Instituto de Investigaciones Filosóficas was very fluid at that time, including Raul Orayen's moving to Mexico in the early '80s), and Brazil, where they participated in the creation, in 1975, of the Centro de Lógica, Epistemologia e História da Ciência (in the Universidade Estadual de Campinas, UNICAMP) and its journal *Manuscrito* (1977). (See Alberto Cordero's chapter in this volume.)

Those who stayed in (or returned to) Argentina organized, once again, reading groups outside the academy. As a result of these activities, the most important philosophical institutions of Argentina were founded, among others, the Sociedad Argentina de Análisis Filosófico (SADAF) in 1972, the only group in which analytic philosophy was developed during this period. Among its founding members were Alchourrón, Bulygin, Carrió, Coffa, Klimovsky, Nino, Orayen, Rabossi, Simpson, and García. In 1981, the journal *Análisis Filosófico* (edited by SADAF) was founded, and is still today the most important analytic journal in Argentina.

Eduardo Rabossi was one of the leading figures during this period, organizing and leading SADAF (in the first years in close collaboration with Orayen), and generating activities to replace the lack of philosophical research in the official circles at the time. Besides his strong commitment to philosophy's institutional life, Rabossi made significant contributions in almost all philosophical fields. Strawson and the philosophy of ordinary language had a strong influence on his philosophy. His first philosophical contributions were in ethics and philosophy of language, but later on he became interested in metaphysics and philosophy of mind. In 1971 he wrote *Análisis filosófico, lenguaje y metafísica* (published in Venezuela in 1975). Its main objective was to eliminate some misunderstandings about analytic philosophy, highlighting the main contributions made to metaphysics, epistemology, philosophy of language, and ethics within this tradition. He examines in detail Moore's and Russell's anti-idealist arguments, the nature of Russell's Platonist commitment, the differences and similarities between Wittgenstein's and Russell's logical atomism, and Moore's ideas about the naturalistic fallacy, among other issues.

In the 1980s he wrote important papers on the foundations of human rights, an issue that was central to both his philosophical and his political life, because he was (just like Klimovsky) a member of the CONADEP, a committee created after the return of democracy, to investigate the violations of human rights during the military regime; Rabossi even became the first undersecretary of human rights during Raúl Alfonsin's government. He defended a non-foundationalist theory of human rights. He was also interested in ways of teaching philosophy (see María Cristina González and Nora Stigol's chapter in this volume) and metaphilosophy. His posthumous book is the best example of this last interest: *En el comienzo Dios creó el canon* (2008), where he develops and argues for three astonishing hypotheses: (1) philosophy, in the way we understand and practice it today, is a young discipline that was born two hundred years ago in Germany during the idealist period, (2) the long life attributed to philosophy is the result of an elaborated historical discourse also created two hundred years ago, and (3) philosophy is anomalous, different to any other discipline, for reasons he presents in detail in the book. He also examines the relationships between philosophy and politics, between central and peripheral philosophy, and between philosophy and its history.

Another important philosopher with great influence abroad was Carlos Nino. He worked in political philosophy and published *Ética y derechos humanos* (1984). (See Eduardo Rivera-López's chapter in this volume for his philosophical contributions.)

The fourth period is the democratic period, from 1983 until the present. It is a time of consolidation, in which analytic philosophy is transformed into a tradition in the country. We find today in Argentina different "generations" of philosophers: there are many analytic philosophers who were trained by the philosophers mentioned above without leaving the country to get their Ph.D.s.

In 1983 analytic philosophers returned to the universities: to give just one example, no analytic philosopher was part of the staff of UBA's Philosophy Department before 1983, and today more than a third of its members are analytic (Gladys Palau teaches logic; Alberto Moretti, logic and philosophy of language; Cristina Gonzalez and Rodolfo Gaeta, philosophy of science; Diana Maffia, epistemology; Samuel Cabanchik, contemporary philosophy; and many others teach courses such as metaphysics, philosophy of history, bioethics, and philosophy of law).

Analytic philosophy has been consolidated during the past twenty-five years, in many different places, not only at UBA. In Córdoba, a group of people including Horacio Faas, Víctor Rodríguez, Carolina Scotto, and Marisa Velasco, among others, have organized every year since 1989 the Jornadas de Epistemología e Historia de la Ciencia, giving a significant impulse to the analytic studies of philosophy of science and logic. There is also an important group of practical philosophers in Córdoba, with people such as Ricardo Caracciolo, Pablo Navarro, and Cristina Redondo, among others. And in other universities across the country there are also more people working within the analytic tradition.

Finally, there are also many philosophers who, at different moments in the history of Argentina, and for different reasons, decided to work in other countries. Among them we should mention Alberto Coffa, Raúl Orayen, Ricardo Gómez, Graciela De Pierris, Ignacio Angelelli, and Horacio Arló-Costa.

Mexico

The history of analytic philosophy in Mexico starts in the 1960s, but we can trace its origins to two philosophers who, although not analytic philosophers themselves, had great influence in the development of this kind of philosophy in the country: Eduardo García Máynez and José Gaos. García Máynez was a lawyer and a philosopher of law who wrote several books on ethics and on legal philosophy. Some of his most important books, such as *Filosofía del derecho* and *Introducción al estudio del derecho*, can be properly called analytic in style, although his main influences came from the German tradition, which was very strong in Mexico in the first half of the twentieth century. He analyzed legal concepts and assessed arguments in a very detailed way, always paying attention to the use of language and to logic; he was a pioneer of deontic logic and was very critical of von Wright's work. Even though he never considered himself an analytic philosopher, when he founded the Centro de Estudios Filosóficos at the Universidad Nacional Autónoma de México (UNAM) in 1940, he invited several analytic philosophers to Mexico. In 1967, the Centro was converted into the Instituto de Investigaciones Filosóficas (IIF), which has been one of the main places in Latin America where analytic philosophy is cultivated.

The other big influence, José Gaos, was a Spanish émigré who went into exile in Mexico after the Spanish Civil War. He had been a student of Ortega y Gasset. Gaos arrived in

203

Mexico in 1938, along with many other Spanish philosophers, and just like most of them, he started teaching at UNAM, in Mexico City. He developed an intense career as an author of a number of original philosophical texts, and as a translator of some of the most important German philosophers, but probably one of his most enduring legacies was his students. A whole generation of Mexican philosophers was trained by Gaos. Some of his students were crucial in the development of analytic philosophy in Mexico, most notably Fernando Salmerón, Alejandro Rossi, and Luis Villoro, who actually reacted against his way of doing philosophy. All of them became members of the IIF, at UNAM, and were decisive in the development of analytic philosophy in Mexico.

Fernando Salmerón had been trained in the neo-Kantian tradition with Gaos, but over the years he got closer to the problems and style of analytic philosophy. In 1966 he became director of the IIF, where he promoted the idea that young philosophers should go to Oxford and to American universities to do their graduate studies. He also invited many analytic Argentine philosophers, such as Rabossi, Alchourrón, and Simpson, to teach brief courses on topics of epistemology, ethics, and the philosophy of language. His main contribution to Mexican analytical philosophy was in the area of ethics, where he published the book *La filosofía y las actitudes morales* (1971). In this book he distinguished between philosophy and conceptions of the world, and he sees these conceptions as expressions of moral attitudes. Salmerón analyzed the concept of attitude as a way of relating philosophy with different conceptions of the world; these two are compatible in practice, he said. Later on he published a collection of his essays in *The Origins of Analytic Moral Philosophy and Other Essays* (1998).

Alejandro Rossi went to Germany to study under Heidegger, but ended up studying in Oxford with Ryle. When he returned to Mexico, he started teaching courses on logic, philosophy of language, and epistemology. He introduced to the Mexican philosophical panorama authors such as Frege, Russell, Strawson, Ayer, and Austin. Rossi was a key figure in training a whole generation of Mexican analytic philosophers. In 1969, he published *Lenguaje y significado*, a collection of his articles on the philosophy of language; particularly influential were those devoted to Russell's theory of descriptions, and to proper names. Many philosophers followed his lead and focused on semantics, working on topics such as proper names, predication, theories of description, and meaning. Olbeth Hansberg, Alejandro Herrera, Hugo Margáin, Raúl Quesada, José Antonio Robles, Margarita Valdés, and Enrique Villanueva were among Rossi's students working in this area. Later on, Rossi decided to explore his analytic interests in more literary essays, which resulted in a celebrated collection of essays called *Manual del distraído* (1978).

Luis Villoro, who by the 1960s had already published a number of books on Descartes, Husserl, and Mexican history, started turning his attention toward analytic epistemology. In 1982, he published the book *Creer, saber, conocer* (translated into English as *Belief, Personal, and Propositional Knowledge*). In this book the transition from a phenomenological to an analytic style of doing philosophy is clear. Villoro analyzes some key epistemic concepts, such as knowledge, belief, and certainty. He examines their relations with justification and truth, on the one hand, and desires, motives, and interests that may distort them, on the other. He conceives knowledge as intrinsically linked to practices: the conditions of the rationality of beliefs are conditions for the realization of a rational and free life. Villoro saw his epistemological work as a way of getting into his interests in political philosophy, specially "the relationship between thinking and forms of domination." Later on he published *El poder y el valor* (1997), where he focused on the concept of domination. He asks: "How is it that human reason, throughout history, operates to reiterate situations of domination, or on the contrary, to liberate us from our subjections?" He then examines different ways in which humanity has tried to realize the ideals of a free, just, and rational society. Villoro also led a group of philosophers who were important in the development of analytic philosophy, such as Wonfilio Trejo and Hugo Padilla, among others.

As members of the IIF, in 1967, Salmerón, Rossi, and Villoro founded *Crítica*, a journal devoted to topics in contemporary analytical philosophy. From its very beginnings, this journal tried to be a meeting point for Mexican, other Latin American, and Anglo-American philosophers in the analytic tradition. Some of the most important analytic philosophers at that time (such as Strawson, Ryle, Quine, Anscombe, Von Wright, and Putnam) contributed articles that were published in their original language. Articles are mainly published in English or in Spanish.

The three Mexican philosophers just mentioned did more for the development of analytic philosophy in Mexico than anybody else. They not only tutored many students in this tradition, but they also helped to create philosophy departments sympathetic to this kind of philosophy. Salmerón was the president of the Universidad Veracruzana, where he supported the development of analytic philosophy, and along with Villoro and Roberto Caso, he also helped to create the Philosophy Department at the Universidad Autónoma Metropolitana in Mexico City in the 1970s, where a significant number of philosophers work in this tradition. Nowadays there are other places where many philosophers are cultivating analytic philosophy, such as the universities in Mérida, Zacatecas, Guanajuato, and Durango, among others. But the IIF has certainly been the center around which most of analytic philosophy in Mexico still revolves.

Later on, other philosophers joined these three founders of analytic philosophy in Mexico. Some were South American philosophers who immigrated in the 1970s for political and other reasons: Mario Bunge, César Lorenzano, Mario Otero, and Ulises Moulines were among the most important. But it was the Argentine philosopher Raúl Orayen who played a more influential role in the development of logic and the philosophy of logic, as well as philosophy of language and ontology in Mexico. His most important work in this area is *Lógica, significado y ontología* (1989), where Orayen analyzes some of the most basic logical notions and, on this basis, defends a conception of logic in which the deductive aspect is given primacy. He focuses on the notion of logical form and analyzes its relations with concepts such as logical truth and valid reasoning. He also analyzes some of the connections of logic with intensional concepts, making an interesting criticism of Quine's attack on these concepts. According to Orayen, there is a tension between this criticism and other parts of Quine's philosophy, in particular his naturalized epistemology. In part due to the influence of Orayen, in recent times there has been an increasing development of the area of logic, where a large number of people work at present.

Someone else who immigrated to Mexico in the 1970s was the Uruguayan philosopher Carlos Pereda, an influential figure in the theory of argumentation. His book *Vértigos argumentales* (1994) warns us about certain theoretical attitudes that may distort good argumentation, such as what he calls the temptations of certainty or of ignorance, of power or impotence, among others. In this book, Pereda also makes a distinction between forms of foundationalism and anti-foundationalism in epistemology, proposing a third option, which he calls "multi-foundationalism." Pereda has also published a number of books on topics of rationality, epistemology, and aesthetics, such as *Razón e incertidumbre* (1994) and *Sueños de vagabundos* (1998).

An important part of analytic philosophy in Mexico has been the study of Wittgenstein's philosophy, where many of the translations into Spanish of this philosopher have been published. Alejandro Tomasini is probably one of the most relevant representatives in this area. He argues that the problems of philosophy are essentially linked to language and that, in the end, they result from misunderstandings about the logic, grammar, and application of signs (of natural or formal languages). For true analytic philosophers, he claims, philosophical problems are pseudo-problems. He develops this kind of Wittgensteinian approach in many books, among others: *Lenguaje y antimetafísica: cavilaciones wittgensteinianas* (2005), *Teoría del conocimiento clásica y epistemología wittgensteiniana* (2001), and *Filosofía analítica: un panorama* (2004), which is one of the few books written in Spanish devoted to the study of analytic philosophy.

Epistemology and the philosophy of science were also two of the areas that saw important development in Mexico after the 1970s (see Alberto Cordero's chapter in this volume). There has also been development of analytic approaches to the philosophy of mind (with a recent expansion in cognitive science and a much more interdisciplinary study of the mind). Ethics has also seen interesting development, but owing to limitations of space, we ask the reader to see Eduardo Rivera-López's chapter in this volume.

The Southern Cone

Brazil is the third place where analytic philosophy has been extensively developed, but this development was slow. It was the first country where manifestations of this kind of philosophy appeared, but it was not until the late 1970s that consistent work on this tradition started. Development was difficult because in Brazil there is a long tradition in the history of philosophy as well as in ethics and political research (dominated in some periods by the Marxist tradition). In the 1940s, the first works in logic appeared: *Elementos de lógica matemática*, by Vicente Ferreira da Silva, and Quine's *O sentido da nova lógica* (who visited the Universidade de São Paulo (USP)) at that time, and in the 1950s the first book on philosophy of science: *Lógica e filosofia das ciências*, by the French philosopher Gilles Granger. But the incipient development of these issues was stopped by a military coup d'état in 1964, which expelled many people from the universities. It was not until the 1970s that some open-minded philosophers again took up the analytic tradition. João Paulo Monteiro, who specialized in Hume and was interested in philosophy of science, and Oswaldo Porchat Pereira, who specialized in Aristotle, both from the USP, invited foreign philosophers who specialized in logic, philosophy of science, and philosophy of language to teach in Brazil. In 1975 Porchat Pereira was designated the chair of the recently created Centro de Lógica, Epistemologia e História da Ciência (CLE) (at the Universidade Estadual de Campinas (UNICAMP)). In 1977 the journal *Manuscrito* was founded, and a bit later *Cadernos de Filosofia da Ciência* (1980).

Porchat Pereira turned his attention to epistemology and devoted his work to skepticism. He published *Vida comun e ceticismo* (1993) and *Rumo ao ceticismo* (2007).

Other analytic philosophers who worked at CLE were Newton da Costa and Marcelo Dascal. Da Costa studied mathematics and later developed several non-classical systems of logic, while also working in philosophy of science and the foundations of physics. He is well known for the development of paraconsistent logic, a system of logic where certain contradictions are allowed (see Newton da Costa and Otávio Bueno's chapter in this volume). His work is well known in the mathematical and philosophical communities. He usually works in collaboration with other mathematicians, philosophers, and logicians; he had many students, and created an important school of logic at CLE. Some of his most important contributions are: *Sistemas formais inconsistentes* (1963), *Lógica indutiva e probabilidade* (1993), *Logique classique et non-classique* (1997), *Elementos de teoria paraconsistente de conjuntos* (1997, in collaboration with J.-Y. Béziau and O. Bueno) and *Science and Partial Truth: A Unitary Approach to Models and Scientific Reasoning* (2003, in collaboration with S. French).

Marcelo Dascal also worked in Campinas, before moving to Israel. He has worked at the University of Tel Aviv since 1967. He is a renowned Leibniz scholar, but his research on the relationship between natural languages and rationality led him to the analytic tradition, and the cognitive sciences. He published *Fundamentos metodológicos da lingüística* (1978), *Pragmatics and the Philosophy of Mind* (1983), and *Interpretation and Understanding* (2003). He remained strongly connected to the analytic community in Brazil and the rest of Latin America. Other important members of the CLE are: Zeljko Loparic (who works in Descartes, Heidegger, Freud and the foundations of psychology), Balthazar Barbosa Filho (who worked on Wittgenstein and philosophy of science, especially social sciences), and Luiz Henrique Lopes dos Santos (who works in logic and philosophy of language, and is now at USP).

There are also many Brazilian analytic philosophers in Rio de Janeiro. Without any doubt, Oswaldo Chateaubriand, who at one point was a colleague of Quine, is one of the major philosophers of Brazil. He works in the philosophy of logic, metaphysics, and philosophy of language, and his contributions address issues such as: logical form, syntax, grammar, logical truth, theory of descriptions, truth theories, metaphysical and ontological issues related to mathematics and logic (senses, facts, states of affairs, properties, sets), modalities, and counterfactuals. His main ideas are presented in *Logical Forms I: Truth and Description* (2001) and *Logical Forms II: Logic, Language and Knowledge* (2005). At the same university, the Pontifícia Universidade Católica do Rio de Janeiro, is Raul Landim Filho who published on Wittgenstein, Kant, Spinoza, Descartes, and Aquinas, studying classical semantic issues with an analytic method. Also in Rio, but at the Universidade Federal do Rio de Janeiro, there are other analytic philosophers such as Danilo Marcondes Filho (philosophy of language, skepticism, and epistemology), Wilson Mendonça (philosophy of mind, ethics and meta-ethics), and many others.

There is an important group of people working at the Universidade Federal de Santa Catarina (Florianópolis) structured around the Epistemology and Logic Research Group (NEL) and who organize every two years an international philosophy symposium addressing issues in philosophy of science, epistemology, logic, and metaphysics. They publish the journal *Principia*. This group includes Newton da Costa, Décio Krause,

207

Luiz Henrique de A. Dutra, and a couple of Argentine émigrés, Alberto Cupani and Gustavo A. Caponi.

The analytic tradition in Chile was almost nonexistent until a few years ago. In the 1950s interest in the new logic arose, but the philosophers who studied logic rejected the analytic tradition as a way of dealing with other philosophical fields, such as metaphysics or philosophy of science (for example, Juan Rivano who was interested in logic and neo-Hegelian tradition). The only exception was Gerold Stahl, a logician who also worked within the analytic tradition, writing about semantic paradoxes, causation, identity of indiscernibles, and truth.

Roberto Torretti was the first Chilean philosopher who adopted the analytic style, but he moved to the Universidad de Puerto Rico in the early 1970s where he developed his work. His book *Manuel Kant: estudio sobre los fundamentos de la filosofía crítica* (Chile, 1967, reissued in Buenos Aires in 1980) is one of the most important contributions to the understanding of Kant's thought in Spanish and it is written in an analytic style. After moving to Puerto Rico, Torretti devoted his work to the foundations of mathematics, especially geometry. His main publications include: *Philosophy of Geometry: From Riemann to Poincaré* (1978) and *Relativity and Geometry* (1983). He remained strongly connected with Chilean philosophy.

As in other Latin American countries, the history of analytic philosophy in Chile has been influenced by political changes. In 1973, a longstanding military regime took power and stopped the development of analytic philosophy. Some incipient work was done before that, for example *Siete escritos sobre logica y semántica de Frege* (1972), written by Alfonso Gómez Lobo who, after the coup d'état, moved to Georgetown University and focused on ancient philosophy. He wrote, with a clear analytic style, and in Spanish, the translation of Parmenides' Poem with an interesting preliminary study published for the first time in Buenos Aires (*Parmenides. Texto, traducción y comentario*, 1985).

There is today a group of people working in logic (both systematically and historically) and in the foundations of mathematics, including Wilfredo Quesada and Manuel Correia, stimulated by the influence of Rolando Chuaqui, who introduced for the first time reflections on the foundations of knowledge in general and science in particular. Every year there is a conference on the philosophy of science and logic in his memory.

In Peru, the history of analytic philosophy starts with Pedro Zulen, who died young in 1924. He studied at Harvard and published the first book about Anglo-Saxon thought in Spanish in 1922: *Del hegelianismo al neorrealismo. Estudio de las ideas filosóficas en Norteamérica*. But apart from this isolated contribution, the main introducer of analytic philosophy in Peru was Francisco Miró Quesada, who published *Lógica* in 1946. He wrote many papers and books mainly in logic, deontic logic, philosophy of mathematics, and also on the social reality of Peru. He was Minister of Education in the 1960s and he was always concerned with the political issues of his country and Latin America. Some of his other books are: *Apuntes para una teoría de la razón* (1963), *Humanismo y revolución* (1969), *Filosofía de las matemáticas* (1976), and *Ensayos de filosofía del derecho* (1986). He conceived logic as a "theory of reason" and hence his logical concerns were always linked to practical questions.

Along with Miró Quesada, another important influence in Peruvian analytic philosophy was Augusto Salazar Bondy. He worked in phenomenology, but he used analytic methods of conceptual clarification in his work. He was also concerned with his political environment, and promoted educational change in his country.

There are some other Peruvian analytic philosophers, such as Edgar Guzmán Jorquera. His posthumous book *Existencia y realidad* (2002) is a collection of his articles about issues in philosophy of logic and ontology, such as Tarski's truth theory, the correspondence theory, predication and existence, and some other epistemological, ethical, and aesthetical questions. Arsenio Guzmán Jorquera works mainly in logic and philosophy of science, and Óscar García Zárate in logic and philosophy of logic. There is also a group of young philosophers, who obtained their doctorates abroad and returned to Peru in recent times. In 2007 they published the first volume of the first analytic journal in the country: *Analítica*.

Uruguay is not an exception in Latin America. Its history is similar to many other countries: an incipient beginning with few people stopped by a military government, forcing many philosophers to emigrate. Among the Uruguayan philosophers living abroad we find Carlos Pereda, in Mexico, and Ezra Heymann, Javier Sasso, and Eduardo Piacenza, in Venezuela.

The first philosopher interested in issues in analytic philosophy, mainly ordinary language, was Carlos Vaz Ferreira. He was an empiricist influenced by the philosophies of life, but also by John Stuart Mill and other Anglo-Saxon philosophers. He died young (in 1958) and had no disciples. The most important Uruguayan analytic philosopher is, without any doubt, Mario Otero. He studied in the United States and in Europe, went into exile in Mexico and then came back to the Universidad de la República (Montevideo). His main interests are philosophy of science and logic; he collected his papers on these topics in *La filosofía de la ciencia hoy: dos aproximaciones* (1977). At the same university is Carlos Caorsi, specializing in philosophy of language, in particular the philosophy of Donald Davidson.

The Northern Part of South America and Central America

Analytic philosophy in Colombia had a late development. Up to the 1960s Colombian philosophy departments were dominated by Heideggerianism and Marxism, which were hostile to analytic philosophy. The latter was introduced by Rubén Sierra Mejía. Even though he was raised in the phenomenological tradition, in 1966 he became Professor of Logic at the Universidad Nacional de Colombia, in Bogotá, where he taught courses on Russell, Frege, Carnap, Popper, Austin, and Strawson. He published a number of papers on these philosophers, mostly in Colombian journals that were then becoming more sympathetic to analytic philosophy, such as *Ideas y Valores*, *Cuadernos de Filosofía y Letras* and *Eco*. He collected his papers in a book entitled *Apreciación de la filosofía analítica* (1985).

Adolfo León Gómez Giraldo also played an important role at introducing analytic philosophy in Colombia. He taught courses on the theory of argumentation at the Universidad del Valle, in Cali. He made use of Perelman's theory of argumentation as well as elements from analytic philosophy of language. He has published several books on this topic, and among the most important ones are *El primado de la razón práctica* (1991) and *Argumentos y falacias* (1997). His work influenced that of Alfonso Monsalve, at the Universidad de Antioquia, in Medellín. In his *Teoría de la argumentación* (1994), Monsalve relates Perelman's theory to classical theories of dialectics and rhetoric.

Along with Sierra Mejía and Gómez Giraldo, Magdalena Holguín is probably one of the most important figures during the period of expansion of analytic philosophy in Colombia in the 1980s. Her work has focused on Wittgenstein's philosophy; in 1997, she published the book *Wittgenstein y el escepticismo*. Holguin's work has been influential on the Colombian philosophical scene and on the increasing interest in Wittgenstein's philosophy. Some of the philosophers who have followed Holguin's lead are Juan Guillermo Hoyos, Jairo Iván Peña, Carlos Cardona Suárez, and others. All this shows that Colombia has one of the most active Wittgensteinian communities in Latin America.

Since the 1990s, the center of analytic activity in Colombia has been Bogotá. At the Universidad Nacional de Colombia, there is a group of philosophers working from an analytic perspective: Juan José Botero is probably one of the most representative analytic philosophers in Colombia today. He has published a number of papers on the philosophies of language and mind, as well as epistemology. One of his main interests the possibility of naturalizing intentionality; on whether it is possible to make a scientific theory of cognitive phenomena.

The development of analytic philosophy in Venezuela was very similar to that of other Latin American countries: from the 1940s to the 1960s there was a big influence of philosophers like Husserl, Heidegger, Sartre and also of Marxism. It was the Spanish émigré Juan David García Bacca who dominated some of the most important changes in the Venezuelan philosophical panorama at that time. One of his students, Juan Nuño, after going to Cambridge to study, started teaching the main topics of logical empiricism and analytic philosophy at the Universidad Central de Venezuela (UCV) in Caracas. In 1965 he published his book *Sentido de la filosofía contemporánea*, which constitutes the first survey of contemporary philosophy written in Latin America, giving analytic philosophy a prominent place. Nuño also got into a polemical debate with some of the most influential philosophical currents in Venezuela during that period. In 1973 he published *Elementos de lógica formal*. Around that time, he formed a small discussion group concerned with analytic topics at the Instituto de Filosofía of the UCV. Nuño published several volumes of his collected papers: *La superación de la filosofía* (1970), *Compromisos y desviaciones* (1982), and *Los mitos filosóficos* (1985) are among the most important ones. He also wrote the book *La filosofía de Borges* (1986), examining, with an analytic spirit, the work of the Argentine writer Jorge Luis Borges.

Among the people linked to the analytic group at the Instituto de Filosofía are Rafael Burgos, Ernesto Battistella, and Li Carrillo, all of whom have written papers on analytic topics. Pedro Lluveres wrote *Ciencia y escepticismo* (1976), an analytic study of Descartes. Little by little, during the 1970s various courses on topics of analytic philosophy were established at the UCV, and its journal *Episteme* turned into a more analytic one.

Someone who also played an important role in introducing analytic philosophy in Venezuela was the Mexican philosopher Adolfo García Díaz, who had been a student of García Bacca in Mexico. In 1959 he moved to Maracaibo, where he founded the Facultad de Humanidades and the Escuela de Filosofía at the Universidad de Zulia. He published a number of papers on topics of metaphysics and ancient philosophy in Mexico and Venezuela; some of them were later collected in his *Investigaciones metafísicas* (1992). The Centro de Estudios Filosóficos (now called "Adolfo García Díaz") publishes the *Revista de Filosofía*, one of the most important philosophy journals in Venezuela.

There is also an important development of Wittgensteinian studies in Venezuela. Sabine Knabenschuh, Nancy Núñez, and Corina Yoris, among others, have published several articles on Wittgenstein's philosophy.

Except for Costa Rica, there are no analytic philosophers in Central America. Analytic philosophy has been cultivated mainly at the Universidad de Costa Rica, where, in the 1960s, Claudio Gutiérrez started teaching and writing on logic. At that time he published several articles on natural deduction systems, and later on he also published on cybernetics and on the philosophy of mind. In the 1970s, Luis Camacho started publishing articles on epistemology and on Wittgenstein; he remains very active working in epistemology and in philosophy of technology, from an analytical perspective. In 2003 he published his book *Introducción a la lógica*. Some of the papers of these philosophers have appeared in the *Revista de Filosofía de la Universidad de Costa Rica*. This journal was founded in 1957 and for a long time published mainly continental philosophy; however, in the past few years it has been publishing significantly more analytic philosophy.

Even though Gutiérrez and Camacho are now retired, some of their students are active working at the Universidad de Costa Rica. This is the case with Max Freund, who has published a number of articles defending conceptualism as a theory of universals, but extended to all meaningful linguistic expressions. He has developed several kinds of logic assuming conceptualism as their philosophical basis, but also a conceptualist theory of computability and of the ontology of possible worlds. He is member of a growing group working in cognitive science in Costa Rica.

Conclusion

We have surveyed here only some of the main figures and developments in analytic philosophy in Latin America up to the 1990s. However, a huge amount of analytic philosophy has been produced in the past 15 years or so. During this time, analytic philosophy has played an important role in some of the main philosophy departments in Latin America. The works considered here are at the center of current discussions by younger generations. Hundreds of people have been trained in this kind of philosophy; many have gone abroad to do graduate studies in Anglo-American universities. Some of them have returned to their countries to contribute to the development of philosophy; others have stayed in the United States or in the UK, where they write and teach. Many of these young Latin American analytic philosophers recently founded the Asociación Latinoamericana de Filosofía Analítica in Mexico in 2007 with the main objective of enhancing the links between analytic philosophers of different countries. Analytic philosophy has a promising future in Latin America: no doubt, it will keep growing in the years to come.

Related chapters: 15 Paraconsistent Logic; 25 Contemporary Ethics and Political Philosophy; 26 Philosophy of Science; 29 Teaching Philosophy; 31 Deontic Logic and Legal Philosophy; 32 Metaphysics; 34 Formal Epistemology and Logic.

References

Alchourrón, C., & Bulygin, E. (1971). *Normative systems*. New York: Springer-Verlag.

Bunge, M. (1961). *Causalidad*. Buenos Aires: Eudeba.

Camacho, L. (2003). *Introducción a la lógica*. Colima, Mexico: Universidad de Colima.

Chateaubriand, O. (2001). *Logical forms I: truth and description*. Campinas: Editora CLE/UNICAMP.

Chateaubriand, O. (2005). *Logical forms II: logic, language and knowledge*. Campinas: Editora CLE/UNICAMP.

Da Costa, N. (1963). *Sistemas formais inconsistentes*. Curitiba, Brazil: Universidade Federal do Paraná.

Da Costa, N. (1993). *Lógica indutiva e probabilidade*. São Paulo: EdUSP.

Da Costa, N. (1997). *Logique classique et non-classique*. Paris: Masson.

Da Costa, N., & French, S. (2003). *Science and partial truth: a unitary approach to models and scientific reasoning*. Oxford: Oxford University Press.

Da Costa, N., Béziau, J.-Y., & Bueno, O. (1997). *Elementos de teoria paraconsistente de conjuntos*. Campinas: Editora CLE/UNICAMP.

Dascal, M. (1983). *Pragmatics and the philosophy of mind*. Amsterdam: John Benjamins.

Dascal, M. (2003). *Interpretation and understanding*. Amsterdam: John Benjamins.

García Díaz, A. (1992). *Investigaciones metafísicas*. Caracas: Universidad Central de Venezuela.

García Máynez, E. (1940). *Introducción al estudio del derecho*. Mexico: Porrúa.

García Máynez, E. (1974). *Filosofía del derecho*. Mexico: Porrúa.

Gómez Giraldo, A. L. (1997). *Argumentos y falacias*. Cali: Universidad del Valle.

Gómez Giraldo, A. L. (1991). *El primado de la razón práctica*. Cali: Universidad del Valle.

Guzmán Jorquera, E. (2002). *Existencia y realidad*. Arequipa: Universidad Nacional de San Agustín.

Holguín, M. (1997). *Wittgenstein y el escepticismo*. Cali: Universidad del Valle.

Lluberes, P. (1976). *Ciencia y escepticismo: aproximación a Descartes*. Caracas: Equinoccio.

Miró Quesada, F. (1963). *Apuntes para una teoría de la razón*. Lima: Universidad Nacional Mayor de San Marcos.

Miró Quesada, F. (1946). *Lógica*. Lima: D. Miranda.

Miró Quesada, F. (1969). *Humanismo y revolución*. Lima: Casa de la cultura.

Miró Quesada, F. (1986). *Ensayos de filosofía del derecho*. Lima: Universidad de Lima.

Monsalve, A. (1994). *Teoría de la argumentación*. Medellín: Universidad de Antioquia.

Nino, C. (1984). *Ética y derechos humanos*. Buenos Aires: Paidós.

Nuño, J. (1965). *Sentido de la filosofía contemporánea*. Caracas: Universidad Central de Venezuela.

Nuño, J. (1973). *Elementos de lógica formal*. Caracas: Universidad Central de Venezuela (2nd edn, 1980).

Orayen, R. (1989). *Lógica, significado y ontología*. Mexico: Universidad Nacional Autónoma de México.

Otero, M. (1977). *La filosofía de la ciencia hoy: dos aproximaciones*. Mexico: Universidad Nacional Autónoma de México.

Pereda, C. (1994). *Vértigos argumentales: una ética de la disputa*. Barcelona: Anthropos.

Rabossi, E. (1975). *Análisis filosófico, lenguaje y metafísica*. Caracas: Monte Ávila Editores.

Rabossi, E. (2008). *En el comienzo Dios creó el canon*. Buenos Aires: Gedisa.

Rossi, A. (1969). *Lenguaje y significado*. Mexico: Siglo XXI.

Rossi, A. (1978). *Manual del distraído*. Mexico: Joaquín Mortiz.

Salmerón, F. (1971). *La filosofía y las actitudes morales*. Mexico: Siglo XXI.

Salmerón, F. (1998). *The origins of analytic moral philosophy and other essays*. Amsterdam: Rodopi.

Sierra Mejía, R. (1985). *Apreciación de la filosofía analítica*. Bogotá: Universidad Nacional de Colombia.

Simpson, T. M. (1964). *Formas lógicas, realidad y significado*. Buenos Aires: Eudeba.

Villoro, L. (1982). *Creer, saber, conocer*. Mexico: Siglo XXI.

Villoro, L. (1997). *El poder y el valor. Fundamentos de una ética política*. Mexico: Fondo de Cultura Económica.

Further Reading

Alegre, M., Gargarella, R., & Rosenkrantz, C. (Eds). (2008). *Homenaje a Carlos S. Nino*. Buenos Aires: Facultad de Derecho (UBA) – La Ley.

Betancourt Delgado, W. et al. (Eds). (1990). *La enseñanza, la reflexión y la investigación filosóficas en América Latina y el Caribe*. Madrid: Tecnos-UNESCO.

Bulygin, E., & Palau, G. (Eds). (2006). Homenaje a Carlos E. Alchourrón. *Análisis Filosófico*, vol. XXVI, 1 and 2.

Garzón Valdés, E., & Salmerón, F. (Eds). (1993). *Epistemología y cultura. En torno a la obra de Luis Villoro*. Mexico: Universidad Nacional Autónoma de México.

Gracia, J. (1984). El análisis filosófico en América Latina [Philosophical analysis in Latin America]. In K. Cramer et al. (Eds). *La filosofía hoy en Alemania y América Latina*. Córdoba: Círculo de Amigos del Instituto Goethe.

Gracia, J., Rabossi, E., Villanueva, E., & Dascal, M. (Eds). (1984). *Philosophical analysis in Latin America*. Dordrecht: Reidel.

Klimovsky, G. (2008). *Mis diversas existencias*. Buenos Aires: AZ.

Makinson, D. (1996). In memoriam: Carlos Eduardo Alchourrón. *Nordic Journal of Philosophical Logic*, 1, 3–10.

Olivé, L., & Villoro, L. (Eds). (1996). *Filosofía moral, educación e historia: homenaje a Fernando Salmerón*. Mexico: Universidad Nacional Autónoma de México.

Peña, L. (1995). Algunos aspectos del desarrollo de la lógica en el Brasil. *Boletim da Sociedade Paranaense de Matemática*, 15, 9–23.

Pérez, D., & Fernández Moreno, L. (Eds). (2008). *Cuestiones filosóficas. Ensayos en honor de Eduardo Rabossi*. Buenos Aires: Catálogos.

Rodríguez, C. (2002). *La filosofía analítica en Colombia*. Bogotá: El búho.

Salmerón, F. (1991). Notas sobre la recepción del análisis filosófico en América Latina. *Isegoría*, 3, 119–37.

Salmerón, F. (2007). La recepción del análisis filosófico en América Latina. In F. Salmerón, *Filosofía e historia de las ideas en México y América Latina* (pp. 195–230). Mexico: Universidad Nacional Autónoma de México.

Several authors. (1993). Special issue on Raúl Orayen's *Lógica, significado y ontología*. *Análisis Filosófico*, XIII, 1.

Several authors. (1994). *Aproximaciones a Alejandro Rossi*. Mexico: Universidad Nacional Autónoma de México/El equilibrista.

Valdés, M., & Fernández, M. A. (forthcoming). La filosofía analítica en Latinoamérica. In E. Dussel, E. Mendieta, & C. Bohórquez (Eds). *El pensamiento filosófico latinoamericano, del Caribe y "latino."* Mexico/Stony Brook/Maracaibo: Siglo XXI/CREFAL.

213

Part II

Current Issues

15

Paraconsistent Logic

NEWTON C. A. DA COSTA AND OTÁVIO BUENO

Introduction

In the past two centuries, logic progressed so much that it became a new domain of inquiry. It is a formal and abstract discipline like mathematics. In fact, it is difficult to separate the fields of logic and mathematics, at least as they are developed in the contemporary scene. There is a permanent interplay between both fields: mathematical ideas and methods are applied to logic, and logical ideas and methods find their way into mathematics.

Logic constitutes, of course, an important tool in the domain of philosophy, particularly in philosophy of science, as well as in all areas of (pure or applied) science. And logic did find applications even in technology. It is also intimately linked to natural reasoning and, in general, to all classes of inference. In this chapter, we will consider logic particularly as it relates to valid, deductive inference.

Our main goal in what follows is to give an idea of a new kind of logic, paraconsistent logic, which has been developed, in particular, in Latin America, and which now has applications in a variety of domains. As will become clear shortly, and roughly speaking, paraconsistent logic is a non-classical logic in which not everything follows from contradictions of the form A and not A. The development of this logic has had a significant impact on the work in logic and its philosophy in Latin America.

Paraconsistent Logic and Latin America

The formulation and development of paraconsistent logic in Brazil eventually led to what has been called the "Brazilian school of paraconsistency," which combines a pluralism about the many existing paraconsistent logics and an interest in applications of these logics to various areas of research (from the foundations of physics to artificial intelligence) with a lack of commitment to the existence of true contradictions. (We will return to these points below.) This proposal is distinct from other approaches to paraconsistency developed, for instance, in Australia, where a commitment to the existence of true contradictions plays a crucial role (see Priest, 2006a). The impact that paraconsistent logic has had on the theoretical landscape in logic and its philosophy

217

in Latin America is significant, although we will restrict our discussion to the Brazilian context.

As part of the development of paraconsistent logic, there has been in Brazil a burst of interest in research in logic, philosophy of logic, and philosophy of science (dealing, in particular, with issues that emerge from inconsistencies in scientific theories). Several generations of philosophers and logicians have been formed in the past four decades in Brazil whose work emerged, directly or indirectly, from concerns that deal with paraconsistency. We will mention just a few examples to illustrate our point.

The late Ayda Arruda was a pioneer with her work on paraconsistent logic and paraconsistent set theory. She also worked on the history of logic (in particular, the history of paraconsistent logic), and intuitionist mathematics without negation (Arruda, 1980).

Walter Carnielli (State University of Campinas, Brazil) has worked in many aspects of paraconsistent logic. In particular, he worked on a framework that offers a semantic interpretation of paraconsistent logic, which is called the possible-translations semantics (Carnielli, 2000). This framework brought new interest in philosophical interpretations of paraconsistent logic. Carnielli also offered a systematic treatment of a large class of paraconsistent logics under the rubric of logics of formal inconsistency. The resulting classification systematizes the variety of paraconsistency logics in an insightful way (see Carnielli & Marcos, 2002).

The work of Itala D'Ottaviano (State University of Campinas, Brazil) has focused on the foundations and applications of non-classical logics, particularly of paraconsistent and many-valued logics. D'Ottaviano has also worked on the development of translations and combinations of logics, and on the history of logic, with special emphasis on the history of non-classical logics, and in particular on the history of paraconsistent logic (see D'Ottaviano, 1990; D'Ottaviano & Feitosa, 2000).

Décio Krause (Federal University of Santa Catarina, Brazil) has worked on many applications of non-classical logics to the foundations of physics. In particular, in collaboration with da Costa, he developed a logic that can be used to capture certain aspects of the foundations of quantum mechanics; it is called Shrödinger logic (da Costa & Krause, 1997). He also developed a set theory, called quasi-set theory, which can be used to treat some aspects of non-relativistic quantum mechanics. After all, as opposed to classical set theories, quasi-set theory does not presuppose that all objects in the theory have well-defined identity conditions (see Krause, 1992; French & Krause, 2006).

Jair Abe has worked on applications of paraconsistent logic to robotics and artificial intelligence, showing the significance that paraconsistent logic has for various branches of technology (see Abe et al., 2006).

This brief selection indicates the variety and scope of some of the work in logic and its philosophy that emerged in Brazil from the development of paraconsistent logic. Researchers in logic and philosophy of logic from several parts of the world regularly visit the country to interact with the Brazilian logic community. Paraconsistent logic is a thriving area of research.

Thinking about Logic

When one talks about logic, it should be pointed out that, normally, any logic L is based on a language L_L, and systematizes the inferences that can be expressed or formulated in that language. The inferences justified by the canons of L are called L-valid; the L-valid inferences are also called L-deductions. From this point of view, L is seen as a deductive logic.

However, in L_L it may be possible to formulate inferences that are not L-deductive in accordance with L, but that, nonetheless, deserve to be codified and analyzed. Such patterns of reasoning can be called L-inductions, and they must display some characteristics that entitle them to be described in this way. For example, the patterns of reasoning should display some degree of plausibility. In this chapter, however, we will discuss only deductive logic, or simply logic. We are mainly interested in deductions as valid inferences, and in related concepts.

The language L_L usually contains connectives: '$\rightarrow$' (if . . . , then . . .), '$\wedge$' (and), '$\vee$' (or), '$\leftrightarrow$' (if and only if), '$\neg$' (negation); quantifiers: '$\forall$' (for all), '$\exists$' (there exists), as well as other components, such as predicate symbols, variables, and the equality symbol: '$=$'. (See, for example, Quine, 1982, and the articles on logic and related topics in Edwards (Ed.), 1972, and Jacquette (Ed.), 2006.)

Of special importance is classical logic. It is one of the most important logics, and the one that is more widely used in the contemporary context. Aristotle, who effectively created logic as a field of study, created what can be called traditional, syllogistic logic. Much later, authors such as G. Boole, G. Frege, B. Russell, and D. Hilbert developed these ideas further, going beyond traditional logic in many ways, and the result is what is now called classical logic. With suitable assumptions, traditional logic can be obtained from classical logic, in the sense that the syllogisms that are considered valid according to traditional logic are considered valid arguments according to classical logic. For this reason, when we talk about classical logic in this chapter, we will consider traditional, syllogistic logic as part of it. (For references and discussion of the history of logic, see Kneale & Kneale, 1988; Edwards (Ed.), 1972; Jacquette (Ed.), 2006.)

From the time of Aristotle to the beginning of the twentieth century, there existed basically one and only one logic: classical logic, which always was *the* logic. But particularly during the twentieth century, numerous new logics were formulated. Some of them *extend* classical logic: for instance, classical modal logic (which introduces modal operators of necessity and possibility), classical tense logic (with introduces time operators), and classical deontic logic (which introduces operators modeling what is permissible and obligatory). Other logics, however, *change or limit* the axioms or the rules governing classical logic. For example, in intuitionistic logic, the principle of excluded middle (namely, $A \vee \neg A$, where 'A' is a proposition or sentence) is not valid in general; in many-valued logic, there are more than two truth-values (for instance, true, false, and indeterminate); in quantum logic, the distributive law (i.e., $P \wedge (Q \vee R) \leftrightarrow (P \wedge Q) \vee (P \wedge R)$, where '$P$', '$Q$', and '$R$' are propositions or sentences) is not generally valid. Logics in the first group, which offer extensions of classical logic, are *complementary* to the latter. Logics in the second group, which challenge the validity of certain principles of classical logic, are *rival* to the latter. They can be considered heterodox logics. We will examine below exactly where in this divide paraconsistent logic belongs.

The Nature of Paraconsistent Logic

One of the historically central principles (or law) of classical logic is the principle of non-contradiction (it is also called the principle of contradiction). The principle has many formulations:

(1) $\neg(A \wedge \neg A)$,

where 'A' is a sentence and '$\neg$' and '$\wedge$' are, as noted above, the symbols for negation and conjunction, respectively. In this formulation, the law of non-contradiction states that it is not the case that a proposition (or sentence) and its negation are both true. So, if 'A' is true, '$\neg A$' is false, and if 'A' is false, '$\neg A$' is true. One commonly says that 'A' and '$\neg A$' cannot be simultaneously true. This is the propositional form of the law.

However, the law also has another formulation: if 'P' is a one-place predicate, 'x' is a variable, and '$\forall$' is the universal quantifier, then it is true that:

(2) $\forall x \neg(Px \wedge \neg Px)$.

That is, an object cannot possess and not possess a property. (The traditional logicians would add: "at the same time and from the same point of view," although this addition is not really necessary.) Thus, there is a second, predicate version of the principle of non-contradiction.

Other formulations are still possible. Consider, for example, the following:

(3) $\forall x \, \forall y \, \neg(Qxy \wedge \neg Qxy)$.

In this case, 'Q' is a two-place relation, and the principle states that objects cannot be both related and not related by the relation Q. (As a rough example: all human beings cannot be both married and not married.)

The last two versions of the principle – (2) and (3) – are the predicate formulations. Version (1), the propositional, in a certain sense implies the predicate forms (2) and (3). So, from now on, when we talk about the principle of non-contradiction, we are making reference to form (1).

One point should be noted, though. Usually, strong logics are stratified in several orders, or levels: first-order logic, second-order logic, . . . , high-order logic, where the latter involves all orders. For this reason, there are various forms of the principle of non-contradiction, depending on the order of the logic.

Some terminology is now needed. In classical logic, a formula of the form:

$A \wedge \neg A$

is called a *contradiction*; sometimes, the pair A and $\neg A$ is also said to be a contradiction. A *theory* T is a set of sentences closed by deduction; that is, T contains all logical consequences of its members (T is, thus, *deductively closed*).

Let T be a theory. T is *trivial* if it does contain all sentences of our language L_L – which, in the case we are discussing now, is the language of classical logic, since at the moment this is the only logic we are considering. (However, the definitions we offer are general, and they cover all logics.) If T is not a trivial theory, T is *non-trivial*. T is *inconsistent* if T has theorems of the form A and $\neg A$; otherwise, T is consistent.

In classical logic, a theory T is trivial if, and only if, T is inconsistent. (This happens in most logics.) The reason for this fact is that, in classical logic, from a contradiction one can deduce any formula whatsoever. Moreover, if A and $\neg A$ are theorems of the theory T, so is $A \wedge \neg A$, and conversely. In synthesis, in classical logic (and in most logics), if a theory T is inconsistent (or, what means the same, contradictory), then T is trivial. Thus, it loses its relevance, given that it is unable, for example, to systematize our experience, and it is practically useless. After all, if a set of premises Δ is inconsistent, any proposition whatsoever can be deduced from Δ. Thus, the presence of contradictions in one's premises or the employment of contradictory sets of premises constitutes a problem – in fact a serious problem – for reasoning.

There are circumstances, however, that motivate one to build a logic that can be the underlying logic of inconsistent but non-trivial theories. The latter are theories that, despite being inconsistent, do not entail everything (that is, they do not have every sentence in the language as a theorem). Clearly, the logic in question cannot be classical logic, or most extant logics, since they are trivialized by a contradiction – in the sense that every sentence in the language can then be derived. These logics do not allow for inconsistent but non-trivial theories.

We have here, then, a syntactic characterization of paraconsistent logic (that is, roughly, a characterization in terms of the formal features of the logic, independently of issues of truth): a logic is paraconsistent if it can be the basic logic of inconsistent but non-trivial theories. But there is also a semantic formulation of paraconsistent logic (that is, a formulation that is ultimately made in terms of truth), and which is loosely equivalent to the syntactic version. Roughly speaking, if the principle of non-contradiction is not valid in general, then there are true contradictions, and conversely. So, a logic L is paraconsistent if the law of non-contradiction is not valid in L.

The syntactic and the semantic definitions of paraconsistent logic are informal, and thus, they are not precise. Nonetheless, they are almost equivalent, and any one of them can be taken as a rough delineation of the domain of paraconsistency. It turns out that there are several (in fact, infinitely many) paraconsistent logics, and all of them satisfy the conditions just offered for paraconsistency (see da Costa, Krause, & Bueno, 2007).

There are numerous situations that motivate the convenience and appropriateness of theories that are inconsistent but non-trivial (that is, paraconsistent theories). This occurs, for instance, in set theory, which taken informally and intuitively is inconsistent, due to Russell's paradox. One may think that for every property there is a set of objects corresponding to that property (namely, the objects that have that property). For example, for the property *is a tiger*, there is a set of objects that have that property: the set of tigers. For the property *is a number*, there is a set of objects that have that property: the set of numbers. What Russell found out, however, is that there are properties for which there is no corresponding set. Consider the property *is a set of sets that are not members of themselves*. Let's call such a "set" *Russell's set* or, more simply, R. Now, consider whether Russell's set is a member of R. Suppose that Russell's set is not a member of R. In this case, given the definition of R, Russell's set *is* a member of R. Alternatively, suppose that Russell's set is a member of R. In this case, given the definition

221

of R, Russell's set is *not* a member of R. Thus, Russell's set is a member of R if, and only if, it is not a member of R. And from this, it follows that Russell's set is a member of R *and* is not a member of R – a contradiction. This shows that our intuitive principle according to which for every property there is a set of objects that have such a property is inconsistent. This is, of course, a big surprise, given that this principle, prima facie, seems to be obviously true.

However, if one adopts an underlying paraconsistent logic, this informal, intuitive set theory is transformed into a paraconsistent theory. In this case, there will be a Russell set, which of course is an inconsistent object, but is not a trivial one, in the sense that it has every property. As any object, Russell's set will have some properties and lack others, and these properties can be studied in a paraconsistent set theory (for details, see da Costa et al., 2007).

There are many other examples in other branches of mathematics, in science, and in philosophy that motivate the need for accommodating inconsistent but non-trivial theories. For example, the early formulation of the calculus in terms of infinitesimals seems to have been inconsistent. An infinitesimal is a positive number (a number that is not zero), but which is smaller than any other number. When the marquis De l'Hospital wrote the first textbook of the calculus, which was published in 1696, his first principle stated that two magnitudes that differ by an infinitesimal are the same. He is here acknowledging that two *distinct* magnitudes are actually *identical* – as long as they differ only by an infinitesimal. It is not surprising that much care was needed when infinitesimals were used in the calculus. And it is interesting to note that, despite the inconsistency, Leibniz, Newton, l'Hospital, and others who worked in the early formulation of the calculus managed to obtain the correct results about the theory. They certainly did not derive everything from their inconsistent principles. In fact, this is an interesting example of an inconsistent, and certainly non-trivial, theory. (For a fascinating discussion of the history of the calculus, see Robinson, 1974.)

The same happens with Meinong's theory of objects, which offers a systematic framework to classify different kinds of objects and their status (Meinong, 1960), and with certain systematizations of dialectics. In both cases, the theories may be inconsistent, but they were certainly non-trivial – not every sentence follows from them. Paraconsistent logic then offers the resources to formulate these theories in a way that preserves some of their central features: their inconsistency, simplicity, and elegance. (The early formulation of the calculus was an elegant theory, and so was Meinong's.) And this is done without logical chaos; that is, without the triviality that emerges from an inconsistent theory formulated in classical logic.

A History of Paraconsistent Logic

The history of paraconsistent logic is a complex and fascinating affair. With hindsight, even the first systematic formulation of logic in Aristotle's hands was already paraconsistent. After all, a syllogism with inconsistent premises does not have any arbitrary sentence of the language in use as a valid conclusion. Consider, for instance, this case: (P_1) No person is mortal. (P_2) Some person is mortal. Therefore, every person is mortal. Clearly, the premises of this argument are inconsistent, but the conclusion does not follow from them according to syllogistic logic. There is a sense of relevance in this logic – a requirement that the premises of a valid argument be relevant to the conclusion – that prevents arguments such as this from being valid. Although Aristotle perhaps would not have put the point this way (given that the concept paraconsistency had not been explicitly formulated at the time), syllogistic theory is indeed paraconsistent.

As part of her account of the history of paraconsistent logic, A. I. Arruda wrote:

> Several philosophers since Heraclitus, including Hegel, until Marx, Engels, and the present-day dialectical materialists, have proposed the thesis that contradictions are fundamental for the understanding of reality; in other words, they claim that reality is contradictory, that is to say, that Hegel's thesis is true of the real world. [Hegel's thesis is the statement that there are true contradictions.]
>
> Clearly, if one accepts Hegel's thesis, one has to employ a new kind of logic (paraconsistent logic), in order to study inconsistent but non-trivial theories. Strangely enough, philosophers who accept Hegel's thesis have not established any formal system of paraconsistent logic. Instead of this, some of them have proposed the so-called *dialectical logic*, whose nature is rather obscure.
>
> According to Lukasiewicz [. . .], Aristotle had already an idea of the possibility of derogation of [that is, the possibility of abandoning] the principle of contradiction, and consequently, the possibility of paraconsistent logic. (Arruda, 1980, p. 6)

It is indeed an interesting feature that from the beginning of the development of logic as a field of inquiry, paraconsistent ideas have been entertained, although they were not, of course, developed at that point. And despite the fact that Aristotle considered the possibility of abandoning the law of non-contradiction in the book Γ of *Metaphysics* (5^b18 9^a6; see Barnes (Ed.), 1984), he ultimately argued against the intelligibility of this move. (Aristotle's arguments, however, are far from being conclusive; see Priest, 2006b, pp. 7–42.)

Arruda continues:

> The first logician to construct a system of paraconsistent logic was S. Jaskowski [in Poland, in 1948 and 1949], following a suggestion of Lukasiewicz. He called his system *discussive (discoursive) logic*. (Arruda, 1980, p. 9)

Arruda also notes:

> Jaskowski had already constructed a paraconsistent propositional calculus, but [the Brazilian] N. C. A. da Costa is actually the founder of paraconsistent logic. Independently of the work of Jaskowski, he started in 1958 [. . .] to develop some ideas which led him to the construction of several systems of paraconsistent logic, including not only the propositional level but also the predicate level (with and without equality), the corresponding calculi of descriptions, as well as some applications to set theory. Da Costa's systems were extended and studied by several authors [. . .]. Da Costa and his collaborators investigated also various other systems of paraconsistent logic, some of them having intimate connections with relevant logic. [Roughly speaking, this is a form of paraconsistent logic that requires that the premises of a valid argument be relevant to the conclusion.] [. . .] In the last years many logicians contributed to the development of paraconsistent logic (some of them quite independently of the works of Jaskowski and da Costa). (Arruda, 1980, pp. 10–11)

It is important to note that some logicians elaborated certain paraconsistent logical cal-culi, although they did not conceive the possibility of paraconsistent logic as a new kind of logic. (This is the case, for instance, of some of the work done by D. Nelson in 1959.)

Paraconsistent logic can be viewed as a heterodox logic, which is then a rival to classical logic. From this perspective, both logics are incompatible. However, para-consistent logic can also be viewed as a complement to classical logic. From this stance, its main concepts and laws are taken to be different from the corresponding ones of classical logic. For example, paraconsistent negation is then distinct from classical negation, obeying proper principles. In general, most heterodox logics can also be conceived as complements to classical logic, since they share several principles. The significance of paraconsistent logic in relation to classical logic depends, thus, on philosophical assumptions about the interpretation of these logics. It is, therefore, an issue in the philosophy of logic.

Many systems of paraconsistent logic have in them classical logic as a kind of "sub-logic." In particular, when paraconsistent logic and classical logic are used to deal with consistent contexts (that is, those that do not involve any contradiction), they yield the same results, in the sense that exactly the same inferences are sanctioned as valid. Thus, the opposition between classical logic and paraconsistent logic is not as irreconcilable as one may think.

Paraconsistent logic, as logic in general, has numerous applications. (a) In philoso-phy, paraconsistent logic is used to systematize certain inconsistent theories, such as dialectics and Meinong's theory of objects, since the latter seems to recognize objects that are neither entities nor non-entities, such as objects that are accessible to our thoughts (Meinong, 1960). Paraconsistent logic also has a role in the philosophical analysis of concepts such as those of negation and implication, and, in philosophy of physics, it shows how to make paraconsistently compatible theories, such as quantum mechanics and general relativity, which are mutually inconsistent. (Of course, the latter applica-tion does not hamper the search for a classical unification of those theories.)

(b) In physics and mathematics, paraconsistent logic finds applications in the formalization of inconsistent theories, similar to Bohr's atomic model and plasma theory, and even the early formulation of the calculus (for a discussion of inconsistent mathematics, see Mortensen, 1995, and da Costa et al., 2007).

(c) Finally, technology offers another domain of application of paraconsistent logic, for example, in traffic control in large cities, in train circulation, in computing, and in artificial intelligence. (A detailed account of paraconsistent logic and topics of para-consistency in general can be found in da Costa et al., 2007.)

Philosophical Aspects of Paraconsistent Logic

Several issues need to be addressed here. In particular, given that there are infinitely many paraconsistent logics (see da Costa et al., 2007), the issues arise as to whether there is a true paraconsistent logic, and how to choose between such logics. As will become clear, the choice between such logics is ultimately a pragmatic and context-dependent matter, largely dependent on the details of the applications at hand. These points will be developed below.

224

In various domains of knowledge, in mathematics, physics, and in philosophical theorizing, inconsistent but non-trivial theories are available. In other words, there are theories in which both a formula A and its negation $\neg A$ are theorems, but not every formula can be derived from these theories. This fact provides an important support for paraconsistency, since it shows that the attempt to accommodate inconsistencies by devising appropriate inconsistent but non-trivial theories is by no means empty or unrealizable. It provides a distinctive perspective on the issues under consideration. Instead of retaining classical logic, and avoiding the inconsistency by rejecting one or another of the premises which generate it – making more or less ad hoc moves – it is possible to retain the inconsistency, change the underlying logic to a paraconsistent one, and study the properties of the "inconsistent object" so generated. The important feature, as a paraconsistent set theory indicates (see da Costa et al., 2007), is that these "inconsistent objects" have certain determined properties and lack others: it is simply *not* the case that "everything goes" with regard to them. So, as opposed to what happens in the case of classical logic, there is a whole new domain of investigation determined by the formulation of paraconsistent logic: the domain of the inconsistent.

Now, the issue arises as to the status of the resulting inconsistent set theory: is it *true?* In other words, are there true contradictions? The answer depends on several considerations. (1) What is the notion of truth used in this context? (2) What kinds of objects are being considered: only mathematical objects, or are physical objects included as well? (3) What notion of existence is assumed? And how are ontological commitments to be spelled out? Of course, the examination of these issues involves particular philosophical moves, and in the context of this chapter, they can only be considered in fairly general terms. But hopefully enough will be said to make clear some of the moves that are available.

According to some authors, the answer to the question *Are there true contradictions?* is affirmative (see Priest, 2006a). The examples given by Priest are the logical and semantic paradoxes, statements about moving objects (objects subject to change), and certain views in the foundations of mathematics and in law. In order to articulate a realist view about true contradictions, Priest advocates (i) a strong notion of truth – truth *simpliciter* understood in the correspondence sense – (ii) a classical view of existence (as the value of our variables in our best theories), and (iii) an extended claim as to the domain of his theory – which incorporates both mathematical and physical objects. (Of course, in order to avoid triviality, Priest adopts a paraconsistent logic: see his system LP, the Logic of Paradox, discussed in Priest, 2006a.) So, Priest's approach countenances classical views about truth and existence, and applies them to a wide-ranging domain. Priest's commitment to several doctrines is by no means fortuitous: in order to be adequately accommodated, inconsistencies require a whole package of logical and philosophical doctrines – indeed, a whole research program is involved. Of course, there are stronger and weaker programs; some are closer to classical proposals, some farther away.

Given that it retains classical notions of truth and existence, Priest's proposal ends up committed to strong metaphysical views. Given the use of truth in the correspondence sense, and the claim that assertions about the world (be it the empirical or the mathematical world) should be true, Priest's view is ipso facto committed to all objects that are posited by these claims. In particular, his proposal seems to be committed to

225

"inconsistent objects" in the physical world: the objects to which inconsistent but true physical theories refer. But how can their existence be established?

The argument to this effect assumes, of course, the classical account of ontological commitment (that is, of which objects are taken to exist): one is ontologically committed to those objects that are required for the best theories to be true. And in the case of inconsistent theories, this criterion leads to the postulation of objects that both have and lack a given property (for instance, the liar sentence is both true and false, the Russell set is both a member of itself and it is not, etc.). And the same goes for theories about the physical world.

However, this argument is not so conclusive. First, the criterion of ontological commitment that is invoked is *not* independent of particular philosophical assumptions. It comes as part of a philosophical program – indeed, Quine's view – and it has built into it, as it were, a given logic: *classical* first-order logic. As such, the criterion is at odds with Priest's own approach, in which a paraconsistent logic is advocated. Moreover, Quine's criterion is *not* independent of logic: if the underlying logic of a given theory is changed, the entities that are quantified over change as well. This can be seen in several ways. For example, consider the move to second-order logic (Shapiro, 1991). This logic allows the quantification over properties and relations. And as the result of second-order logic's strong expressive power, several mathematical theories can be better formulated in this setting (in particular, as is well known, arithmetic and analysis are categorical in a second-order context). Because of this, several nominalist proposals, such as those developed in Field (1980) and Hellman (1989) – and which avoid being committed to the existence of mathematical objects (such as numbers) – have adopted second-order logic as part of their nominalization strategies of science and mathematics. The idea is that, by increasing the strength of the logic, it is possible to decrease ontological commitments; that is, in this case, nominalists need not take mathematical objects to exist. Secondly, using paraconsistent logic, it is possible to quantify over certain constructions (such as the Russell set) that are impossible in classical logic, given the latter's identification of inconsistency and triviality.

The point here is that Quine's slogan – to be is to be the value of a variable – can only have any force once a particular logic is admitted. Quine knows that, of course. The problem is that his view assumes a logic (classical first-order logic) that is not the most adequate to deal with inconsistencies in a heuristically fruitful way.

But there is a different way of addressing the inconsistency issue. It is possible to explore the rich representational devices allowed by the use of paraconsistent logic in inconsistent domains, but withholding any claim to the effect that there are "inconsistent objects" in reality. Whether the world is indeed "inconsistent" – assuming there is a sensible formulation of this claim – is something one can be *agnostic* about. Just as empiricists (such as van Fraassen, 1980) are agnostic about the existence of unobservable entities in science, it is possible to be agnostic about the existence of true contradictions in nature. And one of the reasons in support of this claim is an *underdetermination* argument. It can be proved that there is a hierarchy of infinitely many paraconsistent logics, which are called *C*-logics (for the technical details, see da Costa et al., 2007). And these logics can be used to accommodate certain "inconsistent phenomena," whether it is an "inconsistent" reasoning or an "inconsistent" theory (see da Costa, Bueno, & French, 1998). But which of these paraconsistent logics reflects *the* logic of the world?

There is no argument on purely observational grounds that could settle the issue. It is possible, of course, to select one of these logics on *pragmatic* grounds, but these grounds are certainly not enough to establish a substantive claim about the world. For instance, if one of these logics makes the modeling of the inconsistency in question easier, why should this be taken as a reason for this logic to be *true*? Simplicity may well be a sensible criterion to adopt on pragmatic grounds, but to claim that a logic selected on this basis is (likely to be) true is to conflate pragmatic and epistemic considerations. Why should the world conform to our cognitive limitations? Of course, it might well do. However, to establish this claim demands an argument that goes beyond the observable: it requires a metaphysical commitment to the simplicity of reality. And, to a certain extent, this is as "strong" as the claim that there are true contradictions. After all, both make substantial assertions about the world that transcend empirical observation. Both are metaphysical claims.

It turns out that an alternative program of interpretation of inconsistencies can be devised in which no commitment to this kind of metaphysics is required. The idea is first to avoid the claim that inconsistent theories are *true*; they are *partially true* (or *quasi-true*) at best. The notion of partial truth can receive a formal treatment (see da Costa & French, 2003). But for the purposes of this chapter, it suffices to note that a sentence S is partially true if it models adequately only part of a given domain D, not offering a complete description of the latter. (In a precise sense, S is consistent with a true description of D.) With regard to inconsistent theories, all that is needed is to determine their partial truth, since one need not be committed (and probably should not be committed) to their full truth. A formal underpinning to agnosticism with regard to true contradictions can then be provided. By replacing the notion of truth by the weaker notion of partial truth, it is possible to withhold the commitment to "inconsistent objects." After all, these objects are not found in all of the structures under consideration.

Descartes once remarked (in his *Principles of Philosophy*, iv, 204) that: "with regard to those things that our senses cannot perceive, it suffices to explicate how they can be." The same can be said about inconsistent theories. With the notion of partial truth, it is possible to accommodate this point formally, since partial truth is strictly weaker than truth, and does not commit one to anything *beyond* the assertion that certain structures are *possible*, given some paraconsistent logic.

At this point, it is worth revising Quine's slogan about ontological commitment, making explicit its dependence on the underlying logic. Depending on the logic that is adopted, different commitments will emerge. In this way, it becomes clear that this slogan is *not* the only criterion to adjudicate between alternative logics.

However, if someone ends up not being committed to an ontology of actual inconsistent physical objects, is that person committed to inconsistent *mathematical* entities? This depends, of course, on how the relevant mathematical theory is interpreted. Does the inconsistent mathematical theory provide a *true* description of the mathematical "world"? Again, if the description of this "world" is made at best in partially true terms, no commitment to inconsistent mathematical entities is forthcoming. There is, of course, a whole story to be told here, but for the present purposes, it suffices to note that it is possible to provide an entirely syntactic formulation of paraconsistent set theory, in which various inconsistent theories can be embedded, such that the only commitment is to a countable language (see da Costa, Bueno, & French, 2005). Thus, in a certain sense, no special commitment to mathematical objects is required either.

Thus, a "package" can be offered to accommodate inconsistencies. It is characterized by (1) the claim that inconsistent theories are *partially true* at best; (2) an agnosticism with regard to the existence of true contradictions and a nominalism about inconsistent mathematical entities; and (3) a reevaluation of Quine's view about ontological commitment, emphasizing its dependence on the underlying logic.

The striking feature of this "package" is its logical pluralism, on the one hand, and the fact that it is possible to adopt it to make sense of paraconsistent logic with no commitment to actual "inconsistent objects." The logical pluralism derives from point (3) above. Depending on the domain under study, different kinds of logic may be appropriate. For instance, if someone intends to model the constructive features in mathematical reasoning, an intuitionistic logic is the best alternative; if someone is concerned with inconsistent bits of information, the use of a paraconsistent logic is the strategic option. In particular, there is *no* rejection of classical logic here: it has its own domains and applications. To this extent, while dealing with distinct domains, paraconsistent logic and classical logic are complementary rather than rivals. (They become rivals only when applied to the *same* inconsistent domain. The rivalry derives from the fact that they provide different accounts of the logical connectives.)

But in the application of paraconsistent logic, for example to formulate the theory of the Russell set and other inconsistent objects, there is no need to be committed to the existence of "inconsistent entities" – this is the point of claims (1) and (2) above. The resources of paraconsistent logic can be invoked to draw consequences from inconsistent theories without triviality, but with no commitment to the *truth* of the theories in question; they can be at best partially true.

In this way, a non-committal (agnostic) interpretation of paraconsistency can be offered. This interpretation uses paraconsistent logic in a way that does not require the existence of "inconsistent objects." These objects, either mathematical or physical, can be accommodated without requiring an ontology that includes them. In particular, inconsistent mathematical theories can be studied in the context of paraconsistent logic, but it is not necessary to countenance the existence of the entities the theories are taken to be about.

Related chapters: 14 Analytic Philosophy; 26 Philosophy of Science; 31 Deontic Logic and Legal Philosophy; 34 Formal Epistemology and Logic.

References

Abe, J., Torres, C., Torres, G., Nakamatsu, K., & Kondo, M. (2006). Intelligent paraconsistent logic controller and autonomous mobile robot Emmy II. *Lecture Notes in Computer Science*, 4252, 851–7.

Arruda, A. I. (1980). A survey of paraconsistent logic. In A. I. Arruda, R. Chuaqui, & N. C. A. Costa (Eds). *Mathematical logic in Latin America* (pp. 1–41). Amsterdam: North-Holland.

Barnes, J. (Ed.). (1984). *The complete works of Aristotle*, vol. 2. Princeton: Princeton University Press.

Carnielli, W. (2000). Possible-translations semantics for paraconsistent logics. In D. Bates, C. Mortensen, G., Priest, & J.-P. Van Bendegem (Eds). *Frontiers of paraconsistent logic* (pp. 159–72). Philadelphia: Research Studies Press.

Carnielli, W., & Marcos, J. (2002). A taxonomy of C-systems. In W. Carnielli, M. Coniglio, & I. D'Ottaviano (Eds). *Paraconsistency: the logical way to the inconsistent* (pp. 1–94). New York: Marcel Dekker.

da Costa, N. C. A., Bueno, O., & French, S. (1998). Is there a Zande logic? *History and Philosophy of Logic*, 19, 41–54.

da Costa, N. C. A., Bueno, O., & French, S. (2005). A coherence theory of truth. *Manuscrito*, 29, 263–90.

da Costa, N. C. A., & French, S. (2003). *Science and partial truth*. New York: Oxford University Press.

da Costa, N. C. A., & Krause, D. (1997). An intensional Schrödinger logic. *Notre Dame Journal of Formal Logic*, 38, 179–94.

da Costa, N. C. A., Krause, D., & Bueno, O. (2007). Paraconsistent logics and paraconsistency. In D. Jacquette (Ed.). *Philosophy of logic* (pp. 791–911). Amsterdam: Elsevier.

D'Ottaviano, I. (1990). On the development of paraconsistent logic and da Costa's work. *Journal of Non-Classical Logic*, 7, 89–152.

D'Ottaviano, I., & Feitosa, H. (2000). Paraconsistent logics and translations. *Synthese*, 125, 77–95.

Edwards, P. (Ed.). (1972). *Encyclopedia of philosophy* (8 vols.). New York: Macmillan.

Field, H. (1980). *Science without numbers*. Princeton: Princeton University Press.

French, S., & Krause, D. (2006). *Identity in physics*. Oxford: Clarendon Press.

Hellman, G. (1989). *Mathematics without numbers*. Oxford: Clarendon Press.

Jacquette, D. (Ed.). (2006). *A companion to philosophical logic*. Oxford: Blackwell.

Kneale, W., & Kneale, M. (1988). *The development of logic*. Oxford: Clarendon Press.

Krause, D. (1992). On a quasi-set theory. *Notre Dame Journal of Formal Logic*, 33, 402–11.

Meinong, A. (1960). The theory of objects. In R. Chisholm (Ed.). *Realism and the background of phenomenology* (pp. 76–117). Glencoe: The Free Press (Original work published 1904).

Mortensen, C. (1995). *Inconsistent mathematics*. Dordrecht: Kluwer.

Priest, G. (2006a). *In contradiction*. 2nd edn. Oxford: Clarendon Press.

Priest, G. (2006b). *Doubt truth to be a liar*. Oxford: Clarendon Press.

Quine, W. V. (1982). *Methods of logic*. 4th edn. Cambridge, MA: Harvard University Press.

Robinson, A. (1974). *Non-standard analysis*. 2nd edn. Amsterdam: North-Holland.

Shapiro, S. (1991). *Foundations without foundationalism*. Oxford: Clarendon Press.

van Fraassen, B. C. (1980). *The scientific image*. Oxford: Clarendon Press.

Further Reading

Batens, D., Mortensen, C., Priest, G., & Van Bendegem, J.-P. (Eds). (2000). *Frontiers of paraconsistent logic*. Philadelphia: Research Studies Press.

Carnielli, W., Coniglio, M., & D'Ottaviano, I. (Eds). (2002). *Paraconsistency: The logical way to the inconsistent*. New York: Marcel Dekker.

Priest, G. (2002). *Beyond the limits of thought*. 2nd edn. Oxford: Oxford University Press.

Priest, G. (2008). *An introduction to non-classical logic*. 2nd edn. Cambridge: Cambridge University Press.

Priest, G., Beall, J. C., & Armour-Garb, B. (Eds). (2004). *The law of non-contradiction: new philosophical essays*. Oxford: Clarendon Press.

16

Language and Colonization

ILAN STAVANS

Some years ago, I wrote an essay called "Translation and Identity" (2000), in which I tackled the role that the Spanish language played during the conquest of the Americas. I pondered the fact that the arrival of the Iberian conquistadors forced a reconfiguration of almost every aspect of life in the New World: political, religious, sexual, military . . . ; but I expressed dismay that another important aspect, language, was seldom contemplated in textbooks. What kind of verbal negotiation took place as conquistadors, explorers, missionaries, and other Iberians interacted with the native population? What was the reaction of the local population to the arrival of a foreign tongue whose cadence was unlike anything they had heard before in the Aztec and Incan empires? I also discussed the strategies used by interpreters such as Melchorejo and Julianillo, and by mistresses like Doña Marina, who functioned as cultural bridges between both civilizations.

My essay concentrated on the campaign by Hernán Cortés in the capture of Tenochtitlán, narrated by, among others, Bernal Díaz del Castillo in his book *The Conquest of New Spain*. My intention now is to take my disquisition a step further, investigating the role that language played during the almost three centuries that constitute the colonial period in the region: from 1521, when the last of the Aztec rulers, Cuauthémoc, is tortured and dies at Cortés' hands, to the first attempt at independence by Father Miguel Hidalgo y Costilla, in Mexico in 1810. But my scope is comparatively smaller: I want to focus almost exclusively on the sixteenth century, when a heated debate on the purpose and future of the Spanish language in the Americas took place.

In other words, I'm interested in the slow penetration that *el español* (Spanish) made among the pre-Columbian population. How did an entire continent submit to the colonizing language? What types of institutions were established to foster the spread of Spanish? How did linguistic resistance manifest itself? And was there code-switching among the mestizos, ladinos, and cholos?

I don't intend my reflections to be solely devoted to the history of Spanish in the New World. I'm interested in an entire philosophy of life. To what extent did language become a conduit in the propagation of European values? How was it employed in the establishments of a mentality that, in the end, owes as much to the Iberian Peninsula as it does to the aboriginal civilization? What philosophical investigations needed to take place for *el español* to become what Borges once called *el orden de las cosas*, the order of things? My hunt springs from a particular curiosity. For a decade, I've concentrated on the history and development of Spanglish, a hybrid form of communication, mainly in the United States, that results from the crash of two tongues, those of English and Spanish cultures, and, ontologically, of two civilizations, Anglo and Hispanic. There are three strategies Spanglish speakers engage in to make themselves understood: (1) code-switching and code-mixing, (2) simultaneous translation, and (3) the coining of a vast number of new terms that are neither in English nor in Spanish (*wáchale, friquiar, marqueta* . . .). Spoken by millions of people, some of whom are monolingual while others are bilingual (Spanglish and Spanish, Spanglish and English) and even trilingual (Spanglish, English, and Spanish), I've come to the realization that the phenomenon is the result of a complex circumstance. Among them is the astonishing demographic growth of the Hispanic minority in the United States (close to 50 million in 2008), its mobility as a result of temporary jobs, the influence of Spanish-language media in the country, and the effect of federally funded Bilingual Education programs whose resources were equally applied to language instruction in English and Spanish. Standard histories of Spanish, mostly by Iberian authors, ignore this multitudinous manifestation. In his later editions of *Historia de la lengua española*, Rafael Lapesa hardly pays notice. And Antonio Alatorre's influential *Los 1001 años de la lengua española*, written from the perspective of a Latin American linguist and translator (Alatorre was born in Mexico), features a section on Anglicisms in Spanish but doesn't contemplate more fully code-switching, code-mixing, and the emergence of Spanglish as a linguistic alternative.

My central thesis is that Spanglish in present-day America (a term referring not only to the country but the continent as a whole) is a state of mind. Among Spanish speakers nowadays, 88 percent describe Spanish as their first language and the remaining 12 percent have it as a second or third language. In Spain, the number of Catalan, Gallego, and Basque speakers has grown since the death of General Francisco Franco and the arrival of democracy. In the Americas, where more than 90 percent of the total number of Spanish speakers live, almost two dozen aboriginal tongues (Guaraní, Aymara, Quechua, Nahuatl, Tolteca, Zapoteca, Mixteca, etc.) play an influential role.

Talking about language purity in the Hispanic world is preposterous. The varieties of Spanish used in Argentina, Chile, Venezuela, Nicaragua, and Guatemala differ from the type used in Spain and also from one another. Furthermore, internally none of these countries has a unified language; there are regional, class, and ethnic nuances. There used to be a time, at the dawn of the colonial period, when that Iberian variety served as the unchallenged model against which the colonies set their standards. In spite of what the scholars of the *Real Academia Española* and purists in the Spanish-speaking world might believe, that is no longer the case. The Hispanic world has grown to be a decentralized entity in a number of areas, language being a crucial one. Richard Renaud's *Diccionario de hispanoamericanismos* offers a rich assortment of *latinoamericanismos* whose importance is global: *burrito, huevada, ñato*, and *simpatía*. Indeed, the frequent complaints by intellectuals this side of the Atlantic against the paternalistic opinions from Spain about the abuse that Spanish undergoes in Buenos Aires, Bogotá, and Mexico City are more strident today than they used to be. Jorge Luis Borges, in his essay called "Las alarmas del doctor Américo Castro," a review of Castro's *La peculiaridad lingüística rioplatense y su sentido histórico* first published in the magazine *Sur* in 1941 and

231

included in *El lenguaje de Buenos Aires* (Borges, 1968), ridicules the Spanish philologist for thinking that Iberians are more refined in their speech.

In any case, I want to shift my attention now from the present to the past. The early part of the colonial period in the Spanish colonies was also fertile ground for linguistic cross-pollination. At the end of the fifteenth century, Castilian, the language brought by the Spanish conquistadors, along with Gallego and Vasco, and of course Portuguese, entered a landscape brewing with native tongues. Was there an equivalent – keeping the distance between environments – to Bilingual Education, a schooling effort to make native students proficient in the conquering language while advancing their knowledge in their mother tongue? Was there cross-fertilization between Spanish and the various aboriginal tongues? Did it amount to a full-fledged phenomenon with recognizable patterns similar to Spanglish?

Before I start, it is essential that I set the proper context. When Columbus embarked on his first voyage across the Atlantic Ocean, Spanish had recently become a unifying force in the Iberian Peninsula. The Catholic Kings, Ferdinand and Isabella, in a process known as *La Reconquista* (the reconquest), were successful in campaigning against "outside" forces (e.g., Arab civilization) to create a unified nation. The nascent country had existed in a Babel-like state. However, by 1492 as a language Spanish had metamorphosed from a regional dialect to the language of the empire. To a large extent, the force behind that transformation was the lexicographer, humanist, and grammarian Antonio de Nebrija (1444–1522), whose academic career evolved first at Universidad de Salamanca, then at Universidad de Alcalá de Henares. Nebrija was the author of influential philological studies as well as bilingual lexicons, such as *Introductiones latinae* (Latin introductions, 1486), *Diccionario latino-español* (Latin–Spanish dictionary, 1492), *Vocabulario español-latino* (Spanish–Latin vocabulary, ca. 1495), and *Tabla de la diversidad de los días y las horas* (Chronicle of the heterogeneity of the days and hours, 1499). His *Gramática de la lengua castellana* (Grammar of the Spanish tongue), released in 1492, just as the Genoan admiral was organizing his first trip cross the Atlantic Ocean, and as the Catholic monarchs, Isabella and Ferdinand, were ready to expel the Jews from the kingdom, established Spanish as a tool in the effort to homogenize the population.

Nebrija had qualms about the pedagogical approach that Spaniards had in his time toward their linguistic heritage. Latin was a tool for education. The educated elite employed it in intellectual debates. But in his view, Spain wasn't rigorous enough about the proper usage of Latin. Thus, his lifelong objective was to reestablish, through a clear-cut pedagogical method, the glories of the Roman language in the peninsula. He wanted priests, writers, teachers, and students to take it more seriously. Plus, Nebrija was eager to fix the rules of the vulgar tongue, *el castellano* (from the region of Castile). By forcing it to abandon its anarchic syntax, his dream was to make it more elitist, less a jargon of ignoramuses. As a Renaissance humanist, he believed that language is the key to who we are. Thus, he worried that Spanish spelling was unsystematic, proving that those who used the language had a penchant for anarchy. His solution was to append the written language to its oral counterpart. Nebrija's motto might be said to be his overall philosophical approach to culture: "*escribir como pronunciamos y pronunciar como escribimos,*" to write how we speak and to speak how we write. He endorsed the opinion that language must represent nature in a simple, straightforward fashion.

In the prologue to his *Gramática de la lengua castellana* (1492), which he wrote for Queen Isabella, Nebrija analyzed the evolution of language from the Tower of Babel to the fifteenth century. The engine behind his vision of history wasn't science but myth. He pondered the development of pre-biblical tongues, then reflected on Hebrew and Greek, and finally reached the topic of Latin, which, in his eyes, was the highest manifestation of perfection. The prologue – in old Spanish – includes the following passage, which I have hereby translated (the italics are mine):

> Whenever I think to myself, much enlightened Queen, and I place before the eyes the antiquity of all things that were written for our remembrance and memory, I come to one single and truthful conclusion: that *language was always a companion of empire*; and to such a degree it accompanied it, that together they were born, grew up and flourished, and their demise came together later on as well. And leaving aside the very old things we barely have an image and shadow of, which belong to the Assyrians, Indians, Socinians, and Egyptians, and with which one could very well prove that which I'm saying, I come to the more recent ones, and those about which we're certain about, and first comes the one belonging to the Jews. (Nebrija, 1989, p. 109)

For Nebrija, hence, the Spanish language is a companion of empire.

What aboriginal tongues were in use in the Americas as the Spanish conquistadors, explorers, and missionaries arrived? An estimate of the overall population varies enormously from one historical source to another. Some historians believe the number to be between 13 and 18 million; others push for a far larger figure of 180 million. The latter is certainly too inflated but is connected to the decimation of the Indians through warfare, malnutrition, and epidemics. Even if the actual number of people from Alaska to the Pampas is around 45 million, it is still bewildering (no adjective does more justice) that, according to Díaz del Castillo, Cortés was able to vanquish the Aztec Empire with only 200 soldiers. (Other chroniclers put it at 670 but the adjective still holds). Similarly, Francisco Pizarro, in his conquest of Peru, had a battalion of equal size: 200 soldiers against the army of Atahualpa of 80,000. How did such reduced forces end up bringing down two powerful empires? The answer is complicated and needs to be approached regionally. First, there was the belief among the Aztecs that Quetzalcóatl would soon return from his cosmic journey and seeing the bearded Cortés in an iron suit justified their assumption; and second, the Iberians were far more technologically developed in warfare, using gunpowder (imported from China) in their colonial quest. The effect was equally fatal in Peru. In his encounter with Pizarro, Hernando de Soto, and the Spanish invaders, Atahualpa acted complacently. A leading historian of the conquest of Peru once said, sarcastically, that while the Inca emperor was planning to have Pizarro for lunch, Pizarro had him for breakfast.

The Aztec and Inca empires at the time of the Iberian invasion were amorphous entities. They themselves functioned as mechanisms where the forces of integration and separation were shaped by their conquering pursuits. The Aztec empire is a misnomer referring to a collation of three powerful Mesoamerican people: the Mexicas and their allies, the Texcocans, and the Tlacopans. The partnership is known as *la triple alianza*, the triple alliance. Its height took place in the hundred years preceding the arrival of Cortés. Together these three entities are often described as Nahuas because of the language they used: Nahuatl, of the classical sort, to distinguish it from the Nahuatl

233

spoken nowadays in enclaves of the Mexican population. Centralized in Tenochtitlán, the partnership, while consolidated in religious, economic, and political terms (they had a tributary system of government), was loose in linguistic terms.

While Nahuatl was the lingua franca of Mesoamerica (with two varieties, one known as *pipiltin* that was used by the nobles, and *mācehualtin* used by in the lower strata), subaltern tongues were in much demand among the Aztecs. It is estimated that in the early part of the sixteenth century there were approximately 2,000 languages in the Americas, 350 of which were in use in Central Mexico alone, the region covered by the Aztec Empire, in and around the Tehuantepec Isthmus onward to the Pacific coast of Guatemala. Like the Greeks, the Aztecs believed that whenever they conquered a neighboring power, the way to submit them to their culture was through translations of the Aztec code of law into their colonized tongue. That was a job done by *nauatlatos*, which in Nahuatl means interpreter.

Compared to the Aztecs, the Inca empire was larger in size, covering more than 772,000 square miles on the Pacific coast of South America, passing through present-day Ecuador, Peru, Bolivia, Colombia, Chile, and Argentina. Its capital was the city of Cuzco. The method it used to dominate other cultures was through peaceful assimilation. The empire should best be seen as a federation. It was divided into four parts called *Suyus*. The complex structure that resulted from invasions allowed for multiple forms of worship. The central command in Cusco encouraged the sun god Inti but other loyalties coexisted in the Andean region. Quechua, which is spoken by roughly 10 million people today (it is one of the official languages in Bolivia and Peru), was the dominant vehicle of communication, followed, in descending order, by Aymara, Puquina, and scores of other tongues.

The arrival of the Spanish forces dramatically changed things. Top in the order of needs identified by Iberian missionaries was a survey of the hierarchy of aboriginal languages. It needed to be done in order for the Catechism to be taught to the Indian population. But first, that hierarchy established the concept of *lenguas generales*, a term used for describing the most sophisticated and frequently used tongues in the colonies. They were Nahuatl and Quechua (although the Jesuits adopted Guaraní in their missions of Paraguay, Bolivia, Brazil, and Argentina). A debate ensued among educators and the centralized imperial power in Spain as to what approach to take to implant "civilized values."

The survey performed by missionaries convinced many of them that teaching Spanish to the natives was an effort destined for defeat. Aside from the discrepancy in numbers – depending on the source, by the mid-sixteenth century the ratio varies from 1 Spaniard for 20,000 Indians to 1 Spaniard for 50,000 – there were also the spiritual implications. The Royal Crown believed it was in the best interest of everyone to use Spanish as the language of business, education, and religious affairs. Linguist Angel Rosenblat, in his essay "La hispanización de América: el castellano y las lenguas indígenas desde 1492" (1964), quotes an *Orden de enseñanza*, e.g., educational law, promulgated by the Emperor Charles V on June 7, 1550, that established the following:

> As one of the main things we desire for the good of this land is the salvation and instruction and conversion to our Holy Catholic Faith of its natives, and that also they should adopt our policy and good customs; and so, treating the means which could be upheld to

this end, it is apparent that one of them and the most principal would be to give the order so these people may be taught our Castilian language, for with this knowledge, they would be more easily taught the matters of the Holy Gospel and gain all the rest which is suitable for this manner of life. (Rosenblat, 1964, p. 206)

Yet scores of friars and other religious leaders chose to ignore this legislation. Recognizing the scope of their endeavor, they often fell prey to disillusionment. In a response sent to the emperor that same year, included in Mariano Cuevas's *Documentos inéditos del siglo XVI para la historia de México*, Fray Rodrigo de la Cruz wrote:

Your Majesty has ordered that these Indians should learn the language of Castile. That can never be, unless it were something vaguely and badly learnt: we see a Portuguese, where the language of Castile and Portugal is almost the same, spend thirty years in Castile, and never learn it. Then are these people to learn it, when their language is so foreign to ours, with exquisite manners of speaking? It seems to me that Your Majesty should order that all the Indians learn the Mexican language, for in every village today there are many Indians who know it and learn it easily, and a very great number who confess in that language. It is an extremely elegant language, as elegant as any in the world. A grammar and dictionary of it have been written, and many parts of the Holy Scripture have been translated into it; and collections of sermons have been made; and some friars are very great linguists in it. (Cuevas, 1914, p. 159)

Other Catholic friars expounded a similar rejoinder. In his book *Empires of the Word*, historian of languages Nicholas Ostler makes a reference to an epistle drafted in 1551 by Fray Juan de Mansilla, General Commissioner of Guatemala, to Charles V. Mansilla explained:

We are too few to teach the language of Castile to Indians. They do not want to speak it. It would be better to make universal the Mexican language, which is widely current, and they like it, and in it there are written doctrine and sermons and a grammar and a vocabulary. (Ostler, 2005, p. 364)

Resistance to the colonizer's tongue was conducted by the Indians in all sorts of ways. Isolated populations in the Yucatán Peninsula, for example, retained Mayan as their private language, which people learned in childhood at home and in school. In the urban centers where Indians congregated for work, only fundamental linguistic tools were adopted, enough to satisfy the master. Whenever they needed to go further, the Indians would pretend to have a short memory. Or they would claim not to have talent or energy to accomplish the task. Their negative reaction is understandable. The pride in their aboriginal culture made them resist. "El Inca" Garcilaso de la Vega, quoting Blas Valera, tells this anecdote in his *Comentarios reales*, I, vii, 3:

Whence it has come about that many provinces, where when the Spaniards entered Cajamarca the rest of the Indians knew this common language (Quechua), have now forgotten it altogether, because with the end of the world and Empire of the Incas, there was no one to remember something so convenient and necessary for the preaching of the Holy Gospel, because of the widespread oblivion caused by the wars which arose among the Spaniards, and after that for other causes which the evil Satan has sown to prevent

235

such an advantageous regime from being put into operation . . . There are some to whom it appears sensible to oblige all the Indians to learn the Spanish language, so that the priests should not waste their efforts on learning the Indian one. This opinion can leave no-one who hears it in any doubt that it arose from failure of endeavor rather than stupid thinking . . . (de la Vega, 2000, p. 238)

Along the same lines, Fray Domingo Santo Tomás, one of the canonical lexicographers of the colonial period, in his treatise on Quechua, *Arte de la lengua general del Perú* (Art of Peru's general tongue, 1560), argues:

It is of note that the Indians of Peru, before we Christians had come to them, had certain and particular modes of swearing, distinct from ours. They had no assertive oaths, such as "by God" or "by heaven" but only execrations or curses . . . e.g., "if I am not telling the truth, may the sun kill me," they said; *mana checcanta ñiptiy, indi guañuchiuancmancha* . . . Once when I asked a chieftain in a certain province if he was a Christian, he said "I am not yet quite one, but I am making a beginning." I asked him what he knew of being Christian, and he said: "I know how to swear to God, and play cards a bit, and I am beginning to steal." (Rosenblat, 1964, p. 193)

Still, the proselytizing effort unfolded even amidst complaints, pushing along with it the spreading of the Spanish language in the region. Even before the conquest of Tenochtitlán, twenty copies of Nebrija's *Arte de la lengua castellana* (Art of the Castilian tongue) were delivered in Hispaniola in 1513, sent from the governmental Casa de Contratación de Indias. But Nebrija wasn't an educator. What the providers of Spanish in the Americas needed was a large artillery of pedagogical material: dictionaries, grammars (known as *artes*), and textbooks in Spanish became a priority of the Royal Crown. Within the next hundred years, almost all the lexicons published in the Americas were from Spanish to other tongues and not the other way around. That is, the emphasis by the Iberian educators was placed on teaching, not on learning. Also significant is the effort by friars to identify speakers of aboriginal languages and use them to decodify the surviving codices and other material from the pre-Columbian past (see Zamora, 1976).

Ostler, in *Empires of the Word*, profiles this need as appearing "the first time in the world." He suggests that, unlike previous empires at the global stage, no civilization had ever taken upon itself as ambitious a task to educate a large mass of people in the use of its imperial tongue. Previous empires like the Phoenicians, Hebrews, Greeks, Romans, Byzantians, Aztecs, and Incas had used their language as a mechanism of usurpation. To various degrees, they forced their subalterns to adapt to their manners by making them become fluent in the colonizer's parlance. But the Spaniards went a step further: they orchestrated a transoceanic campaign to educate by means of the importation of printed books, which in turn were disseminated by the Catholic missionaries. These educators weren't always Iberian dwellers. Scores of them were creoles and *mestizos*, such as "El Inca" Garcilaso and Fernando de Alva Ixtilxóchitl, a descendant from the Texcoco kings.

The printing press, first established in *Nueva España* (Mexico today) in 1535, fostered the spreading of manuals and translations designed to enable the aboriginal population to become acquainted with the colonizer's *Weltanschauung*. Immediately, there appeared volumes in Nahuatl, Quechua, and other native tongues. For instance, the first book published in what is today Mexico was *Breve y más compendiosa doctrina cristiana* (Brief and more compendious Christian doctrine, 1539), which appeared in *lengua mexicana*, a code name for Nahuatl. It was followed by Fray Alonso de Molina's *Doctrina cristiana breve traducida en lengua mexicana* (Brief Christian doctrine translated in the Mexican tongue, 1546) and Fray Andrés de Olmedo's *Arte de la lengua mexicana* (Art of the Mexican tongue, 1547).

Not only schooling was used in the imposition of Spanish. The Royal Crown understood that the domestic realm was a fundamental habitat wherein to implement language loyalty. At this level, the topics of ethnicity and language become juxtaposed, for racial miscegenation was a desired goal. In 1503 the Royal Court recommended to the governor of Hispaniola that some Christians should marry some Indian women, so that "they may communicate with and teach one another." Clearly, the connection between marriage and schooling was appreciated in the Iberian Peninsula as essential to the spreading of Catholic values. And, indeed, the rise of *mestizaje* that resulted from the crossbreeding of Spaniards and Indians is a byproduct of the sixteenth century.

Arguably the most significant system implemented by the Spanish conquerors was the *encomienda*. A conquistador was granted a trusteeship over a group of aboriginal people. This was a form of economic property. The relationship between the *encomendero* and his Indians served as an obstacle in the process of integration between Europeans and natives. But it also fostered an atmosphere whereby Indians needed to know basic Spanish in order to respond to their requests. The phenomenon of *mestizaje* fostered enough ambivalence for the duality of cultures, Iberian and aboriginal, and gave place to a third option: a local concoction nurturing from these two sources yet also self-sufficient. The formation of a native Spanish was also a byproduct of the same phenomenon. Words like *mezcal*, *hamaca*, *piñata*, *canoa*, *elote*, and *platicar* defined its idiosyncrasy. *El español mejicano* (Mexican Spanish) is a manifestation of the *mestizo* self. Likewise the *cholo* variety used by Peruvians.

Our knowledge of languages in contact allows us to deduce that depending on the location, the Indians engaged in code-switching and code-mixing, forming misconstrued sentences whose syntax alarmed their educators. Regrettably, there's a scarcity of primary sources allowing us to appreciate the verbal negotiations that took place on the private and public realms. Still, the work of chroniclers like Fray Bernardino de Sahagún and Fray Toribio de Benavente "Motolonía" (in Nahuatl, "the poor one") is useful in determining the cross-pollination. Sahagún's *History of the Things of New Spain* (1579), published bilingually in Nahuatl and Spanish, was designed as both an evangelical and ethnographic resource to convey the Aztec past and to explain it to the native population. Motolinía believed that world salvation would ultimately happen in the Americas. His interest in language showcases the transition he hoped the aboriginal population would make to Spanish in order to be redeemed. Interestingly, unlike what happened in the British colonies, where the Old Testament was translated by John Eliot in 1659 (and published in 1663) from Latin into aboriginal languages, the project of rendering the biblical text in Nahuatl and Quechua wasn't part of the agenda of the Royal Crown. Such endeavor was controversial in the Holy Office of the Inquisition, where translation was judged to be a heretical act. Even having Hebrew and Latin transferred to Spanish provoked strong reactions (see Stavans, 2004).

237

I'm fascinated by this question: Was there an equivalent of Spanglish, a hybrid tongue mixing Spanish and the *lenguas generales* (general tongues) or other native parlances? I have little doubt about it. Where two clearly defined linguistic groups come into intense contact for an extended period of time, a third verbal option is born among young, inexperienced speakers. But the missionaries disregarded the evidence because for them the in-between vehicle of communication was an abomination, neither here nor there and, hence, unworthy of attention. Whenever a Nahuatl speaker faced the problem of not knowing a Spanish word, he would insert a Nahuatl noun and then use a modifier. A pirate was described as an *acalco tenamoyani*, "one who robs people on a boat." Similarly, the law became *tlamelahuacachihualiztli*, "doing things straight." The linguistic negotiation became even more intense. In their native Nahuatl, speakers incorporated Spanish words. A *caja* was a wooden chest, *puerta* became a swinging door, and a church was a *santa iglesia*. Quechua also engaged in similar exercises. Furthermore, "El Inca" Garcilaso described the way the Indian population lived in one language but communicated in another. He offers samples of Quechua terms incorporated into *el español* and vice versa (Sokolow, 2003, p. 132).

Did such back-and-forths result in a perfectly delineated third option? It's hard to say. More evidence is needed to assert such a claim. However, an adaptation of the Iberian mind to the landscape is already evident in translations done in the Americas, which often adapted material to a regional setting for the benefit of the reader. In 1579, a rendition into Nahuatl of a Latin version of Aesop's fables was published. In the Latin original, it says that "a lion once heard a frog croaking; he turned toward the noise thinking it was some great beast; when he saw the frog by the pond he went up and squashed it." In Nahuatl, it reads: "A jaguar once heard a frog, screaming and croaking a great deal. The jaguar was frightened and thought that it was a large animal. To quiet his heart, he looked around him in all directions. When he came to the water's edge, the jaguar was very angry and ashamed of being frightened by such a small creature" (Sokolow, 2003, pp. 133–4).

Should Spanish then be seen as a great equalizer during the colonial period in the Americas? Only to a certain extent. It enabled Catholicism to set roots. Yet its propagation wasn't achieved without numerous obstacles. The defiance and lack of enthusiasm of the natives generated dismay in the Royal Crown, which responded by changing its views as it went along and depending on who was in power. That the aboriginal population was reluctant to become fluent in Spanish repeatedly frustrated legislators. In 1578, King Philip II ordered that religious educators appointed to teach Indians should have some knowledge of their tongue, at the very least one of the *lenguas generales*. And in 1560, he established chairs in indigenous languages in Mexico City and Lima, announcing that "knowledge of the general language of the Indians is essential for the explanation and teaching of Christian doctrine."

As mentioned before, in his classic *Historia de la lengua española*, first published in 1942 (its eleventh edition appeared in 1981, a decade before the author's death), Rafael Lapesa devoted the last section of a chapter entitled "*El español actual*" to the Spanish used in the Americas. Lapesa's succinct appreciation doesn't allow a complete picture of the challenge faced by the regiment of Iberian lexicographers at the outset of the colonial period. Nor does it explain the debate between *el español* and the *lenguas generales*. This isn't unique. A wide-ranging historical analysis of the disputes of the time is essential for a consideration of linguistic identity in the Americas. Especially now that the explorations surrounding Spanglish in the United States have shed light onto the linguistic cross-fertilization of a large minority population, it is crucial to recognize the path that Spanish took on its search for continental domination. How is it that from a tongue of a minuscule army, it metamorphosed during the so-called Age of Independence into the common language of millions of people? It is estimated that in 1810, the year marking the first attempt at secession from Spain, there were 6.7 million inhabitants in the Americas. Approximately 45 percent of them (more than 3 million) were either Spaniards or *mestizos* for whom Spanish was their first language.

By the beginning of the seventeenth century, the social, political, and linguistic landscape in the Americas had been transformed. When Shakespeare staged his play *The Tempest* in 1611, set in a Caribbean island (i.e., Carib), it was widespread know-ledge that the European languages were the instrument of control in the colonies. Shakespeare has Caliban complain to Prospero (act I, scene 2): "You taught me langu-age, and my profit on't Is, I know how to curse." Yet Spanish didn't quite take hold in a homogenized manner throughout the colonies, at least not to the degree the colonizers were wishing for. The *lenguas generales* didn't altogether disappear. On the contrary, literature in Nahuatl, Quechua, Aymara, and other tongues flourished in the form of religious poetry and plays (known as *autos sacramentales*). The fact that they are still in use is proof of the duality of the endeavor. But Spanish, of course, is the true success story: with more than 400 million speakers today, it's the third most popular language in the world after Mandarin and English.

Related chapters: 1 Pre-Columbian Philosophies; 2 The Rights of the American Indians; 22 Philosophy, Postcoloniality, and Postmodernity; 24 Latin American Philosophy.

References

Alatorre, A. (2002). *Los 1001 años de la lengua española*. Mexico: Fondo de Cultura Económica.

Borges, J. L. (1968). *El lenguaje de Buenos Aires*. Buenos Aires: Emecé.

Castro, A. (1941). *La peculiaridad lingüística rioplatense y su sentido histórico*. Buenos Aires: Losada.

Cuevas, M. (1914). *Documentos inéditos del siglo XVI para la historia de México*. México: Editorial Porrúa.

Lapesa, R. (1942). *Historia de la lengua española*. Madrid: Gredos.

de Nebrija, A. (1989). *Gramática de la lengua castellana*. Madrid: Centro de Estudios Ramón Areces (Original work 1492).

Ostler, N. (2005). *Empires of the word*. New York: HarperCollins.

Renaud, R. (1997). *Diccionario de hispanoamericanismos*. Madrid: Cátedra.

Rosenblat, A. (1964). La hispanización de América: el castellano y las lenguas indígenas desde 1492. In *Presente y futuro de la lengua española: Actas de la Asamblea de Filología del I Congreso de Instituciones Hispánicas* (pp. 189–216). Madrid: Ediciones Cultura Hispánica.

Sokolow, J. A. (2003). *The great encounter: native peoples and European settlers in the Americas, 1492–1800*. New York: M.E. Sharpe.

Stavans, I. (2000). Translation and identity. In *The essential Ilan Stavans* (pp. 231–40). New York and London: Routledge.

239

Stavans, I. (2004). *"La imaginación restaurada,"* *El español en el mundo* (pp. 107–25). Barcelona: Círculo de Lectores.

de la Vega, "El Inca" Garcilaso. (2000). In M. Serna (Ed.). *Comentarios reales.* Madrid: Castalia.

Zamora, J. C. (1976). *Indigenismos en la lengua de los conquistadores.* Río Piedras, Puerto Rico: Editorial Universitaria de Puerto Rico.

240

17

Ethnic-Group Terms

SUSANA NUCCETELLI AND RODERICK STEWART

Latin Americans and their descendants abroad have often thought about their identity as an ethnic group. In connection with this, a number of Latin American philosophers and social scientists working in the United States have independently questioned
which term, if any, is adequate for reference (and self-reference) to that group. In their
attempt to come up with correct answers, they have developed three clearly identifiable views. One is "nihilism," a view sometimes favored by social scientists, according
to which there is no good reason justifying the use of any ethnic-group term – not even
those currently popular in the United States such as 'Hispanic,' and 'Latino.' But
nihilism is not widely spread among Latin American philosophers, who have offered
several arguments for one or the other of these common terms. As we shall see, proponents of this view have brought into the debate some political and moral arguments
that will be discussed here. But there is also an alternative view according to which it
doesn't really matter which terms are used provided that they lack morally objectionable connotations.

Not surprisingly, the issues at stake in these debates are of interest not only to Latin
Americans and their descendants abroad, but more generally to anyone concerned with
semantic and pragmatic analyses of terms for groups of people, including ethnic-,
racial-, nationality-, and religious-group terms. By raising the issues about ethnic-group
terms that will concern us here, Latin American philosophers can be said to have made
an important contribution to the understanding of a sort of term largely ignored in traditional philosophical semantics and political philosophy. We'll first consider the issue
of whether ethnic-group terms should be considered names or predicates. Next, we'll
turn to their semantic properties, reconstructing some of the theories on their meaning and denotation recently advanced by Latin American philosophers. Finally we'll
look closely at normative issues involving the use of ethnic-group terms, and a recent
controversy about the use of 'Hispanics' and 'Latinos' that will bring into consideration the political and moral reasons mentioned above.

Names or Predicates?

What's the contribution an ethnic-group term makes to the proposition in which it occurs?
Is it that of a name or of a predicate? These questions concern syntax and logical form.

Any attempt to answer them must examine both the prevalent view and evidence of the role of such terms in sentences ordinarily uttered by members of a speech community. It is possible that evidence points to their being always proper names (i.e., singular terms) or always predicates (i.e., general terms). But it could also point to their being sometimes proper names and other times predicates. The resulting logical form of the sentences containing those terms would therefore vary accordingly.

Let's first consider the most common view: viz., the assumption that ethnic-group terms are proper names. Is there any reason for this assumption? One such reason stems from ordinary parlance, where that's precisely what they are called – though sometimes they are also referred to as 'labels' (see, for example, Schmidt, 2003). Let's define a 'default position' as the view that takes literally the ordinary parlance of ethnic-group terms as "names." But note that it is not difficult to find this position beyond ordinary parlance, for it is also pervasive in the writings of academics, including some Latin American philosophers (e.g., Gracia, 2000, 2008; Alcoff, 2005) and social scientists (e.g., Gimenez, 1989; Oboler, 1992). Since regarding them as *names* is not the only option for this sort of term, we need reasons backing up the default position beyond a mere appeal to ordinary parlance. After all, as we show below, there are a number of objections facing that position.

But before turning to such objections, let's look closely at a philosophical reason for the default position that has been brought into the discussion by Susana Nuccetelli (2004): namely, that Gottlob Frege, one of the founders of contemporary philosophical semantics, held a view consistent with the default position (1952, p. 45). For, according to Frege, the logical form of the proposition expressed by the sentence, 'The Turk besieged Vienna,' stands in sharp contrast with the logical form of the proposition expressed by sentences such as, 'The horse is a four-legged animal.' Of the two, Frege contends, it is only the former that features a singular term. In fact, he claims that 'Turk' is the *name of a people*, not, as some might expect, a quantified predicate at all. Now, although it is true that 'Turk' is a nationality term, Frege's conclusion, if well supported, could easily be extended to apply to terms of the kind that concern us here.

Frege's argument, however, is far from unassailable. Nuccetelli argues that there are several reasons for thinking that ethnic-group terms should instead be treated as having the function of predicates or general terms. First, in the proposition expressed by 'The elephant crossed the Alps,' the term 'elephant' appears to have the logical function of a predicate, and the example is relevantly analogous to Frege's sentence containing 'Turk.' But if so, then there are grounds for maintaining that each of these terms should be understood as existentially quantified predicates. Furthermore, such a conclusion would also be supported by certain grammatical features of ethnic-group terms. For one thing, they are usually considered in the same category with count nouns (e.g., 'horse,' 'lemon,' 'elm') which, unlike other common nouns (mass terms such as 'water,' 'sodium,' and 'nicotine'), divide their reference. And unlike proper names, ethnic-group terms can be genuinely predicated of individuals. Finally, ethnic-group terms admit genuine singular/plural variations; they may occur in generalizations with 'all,' 'most,' 'a few,' and other quantifiers; they can form nouns phrases preceded by 'that,' 'these,' 'the,' and other determiners, and have adjectival forms. No singular term commonly shows such grammatical features. If these and other reasons offered by Nuccetelli are sound, then ethnic-group terms turn out to be predicates.

Given that it is controversial whether ethnic-group terms are names or predicates, to avoid begging the question here we have adopted for them the neutral expression "ethnic-group *terms*," which does not commit us to their being either names or predicates. At the same time, since the question would be begged by anyone advocating a *literalist* construal of the default position, should we say that Jorge Gracia's (2000) and Linda Alcoff's (2005) talk of "ethnic names" commits this fallacy? Not necessarily, for charity in interpretation recommends that we interpret their talk as being non-technical. On our view, that talk is fine provided it is cashed out as metaphorical or figurative – parallel in this respect to saying that the sun rises and sets.

The Semantics of Ethnic-Group Terms

Recent work in Latin American philosophy features two seemingly incompatible accounts of the semantic properties of ethnic-group terms. They illustrate one or the other of two well-known semantic theories of the building blocks of propositions: on the one hand, a broadly Fregean view, often referred to as "description theory," which includes the so-called cluster theory; and on the other hand, a broadly Millean view, here called "referentialism," which includes at least a causal account of the reference of proper names and natural-kind terms. Gracia (2000, 2008) represents what we regard as a description theory of ethnic-group terms, while Nuccetelli (2002, 2004) exemplifies referentialism about those terms. Before looking closely at the details of their views, the following clarification point is in order: Gracia and Nuccetelli both agree that, by contrast with empty terms such as 'Lilliputian,' 'Atlantian,' and 'Hobbit,' the sorts of word in need of an account are non-empty terms such as 'Hispanic' and 'Latino.' Of course, any correct account of the semantic properties of these, by extension, would be of help in accounting for the properties of other genuine ethnic-group terms. Besides this point, the offered accounts run along seemingly opposite lines. We shall now take up each of them in turn.

In Gracia's work (2000, 2008), the semantic issues of concern arise in connection with a discussion of which, if any, should be the ethnic-group term used for reference (and self-reference) to Latin Americans, their descendants abroad, and the Iberians. Against those who reject the adoption of any ethnic-group term and those who favor 'Latino' (more on both views later), Gracia argues that adequate terms such as 'Hispanic' could in fact have some desirable consequences for the designated group of people: e.g., they could bring empowerment and pride to them, and even help them overcoming relations of dependence (2000, chapter 3). Claims of this sort are, of course, pragmatic since they bring into the discussion questions about the use of ethnic-group terms. We shall have more to say about them later. But in the course of substantiating those claims, Gracia outlines an account of the meaning and denotation of those terms that we regard as sympathetic to the description theory. In fact, it exemplifies one of its well-known versions, the so-called cluster theory. Any such theory holds two theses: (1) that ethnic-group terms have meanings, cashed out as conceptions of the denoted groups in the minds of competent users of those terms, and (2) that the denotation of any genuine ethnic-group terms depends on the meanings that speakers associate with the denoted groups.

243

It is not difficult to show that Gracia does hold that ethnic-group terms have meanings. For example, in some remarks about questions involving a controversy with Alcoff in the late 1990s (more on this later), he maintains,

> [B]oth 'Latino' and 'Hispanic' are helpful when thinking about various dimensions of the Latino experience, because each brings out something the other misses and therefore helps to increase our understanding. *'Latino' connotes the marginal and colonial situation of Latinos, whereas 'Hispanic' brings out the historical and cultural connections between Iberia and Latin America. Both are helpful for understanding who we are.* (Our emphasis, 2008, p. 73)

Other passages suggest, however, that Gracia holds thesis (1), that ethnic-group terms have meanings, in conjunction with thesis (2), that those meanings are what determine their denotations. In fact, Gracia takes the correct semantics for ethnic-group terms to run along lines parallel to a description theory of ordinary proper name such as 'Socrates': in both cases, the correct semantic account rest on theses (1) and (2). As a result, on this view success in communication by means of such terms must be contingent upon the availability of certain descriptions to those who use them. "We learn who is called 'Socrates,'" Gracia writes, "learning that he is the main speaker in the Symposium as well as Plato's teacher and that he was married to a scold. Thanks to these descriptions we are able to use the name 'Socrates' effectively in communication" (2008, p. 70).

A further motivation for the cluster theory of ethnic-group terms seems to stem from the observation that users of 'Hispanic' may have in mind different properties of the designated group. Gracia is committed to this claim, since according to him a virtue of his theory is that it avoids essentialism – for it denies the existence of a single property Hispanics have in common. (Note that sharing a past marked by certain historical events, something upheld by Gracia, may turn out to be an essential property of Hispanics after all.) In any case, a description theorist maintaining that there is no single property of members of this group must allow for more than one description or meaning that speakers associate with the denotation of an ethnic-group term. It must, then, be possible that different users of the term 'Hispanic' have in mind different conceptions of the denoted group. And this is consistent with Gracia's appeal to a family of resemblance in the context of discussing the identity of Hispanics as a group (for more on the topic, see Lawrence Blum's chapter in this volume).

The cluster theory of ethnic-group terms faces, however, a number of difficulties. For one thing, given this theory and the claim that those denoted by any term such as 'Hispanic' have no single property in common, ordinary communication by means of that term would often fail. This would be the case because the cluster theory requires for success in communication by means of any ethnic-group term that speakers have at least one description they all associate with the denoted ethnic group. But the evidence from ordinary communication by means of such terms points to success rather than failure even in cases where no common conception seems at work (for more on this objection, see Nuccetelli, 2001).

In addition, the description theory rests on the thesis that it is the speakers' conception of an ethnic group that determines the property picked out by their tokens of the corresponding ethnic-group term. This thesis has the implausible consequence that whenever the speakers' only conception of the property denoted by an ethnic-group term is true, not of all and only the members of the intended group, but of the members of some other group, then the denotation of their tokens of the corresponding ethnic-group term would be the property of belonging to the other group. Consider Nuccetelli's (2001) thought experiment: First, imagine speakers whose only conception of Spaniards is that of being the first Europeans who arrived by sea to the New World. Now, when those speakers utter sentences containing the word, 'Spaniard,' given the description theory, they would be talking not about Spaniards but the Norsemen – which is implausible. Moreover, this line of Kripkean objection can also be run for cases involving speakers who have erroneous and even opposite ways of thinking about the property of belonging to certain ethnic groups. Yet none of these objections is conclusive, since each rests on intuitions about certain scenarios that description theorists like Gracia may deny.

On the other hand, in the absence of convincing counterarguments for dismissing such intuitions, the above objections appear to provide indirect support for a rival view of the semantic features of ethnic-group terms – the causal theory. In her 2004 work, Nuccetelli offers a causal theory of the reference of those terms that departs from the strong referentialism she proposed in 2001. She regards her new version of referentialism as falling short of maintaining that such terms are rigid designators or directly referential, and as holding instead that their semantic properties are in many respects similar to those of natural-kind terms. If so, a causal account of the latter that is weaker than, but broadly inspired by the accounts developed by Kripke and Putnam in the 1970s for natural-kind terms could be adapted to account for the semantic properties of ethnic-group terms.

By contrast with the description theory, the causal account of ethnic-group terms appears to face no problem in accommodating cases of successful communication involving speakers who have no common conception of the property picked out by their tokens of 'Hispanic,' 'Latino,' and the like. Referentialists could agree that descriptions or conceptions of the denotation of those terms in the speakers' minds play an initial role in the grounding of the extension of those terms, even when they would insist that such descriptions fall short of determining their denotation. Nuccetelli (2001) appeals to a historical case to illustrate the role of descriptions and misdescriptions in grounding the denotation of an ethnic-group term. History has it that in the sixteenth century some Spaniards exploring South America saw oversize footprints of a people and dubbed them 'Patagones,' which in the vernacular meant *people with giant feet*. That was, of course, a false conception of the so-called Tehuelches, since what the Spaniards saw were in fact footprints of their feet wrapped in fur. Yet arguably that description grounded the extension of 'Patagones,' a term that nonetheless caught on among other speakers to refer to the Tehuelches (and continued to do so centuries after the associated description was proven false). Nuccetelli argues that cases of this sort appear analogous to situations involving natural-kind terms that are successfully used in speech communities even when the speakers' conceptions of the properties denoted by their tokens is incomplete or seriously flawed. Consider, for example, 'water' or 'whale,' each successfully used in communication before the rise of modern chemistry and biology – that is, before anyone could have had what we now regard as an accurate conception of the nature of the substance or species denoted by tokens of those terms.

245

This causal theory is compatible with the fact that future speakers may come to have other descriptions associated with the denotation of those terms.

But how far can Nuccetelli take the analogy between ethnic general terms and natural kind terms? In contrast with natural-kind terms, speakers introducing ethnic-group terms seem to have *no* causal contact with anything "essential" about all and only the members of a certain ethnic group – as demonstrated by countless ethnic groups who include diverse peoples. If the causal account of ethnic-group terms is vulnerable to this objection, that would clearly count as an indirect reason for Gracia's alternative theory of those terms. To meet this objection and to accommodate the fact that no essential property seems to underlie ethnic groups, Nuccetelli defends her causal theory by appealing to external factors involved in the original "baptismal" event. Recall that, for the causal theory, it is the causal contact with the denoted peoples during the introduction of those terms that grounds their denotation. The speakers' deference to a referential usage going back to the interaction of initial users of the term with those people accounts for later uses of them with the same semantic features. This is compatible with an externalist view of those terms according to which: (1) members of ethnic groups share a complex external property determined by a certain *history* of relations within their own group, with others, and with the environment; (2) such shared relations are responsible for the distinguishing traits of the ethnic group; and (3) the content of sentences containing ethnic-group terms is in some ways dependent on those historical relations. Thus supplemented, the causal account concedes that descriptions may have the role in fixing the reference when an ethnic-group term is introduced. But the account is still incompatible with a description theory since it is only the latter theory that makes the reference of such terms contingent upon descriptions in the speakers' minds. Note, however, the following consequence of the causal account: as far as semantics is concerned (as distinguished from, e.g., pragmatics), it doesn't really matter which terms are used to secure reference for a certain ethnic group – though in order to reject the use of an established term, the theorist may include pragmatic considerations and invoke practical and moral grounds.

Nihilism about Ethnic-Group Terms

Is there any good reason justifying the use of 'Hispanic,' 'Latinos,' and the like? Let us call 'nihilism' the view that there is no such reason. Nihilism of this sort makes two claims, one metaphysical and the other normative. The former amounts to a form of anti-realism about ethnic groups, the latter to the injunction that no ethnic-group terms should be used. In connection with the metaphysical claim, nihilists acknowledge the existence of nationality groups such as Venezuelans, Puerto Rican, Mexican, and so on, but they maintain that there is no mind- or language-independent group that could be the denotation of 'Hispanic' or 'Latino.' In addition, since nihilists think that ethnic-group terms misclassify groups of people, and have been used for evil purposes such as control and stereotyping, therefore, it is not only practically but also morally wrong to use them. If so, then there are no good reasons justifying their use. As noted before, although nihilist positions are not common in Latin American philosophy, they are often held in Latin American studies and social science (Gimenez, 1989; Oboler, 1992;

Schmidt, 2003). By contrast, nihilism is not at all uncommon in other branches of philosophy, where it is sometimes called 'irrationalism.'

Thus construed, nihilism is often found among social scientists (e.g., Gimenez, 1989) and rests on a common extended argument. First, nihilists make the universal generalization that no good reason has yet been offered justifying the adoption of any term for Latin Americans and their descendants in other parts of the world. After all, available terms proposed to pick out all and only the members of these groups have so far been too broad, too narrow, or too broad and too narrow. Besides, ethnic-group terms have commonly been used for social manipulation and other evil purposes. Given these considerations, as far as nihilists are concerned, the use of any term for Latin Americans and their descendants in other parts of the world is unjustified.

It is not difficult to argue that no available ethnic-group term (i.e., neither 'Hispanics,' 'Latinos,' nor 'Latin Americans') has associated descriptive meanings that are true of all and only the members of the group thus designated. After all, there is nothing they all have in common such as a geographical location, political style, language, culture, or race (Oboler, 1992; Nuccetelli, 2001). Consider 'Hispanics': the associated description, if construed literally, picks out people related in some fundamental ways to Hispania, an Ancient Roman territory in what is now Spain and Portugal. This is clearly too narrow, since it excludes, for instance, indigenous peoples – and it is also too broad, since it includes Europeans (viz., the Spaniards and Portuguese). But the associated description of 'Latino,' being people related in some fundamental ways to Latin countries, is not better off since it is clearly too broad – so as to include, when taken literally, for instance, the Italians – and also too narrow – given that it leaves out not only the indigenous peoples but also Latin Americans of non-Latin descent. Finally, 'Latin Americans' presents similar problems: *literally* speaking, it picks out for example French Canadians, while obviously excluding actual members of the group – e.g., Latin Americans of African descent.

So nihilists might have a point here. Besides, there might be social and moral reasons for rejecting the use of such terms. For example, Latin Americans may resent being called 'Hispanics' or 'Ibero-Americans': why should the victims of colonialism agree with words for reference and self-reference that associate them with their former oppressors? Moreover, as noted by Gracia (2000), those terms are often associated with bad traits of character or impoverishment such as laziness, shiftlessness, lack of education, etc. And similar moral grounds would undermine the acceptance of any other ethnic term. Now nihilists are in a position to conclude that, in the absence of a reason outweighing these considerations (which again, are not difficult to find in the literature of the social sciences), their view is plausible.

Note that, if sound, the nihilist argument would undermine not only some proposals for the adoption of one term over another ('Hispanic' for Gracia and 'Latino' for Alcoff), but also the view that any term could be adopted as long as it is not a slur deemed offensive by the group to which the term is applied (Nuccetelli). But the nihilist argument is far from being sound. For one thing, it assumes descriptivism about ethnic-group terms, since it holds that it is the descriptions associated by speakers with the referent of any such term that fails constantly to be true of all and only those designated by the term (thus rendering it susceptible to the criticism that it is either too broad, too narrow, or too broad and narrow). But more importantly, as we saw, a crucial premise

247

in the nihilist argument is a universal generalization to the effect that no good reason has yet been offered justifying the adoption of any term for Latin Americans and their descendants in other parts of the world. None of the considerations so far adduced by nihilists could back up this premise. Descriptivism need not, after all, equate associated descriptions with literal meaning at the "baptismal" origin of words. Besides, even when it is true that some such terms have morally objectionable connotations, this fails to entail that *all* terms of that sort do have them.

Moreover, the use of ethnic-group terms is a common practice that, as we shall now see, may be well supported. Gracia (2000) has in fact pointed out that the adoption of an ethnic-group term could have some desirable consequences such as empowerment, pride, and liberation from relations of dependence (see, e.g., chapter 3). But here there is logical space for nihilists to reply that the practice of labeling groups of people has often been an essential tool in notorious cases of ethnic discrimination and racism. There are grounds for an open-ended discussion about whether adoption of those terms really help or hurt those denoted by them. On our view, questions of this sort cannot be settled by philosophical argument alone, since they are empirical. If we are right, philosophers can merely hope that a mature social science will at some point contribute to resolving those questions. In any case, the above argument against nihilism suggests that more reasons are needed to back up that position.

The Political Pragmatics of Ethnic-Group Terms

Many of us grow up in communities with all sorts of traffic signs. Some are the thin rectangular green ones with white lettering on every street corner that tell us the name of some street. Others (especially the yellow triangular and red octagonal ones) are intended to constrain how, where, when, and in which direction we may drive or park. Most of us grow up accepting these differences in "signage" as a more or less reasonable way of finding our ways about town, one that minimizes the risks of collisions and maximizes our way-finding efficiency. But suppose that, as we grow up, we start to notice that this signage system is not quite the same in all neighborhoods. For example, we discover that, *historically*, traffic gets routed to and around various neighborhoods; or that only representatives of some neighborhoods get to decide which names to give the streets. Or, we come to see that, *historically*, decisions about "signage" are correlated with more basic *political* decisions about which neighborhoods get their streets repaired, widened, upgraded more frequently, and, further, how these decisions in turn are tied to decisions about sewage systems, the placement of local schools, and eventually to what sorts of stores we have available locally. When we ask about all these differences, we are told not to be impatient, that changing such complex systems takes time. Occasionally, we might even be encouraged by our city government to change the *name* of one of the main streets in our neighborhood to honor a beloved neighborhood activist. But we must still be patient about repairing the streets, sewers, and school buildings. Not unreasonably, some of us start to suspect that not all neighborhoods are equal here, and that our problematic signage system is just the tip of some iceberg.

The previous parable might serve as a way to begin to think about a recent and important debate between Gracia and Alcoff on the appropriateness of various ethnic-group terms for the people of Latin America and their descendants abroad. Both of these philosophers take seriously the interplay of history and politics in how ethnic-group terms are used and come into being. Both of them think that with the proper account of such terms we can reveal problematic features of our social world that would otherwise be invisible and not receive their due attention.

Gracia (2001) argues for a "familial-historical" view of ethnicity and ethnic-group terms that attempts to avoid essentialism about such groups, to allow for naturally vague or indeterminate boundaries in defining them, and to reject any ideas of internal homogeneity and purity. (See also Lawrence Blum's chapter in this volume for more analysis of Gracia's position, especially as it is discussed in Gracia [2005] and Alcoff [2006].) It is also fair to say that Gracia adopts a realist view of ethnic groups themselves, thus rejecting any form of social constructivism, nominalism, and anti-realism (including nihilism). On the basis of a Wittgensteinian, "family-resemblance" model, Gracia then makes a case that the term 'Hispanic,' for now, is the more adequate descriptive and explanatory term for the new historical family that was formed as a result of the collision of cultures between (among others) Iberians, Africans, and New World indigenous peoples after 1492, an ethnic group whose constitution is still ongoing and open-ended. On Gracia's view, members of the group Hispanics need share no single similarity (such as language, religion, race, class, ancestry, nationality) other than being part of such historical developments.

Note that given the familial account of 'Hispanic,' the term ranges at the very least over Hispanics/Latinos in Latin America, the United States, and the Iberian Peninsula. At the same time, the account aims to accommodate the fact that, like members of any actual family, one individual can have overlapping memberships in other groups: e.g., she could be Hispanic while also Catalan, Argentine, Mexican, *criolla* (person of Spanish ancestry born in Latin America), Mexican American, *indígena*, Pentecostal, an immigrant to Australia, a veteran of WWII, etc. Individuals reasonably *not* included in this historical web could include those who existed in Iberia, Africa, or the Western hemisphere *before* 1492, or Filipinos *after* the Spanish–American war. There can also be borderline cases: Gracia cites the cases of Angola and Mozambique in Africa and Goa in India, whose relationships to Portuguese colonial and postcolonial language and culture are more blurred. On this historical account, what matters first and foremost for preferring one ethnic-group term over another is the *web of historical relations* captured by the term. As fallible historians, we want terms that can function adequately in our explanations and descriptions of the denoted group (let's keep in mind here that Gracia's first academic training was as a historian). On this historical account, a consensus about such a term could put those denoted by it in a better position to address current issues of "identity politics" than rival views.

Indeed, Gracia (2000, chapter 3) takes on some of these political questions. He argues that using ethnic-group terms can be beneficial if three conditions are met: if the group in question does its own naming and defining (including acts of re-signifying as in the Black Power movement); if the resulting definitions are positive, e.g., by avoiding (historical) stereotypes; and if the definitions are not overly narrow or rigid (e.g., tied only to religion, language, class, culture, or ancestry). Given his familial-historical theory and these three conditions, Gracia argues against using 'Latinos/as' (2000, chapter 1) as the preferred ethnic-group term for the people he has in mind. First, often the use

249

of 'Latinos/as' is intended *politically* to mark off those who were the victims of Iberian oppressors. Gracia points out, however, that such a gesture would also exclude the descendants of Iberians (*criollos* and non-*criollos*) who have lived in Latin America for centuries and thus leave out people who need to be referred to in such a history. Second, why should the European origin of 'Latinos/as' (especially by French colonial administrators) continue to be privileged in our current acts of political naming over Amerindian or indigenous terms? Third, 'Latinos/as' can also be read as too broad a designation since one could just as well argue on historical grounds that it designates anyone whose origins go back to Rome and the people of Latium (which could conceivably include speakers of all Romance languages. See discussion above). Moreover, in the Middle Ages, those who used the Latin language were contrasted with the Muslims and Jews who did not. Depending on the historical web selected here, then, 'Latinos/as' could easily be attached to a history of oppressors. While no single group term will capture all possible historical webs and contexts, Gracia (2000) concludes that for now 'Hispanic' does the best overall job historically and politically for the "identity politics" that currently confronts a wide range of diverse people linked to the Americas today. More recently, Gracia (2008) has addressed again the "politics" of ethnic-group terms and argued against Alcoff's (2005) proposal of replacing 'Hispanic' with 'Latino' on the basis of political considerations (more below). On his latest view, "both 'Latino' and 'Hispanic' are helpful when thinking about various dimensions of the Latino experience, because each brings out something the other misses and therefore helps to increase our understanding. 'Latino' connotes the marginal and colonial situation of Latinos, whereas 'Hispanic' brings out the historical and cultural connections between Iberia and Latin America" (2008, p. 73).

In response to Gracia (2000), Alcoff (2005) advocates the use of 'Latino' on the basis of her close scrutiny of the relationship between historical context and politics when dealing with ethnicity in the Americas. First, Alcoff is concerned that Gracia's account is too metaphysical, in that it all too easily separates the *semantic-epistemic tasks* of securing the reference and descriptive adequacy of ethnic-group terms through careful historiography from the *political task* of establishing solidarity and identity in marginalized groups. Alcoff argues that because there is always more than one story that can be told that gels with the lived experiences of marginalized groups, any criteria of descriptive adequacy will under-determine the question of terms. For Alcoff, then, any historical account (no matter how neutral it tries to be as history) will end up privileging some political vision of group identity at the expense of some other vision. This includes Gracia's familial-historical account.

Building on this first point, Alcoff then argues that Gracia's particular historical account overemphasizes the original encounter between peoples in the New World and thereby pays insufficient attention to lived experiences of more recent colonial and post-colonial relations that have structured the Western hemisphere. If this is the case, then Gracia's account turns out to be not only descriptively and explanatorily incomplete, but politically too naïve. In contrast, then, to Gracia's proposal to take 1492 as the key historical marker, Alcoff argues that we should focus from 1898 to the present, when Spain left the hemisphere and the United States ascended as the new imperial and colonial power (Guantánamo Bay; Puerto Rico; Panama; the Phillipines; the CIA in Chile; etc.). In short, Gracia's proposal overemphasizes *more distant* historical, cultural, and linguistic ties to the "historically impotent colonialism of Spain" at the expense of *more recent* lived experiences with the "all too potent" conditions of U.S. colonialism and racial and cultural supremacist ideology. Alcoff concludes, then, that 'Latinos/as' would better pick out the lived experiences of marginalized groups in this more recent historical context and thus foster the political solidarity that is needed today to resist U.S. hegemony.

In the set of replies that follow Alcoff (2005), four points merit mention here. First, both Gracia and Alcoff come to agree that 'colonialism' is probably an unhelpful and overused term to describe the historical relations with the North that Alcoff wants to highlight, since other than the colonies of St. Kitt and St. Martens, the United States has no traditional colonies in Latin America. Gracia suggests that it would be better to invoke here concepts such as cultural and economic imperialism. Second, while Alcoff gladly accepts this point, she replies that even 'imperialism' will not cover such relationships as the United States and Puerto Rico or the U.S. government's overt and covert roles in Chile, the Dominican Republic, Jamaica, Guatemala, and El Salvador. For the latter cases, Alcoff finds 'neo-colonial' to be the more revealing term historically and politically. Third, both acknowledge the point that any big-tent model of ethnicity and its accompanying pan-ethnic "signs" run the political risks of eliding and erasing the internal heterogeneity of histories in Latin America. Finally, in the end it seems that both Gracia and Alcoff seem more than willing to admit that there are political advantages and disadvantages to the use of both 'Hispanic' and 'Latinos/as.' To adapt an idea from Lawson (1992), we may say that both agree that there is an important "functional lexical gap" in social and political theory that needs filling here and that it will likely take more than one group term to do this. Indeed, as we have already noted, Gracia (2008) grants that both 'Latino/a' and 'Hispanic' bring out historical conditions the other term misses.

But, while both Gracia and Alcoff wish to avoid any "essentialism" about ethnic groups and their names, an important epistemological difference remains between them. Alcoff's epistemic approach, which (inspired in part by Mignolo, 1995, 2000) she calls "pluritopic hermeneutics," sees group identity as emerging from "multiple traditions [places or *topoi*] that are at play in the political contestation over meanings in a postcolonial world" (Alcoff, 2006, chapter 4, p. 125). On this sort of view, even the *ideal* of a politically neutral account or history of some social phenomenon (from *one* intellectual tradition at some ideal limit) likely keeps us from seeing the privileged assumptions that are at work in every actual, dominant conceptual framework. For Gracia, such a (postcolonial) "hermeneutics of suspicion" is overly pessimistic. In contrast, Gracia defends a (fallibilist) "framework approach" where politically neutral conceptual maps or frameworks are not given at the outset, but still may reasonably be assumed as a (regulative) *ideal* (Gracia, 2008, chapter 9). To put this difference in terms of the above parable: where Gracia sees fallible, historical grounds for distinguishing in principle a "semantic realism" about descriptive "green street signs," Alcoff cautions us always to see the "semantics" of our descriptive signs against the likely pragmatic backdrop of hegemonic stop signs, one-way signs, and suspicious detours.

Related chapters: 16 Language and Colonization; 18 Identity and Philosophy; 19 Latinos on Race and Ethnicity: Alcoff, Corlett, and Gracia; 20 *Mestizaje* and Hispanic Identity.

References

Alcoff, L. (2005). Latino vs. Hispanic: the politics of ethnic names. *Philosophy and Social Criticism*, 31, 395–408.

Alcoff, L. (2006). *Visible identities: race, gender, and the self*. New York: Oxford University Press.

Frege, G. (1952). On concept and object. In P. Geach & M. Black (Eds). *Philosophical writings* (pp. 42–55). Oxford: Blackwell.

Gimenez, M. (1989). 'Latino?/Hispanic?' Who needs a name? The case against a standardized terminology. *International Journal of Health Services*, 19, 557–71.

Gracia, J. J. E. (2000). *Hispanic/Latino identity: a philosophical perspective*. Oxford: Blackwell.

Gracia, J. J. E. (2005). A political argument in favor of ethnic names. *Philosophy and Social Criticism*, 31:4, 409–17.

Gracia, J. J. E. (2008). *Latinos in America: philosophy and social identity*. Oxford: Blackwell.

Lawson, B. E. (1992). Moral discourse and slavery. In H. McGary & B. E. Lawson (Eds). *Between slavery and freedom: philosophy and American slavery* (pp. 71–89). Bloomington: Indiana University Press.

Mignolo, W. (1995). *The darker side of the Renaissance: literacy, territoriality, and colonization*. Ann Arbor: University of Michigan Press.

Mignolo, W. (2000). *Local histories/global designs: coloniality, subaltern knowledges, and border thinking*. Princeton: Princeton University Press.

Nuccetelli, S. (2001). 'Hispanics,' 'Latinos,' and 'Iberoamericans': naming or describing? *Philosophical Forum*, 32, 175–88.

Nuccetelli, S. (2002). *Latin American thought: philosophical problems and arguments*. Boulder, CO: Westview Press.

Nuccetelli, S. (2004). Reference and ethnic-group terms. *Inquiry*, 47, 528–44.

Oboler, S. (1992). The politics of ethnic construction: Hispanic, Chicano, Latino . . . ? *Latin American Perspectives*, 19, 18–36.

Schmidt, P. (2003). The label 'Hispanic' irks some, but also unites. *The Chronicle of Higher Education*, 1:14, A9, November 28.

Further Reading

Appiah, K. A. (1996). Race, culture, identity: misunderstood connections. In K. A. Appiah & A. Gutmann (Eds). *Color conscious: the political morality of race* (pp. 30–105). Princeton: Princeton University Press.

Gracia, J. J. E. (1993). Hispanic philosophy: its beginning and golden age. *Review of Metaphysics*, 46, 475–502.

Gracia, J. J. E., & De Greif, P. (2000). *Hispanics/Latinos in the United States: ethnicity, race and rights*. New York: Routledge.

Mills, C. W. (1998). 'But what are you really?' The metaphysics of race. In *Blackness visible: essays on philosophy and race* (pp. 41–66). Ithaca, NY: Cornell University Press.

Taylor, P. C. (2004). What races are: the metaphysics of critical race theory. In *Race: a philosophical introduction* (pp. 70–118). Malden, MA: Polity Press.

18

Identity and Latin American Philosophy

JORGE J. E. GRACIA

The question of identity and Latin American philosophy has been a topic of intense discussion among Latin Americans. It has two major parts. The first concerns the identity *of* Latin American philosophy itself; the second concerns how identity has been discussed *in* Latin American philosophy. The first may in turn be divided into at least two sub-topics: whether in fact there is such a thing as Latin American philosophy and how best to conceive it. The division of the second depends on the identity of which things have been discussed by Latin American philosophers. Most important among these is the identity of the Latin American peoples, and especially of ethnic, racial, and national identities. This chapter concentrates on views about the identity of Latin American philosophy, but it adds some historical discussion of positions Latin Americans have taken with respect to an overall Latin American identity, as opposed to particular ethnic, racial, or national identities. The chapter begins with a discussion of identity, and then moves on to the problem posed by the notion of Latin American philosophy, four general approaches dealing with the problem, and a brief historical account of how the problem has been discussed in Latin America.

Identity

In spite of widespread use in common parlance, the term 'identity' is erudite in origin. It is a transliteration of the Latin *identitas* (in turn a derivative of *idem*). The corresponding term of English (Old Norse) origin is 'sameness' (in turn a derivative of 'same'). For all intents and purposes, these terms are equivalent in meaning. Whether one says that something is identical to something else or says that something is the same as something else generally makes no difference.

Identity is one of the most versatile notions in our ordinary conceptual framework. We apply it to all sorts of things, such as colors, persons, times, spaces, relations, essences, experiences, events, and concepts. We speak of persons or their lives as being identical or as being of an identical type; we say that a daughter is identical to her mother with respect to this or that characteristic; we refer to the use of identical concepts in thought; we agree that sometimes we have identical experiences; and we talk about being in identical places at the same time, being essentially identical, and witnessing

253

identical events. In contemporary philosophy in particular, identity is most often discussed in the context of persons. In short, a very large number of examples could be given here to illustrate the usefulness and pervasiveness of this notion in everyday discourse, but for our purposes the examples provided should suffice.

The notion of identity is obviously related to the notion of similarity. Indeed, it is not unusual to find authors who use 'identical' (or its rough synonym, 'same') and 'similar' interchangeably. This is so because in ordinary language we do use these terms interchangeably on some occasions. For example, we sometimes say that two red-colored objects have identical color, even though the shades of red in question might be different. In this sense, there is no difference between identity and similarity. But it is likewise true that we often entertain and use notions of identity and similarity which are not quite equivalent. Indeed, in the very example just used, we also say that the two red-colored objects are similar in color precisely because the particular shades of red are different.

Important distinctions can be made between the notions of identity and similarity. Perhaps the key distinction is that similarity occurs always in the context of difference. For two things to be similar, they must also be different in some respect, although the difference in question must refer to aspects other than those on which the similarity is based. One may speak of two persons as being similar provided that they differ in some way. If they do not differ in any way, then they are regarded as identical, i.e., as the same person. The conditions of similarity of two things, say X and Y, may be expressed in the following way:

> X is similar to Y if and only if X and Y: (1) have at least one feature that is identical in both and (2) also have at least one feature that is not identical in both.

For the sake of convenience, features are understood very broadly in this formulation. They may include anything that may be said of a thing and thus not only qualities, but also relations, position, temporal location, states, and actions.

In contrast with similarity, identity does not require – indeed it precludes – difference. This does not mean that two things could not be regarded as identical with respect to some feature and different with respect to something else. A daughter, for example, may be identical to her mother with respect to hair color while being different with respect to personality. The point is, however, that for the daughter and the mother to be identical with respect to hair color, their hair color must not involve any difference whatsoever. If there were some difference, so that one were, say, lighter than the other, one would more properly speak instead of a "similarity of hair color." We might express this understanding of the identity of two things, say X and Y, and the identity of their features in the following two propositions:

> X is identical to Y, if and only if there is nothing that pertains to X that does not pertain to Y, and vice versa.
>
> X is identical to Y, with respect to a particular feature F, if and only if there is nothing that pertains to F in X that does not pertain to F in Y, and vice versa.

254

The first formula expresses what might be called *absolute identity*, because it applies to the whole entity in question; the second expresses what might be called *relative identity*, because it applies only to some feature(s) or aspect(s) of an entity.

Part of the reason for the frequent blurring of the distinction between identity and similarity in English discourse is that a single term, 'difference,' is often used as the opposite of both, even though there exists another term that more properly expresses the opposite of similarity: 'dissimilarity.' Similar/different and identical/different are generally regarded as pairs of opposites in English. This usage does not necessarily extend to other languages, however. In the Middle Ages, for example, a concerted effort was made to keep the notions of similarity and identity separate, and this was supported by the use of two opposite terms for each. 'Difference' (*differentia*) was used, at least in most technical philosophical discourse, as the opposite of 'similarity' (*similaritas*), whereas 'diversity' (*diversitas*) was used as the opposite of 'identity' (*identitas*).

The notions of identity and non-identity presuppose each other; they are interdependent in the same way that the notions of cat and non-cat are. Cat is significant as long as non-cat is, and vice versa. If in fact there were nothing that could not be a cat, the very notion of cat would lack relevance. Indeed, in a world of multiplicity such as ours, the identity of something implies its non-identity with something else.

Not all identity about which we speak is of the same sort, however. There are at least four fundamental but distinct kinds of identity: *achronic, synchronic, diachronic*, and *panchronic*. *Achronic identity* is identity irrespective of time, whereas synchronic, diachronic, and panchronic identities have to do with time: *synchronic identity* applies at a particular time; *diachronic identity* applies at two (or more, but not all) times; and *panchronic identity* applies at all times.

These four kinds of identity generate four different problems that apply to Latin American philosophy. One is atemporal: What makes Latin American philosophy what it is? A second is temporal, but abstracts from the passage of time: What makes Latin American philosophy what it is at time t (where t is replaced by any particular time that is appropriate: now, last year, or two hundred years ago)? A third both is temporal and takes into account the passage of time: What makes Latin American philosophy what it is at times t_n and t_{n+1}? And a fourth is temporal but applies to all times: What makes Latin American philosophy what it always is?

In all four cases what is sought are sets of conditions: necessary conditions without which Latin American philosophy is not what it is, and sufficient conditions that distinguish Latin American philosophy from other things. In principle, the sets of conditions for achronic, synchronic, diachronic, or panchronic identity could be different, and whether they are or not is part of the debate. From what was said earlier, it follows also that, if there is such a thing as Latin American philosophy, then there is also something that is not; for what constitutes the identity of something is also presumably what sets it apart from others. Identity is bound up with difference. Now, this claim should be understood both metaphysically and epistemically: Metaphysically, it means just what it says, that identity and non-identity (or difference) are interdependent; epistemically, it means that the understanding of identity is bound up with the understanding of non-identity.

255

Identity of Latin American Philosophy

The notion of a Latin American philosophy has been a subject of heated controversy for most of the twentieth century. In order to understand the issues involved in this controversy, we may begin with a question: Why ask what Latin American philosophy is? The reasons why we ask questions vary considerably. Questions have many purposes, and their purposes often reveal something about the kind of answers that those who ask them seek to provide. Aristotle noted long ago that the purpose, that is, what he called *telos*, determines both what something is and its function. The *telos* of a human being, for example, is the acquisition of a certain kind of knowledge. This *telos* determines both what is distinctive of humans (rationality) among other similar beings (animals) and their function (to reason). If we take this idea seriously in the case we are considering, we should expect that there might be differences in what is considered Latin American philosophy among those who study it, depending on the purposes they have in mind. Teachers will primarily have a pedagogical aim, and consider their object of study differently perhaps than historiographers. And something similar could be said about those who have an ideological aim or those who search for validation and authenticity.

In the case of some other subjects, perhaps there might not be significant differences, because the objects of study have fairly well-established boundaries and the goal pursued is also agreed upon. When we are concerned with cancer, for example, matters appear easier, at least in principle, insofar as the overall aim of the study of cancer is to cure and eradicate the disease. Anything that contributes to this aim is fair game to the investigator.

But Latin American philosophy poses difficulties, because the purpose in studying it is not so clear or uniform, and what qualifies as Latin American philosophy is not well established. True, some authors and texts are clearly part of Latin American philosophy in the broad sense I am using here and regarded as such by everyone. No one disputes that Antonio Caso, Risieri Frondizi, Leopoldo Zea, and Francisco Miró Quesada are Latin American philosophers. Although there are disagreements as to the value and originality of their work, this work is uniformly accepted as philosophical and belonging in the canon of Latin American philosophy. Hence, any course on Latin American philosophy can, and perhaps should, include the study of these figures without apology, and the same goes for historiography. Even those motivated by ideology or validation consider them part of the canon, and either use them to support the case they want to make or consider them exceptions of one kind or another to whatever principles they wish to peddle.

It is equally clear that many philosophers do not qualify as Latin American and their work is not part of the corpus of Latin American philosophical texts. Aristotle, Thomas Aquinas, René Descartes, and Jürgen Habermas, for example, do not, and no one working on Latin American philosophy would be taken seriously if he or she said that they were part of Latin American philosophy, even though some Latin American philosophers have been heavily influenced by their ideas. References to these authors in works or courses on Latin American philosophy are acceptable, but their philosophy is not studied as Latin American. To understand Frondizi's views on the self, for example, references to Christian von Erhenfels are essential, for Frondizi used this philosopher's ideas about value and *Gestalt* to develop his own views. But it is obvious that whereas Frondizi is clearly a Latin American philosopher, and part of the Latin American philosophical canon, von Erhenfels is not.

The authors I have mentioned pose no problems for the pedagogue or historiographer of Latin American philosophy. But problems surface when we consider texts and authors such as the *Popol Vuh*, Bartolomé de las Casas, Sor Juana Inés de la Cruz, Frantz Fanon, and José Gaos.

The problem with the *Popol Vuh* (the book that contains the Maya myth of creation) is twofold. First, it is not a clearly philosophical text in the most widespread Western understanding of the term. After all, there are many texts like this in the Western tradition and they are never included in the philosophical canon. Consider, for example, the Egyptian *Book of the Dead* and the biblical books of Genesis and Job. Even the *Iliad* and the *Odyssey* are not generally included in courses on the history of philosophy except to illustrate the change that historians of philosophy see between religious and literary texts and the work of the pre-Socratics. If this is so, then why should we include the *Popol Vuh* in the study of Latin American philosophy? Perhaps for the sake of validation, to render philosophical legitimacy to the peoples of Latin America before the Iberians arrived? Or perhaps the issue is ideological, namely, that one wishes to change the way we generally think of philosophy in the West because one has some other idea in mind about the nature of philosophy and its role in the social context.

Bartolomé de las Casas poses a different problem. He is a Spaniard who lived part of his life in Latin America and applied the scholastic philosophy developed in the Middle Ages and practiced during his time in the Iberian Peninsula to the Latin American context, particularly to the question of the humanity and rights of conquered peoples. His place of origin and the philosophical framework that he used count against him being part of the Latin American philosophical canon, but his concern with issues arising from the Latin American context, his advocacy for the wellbeing of Amerindians, and the influence he exerted in the way both Latin Americans and non-Latin Americans think about these issues suggest that he should be included in the canon. Besides, no one can doubt that las Casas's scholastic mode of argumentation fits what is considered philosophical in the West, and the philosophical issues raised by the conquest cannot be raised without mentioning las Casas or his work. His thought is clearly philosophical and inspired by the Latin American situation. Are there other reasons why we should include him in Latin American philosophy? Should we include him for ideological reasons, because he mostly said the right things and defended oppressed Amerindian populations? Should we include him because otherwise Latin American philosophy would not exist at the time, or would not make sense without reference to him? So what do we do with him and why?

The case of Sor Juana is difficult in a different way. She was prevented from writing philosophy in the way that was common at the time because she was a woman. So in a sense we do not have any work from her that can be classified as philosophical, strictly speaking. Yet this prohibition did not prevent her from precisely making a case against the prohibition in rational and rhetorical terms. She also wrote poems that have ethical or moral relevance, although her style, as a humanist, was not what counts as strictly philosophical in the West. Keep in mind that Renaissance humanists have a hard time being included in the Western philosophical curriculum or the philosophical

257

research canon. When was the last time you saw a course in philosophy that discussed the work of Lorenzo Valla, or a history of philosophy that does more than mention his name as a humanist? So, on what basis should we include Sor Juana in a course on Latin American philosophy, or include her as a figure to be studied in the historiography of Latin American philosophy when similar authors in Europe are generally excluded from consideration in courses and studies of European philosophy? Because she is a woman and we want to validate women's philosophical capacity? Because there is a certain ideological ax that we want to grind? Because the history of Latin American philosophy makes no sense without reference to her?

The case of Frantz Fanon is even more complicated. He wrote in French and was born in Martinique. Does Latin America include this part of the world? Since the French created the term 'Latin America,' I am sure they would answer affirmatively, but few authors take this French part of the Americas into consideration when studying Latin American philosophy, and no anthologies of Latin American philosophy include the work of authors from this part of the Americas. There is, of course, a very serious bias against any author who is not Spanish-speaking. Even Brazilian authors have problems of inclusion. Moreover, anything outside of the Iberian sphere of influence is almost automatically excluded. So, on what basis do we include Fanon: ideology, validation, an expanded version of Latin America?

José Gaos is also a difficult case. He came to Latin America as an older person, fleeing from political instability in Spain, but his impact on Mexico in particular was enormous. No history of Mexican philosophy makes sense without examining this impact, and perhaps no history of Latin American philosophy does either. Moreover, he also appropriated much that could be considered as arising from the Mexican situation; one could argue that he philosophized from a Mexican context. But should we, then, include José Ortega y Gasset (who also had an enormous influence on Latin American philosophy) and Ginés de Sepúlveda (who had no influence but engaged las Casas in a philosophical controversy arising in Latin America)? Can we consider Gaos in the same category as Caso or Frondizi?

Clearly we have no problem including Caso and Frondizi in, or excluding Descartes from, Latin American philosophy, but when we get to las Casas or Sor Juana matters become more difficult. So, what should we do? Who is to be included in Latin American philosophy, what criteria are we going to use to determine inclusion, and how are we going to conceive this philosophy in order to answer these questions?

Four Approaches

Latin Americans themselves, whether residing in the United States or in Latin America, have been concerned with the identity of Latin American philosophy. Two topics are pertinent for our discussion here. One is framed in terms of a question: Is there a Latin American philosophy? Another concerns itself with distinguishing what is frequently called academic and non-academic philosophy, although other terms are also used, such as Western and non-Western, European and autochthonous, genuine and imported, authentic and inauthentic, and so on. Both topics involve an understanding of philosophy in general and of Latin American philosophy in particular. The three most common approaches to the first topic are the universalist, the culturalist, and the critical, to which I add a fourth, the ethnic, that I have recently proposed.

Universalists such as Risieri Frondizi view philosophy as a universal discipline and not different from science (Frondizi, 1949). Philosophy, like mathematics or physics, has an object that it studies and a method it employs in doing so. But neither the effectiveness of the method nor the truth value of the conclusions it reaches depend on particular circumstances or perspectives. Either material objects are composed of matter and form or they are not, and so Aristotelian hylomorphism is either true or false. The question of whether there is a Latin American philosophy, then, depends on whether Latin Americans have been able to produce the kind of universal discipline that one expects when one has science as a model. Its problems are common to all humans, its method is also common, and its conclusions are supposed to be true, regardless of particular circumstances. Just as water is composed of a certain proportion of hydrogen and oxygen, so there are certain conditions that determine the identity of an artifact over time. Most universalists see Latin American philosophy as largely a failure in this respect.

Culturalists like Leopoldo Zea think, on the contrary, that truth is always perspectival, dependent on a point of view and that the method to acquire it is always contingent on a cultural context (Zea, 2004). Philosophy is a historical, non-scientific enterprise concerned with the elaboration of a general point of view from a certain personal or cultural perspective. But is there a Latin American philosophy? Why not, culturalists ask? If Latin Americans have engaged in developing views from their perspective as individuals or as Latin Americans, and using whatever means they have found appropriate to do so, there cannot but be a Latin American philosophy.

A third critical approach, articulated by Augusto Salazar Bondy and other critics, considers philosophy a result of social conditions and closely related to those conditions (Salazar Bondy, 1969). Some conditions are conducive to the production of philosophy, or what is sometimes called authentic philosophy, whereas others are not. So, is there a Latin American philosophy? For most critics the conditions operative in the area preclude the development of philosophy, because all the philosophy developed by Latin Americans is inauthentic and therefore not true philosophy. The dependence of Latin America on ideas imported from elsewhere, or its situation as dominated, prevents it from being authentic; it is a borrowed, subservient philosophy.

The second topic that has dominated discussions of Latin American philosophy by Latin Americans is concerned with the kind of philosophy that is practiced by Latin Americans. One is the philosophy developed in the academy, similar to what the scholastics developed in schools. It is a result of school activities and developed for academic purposes, the solution to puzzles of interest primarily to academics. The other is the philosophy developed outside the academy, and this responds to the needs and conditions under which it is developed. Its mode of expression is not academic, so it is frequently literary or polemical, and its concerns are not scholarly but real problems and issues confronted by Latin Americans.

Often culturalists and critical philosophers accuse universalists of being academic philosophers, and therefore of not being authentic or responsive to the practical and social needs of Latin Americans. Universalists respond by accusing culturalists and critical philosophers of not doing philosophy at all, but rather of developing the kind of personal or cultural narrative that has no scientific or universal value.

259

It should be obvious that these positions beg the question insofar as they begin with pre-established conceptions of philosophy that de-legitimize others. The issue, then, does not have to do with Latin American philosophy as such, but with the nature of philosophy. It should also be clear that the answer given to the questions we have asked is not descriptive but prescriptive: We are normatively told what is or is not Latin American philosophy, and therefore how we should think about it, and deal with it, in the classroom and as historiographers.

So far little headway has been made when it comes to answering the question we have raised concerning the identity of Latin American philosophy in a way that does not beg the question or even is useful for understanding the issues involved. Elsewhere, I have proposed a fourth approach that claims to avoid some of the problems that have resulted in an impasse (Gracia, 2007). This approach conceives Latin American philosophy as ethnic and serves to understand how Latin American philosophy is both different and similar to other philosophies, including scientific or universalist philosophy. It also helps us decide what to include in courses on Latin American philosophy and in its historiography.

An ethnic philosophy is the philosophy of an ethnos. This requires both the existence of the ethnos and a certain conception of philosophy by the ethnos. The ethnos, just as its philosophy, is not conceived in essentialist terms; there is no need for the ethnos or its philosophy to have a set of properties that are constant throughout their existence. Ethne are conceived in familial-historical terms; they are groups of people who have been brought together by history (Gracia, 2005). The model of a family is used as a metaphor to understand how an ethnic group can have unity without having all the members of the group necessarily share some first-order properties at any particular time in their history or throughout that history. Not all of them need have the same height, weight, eye color, degree of intelligence, customs, or even ancestry. Ethne are like families in that they originate and continue to exist as a result of historical events, such as marriage, but their members need not share common properties, although they may in certain circumstances do so, and certain ethnic groups require it. Indeed, some ethne require descent for membership, for example, a fact that has led some philosophers and anthropologists mistakenly to argue that descent is necessary for membership in all ethne, including the Latino/Hispanic ethnos (Corlett, 2003). Particular ethnic groups have much to say about criteria of membership, but these criteria are not always the same for all ethne.

An ethnic conception of Latin American philosophy conceives it as the philosophy of the Latin American ethnos (Gracia, 2007). This means that, just as the ethnos that produces it, Latin American philosophy need not have essential characteristics that, first, are shared by everything considered to be part of Latin American philosophy and, second, separate it from all other philosophies. It is only necessary that Latin American philosophy be whatever the historical circumstances that originated it and the ethnos that produced it made it. Because the unity of Latin American philosophy is historical and contextual, it becomes easier to account for its variety and for the inclusion in it of texts and figures that traditional Western philosophy might not consider philosophical, such as the *Popol Vuh* or the poems of Sor Juana. The criteria for inclusion are historical and contextual, and open to change and development.

260

History of the Controversy

Apart from the general characterization of the four approaches discussed, an understanding of Latin American philosophy can profit from an account of the historical development of the controversy in Latin America.

Explicit questions about a Latin American philosophy were first explored in the writings of Leopoldo Zea (1912–2004) and Risieri Frondizi (1910–83) in the 1940s. The growth of philosophical literature until then seemed to justify, and perhaps even require, an investigation of the nature, themes, and limits of this philosophical activity. The character and future of Latin American philosophy had been addressed before Zea and Frondizi explicitly raised the question of the identity of Latin American philosophy. The first author to do so was the Argentine Juan Bautista Alberdi (1810–84). He developed his ideas under the influence of a liberalism closely allied with philosophical rationalism, anticlericalism, and optimism about industrialization that was so characteristic of nineteenth-century Latin America (Alberdi, 1895–1901).

According to Alberdi, Latin American philosophy must have a social and political character intimately related to the most vital needs of the region. Philosophy is an instrument that can help introduce an awareness about the social, political, and economic needs of Latin American nations. This is why Alberdi categorically rejected metaphysics and other "pure and abstract" philosophical fields, which he viewed as alien to urgent national needs.

Followers of the universalist perspective, many of whom view metaphysics as the highest expression of philosophical thought, have questioned the validity of the Alberdian postulates, suggesting that they are merely politico-practical and therefore alien to philosophy. Those who adopt the culturalist approach, on the contrary, have seen in Alberdi the founding father of Latin American philosophy, owing to his insistence in the adjustment of philosophical thought to the needs of the region. They argue that Alberdi laid out the basis for a genuinely Latin American philosophy. Both perspectives ignore the historical situation surrounding Alberdi's thought, and interpret Alberdi's work on the basis of their own conceptions of philosophy, without paying sufficient attention to either the objectives of this author or the context of his ideas.

Alberdi's views coincide with the basic tenets of positivism, the most popular school of thought in Latin America in the second half of the nineteenth century. Positivism advocates the development of science and technology, rejects religion and metaphysics, and sees the native population as responsible for the economic backwardness of Latin America. While fighting to introduce the teaching of science in the system of education, and defending the industrialization of the region, positivism also produced a series of racial theories which attempted to explain the "inferiority" of the native population. The reasons for this emphasis on race are intimately connected with the identification, common at the time, of technology and the Anglo-Saxon race. To many positivists, and also to many liberals, the great obstacle to the industrialization of Latin America came from the predominantly Latin and native populations of the area, and their alleged resistance to technological development.

The positivist model for social and economic development received one of its first attacks from José Enrique Rodó (1871–1917). This Uruguayan thinker understood the distinction between technology and culture in terms of the Ariel–Caliban distinction made

261

popular by the French philosopher Renan, who had borrowed it from Shakespeare's play *The Tempest*, and used it as an instrument for social analysis (Rodó, 1988). Rodó represented a reversal of the Alberdian optimism with respect to industrialization, although he legitimized this phenomenon as a genuine concern for Latin American philosophers. According to him, technology not only embodies the gross features of Caliban, but it also represents the utilitarian democracy of the United States.

Whereas Alberdi viewed the elimination of the backward features of Latin American culture by means of industrialization and technological development positively, Rodó was strongly opposed to them, favoring instead the very culture rejected by Alberdi. Rodó underlined the positive features of the race, which he viewed rather romantically, and ascribed to it a spirituality capable of effectively opposing the utilitarian character of the industrial phenomena introduced by Anglo Saxons. Rodó's rejection of industrialization and its cultural implications, however, did not lead him to defend, or identify himself with, the Latin American native population.

This defense and identification, however, is central in the work of the Mexican philosopher José Vasconcelos (1882–1959). He adopted many of Rodó's views, but especially the dichotomies of technology–culture, Latin–Saxon, and foreign–autochthonous, turning them into the very core of the question of Latin American cultural identity (Vasconcelos, 1997). A proponent of a racial and cultural Pan-Americanism, Vasconcelos was confident that the region would find a cultural unity based on the amalgamation of its racial variety. The synthesis of the different cultures and races of Latin America provides, for this author, the very basis of the region's cultural identity, a feature which he opposes to the Anglo-Saxon spirit embodied by the British and North Americans alike. In fact, Vasconcelos believed this latter spirit to be limited to the white race and he argued that the Latin American race, because of its higher spirituality and richness, could successfully confront the narrow Anglo-Saxon spirit and its brainchild, technology.

Vasconcelos interpreted the Latin/Anglo-Saxon conflict as "a conflict between institutions, purposes, and ideals." A critical point of this conflict is the white Anglo-Saxon's attempt to "mechanize the world," whereas the Latin strives to integrate the components and virtues of all existing races into the one synthesis which Vasconcelos called the "cosmic race." This race will be the agent for the creation of the highest possible level humanity can attain: a spiritual-aesthetic stage where technology plays only a subordinate role (Vasconcelos, 1997).

Vasconcelos' emphasis on the cultural peculiarities of different ethnic groups attracted the attention of many intellectuals during the first half of the twentieth century, especially in Mexico, where the revolution was seeking to vindicate socially, economically, and culturally the native segment of the population. Not only did art and literature begin to concern themselves with the racial component of the region, but also philosophy and the essay of ideas in general.

Samuel Ramos (1897–1959), an associate of Vasconcelos at the Ministry of Education in Mexico, was perhaps the leading figure among the intellectuals who were inspired by Vasconcelos' thought. Like Vasconcelos, Ramos rejected the positivism of pre-revolutionary Mexico, though not as much in spiritual and aesthetic terms as in humanistic ones. He pointed out that the conspicuous lack of humanism in Latin American thought was due to a large extent to the legacy of positivism (Ramos,

1962). The growth of this humanism, which he believed to be an essential component of any genuine Latin American thought, was impeded by "the universal invasion of machine civilization," by which he meant industrialization. In this way, Ramos contrasted humanism, which he viewed as the vehicle for the liberation of Latin Americans, with the pervasive technology which was beginning to characterize modern civilization. Mechanistic civilization, according to him, rather than helping human development, constitutes a "heavy burden" which threatens to "denaturalize" humanity.

Samuel Ramos inaugurated a new trend which emphasized autochthonous and national characteristics as the basis for philosophical activity. In contrast with Vasconcelos, who understood cultural identity in Latin American terms, Ramos placed emphasis on the national level, and only by inference, on Latin America in general. The study of *lo mexicano* (the properly Mexican) acquired full expression with Ramos, providing the basis for a culturalist view of philosophy. Students of Ramos's thought, however, have understood *lo mexicano* in more optimistic terms than those envisioned by Ramos himself. Ramos's view that an "inferiority complex" constitutes the fundamental feature of the Mexican character, and his skepticism concerning the integration of marginal segments of the Mexican population into the mainstream of Mexican society, are far from expressing an unqualified optimism with respect to *lo mexicano*.

The Chilean Félix Schwartzmann (b. 1913) understood the cultural impact of industrial development as a phenomenon which is not restricted to Latin America, but which affects the entire planet. Contrary to the positions taken by his predecessors, for Schwartzmann this phenomenon constitutes a cultural reality of its own and he suggested that the reaction against modernity and technology provides some of the most distinctive features which constitute the cultural identity of the region (Schwartzmann, 1950). The loneliness, impotence of self-expression, and search for genuine human bonds are some of the traits which Schwartzmann viewed as Latin American responses against the universal phenomenon of modernity, whose main feature is impersonalism. In search for these peculiar traits, Schwartzmann analyzed literature, poetry, and essays of ideas in the region, and found that both autochthonous and universal traits combine to produce a unique cultural expression which he called "the sentiment of the human in America."

The decade of the 1940s was a period in which intellectuals looked back on Latin American culture and attempted to use it as the basis of philosophical thinking. A generation of Mexican authors inspired by José Ortega y Gasset's perspectivism, introduced in Latin America by the *transterrados*, or Spanish exiles, and particularly by José Gaos, suggested that the cultural "circumstances" of the region provided the basis for the development of an original philosophy (Gaos, 1952). Leopoldo Zea, the leader of these intellectuals, claimed that any type of philosophical reflection emerging in the region could be classified as Latin-American philosophy by virtue of the intimate relationship between philosophy and culture. He also suggested that this philosophy had a historical foundation, owing to the fact that Latin Americans had always, in Zea's judgment, thought of their situation from a vital perspective. In this sense, even philosophical reflection lacking originality, resulting from mere imitation, could qualify as Latin American philosophy by virtue of its historicity and of the fact that it emerged in response to particular vital circumstances (Zea, 2004).

263

The nationalistic sentiment that characterized the politics of most Latin American nations at the time, but particularly Mexico, helped to promote Zea's views concerning the existence and nature of Latin American philosophy. Advocates and detractors of his conception made their voices heard quite quickly throughout the region. For Frondizi, who opposed Zea, philosophy must be distinguished from cultural nationalism and should be considered independent from geographical boundaries. One should speak of philosophy *in* America rather than of a philosophy *of* America (Frondizi, 1949). Philosophy, as Francisco Romero had pointed out earlier, has no last names; that is, it must be understood as a discipline with universal characteristics.

Vasconcelos himself, whose work in many ways reflected a culturalist perspective, adopted a universalist position when discussing the nature of philosophical activity. He went so far as to deny explicitly the existence of a peculiarly Latin American philosophy on the grounds that the discipline was universal in character, although he conceded that it was the prerogative of each culture to reconsider the great themes of universal philosophy (Vasconcelos, 1958). Philosophical nationalism had no place in his thought.

The polemic that suddenly surrounded the question of the existence of a Latin American philosophy in the '40s had the effect, in many cases, of undermining the focus on cultural identity that had characterized Latin American philosophical thought prior to the dispute, and which in many respects had prompted it. The controversy set a precedent for discussions of culture that became increasingly separated from the actual analysis of Latin American cultural phenomena. The culturalists themselves, who based their conceptions on a cultural perspective, have left few detailed accounts of the region's cultural ethos, and frequently refer to culture in very general terms.

Eduardo Nicol (1907–90), one of the members of the generation of *transterrados* to settle in Latin America during the Spanish Civil War, was among the first to return to the search for an ethos that would define Latin American culture. He proposed the notion of *hispanidad* as the core of both Spanish and Latin American cultural identity (Nicol, 1961). This concept, according to Nicol, unites linguistic and cultural aspects in both geographical areas, giving a distinctive character to these regions. Still, he did not see these regions as separated from the rest of the world. In a complete turnabout from the pessimism with which many intellectuals before him had viewed technological development, Nicol suggested that whatever unity the world has is due to science and technology. Technology provides an opportunity for world integration, which both Orteguean perspectivism and existentialism, products of a culture of crisis, are unable to muster. These philosophies, according to Nicol, supply a rationale for cultural regionalism and separatism in the midst of a world increasingly unified by science and technology.

Nicol's attack against one of the byproducts of cultural regionalism, namely, *indigenismo*, led him to justify and even minimize the politically sensitive question of the effects of Spanish colonization in Latin America. Echoing themes already sounded by Alberdi, he charged this movement with presenting an obstacle to the economic and technological integration of the region. Followers of this movement feel threatened, he suggested, by the integrating might of science and technology, which cannot but produce a "mutation" or upsetting of the "vital foundations" prevalent in Latin America. But Nicol did not see anything negative in this process. On the contrary, he saw it as a positive step leading to a "meditation on one's own being" which will ultimately help establish a cultural ethos based on *hispanidad*. This, in turn, should produce a positive attitude in relation to technology and a subsequent end to the economic backwardness of the region.

Phenomenological views of a Heideggerian variety represented in Latin America by Ernesto Mayz Vallenilla (b. 1925) have also been used in the philosophical analysis of the continent's cultural identity. According to Mayz Vallenilla, Latin American culture is historically based on "the Latin American man's expectation to become" (Mayz Vallenilla, 1959). This expectation provides a peculiar state of consciousness which defines the most fundamental nature of human beings in the region. Mayz Vallenilla's definition represents an attempt to understand culture in ontological terms, an attempt which exempts him from examining in detail literary, artistic, and social expressions. In a subsequent work, *Latinoamérica en la encrucijada de la técnica* (Latin America at the crossroads of technology) (1976), however, he picked up the thread which explicitly relates technology and culture, suggesting that technology, which has among its outstanding features certain tendencies toward fostering "anonymity" and "homogeneity," is bent on destroying a Latin American ethos based on peculiarity, originality, and an "expectation" about the future. Consequently, he understands the confrontation between the Latin American cultural ethos and technology as a true "challenge."

None of the different interpretations of the cultural identity of Latin America have become established, a fact which should not surprise us. For neither the "inferiority complex" in terms of which Ramos used to refer to the Mexican character, nor the "cosmic race" of Vasconcelos, nor a particular sense of the human proposed by Schwartzmann, nor the *hispanidad* of Nicol, nor the "expectation" of Mayz Vallenilla, are susceptible to ultimate verification. The lack of consensus about the notion of Latin American culture extends also to the notion of philosophy. This is the reason why during the 1960s a number of authors readdressed this problem, although this time not in terms of either universalism or culturalism. It was at this time that the critical position discussed earlier arose. Augusto Salazar Bondy (1926–74), for instance, viewed philosophy in Latin America as the province of intellectual elites. These elites have borrowed European cultural forms uncritically, lacking an identifiable and rigorous methodology and an awareness of the situation of other social groups. Viewed in this light, the problems of culture and philosophy have been problems for only a small minority of intellectuals alienated from the rest of society, and from economic, social, and political problems (Salazar Bondy, 1969). This position, which has also been shared by Juan Rivano (b. 1926) among others, suggests that the history of the controversy concerning the existence and nature of Latin American philosophy epitomizes a lack of concern among intellectuals with the most urgent problems of their respective communities (Rivano, 1965).

Universalists reacted quickly to this new philosophical challenge. Among them was Fernando Salmerón (1925–97), who, in spite of having developed "culturalist" themes at the beginning of his philosophical career, in subsequent years rejected both the culturalist and the critical postures. According to him, two different conceptions of philosophy must be distinguished. The first conceives it as "wisdom or a conception of the world that, strictly speaking, is nothing but the expression of a moral attitude" (Salmerón, 1969). In this sense, it is possible to adopt a position like that of Salazar

265

Bondy, for example. But the word 'philosophy' is also understood more strictly "to refer to a determinate intellectual enterprise, analytic and theoretical, which, guided by an appropriately scientific energy, confronts problems of various types – for example, logical, epistemic, semantic – making use of certain methods about which there is general agreement." If philosophy is understood in this way, neither the culturalist nor the critical positions make sense.

Another dimension of the controversy surrounding Latin American philosophy has been the attempt to understand and locate it in historical terms, as well as to study its origins, limits, and themes. Francisco Miró Quesada (b. 1918) is among the most important thinkers who have propounded this type of study. He has analyzed the causes, results, and future of, and the views proposed on, this issue. The situation which originated this controversy, according to him, is a so-called "sense of disorientation." The effort to overcome this disorientation, he suggests, "is the key for understanding Latin American philosophical activity" (Miró Quesada, 1976). His concern is not with the question of whether there is, or can be, a Latin American philosophy, but rather with the study of the preoccupation for the topic and its future.

The controversy has continued to grow and attract much attention among members of practically every philosophical tradition, with the exception of philosophical analysis. Existentialists, phenomenologists, Thomists, Kantians, and Ortegueans have felt compelled to explore this issue. But since none of the different interpretations of the cultural identity of Latin America has become widely accepted, it has been impossible in turn to establish a consensus on the notion of Latin American philosophy.

It is in this milieu that the movement known as "the philosophy of liberation" appeared in the 1970s. For philosophers like Enrique Dussel (b. 1934), Horacio Cerutti Guldberg (b. 1950), and Arturo Andrés Roig (b. 1922), the fundamental task of philosophy in Latin America consists in the social and national liberation from the unjust relations such as that of dominating–dominated that have traditionally characterized Latin America. For Roig in particular, this implies an integration of the Latin American peoples based on the consciousness of the historicity of the American man and of the history of philosophy in Latin America. His position rejects the formalism and ontologism characteristic of traditional academic philosophy, favoring instead a philosophy of commitment that seeks integrating concepts in Latin America (Roig, 2004). The novelty of this philosophy will be founded in the political discourse of the marginal and exploited segments of society, developing an authentic thought that may serve to give rise to "man's humanity."

Conclusion

The discussion of the identity of Latin American philosophy has been intense and since the nineteenth century it has become one of the most common topics of discussion in Latin American philosophy. But even before the nineteenth century, Latin American intellectuals were concerned with issues of identity that apply beyond philosophy, to the peoples of Latin America themselves. The concern with identity reveals much about Latin Americans and what they think about themselves and their place in the world. But it also serves to tie Latin American thought to that of other peoples who have been or have become preoccupied with matters of identity, including various ethnic groups all over the world, and in particular, of Latinos/Hispanics in the United States.

Related chapters: 3 Colonial Thought; 5 Early Critics of Positivism; 9 'Normal' Philosophy; 10 Ortega y Gasset's Heritage in Latin America; 13 Liberation Philosophy; 19 Latinos on Race and Ethnicity: Alcoff, Corlett, and Gracia; 20 *Mestizaje* and Hispanic Identity; 24 Latin American Philosophy.

References

Alberdi, J. B. (1895–1901). Ideas para presidir la confección del curso de filosofía contemporánea. In *Escritos póstumos de Juan Bautista Alberdi*, vol. 15. Buenos Aires: Imprenta Europea.

Corlett, J. A. (2003). *Race, racism and reparations*. Ithaca, NY: Cornell University Press.

Frondizi, R. (1949). Is there an Ibero-American philosophy? *Philosophy and Phenomenological Research*, 9, 345–55.

Gaos, J. (1952). *En torno a la filosofía mexicana*. Mexico City: Porrúa y Obregón.

Gracia, J. J. E. (2005). *Race, ethnicity, and nationality: a challenge for the 21st century*. Lanham, MD: Rowman & Littlefield.

Gracia, J. J. E. (2007). What is Latin American philosophy? In George Yancy (Ed.). *Philosophy in multiple voices* (pp. 175–96). Lanham, MD: Rowman & Littlefield.

Mayz Vallenilla, E. (1959). *El problema de América*. Caracas: Universidad Central.

Mayz Vallenilla, E. (1976). *Latinoamérica en la encrucijada de la técnica*. Caracas: Universidad Simón Bolívar.

Miró Quesada, F. (1976). *El problema de la filosofía latinoamericana*. Mexico City: Fondo de Cultura Económica.

Nicol, E. (1961). *El problema de la filosofía hispánica*. Madrid: Editorial Tecnos.

Ramos, S. (1962). *Profile of man and culture in Mexico*. (P. G. Earle, Trans.). Austin, TX: University of Texas Press.

Rivano, J. (1965). *El punto de vista de la miseria*. Santiago de Chile: Universidad de Chile.

Rodó, J. E. (1988). *Ariel*. (M. S. Peden, Trans.). Austin: University of Texas Press.

Roig, A. A. (2004). The actual function of philosophy in Latin America. In J. J. E. Gracia & E. Millán-Zaibert (Eds). *Latin American philosophy for the 21st century: the human condition, values, and the search for identity* (pp. 357–68). Buffalo, NY: Prometheus (Original work published 1976).

Salazar Bondy, A. (1969). *The meaning and problem of Hispanic American thought*. (J. P. Augelli, Ed.). Lawrence: Center of Latin American Studies of the University of Kansas.

Salmerón, F. (1969). Notas al margen del sentido y problema del pensamiento hispanoamericano. In A. Salazar Bondy (Ed.). *Sentido y problema del pensamiento filosófico hispanoamericano*. Kansas City: University of Kansas Center for Latin American Studies.

Schwartzmann, F. (1950). *El sentimiento de lo humano en América* (2 vols.). Santiago de Chile: Editorial Universitaria.

Vasconcelos, J. (1958). El pensamiento iberoamericano. In *Obras completas, vol. 2: Indología*. Mexico City: Libreros Mexicanos Unidos.

Vasconcelos, J. (1997). *The cosmic race*. (D. T. Jaén, Trans.). Baltimore: Johns Hopkins University Press.

Zea, L. (2004). The actual function of philosophy in Latin America. In J. J. E. Gracia & E. Millán-Zaibert (Eds). *Latin American philosophy for the 21st century: the human condition, values, and the search for identity* (pp. 401–13). Buffalo, NY: Prometheus (Original work published 1942).

Further Reading

Gracia, J. J. E. (2008). *Latinos in America: philosophy and social identity*. Oxford: Blackwell Publishers.

Gracia, J. J. E. (2000). *Hispanic/Latino identity: a philosophical perspective*. Oxford: Blackwell Publishers.

Gracia, J. J. E., & Millán-Zaibert, E. (Eds). (2004). *Latin American philosophy for the 21st century: the human condition, values, and the search for identity*. Buffalo, NY: Prometheus.

Mendieta, E. (Ed.). (2003). *Latin American philosophy: currents, issues, debates*. Bloomington: Indiana University Press.

Nuccetelli, S. (2002). *Latin American thought: philosophical problems and arguments*. Boulder, CO: Westview Press.

Schutte, O. (1993). *Cultural identity and social liberation in Latin American thought*. Albany, NY: State University of New York Press.

19

Latinos on Race and Ethnicity:
Alcoff, Corlett, and Gracia

LAWRENCE BLUM

J. Angelo Corlett, J. J. E. Gracia, and Linda Martín Alcoff have each developed distinctive approaches to the nature of race and of ethnicity.

Corlett

In *Race, Racism, and Reparations* (2003), Corlett rejects race as a coherent and intelligible notion, and provides several arguments against 'primitive race theories,' that is, race as a biologically and genetically significant category. He replaces race with ethnicity, as there can be a coherent account of ethnicity. Corlett does acknowledge that the idea of race might be of some value in understanding racism and therefore in providing justice for groups that have suffered from racism. But ultimately he feels that the appropriate categorization of such groups is better captured by ethnic than racial concepts.

Corlett's conception of ethnicity is quite complex. He makes a distinction between metaphysical and public policy analyses of ethnicity; the latter provide categories that are usable and appropriate in public policy contexts, that is, primarily for reparative justice for groups. Metaphysical analyses are more ambitious and aspire to capture something of the full range of human concerns that attach to ethnicities. Although Corlett sometimes lumps ethnicity together with race as concepts for which he rejects metaphysical analyses, it is appropriate to see him as providing both metaphysical and public policy analyses of ethnicity.

Corlett's genealogical conception of ethnicity

For the public policy analysis (which he also refers to as "ethical"), Corlett says that descent – genealogical ties to an ethnic group – is both necessary and sufficient for ethnic membership. Thus the child of French immigrants to Mexico who grows up speaking Spanish as her native language and embraces Mexican culture does not count as Latino, as she is descended from French persons, not Latin Americans (2003, p. 129): her Mexican ethnoculture does not confer ethnic membership. Corlett sees this genealogical account as useful for public policy in two ways. On a practical level, it is

269

much easier to know someone's genealogy than to be able to assess whether she possesses cultural knowledge, respect for the culture or language, self-identity as a member of the group, or other purported non-genealogical criteria of ethnic membership. It would be very difficult to administer programs aimed at justice for such groups if they required assessing whether a sufficient degree of these subjective criteria had been attained by a given individual. Second, Corlett suggests that ancestry rather than culture triggers racist mistreatment. It is this mistreatment that public policy should attempt to rectify.

This privileging of ancestry in Corlett's account ironically makes his view of ethnicity closer to that of standard accounts of race (including Gracia's) than do ones that privilege culture or language. It also reflects his focus on the United States that is not shared, or at least to nothing like the same extent, by Gracia. It is in the United States that Latinos are treated as at least a semi-racialized group (a feature analyzed by Alcoff), and this provides a reason for privileging that aspect in the context of justice. However, in the United States, Latinos are also demeaned and discriminated against for speaking Spanish; that is, they are discriminated against as an ethnocultural group (a point that Corlett recognizes in other contexts), not only as a (semi-)racialized one.

Corlett acknowledges a scalar dimension to his ancestry criterion. Someone's ancestry can be ethnic group E to a certain degree and ethnic group F to another degree; and Corlett says at one point that virtually everyone has mixed ethnic ancestry. Corlett does not work through the problem this mixedness presents for the public policy use of the genealogical account; but he does suggest that most people will have one predominant ethnicity, and presumably this can serve the required policy purposes. Gracia (2005, p. 40f.) criticizes Corlett's genealogical view for its apparent circularity. 'Being descended from ethnic group G' works as a criterion for membership in G only if one has some other criterion for identifying ethnic group G, or at least some members of it, from whom the others can be descended and thereby acquire membership in G. Corlett acknowledges the circularity but does not think it vicious; the constructedness of ethnicity makes it impossible to pin down a definite criterion of G (p. 227). This simply sidesteps the problem. Nevertheless, Gracia takes his argument against Corlett to show that descent is not central to ethnicity; yet Corlett is surely right to say that descent is central to ethnicity, even if he is wrong to think it can stand alone as a necessary and sufficient condition.

Corlett refers to the public policy definition of ethnicity as "broad" and the metaphysical one as "narrow." That is, persons who satisfy the genealogical condition in the broad definition might not satisfy the narrower one, which provides other conditions that must be satisfied in order for someone to be classified as a Latino/a. Corlett does not discuss these other conditions in great detail, but he does at one point provide a list of them: speaking an Hispanic language (Spanish or Portuguese), possessing and respecting a Latino name, respecting and engaging in significant elements of Latino culture(s), perceiving oneself as Latino/a, being perceived by Latino/as as Latino/a, and being perceived by non-Latino/as as Latino/a (2003, p. 129). Some and perhaps all of these conditions are scalar, and Corlett says that their possession to different degrees makes one a Latino to that degree (p. 39).

Corlett regards this scalar metaphysical account as falling under his category of 'genealogical conception' since the descent condition is still necessary and sufficient

270

for Latinohood. No matter how fully one satisfies the cultural/identity conditions, one is not Latino unless one also satisfies the descent condition.

Corlett's account provides a rationale for common expressions about ethnicity – "Angela is very Latina," "Joe is Irish but not as much as Liam," and so on. Indeed it seems both coherent and accurate to recognize that we do accept the idea of degrees of ethnicity, even if this does not replace but only complements a binary conception of it. That is, we can ask *whether* someone is Latina, but also *how* Latina she is. Corlett does not discuss scalar (narrow) ethnicity in great detail, and many questions remain unanswered, such as exactly what the scalar criteria are, how to compare the different scalar criteria in some sort of common metric, and how to translate that metric into an appropriate degree of ethnicity.

Corlett's account of ethnicity, then, recognizes two types of scalarity – one of the degree of purity of descent from recognized ethne, the other a series of ethnocultural and identity features that can be possessed to greater and lesser extents. He treats these two in different ways. Regarding descent, he (implicitly) proposes a threshold above which an individual becomes a member of the ethnic group and below which she does not. But in the case of the cultural/identity features, he treats the scalar possession of them as translating into a scalar form of the ethnicity itself.

Gracia

Gracia develops his metaphysical accounts of race and ethnicity (that is, accounts of racial and ethnic membership) against a background in which both notions have been challenged on several distinct grounds – conceptual, metaphysical, epistemic, moral, and political. He takes up these challenges systematically, and argues that race and ethnicity are coherent and consistent concepts that apply to the world and reveal features of the world that would be invisible without these concepts. The accounts are meant to "be descriptive in that they reflect the most fundamental principles that underlie the ways in which we think about race, ethnicity, and nationality because these ways are based on a common, collective experience of the way the world is" (2005, p. 37). His book *Surviving Race, Ethnicity, and Nationality: A Challenge for the Twenty-First Century* (2005) is the main locus of this philosophical account, but his earlier work *Hispanic/Latino Identity: A Philosophical Perspective* (2000) is relevant as well.

Gracia notes that philosophers have only recently come to pay attention to these notions, especially ethnicity, and he suggests that a philosophical approach is superior to that of the disciplines most commonly associated with them (e.g., sociology) in aspiring to "put together as complete a picture of the world as possible" and thus necessarily being interdisciplinary and so lacking "a specific methodology" (2005, p. xvi). But Gracia's philosophical approach to race and ethnicity does draw on his background in metaphysics, philosophy of language, and history of philosophy, as well as involving great care in constructing arguments for the claims he makes and in seriously addressing important challenges to his views.

Gracia is particularly concerned to distinguish between race and ethnicity, and thinks they are often confused with one another, with deleterious conceptual and moral consequences, such as confusing cultural and genetic characteristics and not

271

recognizing that ethnic groups can change over time. At the same time, once he has
clarified the conceptual distinction, he believes that race and ethnicity can overlap, both
in the sense that the same group, or portions of the same group, can be both racial and
ethnic (as are African Americans), and that race can itself be one marker of ethnicity
for particular ethnic groups at particular historical periods.

Gracia also regards certain general but false views of both race and ethnicity as obstruct-
ing the possibility of a coherent account of them. One is what he calls "essentialism"
– the assumption that all the individual members of a racial or ethnic group possess
individual properties (such as psychological characteristics of temperament and character, or the sort of characteristic Corlett adverts to in his account, such as speaking
a particular language) that are necessary and sufficient for membership in that group.
But, Gracia argues, members of a given ethnic group do not share such features with
all other co-members. Gracia argues, however, that certain *relational* properties characterize both race and ethnicity (different ones for each), so that he is proposing what
he takes to be a non-essentialist account of race and ethnicity.

A second false assumption is that races and ethnicities have clear boundaries so
that it is always clear whether a given individual is or is not a member of the race
or ethnicity in question. Gracia points out that many of our most important human
concepts do not have clear boundaries in that sense; for example, it is often not clear
if someone should be thought of as "dead" or "healthy." We should be able to accept
the same indeterminacy with respect to both race and ethnicity.

The third assumption is that racial and ethnic groups are internally homogeneous.
This assumption leads to inappropriate and harmful stereotyping of such groups, and
has led some to reject the possibility of a coherent and socially useful account of race
and ethnicity entirely. Gracia's accounts of both concepts explain why neither racial
nor ethnic groups are generally internally homogeneous in this sense.

Gracia's account of ethnicity

Gracia calls his account of ethnicity the "familial-historical" view. He gives much more
attention to the familial than the historical aspect. But by the latter he appears to mean
that an ethnic group is a group that exists over time, and that it has a history and a
changing membership over time as some members die and others are incorporated
through birth and other ways (that will be discussed later). Members of the same
ethnic group stand in "historical relationships" to one another.

Hispanic/Latinos, the group to which Gracia devotes most of this attention, began
to exist as a result of the encounter of the Iberians and the indigenous peoples of
the Americas, and, slightly later, African slaves, beginning in 1492. Prior to this point
there were no "Hispanics," only groups that came to be Hispanic subsequent to 1492,
such as Castilians and Aztecs (not that they necessarily or typically lost these prior
identities).

One meaning of 'historical' that Gracia definitively rejects is that descent or ancestry is a necessary feature of ethnic membership. He rejects descent because, on his view,
people who have no descent relationship to other Hispanics can come to be Hispanic;
for example, if they are Welsh immigrants to Argentina, and then their offspring
migrate to the United States, the latter are Hispanic, though none of their ancestors

are (on his view). He rejects descent as sufficient because someone definitively descended from Hispanics but "who has not lived in a Latino country, has not associated with other Latinos, and does not share with them any perceptible traits" is not Latino (2005, p. 41). This view contrasts with Corlett, who would employ such facts as indicating "degree of Latinoness" but not membership itself.

So Corlett and Gracia's ethnic groups have different membership, not merely different accounts of the same membership. For Latinos, Corlett accepts anyone descended from certain Latin Americans, but Gracia excludes those of this group who have given up their cultural or identity ties to Latin America. But Gracia includes any Latin American national, or at least her descendants, while Corlett excludes some of these, for example, "pure" descendants of more recent European immigrants (and descendants of Asians as well). As Alcoff points out, Corlett's criterion has the effect of excluding a fair number of Latin Americans and their descendants, since parts of Latin America are major immigration ports for Europeans and Asians (Alcoff, 2007, p. 235). But Corlett's account makes sense (at least with respect to Europeans) in terms of his focus on Latinos as a victimized or discriminated-against group in the United States, as it is plausible to think that the people of Latin American origin who are perceived to be 'European' are less likely to be discriminated against as Latin Americans than those not so perceived.

Gracia on family and ethnicity

Gracia gives a good deal of attention to the 'familial' dimension of ethnicity, which he draws from Du Bois, who predicated it of races, although at that time (1897), Du Bois thought of races as possessing what we would think of as ethnic characteristics (Du Bois, 1897). The idea of 'family' is put to several distinct, if related, uses by Gracia, that he does not clearly distinguish. One is to invoke Wittgenstein's notion of 'family resemblance' to say how different persons can be members of the same ethnic group (like the same family) without sharing a common property, but different ones sharing different properties. A second is to illustrate the idea that ethnic membership can come about through more than one relationship. That is, membership in families can come through a diverse set of relationships – marriage, birth, adoption. Similarly, Gracia wants to say, membership in ethnic groups comes about through differing sorts of relationship. There is no one relationship that constitutes ethnicity, as there is no one relationship that constitutes family.

Gracia never attempts to spell out what those ethnicity-making relationships are in a systematic way. Some of them are (some of) the same ones as familial relationships, and this is the third use of 'family' in relation to ethnicity. That is, Gracia thinks that birth is one way of acquiring ethnicity, as is adoption. Some would question, however, whether a Vietnamese adoptee of a Russian-American couple becomes 'ethnically Russian' by being brought up in a Russian-American cultural environment, as Gracia's view asserts, although perhaps fewer would deny that she is 'culturally Russian(-American).' Gracia believes that he has a principled reason for not spelling out the relationships that constitute ethnicity – namely that they can be spelled out only for particular ethnicities in particular historical contexts. "[P]ractically any feature can count toward uniting an ethnos, including racial and national ones" (2005, p. 55). For example, Gracia says, in a particular region, say of the United States,

273

Mexican Americans may be the only Catholics and also the only people with a certain skin color, and so could be distinguished by those features (2005, p. 64). But without giving us some idea of the relationships that constitute ethnicity, we have no basis for differentiating empirical *correlates* with ethnicity in a particular context from characteristics that actually *constitute* ethnicity in that context. Suppose, for example, Mexican Americans in a particular city are confined to one particular neighborhood, so that residing in that neighborhood becomes a way to pick out Mexican Americans in that context. This would not make "residing in X neighborhood" a feature of Mexican American ethnicity. Gracia's stated view provides no basis for seeing the Spanish language but not residential patterns as internally related to Mexican ethnicity (as Corlett holds), although neither one is actually *required* for ethnic membership (a Mexican American need not speak Spanish), and both allow us to pick out particular groups in certain particular contexts.

Returning to the issue of 'family' in his account, Gracia wants family to be more than an analogy to ethnicity. He says that ethne are themselves a *kind* of family, and this is a different use than the two so far mentioned. But what kind of family? Gracia gives this summary of his position:

> An ethnos is a subgroup of individual humans who satisfy the following conditions: (1) they belong to many generations; (2) they are organized as a family and break down into extended families; and (3) they are united through historical relations that produce features that, in context, serve (i) to identify members of the group, and (ii) to distinguish them from members of other groups. (2005, p. 54)

The idea that ethnicities are comprised of extended families is questionable; people who marry a member of an ethnic group are not generally thought of as becoming members themselves, even if they embrace its ethnoculture. Moreover, most ethnic groups are large and range over a wide, often dispersed, geographic area, and are not 'organized' in any overall sense at all, though there may be ethnicity-based organizations. An ethnic group is not really like an actual family, no matter how extended.

Ethnicity, nationality, and sub-nationality

Gracia regards it as arbitrary to confine ethnic membership to national borders. Indians in the UK have historical relationships to Indians in India, so why confine Indian ethnicity to groups that are a minority in a non-Indian nation, and Polish ethnicity to Poles not in Poland? And his account of Hispanic/Latino ethnicity embraces Salvadorans in El Salvador as well as in the United States

Gracia uses the expressions 'Hispanic,' 'Latino,' and, more rarely, 'Hispanic/Latino,' but says in a footnote that he prefers 'Hispanic,' because he regards it, as do many but not all commentators on this terminological issue, as being more inclusive in including residents of the Iberian Peninsula as well as Latin Americans (and their descendants). But it is not clear why inclusiveness is a virtue in this context. Others (e.g., Corlett) favor 'Latino' precisely on the grounds that it captures the European colonial status that unites Latin America and distinguishes it from the colonial powers. The fact that one term includes more people than another does not clinch the issue as to whether it is preferable to the less inclusive term.

Gracia's open-ended and expansive conception of ethnicity does not comport with one aspect of his rationale for his accounts of ethnicity and race, namely that they are meant to help us to see aspects of reality that we would not see were we not in possession of these concepts. This point is a useful antidote to a profligate 'social constructionism' that Gracia rightly rejects; ethnic groups might be historical accidents and human constructs that might even disappear, but they are nevertheless real features of our social world, real human groups that are meaningful to people in and outside of them, and that affect social well-being in various ways. But in light of this, the usual notion of ethnicity that distinguishes between Mexican Americans and Mexicans, with the latter being a *national* and the former an *ethnic* group, is pointing to precisely this feature of our social world. Being an ethnocultural sub-national group (i.e., what Gracia recognizes is ordinarily meant by an 'ethnic group') is a distinct and significant social location; it is not the same as the national identity from which the original immigrant group arose, even if there are cultural connections between the two. Gracia himself provides a striking example of this very point in *Hispanic/Latino Identity*. A Mexican author is speaking to a group of Mexican Americans and making clear to them the difference between being Mexican and being Mexican American, when the audience was hoping she would connect them more closely. In this sense, ethnicity understood as an ethnocultural minority is something quite different from nationality, even when the latter is understood culturally rather than politically. This familiar (in the United States at least) view of ethnicity, in contrast to Gracia's, seems to satisfy Gracia's overarching criterion of adequacy for a view of ethnicity, that it "reflect the most fundamental principles that underlie the ways in which we think about . . . ethnicity, and nationality" (p. 37).

Gracia's genetic common-bundle view of race

Garcia also sees races as a type of family. He recognizes the scientific challenge to the idea of race that many philosophers, including Corlett, have also accepted as showing that there are no races. Gracia gives special attention to K. A. Appiah's attempt to retain a notion of racial identity while jettisoning the notion of race (Appiah, 1996), and Gracia rightly sees this as a confused and unacceptable view. But Gracia also thinks, in contrast to Corlett, that a coherent and scientifically respectable view of race can be resurrected that abandons the implication of large genetic differences between 'races' implied in the discredited scientific view.

Gracia's account of race has two necessary conditions for membership. The first is descent; each member of a race is linked by descent to another member of the group, who is in turn also linked by descent to at least some third member of the group. The second is phenotype; each member of the group has one or more physical features that are (i) genetically transmittable, (ii) generally associated with the group, and (iii) manifest to the senses (what Gracia calls 'perspicuous').

Gracia's phenotypic condition is characterized as 'the common bundle view,' that there exists a bundle of phenotypic characteristics, the possession of some of which

275

render someone a member of the race in question. For blacks, for example, it involves a certain skin shade, hair texture, facial features, and so on.

The descent condition for race is meant to contrast with Gracia's rejection of that condition for ethnicity. It may seem that Gracia is not vulnerable to the circularity problem regarding race of which he accuses Corlett regarding ethnicity, since the phenotypic criterion can provide a non-descent condition to save descent from circularity or infinite regress. But this will not work, since, for example, some Australian aborigines have the same phenotypic characteristics as 'blacks' but are not generally regarded as being of the same race as they. Gracia may ultimately have to rely on a continental origin criterion to replace or at least supplement the phenotype one – Africa for 'blacks,' Australia for (Australian) aboriginals, Europe for 'whites' – to allow the descent dimension to do the work he wants it to do.

Gracia treats his phenotypic and descent criteria as equally operative, thus explicitly rejecting the prioritizing of ancestry over phenotype that characterizes the U.S. view of race, captured in the notion of the 'one-drop rule' – that is, that any degree of African ancestry renders someone 'black,' independent of phenotype. Gracia rejects this rule because he sees it as inconsistent; it cannot be applied equally to all races. It is inherently asymmetrical; black ancestry trumps white, but not vice versa. On Gracia's view, no ancestry is privileged over any other; the degree of ancestry generates a comparable degree of membership in the given race, independently of the phenotype condition. But if a person with half African and half European ancestry looks like what most people take to be "white," on Gracia's view he is white, because of the phenotypic criterion.

Gracia describes a view of race, or at least of phenotype and ancestry, common in Latin America, that contrasts with that in the United States; in the former, there are many terms describing varying combinations and degrees of mixture (of both phenotype and ancestry), such as mestizo and mulato. All parts of the phenotypic and ancestral heritage are recognized in this terminology. This Latin American view is much closer to Gracia's own conception of race than is the U.S. view, for it jettisons the one-drop rule and is symmetrical across races. However, it is not quite the same as Gracia's, since his still retains a small number of racial group terms; racially mixed persons are not seen as falling in a classificatory group of those with that particular racial mixture (as in the Latin American conception) but rather as falling within multiple but a small number of standard racial groups corresponding to the distinct elements of their mixture.

There is an inconsistency between Gracia's account of race and what we saw that he wants his accounts of race and ethnicity to do, namely track the socio-historical, experiential reality of race. He imposes a purely intellectual requirement of symmetry across races, which is independent of the shared historical and experience of race. But in the United States 'race' was, historically and experientially, never a symmetrical concept. Its purpose was to validate the superiority of whites and the inferiority of all other races. This asymmetry is part of the meaning of race in the United States. The one-drop rule reflects how U.S. Americans understood both the concept and the social reality of race. The rule had an intelligible, if complex, rationale, viewed historically. First, by declaring the offspring of slave masters and slave women 'black,' these offspring were deprived of a claim to the superior status of 'whites,' or at least non-blacks. The rule increased the number of slaves, and facilitated slave masters' not acknowledging their liaisons with slave women. The rule also helped to preserve, in the eyes of whites, a social correlate for the view of race that Gracia recognizes as under attack by recent scientific developments, that of a permanent and unalterable biological subdivision of the human species. And after Emancipation in 1865, the one-drop rule also had certain advantages for 'blacks,' and was explicitly discussed and contested within the black community. It prevented divisiveness between 'mixed' and 'unmixed' blacks (that there could not in reality be a clear phenotypic distinction between these two groups only supports this point); made it more difficult for whites to use 'mixed' blacks as a middle group to discipline blacks; and forged ties of solidarity based on the experience of discrimination shared (even if to different extents) by mixed and unmixed blacks. Abandoning the one-drop feature of the U.S. idea of race means abandoning something Gracia says he seeks – to reveal aspects of reality that would be hidden were we to lose or abandon those concepts, and to capture the principles underlying the way (non-Latino/a) U.S. Americans think about race.

Alcoff

Alcoff's approach to race and ethnicity occupies a different conceptual terrain than Corlett's and, even more so, than Gracia's. She is not interested in their shared concern to examine whether race or ethnicity can be given coherent meanings, and, if so, what are the criteria for membership in racial and ethnic groups. Rather she is interested in race and ethnicity as lived realities in society and history. That is, she is interested in race and ethnicity as *kinds of experience*, and as *historical and social processes*. Corlett is also interested (more so than Gracia) in historical racism, primarily as a basis for judgments about justice and injustice that can drive public policy (the "Reparations" in the title of his book). But he does not frame this concern as something internal to the idea of race itself, as Alcoff does.

Even if the concept of race cannot stand up to scrutiny as the intellectually viable notion it has pretended to be, nevertheless race as an historical process has had a profound effect on human social life, and it is this effect with which Alcoff is concerned. Although she nowhere lays out a systematic account of race, or ethnicity, she does provide accounts of both along the way, and sees them as distinct social processes, doing different kinds of social, political, and ideological work.

In her book, *Visible Identities: Race, Gender, and the Self* (2006), which collects, updates, and connects various previously published and in some cases already influential articles, Alcoff is more centrally interested in race than ethnicity. Along with gender, she sees race as having a necessary relationship to the body. This gives race a particular salience and inescapability. "[R]ace operates differently from ethnic or cultural identities, which can be transcended, with enough effort. Inherent to the concept of race is the idea that it exists there on the body itself, not simply on its ornaments or in its behavior" (p. 196). But race, Alcoff says, is not only about bodily features; it is also about attributing inherent and inescapable psychological or behavioral characteristics to a group, and seeing the bodily features as signs of the possession of such characteristics. Alcoff also includes a third feature, not quite as definitively, that the attributed traits are taken to mark the group in question as superior or inferior to other

277

such groups. Thus, for Alcoff, race marks characteristics that *are attributed to* groups; she does not see those characteristics as actually belonging to those groups. By contrast, Gracia looks for characteristics actually possessed by (racial and ethnic) groups to ground an account of them, and Corlett rejects the possibility of an account precisely on the basis that no such attributes can be found.

Alcoff on Latino/as

Like Corlett and Gracia, Alcoff is particularly concerned with Latinos as an ethnic group; but unlike them, her discussion of Latinos is not part of an attempt to come up with a general account of ethnicity in general. On the contrary, she sees 'Latino' as being an importantly distinct kind of ethnicity in the United States, differing in important ways from other ethnic groups. Although she sees 'Latino' as having a basic ethnic meaning, she thinks that the group to which this term refers has been seen and treated, at least in part, in a *racial* manner as well. Latinos thus have a complex relationship to both race and ethnicity, and Alcoff is concerned to understand this relationship. But she is also concerned with the political and ethical question how Latinos *should* position themselves within U.S. society in relation to both race and ethnicity, and she sees the answer to this question (only) partly constrained by the current and historical ways that Latinos have been both ethnicized and racialized.

Alcoff very clearly recognizes that 'Latino' is not an ethnic identity in the way that nationally based ethnicities – such as Mexican American, Dominican American or Salvadoran American – are. Rather it is a *pan*-ethnicity, an umbrella of many distinct ethnocultural groups into one super ethnicity. She shows how Latino pan-ethnicity is created in the United States by several different factors – the pluralizing of Latin American ethnic populations, especially in cities that had been formerly dominated by one ethnonational group (Mexicans in Los Angeles, Puerto Ricans in New York, Cubans in Miami); the creation of a pan-Latino marketing niche; the increasing of mixed ethnic coupling and families; the political value of strength in numbers; the model of African Americans as a 'minority group' agitating for its interests; and the administrative convenience of the 'Hispanic/Latino' category. For these reasons, Alcoff says, Latino pan-ethnicity can feel artificial and 'constructed' in a way that ethnic, that is, ethnocultural, identities do not. Nevertheless, although pan-ethnicities lack the cultural substance that ethnicities like Mexican American possess, Latino pan-ethnicity has come to be a genuine social identity in the United States, one that is personally meaningful to many Latinos. The language of "ethnicity" can be used for both ethnocultural and pan-ethnocultural groups, and the distinction between them does tend to get lost in Gracia's account, while Alcoff's highlighting of pan-ethnicity is salutary in this respect.

The racializing of Latinos

Latinos in the United States, especially immigrants, are often racialized in a way that is unfamiliar in their home countries. In this context, Alcoff means two distinct things by 'racialize.' One is that Latinos are treated as non-white and are stigmatized or seen as inferior in that respect. The other is that Latinos are pressed to claim a racial identity, which can include "white," in terms of standard US racial categories – white, black,

Asian, and so on. There is some evidence that this latter push to claim a racial identity has led some Latinos to claim "Latino" itself as a kind of racial identity, distinct
from and alternative to standard U.S. racial categories (Haney Lopez, 2005). The second form of racialization does not necessarily inferiorize, since some (indeed many) Latinos
can choose to be 'white.' But doing so can still be alienating and unwanted since
it implies a demoting of their ethnocultural or panethnic identity in favor of a racial
one to which they may well not feel a genuine affinity. The two forms of racialization
operate at different levels, and so can coexist. For example, as a *group* Puerto Ricans
might be racialized as (some type of) 'non-white,' but an *individual* light-skinned
Puerto Rican might be seen as 'white.'

Regarding the 'non-whitening' form of racialization, Alcoff says that different
Latino ethnonational groups are treated differently, a difference also sensitive to geographical location (2006, p. 241). So Mexican Americans are more likely to be seen
racially by others, especially whites, than are, say, Argentine Americans; and this is also
more likely to be so when the Latino population of a certain area (say the Southwest)
is predominantly Mexican American. Alcoff credits Gracia with recognizing that the
category 'Latino/Hispanic' carries ethnically distinct associations in different parts of
the United States ("tacos in California, *arroz con gandules* in New York" [p. 241]); she
adds to his point that it is differently racialized as well.

Alcoff asks how Latinos should respond to the forms of racialization she has described. That is, she assumes that while Latinos cannot necessarily stop either the non-
whitening or the 'choosing a race' processes from taking place, they can assert some
agency in the face of these forces. She mentions three different options. One is to embrace
the non-whitening racialization but attempt to reverse its valuation – for example, by
accepting or adopting a 'brown' racial identity but revaluing it as positive rather than
negative, on the model of what U.S. blacks have attempted to do. A second option is
to attempt as much as possible to take on a 'white' racial identity and thereby avoid
racial stigma; or, to put it another way, to assimilate into white society, the way that
the early twentieth-century waves of Southern and Eastern Europeans managed to do
by the 1950s or so (see Jacobson, 1998; Roediger, 2005).

The third option, to which Alcoff devotes the most attention, is the 'ethnic option,'
which she sees as attractive yet ultimately misguided. This option involves resisting
both modes of racialization by asserting that 'Latino' is a (pan)ethnic rather than a racial
identity and that Latinos wish to privilege that (pan)ethnic identity (and perhaps their
particular ethnocultural identities as well). Alcoff associates this option with Corlett's
rejection of race in favor of ethnicity, but this is somewhat misleading as Corlett favors
ethnicity over race because he does not see race as intellectually coherent, not (as Alcoff
does) as politically problematic.

How should Latinos respond to racialization?

In favor of the ethnic option, Alcoff notes that racial terminology tends to carry historically sedimented associations of inherent natures and group hierarchies of worth,
even if many users of that terminology believe themselves to be using racial language
in a neutral, merely classificatory way. Ethnic terminology does not generally carry
these deleterious associations. Alcoff also sees the ethnic option as an advantage because

ethnicity highlights a group's agency – creating its own ethnoculture – while race is an identity imposed from outside the group, and, with the implication of an essential and inherent nature, invokes passivity and determinism (2006, p. 236). Indeed, Alcoff suggests that U.S. blacks have attempted to self-ethnicize by affirming 'African American' as a label of choice over the more distinctly racial 'black,' thereby adding an ethnic association to the group's raciality. Finally, Alcoff points to Latinos being comprised of all of the conventional racial groups (Europeans, Africans, indigenous people, and a smaller number of Asians), and generally a mixture of the first three. So how can they be a 'race' in the U.S. sense?

Alcoff agrees with these positive arguments in favor of the ethnic option; but she nevertheless rejects it as a path for Latinos. First, there is a self-deceptive aspect to it. Just because one embraces an ethnic label does not mean that others will thereby stop seeing one racially. She contrasts Latinos (and Asian Americans) with white ethnics (Polish Americans, Italian Americans) in this respect. The latter groups, she says, managed through ethnic assertion eventually to avoid (group) racialization; but Latinos' ethnic assertiveness tends to evoke guilt and resistance in the white population "because [it] invoke[s] the history of colonialism, annexation, of lands, slavery, and genocide" (2006, p. 243). These associations pull toward a racializing (non-whitening) of these populations and thus prevent Latinos' and Asian Americans' ethnic (or pan-ethnic) assertion from having a deracializing effect.

Both Alcoff's arguments here are problematic. It is true that white ethnics were deracialized in the sense that they stopped being seen by other whites as inferiorized populations with inferior inherent characteristics – a process documented in recent scholarship (Roediger, 2005; Jacobson, 1998). But they accomplished this precisely by coming to be seen definitively and unproblematically as *white*; so they were not deracialized in the sense of not being seen racially, as the 'ethnic option' tries to do. Although current white ethnics often attempt to distance themselves from a white identity by foregrounding their ethnicity, they are still very much thought of as, and recognize themselves to be, white (see Waters, 1990). Alcoff's claim about the historical associations white Americans have with Latinos and Asians and their ethnic assertion is also questionable. Most whites are too unaware of, or deluded about, that history to make those associations of colonization, land-grabbing, and genocide.

But Alcoff's primary argument against the ethnic option is that it is more fruitful for Latinos not to resist North American racialization, since it is essentially impossible to do so, but rather to change the terms of that racialization by attaching more positive meanings to race. She is not naïve about this daunting task; the negative meanings of race are deeply culturally embedded and cannot be willed away. But she takes heart from the work of Paul Gilroy, Robert Gooding-Williams, Lewis Gordon, bell hooks, Patricia Williams, and others, who have looked to an expansive, diasporic notion of blackness that is more cultural and less biologistic and geneticist in character, often rooted in cultural expression, interchange, and historical memory in "the Black Atlantic" (Africa, the United States, the UK, and the Caribbean, as in the concept developed by Gilroy, 1993). (Literature on "the Black Atlantic" has tended, until fairly recently, to omit the black presence in Latin America.) "[T]he meanings of race are subject to some movement. Only a semantic essentialist could argue that race can only mean biological essentialism; in reality, this is not the way meaning works" (Alcoff, 2006, p. 244).

280

While this solution to the problem of what Latinos should attempt to do about racialization is realistic in recognizing the power of race in U.S. life, Alcoff makes the search for a positive racialization harder for herself because of the way she thinks about racial 'blackness.' She looks to a *cultural* blackness provided by the diasporic perspective to supply a sense of agency and avoid the implication associated with racial(ized) blackness of inherent psychological qualities constituting an inferior nature. What Alcoff largely misses here is that the process of racialization itself, independent of its diasporic development, has always included a component of agentic resistance by 'blacks' to the inferiorizing and essentializing aspects of racialization. That is, a continual theme in African American thought, and in pan-African thought more generally, has been to challenge the inferiority in humanity, dignity, capability, and intellect that has been attributed to them. So the agentic challenge to racialized inferiority can arise from within, and be a product of, racialization itself, arising from within a racialized ethnos; it does not have to be sought, as Alcoff does, solely in ethnicity or culture (although it can be found there as well, though perhaps in a less politically focused form).

Another way to put this point is to say that Alcoff's account of race fails to see a politically progressive racial solidarity as standardly arising from racialized groups, racialized ethne. While the point of Alcoff's book is to defend the importance of racial identities as a source of politics, she locates that importance primarily in social and historical power relationships, epistemic perspectives, expressivist concerns, and the need for identity-based representation. Surprisingly absent is that, in the United States and elsewhere, black racial identity has in addition given rise to a sense of politicized (racialized) peoplehood and solidarity – a solidarity that has itself challenged the negative attributes and the inferiorized social position associated with blackness. Exploring the possibility of a similar racialized agency for Latinos in challenging the inferiorization and racial essentializing to which that group is and has been subject might facilitate Alcoff's search for an agentic and political identity that accepts the inescapable fact of racialization.

Alcoff also discusses *mestizaje* – an idea common to the national self-images of several Latin American countries. *Mestizaje* means 'mixedness,' and generally connotes both 'racial' and cultural mixing among the founding populations of Latin America – indigenous peoples, Europeans, Africans. This idea has been used, especially in Brazil where it is called 'racial democracy,' to deny or downplay continuing inequality between a disadvantaged population of people of predominant indigenous or African origin, and a privileged one of predominant European ancestry. Alcoff decries this masking of inequality and of the continuing stigmatizing of African and indigenous peoples in Latin America. She calls attention to this racism, although she does see the idea of *mestizaje* as having some liberatory and cosmopolitan potential. Nevertheless, Alcoff shares with Gracia a denial of anything positive in the U.S. system of racial classification, which denies or downplays mixedness in favor of grouping all people of African ancestry into the 'black' group. But the expanded black solidarity enabled by the one-drop rule is precisely a way to avoid the mystifications of *mestizaje* and to foreground racial injustice.

Related chapters: 7 Darwinism; 17 Ethnic-Group Terms; 18 Identity and Philosophy; 20 *Mestizaje* and Hispanic Identity.

References

Gilroy, P. (1993). *The black Atlantic: modernity and double consciousness.* Cambridge, MA: Harvard University Press.
Gracia, J. J. E. (2000). *Hispanic/Latino identity: a philosophical perspective.* Malden, MA: Blackwell.
Gracia, J. J. E. (2005). *Surviving race, ethnicity, and nationality: a challenge for the twenty-first century.* Lanham, MD: Rowman & Littlefield.
Haney Lopez, I. (2005). Hispanics and the shrinking white majority. *Daedalus,* 134:1, 42–52.
Jacobson, M. F. (1998). *Whiteness of a different color.* Cambridge, MA: Harvard University Press.
Roediger, D. R. (2005). *Working toward whiteness: how America's immigrants became white.* New York: Basic Books.
Waters, M. C. (1990). *Ethnic options: choosing identities in America.* Berkeley: University of California Press.

Further Reading

Bay, M. (2000). *The white image in the black mind: African-American ideas about white people, 1830–1925.* New York: Oxford University Press.
Corlett, J. A. (2007). Race, ethnicity, and public policy. In J. J. E. Gracia (Ed.). *Race or ethnicity? On black and Latino identity.* Ithaca, NY: Cornell University Press.
Du Bois, W. E. B. (1997). *The souls of black folk.* R Gooding-Williams & D. Blight (Eds). New York: St. Martin's Press (Original work published 1903).
Garcia, J. L. A. (2007). Racial and ethnic identity? In J. J. E. Gracia (Ed.). *Race or ethnicity? On black and Latino identity* (Ithaca, NY: Cornell University Press).
Goldberg, D. T. (1993). *Racist culture: philosophy and the politics of meaning.* Oxford: Basil Blackwell.
Gooding-Williams, R. (2006). On Jorge Gracia's *Hispanic/Latino identity.* In *Look, a negro! Philosophical essays on race, culture, and politics.* New York: Routledge.
Gordon, L. (1995). *Bad faith and antiblack racism.* Atlantic Highlands, NJ: Humanities Press.
Gracia, J. J. E. (2007). Individuation of racial and ethnic groups. In J. J. E Gracia (Ed.). *Race or ethnicity? On black and Latino identity.* Ithaca, NY: Cornell University Press.
Gracia, J. J. E. (Ed.). (2007). *Race or ethnicity? On black and Latino identity.* Ithaca, NY: Cornell University Press.
Patterson, O. (2005). Four modes of ethno-somatic stratification. In G. Loury, T. Modood, & S. Teles (Eds). *Ethnicity, social mobility, and public policy.* New York: Cambridge University Press.
Telles, E. (2004). *Race in another American: the significance of skin color in Brazil.* Princeton: Princeton University Press.
Williams, P. (1997). *Seeing a color-blind future: the paradox of race.* New York: Farrar, Straus, Giroux.

20

Mestizaje and Hispanic Identity

GREGORY VELAZCO Y TRIANOSKY

The struggle to define their identity has been a part of the experience of Latin Americans and people of Latin American descent since the beginning. During the colonial period, influenced strongly by developments in Spain itself, this struggle took on the form of defining racialized identities. In the Viceroyalties of Mexico and Peru, which covered substantial parts of Spain's New World territories, racial identity was refined through the *casta* system, which mapped a highly ramified terminology onto a set of identities rigidly distinguished through birth and heredity (Katzew, 2005). Even more widely used during the period, and surviving in one way or another until the present day, was the more generalized terminology of *mestizo* and *mulato*, referring to those who were by birth of mixed indigenous and Spanish heritage, and of mixed African and Spanish heritage, respectively.

It was during the independence period, spanning roughly one hundred years from the early nineteenth century to the early twentieth, that the term *mestizo* came to be used more broadly by nationalist and pan-nationalist writers like Bolívar and Martí to refer to people of mixed European and either indigenous or African descent, in service of the claim that it is this range of racial mixtures which is characteristic, or indeed definitive, of the peoples of Latin America. Despite this explicit broadening of the term, however, and despite the widespread importation of African slaves throughout much of South America and Mexico as well as the Caribbean during the preceding 300 years, in much of the literature of this period the African presence is unmentioned or even ignored. The choice of the term *mestizo* in the independentist literature thus hints at one continuing challenge in the struggle over Hispanic identity, namely, to accord an appropriate place in the mix to African heritage and African-influenced cultural forms throughout the Americas.

Vasconcelos and Essentialist Conceptions of *Mestizaje*

Although the work of José Vasconcelos appeared after the independence period had come to an end, it represents many of its major trends and their nineteenth-century European context. Vasconcelos' work mixes nationalist strains with an explicit pan-nationalist ideology. Unlike some earlier writers in this period, Vasconcelos explicitly

283

defines the racial mix he holds to be characteristic of Hispanic people as including African elements as well as indigenous and Spanish ones, and indeed, at least in some passages, a variety of other elements as well (Vasconcelos, 1997, p. 22, but see p. 26 for an important qualification with respect to the presence of black people). Vasconcelos famously holds that this mixing of the races will give rise to a newly emergent race, the *raza cósmica* (cosmic race), which is well suited to take the lead in the new age of love and "brotherhood" into which the world is emerging:

> In Spanish America, Nature will no longer repeat one of her partial attempts. This time, the race that will come out of the forgotten Atlantis will no longer be a race of a single color or of particular features. . . . What is going to emerge out there is the definitive race, the synthetical race, the integral race, made up of the genius and the blood of all peoples, and, for that reason, more capable of true brotherhood and of a truly universal vision. (Vasconcelos, p. 20)

Like the early Du Bois and many of his nineteenth-century compatriots in the United States, Vasconcelos regards each of these races as having certain essential qualities – a "gift" or "genius" that it brings to the mix. Even aside from his mysticism, much of Vasconcelos' writing expresses classic European conceptions of racial essences, complete with Orientalist tropes (Vasconcelos, pp. 21–2).

The notion of race he deploys is an *essentialist* one: it supposes that race membership is conferred in the first instance by descent, and that descent always carries with it a predisposition to certain traits of character and personality, if not phenotype, in the individual case; and a predisposition to certain cultural forms, in the case of the group taken as a whole. This notion is a familiar one in the eighteenth and nineteenth centuries, in Latin America as in the United States and Europe. What is distinctive of the strand of Latin American thought under discussion is first, the insistence that the mixing of races can itself generate a new race (and not merely a group of "mongrel" or "half-breed" peoples, as conventional nineteenth- and early twentieth-century European and North American wisdom held); second, a corresponding attempt to valorize *mestizaje* so conceived; and finally, the attempt to link *mestizaje* thus interpreted to an explicitly Hispanic nationalist or pan-nationalist understanding of identity.

Beginning in the 1930s, shortly after publication of *La raza cósmica*, and continuing until the present time, a network of criticisms of the essentialist understanding of *mestizaje* and its deployment in an account of Hispanic identity have been raised. In brief, critics have argued that the essentialist understanding of *mestizaje* provides a foundation for narrowly defined, utopian nationalist or pan-nationalist ideals that support intolerance and the marginalization of difference, both within *mestizaje* culture and between it and its component groups. (See sources cited in Miller, 2004.)

First, it has been pointed out that the "gifts" of the races were plainly specified in very unequal terms, as the above quotation from Vasconcelos should suggest. The "White" or European contribution to the mix is "superior ideals," "superior traits of culture and nature," or more specifically, "clear mind," "science," "control of matter," rationality, intellect, reason, and "practical talents," issuing in "railroads, bridges, and enterprises." However much these need to be modulated by spirituality, emotion, and a concern for justice and non-violence, it is "the Whites" who are "a race full of vigor and solid social virtues," and it is the other races that "might be considered inferior" (Vasconcelos, pp. 17–26). Thus it is the civilization of "the white race" which "sets the moral and material basis for the union of all men into a fifth universal race" (Vasconcelos, p. 9). Consequently it is Europeans, or the "White" elements in Latin America, that are expected to take the lead, both politically and in setting the broad agenda for education and cultural development. It is the "superior ideals" of "the Whites" that are to be propagated, although not by the "harsh law of [racial] domination . . . and extinction" characteristic of North American colonial practices (Vasconcelos, p. 25). Moreover, even though the hallmark of the Cosmic Race is its mestizo character, Spaniards are characterized as already-mixed; and it is the Spanish method of "the abundance of love that allowed them to create a new race with the Indian and the Black" (Vasconcelos, p. 17) that is valorized in his writings, in contrast with the violent and genocidal methods of "the Anglo-Saxon" (Vasconcelos, p. 18). Thus the gifts of the already-mixed Spaniards define both the "ideals" and the methods of their propagation for the emergent Cosmic Race. In this respect it was easy to see the essentialist use of *mestizaje* as simply old wine in new bottles: a validation, if not a valorization, of the old colonial structure of social and political oppression; underwritten by an ideology that only seemed innovative.

Second, critics pointed out that the very notion of a *raza cósmica* as inherently superior in its synthesis of racial "gifts" privileges those identified as mestizo over those who are identified – or who self-identify – as "black" or "Indian." Indeed, given the tie to a nationalist or pan-nationalist conception of identity, such people are by definition marginal if not inimical to the nationalist or pan-nationalist project. Thus policies designed to support or protect their communities must, unless they are assimilationist in intent (like what is called transitional bilingual education in California today), be a threat to the project itself. Here again the essentialist understanding of *mestizaje* appears to support the continuing marginalization of the poorest and most discriminated-against segments of Latin American society, defined once again, as in the colonial period, as the racial Other.

This difficulty reveals a second important challenge in the continuing debates over Hispanic identity, namely, to define that identity in a way that does not ratify the continuing marginalization and unjust treatment of indigenous peoples and indeed peoples of African descent as well. The negritude or *negrista* movement in the Caribbean, and to some extent *indigenista* movements in various parts of Latin America as well, rejected the terms of this challenge by seeking to valorize the stereotypical traits assigned to these marginalized communities: in the case of Afro-Hispanic communities, for example, "unbridled lust" (to use Vasconcelos' phrase), the exaltation of emotion over reason, music, rhythm, the associations with the supernatural vision of *santería* and *vodún*. The poetry of Nicolás Guillén or Luis Palés Matos is typical in this respect. But in so doing, these movements seem to endorse the essentialist understanding of race that underlies the conception of *mestizaje* under discussion, thus giving credibility to the complaint that they only succeed in imprisoning black or indigenous communities in the traditional stereotypes, independently of any positive value these are taken to have.

Third, it is sometimes claimed that the deployment of the notion of *mestizaje* in the project of developing a nationalist or pan-nationalist identity is a utopian one. Even

285

setting aside Vasconcelos' mystical bent, the project itself is certainly utopian in a literal sense, since it is clearly envisioned by many of its advocates, past and present, both in North and in Latin America, as defining a valued future state. More deeply, however, when underwritten by an essentialist conception of *mestizaje*, the project seems to regard the erasure of biological and cultural difference via the blending of the races as the key to social harmony. From the point of view of the essentialist version of the ideal, at any rate, current biological and cultural differences must therefore be dysfunctional. The superiority of homogeneity is in this way implicit in the utopian ideal of social harmony. If this is the case, then intolerance and repression of difference, and even genocide, may seem, and indeed in many cases in the history of Latin America have seemed, the proper response, even if the ideal itself does not explicitly include or endorse them.

It must be said, however, that the validity of these criticisms may turn not on the project of linking some conception of *mestizaje* to nationalist or pan-nationalist ideas of Hispanic identity so much as it turns on the commitment to an essentialist understanding of *mestizaje* itself. Historically acute though these critical observations are, perhaps their force as objections to the project in question could be blunted if one were willing to adopt an anti-essentialist approach on which mestizo cultural and perhaps even racial identity were conceived as more open-textured and multi-vocal (Velazco y Trianosky, 2002). Here, then, is, if not necessarily a third challenge to any discussion of Hispanic identity, at least a central challenge for those who advocate the project of grounding that identity in some conception of *mestizaje*: to do so without being drawn into the essentialist quagmire.

Gloria Anzaldúa: The New *Mestizaje*

In the twentieth and twenty-first centuries, as increasingly large and diverse Hispanic populations have emigrated from Latin America to the United States, the question of Hispanic identity has taken on a new dimension. In the United States the question is not typically posed in nationalist or even quite pan-nationalist terms; but instead in terms of the common identity of strangers who, to one degree or another, have made, or found, their homes in a strange land.

Perhaps because it is free from the nationalist project, the work of recent American theorists of *mestizaje* like Gloria Anzaldúa turns attention away from the essentialist search for common ancestry or mixed lines of descent. For Anzaldúa, identity is grounded instead in the concrete experience of Chicanas (Mexican American women) as women who live between traditional Mexican culture and the dominant Anglo culture of the United States. In the first instance, therefore, her work is a study in the logic of the identity of a particular sub-group of Hispanics. Nonetheless, her conception of *mestizaje* as grounded in the experience of living "in between" is often regarded as a prototype for Hispanic identity in the United States, and it will be so regarded here. This general way of understanding mestizo identity is sometimes called "the New *Mestizaje*," a label which will be adopted here.

To live between cultures, for Anzaldúa, is to experience ambiguity on a daily basis. The person living in between recognizes, willingly or unwillingly, the authority of two

286

conflicting sets of norms. For the mestizo, the norms of the dominant culture constitute, not simply the alienated external forces that must be reckoned with by every stranger who visits a strange land, but internalized requirements and expectations that shape to some extent their outlook, habits, and choices in ways not altogether unlike the ways that these are shaped by the norms of the "home" culture from which they, or their family, have come. To be mestizo is thus to live a life, whether as an immigrant or as a resident of a territory now dominated by an alien culture, in which there is an internal *split* in one's day-to-day experience, and not just a discontinuity from one time or place in one's life to another (cf. Anzaldúa, 1987, pp. 2–3).

The immediate result of living in between, so described, is the experience of a kind of second-order ambiguity as well, involving moments of clarity and distance from both of one's two cultures, in which one's detachment enables one to think creatively both about who one is, and about how to regard others. For this reason, Anzaldúa sees the mestizo experience as potentially a liberating one (Anzaldúa, 1987, pp. 22, 55, 79–80).

In contrast to the traditional Latin American understanding, then, *mestizaje* is constituted for Anzaldúa not in terms of mixed blood, but in terms of the multiply-ambiguous experience of daily life. There is a twofold shift in the theorizing of *mestizaje* involved in her approach. First, there is a substantive shift from a putatively objective understanding of *mestizaje* in terms of mixed blood to a subjective account in terms of mestizo experience. This shift is of great importance in the discussion of *mestizaje*, supported as it is by increasingly widespread skepticism about the idea of race as a legitimate scientific category. Second, there is a rhetorical shift, from the notion of a mestizo as someone who is half one thing and half another – a bronze alloy composed of two distinct elements, to use one of Vasconcelos' metaphors – to the notion of a mestizo as someone who is fully neither. For Anzaldúa, to be mestizo is to be "*ni chicha ni limonada*," as the saying has it (rendered colloquially: neither fish nor fowl). Mestizos are alienated, not fully identified with either culture. With respect to both cultures, they find themselves experiencing moments of distance and moments of identification.

Anzaldúa's approach has been widely viewed as providing a foundation for a progressive discussion of practical and moral problems of justice, resistance, and assimilation – new versions of the very problems discussed above as challenges to the essentialist accounts. Influential as Anzaldúa's work has been, however, there are some risks involved in deploying this understanding of *mestizaje* to define Hispanic identity, or for that matter, more specific notions like Chicano/a identity. For one thing, there is always the danger of homogenizing the experience of being in between. If the notion of *mestizaje* is to be conceived experientially, it is important to emphasize that there are many different ways of being mestizo. Some of them may be more uncomfortable and damaging to the subject of experience, or perhaps more creative and energizing, or perhaps all of these. Some ways of being in-between cultures may only create discomfort in certain circumstances. Some ways of being "in between" may allow one to be more or less at home on both sides of the (literal or figurative) border, while still others may ensure that one is never at home anywhere. To be in between is, as characterized above, simply to be in a certain position with respect to the norms of two very different cultures. It would be an all-too-familiar mistake, echoing the criticisms of Vasconcelos given above, to suppose that there is only one way, or indeed only one correct or "authentic" way, of living this position.

Hidden below the surface of this mistake is of course the danger of essentializing the position of being in between, conceiving the mestizo as some third type of being. This would be to return to the Vasconcelos position. But the power of Anzaldúa's work is that it shows us the potential that being Chicana in America, for example, can have to liberate those so identified from the deadening weight of both the culture of origin and the dominant culture by giving them a potentially creative distance on each. Her idea, generalized to yield an account of Hispanic identity, is that to be Hispanic is to have the potential to refuse two cultural traditions and the identities that each defines; and to have in consequence the potential to act creatively to define new ways of living. It is precisely not, therefore, to have some particular, "third" nature. Instead, on her view as here generalized, it is to be free to create one's own. To be sure, this creation is not ex nihilo; it is grounded in the sense of alienation from each of two cultures, in tension with the very internalization of the norms of each that defines being in between.

On the other hand, there is no special magic that flows with necessity from living between. The middle is what one makes of it; and Anzaldúa shows us how Chicano/as can draw on certain resources in Mexican culture and mythology to make it a site of resistance. This liberatory potential for providing creative insight and resistance, however, may or may not be realized by those who live between. The mestizo position therefore should not be romanticized, as though by its very nature it made one superior, regardless of the character of one's choices and moral views.

There is another danger, however, that Anzaldúa herself may not always fully appreciate. It is undoubtedly very difficult to live suspended in between for long, and the development of Chicano/a culture itself points up the result. Over a single generation, Mexican immigrants in the United States responded to the experience of being in between by creating a third culture of their own, Chicano/a culture. This sedimentation of the experience of immigrants into a full-blown culture is probably unavoidable. Many immigrant groups tend to settle, and, in so doing, create new variants on the old ways, influenced by new surroundings and customs. This is why "going back" after even a few years can seem strange and disorienting. This tendency to create or re-create culture undercuts the experience of living in between.

It is true that, depending on one's criteria for the individuation of cultures, one might reasonably regard Chicano/a culture not as a distinctively new culture, but rather as a continuation of both Mexican culture and Anglo-American culture at the same time. After all, in any culture each generation is always engaged in the creative reinterpretation of the norms it has internalized. In any case, there has grown up in the United States a Chicano/a culture which, however heterogeneous it may be, embodies like any other culture a set of norms against which Chicano/as can react, and between whose demands and the demands of Anglo culture they can, once again, find themselves living. (Anzaldúa's discussion of sexism and homophobia in Chicano/a culture, pp. 16–21 in the work discussed above, should make this clear.) In short, the position of living in between is so far from being essential to the experience of Chicano/as that it may in fact be inherently ephemeral, almost inevitably giving way to the creation of a new or perhaps re-elaborated culture.

Linda Alcoff has argued in favor of a rather different way of understanding Hispanic identity in the United States. She tentatively rejects Anzaldúa's rhetorical shift, mentioned at the outset of this section, from conceiving *mestizaje* as "both combined" to conceiving it as "neither/nor." In a generalization of the notion of Chicano/a culture as a continuant of both Mexican and Anglo-American cultures, Alcoff proposes that to be mestizo in the United States is to possess a kind of cultural dual citizenship, to be at the same time fully a member of both the dominant American culture and of the Latin American culture of one's country of origin. She regards this proposal as grounding a legitimate but dual identity that the cultural mestizo can embrace, constituting "an alternative positive articulation of *mestizo* consciousness and identity," thus undercutting the psychological discomfort and dislocation of the experience of being in between (Alcoff, 2006, p. 280, in reference to one aim of Anzaldúa's work, shared by Alcoff).

In order for this notion of double identity to be successful, however, Chicano/as, for example, must be able to regard themselves as fully Mexican, and as fully American. This has the consequence that there will be Mexicans – many third-generation immigrants to the United States, for example – who do not speak Spanish or ever visit Mexico, and who may not even know of any living relatives still in that country. As suggested above, whether this is plausible depends on one's account of culture and cultural continuity. For example, if one rejects essentialist understandings of culture, as Alcoff does, and if one defends instead both a historical understanding of what it means to be a member of a particular culture, and fairly porous criteria of cultural identity or continuity through change (Gracia, 1999, pp. 44–69), then it may not be unreasonable to see Chicano/as as Mexican, and, mutatis mutandis, as American as well. This does not mean, however, that many of the conflicts that are now experienced by mestizos in the United States insofar as they conceive themselves as being between cultures will necessarily disappear. Perhaps they will simply be recast as intra-cultural conflicts between those "here" and those "back home," similar to the inter-generational conflicts referred to above and familiar in many cultures. Moreover, it remains to be seen how such an account can ground the liberatory function of *mestizaje* so strongly emphasized by Anzaldúa, namely, that of creating a critical vantage point from which culture, its values, and its constructions can be questioned. (See Velazco y Trianosky, 2002, for a discussion of how such an account might serve this purpose.)

María Lugones: *Mestizaje* and Hybridity

Lugones's work provides a highly theorized conception of *mestizaje*, not intended to apply merely to the case of Hispanics, and in fact, not intended specifically to answer the traditional question about what it is to be a Hispanic at all. Lugones is concerned instead to explore the logic of resistance to oppression through a more nuanced understanding of the nature of "interlocking oppressions," or different forms of oppression that intersect to limit our understanding (and their own) of the identity of the oppressed, and of their options. Ultimately her objective is to find ways for oppressed and marginalized peoples to build true and lasting coalitions. The challenges of justice, repression, and assimilation that appeared in response to Vasconcelos' work, and that drove much of the recent work by Anzaldúa and others, reappear as a driving force in the work of Lugones.

289

Her work focuses on conceptions of cultural separation and purity, organized around the trope of emulsion as expressing the kind of mixed or mestizo identity that many people in many cultures and sub-cultures have: a mixture that, if it separates at all, separates impurely, with traces of each element remaining in every portion of the mix (Lugones, 2003, pp. 121–6). Here again there is a rhetorical shift that enriches the discussion of *mestizaje*, one that perhaps underwrites a new approach to the practical and moral issues of continuing concern in discussions of *mestizaje*.

Her most influential idea in this vein has been the notion of *mestizaje* as involving the experience of "world-traveling," or crossing from one sub-culture to another, where different "selves" or, one might say, different aspects of one's identity, function in each sub-culture. On her view, for a "world-traveler" resistance to oppression involves (a) resisting the pressures to identify oneself purely with any one of these "selves," particularly when the interests of these selves are conceived "thinly" (Lugones, 2003, pp. 85–98); and (b) using the "impure" aspects of oneself to disrupt the homogenizing expectations of many of the "worlds" one inhabits (Lugones, 2003, pp. 126–34).

It is tempting to say that Lugones's work is too highly theorized and not sufficiently attentive to the highly variable details of concrete experience. The turn to abstraction is evident even in the final chapter of Lugones's book, which is entitled, "Tactical Strategies of the Streetwalker," where she tries to develop a theoretical framework for understanding resistance and organization "on the street." At another level, however, Lugones's work shows how one can write as a Hispanic, conscious of how one draws upon the unique Hispanic experience with *mestizaje*, to address more general questions of coalition and resistance. It can thus be seen as pointing the way beyond the preoccupation with questions of Hispanic identity to broader issues of identity and culture, and the concerns about justice and repression that frequently animate them.

On the other hand, Lugones and quite a number of other post-nationalist, postmodernist writers frequently seem not to appreciate fully the distinction between the concept of *mestizaje* and broader notions like hybridity or nomadic subjectivity (Alcoff, 2006, pp. 275–7; Miller, 2004, p. 144f.) If hybridity is a term of art drawing our attention to the porous or heterogeneous nature of culture, then it describes something to be found in every experience of prolonged cross-cultural interaction, cultural conflict, cultural blending, or domination. It is, if not the common lot of most peoples in most times and places, then certainly, as many proponents of the notion have claimed, the common lot of almost all peoples in today's increasingly globalized economy. But to see *mestizaje* as simply the local instantiation of the pervasive phenomenon of hybridity risks losing what is distinctive about Hispanic cultures, even in the postmodern world, namely, that for much of their history and across otherwise great changes and variations in culture, the concept of *mestizaje* has played an explicit and powerful organizing role in social and political institutions, everyday practices, and people's understanding of themselves and others. The concept is therefore not in the first instance a theoretical one, but a quotidian one. It is self-consciously deployed by Hispanics themselves in order to understand and regulate themselves and those around them. Consequently a theory of *mestizaje* should be seen as first and foremost a theory rooted in the self-understanding of Hispanics, with all the risks and the potential benefits that critically examining a cultural self-understanding promises.

Implicit in these remarks is a second point of difference between hybridity in general and *mestizaje* in particular. It does not suffice to make the distinction between the two merely to point out that the use of the latter concept is self-conscious and quotidian, while the use of the former concept is theoretical and removed. *Mestizaje* is not simply a folk version of a theoretical construct. Talk of mestizo identity is specific to a particular quotidian cultural context or range of contexts. It is the specifically Latin American version, where the hybridity in question is constituted by the gamut of individual and cultural experiences of living in between cultures of Spanish and Portuguese origin, on the one hand; and cultures of either African or American Indian origin (or both), on the other. The salience of these particular forms of living in between, in turn, is a function of the sui generis place of black and Indian racial categories in the American imaginary, both in Latin America and in North America, and the various ideologies that have grown up around the two corresponding, pervasively American forms of race mixing.

The New *Mestizaje* and Race

The departure from essentialist understandings of *mestizaje* has opened up a variety of new and important lines of inquiry, but it may appear that what has been left behind is the notion of *mestizaje* as a type of racial identity. Indeed, the various rhetorical and substantive shifts described above might be read as movements away from racial categories, seen as embodying putatively objective claims about biological nature, and toward categories of self-identification, seen as embodying subjectively grounded claims about self-understanding against a particular cultural background.

To reject the sort of biological essentialism about race represented here by the work of Vasconcelos, however, is not necessarily to reject any and all accounts of what race and racial categories are. The paucity of attempts to integrate alternative understandings of what race is into the contemporary discussion about *mestizaje* is therefore noteworthy. (But see Bernasconi, 2007, p. 135.) Many writers in race theory today hold that, though racial categories may present themselves as embodying claims about biological nature, as a matter of fact they designate and define socially constructed kinds. On this constructionist view, the real issue about whether *mestizaje* constitutes a racial category is an issue about whether it does or should figure in the socially constructed frameworks that define racial categories in a particular time and place. Of course, to the extent that these frameworks are variable, the answer to such a question may likewise be variable. In any case, there is recent work in race theory suggesting that subjective elements have a central place in the social construction of race.

Robert Gooding-Williams has drawn a distinction, in effect, between one's meeting the socially defined criteria for membership in a particular racial category ("being black," in the case of interest for his discussion), and one's self-identifying as a member of that racial category ("being a black person," in his terminology) (Gooding-Williams, 1998. Compare Bernasconi's discussion of Alain Locke's "dynamic conception of group identity" in the work mentioned above.) One might say that the question of what racial *category* one belongs to is a matter of objective fact, with the understanding that the categories are socially constructed (compare "being from Texas"); and the question of whether one *self-identifies* with some socially sanctioned racial categorization is a subjective one (compare "being a Texan," or perhaps "being a real Texan").

Moreover, to use terminology that is not quite Gooding-Williams' own, one might say that one is *fully* self-identified with the racial category in which one is placed only under certain conditions. Gooding-Williams says that one "becomes a black person," i.e., has one's identity at least partially constituted by one's being socially classified as black, only if (1) one begins to identify (classify) oneself as black and (2) one begins to make choices, to formulate plans, to express concerns, etc., in light of one's identification of oneself as black (Gooding-Williams, p. 23). He later appears to add a third condition to what is here called full self-identification: (3) the "meanings and understandings" that one assigns "to being black" are ones that have been assigned in awareness of the fact that one lives "in a society that has been shaped by black slavery and anti-black racism" (Gooding-Williams, p. 32).

Gooding-Williams does not regard this kind of self-identification as simply a psychological epiphenomenon supervening on already-constructed racial categories. Instead, he says, "Individuals so classified contribute to the construction of their racial identities" through "the identifications by which they shape their projects [and their self-understandings] in light of the racial labeling and classifications to which they have been subjected" (Gooding-Williams, pp. 22–3). On this account, one might say, the ontology of racial categories contains both subjective and objective elements; and the relation between subjective self-identification and objective socially-constructed categories should be conceived as a dynamic one. The racial categories, their history, and their context ground self-understanding and, in turn, the self- and communal understanding of those who are defined, e.g., as black can in turn help to shape the criteria of application for the category of blackness, or perhaps even the content of the concept itself. (Cf. Alcoff, pp. 182–6.)

This account suggests an approach to the relation between race and *mestizaje*, but with one qualification. Notice that Gooding-Williams' view, at least as reconstructed here, seems to contain a conservative element: black self-identification requires seeing oneself as a member of the currently-established racial category, "black." Though of course the experience and the responses of self-identified "black persons" may over time alter the shape of the category, the starting-point for black self-identification is the category as currently given. For the self-identified "black person" the category itself is, in this respect, uninterrogated.

With respect to *mestizaje* the situation in the United States is quite different. It has certainly been argued that "Hispanic" is, or is becoming, a racial category here (see, e.g., the sources quoted in Alcoff, pp. 241–2). The specific question at hand, however, is whether Hispanicity understood in terms of *mestizaje* has been established as such; and it is probably correct to say that, at least in the twentieth and twenty-first centuries, there is no generally accepted racial category in the United States that corresponds roughly to the range of contemporary Hispanic conceptions of *mestizaje* rather than to some more general notion of mixed race. It appears, therefore, that *mestizaje* subjectively understood creates an identity orthogonal to the current socially constructed American racial categories. Fully to self-identify as mestizo in the United States is thus explicitly to reject exclusive classification in any one of the available racial categories. And, of course, for writers like Anzaldúa, this is precisely the point: to be mestizo in the United States is to have a certain subjective understanding of one's place in refer-ence to the dominant racial schema that is not supported by its objectively established racial categories. One might say, to adopt a term of Falguni Sheth's, that *mestizaje* so understood is inherently an unruly identity (Sheth, 2009, chapter 1).

It could be argued that it counts as a racial identity nonetheless, for two reasons: First, it is a self-identification built on racial categories, albeit orthogonally. All the accounts of the New *Mestizaje* discussed thus far locate the mestizo subject with respect to racial categories: as neither one nor the other; or as partially one and partially the other; or as fully both; etc. Second, there is no reason to think that every subjectively defined racial identity must fit one and only one of the socially available, objective racial cate-gories, unless one assumes that the fundamental racial categories must necessarily be exhaustive and mutually exclusive. But these are exactly the assumptions that the idea of a mestizo racial identity seeks to challenge. Indeed, perhaps a significant part of the potential power of the notion of *mestizaje* as a racial identity, deployed in the American context, is its presupposition that racial identities need not track racial categories one-to-one. On the other hand, provided these two points are conceded, perhaps whether one insists on calling it a category of racial identity rather than, say, a category of ethnicity or even of counter-cultural or counter-racial identity does not matter. (But see the discussions in Gracia, 2007.)

Of course, there remains the challenge facing any social-constructivist account of race of how to reinterpret or replace North American and Latin American essentialist notions of descent as the mode of transmission for racial identity. This echoes the last challenge mentioned in the discussion of Vasconcelos above, although the problem is not unique to constructivist attempts to frame *mestizaje* in particular as a racial iden-tity. The work of Gracia, Corlett, and others suggests that it may be useful to explore historically oriented accounts of racial continuity between generations for this purpose (Gracia, 1999; Corlett, 2003).

A more difficult question, perhaps, has to do with how regarding *mestizaje* as a racial identity might affect its liberatory potential. The insight guiding the writers who offer a subjective understanding of *mestizaje* is that this potential is rooted in the nature of the experience of living in between. In the United States *mestizaje*, subjectively understood, clearly begins from a potentially liberatory perspective since, as suggested above, to self-identify as mestizo is to begin from the experience of a kind of racelessness. But what are the conditions under which *mestizaje* so understood can sustain this potential?

First, full-self-identification as a mestizo must involve an understanding, not only of the history of the treatment of the peoples so classified (parallel to Gooding-Williams's third condition), but also of the fact that the racial categories out of which an objec-tive category of *mestizaje* might be built in the United States, and out of which it has been built in Latin America, are socially constructed. *Mestizaje* cannot retain its liberatory potential so long as self-identified mestizos see themselves as frozen into a certain in-between range of character and culture by virtue of their mixed descent. On one view, the history of the negritude movement shows how an attempt to liber-ate by exercising the power of racialized self-understanding can fail when it is under-written by essentialist notions of race. Thus the notion of full self-identification required for the subjective account of *mestizaje* to do its job must be even stronger than the one here attributed to Gooding-Williams.

293

Second, full self-identification must involve a disposition to resist the sedimentation of living in between into a full-blown culture, for the reasons given above in the discussion of Chicano/a culture. It is this refusal of a defining culture, along with the New *Mestizaje*'s underlying refusal of the currently established racial categories, that opens up the possibility of the sorts of rhetorical shifts in thinking about racial identity that appear in the work of Anzaldúa, Lugones, and Alcoff.

Finally, and for the same reasons, insofar as racial categories in the United States begin to change so that mestizo itself becomes an available socially constructed racial category on a par with being black or being white and with which one can identify, the fully self-identified mestizo must reject that as well. After all, much of the writing of Anzaldúa, Lugones, Alcoff, and others focuses precisely on the way in which the liberatory potential of *mestizaje* comes from its resistance of the imposition of any socially defined racial category, old or new, onto the experience of living in between.

The above conditions are difficult to satisfy, and consequently the liberatory potential of *mestizaje* will be difficult to maintain, to the extent that it is conceived as a racial identity. The full weight of two sets of socially constructed racial categories (Latin American and those of the United States) militate against the satisfaction of these conditions, as do the pervasive sociocultural pressures toward regulating and controlling the experience of living in between. Perhaps it is best to think of the experience of living in between as defining a powerful and demanding kind of ideal, toward which some who live between Latin American cultures and Anglo-American culture will aspire, and which, on some occasions at least, will characterize the day-to-day experience of many more. On the other hand, an analogous set of conditions do appear to be satisfied by the increasingly widespread forms of self-identification described in much of the popular literature of the mixed-race movement.

Mestizaje and Pan-Hispanic Identity

Clearly much, though by no means all, of the discussion of *mestizaje*, both in the more traditional essentialist mode and among the proponents of the New *Mestizaje*, has been motivated by the hope that in some form or other it can be used to define a pan-Hispanic identity.

There are a variety of ways in which this might be accomplished in the United States, provided that one expects no more precision than is appropriate to the subject matter of group identity-claims. For example, one might delimit, very roughly, a group of people who either (a) have emigrated from their homes in Latin America to, or otherwise found themselves in, the United States, or (b) are descended from people who have so emigrated or so found themselves. Such a broad, objective delimitation might also suffice to pick out a group who are to some extent disposed, in virtue of tradition and upbringing, to deploy variants of some subjective notion of *mestizaje*, already familiar to one degree or another from its use in Latin American contexts, in order to understand their own racial and cultural experience in the United States. Hispanics would then be those people whose lives and histories displayed both this objective feature and a disposition toward such a subjective form of self-understanding. (Cf. Corlett, 2003.)

294

Naturally, this approach will legitimize a correspondingly broad range of experiences of being in between as legitimately mestizo experiences, underwriting in turn a wide range of interpretations and understandings of what is involved in subjectively self-identifying as Hispanic. But perhaps this is as it should be. Perhaps the real question of what interests – or indeed what cultural forms and values – Hispanics in the United States have in common on any particular occasion or issue should be left open for debate by an account of Hispanicity. Moreover, by leaving these questions open, the proposed account undercuts the frequently heard objection to embracing a pan-Hispanic identity, namely that it involves the erasure of national, ethnic, linguistic, and other differences among Hispanics.

Whether a similarly broad approach in which perhaps geography or overlapping cultural histories, together with a tendency to deploy some notion or other of *mestizaje* in the understanding of self and other, could underwrite a workable conception of Hispanicity in Latin America is a question best left for another time. Suffice it to remark that the longstanding presence in Latin America of powerful, entrenched, and largely ahistorical objective categories of mestizo identity make this a much more difficult question, at least if a mestizo conception of Hispanicity is not simply to reinscribe the history of intolerance, injustice, and marginalization that have traditionally marked the deployment of essentialist notions of *mestizaje*. In Latin America, to be mestizo is clearly not to begin from the experience of racelessness. In this respect the Latin American struggle to liberate oneself and one's community through the subversive reinterpretation of mestizo identity is much more akin to the struggles of African Americans than it is to the in-between experience faced by Hispanic immigrants to the United States.

Related chapters: 3 Colonial Thought; 5 Early Critics of Positivism; 18 Identity and Philosophy; 19 Latinos on Race and Ethnicity: Alcoff, Corlett, and Gracia; 24 Latin American Philosophy.

References

Alcoff, L. M. (2006). *Visible identities: race, gender, and the self.* Oxford: Oxford University Press.

Anzaldúa, G. (1987). *Borderlands/la frontera: the new mestiza.* San Francisco: Spinsters/Aunt Lute Press.

Bernasconi, R. (2007). Ethnic race. In J. J. E. Gracia (Ed.). *Race or ethnicity: on black and Latino identity* (pp. 123–36) Ithaca, NY: Cornell University Press.

Corlett, J. A. (2003). *Race, racism, and reparations.* Ithaca, NY: Cornell University Press.

Gooding-Williams, R. (1998). Race, multiculturalism and democracy. *Constellations*, 5, 18–41.

Gracia, J. J. E. (1999). *Hispanic/Latino identity: a philosophical perspective.* Oxford: Blackwell.

Katzew, I. (2005). *Casta painting: images of race in eighteenth-century Mexico.* New Haven: Yale University Press.

Lugones, M. (2003). *Pilgrimages/peregrinajes: theorizing coalition against multiple oppressions (feminist constructions).* New York: Rowman & Littlefield.

Miller, M. G. (2004). *Rise and fall of the cosmic race: the cult of mestizaje in Latin America.* Austin: University of Texas Press.

Sheth, F. A. (2009). *Toward a political philosophy of race.* Albany, NY: SUNY Press.

Vasconcelos, J. (1997). *The cosmic race/la raza cósmica*. Baltimore: Johns Hopkins University Press.
Velazco y Trianosky, G. (2002). Beyond *mestizaje*: the future of race in America. In Herman DeBose & L. Winters (Eds). *New faces in a changing America: multiracial identity in the 21st century* (pp. 176–93) Thousand Oaks, CA: Sage.

Further Reading

Bernasconi, R., & Dotson, K. (Eds). (2005). *Race, hybridity, and miscegenation*. New York: Thoemmes Continuum.
Cruz, I. Z. (1974–55). *Narciso descubre su trasero: el negro en la cultura Puertorriqueña* (2 vols.). Humacao, Puerto Rico: Editorial Furidi.
Forbes, J. D. (1993). *Africans and Native Americans: the language of race and the evolution of red-black peoples*. Champaign: University of Illinois Press.
Gracia, J. J. E. (2008). *Latinos in America*. Oxford: Wiley-Blackwell.
Root, M. P. P. (Ed.). (1986). *The multiracial experience*. Thousand Oaks, CA: Sage.
Zack, N. (1994). *Race and mixed race*. Philadelphia: Temple University Press.
Zack, N. (1995). *American mixed race: the culture of microdiversity*. New York: Rowman & Littlefield.

21

Liberation in Theology, Philosophy, and Pedagogy

IVÁN MÁRQUEZ

The identity, reality, and history of Latin America are inextricably tied to three constitutive factors: (1) its discovery, conquest, and colonization by Western Europe, (2) its relative underdevelopment compared to First World nations, and (3) its highly unequal internal economic distribution of land and wealth. This has marked the horizon of thought for most (if not all) Latin American thinkers since the sixteenth century. However, some of these thinkers have turned this horizon of thought into its very locus of concern. For these thinkers, the important task of thought is the overcoming of this very horizon of thought and its underlying realities.

Since the 1960s, a segment of Latin American intellectuals have embraced the notion of *praxis*, by which they meant that theory and practice form a nexus that ultimately shapes lived reality and that thinking should privilege critical reflection on that lived reality. They then took as their aim the development of a liberatory praxis, each starting out from his or her own place within reality. The collective efforts of this kind of thinking-in-action have generated several movements which have received worldwide recognition, among them liberation theology, philosophy of liberation, pedagogy of the oppressed, and dependency theory. This chapter will sketch out the first three of these approaches to liberation in Latin America.

Liberation Theology

There are many kinds of liberation theology, including Christian, Jewish, and Islamic. Here the discussion will be framed within the tradition of Christianity. The history of Christianity has been to a large extent a series of attempts to come up with an understanding of what it means to be a Christian and to live out this understanding in the world. These Christian efforts have often included questioning and denouncing the discrepancies people perceive between the world they inhabit and their understanding of the good Christian life, and also attempting to bridge the gap between the two. For instance, in the eyes of some Christians, the conquest, colonization, and evangelization of the New World by Spain and Portugal in the sixteenth and seventeenth centuries called in question the consonance between colonialist practices and Christian teachings. The Spanish Dominicans, Antonio de Montesinos (ca. 1480–1545) and

Bartolomé de las Casas (1474–1566), and the Portuguese Jesuit, António Vieira (1608–97), vehemently denounced the treatment of and general colonial policies toward the indigenous people, championing reform throughout their lives. Among other examples, in the nineteenth century the Brazilian Carmelite, Joaquim do Amor Divino Rabelo Caneca (1779–1825), fought for the independence of Brazil from Portugal.

In the 1960s the Catholic Church's Second Vatican Council (1962–5) and especially its pastoral constitution on the church in the modern world, *Gaudium et spes* (1965), served as a catalyst for a whole series of initiatives around the world aimed at rethinking the message of Catholic Christianity. At its core, the Christian message was taken to be one of the construction of the kingdom of God on earth and of what came to be defined in Latin America as a "preferential option for the poor" (Boff, 1985, p. 8) and marginalized. This gave centrality in the Christian life to the love for and solidarity with the poor and to the active struggle for justice and human rights. This interpretation of the message of the Bible (particularly the Gospels) was enthusiastically embraced in Latin America, especially, but not exclusively, by the Jesuits. The second general conference of the episcopate of Latin America held at Medellín, Colombia, in 1968 and the third general conference held at Puebla, Mexico, in 1979 can be taken as focus points in the development and organization of this "liberation theology" in Latin America.

Liberation theology is not otherworldly. It moves away from a salvation project of personal chastity as entryway to heaven and toward one of personal engagement with the world to construct a society of brotherly and sisterly love and justice for all. This Christian engagement, however, cannot be seen as simply depending on benevolent empathy with the poor and generous charity coming from the people who are better off. Solidarity with the poor means to live among the poor and to share their own struggles, not simply to love them and help them from afar. The emphasis is not on compassion (from the Latin *compati*, i.e., to bear or suffer with) but instead on communion (from the Latin *communis*, i.e., mutual participation) with them in a collective life-project to construct a world ruled by Christian love and respect. The intention is not to passively accept the sufferings of life in the Augustinian earthly city of man in the vale of tears and to hope for a better life in the heavenly city of God. It is to construct the heavenly city of God on earth. And to the extent that this is the case, this Christian life-project is life-affirming rather than life-denying.

Liberation theology sees Christ as catalytic liberator and not as fatherly savior. He works with us and through us, but not in place of us. As life-project, the Christian future can be seen in historical terms. Humans have the capacity and the choice to make a better world. The future as historical project is seen as a new exodus in search of the Promised Land, a notion that designates a space of possibility and actualization that is more social, political, moral, and economic than geographic.

This proposal for an act of engagement in a new way of being-in-the-world as a Christian takes into consideration the contemporary state of knowledge in the natural and social sciences. Thus, it understands and takes for granted the inextricable link between theory and practice, agent and structure, consciousness and ideology, subject and historicity. To change the world, we have to understand the world, ourselves, what can be done, what should be done, and how to do it. Last but most importantly, we have to do it: to change ourselves and to change the world.

Given its very historical consciousness, liberation theology does not conceive of its goal as one having a definite endpoint in history. The history of the world, of humanity, and of the church is a history with no determinate endpoint and no terminus. The idea of the kingdom of God is a regulative idea, a horizon of thought, action, and interpretation. So, in a way, humanity will always be nomadic – wandering in search of the Promised Land – making itself at home only in the consciousness, hope, and faith that it is really trying to approximate an endpoint, while fully conscious of the very impossibility of getting there and staying there, in an all-too-human journey defined at best by an asymptotic curve.

Gustavo Gutiérrez's "Toward a theology of liberation" (1968) is widely considered to be the founding text on liberation theology. In this essay the Peruvian Dominican theologian, Gutiérrez, explains the theological meaning of faith and commitment to God and human beings from the point of view of the Catholic Church's Second Vatican Council, especially *Gaudium et spes* (1965) and Pope Paul VI's encyclical letter on the development of peoples, *Populorum progressio* (Catholic Church and Pope Paul VI, 1967). The essay establishes an explicit connection between the theological meanings of salvation and the kingdom of God and human emancipation in the social, political, and economic orders. It makes the commitment to God a commitment to historical progress understood as the progressive integral development of humans individually and collectively. It ends by taking on Marx's challenge in his critique of Christianity. Either Christianity passively accepts and legitimizes the way the world is or it denounces its injustices and actively engages in a positive process of change. The first path makes it an "opiate of the people." The second path makes it a force of human liberation and development. Gutiérrez takes on the second path in his classic *A Theology of Liberation* (1973), where he develops an understanding of theology as critical reflection on praxis, starting from Latin America's condition of underdevelopment and poverty. He elaborates a proposal for the church in history as a force of liberation, while also reinterpreting the role of lay persons, clergy, and theologians in a process of worldly salvation.

One of the most influential and controversial critical reflections on praxis that has come out of liberation theology is Leonardo Boff's *Church: Charism and Power* (1985). In it, the Brazilian theologian, Boff, critically analyzes the actual and possible roles of the institutional church in the late twentieth century. First, Boff defends the church's involvement in politics, insofar as politics is defined as the search for the common good. In this guise, Christian faith is directly connected to political action, to the extent that Christian faith directly implies an active commitment to uphold, defend, and promote justice, human dignity, and truth. Furthermore, Boff expands the meaning of the institutional Catholic Church explicitly to include not only the clerics but also and centrally the laity. In practice, according to Boff, the Christian commitment will entail an option for the poor and an option for integral liberation – a movement toward complete humanization, i.e., the development of full human potentiality in the image of God and with Christ as the model.

Boff sees the church hierarchy as engaged in a contradiction between message and practice. The gap between its words and actions are shown in its passivity, and sometimes complicity, regarding the earthly reality of injustice, and in its traditional (i.e., historical) allegiance with the socially and politically powerful at the expense of the disempowered and marginalized. Boff believes that the church should look back at its origins and restore the spirit and practices of the early (or primitive) church, especially its communal organization of life, its more open practices of leadership, and its existence at the center of (and for) the daily life of common people. Finally, along this renewed commitment to live the Christian life in ways that evoke, if not outright imitate, the experience of the early church, Boff explains the structure and function of the new grassroots center of the Catholic Church – the base ecclesial community (BEC). The BEC is the community of laity who self-organize to reflect on and live out their faith. The concept of the BEC challenges the hierarchical and patriarchal structure of the institutional church. Some of the central principles of this model are (1) giving preeminence to the lowest level of the institutionalized church, (2) taking daily life as the central locus of Christian reflection and engagement, (3) taking the church as event and experience rather than as doctrine and structure, and (4) taking the community of the poor and marginalized as the preferential site for the "experience of Church" (1985, pp. 125–30). In these base ecclesial communities, the kingdom of God is built by means of a communal and democratic dialogue and action that (1) helps people acquire consciousness of themselves and their situation, (2) helps them see others as brothers and sisters in the fellowship of Christ, and (3) allows them to bridge the gap individually and collectively, between doctrine and practice, and between sacrament and daily reality.

In *The Gospel in Solentiname* (1976) the Nicaraguan poet and theologian, Ernesto Cardenal, documents the experience of faith in a Nicaraguan base ecclesial community. It serves as concrete church exemplar, allowing non-participants a glimpse into this alternative way of Christian living in the modern world. One of the cornerstones of many Christian base communities is the group reading of and reflection on the Bible. The process, as seen by the BECs, is one of consciousness-raising that develops persons as Christians, enhances their consciousness as subjects, empowers them as agents, and helps them build community. Cardenal sets himself the task of reconstructing many of such encounters within a particular BEC.

Although liberation theology is a predominantly Latin American Catholic phenomenon, founded by the proponents discussed above, plus others such as Juan Luis Segundo, Hugo Assmann, Ignacio Ellacuría, and Jon Sobrino, Protestants such as Emilio Castro, Julio de Santa Ana, Rubem Alves, José Míguez Bonino, and Franz J. Hinkelammert also contributed to its development from the outset. In addition, a version of liberation theology can be found in the United States in the Protestant black theology of prominent theologians and pastors such as James H. Cone and Jeremiah A. Wright, respectively.

Almost from the beginning there were efforts by Latin American women to develop their own contributions to liberation theology; for example, there is feminist theology, exemplified by María Pilar Aquino, Ivone Gebara, and María Clara Bingemer (Catholic), Elsa Tamez (Protestant), and *mujerista* (womanist) theology, exemplified by Latina female theologians such as Ada María Isasi-Díaz and Yolanda Tarango (Catholic). Finally, there are some white North American feminist theologians who have done work that can be seen as falling under the general rubric of liberation theology, such as Elizabeth Schüssler Fiorenza and Rosemary Radford Ruether (Catholic), Mary Daly (post-Christian), Judith Plaskow (Jewish), and Letty M. Russell (Protestant).

A second-generation liberation theology has been developed by Antonio González (2005) and Ivan Petrella (2008) among others. Their aim is to move beyond an identity politics model of liberation theology, where one develops theological reflections from particular experiential loci, such as the experience of the poor, women, Hispanics, African Americans, toward an all-embracing planetary theology of liberation whose central mission at the moment is to conceive of a new historical project for the post Cold War, global world.

It should be noted that there has been strong criticism and reaction against liberation theology. The Vatican has been officially critical of diverse aspects of liberation theology and has silenced, admonished, chastised, relieved from their roles, or otherwise disapproved of many of its practitioners including Gutiérrez, Cardenal, Boff, Ellacuría, Gebara, and Sobrino. Also in 1989 Special Forces of the El Salvador's army assassinated the Spanish-Salvadoran Jesuit liberation theologian and philosopher, Ignacio Ellacuría, and five other Jesuit priests in their residence at the Universidad Centroamericana. They were targeted for their public denunciation of the government during El Salvador's 1980s civil war.

Philosophy of Liberation

The philosophy of liberation developed in Latin America shares some of the features of the theology of liberation while also creating a distinct approach and unique contribution to philosophy.

Philosophy of liberation shares with liberation theology its historicity, its commitment to human development from the locus of the poor or otherwise oppressed, its emphasis on praxis, and its intent to elaborate theoretical and practical proposals that arise from and reflect the lived reality in Latin America, and that serve as adequate responses for its specific challenges, possibilities, and place in time.

More specifically, philosophy of liberation aims to tackle two problems. The first problem is Latin American philosophy's intellectual dependence on Western-European philosophy. This problem arises in that, allegedly, since the Europeans' arrival to the American continent five hundred years ago, Latin Americans have internalized ideas, methods, and aims coming from the European continent and, thus, have not yet developed their own distinctive philosophical tradition corresponding to Latin America's own history and reality. The proposed solution to this first problem is to develop an awareness of the nature and extent of this dependence and to develop new concepts, methodology, aims, and a new locus of philosophical thinking that starts from the most important problems in Latin America. The second problem addressed by the philosophy of liberation is that of economic and social oppression. Within this larger category, those philosophers whose work crosses over into the theology of liberation such as Enrique Dussel focus extensively on the problem of massive and abject poverty within an oppressive socioeconomic system controlled to a great extent by North American and European interests and power groups.

Simply put, philosophy of liberation's primary concern is to understand the interrelationships between Latin America's problems of cultural-intellectual dependence and

301

socioeconomic dependence, and to elaborate transformative proposals for liberation from both of these conditions.

The philosophy of liberation emerged in Argentina in the 1970s and includes philosophers as diverse as Arturo Andrés Roig, Horacio Cerutti Guldberg, Osvaldo Ardiles, and Juan Carlos Scannone (Schutte, 1993, pp. 175–205). However, the foremost exponent of liberation philosophy is the Argentine theologian and philosopher, Enrique Dussel. Cerutti, Dussel, and Roig were forced into exile in the mid-1970s during the years of political repression in Argentina because of their ideas on liberation.

Roig and Cerutti have formulated post-Hegelian, historicist versions of philosophy of liberation. According to Roig, the task of philosophy of liberation is to clarify the situatedness of the Latin American subject to him or herself. In order to do this, a sense of the historicity of the Latin American subject must be developed. This is done through a historical-hermeneutical inquiry – a broad-reaching history of ideas – having two related functions: (1) to discover the collective sources of meaning, affective relation, and valuation – the historical a priori (Foucault's term) – of a given group and (2) to unmask the sometimes imposed and oppressive totalities that serve as objective frames of mind for that given group. Once this is achieved, philosophy of liberation proceeds to an elaboration of integrating categories that allow subjects to reintegrate themselves with themselves and with their historicity in a non-alienated way, thus helping in the process of Latin American liberation (Roig, 1981).

For Cerutti, philosophy of liberation defines a philosophy in tune with, and thus able to face, the challenges of Latin America. Such a philosophy must start with the dual aim to understand reality immanently and its own situatedness within that same reality. In order to effectively contribute to the praxis of liberation, this philosophy must work in partnership with the social sciences and must have a critical eye for the ideological function of language. Latin American philosophy does not have to be original but it must be genuine and appropriate to its place. It should not start from zero but rather should take anything useful from all philosophical traditions and from its own philosophical past to tackle the task at hand. Philosophy's long-term effectiveness in this praxis of liberation hinges on its own capacity to remain critical of reality and, most importantly, self-critical and open to renewal (Cerutti Guldberg, 1983).

Dussel's earliest formulation of philosophy of liberation (1973a) takes Heidegger's ontological existentialism and Ricoeur's phenomenological hermeneutics as its points of departure to understand the reality of Latin America. Under this guise, liberation philosophy takes on the task of thinking from Latin America. That is, its aim is to develop a way to make conscious and discursively explicit the ways of being-in-the-world in Latin America. The difficulty with this task, according to Dussel, is that Latin America's present is the result of a 500-year historical process that includes two silencings and cover-ups. First, there is the silencing and cover-up of the whole array of pre-Columbian cultures: Mayan, Aztec, Inca, Quechua, Aymara, Mapuche, etc., by the European cultures after 1492. Secondly, there is the silencing and cover-up of the *mestizo* culture (and I would add mulatto culture) – a mixture of pre-Columbian Native American ethnic groups and European ethnic groups (and African groups) – that constitutes the current reality of being Latin American for the majority of the continent's inhabitants. Latin American culture is estranged from itself owing to the hegemony of European and now North American models of cultural-intellectual and

302

socioeconomic development, the result of five centuries of European dominance and one century of U.S. influence in Latin America, and the concomitant Latin American dependence on both.

The task of the liberation philosopher is one of phenomenological disclosure and hermeneutical disentanglement, helping Latin Americans see themselves and their collective history in their own terms, but also in a historical relationship to diverse others. Latin American philosophy of liberation tries to liberate Latin American consciousness so that it can simultaneously realize and become aware of its own distinct identity and destiny vis-à-vis Europe and the United States.

Dussel's encounter with the work of the French-Jewish philosopher, Emmanuel Lévinas, especially his book *Totality and Infinity: An Essay on Exteriority* (1961), made him revise his general approach, going beyond a Hegelian–Heideggerian ontological approach that conceives of Being as an absolute unity – a totalizing totality – to a Schellingian–Lévinasian metaphysics of exteriority that acknowledges the ultimate irreducibility of alterity – of the Other.

Under this metaphysical (and ethical) rather than ontological formulation, liberation philosophy aims to analyze Western onto-metaphysics with an eye to discovering the extent to which it creates a normative reality – a closed "totalizing" totality – that absorbs all alterity (Dussel, 1972, 1973b, 1985). Such totalizing silences others (i.e., other realities, experiences, subjects, agents, objects), makes them invisible, inscrutable (i.e., either exotic, ineffable, a fetish, mystifying, sublime, or monstrous), or reduces them to itself or to the negation of itself, a negation defined as absence or lack, in the limit case turning them into nothing – non-existent, unreal.

Following Lévinas, Dussel argues that this recurrent phagocytic tendency in Western metaphysics points to its very resolution in an ethical foundation for itself, based on an affirmation of life, and on the irreducibility of the Other into the Same or the denial of its full absorption (without residue) into the Totality. Thus, in this understanding of the philosophy of liberation neither metaphysics nor epistemology constitutes proper foundations for philosophy; only ethics presents us with an adequate starting point for thought, because only ethics can regulate metaphysics and control the advance of any totalizing efforts.

In the best-known text of Dussel's Lévinasian period *Philosophy of Liberation* (1977), philosophy is placed in space and time and it is made part of the lifeworld. The inextricable relation between theory and practice is taken for granted. The ethical foundation of philosophy and its historicity become fused in the notion of a philosophy of praxis, that is, of a liberatory praxis as *prima philosophia* (first philosophy). The contemporary philosophical scene is analyzed in terms of a hegemonic philosophical discourse that draws the contours of the world. The relative autonomy of the act of philosophizing is placed within the context of a hegemonic system of cultural production and reproduction that marginalizes the spaces for alternative, non-hegemonic discourses. The normative adequacy of the relative autonomy of philosophy is taken as essential to any liberatory philosophy (1985, pp. 183–8). Thus, the need for the construction of alternative spaces for the production and reproduction of non-hegemonic philosophical discourses is affirmed and its possibility is explained. Dussel hints at a global geopolitics of philosophical production that approximates the geopolitics of material and symbolic production and postulates the existence of an international division of philosophical

303

labor. This division of philosophical labor has a tendency to reproduce the very same world that it describes but, according to Dussel, it can equally be redirected to establish a global anti-hegemonic apparatus, one that could lead to a global philosophical praxis of liberation, with philosophical allegiances and ties of solidarity being built between philosophers of rich and poor countries.

Dussel's philosophical weapon, which he will continue to deploy in his subsequent reformulations of philosophy of liberation, is the *analectical* (or *anadialectical*) *method*. According to Dussel, the analectical method is a non-reductive thinking from the exterior of the hegemonic, totalizing system, and an antidote to the totalizing tendencies of the dialectic method. Analectics allows us to think the Other in terms that do not reduce it to the hegemonic One, thus, giving the Other its true voice.

Following his development of philosophy of liberation along Lévinasian and, to some extent, Heideggerian lines, but also using theology of liberation and dependency theory, Dussel undertook a serious study of the complete works of Marx, especially, Marx's *Grundrisse* and the manuscripts of the four drafts of *Capital* (Dussel, 1988). What emerges from these studies is a new interpretation of Marx. Dussel sees Marx not as a dialectician and heir of Hegel, but as an analectic thinker who tries to fight the totalizing efforts of the most important totality of his time, i.e., capitalism. At the heart of Dussel's interpretation in the 1980s is Marx's opposition of living labor (*lebendige Arbeit*) and capital. On the one hand, living labor is seen as the effort of human life to survive, to sustain itself, to develop itself, and to reproduce itself. On the other hand, capital is seen as objectified labor, as the result of the appropriation by a few of everyone else's life-force, and thus, ultimately, a stealing of the actual life of the many by the few. Contrary to the conventional European and Soviet interpretations of Marx, Dussel's reading gives us a portrait of a profoundly humanistic and ethical thinker, exhibiting a remarkable continuity of fundamental outlook throughout his *oeuvre*. It also aligns Marx with the preferential option for the poor found in the theology of liberation.

From his Lévinasian–Marxist perspective, Dussel (1995) performs a critical analysis of the process of development of European modernity and its relationship to the European discovery, conquest, and colonization of Latin America, a theme he has addressed since the 1970s. Dussel's aim is to show how modernity had its origins in 1492, when Columbus's discovery of a whole new continent paved the way for Europe's brutal exploitation of its human and other natural resources, allowing Western Europe to emerge as a world global power for the first time in history. The conquest of America, according to Dussel, is essential to European modernity as its "other face."

Dussel writes a critical history of European modernity and of its efforts to construct a self-legitimazing image, with strong claims to objectivity and universality, as the endpoint of a "universal history" and of human civilization. Dussel's critical history questions the metanarrative of European modernity – which casts Western Europe in Hegelian terms, as the beginning and end of the history of reason – especially its cultural claims to moral exceptionalism, radical innovation, and unabated civilizing zeal. Dussel marshals an array of historiographical and archeological sources to show the very problematic relations between modernity and plunder, civilization and barbarism, Prospero and Caliban. Out of Dussel's critical history of modernity and its universal history comes a more balanced picture of the place of both Europe and Latin America in world history. Also, this critical history simultaneously provides a new hermeneutical framework to understand Latin America in its own terms and allows us to move from the modernity versus postmodernity impasse, toward an embrace of Dussel's notion of trans-modernity, i.e., a transcending of modernity in which both modernity and its negated alterity (the victims) co-realize themselves in a process marked by mutual creative fertilization and solidarity (1995, pp. 133–40). But, according to Dussel, in order to embrace trans-modernity, modernity must come to terms with the irrational violence marking its birth and development, while the "other face (or underside)" of modernity must discover itself as the innocent victim of this irrational violence.

Dussel also draws the connection between the philosophical critique of meta-physical totalizing totalities and the critique of political economy, i.e., a critique of the evolving capitalist system of exploitation of people and resources on a global scale, char-acterized by one or more dominating centers and dominated peripheries (2001a). Hence, the metaphysical Being–alterity dyad is critically investigated as it is instanti-ated politically and economically in the center–periphery dyad. In this way, Dussel links the concerns of philosophy of liberation to those of dependency theory, a theory devel-oped in the 1960s and 1970s by Latin American sociologists and economists, such as Enzo Faletto, Fernando Henrique Cardoso, Theotonio dos Santos, and Ruy Mauro Marini. Dependency theory tries to explain how the global capitalist system is con-stituted by a structure of unequal development, in which the development of the First World center is predicated upon the underdevelopment of the Third World periphery, creating a situation of chronic structural dependence of the periphery on the economic imperatives of the center.

During the 1990s Dussel critically engages with the universal pragmatics and discourse ethics of Karl-Otto Apel and Jürgen Habermas (Dussel, 1996). Apel and Habermas try to overcome the problems with the philosophy of the subject (con-sciousness) lying at the heart of Kantian deontological ethics by recasting this ethics in terms of the formal conditions for the existence of a public discourse that has as its goal intersubjective agreement about norms of action, or what Habermas calls "communicative action." Dussel agrees with Apel's and Habermas's new approach to formal ethics but finds it lacking a material principle as ground. Dussel argues that this linguistic-pragmatic turn in philosophy, in general, and ethics, in particular, away from private consciousness and toward public language is necessary but not sufficient. This abstract and formal model of ethics obscures the material realities of the linguistic subjects, just as the previous philosophical systems had hidden what was outside of or did not pertain to the hegemonic, cognizing subject – the *ego cogito*. According to Dussel, before anyone can participate in a public conversation about values and norms, one has to be in a position to take care of one's basic survival needs. One has to be alive and not struggling for survival before one can engage in this kind of rational, consensus-generating dialogue. Life is the material condition of possibility of all communicative action and not vice versa (1996, pp. 12–13). Furthermore, Dussel argues that the public community of discourse cannot claim to be a community of equals, where every-one's voice is of equal value, when the majority of humans are de facto placed radic-ally differently within material-social reality, as it is the case in Latin America. In many instances, the Other is de facto excluded from the empirical community of discourse just as s/he is excluded from the economic community of reproduction of life. This is

305

especially true for the "poor," for whom discursive and economic marginalization go hand in hand.

Dussel's attempt to overcome the shortcomings of discourse ethics is the reformulation of an ethics of liberation (1997). This ethics of liberation is a tripartite ethics consisting of (1) a material aspect, concerned with the reproduction and growth of human life – of survival – as basic ethical ground, (2) a formal moment, representing the procedural dimension of the application of the material principle of survival, according to a formal consensual rational principle of intersubjectivity, yielding moral validity in the form of legitimate norms and principles, and (3) a feasibility moment, when the material-ethical principle of survival and the formal-moral principle of normative legitimacy come together in the form of criteria of application of principles capable of transforming reality, with the aim of fulfilling "the good" in concrete contexts.

According to Dussel, an ethics of liberation along these lines would enable the majority of the oppressed to form an anti-hegemonic communicative community that takes on the leading role in the production of the new intersubjectivity of a future ethico-moral validity. It then proceeds to criticize the hegemonic, ruling, valid consensus of the older dominating intesubjectivity by an appeal to the universal material-ethical principle of survival. This, Dussel claims, constitutes the process of liberation at the formal-discursive level. And from this initial formal-discursive process, a praxis of liberation gets established that eventually leads to a new democratic institutionalization of the future "valid-good" (1997, pp. 289–94).

Dussel's latest turn is toward an elaboration of a "critical politics," defined among other things as an inquiry into the organization of power and its process of liberation, aiming to make real the promise of the ethics of liberation (2006). Here, he begins with an account of politics as a biopolitics of the "will to live," with communitarian overtones, and a Spinoza-influenced notion of the field of power. Power (*potentia*), he claims, lies naturally in the community. But as politics becomes institutionalized, this power (*potentia*) is passed on to institutions as institutional power (*potestas*). Here is where the conflict begins, given that oftentimes *potestas* claims and acts as if it was the ultimate source of *potentia* (2006, p. 41).

Political corruption leads to a notion of power as domination, which has become axiomatic for most of the history of Western political thought. Dussel accuses this tradition of political thought of being a legitimator of minority interests, obscuring the fact that the original source of power lies in the community, and conferring a natural, universal, normative status to the current states of affairs, thus, stealing the rightful place of *potentia*, away from the community toward institutions (2006, p. 42).

Taking its cue from the 1994 Zapatista uprising in Chiapas, Mexico, Dussel proposes a notion of an "obeying power" (*poder obedencial*), a power that stays in line with its original sovereign, the people (*el pueblo*), and that is immune to the widespread, corruptive tendency of a fetishism of power (2006, pp. 38–9). Ultimately, Dussel wants to articulate a political theory that moves us away from a notion of power as domination toward a notion of power as creative solidarity – with the people, with the community, and, in the last instance, with life – one that describes the whole contemporary political landscape and its history in these terms, and that points out available resources and ways to engage in praxes of liberation at the political level in our place and time.

306

It should be noted that Dussel has been collaborating since the mid-1990s with the Argentine and U.S. theorist, Walter Mignolo, and has had a strong influence on a new generation of Latino philosophers in the United States, most notably, Eduardo Mendieta and Nelson Maldonado-Torres.

Pedagogy of the Oppressed

In the 1960s a pedagogy of the oppressed arose in Latin America, sharing significant features with liberation theology and philosophy of liberation. In this case, the discourse and the movement can be tracked down to the work of a single individual, the Brazilian educator, Paulo Freire (1921–97).

In the early 1960s Freire took on the task of conceiving, organizing, and executing a nation-wide adult literacy program. Brazil in the 1950s and early 1960s was a resource-rich country in the process of modernization and democratic nation-building but with high levels of adult illiteracy. Freire and many others in the state and civil society held that these two processes could only advance if the Brazilian population became literate. However, Freire's notion of education took a form that transcended any narrow instrumental notion of competencies, skill-sets, or basic knowledge. For him, education was inextricably linked to the exercise of freedom, and the exercise of freedom to the development of structures of civil society, practices of popular (not populist) governance, and ultimately to the advent of a robust culture of real democratic politics (as opposed to legalistic formal democracy).

The literacy program implemented by Freire was successful and constituted one dimension of an explosion of activity in Brazilian civil society in the late 1950s and early 1960s, especially in the urban areas. The expansion of civil society that occurred at this time, brought about in part by this literacy program, proved to be great enough to elicit a reaction from the hegemonic powers in the form of a military coup in 1964. After the coup Freire was arrested twice in connection with his government-endorsed, national educational campaigns. Upon his release, Freire was exiled, living in Santiago, Chile (1964–9), Cambridge, MA, USA (1969–70), and Geneva, Switzerland (1970–9), and doing educational reform work worldwide, but especially in Chile, Cape Verde, Angola, and Guinea-Bissau. Freire was allowed to return to Brazil in 1980 and spent the last seventeen years of his life continuing the educational initiatives that had been abruptly terminated sixteen years before by the military government.

A true believer in the Baconian dictum that "knowledge is power," Freire took education as the generative center of any efforts to build a better society. Change must begin from the inside of people and from the majority of people that experience the negative effects of the socioeconomic arrangements that we ourselves reproduce. For him violent coups and top-down initiatives both have a tendency to reproduce, inside individuals and between them, the very structures that need to be changed.

Following a similar logic of oppression claimed by Frantz Fanon, in his (*avant la lettre*) postcolonial classics, *Black Skin, White Masks* (1952) and *The Wretched of the Earth* (1961), Freire affirms that the oppressor and the oppressed form a psycho-social functionally inextricable dyad. Hence the oppressor is in no a priori privileged condition/position to help the oppressed because both oppressor and oppressed produce and reproduce the very same reality that in turn shapes them. Freire thus recommends a pedagogical program that establishes a teacher–student relationship aiming to discover/uncover the reality of the oppressed.

Adult literacy programs are an ideal site for this type of self-generative, consciousness-raising work, because it gives those illiterate people, who in the twentieth and early twenty-first centuries are by definition socially and economically marginalized, a space from which to name their world for the first time, to take possession of it in their own terms, and to own up to themselves. The medium of the written word and the gradual mastery of it offers these people, at the very least at the level of consciousness, an opportunity of mastery over this very same world.

The very act of learning to use the written language gives these people an opportunity to call things by their right names, so to speak. This rechristening of the world allows for a development of one's own voice, hopefully one that represents one's own internal and external reality. The pedagogical process thus produces an increasingly self-conscious subject and an increasingly self-determining agent. Ideally, therefore, it produces an empowered human being.

Once seen from this point of view, pedagogy of the oppressed and the process of *conscientização* (defined in English as "conscientization") are nothing but a self-edifying practice to generate subjects-agents who alternately can be conceived of as (1) Kantian autonomous selves who are ends-in-themselves rather than means-to-an-end, (2) Marxian non-alienated, non-objectified subjects and historical actors, or (3) Aristotelian active, creatively productive, self-realized beings rather than passive, reproductive, underdeveloped beings – disposable commodities and passive consumers in the global market.

Obviously the liberatory potential of this practice hinges on the nature of the teacher–student relationship, and this can be deduced from the concept of education embodied by the teacher–student relationship in any given educational environment. In Freire's paradigm-generating book, *Pedagogy of the Oppressed* (1997 [1968]), he opposes a 'banking' concept to a 'problem-solving' concept of education, rejecting the former while affirming the latter. The banking concept of education is characterized by the teachers' deposit of information into students' minds, the latter considered passive receptacles of information. The problem-solving concept of education is instead predicated on the primacy of the generation of acts of cognition over the reception of bits of information. Furthermore, Freire argues that while the banking concept presupposes a ready-made world that the student needs to learn to fit in through an education process of socialization that, in the words of Erich Fromm, ends up being "necrophilic," the problem-solving concept presupposes instead a human-made world that needs to be understood in order to be changed in the ways that the student cognizers come to see fit. The latter is an educational process aimed at individual and collective realization, what Freire calls "humanization," which by its very life-affirming nature is "biophilic" rather than "necrophilic" (1997, p. 59).

If the problem-solving concept of education, as understood above, is the one regulating the teacher–student relationship, then the educational practice will be conducted in a space constituted by teachers-as-students and students-as-teachers. And the more we can assure that these conditions are actually in place in any given educational environment, the more we can expect that a liberatory pedagogical practice is taking place.

308

To the extent that education is connected to knowledge and knowledge is connected to power and the freedom that comes with it, to the extent that we live inside societal structures that produce and reproduce a social reality with differential levels of powers and freedoms among the human beings living in that reality, and to the extent that societal structures are changed through political acts, then any education that is truly so will be (also) a political (not "politicized") education.

Freire's work is widely read and it is generally acknowledged to be the foundation of the contemporary critical pedagogy approach to education in the United States, which counts bell hooks, Stanley Aronowitz, Peter McLaren, Henry Giroux, Ira Shor, Joe L. Kincheloe, Michael Apple, Rich Gibson, and Donaldo Macedo among its practitioners.

Conclusion

The end of the bipolar world of the Cold War, brought about by the fall of the Berlin Wall in 1989, plus *Perestroika*, *Glasnost*, and the collapse of the Soviet Union in 1991, together with the dissolution of the Sandinista revolution in Nicaragua in 1990 and the end of civil war in El Salvador in 1992, meant the waning of utopian energies and radical politics throughout Latin America. With the new unipolar world of global capitalism came a new emphasis on reformist, neoliberal pragmatism. Within this new historical period – which some called the "end of history" – the notion of a praxis of liberation seemed naïve and outdated.

However, after almost twenty years of neoliberalism and globalization, the unresolved problems of war, religious conflict, poverty, climate change, environmental stress, and continued (and in some cases increased) social marginalization of very large numbers of people are making some people take a second look at the prospects of coming up with new broad frameworks and proposals for radical change.

Furthermore, the push of neoliberalism and globalization has brought about a real expansion of democracy and civil society in many countries. The number of grassroots movements has multiplied exponentially and the internet and World Wide Web have greatly facilitated the cooperation, coalition, and coordination among these groups. It appears that a plethora of liberation praxes are being enacted everywhere, inside and outside Latin America. People are not waiting for the governments of their nation-states to lead the way, but rather, they are taking their own lead at all levels in the sphere of everyday life.

Religion, philosophy, and education are fundamental areas of human edification and, thus, primary sites for any liberatory praxis. Owing to the nature of our current planetary challenges, and current trends in democratization and civil society, we are witnessing a worldwide reception and appropriation of aspects of liberation theology, philosophy of liberation, and pedagogy of the oppressed, signaling that some late twentieth-century Latin American approaches to liberation are going global in the early twenty-first century.

Related chapters: 13 Liberation Philosophy; 22 Philosophy, Postcoloniality, and Postmodernity; 23 Globalization and Latin American Thought; 30 Cultural Studies.

References

Boff, L. (1985). *Church: charism and power: liberation theology and the institutional church.* (J. W. Diercksmeier, Trans.). New York: Crossroad (Original work published 1981).
Cardenal, E. (1976). *The gospel in Solentiname.* (D. D. Walsh, Trans.). Maryknoll, NY: Orbis (Original work published 1975).
Catholic Church, & Pope Paul VI. (1967). *Populorum progressio.* London: Catholic Truth Society.
Catholic Church, & Vatican Council II. (1965). *Gaudium et spes: pastoral constitution on the Church in the modern world.* Washington: National Catholic Welfare Conference.
Cerutti Guldberg, H. (1983). *Filosofía de la liberación latinoamericana.* Mexico: Fondo de Cultura Económica.
Dussel, E. D. (1972). *Método para una filosofía de la liberación. Superación analéctica de la dialéctica hegeliana.* Salamanca: Sígueme.
Dussel, E. D. (1973a). *América Latina, dependencia y liberación. Antología de ensayos antropológicos y teológicos desde la proposición de un pensar latinoamericano.* Buenos Aires: Fernando García Cambeiro.
Dussel, E. D. (1973b). *Para una ética de la liberación latinoamericana* (2 vols.). Buenos Aires: Siglo XXI.
Dussel, E. D. (1985). *Philosophy of liberation.* (A. Martinez & C. Morkovsky, Trans.). Maryknoll, NY: Orbis (Original work published 1977).
Dussel, E. D. (1995). *The invention of the Americas: eclipse of "the Other" and the myth of modernity.* (M. D. Barber, Trans.). New York: Continuum (Original work published 1992).
Dussel, E. D. (1996). *The underside of modernity: Apel, Ricoeur, Rorty, Taylor and the philosophy of liberation.* (E. Mendieta, Ed. & Trans.). New York: Humanities Press (Original work published 1994).
Dussel, E. D. (1997). The architectonic of the ethics of liberation: on material ethics and formal moralities. (E. Mendieta, Trans.). In D. Batstone, E. Mendieta, L. A. Lorentzen, & D. N. Hopkins (Eds). *Liberation theologies, postmodernity, and the Americas* (pp. 273–304). London: Routledge (Original work published 1995).
Dussel, E. D. (2001a). *Hacia una filosofía política crítica.* Bilbao: Editorial Desclée de Brouwer.
Dussel, E. D. (2001b). *Towards an unknown Marx: commentary of the manuscripts of 1861–1863.* (F. Moseley, Ed. and Y. Angulo, Trans.). London: Routledge (Original work published 1988).
Dussel, E. D. (2006). *20 tesis de política.* Mexico: Siglo XXI.
Fanon, F. (1965). *The wretched of the earth.* (C. Farrington, Trans.). New York: Grove Press (Original work published 1961).
Fanon, F. (1967). *Black skin, white masks.* (C. L. Markmann, Trans.). New York: Grove Press (Original work published 1952).
Freire, P. (1997). *Pedagogy of the oppressed.* (M. B. Ramos, Trans.). New York: Continuum (Original work published 1968).
González, A. (2005). *The gospel of faith and justice.* (J. Owens, Trans.). Maryknoll, NY: Orbis.
Gutiérrez, G. (1973). *A theology of liberation: history, politics and salvation.* (C. Inda & J. Eagleson, Trans.). Maryknoll, NY: Orbis (Original work published 1971).
Gutiérrez, G. (1990). Toward a theology of liberation. (A. T. Hennelly, S.J., Trans.). In A. T. Hennelly (Ed.) *Liberation theology: a documentary history* (pp. 62–76). Maryknoll, NY: Orbis (Original work published 1968).
Lévinas, E. (1969). *Totality and infinity: an essay on exteriority.* (A. Lingis, Trans.). Pittsburgh: Duquesne University Press (Original work published 1961).
Petrella, I. (2008). *Beyond liberation theology; a polemic.* London: SCM Press.

Roig, A. A. (1981). *Teoría y crítica del pensamiento latinoamericano*. Mexico: Fondo de Cultura Económica.

Schutte, O. (1993). *Cultural identity and social liberation in Latin American thought*. Albany, NY: SUNY Press.

Further Reading

Márquez, I. (2008). *Contemporary Latin American social and political thought: an anthology*. Lanham, MD: Rowman & Littlefield.

22

Philosophy, Postcoloniality, and Postmodernity

OFELIA SCHUTTE

In this chapter I discuss three theoretical approaches of significance to Latin American philosophy. Widely known in the 1990s and carrying over their influences into the twenty-first century, they are Latin American subaltern studies, post-Occidentalist border thought, and feminist cultural criticism. These theoretical approaches appeal to new conceptual models to address important sociopolitical and cultural changes affecting Latin American societies since the 1980s.

The global policies of capitalist neoliberalism were unleashed in the 1980s during the conservative administrations of Ronald Reagan and Margaret Thatcher. Neoliberalism's focus on the privatization of state and public-sector resources, among other features, contributed to a fragmentation of social identities. Neither the Enlightenment paradigm of the universal citizen nor older Marxist paradigms of working-class/peasant consciousness seemed ready to address the actual complex conditions of those disempowered by race, ethnicity, sex/gender classifications, age, migration status, or sheer poverty, including the multiple effects of more than one of these factors. In the wake of important movements for human rights that had confronted the dictatorships of the 1970s, transitions to democracy took place primarily in the 1980s (and up to the early 1990s in Central America). The new social movements, such as the women's and the indigenous people's movements, added new vigor to the transitional democracies as various sectors of society mobilized on behalf of their constituencies. The political advantages brought about by democratic change, however, were limited by the negative economic effects of neoliberalism, since neoliberal policy resulted in great increments of wealth for a minority while poverty increased across the continent.

A question facing many intellectuals in Latin America and specialists in Latin American studies in these years was how to address these complex factors theoretically, keeping in mind the goals of making democracies more inclusive and egalitarian; in other words, how to keep alive the ideals of social justice that had energized the emancipatory political projects of the region for decades prior, if not centuries.

The important role played by poststructuralist theory in Latin America at this time is not a mere coincidence deriving from the theory's popularity in the United States and parts of Western Europe. If we look more closely at the sense of disillusionment with existing Leftist models for democratization and social change affecting some Latin

Americans in the 1980s and early 1990s, we will note that it is comparable in some respects to the disappointment with existing conceptual models for political change experienced by philosophers in France following the defeat of the Paris student and worker rebellions of 1968. It was at that time that a number of those who would become leading poststructuralist philosophers (Derrida, Lyotard, Foucault, Deleuze, Kristeva) developed new theories to conceptualize cultural and democratic change from a post-Enlightenment perspective. It is these philosophical theories that many call "postmodern," although technically they should be considered poststructuralist, leaving the term "postmodern" as a designator of cultural, economic, mass-mediatic, and historical conditions brought about by the accelerated expansion of global technologies and of capitalist globalization processes in the last half of the twentieth century. The term "poststructuralism" is widely acknowledged to elude definition. In practice, the emergence of the poststructuralist philosophies emphasized, among other interests, the question of nonlinear processes of reasoning, critiques of metaphysical essentialism, attention to the phenomenon of discursive domains and their margins, and attention to the complicity between academic knowledge and the sociopolitical empowerment or disempowerment of marginal voices (as the case may be). Given this chapter's space limitations, for the purposes of the following discussion the terms "poststructuralist" and "postmodern" (when referring to theory) will be used interchangeably unless further specificity is required.

With the new interest in the voices of marginality taking hold in the North, a new opportunity but also a dilemma arose for some Latin American theorists. The rising popularity of looking out for marginal and subaltern perspectives awoke a new desire in the North to learn more about Latin American issues and voices. The problem was that, as Nelly Richard and others noted, the theoretical framework that impelled this attention toward them was produced outside of Latin America (Richard, 1995). The inclusion, such as it was, was determined under theoretical paradigms crafted elsewhere. This was the case even with postcolonial theory whose growth in the United States stemmed from the work of the Palestinian critic Edward Said and the theorists Gayatri Spivak and Homi Bhabha (both from India). Although a main goal of postcolonial theory is to question what used to be called "cultural imperialism," or the cultural dominance of the global North over the global South, its research focus was far remote from the local experiences of South American cultural critics and usually excluded mention of Latin America's colonial and postcolonial history.

In short, a rich and at the same time conflictive intellectual climate explains the priorities felt by these Latin American critics, both in the region and in the diaspora, to come up with theoretical paradigms developed closer to the home ground of Latin American societies and cultures, and the extraordinary impetus to make these known among themselves and to their Anglophone colleagues and readers in the North (Beverley, Oviedo, & Aronna, 1995). Along with Latin America being the importer of Western European and Anglo-American culture, it was now time for Latin Americans to become exporters as well of cultural theory. The processes of globalization, conflictive and disparate as they are in terms of their effects, allow a window for this reverse form of political action and cultural consumption. The emerging field of Cultural Studies in Latin America – marked by its critical distance from its counterpart field in the United States – served as an inter- and trans-disciplinary site for debates regarding

313

the role of Latin American cultural theory in this new postmodern, global, transnational, neoliberal age (Del Sarto, Ríos, & Trigo, 2004). Along with cultural studies, trends in poststructuralist theory, feminism, and postcolonial studies, traversing the Americas and mediated by local conditions in the South, interacted with existing approaches to cultural theory since the 1960s in the Caribbean and Latin America, as already developed by philosophically oriented literary theorists such as Roberto Fernández Retamar (Cuba), Angel Rama (Uruguay), and Antonio Cornejo Polar (Peru).

A new round of debate broke out following the 1989 publication in Spanish of Néstor García Canclini's *Hybrid Cultures* (2005). García Canclini offered an optimistic assessment of the opportunities brought about by globalization market processes, viewed from the standpoint of the social sciences in alliance with a defense of popular culture. His book initiated an important debate due to its optimistic reading of the new globalizing conditions – a position from which the author has retrieved a moderate amount of enthusiasm since then. Nonetheless, and going back to his original argument, Canclini introduced the term "hybrid," or more precisely "processes of hybridization," as a way to mark the shift to a new way of thinking about processes of cultural formation and production in Latin America (both traditional and contemporary) in keeping with an anti-foundationalist postmodern sensitivity. The "processes of hybridization" paid attention to "the instability of the social and semantic plurality" (García Canclini, 2005, p. 249). Indeed, the postmodern hybrid manifests the tensions at the boundaries of cultural clashes and interactions as well as the porousness of contemporary subjective experience and of cultural processes (particularly urban ones) to transcultural exposure and influence (2005, pp. 243–9). Canclini also offered the notion of "processes of hybridization" as the most apt and inclusive category in and through which to analyze and further problematize the many varied phenomena of cross-cultural mixing occurring in Latin America, such as *mestizaje* (2005, p. 11).

In the second edition of *Hybrid Cultures* Canclini distinguishes more explicitly between a descriptive and an explanatory use of the category of hybridization. He continues to defend its explanatory potential, but acknowledges the need for more conceptual work on the subject. Citing some criticisms offered, among others, by the British cultural critic John Kraniuskas and by the Peruvian Antonio Cornejo Polar, Canclini no longer puts forward the category of "the hybrid" as a way of replacing "mestizaje," "syncretism," and other older analytical frameworks in this "family of concepts" such as Fernando Ortiz's "transculturation" (García Canclini, 2005, pp. xxiv–xxxiv, xli). Instead, he proposes to include "the hybrid" alongside them, so as to make the world "more cohabitable in the midst of differences" (2005, p. xliii).

Canclini's initial optimism toward the phenomenon of recent forms of hybridization – groundbreaking as it was, in its mastery of postmodern approaches to cultural analysis in the new age of neoliberal globalization – met with skepticism from a number of cultural critics in the humanities, who framed their thoughts in a firmer climate of opposition to the politics of neoliberalism. The remainder of this essay analyzes some of the major positions developed by some of these critics particularly since the 1990s, beginning with subaltern thinking (the Latin American Subaltern Studies Group) and moving on to post-Occidentalist border thought (Walter Mignolo) and cultural criticism (Nelly Richard).

314

Latin American Subaltern Studies

Latin American Subaltern Studies came into being after the defeat of the Sandinistas in the 1990 election in Nicaragua. At that time, there was a deep sense of disillusionment within the Left with existing models of theorizing social change. In the late 1960s and throughout the 1970s, not just Marxisms but the theology of liberation and proponents of "dependency theory" had pointed to serious structural problems in capitalist-dependent societies, which demanded solutions to poverty beyond unfettered capitalism. With the defeat of the Sandinistas in Nicaragua's 1990 elections, it seemed that the paradigms of emancipation that had fueled those struggles had also failed. Conditions were favorable, however, for new approaches that would incorporate some postmodern ideas without giving up hope for social justice and addressing the plight of the most marginal, forgotten sectors of society.

Despite the stereotypical view one hears repeatedly in philosophy discussions about Latin America, that postmodern thinking must be rejected either because it is inevitably Eurocentric or because it rejects humanism and the ideals of human emancipation, in fact the effects and incorporation of postmodern themes and ideas in various parts of Latin America are both diverse and complex. Suffice it here to refer to the Cuban critic Margarita Mateo who states regarding one specific case: "Cuban postmodernism is expressed through a very broad range of ideo-esthetic positions and nuances . . . In general it sustains a commitment to subvert its social context . . . , to promote dialogue and confrontation with history, [and] to search for a new ethics and an emancipatory project adequate to the new times" (2005, p. 180; my trans.). Or, as the Colombian philosopher Santiago Castro-Gómez has aptly stated, "postmodernity does not entail the abandonment of the emancipatory ideals of modernity . . . but instead the rejection of the totalizing and essentialist language in which those ideas have been articulated" (2001, p. 139).

The founding members of the Latin American Subaltern Studies Group (LASSG) held that new models were needed for theorizing socialisms – models more attentive to grassroots democratic change and to constituencies that were historically left out of power. They reasoned that socialist and left-wing alliances prior to the 1990s had failed not solely because of various political contingencies but also due to limitations in the theoretical models themselves. LASSG founders adopted a new theoretical model calling for "divestment" (my metaphor) in the authority and self-assurance of academic knowledge vis-à-vis Latin American socio-historical and cultural realities. They looked for a theoretical model capable of showing the limits of academic theory, assuming that with respect to the non-academic, or at least the "popular" sectors of society, academics stood in a position of privilege and power. The idea of a self-critical model capable of inverting its glance on itself replaces the authority of the privileged theorist (Beverley, 1999). Specifically, LASSG sought to make room for the perspective of the poorest and most neglected members of society – the "subaltern" – if only these could be heard or understood. For this task, they found theoretical and political inspiration in a group of historiographers in India who, under the leadership of historian Ranahit Guha (b. 1923), had founded the South Asian field of "Subaltern Studies" in the early 1980s (Chakrabarty, 2000, p. 467). Their writings gradually caught international attention

315

as postcolonial studies grew in importance in Britain and the United States. Along with the Italian Marxist Antonio Gramsci (1891–1937), Guha would become a leading theoretical influence on LASSG. The primary question retained from Gramsci was how to formulate a contemporary analysis of the relationship between the nation and the people, more technically known as the "national-popular" question, so that those who were out of power (the subaltern) would join forces to gain it. From Guha LASSG founders sought a new approach to historiography. Guha's insightful analyses of peasant rebellions in India demonstrated the limits of using a linear model of temporality, progress, and development as a basis for understanding historical change. As LASSG founding member Ileana Rodríguez states, "in the nineties, we perceived in the South Asian group a new kind of social sensibility that, coupled with a theoretical stubbornness and a spirit of academic militancy, was very much in agreement with what we called a 'new humanism.'" (Rodríguez, 2001b, p. 3). By "new humanism" Rodríguez means continuing to care for "the struggles of the poor" in the absence of viable political models enabling to make their plight visible.

Founded in 1992, LASSG's initial core members were Ileana Rodríguez, John Beverley, Patricia Seed, Javier Sanjinés, José Rabasa, Robert Carr, and María Milagros López (d. 1997) (Beverley, 1999). A more detailed description of the group's stages, members, and close collaborators is offered by Ileana Rodríguez in an important anthology that gathers some of their most representative writings during this period (Rodríguez, 2001b, pp. 1–30). LASSG was composed primarily of literary critics, several of whom also worked in cultural studies. Other fields represented were history, sociology, cultural anthropology, and women's studies. Among its more philosophically oriented members were John Beverley, Walter Mignolo, Alberto Moreiras, and John Kraniuskas. LASSG was dissolved in the year 2000. Despite its brief existence LASSG galvanized the question of the subaltern as central not just to the humanities and politics but to the philosophy of culture. The repercussions of this question continue to be of interest across the disciplines today.

In its Founding Statement, LASSG accepted Guha's definition of "subaltern" as "a name for the general attribute of subordination in South Asian [and analogously in Latin American] society whether this is expressed in terms of class, caste, age, gender, and office or in any other way" (Latin American Subaltern Studies Group, 1995, p. 135). The subaltern are basically those who lack access to discursive (but also political) representation in their own terms. For example, in historical narratives, accounts of indigenous uprisings are usually told on somebody else's terms. The *testimonio* (testimony) genre in Latin America, with its accounts of oppression told at least partially in the voices of the marginalized, became a privileged site of interest for LASSG and other subalternists. This shift in the epistemic authority granted to marginalized speakers by academics (and contested in academic controversies) signaled a major departure from the usual account of the nation prevalent in higher education. In the past, the interlocutors of the dominant concept of the nation and its identity had normally been the *letrados* (lettered), a class indispensable to the rule of what Angel Rama had called "the lettered city" (Rama, 1996; originally published 1984).

An important debate in Subaltern Studies (beyond LASSG itself) arose from the question raised by Gayatri Spivak in her famous essay "Can the Subaltern Speak?" (Spivak, 1988). She initially argued that whether "representation" is taken to mean "speaking about" or "speaking for, or on behalf of," the subaltern are necessarily silenced by the representation made about them or on their behalf (cf. Rodríguez, 2001b, pp. 10–11). Spivak's point is that by the time the subaltern speaker can be heard or understood by the corresponding dominant structure, s/he is not heard *as subaltern* but only insofar as the dominant hermeneutic horizon (or discourse) imprints its own epistemic stamp, as it were, on what the subaltern has said or done. In Spivak's terms, this dynamic characterizes the process of epistemic violence prevalent in colonial and, to a great extent, postcolonial societies that exercise it toward its disenfranchised members. How then can the actions, motivations, or needs of the subaltern be known, assuming, for the sake of the argument, that they cannot be represented? Among the principal strategies LASSG proposed (in affinity with deconstructive theory and psychoanalysis) is looking for interruptions, holes, or cracks in the dominant narratives. These are thought to point to the *effects* of subalterns on dominant discourse. Another strategy is to study the notion of citizenship and check the extent to which it disenfranchises the subaltern (who as Guha indicated can refer to groups subordinated by age, gender, caste, class, or any other way). Ileana Rodríguez argues that if one takes the notion of governability, including propriety, and then considers those thought to transgress its categories – often cast in the role of servants or uneducated characters – this is one way to find the subaltern (Rodríguez, 2001a, pp. 362–4).

There is a tension in these subaltern studies between a type of hermeneutical approach to let the subaltern be seen and heard, as one might do as a literary critic by bringing attention to marginal subaltern characters in a work of fiction, and acting politically to empower the subaltern. I would associate the hermeneutical approach with the practice of "letting be" in relation to listening with respect and care to a marginally positioned interlocutor. In the subalternist case "letting be" could be understood as requiring a phenomenological shift of perspective from the ordinary, say, male-dominant or class/race stratified society, to standing back and allowing the humanity of the subaltern to speak to us. This shift of perspectives would be a shift away from the customary and often unnoticed violence that silences or covers up the humanity of these others. The focus on "letting be" also allows for a shift away from linear thinking, even if for a few moments only. Within this perspectival shift it is also possible to locate the experience of inverting the glance that Beverley considers crucial to subaltern studies. The glance is inverted because the dominant person may pause to consider how the subaltern sees her or him. This approach, I suggest, may work alongside, but is still quite distinct from, political action or militancy on behalf of the subaltern, or with political action by the subaltern themselves to overcome the hegemonies that oppress them. A careful balance between "letting be" (or decentering one's views to hear those from the margins) and forming alliances to overcome oppressions of various kinds appears necessary to carry on the spirit of subaltern studies.

Post-Occidentalism and Border *Gnosis*

Retaking the matter of the debate arising from García Canclini's optimistic conceptualization of the hybridization of cultures in postmodern times, one alternative that has enjoyed considerable academic influence, especially in the United States, has been

317

the "post-Occidentalist" reading of Western colonialism in Latin America offered by Walter Mignolo, a leading expert in the colonial era and, more recently, in global studies. From a perspective such as Mignolo's, the concept of hybridization, or for that matter any other concept, such as *mestizaje*, needs to be analyzed in the context of a decolonizing epistemology. Mignolo has been developing and at times modifying the basic premises of this conceptual framework since the 1990s.

Mignolo's *The Darker Side of the Renaissance* (2003; originally published 1995) relies on the notion of a "pluritopic hermeneutics" to analyze the effects of the Spanish conquest and colonization in a non-Eurocentric way while also pointing to a blind spot or lapse in colonial thinking. He argues that the typical Western historiographical narrative, in which time is conceived as linear and space is subordinated to time, uses a time-space imaginary in which history is seen as moving from past to future, with Western civilization symbolizing the higher end of progress toward the future. As a result, other cultures or civilizations are projected symbolically toward the primitive times of the past. He holds that whereas the landing of Europeans in what came to be known as "America" may be theorized in terms of two or more coexisting societies in time, differentiated by a nonhierarchical "pluritopical" view of place, the indigenous societies in what became known as the "Indias Occidentales" (Western Indies) and later "America" were cast into a singular time-space framework of linear thought. In such a narrative, or perhaps we should say metanarrative, European culture came to be identified with progress or the forward-looking force of history, while non-Europeans occupied the time-space of the less developed, the primitive, the uncivilized, and the historical past.

Mignolo's notion of a "pluritopic hermeneutics" reverses the established Eurocentric linear thinking with an interpretive counterstance in which concepts of time and space held by various indigenous societies could be cognitively mapped in a type of side-by-side relation to those of the Iberians, rather than subordinating the former to the latter. In this view, the adoption of a pluritopic hermeneutics performs a valuable role in allowing for a decolonization of the interpretive methods by which one may come to understand indigenous thinking and cultural practices (as they would no longer be subsumed by an alien imaginary and symbolic order). Mignolo defines "colonial semiosis" as a new approach to linguistics featuring the interpretive method of such a pluritopic hermeneutics, which opens up new intellectual horizons for research and empowers the agency of those formerly marginalized or excluded by colonial legacies. This hermeneutical approach also allows Mignolo to present what perhaps turns out to be an even more powerful epistemic concept, which he names "the colonial difference." He develops the latter concept in his next book (Mignolo, 2000).

Mignolo's concept of the "colonial difference" acts as an epistemic filter through which to diagnose what modern (and later, European postmodern) discourse pushes out to the margins of thought in the social sciences and the humanities (as in modern culture more generally). It is a signifier of that which is assimilated with difficulty or through violence when theories of modernity are articulated out of the colonial experience; but it is also a reference to those marginalized or expelled speaking positions from which challenges to the hegemony of modern/colonial/Eurocentric thought may be carried out. The colonial difference reveals "the dark side of the Renaissance" (that is, the domination and conquest of non-Europeans) as his former study diagnosed. But it also reveals the discursive effects of colonialism in modern epistemology and Western scholarship, while it empowers those who challenge such paradigms through alternative epistemic practices. Specifically applied to the United States, the colonial difference reveals the marginalization or subordination of the cultures or voices of African Americans, Latinos/as, native Americans, and others. Out of these groups, Latinos/as, and particularly Chicanos/as in the United States, become the major signifiers of what Mignolo calls "border thinking," or "border *gnosis*." Border thinking, in turn, is aimed at a displacement of modern epistemology and hermeneutics, both of which Mignolo now charges with being irredeemably Eurocentric (2000, p. 12). Contrary to modern epistemology's "territoriality," Mignolo describes border thinking as mobile, enactive, and performative (2000, p. 26). In this view, the latter's *locus* (place) of enunciation becomes a marker for the shifting borders and tensions between subaltern and mainstream or hegemonous thought.

Another epistemic framework developed by Mignolo in the 1990s is that of "post-Occidentalism." As a challenge to Anglophone postcolonial theory, which followed Edward Said's critical analysis of Orientalism as a Eurocentric paradigm used in the Western study of the East and Middle East (Said, 1978), Mignolo adopts the terms *Occidentalism* and *post-Occidentalism* to indicate a shift of epistemic perspective for his postcolonial approach to Latin American studies. Mignolo argues that unlike the East which, as Said showed in *Orientalism*, was conceived as Europe's opposite other, the Americas appeared as far back as the colonial period as an expansion of Europe or, if different, a difference subject to "annexation" (Mignolo, 1996, p. 687). For example, Columbus named the islands he found "Indias Occidentales" (Western Indies) and centuries later Hegel's philosophy of history shows the Idea moving from East to West, with the Americas treated as a Western expansion of Europe. Following this thread we see that the paradigm of Occidentalism (including the notion of Western superiority) serves to justify the conquest of America both materially and culturally. It helps to explain the subjugation of the native indigenous population of the Americas and the enslavement of Africans brought to this hemisphere. If a postcolonial perspective is to be applied to Latin America and the Caribbean, Mignolo argues, its cartography should be mapped, specifically, as a *post-Occidentalist* perspective – one from which it is possible both to criticize and overcome the paradigm of Occidentalism along with its racial and ethnic prejudices.

Mignolo took the term *post-Occidental* from the Cuban Marxist literary critic Roberto Fernández Retamar (Mignolo, 2000, pp. 94–5, 107–8; Fernández Retamar, 1986, p. 17). He disassociates the term, however, from Retamar's Marxist reading, updating it via the U.S./Venezuelan anthropologist Fernando Coronil's reflections on Occidentalism (Coronil, 1996) and Chicana feminist Gloria Anzaldúa's groundbreaking work in *Borderlands/La Frontera* (1987). In Mignolo's view, *border thinking* takes on the protagonist role as the epistemic site of resistance or *locus* (place) of enunciation in a post-Occidentalist epistemology.

Mignolo's conceptual framework is populated by spatial over temporal metaphors (pluritopic, border, place of enunciation, and so on). In the earlier (mid-1990s) formulation of his hermeneutic framework, his approach shows some affinity with that of Homi Bhabha (1994) whose own articulation of postcolonial theory was influenced by deconstruction and psychoanalysis. Without altogether abandoning some uses of ambiguity,

319

non-linear thinking, or localized adaptations of Foucault's concept of power/knowledge, toward the latter part of the 1990s, however, Mignolo transfers some of his earlier methods and concepts, such as "pluritopic hermeneutics," and reinserts them in a different conceptual framework. The new framework, he states, emerges out of his approximation to the ideas of Argentine philosopher Enrique Dussel and the critique of colonial power articulated by the Peruvian sociologist Aníbal Quijano (Mignolo, 2000, pp. 49–55).

In his influential analysis of colonial power (which is the structure of power imposed on the Americas by European domination) Quijano argues that "the coloniality of power" (or the colonial use of power) consists of three principal features. At the material level, there is class exploitation; at the level of social/demographic classification, there is the introduction of the category of race to mark the exploited populations; at the intersubjective or cultural level, there is a fierce Eurocentrism (Quijano, 2000). Following Quijano and Dussel, Mignolo accepts, as his point of departure, a version of Immanuel Wallerstein's sociological analysis of "the modern [capitalist] world-system" beginning in the sixteenth century (see Quijano & Wallerstein, 1992; Dussel, 1998; Wallerstein, 2004). Dussel's idea of situating the production and interpretation of philosophy within a global geo-politics (Dussel, 1985) easily fits within this paradigm. The "geo-politics of knowledge," Mignolo elaborates, involves a series of "global designs" against which a set of local knowledges can be enlisted (Mignolo, 2000; cf. Mignolo, 2005, p. 43). Mignolo also appeals both to subaltern studies and to Foucault's idea of unearthing "subjugated knowledges" as he grounds his project in support of legitimating local ways of knowing (Mignolo, 2000, pp. 19–20; Foucault, 1980, pp. 80–2).

By incorporating Quijano's structural analysis of the coloniality of power into his notion of "the colonial difference" Mignolo sets up the framework of "the modern/colonial world system" against which all theories except the border knowledges that contest it may be judged for the extent of their participation in a racially stratifying, exploitative global system (2000, pp. 3–45). He also recalls the influence of dependency theory on Quijano and Dussel (Mignolo, 2000, p. 54). In the late 1960s and the 1970s, Latin American dependency theory argued that it was not possible to overcome underdevelopment through development because underdevelopment was caused by development; it was its other side. Using similar reasoning, Mignolo now argues that it is not possible to overcome coloniality through modernity because coloniality is required by modernity. "Coloniality cannot be overcome by modernity, since it is not only its darker side but its very raison d'être" and, moreover, "epistemic modernity . . . simultaneously became the very foundation of coloniality: the erasure and suppression of *other* knowledges" (Mignolo, 2003, p. 456). Subsequently, the Argentine/U.S. Latina feminist philosopher María Lugones has argued that the modern/colonial system also imposed a rigid heteronormative and violent binary of sex–gender identity which in many instances went contrary to the sexual practices and multiple understandings of sex differences found in indigenous societies (Lugones, 2007).

A point that remains ambiguous in Mignolo's presentation of border knowledges is the degree of compatibility he thinks such ways of thinking have vis-à-vis post-structuralist theory in Latin America and its diaspora. While Foucault and subaltern studies offer a poststructuralist approach to knowledge (or at least one influenced by poststructuralism, in the case of subaltern studies), Wallerstein, Dussel, Quijano, and

320

world-systems analysis do not. This is because world-systems theory, as developed by Wallerstein and adopted with modifications by Dussel and Quijano, basically offers a tightly structural analysis of the development of capitalism since the sixteenth century as a "world-system." Since Mignolo incorporates elements from all the above sources, including Foucault and subaltern studies, into his overall analysis, it cannot be inferred that he stands in strict opposition to poststructuralist theory. Part of the ambiguity results from a lack of specificity in the use of the relevant terms. Mignolo usually refers to *European* poststructuralist philosophers as *deconstructionist* or *postmodern*, whereas he refers to *global South* poststructuralist/deconstructive theorists as *postmodern* and/or *postcolonial* (cf. Mignolo, 2000, p. 201). Criticizing the Europeans, he holds that "deconstructive strategies are blind to the colonial difference" (2000, p. 38). But this cannot be right about deconstruction without qualification since it misses the point of the effective uses of deconstructive methodology by leading postcolonial critics including Spivak and Bhabha. It seems that Mignolo would like to find a kind of epistemic point, or bridge, where the set of global South theories (whether poststructuralist or not) will meet with the European theories so far blinded to their postcolonial others, out of which encounter a transformation of knowledge can occur. In this spirit he seems to indicate that "decolonization should be thought of as complementary to [Derridean] deconstruction" (2000, p. 326) and to offer his conception of border thinking "in dialogue with . . . Foucault's notion of 'insurrection of subjugated knowledges'" (2000, p. 19).

The Colombian-born U.S. Latino philosopher Eduardo Mendieta has pushed the dialogue agenda forward, especially in his editorial work (Lange-Churión & Mendieta, 2001; Mendieta, 2003). His own interest lies primarily in the question of postmodernity as a geohistorical, global phenomenon, not in providing close readings of particular theories or philosophers (Mendieta, 2007, pp. 60–5). In contrast, the Colombian philosopher Santiago Castro-Gómez appeals to a poststructuralist approach in order to criticize dependency theory, world-systems analysis, the philosophy of liberation, and traditional Marxisms. He points to the problems found in dependency theory and the philosophy of liberation insofar as they subordinate the analysis of smaller-scale phenomena into totalizing, all-inclusive categories and "dualistic hermeneutical structures" (like oppressor/oppressed) which actually "cover up struggles that need to be understood in their particularities" (Castro-Gómez, 2001, pp. 142–3). Mignolo has defended his own formulation of border thinking from this kind of charge, arguing that although criticism cannot give up a certain use of macronarratives, it is possible to conceptualize the objects of investigation as networks of "local histories" or "multiple local hegemonies," not as totalities (Mignolo, 2000, p. 2). Next, a look at the Chilean cultural critic Nelly Richard's deconstructionist *and* feminist approach to decolonizing knowledge will serve to reveal "the border of the border," if one may speak in such terms.

Cultural Criticism

Nelly Richard is best known as a cultural critic and as the founder and editor of the *Revista de crítica cultural* (1990–2007). Born in France and educated at the Sorbonne, she has lived in Chile since 1970. Her expertise extends to art criticism and literary theory. Richard's critical position traverses multiple areas of sociopolitical and cultural criticism. This discussion highlights her role as a feminist cultural critic.

Richard played a major role in organizing the First Congress of Latin American Women's Literature (Primer Congreso de Literatura Femenina Latinoamericana), an extraordinary event held in 1987 in Santiago, Chile, under the dictatorship of Augusto Pinochet. In the paper she delivered there, she laid the ground for interpreting "the feminine" as a disruptive and transgressive sign that may be mobilized against a masculine, authoritarian culture (such as the one instantiated by the dictatorship). She rejects those senses of "the feminine" that link it to an essence or to a "fixed identity" (*identidad fija*) at the same time that she expresses concern for "the double colonization of the female Latin American subject" (1990, pp. 50–1; my trans.). Richard takes a poststructuralist approach to the text, seeing it not as an independent universe of self-contained meaning but rather as inscribed by a multiplicity of social meanings (codes) and likewise yielding multiple potential interpretations. She also notes the importance that parody can assume when undermining the authority of colonial or masculine-dominant discourse.

A first principle of Richard's critical approach is the disentanglement of "the feminine" as a sign of passivity or compliance before the paternal law. This position allows Richard sufficient ground to criticize Leftist cultural theorists whose cartographies of knowledge appropriate women, the feminine, or feminism for their own purposes within their metanarratives regarding liberation, democracy, or decolonization. In this view, the degree to which a hermeneutic or conceptual framework is friendly toward feminist critique depends on the degree of feminine discursive transgressiveness it is able to tolerate without either the framework or its challenger receding into some form of dogmatism.

In releasing the notion of the feminine from a sign of domestication or, at best, complementarity to the masculine, and enabling it to take on an active role against the authority of the phallic signifier, Richard associates the signifying action of the feminine with a stance against the totalization of meaning. Although the preeminent target of Richard's criticism remains the Pinochet dictatorship (even after its demise), her aim is not to let the cultural critic's guard down as if the postdictatorial era were immune from the continued deployment, even if less centralized, of authoritarian thought and practices.

In a later study Richard observes that the 1973 coup dismantled past "structures of collective representation" leading to widespread feelings of "dispossession" (2004b, p. 45). In such circumstances many artists felt morally bound to put the shattered pieces together by trying to restore the lost sense of community. Yet she criticizes the politics of art that sought its grounding in "the messianic fundamentalism of utopias" and a re-elaboration of the "national-popular" vision of government for Chile (2004b, p. 45). These themes energized what Richard calls "the traditional left." With the benefit of hindsight we can say that she is referring to the Left that has so often dominated the political imaginary of Latin America, with populist-oriented masculine leadership and proclamations of national liberation that sooner or later become cemented in reconfigured authoritarian practices. In stark contrast to this political orientation, she explains that the *avanzada* or "new scene" (a type of art and aesthetics appearing in Chile in 1977), also born from the Left but with a very different approach, immersed

322

itself in the experience of shattering and fragmentation, addressing it in its art and writing. Here historical narrative loses its linear sequence, the "I" is no longer represented as unified and continuous, the sense of indeterminacy explodes the binaries of feminine and masculine, and writing itself displays the impact of violence – in short, art comes to defy the stabilization of meaning suitable for collective, even if oppositional, identities (Richard, 2004b, pp. 46–7). I think it is fair to say that despite the apparent nihilism of such art and writing, the aesthetics advanced by the "new scene" sets the stage for an explosion of meaning out of which new ways of thinking and relating can arise beyond dictatorship. In Richard's view, one important indicator for the possibility of democratic political change is what transpires in our discursive practices. Hence her constant emphasis on recognizing the interruptions, inversions, and excesses of meaning at every register of interpretive activity: imaginary, symbolic, corporeal, and so forth.

In the case of geopolitical centers and margins, Richard does not let the fact that poststructuralist theory emerged in Europe deter her from engaging with it from a local or peripheral position in Latin America. The first step of her argument is to recall that postmodernism does not have a univocal meaning so it is important to be precise regarding what one wishes or not to salvage out of its plural and even contradictory formulations (Richard, 2004a, pp. 55–60). She notes, more precisely, that the specific crisis of the modern paradigm of subject–reason–historical progress to which the center's postmodernism speaks also empowered the center's institutions and intellectuals to mediate their own identity crisis (1995, p. 218). If, philosophically, postmodern thought addresses this crisis by decentering the subject and allowing more attention for "the other," alterity, the margins of discourse, or the underrepresented in Western history, a major problem for Latin Americans is that the redistribution of emphasis between center and margins, subject and other, is determined by the center's intellectuals and institutions, not by those of the periphery. The asymmetrical relations of power between center and periphery continue to exist even when the center advocates for the inclusion of the margins. Nonetheless, argues Richard, the theoretical opening toward Latin America and other peripheral cultures and peoples provides the opportunity for these "others" to call for recognition on their own terms.

Again, when referring to a peripheral subject's terms, it is not a case of homogenizing all Latin Americans, or women, as if they could speak in some sort of essentialized voice. On the contrary, Richard holds that given the uneven sociocultural conditions and internal differences characterizing Latin American societies across the board, the local adaptations and engagements with postmodern thought will undoubtedly be marked by the multiplicity of influences affecting theorists in the periphery. Just as there are internal differences and a wide range of intersectional configurations of cultural and social positions in the center, so there are in the periphery. Her basic strategy is to link up "the new antiauthoritarian modulation of a postmodernity finally respectful of diversity" in the center with her long-held emphasis on the need for antiauthoritarian discourses in the periphery (Richard, 1995, p. 221). But this requires that the marginal subject, that is, the subject of difference, has "the right to negotiate its own conditions of discursive control" and that the center's intellectuals stop defining the categories and classifications in accordance to which the "differences" marking "the Latin American" and "the feminine" are to be known in academia's Northern institutions of prestige (Richard, 1995, pp. 221–2). Despite the increased recognition given to global South intellectuals in recent years, Richard's concern continues to be legitimate. It is important to note, however, that all scholarship involves a reconfiguration of previously published material. This qualifier granted, her point simply is that given the asymmetrical power relations between North and South, the former enjoys a privileged position in its capacity to define the latter and thereby to misrepresent the other according to its own interests, which may range from a constructive sense of affinity with the other to epistemic violence and abuse.

Richard also clarifies what she takes to be the optimum relationship between the postmodernisms of the center and the feminisms of the periphery. Again, warning that while it is true that some forms of postmodernism (to which she refers as postmodernisms of "reaction") have served to legitimate the neoconservative political agendas of the center by promoting skepticism or nihilism toward progressive social change, there are also postmodernisms of "resistance" whose critique of imperial, colonial, Eurocentric, and phallocentric rationality allow for important bridges to be built with local forms of feminism in Latin America (Richard, 2004a, pp. 55, 66). In particular, she calls attention to the postmodern deployment of the margins of discourse in order to destabilize the hegemony of what used to be called the subject of universal history and likewise the "sole possessor of knowledge . . . whose authority was based on the primacy of the white-male-lettered-metropolitan subject" (2004a, p. 60). She holds that it is precisely from the margins of discourse in the global periphery that the voices of women will challenge such a limited/limiting paradigm of knowledge and universality. She therefore encourages Latin American feminists to intervene critically and constructively in the debate over the local relevance of postmodernism, since the latter's emphasis on reclaiming the margins of discourse can be seen as an ally of women's creativity and feminist criticism as well as of all those who care deeply about moving beyond authoritarian thinking and practices.

Concluding Thoughts

Poststructuralism in European continental thought and philosophy introduced a major shift of theoretical perspective away from linear accounts of historical progress, Cartesian conceptions of the transparency of consciousness, totalizing conceptions of knowledge, mass culture, and social reality in social science methodologies, and monological accounts of the meaning of texts in literary theory. Unlike empiricism, which may appeal to (counter)factual information to displace outdated facts and concepts without altogether displacing the larger paradigms that hold their meaning, and unlike much standpoint epistemology, which sets up a firm positional epistemic model from which to challenge what counts as universal knowledge, poststructuralism tends to destabilize the ruling paradigms themselves, especially those paradigms that foreclose experimentation and the radical questioning of meaning. Poststructuralist theory is especially well equipped to analyze critically the irruptions, accelerated changes, displacements, and discontinuities characteristic of the postmodern historical conditions which have impacted and continue to affect the lives of people throughout the world in this global age, often leading to the need to revise prior understandings of the "world" which are no longer persuasive given changing contexts and experiences. Subaltern studies, border thinking, and cultural criticism are three distinct ways in which such new worlds of understanding have emerged in recent times, challenging new global hegemonies and allowing perspectives from the margins to sharpen our conceptual approach to Latin American philosophy thanks to the critical adaptation of some post-structuralist ways of thinking.

Related chapters: 11 Phenomenology; 13 Liberation Philosophy; 21 Liberation in Theology, Philosophy, and Pedagogy; 28 Feminist Philosophy; 30 Cultural Studies.

References

Anzaldúa, G. (1987). *Borderlands/la frontera: the new mestiza*. San Francisco: Aunt Lute.

Beverley, J. (1999). *Subalternity and representation: arguments in cultural theory*. Durham: Duke University Press.

Beverley, J., Oviedo, J., & Aronna, M. (Eds). (1995). *The postmodernism debate in Latin America*. Durham: Duke University Press.

Bhabha, H. K. (1994). *The location of culture*. New York: Routledge.

Castro-Gómez, S. (2001). The challenge of postmodernity to Latin American philosophy. (E. Mendieta, Trans.). In P. Lange-Churión & E. Mendieta (Eds). *Latin America and post-modernity* (pp. 123–54). Amherst, NY: Humanity.

Chakrabarty, D. (2000). A small history of subaltern studies. In H. Schwarz & S. Ray (Eds). *A companion to postcolonial studies* (pp. 467–85). Malden, MA: Blackwell.

Coronil, F. (1996). Beyond Occidentalism: toward nonimperial geohistorical categories. *Cultural Anthropology*, 11:1, 52–87.

Del Sarto, A., Ríos, A., & Trigo, A. (Eds). (2004). *The Latin American cultural studies reader*. Durham: Duke University Press.

Dussel, E. (1985). *Philosophy of liberation*. (A. Martinez & C. Morkovsky, Trans.). Maryknoll, NY: Orbis.

Dussel, E. (1998). Beyond Eurocentrism: the world-system and the limits of modernity. In F. Jameson & M. Miyoshi (Eds). *The cultures of globalization* (pp. 3–31). Durham: Duke University Press.

Fernández Retamar, R. (1986). Our America and the West. *Social Text*, 15, 1–25 (Original work published 1974).

Foucault, M. (1980). Two lectures. In C. Gordon (Ed.). *Power/Knowledge: selected interviews and other writings 1972–1977 by Michel Foucault* (pp. 78–108). New York: Pantheon.

García Canclini, N. (2005). *Hybrid cultures: strategies for entering and leaving modernity*. 2nd edn. (C. L. Chiappari & S. López, Trans.). Minneapolis: University of Minnesota Press (Original work published 1989).

Lange-Churión, P., & Mendieta, E. (Eds). (2001). *Latin America and postmodernity*. Amherst, NY: Humanity.

Latin American Subaltern Studies Group. (1995). Founding Statement. In J. Beverley, J. Oviedo, & M. Aronna (Eds). *The postmodernism debate in Latin America* (pp. 135–46). Durham: Duke University Press.

Lugones, M. (2007). Heterosexualism and the colonial/modern gender system. *Hypatia*, 22:1, 185–209.

Mateo, M. (2005). *Ella escribía poscrítica*. La Habana: Editorial Letras Cubanas (Original work published 1995).

Mendieta, E. (Ed.). (2003). *Latin American philosophy: currents, issues, debates*. Bloomington: Indiana University Press.

Mendieta, E. (2007). *Global fragments: globalizations, Latinamericanisms, and critical theory.* Albany, NY: SUNY Press.

Mignolo, W. D. (1996). Posoccidentalismo: las epistemologías fronterizas y el dilema de los estudios (latinoamericanos) de áreas. *Revista Iberoamericana*, 62:176–7, 679–96.

Mignolo, W. D. (2000). *Local histories/global designs: coloniality, subaltern knowledges, and border thinking.* Princeton: Princeton University Press.

Mignolo, W. D. (2003). *The darker side of the Renaissance: literacy, territoriality, and colonization.* 2nd edn. Ann Arbor: University of Michigan Press (Original work published 1995).

Mignolo, W. D. (2005). *The idea of Latin America.* Malden, MA: Blackwell.

Quijano, A. (2000). Coloniality of power, Eurocentrism, and Latin America. *Nepantla: Views from South*, 1:3, 533–80.

Quijano, A., & Wallerstein, I. (1992). Americanity as a concept, or the Americas in the modern world-system. *International Journal of Social Science*, 134, 549–59.

Rama, A. (1996). *The lettered city.* Durham: Duke University Press (Original work published 1984).

Richard, N. (1990). De la literatura de mujeres a la textualidad femenina. In C. Berenguer et al. (Eds). *Escribir en los bordes* (pp. 39–52). Santiago, Chile: Cuarto Propio.

Richard, N. (1995). Cultural peripheries: Latin America and postmodernist de-centering. In J. Beverley, J. Oviedo, & M. Aronna (Eds.), *The postmodernism debate in Latin America* (pp. 217–22). Durham: Duke University Press.

Richard, N. (2004a). *Masculine/Feminine: practices of difference(s).* (S. R. Tnadeciarz and A. A. Nelson, Trans.). Durham: Duke University Press (Original work published 1993).

Richard, N. (2004b). *The insubordination of signs.* (A. A. Nelson & S. R. Tandeciarz, Trans.). Durham: Duke University Press (Original work published 1994).

Rodríguez, I. (2001a). Apprenticeship as citizenship and governability. In I. Rodríguez (Ed.). *The Latin American subaltern studies reader* (pp. 341–66). Durham: Duke University Press.

Rodríguez, I. (2001b). Reading subalterns across texts, disciplines, and theories: from representation to recognition. In I. Rodríguez (Ed.), *The Latin American subaltern studies reader* (pp. 1–31). Durham: Duke University Press.

Said, E. W. (1978). *Orientalism* (New York: Vintage).

Spivak, G. C. (1988). Can the subaltern speak? In C. Nelson & L. Grossberg (Eds). *Marxism and the interpretation of culture* (pp. 271–313). Urbana: University of Illinois Press.

Wallerstein, I. (2004). *World-systems analysis: an introduction.* Durham: Duke University Press.

23

Globalization and Latin American Thought

A. PABLO IANNONE

The Colombian historian and educator Germán Arciniegas once wrote of Latin American life: "For the moment our life moves within a gamut that ranges from the almost primitive aspects of the Amazon jungle to the refinement and culture of the great cities" (Arciniegas, 1944, p. viii). Yet, he added, "It is not in the light of the present but of the future that the importance of Latin-American nations must be evaluated." Arciniegas foresaw that these countries would soon increase communications, transportation, and energy availability (Arciniegas, 1944, p. vii), reshaping Latin American life (Arciniegas, 1944, p. 223) and, as he unyieldingly hoped, causing the demise of Latin American dictatorships (Rother, 1999).

Since Arciniegas made these statements, some of the future he foresaw has come to pass, though not always in the ways or with the positive results he envisioned. Communications, transportation, and energy availability have increased together with business and amenities in the cities, some of which have grown exponentially. Yet, poverty is still rampant in the region, and dictatorships have not quite seen their demise or, where they have, they all-too-often have been replaced by authoritarian governments where the judiciary has little or no independence and the executive has little or no restraint. What went wrong?

This is a matter of much debate among Latin American thinkers who, whatever their disagreements, by and large agree with Arciniegas's warning: "Everything in the New World requires original defenses and its own care, a deeper knowledge of the history of Europe and the history of the Americas . . . The inequality in economic development between the different parts of the hemisphere requires a more exquisite care of the economic interests and moral and material defenses in order to resist the complications of international life" (Cardoso Ruiz, 2006, p. 8 [my translation]). Accordingly, the following questions arise: To what extent and in what ways have economic development and political freedoms taken root in Latin America since the mid-twentieth century? What other developments, not envisioned by Arciniegas, have accompanied or resulted from those he did envision? How are the latter related to processes of globalization and how should globalization be understood? What challenges does the current situation concerning globalization in Latin America pose? How should they be addressed?

Philosophical and Scientific Approaches to Globalization in Latin America and Abroad

The globally integrative forces of transnationalism, cosmopolitan culture, and modernity elicit romantic enthusiasm among some Latin Americans and cautious skepticism – when not outright fear and anger – from others. In a parallel manner, the globally disintegrative forces of nationalism, local culture, and tradition also elicit romantic enthusiasm among some Latin Americans and cautious skepticism – when not outright fear and anger – from others. There are those who hail the globally integrative forces affecting Latin America as a way out of widespread poverty, legal and political sectarianism, cultural stagnation, and longstanding oppression of traditionally disenfranchised groups – say, the poor living in Brazil's favelas, and Argentina's Villa Miserias. Others argue that those globally integrative forces are regionally, locally, and even globally disintegrative and a sure way to economic and political dependence, cultural decadence, loss of national identity, and the destruction of traditionally disenfranchised groups – say, the Amazonian Yanomani, Nambi-kwara, Kayapo, Uru-Eu-Wau-Wau, and Xingu, and the remaining Mapuches, still pursuing a traditional way of life (Vargas Llosa, 2001). Let us briefly review the very notions of globalization involved in these and related views, and the theoretical approaches – some philosophical, others scientific – in which they are embedded.

Until recently, theories of globalization formulated in the social studies outside of Latin America – e.g., the commodity-chain, dependency, imperialism, modernization, and world systems conceptions (Iannone, 2007, p. 226) – approached globalization primarily focusing on the relations between nation-states, where the units of study are largely countries, and the relations studied are primarily bilateral or multilateral relations between countries. Only recently have theorists begun to focus on transnational practices, even some who think globalization will bring about a restructuring, not the demise of nation-states (Iannone, 2007, p. 226).

As for philosophical discussions, they have followed lines parallel to those of the social studies. Most scholars have traditionally focused on international relations primarily using countries as the units of study, and emphasizing bilateral or multilateral relations between countries. Others have not, and have even abstracted from the geographic and geopolitical context – local, regional, national, or global – in which policy and decision making take place. Still others have focused primarily on a particular country or small group of countries. Transnational approaches have appeared only lately (Iannone, 2007, p. 126).

With regard to Latin American thinkers, since the 1970s, they also have by and large addressed issues of globalization along the lines of international relations. Yet, the terms of these relations have been, on the one hand, non-Latin American countries, firms, or other organizations, and on the other, Latin American countries. This has been typically accompanied by the belief that the driving forces of globalization affecting Latin America were primarily if not exclusively foreign. A most notable contrast with many non-Latin American thinkers, however, is that Latin American thinkers primarily focused on globalization as correlated with poverty (which they – often without argument – considered an effect of globalization), and addressed it from a critical standpoint which interprets globalization as a struggle between those doing the globalizing and those being globalized. Their approach, though, was not a merely political or economic critique: It also emphasized moral and humanistic concerns. Let us consider some influential versions of this approach and the conception of globalization it involves.

The Philosophy of Liberation, Globalization, and Oppression

Influenced partly by Marxism and its conceptions of social class and class struggle, partly by the problematic of the contemporary Mexican philosopher Leopoldo Zea who conceived of philosophy as a non-scientific enterprise aimed at the elaboration of a world-view from a personal or cultural standpoint, partly by traditional Catholic ideas concerned with the plight of the poor and the absolute value of the human person, Latin American thinkers in the 1970s formulated the philosophy of liberation, which was aimed at improving the situation of the oppressed. Most notable among its representative works are *Filosofía de la liberación* (1977) by the Argentine philosopher Enrique Dussel (who, since then, has been active in Mexico), and *Filosofía de la liberación latinoamericana* (1983) by the contemporary Argentine philosopher Horacio Cerutti Guldberg, who has also been active in Mexico. These thinkers initially criticized the theories of developmentalism (partly involved in the previously cited remarks by Arciniegas); but, since the 1990s, they have turned to a critique of neoliberal ideas of globalization. In this critique, the term "globalization" tended to become simply a synonym for the term "imperialism," roughly understood as the subordination and domination of one or more states or peoples by agents of another.

In the early 1990s, however, other philosophers of liberation began to emphasize the fact that the oppression being faced by Latin America is partly caused by domestic forces in postcolonial societies, where the European colonial metropolises have been replaced as colonial centers by the metropolises of the old colonies, e.g., by Buenos Aires in Argentina, and Mexico City in Mexico. This is sometimes hailed as a recent social studies discovery; but, to be fair, this fact was already being pointed out in the late 1960s by various U.S. social scientists and historians – at least by those social scientists (e.g., Luigi Einaudi) and historians (e.g., James Lockhart) who where my teachers at UCLA between 1967 and 1969. They also pointed out that Latin America was, as some of them said, the grave of Western (including Marxist) political theory and that the notion of social class either needed sharp revisions or had to be abandoned to make room for more realistic hence applicable notions, e.g., that of interest groups.

Beyond recognizing the significant role of globalization's domestic agents and adapting the theory accordingly, however, the version of the philosophy of liberation just described continued to criticize globalization primarily or exclusively from its underside, for example, in Dussel's *Ética de la liberación en la edad de la globalización y de la exclusión* (1998) and in Eduardo Mendieta's "Beyond universal history: Dussel's critique of globalization" (2000). To be sure, this focus does help clarify some important aspects of the problems and issues associated with and enhanced by globalization processes. Most important among these aspects are societal and individual changes associated with globalization, the shortcomings of traditional strictly economic or strictly political or strictly cultural approaches to study globalization, and the multifaceted

329

interdependence between the globalizing agents and those individuals and regions constituting the globalized victims. Yet, the said more recent version of the philosophy of liberation goes no way toward characterizing globalization in a comprehensive instead of one-sided and polemic way. Nor does it go any way toward seriously invest-igating the causes of globalization, and the wide range of very mixed social and indi-vidual developments associated with it. Nor does it, consequently, go any way toward articulating workable and specific ways of dealing with the wide range of problems and issues globalization involves – from poverty, to dislocations in people's self-conception, to environmental degradation, to oppression. As a result, it does not help make progress toward determining how to deal with globalization processes in an effective and morally acceptable way. Its contribution is useful but largely negative.

The Philosophy of Liberation, Globalization, and Interculturalism

Another trend in Latin American thought on globalization has attempted to over-come the limitations of Leopoldo Zea's culturalism, which conceived of philosophy as a non-scientific enterprise aimed at the elaboration of a worldview from a personal or cultural standpoint. An example of this new trend in the philosophy of liberation is the work of Raúl Fornet-Betancourt, most notably, his *Interculturalidad y globalización* (2000). Born in Cuba, Fornet-Betancourt has resided in Germany since 1972. His approach addresses philosophical thinking in its cultural context and, through an intercultural dialogue, aims at transforming both the conception and practice of philosophy. The dialogue it encourages assumes the universal value of human life, whose specific application to each culture is to be formulated by each culture which, from that standpoint, is to engage in the said intercultural dialogue.

There are, no doubt, positive aspects to this approach too. Yet, like the previous version of liberation philosophy, it primarily, if not exclusively, focuses on what is wrong with globalization, still without making any substantial headway toward at least tentatively characterizing it or, more crucially, investigating its causes (since it largely bypasses the social studies). As a result, this approach merely indicates some very general vision – the liberation and realization of all cultural universes. Its articulation in the actual world is at best addressed in a sketchy manner. This can be criticized as utopian and Adolfo García de la Sienra (2003) so criticized it.

Indeed, such an approach does not help make progress toward determining how to deal with globalization processes in an effective and morally acceptable way *now*, when those suffering need it the most. Its contribution, though suggestive and useful, is largely negative. Besides, the dialogue Fornet-Betancourt proposes is not sufficiently open. For it *assumes* the universal value of human life, an anthropocentric assump-tion which automatically excludes the many – both Latin American and non-Latin American – voices which uphold non-anthropocentric views.

An emphasis on intercultural dialogue, however, makes room for fruitful dialogue with cognate approaches developed by philosophers and social scientists outside Latin America. North American examples of these are David Braybrooke and Charles Lindblom's *A Strategy of Decision: Policy Evaluation as a Social Process* (1963), David Braybrooke's *Meeting Needs* (1987) and Iannone (1994 and 1999), among others.

Globalization, Philosophy, the Other Humanities, and the Sciences in Latin America

One can adopt what I have called the *transcultural and transnational dialogue and interactions* approach which, in principle, makes room for a great diversity of peoples, initiatives, values, and ways of doing things. In this approach, the only common ground needed is that which furthers meaningful dialogue and interactions among the states, groups, organizations, and individuals involved. No less, but no more.

Saying this has the implication that some conceptions of philosophy, whether originally developed outside Latin America as *the study of large unsolvable problems*, or as *a dialogue about fundamental problems*, or as *the task of underlaborers* of the sciences, or originally developed inside Latin America as those previously discussed, are too narrow and constrictive. So are mere interdisciplinary – hence merely academic – approaches, which by their very (merely academic) nature fail to engage the larger society, and so do not help deal comprehensibly with globalization problems and issues, which to be sure are not merely academic. Nor do they help deal with the networks of ideas or outlooks that range not merely over the community of philosophers, or even over the wider community of intellectuals, but over Latin American and global society at large.

These tensions had already begun to be addressed by Latin American literary authors during the last part of the twentieth century, for example, by the Peruvian novelist, essay writer, and 1990 presidential candidate Mario Vargas Llosa (2001). He accepted the view that our times are and will become less picturesque than previous ones; but argued that this is the result of modernization, not of globalization. He, however, added that this process is unavoidable – which is questionable given that globalization processes are partly the result of policies and decisions about a variety of institutions (from business and technology to government and education), and policies and decisions lack logical or historical necessity.

Vargas Llosa also argued that modernization causes globalization, not the other way around, and that the individual and social effects blamed on globalization are caused by modernization. This latter position, however, needs more argument than he provided. For even if modernization is a cause of globalization, globalization is caused only partly by modernization, which is by itself insufficient to explain the extremely widespread, sometimes planetary or quasi-planetary diffusion of business practices, scientific protocols, uses of technology, and multi-centered expertise and cultural expressions characteristic of globalization. To explain the latter, one needs also to appeal to business, technological, scientific, or cultural interests (usually to a mutually interactive combination of these) and a variety of conditions in which they come into play. In short, the causes of globalization are many and interconnected. Further, given its characteristic wide scope, globalization contributes to cause some effects too, namely, wide-reaching consequences (from bureaucratic or economic breakdowns, through environmental overload, to political conflicts) which modernization does not cause by itself. For the consequences, first, often involve large numbers of people's perceptions of, and their resulting responses to, the enormous scope of the changes characteristic of globalization; and, second, the consequences sometimes simply result from the

331

various forms of overload (from issue overload to information overload) which globalization causes – a matter discussed in my work (Iannone, 1994, 2007). In short, globalization's large-scale features at least contribute to cause ecological, social, and even psychological changes.

The question, however, arises: Even if the views just discussed are – as they should be – addressed in the previously outlined open dialogue, will this ensure success so that the eventual result does not end up being the mere mutual acknowledgment of differences where anything goes? The answer is no, it will not *ensure* it – failure is possible; but the approach just outlined opens up possibilities of success where other approaches have led to dead ends because they are either dogmatic, too vague, or too narrow. What conception of globalization should be used in order to avoid these shortcomings?

A Working Characterization of Globalization

As our previous discussion indicates, globalization involves various general types of relations, none of which should be excluded or disvalued by definitional fiat at the outset – and we are very much at the outset – of the inquiry and dialogue on the topic. Among the said general types of relations are, first, those between global business firms and other global, regional, national, or local firms (e.g., those involved in import–export trade); second, relations between global firms and countries (say, those discussed below between the Scandinavian paper mill or the Rio Tinto company and the government of Uruguay in 2008); third, relations between global firms, countries, and a variety of groups: from scientists and engineers (as in the case of genetically modified potatoes produced by Argentine scientists and tested in Brazil and Chile), through importers of iron or gold ore (as in the Rio Tinto case), to journalists upholding freedom of the press, or groups or entire countries (say, France) attempting to preserve their cultural identity, or environmentalists opposing pipeline-building and related engineering activities across Bolivia and Northwestern Argentina or elsewhere; and fourth, relations between civic sector organizations – say, The Nature Conservancy – or governmental or quasi-governmental organizations – say, the Canadian International Development Agency – and various interest groups, e.g., the International Council for Local Environmental Initiatives (ICLEI) or its associated Campaña Ciudades por la Protección Climática (CCP). That is, not only are the relations involved of various kinds, but they involve a wide range of human activities and concerns – economic, scientific, technological, legal, political, and cultural.

None of these should be excluded or disvalued by definitional fiat at the outset. Yet, unilateral definitions of globalization abound. A number of them – the commodity-chain, dependency, imperialism, modernization, world systems, and transnational practices conceptions – were mentioned at this article's outset, and some of them have been indicated in the preceding discussion of liberation philosophies. They are either exclusively macroeconomic, financial, commercial, political, institutional, technological, informatic, or, of late, focused on sustainability (Guimaraes, 1999). How can globalization be characterized without excluding or disvaluing one of these types of relations, activities, and concerns by definitional fiat? I propose a working characterization of globalization as the spreading interconnectedness of business, science, technology, politics, and culture through large regions or the entirety of the world. On this basis, one can proceed to examine a variety of controversial matters that appear to have some claim to be considered instances of globalization, in that, with good reason, they are ordinarily considered globalization developments. Examples include transnational corporations' involvement in global development, the growth of global or regional supranational production chains and markets, the globalization of scientific protocols, the globalization of expertise, the attempts by countries and localities to access global markets, and the attempts by ethnic groups or nations to preserve their traditions or languages when the globalization of other cultural traditions (e.g., the growing global spread of fast food chain outlets) or languages (e.g., the growing global use of English, perhaps next Chinese?) threatens to undermine them.

By adopting this approach, it will be possible for the discussions to highlight the issues at stake, thus developing reasons for adopting a concept of globalization that is sensitive to real issues. This sensitivity is essential if a notion of globalization is to be of any use in discussing moral controversies related to globalization processes. It is equally essential to become keenly aware of the facts, especially of the nature, complexity, and magnitude of the globalization processes involved, so as to avoid the ineffective, hence unwarranted and, because of the undesirable when not disastrous consequences and correlative violations of individuals rights such ineffectiveness involves, morally objectionable approaches to globalization. Let us then, for this purpose, turn to a discussion of a salient Latin American case involving globalization processes and the host of moral and policy and decision problems and issues it poses.

Amazonian Development and Its Socio-Ecological Consequences

The most conspicuous example of gigantic highway construction in Latin America since the mid-twentieth century is the Transamazon Highway system. It runs across Brazil's Amazon jungle and merges into the Transoceanic Highway, which is projected to end in the state of Acre and from there connect with the Peruvian ports of the Pacific. Its construction was part of "operation Amazon," a series of legislative acts and decrees aimed at developing, occupying, and integrating Amazonia into the rest of Brazil (Mahar, 1976, p. 358). However, rather than being hand in hand with political freedoms in accordance with Arciniegas's dreams of development conjoined with democracy, it was instituted and seen well on its way by the military government which came to power in 1964, starting a parade of military presidents which would last until the 1980s (Knippers, 1993, pp. 1–2). It has also had significant and worrisome ecological and social consequences. Let us next turn to these.

The social consequences of Amazonian development are as complex as its ecological consequences. After beginning with the building of the new capital, Brasilia, by the Juscelino Kubitschek administration (1956–61) in the state of Goias, the pace quickened with the construction of the Transamazon Highway. During the mid-1970s, the government offered incentives for clearance of the rainforest and tax shelters to major corporations. The offers drew large numbers of individuals from the Northeast and

Southeast who helped clear the land and start small farming operations. Also, a free-trade zone was created in Manaus, a city that had decayed when its rubber industry had lost markets to synthetic-rubber and its byproducts. As a result, the population of Manaus grew exponentially to over a million. Ranching, logging, and public and private mining ventures also were undertaken, accompanied by infrastructure projects to build roads, bridges, and dams, at an increasing pace since the 1980s (Knippers, 1993). Huge electric dams were built covering millions of acres of forest with water and providing electricity to whole sections of the jungle. An area the size of Belgium was cut or burned down – with the concomitant enormous release of smoke into the atmosphere – for the sake of growing cocoa and raising cattle.

In the process, various Native American tribes – the Yanomani, the Nambi-kwara, the Kayapo, the Uru-Eu-Wau-Wau, and the Xingu – were uprooted. Only about 200,000 of Brazil's indigenous tribal peoples are estimated to have survived, with perhaps 50,000 of them still living deep in the rainforest. And many lives were lost to malaria, yellow fever, typhus, diarrhea, and other diseases. Further, within ten years after this experiment started, much of the Transamazon Highway had been washed away by torrential rains, or taken back by the jungle. The small-farm concentrations were practically empty, some totally abandoned. The soils, leached by tropical rains, stopped producing crops. Since the soil is often so infertile, farmers and corporations earned more from tax write-offs than from anything cultivated.

Forest clearance incentives were revoked in 1987, in response to international pressures, but land speculation continues. Some farmers returned to the cities looking for work. Others proceeded to search for gold, and were joined by additional migrants from the cities, further into the jungle where over one million miners are estimated to have staked claims, digging holes, clearing more forest, dredging rivers and pouring mercury into them, while leading Brazil to become the world's third largest gold producer. On the other hand, by the 1980s, many peasants had become an itinerant labor force, primarily located in instant slum towns on the margins of the land they had cleared. This process has continued to expand, leading to conflicts between neighboring countries. One such conflict is that between Argentina and Uruguay, concerning the Scandinavian paper mill operations on the shores of the Uruguay River shared by both countries but, according to Argentina's claim before the International Court of Justice, in violation of both countries' accords. Another is a related conflict between the same countries concerning the imminent plans by British and Australian enterprises associated with the Rio Tinto Company to build a port terminal in the La Agraciada area to export tons of iron and coal from Brazil.

The Amazonian development case gives ample evidence of the nature, complexity, and magnitude of the host of moral and policy and decision problems and issues facing Latin America (and arguably the world) just with regard to the development of Amazonia, and of the extent to which globalization processes are involved in it. We have also previously outlined some suggestions for addressing the problems and issues – proceeding with the critique of development in a more open way and not merely from the standpoint of the victim, and engaging in dialogue with those affected. Yet, those suggestions are still too general. What are Latin American thought's contributions and prospects for formulating and help implementing a more articulated approach?

Dealing with Globalization Issues in Latin America

Let us begin by examining a procedure developed in Brazil that found favorable echoes among U.S. philosophers of a variety of theoretical persuasions. Called *empate*, in English *tie* [my translation], it is a kind of nonviolent adversarial approach used by Chico Mendes and other tappers to save Amazonian rainforest areas scheduled for logging in order to make room for ranching concerns in the late 1980s. Having learned where future logging was planned, Mendes, with other tappers union leaders and members, would march to the site to have a calm discussion with the loggers, possibly indicating how cutting the trees would threaten the loggers' future. Typically, the loggers peacefully abandoned their chain saws and left while the tappers destroyed their camp. As a result, two of Brazil's largest ranchers left the area (Iannone, 1999, p. 70).

This social decision procedure, which involved meaningful dialogue between tappers and loggers, worked in the Amazonian rainforest so long as the situation did not become predominantly confrontational with the ranchers. Eventually, however, the ranchers were so enraged that the situation became confrontational, meaningful dialogue lost predominance, and the *empate* became ineffective – in fact leading to some ranchers' goons killing Chico Mendes, and to further logging. That is, the *empate* has some, but limited, effectiveness in dealing with Amazonia's issues, though other approaches involving meaningful dialogue and interactions between different groups or at other societal levels may still be effective. Let us next consider additional procedures often advocated by Latin Americans and non-Latin Americans alike.

Virtues and Limits of Legislation

Globalization issues have prompted a variety of responses in the form of international agreements. Examples include the 1997 *Kyoto Protocol* (United Nations, 1998), which entered into force on February 16, 2005, ratified by 175 parties, but not the United States, and *The Millennium Development Goals Report 2007* (United Nations, 2007), developed out of the eight chapters of the *United Nations Millennium Declaration*, signed in September 2000 (United Nations, 2000). Do these primarily legalistic global attempts work? How helpful are they in addressing globalization issues? Does soundly addressing these issues call for a shift in emphasis, away from an exclusive or primary focus on legislation and treaties? What alternative and plausible approaches are there?

The history of international treaties offers more evidence of hopes and wishes than of actual commitments. Concerning poverty and the globalization processes often associated with it, for example, *The Millennium Development Goals Report 2007* evidences a mixed record seven years after the signing of the *United Nations Millenium Declaration*. This is not to say that the treaties are useless. Yet, they are merely opening moves in a policy-making process that can hardly succeed along exclusively legalistic lines. In fact, this is exactly what the Kyoto Treaty indicates when it refers to flexibility in the execution timeframe for attaining its goals as the first commitment period (United Nations, 1998, art. 6 and 7).

As for tensions between globalization and democracy, the Uruguayan philosopher Yamandú Acosta has suggested that they can be resolved only if efforts are guided by

335

the regulative ideal of world-citizenship and its correlate, a world-state which treats individuals as citizens and not mere subjects of separate nation-states (Acosta, 2000, pp. 229–32). But progress toward resolving issues concerning oppression cannot wait until world-citizenship and its correlative world-state are established. Nor can measures aimed at resolving those issues and their frequent correlates, poverty, environmental degradation, and dislocations in people's self-conception, take a back seat behind measures aimed at promoting eventual world-citizenship. Acosta's suggestion, like those previously discussed, is focused on global legislation and suffers from the same (or, given its scope, greater) limitations as those affecting the global legislation approaches previously discussed.

The limitations of any legalistic approach are not merely failures of enforcement, will, or vision. Such failures exist. Yet, implementation failures also occur, and are likely to continue so long as human resources are scarce and various details – some legalistic, other not – fail to be worked out. This can be established by examining policy implementation at the national level.

Latin American efforts to produce enough capital to benefit fully from the division of labor in international and now in global markets have failed recurrently. The Peruvian economist (with a philosophical bent), Hernando de Soto, has poignantly reminded us that at least four times since they became independent from Spain in the 1820s, Latin Americans have unsuccessfully tried to become part of global capitalism. They have restructured their debts, stabilized their economies by controlling inflation, liberalized trade, privatized government assets, undertaken debt equity swaps, and overhauled their tax systems. Yet, they have recurrently failed to produce enough capital to benefit fully from the division of labor. De Soto attributes it to the fact that most people in the region do not have property rights because the assets of many are not properly documented by a property bureaucracy and, hence, they cannot raise capital – e.g., outside of their narrow circles where people trust them, they cannot use their possessions as collateral to get loans to make their ideas marketable or to work competitively the land where they have lived for generations (De Soto, 2000, pp. 6, 210–11).

This is not just a rural problem in developing countries (recall the aftermath of Hurricane Katrina in New Orleans). At any rate, De Soto's conception of property rights goes beyond traditional conceptions of property, which equated property to ownership. He quotes Michel Foucault's conception of reality organized in a conceptual universe (la région médiane) that provides a system of switches or basic codes (codes fondamentaux), and says "I see formal property as a kind of switchyard that allows us to extend the potential of the assets that we accumulate further and further, each time increasing capital (De Soto, 2000, p. 221). He likens this view to Popper's notion of World 3 – a separate reality from World 1 of physical objects and World 2 of mental states – "where the products of our minds take on an autonomous existence that affects the way we deal with physical reality" (De Soto, 2000, p. 221). In fact, this notion is a legal fiction – just like that of a corporation, which allows individuals and societies to deal with very real risks and opportunities. That is, De Soto conceives of property as virtual in nature but very real in purpose: to help redress what globalization fails to redress – indeed hurts – when the legal bureaucracy of property is not developed to help the poor access credit (De Soto, 2000, p. 222). He further adds that simply focusing on the macroeconomic factors – as most projects, including the Amazonian one, have done – in the midst of globalization is insufficient and plays into the hands of those who want to replay the old struggle between haves and have-nots (De Soto, 2000, p. 211).

De Soto's suggestions are theoretically significant, not merely because he formulates a new conception of property, but because this conception makes it possible to characterize social classes in new and fruitful ways, e.g., though he does not say it, on the basis of access, through ownership and concurrent credit worthiness, to the means of wealth creation. Or, from a more comprehensive standpoint, one could characterize social classes on the basis of access to the means of flourishing – a conception that includes but has wider scope than current conceptions of social classes based on power and focused on the distinction between the powerful and the powerless (Kerbo, 2000, *passim.*)

De Soto's suggestions are also practically significant, because they are likely to help soundly address issues about globalization and poverty. But they are not sufficient, because the issues are complex and not, as many tend to assume, merely economic or governmental – a matter that De Soto himself acknowledges (De Soto, 2000, pp. 225–6). As De Soto makes plain, appealing merely to markets does not work. Nor does it work to advocate or engage in merely adversarial approaches such as those previously discussed. Nor does it work to appeal merely to governmental action, as the limitations in merely legalistic approaches indicate. These are all tunnel-vision approaches. Fortunately, more can be and has already begun to be done outside of and, to a lesser extent, in Latin America. Let us see what.

Beyond Tunnel-Vision Approaches

To be sure, the adversarial approaches we discussed give negotiation and bargaining power to those who advocate for the poor, the oppressed, or ecosystem stability, and learn to use the legal challenge process to win commitments from a variety of institutions, often in the form of negotiated settlements to the dispute. But the settlements are parasitic on legal challenges, hence on adversarial approaches to dealing with non-compliance and, when enforcement is lax or when legislation is weaker (or absent) and its implementation limited, there is less, or no, legal leverage for negotiating similar settlements. Further, another limitation is that the said challenges typically occur *after* the fact, when personal, social, or environmental damage has already occurred, or momentum toward personal, social, or environmental damage has already been built.

Since advocating the exclusive use of any of the types of approaches just discussed is likely to be ineffective, attention is now focused on such social decision procedures as negotiation, bargaining, mediation, consensus building, and various forms of convention settling, and on the civic sector, also called the non-profit sector and, by contrast with the market and government, the third sector.

Civic Sector Partnerships

One – though by no means the only – helpful additional procedure is to form *civic sector partnerships* between affected institutions and local communities. The Argentine

337

philosopher and physicist Mario Bunge has recently advocated the civic sector as offering not a sufficient, but a useful alternative to mere reliance on markets or on government. Indeed, he pursued a civic sector project when, in 1938, he helped organize the
Universidad Obrera Argentina, which operated for five years, reaching an enrolment
of 1,000 students, but was shut down by the then Axis-leaning dictatorial government
in 1943 (Vidal-Folch, 2008).

The preceding discussion offers a somewhat detailed idea of the approach and
institutions jointly suitable to address globalization problems and issues, and of their
effectiveness and moral justifiability, both in Latin America and beyond. As the saying
goes, however, the proof of the pudding is in the eating.

Related chapters: 13 Liberation Philosophy; 21 Liberation in Theology, Philosophy, and
Pedagogy; 22 Philosophy, Postcoloniality, and Postmodernity.

References

Acosta, Y. (2000). Democratización en la globalización. In A. Rico & Y. Acosta (Eds). *Filosofía
latinoamericana, globalización y democracia* (pp. 229–32). Montevideo: Editorial Nordan-
Comunidad.

Arciniegas, G. (1944). *The green continent.* New York: Alfred A. Knopf.

Braybrooke, D. (1987). *Meeting needs.* Princeton: Princeton University Press.

Braybrooke, D., & Lindblom, C. E. (1963). *A strategy of decision: policy evaluation as a social
process.* New York: Free Press.

Cardoso Ruiz, R. P. (2006). *Perspectivas y retos de la filosofía latinoamericana.* San Juan de Pasto,
Colombia: Facultad de Filosofía y Letras – UNAM.

Cerutti Guldberg, H. (1983). *Filosofía de la liberación latinoamericana.* Mexico City: Fondo de Cultura
Econónica.

De Soto, H. (2000). *The mystery of capital: why capitalism triumphs in the West and fails everywhere
else.* New York: Basic Books.

Dussel, E. (1977). *Filosofía de la liberación.* Mexico: EDICOL.

Dussel, E. (1998). *Ética de la liberación en la edad de la globalización y de la exclusión.* Madrid: Trotta.

Fornet-Betancourt, R. (2000). *Interculturalidad y globalización.* San José, Costa Rica: Editorial
DEI – Departamento Ecuménico de Investigaciones.

García de la Sienra, A. (November 2003). Neoliberalismo, globalización y filosofía social.
Diánoia, 48:51, 61–82.

Guimaraes, R. P. (1999). Aspectos políticos y éticos de la sustentabilidad y su significado para
la formulación de políticas. *Persona y sociedad*, 13:1, 157–83.

Iannone, A. P. (1994). *Philosophy as diplomacy: essays in ethics and policy making.* Atlantic
Highlands, NJ: Humanities Press.

Iannone, A. P. (1999). *Philosophical ecologies: essays in philosophy, ecology, and human life.*
Atlantic Highlands, NJ and Amherst, NY: Humanities Press and Humanity Books.

Iannone, A. P. (2007). *Los negocios y la sociedad global.* Lima, Perú: Fondo Editorial de la
Universidad Inca Garcilaso de la Vega.

Kerbo, H. R. (2000). *Social stratification and inequality: class conflict in historical, comparative, and
global perspective.* Boston: McGraw-Hill.

Knippers, J. (March 1, 1993). Limits of boom-and-bust development: challenge of the Amazon.
USA Today Magazine, 121:2574, 34–6.

Mahar, D. J. (August 1976). Fiscal incentives for regional development: a case study of the Western Amazon basin. *Journal of Interamerican Studies and World Affairs*, 18:3, 357–78.

Mendieta, E. (2000). Beyond universal history: Dussel's critique of globalization. In L. Alcoff & E. Mendieta (Eds). *Thinking from the underside of history*. Lanham, MD: Rowman & Littlefield.

Rother, L. (December 5, 1999). Germán Arciniegas, 98, critic of Latin American dictators. *The New York Times*, p. 62.

United Nations. (1998). *Kyoto protocol to the United Nations convention on climate change*. New York: United Nations.

United Nations. (2000). *United Nations millennium declaration*. New York: United Nations.

United Nations. (2007). *The millennium development goals report 2007*. New York: United Nations.

Vargas Llosa, M. (February 2001). The culture of liberty. *Foreign Policy*, 122, 66–71.

Vidal-Folch, I. (April 4, 2008). Mario Bunge: filósofo y físico. Madrid: *El País*, Cultura, p. 46.

Part III

Disciplinary Developments

24

Latin American Philosophy

SUSANA NUCCETELLI

Latin American philosophers have often thought about whether there *is* a Latin American philosophy. Although, as raised by them, the question might at first appear idiosyncratic, even self-defeating, this chapter will show that it is neither, at least when certain conditions are satisfied. Such appearances can be explained away by pointing to the ambiguity and vagueness of the expression 'Latin American philosophy.' Given its ambiguity, at least two construals, which I shall call "universalist" and "distinctivist," are possible. Given its vagueness, for some cases it is difficult to determine whether certain works fall under a philosophy of that sort. But parallel semantic shortcomings affect other areas of philosophy, which, as we shall see, may likewise not only be construed in the universalist or distinctivist way, but also have borderline cases.

1. The Question of Whether There Is a Latin American Philosophy

When a question is ambiguous, seemingly contradictory answers can be offered without inconsistency or relativism. Compare, 'Is there a Latin American Thomism?' – which admits of several different readings such as 'Is there Thomism *in* Latin America?', 'Is Thomism one of the traditions in Latin American philosophy?' and 'Is there a *characteristically* Latin American Thomism?'. As a result, accepting the proposition expressed by one of these questions is consistent with rejecting, or suspending judgment about, the proposition expressed by one of the others (Nuccetelli, 2002).

Similarly, Latin American philosophers have understood and answered the question of concern here in a number of ways. Some endorse versions of 'SU' (strong universalism), according to which

SU   All theories, methods and topics philosophy are universal.

Given SU, no philosophical theory, method or topic is distinctively Latin American. Views along these lines are not at all uncommon among Latin American philosophers. For example, Mario Bunge (a prominent Argentine philosopher of science working in Canada) has recently declared: "I don't think that Latin America constitutes a distinct area of philosophy. Latin America is philosophically just as pluralistic as North America, Western Europe, India, or Japan" (Gilson, 2006, p. 10). But SU, as held by Latin American philosophers, faces serious objections, such as the charge of being self-defeating or leading to a skeptical view about Latin American philosophy. We shall later discuss these objections in connection with the work of two proponents of the doctrine. Note that the plausibility of SU is contingent upon the failure of weaker versions of universalism and distinctivism.

Other universalists embrace weaker theses that are in fact consistent with distinctivism. For example,

WU   Some of the theories, methods and topics of philosophy are universal.

Given WU, there is logical space for some such theories, methods, and topics to be distinctively Latin American in some sense. Weak universalists may take the existence of Latin American philosophy to depend entirely on whether the discipline of philosophy, with at least some of its standard manifestations (schools, professional associations, spaces in the academy, and so on), exists in the subcontinent – without excluding the possibility of a characteristically Latin American philosophy, about whose possibility they could keep an open mind.

Jorge Gracia has recently expounded a view which amounts to a form of weak universalism. On this view, Latin American philosophy is 'ethnic philosophy', understood as follows:

> [A]n ethnic philosophy is the philosophy of an ethnos, and insofar as it is so, and members of ethne do not necessarily share features in common, then what the philosophy of a particular ethnos is exactly will not require any features in common with other philosophies outside the ethnos or even within the ethnos throughout its history. This, I claim, is the best way of understanding the unity of Latin American philosophy. (2008, p. 140)

The view clearly accommodates the notion that some philosophical theories, methods, and topics are universal while others aren't. One of its advantages, Gracia contends, is that it allows the inclusion in Latin American philosophy of works that cannot be counted in either the philosophy of any other ethnic group, or in universal philosophy, which Gracia equates with 'scientific' philosophy. Latin American 'ethnic' philosophy can make room for works that fit Gracia's qualifying conditions, whether they be nonstandard ones such as those by Bartolomé de las Casas and Jorge Luis Borges, or mainstream ones such as those by Hector Neri-Castañeda and Ernest Sosa.

But in the end it is far from clear which works are included or excluded. For example, as we shall see later, the view doesn't help in deciding whether a well-known Maya folk-cosmology, *Popol Vuh*, belongs to Latin American philosophy. Gracia provides only a sketchy conditional criterion according to which it should be included if and only if the Maya are part of the Latin American people. But that will be shown to leave us with a difficult dilemma instead of an answer to the question of the place of works such as *Popol Vuh* in Latin American philosophy. Another apparent advantage of construing the discipline as ethnic philosophy is in avoiding relativization to "some exclusively external standard of rationality, topical relevance, or methodology" (p. 142). This,

344

however, is puzzling. For one thing, it is unclear which alternative proposals, if any, would entail relativizing Latin American philosophy to an "external standard of rationality." Furthermore, obviously any account of the discipline must have a relativization of some sort (at least, to *Latin America*). Gracia's account in fact relativizes philosophy to a certain ethnic group. In addition, both a discipline's topics and methodology are factors internal, not external, to that discipline. Hence something more is needed to understand what an ethnic philosophy is, whether Latin American philosophy is such a discipline, and how that could help to resolve some of the matters in dispute.

Another example of weak universalism is my own 2002 proposal, which may labeled an 'applied-philosophy' view. On this view, universalism and distinctivism are compatible, given that a philosophy is *characteristically* Latin American just in case it develops

1   original philosophical arguments, and
2   topics that are at least in part determined by the relation its proponents bear to cultural, social, and/or historical factors in Latin America.

Construed in this way, there is ample evidence of the existence of a characteristically Latin American philosophy in the works of Latin American thinkers – including both the 'amateur philosophers' and the professional ones – many of whom plainly score high in both originality and sensitivity to the cultural, social, and historical context.

At the same time, the applied-philosophy view agrees with universalism on one important point: that there are some issues, such as the problem of knowledge, the mind–body problem, and whether belief in God can be justified, that have a universal import grounded in the tradition of Western philosophy. There is, then, a core of fundamental questions of this sort that belong to universal philosophy. And Latin American philosophy is related to this core of philosophy in the same way that other branches of applied philosophy are, such as medical ethics, environmental ethics, feminist philosophy, philosophy of biology, and philosophy of law.

Weak universalism of this or other sort avoids the threat of a strong ad hominem facing strong universalism. For note that the latter is committed to cash out 'Latin American philosophy' as 'philosophy *in* Latin America,' but once it does that, it must accept the existence of a Latin American philosophy in that sense, or face the objection of holding a self-defeating view. Were they to say that there is no such a philosophy, what exactly would be what they themselves are producing? Yet universalists often reject the existence of a Latin American philosophy without noticing that by doing so their view is either self-defeating or implicitly distinctivist. We shall now consider what this means. Distinctivists claim that,

D   The theories, methods and topics of Latin American philosophy are *characteristically* Latin American.

Although compatible with WU, D conflicts with SU. On some versions, D is a thesis about the possibility (rather than the actuality) of a characteristically Latin American philosophy. But those who hold a thesis along D's lines seem committed to providing a plausible account of a philosophy of that sort in order to make their view acceptable. Distinctivists are especially constrained to account for what 'characteristically' stands

345

for. Clearly, the term must pick out a certain virtue of philosophical theories, methods, and topics developed by Latin American philosophers, whether in Latin America or abroad. For distinctivism, the debate is not about whether a Latin American philosophy exists at all, but rather about whether an x Latin American philosophy exists – where 'x' stands for being original, authentic, autochthonous, and the like (more on these later).

All this suggests that the question of concern here is affected by *ambiguity* (roughly, more than one meaning) and *vagueness* (roughly, indeterminacy about reference). But such semantic shortcomings fall short of rendering the question of concern here idiosyncratic or self-defeating, as suggested by analogous metaphilosophical questions about the existence of other areas of philosophy. Consider, 'Is there a French philosophy?' Here a universalist reading would individuate the relational property *being a French philosophy* by invoking only certain geopolitical factors, so that the question turns on whether there is philosophy *in* France. But a distinctivist reading would proceed differently – for example, by taking its answer to turn at least in part on whether there are certain theories, methods, or topics that are *typical of the sort of philosophy* currently done in France. Once again, then, some apparently conflicting answers are in fact consistent. One might accept the existence of philosophy in the geopolitical entity called 'France,' and at the same time consistently deny the existence of a philosophy with distinctively *French* theories, methods, or topics.

Even questions such as 'Is there a Greek philosophy?' seem susceptible of different construals along these lines. In the universalist reading, a Yes answer would depend on whether the discipline of philosophy exists in Greece; while in the distinctivist reading, it would depend on whether there is a philosophy that is characteristically Greek. Elsewhere I have argued (2002) that, under certain construals of the latter, the correct answer is 'No.' Even if we take into account only ancient philosophy, there is nothing *typically* Greek in the works of Plato, Aristotle, etc. (Indeed, it is often said that it's their very *universality* that partly accounts for their enduring appeal and relevance to our lives.) By contrast, it is of course undeniable that these do make up a body of *original* philosophy, so that the existence of a *characteristically* Greek philosophy in that sense is beyond doubt.

If this is correct, then the ambiguity of the question, 'Is there a Latin American philosophy?' seems no more likely to invite equivocation than some parallel questions involving a number of other philosophical disciplines. Since it's crucial in philosophical disputes to avoid ambiguity whenever possible, I'll make plain hereafter which of these two readings of the question is at stake whenever possible. Although these readings are different, as pointed out before, they are not exclusive, since it is also possible to ask about the existence of a *characteristically* Latin American philosophy *in* the subcontinent. And they are not contradictory, since the correct answer could be either assent or dissent in both readings of the question.

2. Is There Philosophy in Latin America?

The question now is about the existence of philosophy *in* a certain geographical area made up of political entities – such as Cuba, Uruguay, Venezuela, and so on. Thus understood, it calls for a straightforward assent that is supported by well-known facts attesting to the existence of the discipline in the subcontinent: viz., a number of institutions, works, and practitioners devoted to philosophy in Latin America. These constitute sound evidence that, in Latin America, Western philosophy not only exists, but appears to be thriving. It is practiced in specialized departments that grant undergraduate, and in some cases graduate, degrees in philosophy. There are scholarly journals, websites, and publications of the usual sorts. Furthermore, philosophical works covering a spectrum of representative topics, treated from a variety of traditions, are commonly available. And, since at least the 1940s, there are regular conferences, workshops, and other public venues of expression of academic philosophy (see, for example, Baschetti, 2005; Villegas, 1963; and González & Stigol in this volume).

   In light of the evidence, then, there is no doubt that philosophy exists in Latin America. As we saw, this conclusion (crucial for universalists willing to avoid self-defeat) triggers the acceptability constraint above, since its acceptance requires a plausible account of what, exactly, Latin American philosophy consists of. In turn, this commits to finding suitable solutions to a number of problems, such as determining the scope, name, boundaries, and historical roots of the discipline.

The scope of the discipline

As noted earlier, by 'Latin American philosophy,' universalists take themselves to mean 'philosophy in Latin America' rather than 'characteristically Latin American philosophy.' As a consequence, the issue of what, exactly, that philosophy consists of is particularly pressing to them. For one thing, they must now determine what to make of the celebrated work of certain Latin American thinkers who have clearly broached philosophically interesting ideas, but are themselves perceived as only 'amateur philosophers.'

   This raises the uncomfortable but unavoidable question: Who counts as a philosopher? In Latin America, it was not until the first half of the twentieth century that philosophy acquired an academic status similar to the one it already had by then in Europe and North America. During the colonial period (roughly, from the late fifteenth century to the early nineteenth century), Iberian rulers imposed in the New World their own scholastic conceptual framework, a paradigm of philosophical thinking that was already obsolete in other parts of Europe. For the most part, Latin American academic philosophers of the period failed to produce original philosophical work within that framework. Even so, during the colonial era, and during the wars of independence and the national organization that followed them, a number of amateur philosophers wrote insightful pieces that bear on various areas of philosophy, ranging from feminism and ethics to social and political philosophy. Though not philosophers by training, they were clearly motivated by philosophical curiosity and developed, in the course of their own reflections on issues related to their careers as generals, politicians, grammarians, librarians, scientists, and literary figures, significant new ideas that can only be called *philosophical*. This group includes, among many others, Juana Inés de la Cruz, Simón Bolívar, Juan Bautista Alberdi, Andrés Bello, José Martí, José Carlos Rodó, Justo Sierra, and José Ingenieros. If we were to exclude from our pantheon thinkers of this caliber as 'insufficiently philosophical,' the risk is that we'd be left with

347

a Latin American philosophy consisting of only a very thin and unoriginal corpus of philosophical work.

This is, however, very far from being a settled issue. Given certain universalists' standards for what is to count as philosophy, amateur philosophy is *not* philosophy. As a result, when faced with an acceptability constraint, those universalists generally offer a severely skeptical account of Latin American philosophy. Once amateur philosophers are excluded, universalists are left with a comparatively short list of contemporary philosophical practitioners and philosophical theories in Latin America – and this leads them to see Latin American philosophy as being 'unsubstantial,' 'imitative,' 'fruitless,' and the like. But note that, in the hands of such 'skeptical' universalists, the question at stake has implicitly the form, 'Is there an *x* Latin American philosophy?' – where '*x*' stands for 'substantial,' 'original,' 'consequential,' and so on. That is, skeptical universalists are in fact asking what *is* in some sense a distinctivist question. If they are right in their answers, then although Latin American philosophy might be of some historical interest, it would not be worth considering for its own sake.

Examples of this universalist approach are not difficult to find. Consider the skeptical universalism of two generations of Latin American philosophers, one represented by the Argentine, Risieri Frondizi (1910–83), and the other by the Mexican, Carlos Pereda (contemporary). In his influential (1949) paper, Frondizi excludes from Latin American philosophy many celebrated works of the amateur philosophers from various historical periods, from the sixteenth century to at least the early twentieth century. On his view, to be eligible for inclusion, those thinkers should have pursued 'philosophy as such' – by which he appears to mean 'philosophy for its own sake' – and a quick look into their work reveals that they certainly did subordinate narrowly philosophical concerns to other nonphilosophical interests, such as literary, social, and political ones. It follows that they must be ruled out as Latin American *philosophers*.

Frondizi is then led to answer his question 'Is there a Latin American philosophy?' in the negative. But the argument offered to support that conclusion suggests that he is in fact asking about the existence of a *substantial, original* philosophy of that sort. With no amateur philosophers included, he is then committed to skeptical universalism, the view that the discipline of philosophy does exist in Latin America but has very little to be said for it. Again, once the amateur philosophers are excluded, Latin American philosophy appears an anemic exercise devoid of significant history, theories, methods, and number of practitioners. It would comprise mostly contemporary works, since academic philosophy began in Latin America only in the early twentieth century, through the efforts of the so-called *fundadores* (founders). Moreover, since those who have the more original views were not these trained philosophers, and so are at best amateurs, the discipline does seem vulnerable to the objection that it is imitative and fruitless.

More recently, Carlos Pereda's reflection on Latin American philosophy, which he calls 'thought,' offers a parallel case of skeptical universalism. Consider Pereda's take on the work of another contemporary Mexican thinker, Luis Villoro (2006): we are told by Pereda that it contributes no less to Latin American philosophy when it applies analytic methods to some universal topics of epistemology than when it addresses distinctive issues concerning the Latin American Indians. But this claim clearly equivocates between the two different construals of 'Latin American philosophy' mentioned earlier. After all, suppose the epistemological work of Villoro, say, on Cartesian skept-icism, is such that it adds nothing *characteristically* Latin American to the discussion of that topic. That work might then count as 'Latin American philosophy' only in the weak sense of 'philosophy in Latin America' – where the relevant discipline is construed universalistically. Another matter is Villoro's (and any other philosopher's) philo-sophical work on the Latin American Indians, which as far as topic is concerned, would clearly count as characteristically Latin American. It would therefore plainly belong to Latin American philosophy, distinctivistically construed. Now since anything that qualifies as *characteristically Latin American philosophy* qualifies as *philosophy* but not vice versa, therefore the two different construals of the question should not be conflated.

Skeptical universalism also fuels Pereda's endorsement of a conception of 'philo-sophy in Latin America,' which takes it to be 'unbridled' in the sense of lacking specific subject matters and welcoming them all. Against what I have called here 'distinctivism,' Pereda writes:

> Outside of the persistence of certain colonial habits, I do not understand why some Latin Americans want to stop the rest from acquiring this wise 'unbridled' character: from 'delving into everything.' This simplifying force has a long history among us, one of whose origins may be found in the claims of Juan Bautista Alberdi. (2006, p. 201 n.10)

But there are two problems in this passage. For one thing, it conflates doing philosophy in Latin America (about which it is plausible to say that it has 'delved into everything') and doing a characteristically Latin American philosophy, a necessary condition of which is having certain distinctive features. Furthermore, it traces back to Alberdi (Argentinean, 1810–84) the view that Latin American philosophy must in some ways be limited to social and political philosophy. Here Pereda has in mind the Alberdi of 'Ideas . . . ,' a short article that appeared in the newspaper *El Nacional* (Montevideo, October 2, 1840), and was not reprinted until the turn of the nineteenth century. To set the record straight, the article does *not* endorse the view that philosophy in the newly independent Latin American nations should be only 'applied philosophy,' with emphasis on autochthonous political and social problems. Rather, as suggested by its title (see references), the piece attempts to provide directions for developing a course in contemporary philosophy that could be offered in secondary schools. Given its purpose, time, and place of publication, it is very implausible that Alberdi's 'Ideas . . .' could have had the distinctivist influences Pereda attributes to it.

The Cuban journalist and poet, Jose Martí, and the Mexican writer, Octavio Paz, might both be counted as amateur philosophers of great talent and acuity, and Pereda praises them as Latin American essayists whose work ought to be admired and whose success ought to be studied and emulated by Latin American philosophers. But he ultimately agrees with Frondizi that these and other amateur philosophers don't belong to philo-sophy in Latin America. As a result, Pereda too is led to a skeptical conclusion about the Latin Americans who *do* count as philosophers: namely, that those practitioners of the discipline in the subcontinent exhibit a number of vices, such as demonstrating 'subaltern fervor' (i.e., being imitative), 'craving for novelty' (i.e., being impressed by the latest philosophical fads) and 'nationalist enthusiasm' (i.e., having narrow-minded

349

distinctivist tendencies). In the end, such pessimistic conclusions don't differ much from Frondizi's. Other well-known arguments for similar conclusions are to be found, e.g., in the work of Augusto Salazar Bondy (1968) and José Carlos Mariátegui (1925, see Pearlman, 1996).

The name of the discipline

The strategy of countenancing a broader discipline, sometimes called 'Latin American thought,' is indeed an option. But it is not available to skeptical universalists unless they were to conceive it as entirely separate – viz., a non-philosophical discipline devoted to the work of amateur philosophers. *There is already* a discipline by that name recognized widely in Latin America, *pensamiento latinoamericano*, but it standardly includes the works of both philosophers and amateur philosophers.

On the other hand, non-skeptical universalists may countenance a discipline of just that sort without being committed to denying that there are some philosophical theories, methods, and topics that are exclusively universal. Different versions of this weak universalist position can be found in Nuccetelli (2002) and in recent work by the Cuban American philosopher, Jorge Gracia (I see Gracia's proposal as agnostic about the inclusion of amateur thinkers; more on this below). Besides 'Latin American thought,' other labels proposed for the discipline more inclusively construed include 'Hispanic-American thought' (Mariátegui, 1925), 'Latino philosophy' (Gracia, 2008), and '*el filoso-far lationamericano*' ('Latin American philosophizing'; Miró Quesada, 1974). Although the last, a quite unusual label, has never caught on, it clearly aims at capturing the distinctiveness of philosophy in Latin America.

The boundaries of the discipline

However called, non-skeptical strong universalists are committed to including in the discipline only philosophical works individuated by reference to certain geopolitical entities: viz., the subcontinent and group of countries that make up Latin America. Recall that for such universalists, the discipline boils down to what we have called 'philosophy *in* Latin America.' Although this expression might be taken to set clear boundaries, it has several shortcomings: it doesn't applying to the proper cases and it doesn't rule out borderline cases (which amounts to saying that *it is indeterminate*, or at least unclear, whether it applies to those cases). One way to interpret the expression is as denoting the property:

(1)   Being philosophy produced *in* Latin America.

But (1) faces problems. Clearly, it doesn't apply to works in Latin American philosophy done by Latin Americans outside the subcontinent, such as Gracia's and my own. And it doesn't rule out *non*-Latin Americans whose works seem either a borderline case, such as Ortega y Gasset's (a Spanish philosopher, 1883–1955, who did some work in Latin America), or not part of the Latin American philosophy corpus of at all (e.g., Larry Laudan, U.S. philosopher of science now working at the Universidad Autónoma in Mexico). So the criterion captures neither necessary nor sufficient conditions. Moreover, it leads to absurd conclusions when the principle is developed further. It comes out as preposterous when we try a similar move for biology, since then the part of Charles Darwin's theory developed in the course of his long travels in South America should come out as Latin American biology!

Another possible interpretation is

(2)   Being a philosophical work produced by a philosopher born in Latin America.

(2) is certainly not necessary, and if sufficient, it would be a very weak criterion indeed, as shown by the cases of philosophers who, though Latin American by birth, have produced important work on theories, methods, and/or topics that bear no especial relation to Latin America. Surely the work of Ernest Sosa (Cuban-born epistemologist, United States) and of C. Ulises Moulines (Venezuelan-born philosopher of science, Germany) is eligible for Latin American philosophy understood as (2), but this is a very weak, uninteresting sense of the term. On the other hand, that (2) is not a necessary condition is shown by, for instance, foreign-born Latin American philosophers who are nonetheless standardly counted in the history of the discipline, such as the Italian-born Rodolfo Mondolfo (1877–1976) who worked extensively in Argentina.

We needn't now continue our search for other simple criteria, such as 'being the philosophical work of those of Latin American descent' and the like, since it's likely that these are vulnerable to similar objections. Let's consider instead a more a disjunctive criterion such as,

(3)   A philosophical work qualifies for Latin American philosophy if and only if it is either
    (a)   produced in Latin America, by a Latin American philosopher or by a foreign philosopher settled in Latin America; or
    (b)   produced outside Latin America, by a philosopher who is Latin American by birth or descent.

This inclusive disjunction featuring some of the above conditions is not, however, without problems. For one thing, it is too liberal since it would count as Latin American philosophy any philosophical work by a Latin American philosopher, *even if it bears no other relation to the subcontinent than the historical connection of its author.* Many would, for example, hesitate to count among the practitioners of Latin American philosophy international figures such as Bunge, an Argentinean philosopher of science who has worked mostly in Canada (beginning with Bunge himself, given what he says in the passage quoted above).

It may be replied that all of these difficulties are just semantic ones: having already accepted that the expression 'Latin American philosophy' has at least two readings – one universalist, the other distinctivist – universalists might invite us to further acknowledge that the expression is also vague. If so, then it is as indeterminate whether the expression applies to the works of figures such as Bunge, Sosa, Ortega, and many others, as it is whether 'tall' applies to George W. Bush or 'young' to Queen Latifah. But that doesn't preclude the expression from determinately applying in other cases.

The historical roots of the discipline

Skeptical universalists often credit the *fundadores* of the early twentieth century with the origins of philosophy in Latin America, who actually did initiate a 'standarization' academic philosophy in the subcontinent (e.g., Alberini, 1927; Cooper in this volume). But many non-skeptical universalists and distinctivists are willing to credit philosophers or thinkers of other periods as well. On a recent proposal (Oviedo, 2005), it is only with the work of José Ingenieros and other nineteenth-century positivists that the discipline began. But proposals of this sort cannot accommodate the evidence of Western philosophy in Latin America during earlier periods such as the colonial one (see Beuchot, 1996).

An interesting problem regarding the origins of the discipline is created by written documents suggesting the existence of pre-Columbian philosophical thought. It has been argued (León-Portilla, 1963, pp. 8–9, 23 and ff.; Nuccetelli, 2002; Maffie in this volume) that certain well-preserved texts are evidence of the existence of philosophical thought among the Maya and Aztec in the form of folk-cosmologies and reflections on problems of epistemology, metaphysics, and ethics. Prominent among the existing documents are the Maya's *Popol Vuh* and their *Books of Chilam Balam* or *Códices* – though there is also evidence from Spanish chronicles of the New World (see Restrepo in this volume).

Needless to say, pre-Columbian thought unfolds in ways that seem utterly alien to our standard conceptions of philosophy. But a strict compliance with such standards cannot be held as a necessary condition of being counted as philosophy. After all, it has been not uncommon in the history of Western philosophy to include as *philosophy* path-breaking works that also flout prevalent standards of format or content. One thinks immediately of the writings of Parmenides, Plato, and Wittgenstein. Moreover, those who wish to exclude pre-Columbian thought from the history of Latin American philosophy cannot argue that such a thought raises issues we would now think not properly philosophical. For in that case the works of nearly all pre-Socratic Greek philosophers would have to be excluded too, since they raise questions that are in fact quite analogous to those in pre-Columbian folk-cosmologies. And, as in the case of Pythagoras, their answers were often also mixed up with myth and religion (see Nuccetelli, 2002).

On the other hand, as in the case of the relation between pre-Socratic thought and Western philosophy, pre-Columbian philosophical works have been taken to make up at least a proto Latin American philosophy – a claim that is consistent with holding that more contemporary philosophical methods are needed *now* to properly discuss the same issues. Among those who reject the parallel, some argue that only in the case of pre-Socratics there is some continuity in the method used (Nuccetelli, 2002). Others suspend judgment: "Latin American philosophy," write the authors of a topical entry in a current dictionary of philosophy, "begins with the Spanish and Portuguese discovery and colonization of the New World" (Gracia et al., 1995, p. 462). Gracia himself appears to be also agnostic on the matter, since when reflecting upon whether the Maya folk-cosmology in the *Popol Vuh* belongs in the discipline, he has this to say:

Is the *Popol Vuh* to be included in Latin American philosophy? The issue now shifts to whether pre-Columbians can be considered part of the Latino ethnos and why . . . Still, you
probably want me to tell you what I think about the *Popol Vuh*: Does it belong or not to
Latin American philosophy? I do not want to answer the question, because I do not find
it philosophically interesting. (2008, p. 142)

Even when professing agnosticism, Gracia clearly provides here what he considers a
condition for the folk-cosmology in the *Popol Vuh* to amount to philosophy: viz., that
"pre-Columbians can be considered part of the Latino ethnos." In other words, the philosophical ideas in the *Popol Vuh* would belong to Latin American philosophy if the Mayans
themselves belong to what Gracia calls 'Latino' people (to whom I'm referring here
as 'Latin Americans,' widely construed to apply also to persons of Latin American
heritage.) But what is meant by 'belonging to a people' is in need of clarification.
For example, it cannot be relativized to actuality only, for that would lead to the implausible conclusion that, for example, Ancient Greek philosophy doesn't count as
European philosophy. After all, *today* the Ancient Greeks are not literally *part of* the
European people. But we don't want to say that Plato's *Republic* is not to be included
in European philosophy. So the relation must allow for historical chains: Ancient
Greeks are in this sense *part* of the European people, and their philosophical works
therefore eligible for inclusion in European philosophy. Now it is beyond dispute that
the *Popol Vuh*, perhaps more than any other pre-Columbian narrative, is part of the
culture of the Maya people today, who have received it mostly through an oral tradition. So, by the above condition, the *Popol Vuh* would qualify for inclusion in Latin
American philosophy unless the Maya do not qualify as Latin Americans. But clearly
they do. After all, consider Rigoberta Menchú, a Maya Quiché Guatemalan who is a
Nobel laureate well known as an advocate of human rights for indigenous peoples.
Surely, in light of the historical, geographical, and cultural facts – e.g., that Menchú
is held in high regard as an honored citizen in Latin America – it would make no sense
to deny that she is Latin American. Likewise, it would make no sense to exclude the
people whom she represents: the Maya.

It follows that, if we reason by Gracia's criterion in the passage above, the *Popol Vuh*
comes out as included in Latin American philosophy. So, it seems that if Gracia
chooses to remain agnostic on the subject, he would now face a dilemma with no plausible solution. On the one hand, he could argue that the *Popol Vuh* cannot be read as
a philosophical or proto-philosophical text at all (i.e., he could simply *deny* our assumption above). On the other, he could insist that the Maya are *not* part of the Latin American
people. But supporting the latter horn would be an uphill battle. And to support the
former would require setting up sound standards for what is to count as philosophy,
an equally unpromising assignment.

But skeptics and agnostics about pre-Columbian philosophical thought often do
include in Latin American philosophy the works of Scholastics such as Antonio Rubio
(Mexican, 1548–1615), whose textbook *Logica mexicana* (*Mexican Logic*) was at the time
also popular in Spain. For this work, the problem would be just the reverse of what
we've had with the *Popol Vuh*: it would pass muster with universalists but not with
distinctivists. From the latter's perspective, to which we now turn, no work can count

as Latin American philosophy unless it clearly shows something characteristically Latin American – and *Logica Mexicana* fails to do this.

Is there a characteristically Latin American philosophy?

Recall that for distinctivists, a characteristically Latin American philosophy is one that has one or more virtues, such as *being original, being authentic,* or *being autochthonous.* Furthermore, weak universalists keep an open mind about such a philosophy, and at some points even strong universalists have had some such qualities in mind when they denied the existence of a Latin American philosophy. Although failure to identify the specific quality at issue in discussions of the existence (or possibility) of characteristically Latin American philosophy is endemic, here is a tentative list of what may be at stake:

(1)   Being an original or novel Latin American philosophy
(2)   Being authentic or genuine Latin American philosophy
(3)   Being an autochthonous Latin American philosophy.

When understood as having property (1), there is a characteristically Latin American philosophy just in case such a philosophy has theories, methods, or topics that are (in some relevant sense) distinct from those of standard philosophy. (1) entails (2), which boils down to the negative quality of avoiding being imitative. But neither of these entails having (3), which amounts to the property of being relevantly related to Latin America. Different parties in the debate have had one or more of these construals in mind. As we have seen, Frondizi's and Pereda's skepticism construes 'characteristically' as (1) and (2). But other skeptics have in mind (2) and (3): among others, José Carlos Mariátegui and Augusto Salazar Body have held a colonial-mentality view according to which Latin America's dependence on the West is an insurmountable obstacle to the development of a characteristically Latin American philosophy in those senses. Yet even so, they are merely *describing* a condition that need not last forever.

On the distinctivist camp, Leopoldo Zea (Mexican, 1912–2004) construes it as (3), for his perspectivism is indifferent about whether Latin American philosophy has (1) or (2). For Zea, philosophical works invariably show the cultural perspectives of those who produce them. Thus, in Latin America, "even in imitation, there was creation and re-creation" (1989, p. 41). Now of course it cannot be denied that Latin American literature did undergo a process of this sort. But in the case of philosophy, textual evidence is needed to support the idea that a philosophy entirely 'borrowed' from foreign sources could be *characteristically Latin American.* In any case, Zea's perspectivism holds:

(i)   There is a characteristically Latin American philosophy.
(ii)   The problems and methods of philosophy are universal.
(iii)   Philosophers' 'circumstances' always shape their theories and methods.

The perspectivist adds (iii) to make (i) and (ii) compatible, since now there is logical space for a universal philosophy that at the same time "permeates" its context. But this

354

perspectivist thesis is quite strong, entailing that no philosophical doctrine of any kind could be *perspective-less* (it is only from within a particular set of social circumstances that a doctrine could be entertained at all). As Zea puts it,

> The abstract issues [of philosophy] will have to be seen from the Latin American man's own circumstance. Each man will see in such issues what is closest to his own circumstance. He will look at these issues from the standpoint of his own interests, and those interests will be determined by his way of life, his abilities and inabilities, in a word, by his own circumstance. In the case of Latin America, his contribution to the philosophy of such issues will be permeated by the Latin American circumstance. Hence, when we [Latin Americans] address abstract issues, we shall formulate them as issues of our own. Even though being, God, etc., are issues appropriate for every man, the solution to them will be given from a Latin American standpoint. (1986, p. 226)

We might reasonably ask whether Zea's argument here can really bear the weight of such an ambitious claim. For philosophers' cultural differences need not affect their theories or methods. Compare visual images: Although people's eyes vary in size, shape, and color across different groups, those variations have no bearing on their visual images. But even if this is not a perfect analogy, Zea's argument would still be in need of support, given the evidence from the history of philosophy. It would be odd, to say the least, to hold that there is something autochthonous in Aristotle's theory of the syllogism, in Descartes' attempted solution to the mind–body problem, or in Hume's skepticism about induction. In addition, perspectivism seems quite liberal: it permits almost any philosophical theory, method or topic at issue in Latin America to count as *Latin American* philosophy.

Related chapters: 1 Pre-Columbian Philosophies; 3 Colonial Thought; 9 'Normal' Philosophy; 18 Identity and Philosophy; 22 Philosophy, Postcoloniality, and Postmodernity.

References

Alberdi, J. B. (1988). Ideas para presidir la confección del curso de filosofía contemporánea. In O. Terán (Ed.). *Alberdi póstumo* (pp. 90–8). Buenos Aires: Puntosur (Original work published 1840).

Alberini, C. (1927). Contemporary philosophic tendencies in South America. *The Monist*, 37, 328–34.

Baschetti, R. (2005). El primer congreso nacional de filosofía en Argentina. *La Biblioteca*, 23, 360–7.

Beuchot, M. (1996). *The history of philosophy in colonial Mexico*. Washington, DC: The Catholic University of America Press.

Frondizi, R. (1949). Is there an Ibero-American philosophy? *Philosophy and Phenomenological Research*, 9, 345–55.

Gilson, G. (2006). The project of exact philosophy: an interview with Mario Bunge, Frothingham Chair of Logic and Metaphysics, McGill University, Toronto, Canada. *APA Newsletter on Hispanic/Latino Issues in Philosophy*, 1, 8–10.

Gracia, J. J. E. (2008). *Latinos in America: philosophy and social identity*. Oxford: Blackwell.

Gracia, J. et al. (1995). Latin American philosophy. In T. Honderich (Ed.). *The Oxford companion to philosophy* (pp. 23–7). Oxford: Oxford University Press.

León-Portilla, M. (1963). *Aztec thought and culture*. Norman: University of Oklahoma Press.

Miró Quesada, F. (1974). *Despertar y proyecto del filosofar latinoamericano*. Mexico: Fondo de Cultura Económica.

Nuccetelli, S. (2002). *Latin American thought: philosophical problems and arguments*. Boulder, CO: Westview Press.

Oviedo, G. (2005). Historia autóctona de las ideas filosóficas y autonomismo intelectual: sobre la herencia argentina del siglo XX. *La Biblioteca*, 23, 76–97.

Pearlman, M. (Ed.). (1996). *The heroic and creative meaning of socialism: selected essays of José Carlos Mariátegui*. Atlantic Highlands, NJ: Humanities Press.

Pereda, C. (2006). Latin American philosophy: Some vices. *Journal of Speculative Philosophy*, 3, 192–203.

Salazar Bondy, A. (1968). *Existe una filosofía de nuestra America?* Mexico: Siglo XXI.

Villegas, A. (1963). *Panorama de la filosofia iberoamericana actual*. Buenos Aires: Eudeba.

Zea, L. (1986). The actual function of philosophy in Latin America. In J. Gracia (Ed.). *Latin American philosophy in the twentieth century*. Buffalo, Prometheus (Original work published 1948).

Further Reading

Ardao, A. (1979). Historia y evolución de las ideas filosóficas en América Latina. *Proceedings of the IX Inter-American Congress of Philosophy*, I, 61–9.

Hurtado, G. (2006). Two models of Latin American philosophy. *Journal of Speculative Philosophy*, 3, 204–13.

Marti, O. (1983). Is there a Latin American philosophy? *Metaphilosophy*, 1, 46–52.

Miró Quesada, F. (1976). *El problema de la filosofía latinoamericana*. Mexico: Fondo de Cultura Económica.

Zea, L. (1976). *El pensamiento latinoamericano*. Barcelona: Ariel.

25

Contemporary Ethics and Political Philosophy

EDUARDO RIVERA-LÓPEZ

Contemporary moral and political philosophy in Latin America can be divided along three dominant trends. The first trend, which characterizes a good portion of the Latin American philosophical profession, is devoted to the study of the history of philosophy or of contemporary philosophers. Scholars in this trend, who can be found at leading universities in Latin America, work on Marxism, existentialism, phenomenology, classical and modern philosophy, structuralism, and postmodernism. I will not focus on this exegetical type of investigation. A second trend represents the so-called "liberation philosophy." This is an attempt to create a radically original perspective, although it has obviously been influenced by European philosophy and theology. This view deserves separate treatment and will therefore not be dealt with in this chapter. The third trend seeks to solve philosophical problems, starting from two methodological premises: first, such problems are universal in essence (albeit not always in application); second, we can discuss those problems by (and only by) appealing to reasons and arguments. This general stance toward philosophical problems includes paradigmatically analytical philosophy, but also goes beyond it. It is not my purpose here to delimit schools of thought or make terminological stipulations. My aim is to review some theories and positions on ethics and political philosophy created by Latin American philosophers that share these two assumptions and that can be considered valuable contributions to the contemporary debate.

Who exactly count as Latin American philosophers is difficult to say. But I shall mean, stipulatively, those philosophers who were either born or educated in Latin American countries and have developed a relevant part of their philosophical activity in Latin American countries (on the difficult issue of defining "Latin American philosopher," see Nuccetelli and Gracia in this volume). Of course, I will only be able to discuss a selection of Latin American philosophers. Indeed, a significant emphasis on the Argentine philosopher and lawyer Carlos S. Nino (1943–93) will be evident in the two first sections of this chapter. This deserves some explanation. Nino's work brings together several features that no other Latin American moral or political philosopher does (at least within the 'reasons and arguments' trend with which we are concerned). First, his work has transcended the Spanish-speaking world (he has published in the most renowned journals and presses in Europe and the United States). Second, he has had an enormous influence in both Latin America and Spain. Third, he has

357

developed several arguably original theories on a range of issues. Examples include a general theory of ethical norms and human rights, a theory of democracy, a theory of punishment, a theory of the constitution, and a theory of legal norms (see Navarro in this volume), among others. Fourth, he has always been committed to Latin America's peculiar political reality; he has participated in politics and written on certain aspects of this political reality (for example, on the average Argentine's reluctance to comply with the law and on constitutional reform). All of this makes him unique among Latin American moral and political philosophers.

Having expressed this caveat, I still hope to offer a representative picture of con-temporary Latin American ethics and political philosophy. Other philosophers besides Nino will therefore be addressed as well. The discussion is organized in three sections. It begins by reviewing the contribution of Latin American philosophers to metaethical issues concerning the nature and ultimate foundation of ethical norms and values. Next, it addresses some normative theories on ethics and political philosophy, with special emphasis on human rights and democracy. Finally, it discusses some applied prob-lems around two issues that are especially relevant in Latin America: bioethics and multiculturalism.

Metaethics: The Foundations of Moral Values and Norms

Metaethics has been of central importance among moral philosophers in Europe and the United States during the first half of the twentieth century. The emphasis on normative issues recovered vigor only after John Rawls's work in the 1960s and, espe-cially, after the publication of *A Theory of Justice* in 1971. Something parallel happened in Latin America, but with peculiarities of its own. Phenomenology has been one of the main varieties of anti-positivistic thought during the first decades of the last cen-tury. Together with Edmund Husserl, Max Scheler and Nicolai Hartmann have had a deep influence on Latin American moral philosophy. José Ortega y Gasset and Eduardo García Maynez contributed decisively to introducing this school of thought. This might explain why the question about the foundations of ethics has often been under-stood as an axiological question: the problem of the objectivity of values.

The first and perhaps most important attempt to go beyond inherited ideas on the nature of values is Risieri Frondizi's (Argentine, 1910–85) axiological theory in his well-known *¿Qué son los valores?* (first published in 1959 and expanded in 1972) and other works. After a careful critical examination of the main theories of contem-porary axiology, Frondizi tries to outline an approach that overcomes the flaws of both subjectivism and objectivism. According to Frondizi, values are, as subjectivists hold, inseparable from valuing. However, they are more than mere projections of our desires. Valuing requires an intentional object (Frondizi, 1972, p. 201), and there are objective qualities that force us to react in a positive or negative way. Such objective qualities are, according to Frondizi, "structural qualities" (Frondizi, 1972, p. 208). A structural property (Gestalt) is constituted by empirical properties but is more than the sum of those properties. Such a property is a concrete and empirical unity, in which the parts are interconnected in a certain way. Moreover, those qualities are not isolated. Rather, they are in a complex interdependence with physical and cultural situations.

Concerning ethical norms or prescriptions, Frondizi holds that they depend upon values. In that sense, Frondizi's moral theory is teleological. For instance, it is because human life is desirable (valuable) that it is forbidden to kill human beings (Frondizi, 1986, pp. 146–7). Frondizi's approach has recently come under criticism and has since been abandoned. A first criticism is that it is unclear whether his "situationalism" really escapes value relativism. If value depends on cultural and historical situations, they are not objective in the required (interesting) way and the attempt to build a unified theory might well fail. Second, many Latin American philosophers have objected to his teleological view of moral rules. Coercive moral norms (typically moral prohibitions) cannot be founded on values like "desirability" but must depend on categorical prescriptions (see Guariglia, 1998, p. 61). Before turning to the more Kantian or constructivist approaches that underwrite such criticisms, I would like to briefly mention two other attempts to reduce metaethical subjectivism to its minimum and, in that way, find some rationality in moral judgments and attitudes.

The first attempt is Fernando Salmerón's (Mexican, 1925–97) view of moral attitudes (see his 1971 work, "La filosofía y las actitudes morales"). After analyzing the concept of an attitude from an historical and empirical (psychological) perspective, Salmerón inquires into the justification of moral attitudes. Being essentially subjective, it seems that they cannot withstand rational scrutiny: "they can be neither refuted nor justified" (1971, p. 154; hereafter, translations are mine). However, moral philosophy can help us to find out whether a moral attitude "can escape criticism by showing the efficacy of its social function, its logical consistency, and its compatibility with scientific statements, and in such a way it would be more justified than other principles" (1971, p. 155). Moral justification is, according to Salmerón, always provisional and incomplete, but not completely arbitrary. It is important to stress that Salmerón's view here is not naturalistic. It is not that moral attitudes are founded on natural or empirical facts. It is rather that natural or empirical sciences, as well as philosophical analysis, help to reveal more rational attitudes: attitudes that are more consistent, both among themselves and with empirical facts.

The second attempt I want to mention is Augusto Salazar Bondy's (Peruvian, 1925–74) view of values. Salazar Bondy first denounces several "axiological confusions," which are closely associated with the naturalistic fallacy criticized by G. E. Moore (Salazar Bondy, 1969). Starting from this non-naturalistic stance, he also objects to metaphysical objectivism. The problem is then what he calls "the difficulty of choosing." On the one hand, choosing seems to be essentially arbitrary and subjective; on the other, it contains an ineradicable imperative element (we choose something because it is good) (Salazar Bondy, 1971, p. 164). Without developing a complete theory, Salazar Bondy suggests that the only way out of this paradox is Kantian: we have to assume the objectivity of values as a precondition of the intelligibility of the practice of valuing (1971, p. 165).

In the rest of this section, I will focus on two kinds of metaethical outlook that have received more attention from contemporary philosophers: constructivism and versions of naturalism. At least the first of them is more ambitious than Frondizi's and Salmerón's views and aspires to offer rational criteria to discover moral truths.

Kantian formalism and constructivism, as represented in the work of philosophers such as Jürgen Habermas and John Rawls, have exerted a good deal of influence in Latin America. Some philosophers have tried to overcome the shortcomings of formalism

359

and find a compromise between Habermas's formal dialogic strategy and Rawls's more substantive, monologic outlook. The most important attempt to do so was made by Carlos Nino, although other philosophers have also made sophisticated contributions (see Guariglia, 1996). I will here focus on Nino's constructivism.

Nino begins his metaethical reflections from a rather naturalistic, Hobbesian, stance: Morality is a social invention designed to "generate actions and attitudes which avoid conflict and promote cooperation" in a world characterized by the "circumstances of justice" envisioned by David Hume, H. L. A. Hart, and Rawls (Nino, 1991, p. 66). Such a social artifact is similar to the law, which serves the same function. Law operates via two means: coercion and authority. However, since the authority of law cannot hinge upon coercion alone, it must provide non-prudential reasons for action. And those reasons, according to Nino, cannot but be moral reasons. Likewise, morality operates as an independent social practice that promotes cooperation, and, for the same reasons, cannot base its functioning on providing prudential reasons alone (for example, through informal sanctions). It must provide moral reasons. The social practice of moral discourse is constituted by the way in which people offer and accept moral reasons for action. Therefore, the ultimate justification of moral norms must arise from an analysis of moral discourse.

At this point, Nino's approach becomes constructivist: moral truth is rooted in the rules of moral discourse. Rawls's Kantian and Habermas's dialogical versions of constructivism strongly influenced Nino. However, Nino's view departs to some extent from each view and tries to find a middle road. According to Nino, Rawls's constructivism is monological: moral truth is based on the reasoning of each moral agent under conditions of impartiality. Habermas, on the other hand, believes that moral truth is constituted by the actual practice of moral discourse under conditions of impartiality. Nino proposes a compromise, which he calls "epistemic constructivism": "moral truth is constituted by the formal or procedural assumptions of a social discursive practice oriented to cooperate and to avoid conflicts" (Nino, 1989, p. 104). One of these assumptions is that a moral principle must fulfill conditions of publicity, impartiality, rationality, and full knowledge (see Nino, 1991, pp. 72–3). On the other hand, access to such moral truth is not monological: "discussion and intersubjective decision is the most reliable procedure to access moral truth" (Nino, 1989, p. 105). As we will see in the next section, this epistemic feature of Nino's metaethical outlook is the bridge toward his normative theory of democracy.

Since Nino's constructivism is epistemic, the ontological question about the nature of moral truths remains open. With regard to this question, Nino defends a peculiar kind of objective naturalism. The nature of moral facts is neither empirical nor metaphysical: it is counterfactual. Moore's famous open question can be answered by claiming that "good" is what would be accepted by an ideal observer under conditions of rationality and impartiality. This criterion about what is good (or right) is, according to Nino, implied by those who take part in the practice of moral discourse to solve conflicts and promote cooperation (see Nino, 1991, pp. 68–9).

This rather positive attitude toward metaethical naturalism has been shared by other Latin American philosophers, although often with substantial differences. Eduardo Rabossi (Argentine, 1930–2005), for example, has attempted to uncover certain basic misunderstandings of Moore's naturalistic fallacy argument (Rabossi, 1979, pp. 83–97) and has defended a sort of empirical naturalism trying to connect factual judgments about basic human needs with normative duties to fulfill those needs (see Rabossi, 1983). Several other Latin American moral philosophers have welcomed the idea that human needs may play an important role in moral theory. Beyond Rabossi, we find a positive stance in Ernesto Garzón Valdés, Salmerón (1998, pp. 48 ff.), and Leon Olivé (2003, pp. 85–9), among others. As we will see, some discussions of normative and applied ethics are strongly influenced by this view.

Normative Principles: Human Rights and Democracy

I turn now from metaethics to normative ethics, and especially to normative political philosophy, which are more well developed in Latin America. Some approaches are valuable contributions to contemporary moral and political philosophy.

The focus of my review will once more be on Carlos Nino's theory, which is, in my view, the most developed theory in the field in Latin America. However, in discussing some of its arguments, I will mention other approaches. Nino's political philosophy addresses two main issues: the principles of justice and the foundation of political authority. Let us consider each issue in turn.

Basic principles and human rights

Nino holds three principles, which represent the basic tenets of a liberal society. At the same time, these principles can be derived a priori from the structure of moral discourse. The first is the "principle of autonomy," which states that "the state may not interfere with the choice and realization of those ideals and plans, limiting itself to the design of institutions that facilitate the individual prosecution of them so as to avoid mutual interference" (Nino, 1991, p. 132). The principle of autonomy is opposed to perfectionism. The second principle is the "principle of inviolability of the person." This principle, which resembles Kant's categorical imperative and is therefore opposed to utilitarianism and other aggregative approaches, makes it wrong "to impose on individuals without their consent sacrifices which do not redound in their benefit" (Nino, 1991, p. 149). Finally, Nino defends a "principle of the dignity of the person," which "prescribes that men should be treated according to their decisions, intentions, and expressions of consent" (Nino, 1991, p. 178). A conception of society that assumes a strong version of determinism is, according to Nino, unintelligible.

How are these principles related to each other? Nino notes that the principle of autonomy is aggregative: it prescribes maximizing autonomy across individuals. The principle of inviolability constrains this aggregative feature by giving each person a right not to be treated as a mere means. However, the combination of these principles does not preclude the existence of conflicts of rights since it does not define the scope of those rights. According to Nino, the solution to the problem depends upon the status of omissions as compared to actions: If we can transgress the inviolability of a person by omission (as well as by action), then the principle of inviolability does not represent a real constraint on the straightforward maximization of autonomy. For when we restrain ourselves from acting in a way that maximizes overall autonomy in order to

361

avoid treating someone as a mere means, we are treating *others* as a mere means by omission. One proposal would be to maintain that actions and omissions are morally different, but Nino denies this and claims (following Jonathan Glover and others) that actions and omissions are on a par from the causal and moral point of view. Therefore, he proposes reformulating the principle of inviolability so as to produce a non-aggregative, egalitarian distribution of autonomy. The reformulated version is as follows: "someone sacrifices another for his own benefit when he restrains the autonomy of the other so that the latter ends up with less autonomy than the former enjoys" (Nino, 1991, p. 215). All this entails a liberal egalitarian criterion for establishing the scope of rights: "maximize the autonomy of each individual separately in so far as this does not imply putting another individual in a situation of lesser comparative autonomy" (ibid.).

Starting from similar assumptions (the value of autonomy), other philosophers have departed from this egalitarian conclusion. For example, Horacio Spector (Argentine) shares the belief that autonomy, which he calls positive freedom, is intrinsically valuable. Negative freedom, on the other hand, is conceptually unstable because it depends upon valuing positive freedom (Spector, 1992, chapter 2). However, his adherence to positive freedom does not lead Spector to embrace an aggregative or maximizing view. Valuing positive freedom does not imply maximizing the satisfaction of positive freedom across individuals. Like Nino, Spector believes that positive freedom (or autonomy, in Nino's terms) must be subjected to deontological constraints based on the moral separateness of individuals. However, Spector's view on deontological constraints is much stronger than Nino's. First, he argues for the priority of negative duties over positive duties to respect positive freedom; second, he defends the incommensurability of values; and finally, he claims that moral duties are agent-relative (Spector, 1992, chapters 4 and 5). In sum, Spector's argument leads to a libertarian position (one that maintains that negative rights prevail over other moral considerations), although its starting point is different from other libertarian theories: an adherence not to negative freedom (as is common to libertarian philosophers) but to positive freedom.

The value of autonomy, as conceived by Nino and Spector, is non-conventional. It has instead a constructivist or a Kantian foundation. In this sense, human rights (crucially, the right to autonomy or to positive liberty) has, on their views, a rational and universal underpinning. Coherently with his more naturalistic metaethics, Rabossi has supported a radically different view of human rights as an historical and conventional product of our time (Rabossi, 1990). The concept of a human right should be "naturalized," according to Rabossi. Philosophical foundations of human rights as moral rights are hopeless and, more importantly, unnecessary. The empirical existence of a "human rights culture" and the legal enactment of human rights at the international and, increasingly, national levels make the search for an a priori justification otiose. Philosophers should work with this social fact as a premise and focus on conceptual clarification or institutional design (Rabossi, 1990, p. 175).

In a less conventional vein, other philosophers have also tried to found norms of justice and human rights on cultural facts or, more broadly, on facts about human existence. Two attempts are especially interesting, because they do not start by postulating some kind of value (such as autonomy or liberty) or some norm of justice (such as equality), but by focusing on *disvalue* and *injustice*. Garzón Valdés (Argentine, working in Germany) has argued that it is possible to reach a consensus about what

s good and right in this negative way: no one denies that torture, genocide, depriva-
ion, famine, among other things, are evils (Garzón Valdés, 1998, pp. 163–5). Luis Villoro
(Mexican) has explored a similar approach by appealing to the experience of exclusion
(Villoro, 2000). In both cases, the aspiration is to find a rational consensus about goodness and justice by rejecting what we all agree is bad or unjust. No detailed argument
or systematic account has been provided for this position, to my knowledge, but the
strategy is certainly promising and, to some extent, original. At least in the case of Garzón
Valdés, the strategy is closely connected to his conception of human needs as the cornerstone of human rights (Garzón Valdés, 1993, pp. 45–50). Unfulfilled basic human
needs are the mirror image of deprivation and their fulfillment defines the set of rights
that neither the market nor democratic decision can override (idem, p. 45).

Government authority and democracy

The second important issue in Nino's work on political philosophy is the justification
of government and of democracy. His starting point is the following puzzle: in order
for the legal authority to give a reason for me to follow its legal rules, these rules must
be justified by moral reasons; but, if those legal rules are morally justified, then the legal
authority (the government) is superfluous (Nino, 1991, pp. 234, 304–5). Nino's way
out of this puzzle is epistemic: Rules enacted by governmental decisions should be taken
in such a way as to maximize the chances of their being morally right. To do so, the
decision procedure must reflect the procedure that, according to the moral theory, leads
to moral truth. At this point, Nino connects his political theory to his constructivist
metaethics by arguing that deliberative democracy is the system that best follows the
rules of moral discourse. In a democracy, those rules are subjected to real-world constraints, especially time constraints, yielding a system of majority rule. On the other
hand, the majoritarian system must be constrained by procedural rules that allow it
to approximate the conditions of ideal moral dialog. These procedural rules (which should
be enshrined as constitutional rules) are, primarily, those guaranteeing impartiality and
careful deliberation (see Nino, 1996, pp. 121–2).

Several Latin American philosophers have objected to Nino's idea that deliberative
democracy is primarily justified by reference to epistemic considerations. Some have
objected that, if it is true that the decision of the majority is more likely to be morally
correct, no right could be provided to the minority against such a decision, whatever
its content (Farrell, 1986, p. 100; Rodríguez Larreta, 1986, pp. 92–3). Further, it is
not clear how the epistemic qualities of the ideal moral deliberation are inherited by
imperfect deliberators in a complex, multitudinous society (Rodríguez Larreta, 1986,
pp. 89–91). In the same vein, Guido Pincione and Fernando Tesón (both Argentine)
have recently developed a far more sophisticated criticism of the epistemic credentials
of deliberative democracy and, more generally, to deliberative democracy overall
(2006). While their objection relies heavily on a public choice theory of democracy,
they go beyond it. Their point is not only that voters in a representative democracy
have incentives to remain ignorant in political matters (rational ignorance), as the traditional economic theory of democracy already holds. The deeper problem in a deliberative democracy is, according to Pincione and Tesón, that the rational ignorance of
voters induces politicians to spread false theories about society in a systematic way.

They call this phenomenon "discourse failure." Since reliable social science (especially economics) is complex and appeals to causal connections that are far from obvious (such as the "invisible hand" of economics), politicians will, publicly, tend to endorse the sort of superficially persuasive and simple (but regrettably unreliable) theories that rationally ignorant voters will "buy." Epistemically sound deliberation is therefore unfeasible in the political arena and, for that reason, deliberative democracy is utopian in a negative sense.

Further discussion on the relative merits of deliberative and public choice theories of democracy is needed among academics both in Latin America and in the developed world. The quality of democracy in Latin America is particularly affected by widespread poverty and illiteracy, populism, hijacking of political power by particular interests, among other vices. Because of this, a theoretical and applied debate regarding the possibilities and nature of democracy in Latin America is of fundamental importance. Pincione and Tesón's challenge to deliberative democracy is especially telling in Latin America. Nino's early death has left us without what might have been an interesting response. In any case, it is crucial for political philosophy not to confine itself to one restricted paradigm (deliberative democracy, social choice theory, or whatever). It is the task of contemporary philosophers to continue the dialogue and discussion.

Applications: Bioethics and Multiculturalism

As my last remarks suggest, it is in applied moral and political philosophy that the peculiarities of Latin American thought are more salient. With the exception of Pincione and Tesón's critique of deliberative democracy, I have, thus far, been discussing moral and political theories conceived for ideal societies. As is well known, John Rawls distinguishes between ideal and non-ideal moral theory. An ideal moral theory tries to discover the principles of a "well-ordered" (or just) society, assuming that everyone will comply with moral and legal norms and institutions, and that social circumstances are fairly favorable. Theories of applied ethics are typically non-ideal in that they discuss or assess social or legal rules within the framework of injustice and unfavorable social or economic circumstances. For non-ideal theories, the context of the practices or institutions to be discussed is highly relevant. Therefore, the special features of Latin American reality are crucial to at least some of those discussions. I will address two issues, bioethics and multiculturalism, from this perspective. Relevant contributions to these topics will be mentioned, but I will give special emphasis to the way in which the peculiarities of Latin American reality shape the debate.

Bioethics

Bioethics has been established as a philosophical discipline in Latin America only in the past twenty years. The classical issues of bioethics require a different treatment in Latin America from the ways in which they are treated in developed countries. This does not mean that the general philosophical discussions lack relevance in Latin America. On the contrary, my own opinion is that they are of fundamental importance. However, the realities of life in Latin America have forced philosophers to modify some assumptions and emphases. I would like to focus on these peculiarities by briefly dealing with two problems: abortion, and medical practice and research with vulnerable subjects. Poverty, exclusion, and vulnerability, endemic in most Latin American populations, permeate these issues more thoroughly than they do other bioethical issues (such as euthanasia, assisted reproduction, organ transplants, cloning, or genetics).

As is widely known, there are two principal philosophical perspectives taken on the morality of abortion (both of the individual act and of its legal permission): the perspective of the pregnant woman and her reproductive rights, and the perspective of the fetus and its right to life. Latin American philosophers have dealt with these issues and made some valuable contributions (see for example Valdés, 2001). However, three features of Latin American reality are especially worth noting: the pervasive influence of the Catholic Church, the existence of restrictive legislation on abortion in most countries, and the lack of sexual and reproductive education and of contraceptive resources (see Valdés, 1997). These combine to shape the discussion of abortion in three ways. First, they make the discussion more case-specific and less general. Rather than dealing with the problem of the status of the fetus and of the rights of women in general, more energy is devoted to discussions of the case of abortion in specific circumstances: anencephaly of the fetus, health risk to the pregnant woman, pregnancy in adolescents or infants, and so on (for good examples of this kind of approach, see the articles in the volume edited by Diniz et al., 2007). Second, the discussion becomes less theoretical. Facing the reality of a hundred thousand deaths per year from botched illegal abortions, questions regarding the moral status of the embryo are frequently dismissed and problems such as how to interpret the (normally severely restrictive) positive law to allow women to undergo safe abortions become more salient. Finally, the debate is less philosophical and more political: Most of the cases under discussion are such that an abortion would be indicated without much discussion in almost every developed country. Therefore, there is no real attempt to understand deep philosophical problems. Rather, the search is for discursive tools to remove, or at least undermine, dogmatic thinking and rules.

The problem of patient autonomy and physician paternalism is slightly different. As in the case of abortion, it is a classical bioethical issue. To what extent the patient's will and decision should be respected, especially in risky circumstances, is a question that might make sense in different social or cultural settings. The same holds for the more specific case where the patient is a subject of biomedical research. In both the normal relationship between physician and patient and the more peculiar one between researcher and subject of research, the autonomy of the patient or subject of research competes with the objective risk–benefit judgment of the physician or researcher, and the consequent paternalistic attitude. Now, when the patient or the subject of research belongs to a vulnerable population, or to a non-individualistic culture, these tensions become more acute and give rise to some genuine philosophical concerns. In this sense, this issue is different from abortion. In the case of abortion, I do not see that the peculiar Latin American cultural or social reality fundamentally changes arguments or perspectives. It is rather a matter of attempting to combat dogmatism and authoritarian impositions on women. On the other hand, in the case of patient autonomy, there is some reason to think that the particular Latin American setting does frame the issue in a more fundamental way. In Latin America, extensive poverty, illiteracy, and

365

traditional cultural patterns seem to prevent individual consent from being taken seriously. Individual consent (more generally, individual freedom) seems to be out of place in a culture in which traditional patterns are non-individualistic and persons lack the capacities to acquire information and to deliberate. Some Latin American bio-ethicists have recently reacted against this seemingly logical position. First, illiteracy does not imply incompetence, the incapacity to understand information and to take decisions according to one's own values (Luna, 1995). Second, it is not true that the particular Latin American cultural patterns are incompatible with the value of auto-nomy (Salles, 2002). I will not pursue this discussion any further. However, it is worth noting that it is deeply connected to the following, broader, issue: whether cul-tural diversity should be respected even when certain traditional cultural values are incompatible with individual autonomy and other liberal rights. Let us now focus on this problem.

Multiculturalism

Cultural and ethnic diversity are pervasive in Latin America. Such diversity is not morally innocuous: it is marked by the experience of colonialism, domination, slavery, and servi-tude. All of this makes the issue somewhat different from the way in which it appears in standard treatments of multiculturalism in developed countries. Several distinctive issues are involved: claims to restitution for past (or, in some cases, present) violations of rights (especially but not only, the restitution of lands), claims to the preservation of cultural identity (sometimes involving claims to collective rights), claims to freedom from poverty and exploitation, and claims to due representation in political bodies, among others.

The most important theoretical contributions to the debate have come from those countries with strong philosophical traditions and, at the same time, a considerable historical influence of native peoples: Mexico and Peru. Three main views compete. One view is that indigenous communities have a legitimate claim to more political auto-nomy, cultural identity, and compensation for past and present domination. As a practical matter, this implies strengthening local communities, empowering them to manage their own problems and conflicts, respecting their own customs, traditions, authorities, and social, political, and economic organization (see Bonfil Batalla, 1989, pp. 237–44). Some go still further and argue for political autonomy in the sense of full exercise of self-government (Díaz Polanco, 1998, pp. 17–18). Others have linked the claim to autonomy and cultural identity to environmental protection and sustainabil-ity. The idea is that native people have ways of dealing with the natural environment (their traditional knowledge) that can prevent degradation and promote a more authentic (or less alienated) culture. Given the particular ties of these peoples, culture and preservation of nature reinforce each other (see Heyd, 2005, for an outline of dif-ferent versions of this view among Latin American social scientists).

From a radically opposite perspective, and focusing specifically on the case of Mexico, Garzón Valdés has argued for a liberal universalistic view (Garzón Valdés, 1993). In accordance with his conception of human rights (see the previous section), Garzón Valdés holds that national authorities have a "duty of homogenization," a duty to satisfy the objective basic needs of all, while indigenous communities (or at least their representatives) have a "duty of dynamization," that is, the duty to accept the changes that homogenization implies (Garzón Valdés, 1993, p. 51).

Other philosophers take a more moderate stance and, partially following Will Kymlicka, argue that cultural identity is not incompatible with universal human rights. Moderate multiculturalists accept some individual, universal rights. One such right is the right to an autonomous life. However, respecting this right requires that cultural identity and, to some extent, collective rights be acknowledged. With some differences in details, advocates of this moderate position argue that choosing a life plan requires a cultural framework. Otherwise, the choice would lack authenticity and meaning. If a cultural framework is a prerequisite for autonomy and autonomy is an individual right, then native peoples have a (collective) right to preserve their culture and traditions, including its economic and social rules (see Villoro, 1998, p. 92; Olivé, 2003, p. 89).

This is not the place to advance an opinion, but it is worth stressing what is at stake in this controversy. Strong communitarians see European culture as responsible for the oppression and exploitation of native peoples. Extreme poverty and cultural alienation are two sides of the same coin. Liberals, on the other hand, believe that the only way to rescue these populations from poverty and exclusion is by incorporating them into Western culture. The debate resembles in some ways the eternal controversy over free will and determinism. Both sides agree that liberal rights and communitarian rights are incompatible. Moderate multiculturalists are compatibilist. They restrict liberal rights to a minimum and try to rescue traditional customs as much as possible to the effect that both (individual and collective rights) can coexist. Whether they are successful in this enterprise is an open question.

Conclusion

As we have seen, Latin American ethics and political philosophy have made many valuable contributions. In metaethics and normative ethics, those contributions are universal in kind, at least within the constraints I described in the introduction. The particular Latin American context affects what we might call the context of discovery, but not the ultimate reasons and arguments. In applied ethics, the context plays a different and more fundamental role. It constrains the kinds of arguments that are relevant since the problems themselves are shaped by particular features of our reality. However, theoretical and practical philosophy are not isolated enterprises. We have seen the strong interplay in a number of places, especially in discussions of the problems of democracy and multiculturalism. It is therefore crucial for Latin American moral and political philosophy to pursue the highest standards of theoretical rigor and sophistication: the standards that are demanded in the international arena. Only in that way will it be able to face its practical, local, political, and ethical problems with philosophical tools adequate to the task.

Related chapters: 2 The Rights of the American Indians; 3 Colonial Thought; 4 The Emergence and Transformation of Positivism; 6 The Anti-Positivist Movement in Mexico; 13 Liberation Philosophy; 24 Latin American Philosophy; 28 Feminist Philosophy; 31 Deontic Logic and Legal Philosophy.

EDUARDO RIVERA-LÓPEZ

References

Bonfil Batalla, G. (1989). *México profundo. Una civilización negada.* 2nd edn. México: Grijalbo.
Díaz Polanco, H. (1998). *La Rebelión zapatista y la autonomía.* México: Siglo Veintiuno.
Diniz, D., Figueroa Perea, J. G., & Luna, F. (2007). Reproductive health ethics: Latin American perspectives. *Developing World Bioethics,* 7, ii–iv.
Farrell, M. D. (1986). En busca de la voluntad de Dios. *Análisis Filosófico,* 6, 97–102.
Frondizi, R. (1972). *¿Qué son los valores?* 3rd edn. México: Fondo de Cultura Económica.
Frondizi, R. (1986). Fundamentación axiológica de la norma ética. In R. Frondizi. *Ensayos Filosóficos* (pp. 138–48). México: Fondo de Cultura Económica.
Garzón Valdés, E. (1993). El problema ético de las minorías étnicas. In L. Olivé (Ed). *Ética y diversidad cultural* (pp. 31–57). México: Fondo de Cultura Económica. Also in E. Garzón Valdés. *Derecho, ética y política* (pp. 519–40). Madrid: Centro de Estudios Constitucionales, 1993.
Garzón Valdés, E. (1998). ¿Puede la razonabilidad ser un criterio de corrección moral? *Doxa,* 21, 145–66.
Guariglia, O. (1996). *Moralidad. Ética universalista y sujeto moral.* México: Fondo de Cultura Económica.
Guariglia, O. (1998). Valor y ética en Risieri Frondizi. *Cuadernos de Filosofía,* 43, 57–62.
Heyd, T. (2005). Sustainability, culture and ethics: models from Latin America. *Ethics, Place and Environment,* 8, 223–34.
Luna, F. (1995). Paternalism and the argument from illiteracy. *Bioethics,* 9, 283–90. Spanish translation: Los analfabetos y el respeto a las personas. In F. Luna. *Ensayos de Bioética. Reflexiones desde el Sur* (pp. 47–58). Mexico: Fontamara, 2001.
Nino, C. (1989). *Constructivismo ético.* Madrid: Centro de Estudios Constitucionales.
Nino, C. (1991). *Ethics of human rights.* Oxford: Clarendon Press.
Nino, C. (1996). *The constitution of deliberative democracy.* New Haven: Yale University Press. Spanish translation: *La constitución de la democracia deliberativa.* Barcelona: Gedisa, 1997.
Olivé, L. (2003). Un modelo multiculturalista más allá de la tolerancia. *Dianoia,* XLVIII:51, 83–96.
Pincione, G., & Tesón, F. (2006). *Rational choice and democratic deliberation. A theory of discourse failure.* Cambridge: Cambridge University Press.
Rabossi, E. (1979). *Estudios eticos.* Valencia (Venezuela): Universidad de Carabobo.
Rabossi, E. (1983). Necesidades humanas y moralidad. In *Actas del II Simposio Internacional de Filosofía* (pp. 31–52). México: UNAM.
Rabossi, E. (1990). La teoría de los derechos humanos naturalizada. *Revista del Centro de Estudios Constitucionales* (Madrid), 5, 159–75.
Rodríguez Larreta, J. (1986). Democracia y moral. Respuesta a Nino. *Análisis filosófico,* 6, 83–95.
Salazar Bondy, A. (1969). Confusiones axiológicas. *Crítica,* 3, 85–100. Afterwards in *Para una filosofía del valor.* Santiago de Chile: Editorial Universitaria, 1971.
Salazar Bondy, A. (1971). La dificultad de elegir. In *Para una filosofía del valor* (pp. 152–65). Santiago de Chile: Editorial Universitaria.
Salles, A. L. F. (2002). Autonomy and culture. The case of Latin America. In A. Salles & M. J. Bertomeu (Eds). *Bioethics. Latin American perspectives* (pp. 9–26). Amsterdam and New York: Rodopi.
Salmerón, F. (1971). La filosofía y las actitudes morales. In *La filosofía y las actitudes morales* (pp. 105–73). México: Siglo Veintiuno.
Salmerón, F. (1998). *Diversidad cultural y tolerancia.* México: Paidós.
Spector, H. (1992). *Autonomy and rights.* Oxford: Oxford University Press.

368

Valdés, M. (1997). Aborto y anticoncepción en México: las actitudes y los argumentos de la Iglesia Católica. In M. Platts (Ed.). *Dilemas éticos* (pp. 53–96). Mexico: Fondo de Cultura Económica and UNAM. English version: Abortion and contraception in Mexico: the attitudes and the arguments of the Catholic Church. In A. Salles & M. J. Bertomeu (Eds). *Bioethics. Latin American perspectives* (pp. 27–52). Amsterdam and New York: Rodopi, 2002.

Valdés, M. (2001). Aborto y personas. In M. Valdés (Ed.). *Controversias sobre el aborto* (pp. 69–88). México: Fondo de Cultura Económica and UNAM.

Villoro, L. (1998). *Estado plural, pluralidad de culturas.* México: Paidós.

Villoro, L. (2000). Sobre el principio de la injusticia: la exclusión. *Isegoría,* 22, 103–42.

26

Philosophy of Science

ALBERTO CORDERO

1. Introduction

Reflection on scientific thought has long mattered in Latin America. Modern attention to the logic, conceptual structure, and epistemology of science took some time to develop, however. It gained momentum in the 1940s, fueled in part by critical reactions to the ways in which philosophy was then practiced in several parts of the region but also by the presence of thinkers recently arrived from Europe, notably Hans Lindemann (a member of the Vienna Circle) in Argentina. When, shortly after World War II, philosophy of science became a professional discipline, some scientists and philosophers in Latin America were able and willing to join in as full players.

This chapter offers an overview of important work conducted at centers in the subcontinent between 1950 and the early 2000s. The primary emphasis is not on work *by* Latin Americans as such but rather on significant contributions produced *within* the region, especially leading local thinkers and their specific contexts. The period, I will suggest, is one of considerable interest. During the second half of the twentieth century, despite negative local circumstances, a number of philosophers of science based in Latin America managed to produce work of the highest international standards, a feat arguably not matched by developments anywhere else in standard branches of philosophy in the developing world.

My focus in this paper is on "mainstream philosophy of science" – broadly analytic in style, centered in the study of knowledge, methodology, and epistemic values, a discipline internationally associated with such major journals as *Philosophy of Science, Erkenntnis, The British Journal for the Philosophy of Science*, and *Studies in the History and Philosophy of Science*. Sections 2 through 7 are devoted to works produced in the region between the 1950s and the beginning of this century. The paper closes with a brief commentary on the past of, and prospects for, the practice of philosophy of science in Latin America. Although I have tried to be even-handed and objective, inevitably the selection involved has been influenced by my own interpretation of the discipline.

2. Argentina

The field already had an active presence in Buenos Aires when philosophy of science established itself as a professional discipline in the United States and Europe in the late 1940s, by which time a branch of The Academy of History and Philosophy of Science was in operation in the city. From early in the 1950s, research and seminars were regularly held by Mario Bunge, Gregorio Klimovsky, and Julio Rey Pastor. Particularly useful in gathering attention to the emerging discipline were discussions of works by Bertrand Russell and the Vienna Circle (as noted, Hans Lindemann had moved to Argentina).

In and around Buenos Aires, the 1950s were a decade of optimism about the academic and cultural possibilities of philosophy of science and its practice. Two very active institutions opened in 1952. One was Círculo Filosófico (The Philosophical Circle of Buenos Aires), led by Mario Bunge, where drafts of many of his early works were presented for discussion, notably the materials for his book *Causalidad*. The other was an organization for higher studies, Instituto Libre de Estudios Superiores, with Gregorio Klimovsky and Rolando García, where discussions about the Vienna Circle and the new positivism were systematically presented to wider audiences. By the mid-1950s Bunge and Klimovsky had managed to secure chairs at Buenos Aires University in philosophy of science and logic, respectively. Through their courses, seminars, and activities philosophy of science became a vibrant field at the university. One major emphasis of Bunge's administrative and cultural efforts during this period was on making professional philosophical activity possible in Argentina. In 1956 a new association for logic and scientific philosophy, Agrupación Rioplatense de Lógica y Filosofía Científica, was launched with the explicit aim of uniting thinkers from Argentina and Uruguay interested in the development of a critical rational approach to the study of philosophy. Its participants included Mario Bunge, Gregorio Klimovsky, Jorge Bosch, Gino Germani, and Rolando García. Klimovsky would later hold the chair in epistemology at Belgrano University. A group of disciples began to form; translations of important analytic works into Spanish flowed from their workshops; the series *Cuadernos de Epistemología* started to provide students in the whole of Latin America and Spain with access to translations of key works in the field.

Between 1959 and 1960 Bunge held seminal lectures and discussions on the shortcomings of the empiricist conception of causality, which he blamed for having promoted much confusion in science and philosophy. Bunge's thoughts in these directions were put together in *Causalidad*, a book published in 1959 with considerable international success. Advocating a realist conception of causality, in this work Bunge distinguishes between causal determination and other forms of determination (statistical, structural, teleological, and dialectical), teasing apart three different ways in which talk of "causality" enters scientific discourse – as a *principle* according to which everything has a cause; as a *relation* between cause and effect; and as a *law* according to which same causes produce same effects. Notably, this and other works begun in Argentina soon found a consistent place in mainstream reading lists in Europe and the English-speaking world. For the first time, philosophy books one may call "classics" were coming out of Latin America.

A major *universalist*, perhaps even *the* universalist philosopher in Latin America, Mario Bunge is also very particularly South American (it is hard to imagine Bunge growing

371

up anywhere else but in cosmopolitan Argentina). Ever since the 1950s, in his native country and elsewhere, he has been an energetic spokesman for the need to maintain in Latin America cultural and educational institutions capable of supporting the exercise of philosophy by minds free from ideological pressure, financial oppression, and political or governmental control of their activity. In Buenos Aires he inspired a demanding sense of professional rigor in students and collaborators, declaring "war" on the relaxed understanding of philosophy he sensed was then in place at the faculty of Philosophy and Letters. His series *Cuadernos de Epistemología* had a considerable impact on scientists, philosophers, and the educated public throughout the Spanish-speaking world. None of this was achieved without friction, however. Also, on the wider scale, the country was deteriorating. By the early 1960s clashes within factions in the Argentine army had started to impinge on civic life. In 1963 Bunge left the country, first to the United States (where he did not find himself at home, partly because of the Vietnam War) and then to Canada, where he remains to this day.

Something constantly present in Bunge's philosophical work is a search for a *vision* worth having. His is a quest for a comprehensive system in which ontology, metaphysics, epistemology, semantics, psychology, and science in general resonate with each other and advance each other coherently. So far Bunge has produced more than fifty books and hundreds of philosophical and scientific articles, mostly in English and Spanish (many of his principal works have been translated into Italian, German, Russian, French, Hungarian, and Portuguese, to mention a few languages). In mainstream philosophy of science his works of greatest impact include *Causality* (1959), *The Myth of Simplicity* (1963), and *Foundations of Physics* (Springer-Verlag, 1967). Then there is Bunge's all-encompassing *Treatise on Basic Philosophy*, published by Springer, an eight-volume wide-ranging work published between 1974 and 1989. In these and other publications, and even more forcefully in his seminars and oral presentations, Bunge has always championed the use of logic as an expediter of clarity of thought, attention to detail, and the evaluation of arguments at hand. His works and lectures are also renowned for the ferocity of his critiques of all cultural and academic positions that belittle either reason, the search for truth, the universality of science, scientific naturalism, or respect for human beings as individuals. Bunge is an enthusiastic continuator of the project of the Enlightenment. He certainly celebrates the way in which the Enlightenment disseminated to the four corners conceptual and moral tools needed to revise and improve human thought and life in general. Bunge's works typically endorse the idea that science can, and often does, provide us with knowledge of the world, which he regards as the only sensible foundation for social and political action.

Most important, in Latin America Bunge has functioned as a much-needed exemplar, a "possibility proof" that philosophers working in the subcontinent could, despite the often surreal difficulties faced by academics, stand up and join the highest level of contemporary philosophical conversation. No Latin American philosopher had achieved anything comparable before.

Philosophy of science marched on in Argentina during the 1960s, but the loss of Bunge was a major blow. The decade was in many ways bad for the country. In 1966, military intervention in the universities led to a diaspora of many of the most talented minds in science and philosophy. Klimovsky remained in Argentina, however, and his presence helped keep the discipline alive during this difficult period. Despite the surrounding turmoil, young talent continued to emerge, as in the case of Alberto Coffa, active at Universidad de la Plata until 1967, when he left for the United States. Nonetheless, as the decade ended, a remarkable period of expansion began, marked by the foundation of Sociedad Argentina de Análisis Filosófico (SADAF), an exemplary institution supported by its own members, in which fellows and especially invited guests meet around topics of philosophical interest, including many of central importance in philosophy of science. The 1970s were also a difficult time in Argentina; it was possible, however, to start a major journal in 1975, *Revista Latinoamericana de Filosofía*, followed in 1981 by another important periodical, *Análisis Filosófico*.

From the 1980s on, there has been a growing revival of activity in the discipline in Argentina. Several researchers and projects are discernible. Jorge Roetti (Universidad Nacional del Sur), whose area of concentration is philosophical logic, also has made contributions to the philosophical history of science and the philosophy of the social sciences. Juan Manuel Torres (Bahía Blanca) is a recognized researcher in the philosophy of medicine and the history and philosophy of genetics and biology. Pablo Lorenzano, back in Argentina after completing a doctorate in Berlin, is now at Instituto de Estudios sobre la Ciencia y la Tecnología, University of Quilmes, Buenos Aires. A specialist in structuralist metatheory and the history and philosophy of formal Mendelian genetics, Lorenzano is a regular contributor in these fields as well as in science studies; his book *Geschichte und Struktur der klassischen Genetik* (Peter Lang Verlag, 1995) has been well received, particularly in Germany and Latin America. These recent developments provide just some examples of the state of the discipline. Philosophy of science seems to be growing country-wide in Argentina now, judging by the amount of teaching and research projects in place at various centers, from the greater Buenos Aires to Córdoba to Santiago del Estero and more. In Córdoba, in particular, annual meetings devoted to epistemology and the history of science (Jornadas de Epistemología e Historia de la Ciencia) have been held for twenty years now under the direction of Víctor Rodríguez, with significant impact in Latin America.

Meanwhile, in neighboring Uruguay, Mario Otero is back in the country after holding important teaching positions at Buenos Aires University and Mexico's National Autonomous University (Universidad Nacional Autónoma). Earlier in his career, he had taught epistemology and chaired the department of philosophy of science at Uruguay University. Now retired, he remains one of the forces behind much of the activity taking place in the country, especially some successful history and philosophy of science encounters organized jointly by several institutions from the Southern Cone of the subcontinent.

3. Mexico

Higher education in Mexico has enjoyed comparatively high governmental support for a very long time. At the forefront of intellectual life is the country's leading state university, Universidad Nacional Autónoma de México (UNAM), a world-class institution in the Spanish-speaking world. Philosophy of science found a fertile soil there, particularly since the 1960s and early 1970s, when Fernando Salmerón and Luis Villoro launched a movement to encourage rigor and clarity in philosophy at the university. They were instrumental in the creation of scholarships to enable students to do postgraduate work in Europe, the UK, and the United States. With Alejandro Rossi, recently back from Oxford, in 1967 they founded the journal *Crítica*, which has become a choice organ of philosophy in Latin America. The following year Salmerón published *La filosofía de las Matemáticas*. World-class seminars and meetings soon became a regular feature at UNAM's Institute for Philosophical Investigations (Instituto de Investigaciones Filosóficas – IDIF). In the 1970s and 1980s this institute hosted some now legendary seminars and short courses led by internationally recognized figures. One of the earliest seminars to get established was an interdisciplinary group devoted to the history and philosophy of science, started by Mario Bunge. During these years IDIF was also the arena of many a spirited philosophical debate – some between Neri Castañeda and Mario Bunge being among the most fondly and vividly remembered. In 1976, with Bunge's help, a lively epistemology forum was established in Mexico, Asociación Mexicana de Epistemología.

The structuralist approach, which had been adopted with special fervor in Germany and other parts of Central Europe, came to Mexico in a big way with Carlos Ulises Moulines, who in the mid-1970s began a fruitful association with IDIF. A Venezuelan former pupil of Jesús Mosterín at Barcelona and Wolfgang Stegmüller at Munich, Moulines's early work displays a fertile interest in the rise of the logical-empiricist approach, particularly the projects of logical reconstruction of the empirical world variously advocated by Bertrand Russell, Rudolf Carnap, and Nelson Goodman. These studies developed into one of his first monographs, *La estructura del mundo sensible* (1973). Around this time the approaches opened by Patrick Suppes in the United States and Gunther Ludwig in Germany were enriching Moulines's research, as some of his articles from this period show, notably "A Logical Reconstruction of Simple Equilibrium Thermodynamics," published in *Erkenntnis* in 1975, and "Approximate Application of Empirical Theories: A General Explication" (published in the same journal the following year and arguably one of his best papers, influenced by the work of Ludwig). Sensitive to the historical turn in philosophy of science, Moulines, like Joseph Sneed in the United States and Stegmüller in Germany, studied the issue of theory change, devoting much of his research during the 1970s and 1980s to the dynamics of theories – their "diachronic" aspects. Moulines applied the resources of structuralist reconstruction and Kuhnian analysis (in terms of disciplinary matrices) to the development of Newtonian mechanics and its subsequent evolution. His labors in these directions found expression in book form in *Exploraciones metacientíficas* (1982).

Moulines quickly became a major intellectual force at IDIF, where he stayed for over a decade, conducting research that confirmed him as a leading figure in the structuralist movement. In Moulines's conception of science, scientific theories are cultural constructs of key philosophical interest; he regards philosophy of science as a theorization about theorizations, a discipline whose epistemology is primarily *interpretive* rather than prescriptive or descriptive. Moulines is one of the most influential philosophers to have worked in Latin America in recent decades, a good part of the activity in philosophy of science conducted at IDIF during his tenure having been directly helped by him. For the purposes of this chapter, an important point to stress is that the work he produced during his Mexican period reached the highest level within the worldwide structuralist movement, of which he remains one of its leaders. In 1984 Moulines left for Bielefeld

University, from which he subsequently moved to Berlin and then to his current chair in Munich, where he has returned as Stegmüller's successor.

From the 1980s to the present, many research seminars at IDIF have been expanded and strengthened. On an impressive scale, a series of "international symposia of philosophy" was put in place, initially with Enrique Villanueva at the helm. These meetings brought together distinguished figures from the United States and from Mexico, the UK, and other parts of Latin America and Europe. The intense and high-quality exchanges these venues generated have proved remarkably fruitful as starting points of much subsequent research activity in Mexico, Argentina, and elsewhere in the subcontinent. Happily, these international symposia continue to the present. The 1980s were also marked by serious investment in specialized research libraries and the strengthening of strong publishing programs at UNAM and elsewhere in Mexico. Generously funded scholarships continued to enable researchers and students to spend appropriate periods at major international centers. Facilities for philosophical research reached at IDIF levels never seen before in Latin America. An important addition during a crucial period was Mario Otero (Uruguay), already mentioned in this chapter, whose work at IDIF helped advance studies in the philosophical history of science. Fruitful activity in philosophy of science began to flow on a regular basis from seminars – general philosophy of science and the philosophy of physics being top beneficiaries, although not the sole ones (as attested for example by Margarita Ponce's work in philosophy of biology during the decade).

From the mid-1980s on, activity in the field has become more diverse at IDIF. Prominent in the reflections about science are investigations into the limits of scientific knowledge. Works in this area include Luis Villoro's critique of scientism. In *Creer, saber, conocer* (Belief, knowledge, learning, published in 1982 by Siglo XXI), Villoro presses on the theme of how human reason has operated throughout history and the extent to which it has led to situations of domination and/or emancipation from subjection; in this book Villoro favors a revaluation of "wisdom," which he characterizes as knowledge drawn from lived experiences, which, in his view, is richly found in the "wise men" of traditional cultures. On the area of value issues in science, technology, and society, Leon Olivé's studies have led to numerous publications, including *Knowledge, Society and Reality* (Rodopi, 1993). A member of IDIF since 1985 and its director for many years, Olivé worked on an interdisciplinary project at Oxford for his doctoral dissertation (*The Significance of Epistemological and Ontological Preconceptions in Three Sociological Theories of the State*). Although his concentration is on value issues, his contributions also include works on realism, relativism, rationality, and naturalism.

Also at IDIF is Sergio Martínez, originally from Guatemala, a prolific philosopher who moved to Mexico in the 1990s after completing a doctorate with Linda Wessels at Indiana University on the philosophy of quantum mechanics, a field in which he has authored some major international papers. Initially interested in the algebraic structure and the foundations of quantum mechanics (particularly the Luders Rule), in the last decade he has broadened his interests toward the study of naturalism and scientific practices – how explanatory patterns play a role in the formation and stabilization of scientific disciplines. His books include *De los efectos a las causas* (PAIDOS, 1997) and *Geografía de las prácticas científicas: racionalidad, heurística y normatividad* (UNAM, 2003). Research on the philosophical history of science continues at IDIF, as shown by valuable work produced in recent years by Laura Benítez and José Antonio Robles; likewise, research on conceptual change, the semantic view, and the debate over realism continues, particularly in the work of Ana Rosa Pérez. On areas close to the life sciences, Carlos López has authored well-received papers published in international journals. Additional work relevant to philosophy of science is also conducted at other UNAM units, for example by Lourdes Valdivia on the interface between neurobiology and the philosophy of mind. Centers of activity outside UNAM include Mexico City's Metropolitan University, Universidad Autónoma Metropolitana, as well as some centers in the provinces.

Mexico in general continues to attract major figures from the wider world – Larry and Rachel Laudan (IDIF) and Evandro Agazzi (in Mexico several months each year) being important cases in point.

4. Brazil

Interest in philosophy of science was encouraged in the 1950s by Gilles-Gaston Granger (a disciple of Gaston Bachelard), who taught at the University of São Paulo (USP) from 1947 to 1953. His work favored a Continental, historically oriented approach, but with room for the analytic style associated with English-speaking countries. In 1955 Granger published an influential textbook, *Lógica e filosofia das ciências*, generally recognized as the first introduction to the discipline in Portuguese. The academic line he started continued to develop through the efforts of Oswaldo Porchat Pereira and others.

University life in Brazil was significantly affected by the military coup of 1966, which led to actions by the de facto regime to eradicate academics of leftist leanings (or suspected of such), among other forms of institutional disruption. Activities in philosophy of science dwindled as a result. Still, in 1970, partly as a response to this challenge, João Paulo Monteiro (University of São Paulo) succeeded in launching *Ciência e Filosofia*, a journal devoted to the study of logic and science from a plurality of perspectives. Philosophy of science was further energized throughout the decade by international visits and courses organized by Porchat, active at USP until 1975, when he moved to Campinas State University to head a newly created research center, Centro de Lógica, Epistemologia e História da Ciência (CLE). Also at Campinas, Zeljko Loparic helped to develop CLE, working there for many years as chief coordinator. Publication of the journal *Manuscrito* started in 1977.

CLE is internationally recognized as the cradle of "paraconsistent logics," a field championed by Newton C. A. da Costa, a leading figure in mathematics, logic, and philosophy of science, with a long-enjoyed international reputation for the originality of his works on non-classical logics and on axiomatization of scientific theories. For many years he was one of the most energetic spirits at Campinas. From its early days, CLE has promoted work in logic and the philosophy and history of science. In its facilities, important research has come to fruition on the character and structure of modern science, its concepts and theories – conducted from a variety of perspectives, including investigations into science teaching and the uses of philosophy of science in education. Academic quality has been further encouraged by regular seminars, distinguished international visitors, research support (particularly for interdisciplinary studies), and the publication of original monographs and translations of major works into Portuguese, as well as the periodical *Cadernos de História e Filosofia da Ciência*. The establishment of a program of postgraduate studies in logic and philosophy of science followed.

In the 1980s, CLE managed to attract some first-class junior faculty from England, particularly Harvey Brown and Steven French. With their help, philosophy of physics, mathematics, and formal approaches to the philosophy of science thrived at the Center. At Campinas, Steven French and Newton da Costa started a long-lasting collaboration that would prove remarkably fertile. It continues to this day, having resulted in influential contributions on such topics as space-time, the philosophy of quantum mechanics, the semantic model of theories, and generalizations of the traditional concept of truth ("pragmatic truth" and "partial truth") – a subject of growing interest in fields ranging from philosophical logic to current debates about realism. In 2003, they coauthored a major book, *Science and Partial Truth: A Unitary Approach to Models and Scientific Reasoning* (Oxford University Press), which has gained much-deserved international recognition. Brown and French virtually adopted Brazil as their own country in the 1980s, and one can't help speculating how different the world geography of the philosophy of physics and mathematics might have turned out from the late 1980s on, had circumstances in Brazil been a little kinder to academic life at Campinas. Brown and French might have stayed. Together with da Costa, and the new breed of talent they began to produce (Otávio Bueno among them), it is hard to imagine their group failing to transform the Center into a world-class place in their combined fields. Nevertheless, Brown and French left – Brown to a distinguished career at Oxford, where he is now professor of the philosophy of physics; and French to the University of Leeds, where he is now professor of philosophy of science and head of its Philosophy Department. Both have since served distinguished terms as presidents of the prestigious British Society for the Philosophy of Science.

In recent years activity in Brazil has been expanding at many other institutions. The University of São Paulo now houses about half a dozen permanent faculty engaged in teaching and research in the history and philosophy of science; this group initially included Newton C. A. da Costa and Jair M. Abe. Da Costa subsequently moved to the Federal University of Santa Catarina in Florianópolis, and Abe is now at the Universidade Paulista in São Paulo. Up north, the Federal University of Rio de Janeiro has a graduate program in epistemology and the history of science, which runs an active program of visiting lecturers (the list of past guests includes Harvey Brown, Steven French, Michel Ghins, Ulises Moulines, Gilles-Gaston Granger, among others). Activity also seems to be on the increase at many other centers, including the Federal University of Rio Grande do Sul, the Federal University of Bahia, and the State University of Feira de Santana. The latter two centers jointly run "Interdisciplinary Studies on Science and Education," a Master's program in History, Philosophy, and Science Teaching, developed by a group of innovative scholars whose members include Olival Freire, André Luís Mattedi Dias, and Robinson Tenório. Also important to mention is the leading role played by Brazilian philosophers in a regional association of growing consequence in Latin America (Asociación de Filosofia e Historia de la Ciencia del Cono Sur), which organizes well-attended biannual meetings.

5. Chile and Puerto Rico

Philosophy of science has benefited greatly in recent years from the return of Roberto Torretti, back in Santiago since the late 1990s. But the discipline is far from new in Chile. Activity began early, as witnessed by the establishment in the 1950s of the Chilean Association for Logic and the Philosophy of Science. During the 1960s the presence of Gerold Stahl, Nathan Stemmer, and Augusto Pescador directed attention to the study of logic, which became a major field in the country. In 1967 Torretti published an admirable book, still in print (third revised edition), *Manuel Kant. Estudio sobre los fundamentos de la filosofía crítica* (Ediciones de la Universidad de Chile). Later in the decade, Torretti's work on Kant led him to fertile topics in the philosophical history of science. However, life in Chile became increasingly difficult. Early in the 1970s the economy collapsed, and ruthless military dictatorship followed. Chile's leading *Revista de Filosofía* ceased publication; it would not resume until 1977. The academic environment was far from good, although quality work continued in logic, as evidenced by world-class contributions from Rolando Chuaqui and others. In 1970 Torretti left for Puerto Rico, where his interest in the philosophical history of science continued to develop, leading to major works on nineteenth-century geometry and the theory of relativity.

Roberto Torretti is an icon of rigor and good philosophical sense, the author of world-class level contributions, virtually always from bases in Latin American soil. His writings are widely celebrated for his insightful commentaries and highly educated perspectives on the rational development of ideas in Galileo, Newton, Leibniz, Kant, nineteenth-century mathematics, Helmholtz, Poincaré, and relativity theory. Torretti's major publications on these subjects have a secure place in the "mandatory" sections of reading lists in the philosophy of physics anywhere. His leading books include *Philosophy of Geometry from Riemann to Poincaré* (1978), *Relativity and Geometry* (1983), *Creative Understanding: Philosophical Reflections on Physics* (1990), and *The Philosophy of Physics* (1999), all magisterial works in the philosophy and the philosophical history of physics. In a recently published extended interview (with Eduardo Carrasco, Universidad Diego Portales, 2006), Torretti reveals himself as a practical philosopher endowed with a refined sense of irony that brings to memory the joie de vivre that prevailed in some parts of South America until well into the 1960s, a way of life at once charmed and serious – marked by optimism about the possibilities of science, literature, art, philosophy, music, the classics, and the political future of the region. In his youth Torretti had shown promising literary talent; he even wrote some short stories with Carlos Fuentes when they were school mates at The Grange – a gracious extension of England's Cheltenham. Torretti's university education took place in Chile and Germany (where he completed a doctorate with Wilhelm Szilasi at the University of Freiburg in 1954). After brief periods at the United Nations in New York and in Puerto Rico, Torretti returned to Santiago, where he remained as a professor of philosophy at Universidad de Chile until 1970, when, as noted, he moved to Puerto Rico. There, at the Río Piedras campus, he led a remarkable career at until his retirement in 1995. During most of this period he was the editor of *Diálogos*, one of the leading philosophy journals in Latin America. In Puerto Rico he became an internationally recognized authority in the philosophy of nineteenth-century mathematics and the philosophy and philosophical

378

history of the theory of relativity, subjects on which he remains a world-class figure. Now back in Chile, his positive influence significantly strengthens activity in the region.

6.   Peru

Peru's leading philosopher, Francisco Miró-Quesada, occupies a special place in the development of the discipline in Latin America, where he has been a source of confidence in the power of human reason since the late 1940s. For more than two decades he taught at Universidad Nacional Mayor de San Marcos in Lima (UNMSM), and then at Universidad Cayetano Heredia and many other centers in the country. Miró-Quesada currently heads an institute for philosophical research at Universidad Ricardo Palma, Lima. He is the author of numerous works in the area of philosophy of science, including a book in the philosophy of mathematics (*Filosofía de las Matemáticas*, UNMSM, 1954). His most heart-felt project, which continues into the present, focuses on the study of human reason, regarded as the capacity to reach truth, broadly understood. In an influential preliminary book, *Apuntes para una teoría de la razón* (UNMSM, 1962), Miró-Quesada outlined how he seeks to clarify rational validity in logic, science, metaphysics, and ethical theory.

Activity in philosophy of science in Peru started early in the 1950s with articles in the weekly literary supplement of *El Comercio* by Oscar Miró-Quesada, Francisco Miró-Quesada, and a number other intellectuals interested in logic, science, and mathematics. During the 1950s and 1960s the main centers of academic activity were UNMSM and Sociedad Peruana de Filosofía. In the early 1970s, the return of faculty trained in Europe and the United States upgraded the quality of philosophical studies of science in the country, particularly at San Marcos. Important contributions were made, in particular, by Luis Piscoya (philosophy of psychology and general philosophy of science), Juan Abugattàs (philosophy of science), Julio-César Sanz-Elguera (philosophy of science), and David Sobrevilla (philosophy of the social sciences). Later in the decade, an innovative program in philosophy of science opened at Universidad Peruana Cayetano Heredia (UPCH), one of the leading research universities in the subcontinent; with Francisco Miró-Quesada at the helm, numerous international workshops, seminars, and courses took place in Lima as part of this venture. Subsequently and through the 1990s, activity continued through a program named *Scientific Thought*, headed by Alberto Cordero, with the collaboration of Sandro D'Onofrio (Catholic University) and José Carlos Mariátegui (UPCH). As the century came to a close, action in philosophy of science shifted again to San Marcos, where a postgraduate program in the discipline was created. Interest has been growing in recent years at other institutions in the country, notably Peru's Pontifical Catholic University (Pontificia Universidad Católica del Perú – PUCP). Although the traditional emphasis at PUCP favors such areas as phenomenology, existentialism, and the history of philosophy, the institutional focus has expanded in recent years thanks to the incorporation of faculty with doctorates from American universities, who are encouraging analytically oriented work at PUCP, chiefly Pablo Quintanilla (a holder of degrees from the University of Virginia and the London School of Economics, currently doing very promising work on naturalism).

7.   Other Centers

Significant activity has also taken place elsewhere in Latin America, at several institutions. Although philosophical work in Colombia remains much influenced by European schools, "analytic" philosophy of science has had some presence since the 1950s, when Mario Laserna at Universidad de los Andes, Bogotá, promoted the study of logic and the scientific philosophy of Hans Reichenbach. Subsequently, local groups, helped by international visitors, have played a consistent role in Colombia. Important in this regard have been regular visits by Gonzalo Munévar, a philosopher of science now based in the United States. Interest in the discipline is currently growing, especially with the addition of young faculty recently returned with doctorates from centers in the United States. An example of this is Andrés Páez, whose work on explanation as a belief revision operation has met with good international reception; his recent book *Explanations in K* (Athena Verlag, 2006) is being followed with interest in various European circles.

Other centers show promising activity as well. In Venezuela philosophy of science has enjoyed a continuous presence at various centers, including Instituto Venezolano de Investigaciones Científicas, Caracas's Central University (Universidad Central), and Carabobo University. In Ecuador courses and activities seem also on the increase, especially at Quito and Cuenca.

There is much more going on in the subcontinent, of course. The above outline is meant to provide no more than a rough picture of the situation.

8.   Concluding Remarks

The practice of philosophy has faced daunting obstacles in much of Latin America over the past half-century. Nevertheless, if the preceding sections are correct, contrary to what the circumstances might have led one to expect, during the period at least four philosophers of science, from bases in the subcontinent, did manage to produce work of the highest international level. It seems difficult to find a comparable development in other branches of standard philosophy in Latin America, or for that matter in the developing world (logic in Latin America being perhaps the runner-up success story in this regard). At highlighted stages in the story, Mario Bunge in Argentina, Roberto Torretti in Chile and Puerto Rico, Newton da Costa in Brazil, and Ulises Moulines in Mexico were able to engage in real and fruitful dialogue with leading members of the discipline, transcending limitations imposed by "received borders." Exercising the dialogical dimension of philosophy from centers in Latin America, these thinkers produced works that have been read, praised, and critically reacted to at the highest levels of the profession. The explanation for this phenomenon is complex, of course, but some factors seem readily apparent. One has to do with the comparative clarity and precision of writing practiced in mainstream philosophy of science. Another has to do with the discipline's initial concentration on themes from physics and mathematics, which facilitated communication and dialogue across linguistic barriers. A third factor may be that philosophy of science arose in Latin America contemporaneously with the discipline's beginnings as a professional field in the developed world. Yet another reason

380

is the centrality of science to contemporary life, particularly after World War II. Last, but not least, of course, are the considerable talents of the philosophers involved.

In the past quarter-century, the technical quality of the best works produced in the region has continued to improve. Although the structuralist program remains strong in Latin America, some critics sense little real prospective progress relative to the approach's original goals (philosophical or scientific). Meanwhile, other projects are gaining momentum, notably research on the antirealist moves started in the 1980s in different but complementary ways by Bas van Fraassen and Larry Laudan (presently living in Mexico, as noted), as well as a trend toward moderate realist positions focused on clarifying and assessing actual scientific theorizing and practices (exemplified by the approaches championed by Ronald Giere on scientific theories, and by Jarrett Leplin and Stathis Psillos on scientific realism).

On the professional side, recent times have seen a surge of sponsored research (including funding for research seminars and international exchanges) in countries with growing financial stability, particularly Mexico, Brazil, and Argentina, where scholars now enjoy much enhanced opportunities. Another key recent improvement throughout Latin America is wide access to electronic libraries, especially in the area of periodicals. Inter-group dialogue within the Spanish- and Portuguese-speaking worlds is good and seemingly on the increase. On the other hand, interactions with the larger world have room for improvement, particularly between Anglo-American and Latin American groups.

Some old problems persist, unfortunately, including the comparative vulnerability of academic careers in Latin America, especially in the humanities. This difficulty seems unlikely to improve until universities and research centers manage to provide appropriate base salaries and reliable facilities on a regular, long-term basis. Remedial measures, increasingly practiced in the region, include salary supplements in the form of specific research grants. While such measures help, survival by grants can be intellectually damaging, particularly when the attached research-load forces faculty away from their authentic philosophical pursuits. Developing proper university positions, earned on the basis of clear academic merit, adequately funded, not conditioned to "guidance" from central administrations, would seem far more promising as a solution to the noted lingering problems.

Related chapters: 14 Analytic Philosophy; 15 Paraconsistent Logic; 24 Latin American Philosophy; 32 Metaphysics; 34 Formal Epistemology and Logic.

References

Bunge, M. (1959). *Causality. The place of the causal principle in modern science.* Cambridge, MA: Harvard University Press.

Bunge, M. (1963). *The myth of simplicity. Problems of scientific philosophy.* Englewood Cliffs: Prentice-Hall.

da Costa, N. C. A., & French, S. (2003). *Science and partial truth: a unitary approach to models and scientific reasoning.* Oxford Studies in Philosophy of Science. Oxford: Oxford University Press.

Moulines, C. U. (1973). *La estructura del mundo sensible.* Barcelona: Ariel.

Moulines, C. U. (1975). A logical reconstruction of simple equilibrium thermodynamics. *Erkenntnis*, 9, 101–30.

Moulines, C. U. Approximate application of empirical theories. *Erkenntnis*, 10, 201–27.

Moulines, C. U. (1982). *Exploraciones metacientíficas*. Madrid: Alianza Editorial.

Torretti, R. (1967). *Manuel Kant. Estudio sobre los fundamentos de la filosofía crítica*. Santiago: Ediciones de la Universidad de Chile.

Torretti, R. (1978). *Philosophy of geometry from Riemann to Poincaré*. Dordrecht: D. Reidel. Corrected reprint, 1984.

Torretti, R. (1983). *Relativity and geometry*. Oxford: Pergamon Press. Corrected reprint. New York: Dover, 1996.

Torretti, R. (1990). *Creative understanding: philosophical reflections on physics*. Chicago: The University of Chicago Press.

Torretti, R. (1999). *The philosophy of physics*. New York: Cambridge University Press.

Torretti, R., with E. Carrasco. (2006). *En el cielo sólo las estrellas: conversaciones con Roberto Torretti*. Santiago de Chile: Ediciones Universidad Diego Portales.

Further Reading

Bunge, M. (1959). *Metascientific queries*. Springfield: Charles C. Thomas Publisher.

Bunge, M. (1960). The place of induction in science. *Philosophy of Science*, 27, 262–70.

Bunge, M. (1961). The complexity of simplicity. *Journal of Philosophy*, 59, 113–35.

Bunge, M. (1961). Kinds and criteria of scientific law. *Philosophy of Science*, 28, 260–81.

Bunge, M. (1961). The weight of simplicity in the construction and assaying of scientific theories. *Philosophy of Science*, 28, 260–81.

Bunge, M. (1962). *Intuition and science*. Englewood Cliffs: Prentice-Hall.

da Costa, N. C. A., & French, S. (1989). Pragmatic truth and the logic of induction. *British Journal for the Philosophy of Science*, 40, 333–56.

da Costa, N. C. A., & French, S. (1990). The model-theoretic approach in the philosophy of science. *Philosophy of Science*, 57, 248–65.

da Costa, N. C. A., & French, S. (1991). On Russell's principle of induction. *Synthes*, 86, 285–95.

da Costa, N. C. A., & French, S. (1993). A model theoretic approach to 'natural reasoning'. *International Studies in Philosophy of Science*, 7, 177–90.

Torretti, R. (1984). Spacetime physics and the philosophy of science. *British Journal for the Philosophy of Science*, 35, 280–92.

27

Philosophy and Latin American Literature

JESÚS H. AGUILAR

Literature is notable among the arts practiced in Latin America for containing artworks that are at the same time universal and distinctively Latin American. Furthermore, the Latin American literary tradition has rich and profound connections with philosophy. This chapter examines some of the most significant ways in which those connections take place. First and foremost, it explores Latin American philosophical literature in the form of contributions to philosophical thinking that are present in key literary artworks. The explanatory strategy here is essentially topical, although attention is given to the historical context that surrounds the production of the literary works that are examined. Moreover, given the riches offered by the Latin American literary tradition, what follows is necessarily selective in its identification of significant works of literature with relevant philosophical content.

Metaphysics and Epistemology

The metaphysical effort to understand issues such as the nature of time, existence, and death begins in many cultures with works that try to make sense of these issues from a religious perspective. Often these works are sacred texts with a high literary value. The Latin American literary tradition is no exception to this phenomenon and contains several early examples of sacred literature with relevant metaphysical content which can be traced back to some of the major indigenous cultures of the Americas. Most of the extant sacred texts of this type were the result of a complex process of transliteration, copying, and editing done by people with diverse cultural backgrounds who lived after the period of European conquest and colonization that begun in 1492. Nevertheless, the central ideas of the sacred texts that have come down to us in this intricate way can trace their origin back to the Amerindian cultures that flourished before the European arrival.

Notable among the extant Amerindian sacred literary works that contain philosophical thoughts are the books of *Chilam Balam* from the Maya of Yucatan, and the *Popol Vuh* (1985) or "Council book," from the Maya Quiché of Guatemala. The *Popol Vuh* is particularly useful as a source of metaphysical ideas related to the ancient Maya's complex sacred account of the universe. A good example is the conception of time present throughout this work. In contrast to Western metaphysics that traditionally conceives time as a linear progression of unrepeatable events, or less commonly as a cyclical progression of repeatable events, the Maya conception of time as contained in the *Popol Vuh* consists in the progression of unrepeatable events that nevertheless follow a cyclical pattern. Such a conception of time is often illustrated by a geometrical figure like the helix in contrast to a straight line or a circle typically used to illustrate the two conceptions of time associated with Western metaphysics. By conceptualizing time in terms of a cyclical yet progressive pattern of events, the ancient Maya were also able to provide a conceptual justification for some of their epistemic practices like prediction and divination, the assumption being that although different in their details, future events conformed to an established pattern of recurrent general events.

A set of related metaphysical ideas also present in the sacred literature of the ancient Amerindian cultures deals with topics associated with the nature of human existence. As in other similar cases found in literary traditions around the world, the works that contain these ideas are part of a systematic effort to make sense of the cosmic laws that govern human existence. However, in at least one ancient Amerindian culture it is possible to find exquisite literary texts that are neither religious nor mythical and that contain this type of existential concern. These texts are the poems written by authors who belong to the Nahuatl indigenous culture that flourished in the central highlands of Mexico before the arrival of the Europeans. Here, poets like Netzahualcoyotl and Netzahualpilli of Texcoco authored a series of highly personal poems about the human condition emphasizing things like the fleetingness of life, the inevitability of death, and the existential anxiety that arises from the realization of this precarious state of affairs León-Portilla (1992). It was to take several centuries before similar metaphysical existential topics found their way once again into Latin American secular literature. However, when the reemergence did occur, it was part of one of the most fertile moments in the history of this literary tradition.

By the beginning of the twentieth century the cultural and literary context in Latin America was ripe for the emergence of a highly individualistic and existentially infused literature. Perhaps the two most influential Latin American poets of this time participated in this literary explosion of works that are marked by an exploration of the human condition in ways that later will be associated in philosophy with the existentialist movement and its literature. The first poet is the Chilean Pablo Neruda who in *Residencia en la tierra* (Residence on earth) began a lifelong poetic expression of personal identity and existence anchored on the earth of the Americas. The second poet is the Peruvian Cesar Vallejo who in his books *Los heraldos negros* (The black messengers) and *Poemas humanos* (Human poems) embarked on a deeply moving poetic exploration of issues like pain, desolation, and authenticity arising from the experience of the Andean people of Peru.

In Mexico the existential approach to literature that occurred during this time in Latin America found its most explicit lyrical practitioners in the work of a group of young poets associated with a journal that gave them their name: "Los Contemporáneos" (contemporaries.) Following an old literary tradition that can be traced back to the Nahuatl poets and reflecting a Mexican cultural obsession, some of their best literary work reflects a topical obsession with death tainted with relevant metaphysical considerations

384

about its nature. Two outstanding poetic works by members of the Contemporáneos group in which death occupies a metaphysical center stage are Xavier Villaurrutia's *Nostalgia de la muerte* (Nostalgia for death) (1938) and José Gorostiza's *Muerte sin Fin* (Death without end) (1939). In the case of Villaurrutia's work, death is conceived not solely as the end of life but also and most importantly as a return into nothingness. That is, death is conceived as a metaphysical state where existence finds its origin and ultimate destination, a metaphysical state toward which the proper attitude must involve a sort of nostalgia. In the case of Gorostiza's long metaphysical poem "Muerte sin fin," death is conceived instead as a continuous falling into nothingness resulting from consciousness becoming aware of its own existential condition. The consequence of such self-awareness is that the external world reveals itself as the only permanent reality in the form of a substantial though empty body constraining the never-ending flux of ephemeral episodes that make up the conscious self.

The metaphysical centrality of death as a trademark of Mexican literature also has its narrative counterparts in novels like Juan Rulfo's *Pedro Páramo* and Carlos Fuentes's *La muerte de Artemio Cruz* (The death of Artemio Cruz). In Rulfo's novel the ontological boundaries between the living and the dead disappear as we follow its main character's descent into the fantastic town of Comala in search of his identity in the symbolic figure of his father Pedro Páramo, only to realize that not only are all of Comala's inhabitants dead but the narrator himself is one of them. In Fuentes's novel we also witness an individual's search for identity through death in the form of the politician Artemio Cruz whose last hours turn out to be a sort of privileged epistemic window into his layered and complex inner self.

The middle of the twentieth century also saw the production of outstanding narrative works expressing existential ideas by a group of South American writers from the urban centers of the Río de la Plata region. Their work took the form of narrative explorations of the urban reality confronted by the inhabitants of cities like Buenos Aires and Montevideo. Although sharing with existential novelists from other traditions an interest in recognizable topics like freedom, alienation, or death, the South American authors were able to approach them from a particular perspective arising from their distinctive regional and cultural conditions. For instance, their fictional characters often exhibit an existential isolation that emerges from the awareness of living in cities surrounded by an enormous expanse of desolate lands or resulting from their status as newcomers to city neighborhoods flooded with the latest wave of immigrants from distant lands. Hence, a general mark of this narrative is the presence of fictional characters that are cut off in the most radical way from their surroundings and from other human beings. Such lack of meaningful connections to reality and to others is often dramatized in the form of characters exhibiting a life of despair in which eccentricity and even murder happens to be the only possible alternative to express their alienating isolation. The novels of Ernesto Sábato – *El túnel* (The tunnel) and *Sobre heroes y tumbas* (On heroes and tombs) (1961) – and those of Juan Carlos Onetti – *La vida breve* (A brief life) (1950), *El astillero* (The shipyard), and *Juntacadáveres* (Body snatcher) – contain many central characters that exhibit this type of alienated existence. Other notable works associated with the Río de la Plata existential narrative are Macedonio Fernández's *Continuación de la nada* (Continuation of nothingness), and Mario Benedetti's *La tregua* (The truce).

385

A further significant Latin American contribution to philosophical literature infused with existential ideas comes from Brazil where the distinctive general topical feature is the centrality given to humor and irony. The best representative of this exploration of the human condition from a humorous perspective is the foundational narrative work by the most important Brazilian novelist of the turn of the twentieth century, Joaquim Machado de Assis. For instance, in his novel *Memórias póstumas de Brás Cubas* (The post-humous memoirs of Brás Cubas) (1881), the main character and narrator begins the story with a eulogy to the worms that have fed from his corpse. The story then develops in such a way that the traditional narrative epistemic boundaries that separate the author, the reader, and the characters are completely undermined. Soon the reader finds himself wondering if he too belongs to a larger and absurd fiction in which, like Brás Cubas, the only way to make sense of it is by bringing in a strong dose of humor and irony. In this way, Machado de Assis's work exhibits a surprisingly early presence of topics, situations, and characters later associated with the literature of the absurd, something that ended up being a determining influence in twentieth-century Brazilian literature.

However, during this same century and just as in other countries of Latin America, Brazil also produced a more austere version of existential literature. Two notable examples of this other approach are some of the works of poetry by Carlos Drummond de Andrade such as *Brejo das almas* (Morass of souls) and *Sentimento do mundo* (Feeling about the world), and some of the narrative works by Clarice Lispector such as *A maçã no escuro* (The apple in the dark) and *A paixão segundo G.H.* (The passion according to G.H.). Drummond de Andrade articulates a vision of human metaphysical isolation by exploring in his poetry the limits of language. Lispector in her narrative also explores such metaphysical isolation but through the exploration of the limits of human consciousness and the possibility of psychological fragmentation.

From a philosophical perspective the uniqueness of the literature produced in South America during the middle of the twentieth century is more evident not so much in those works that exhibit existential topics but rather in works that went beyond a purely realistic type of literature and moved into the world of the fantastic and bizarre. Most of the authors associated with this type of literature tended to favor the use of short stories. Among the key books containing these stories are Jorge Luis Borges's *Ficciones* (1944) (Fictions) and *El aleph* (1949) (The aleph); Felisberto Hernández's *Nadie encendía las lámparas* (Nobody lit the lamps) and *La casa inundada* (The inundated house); and Julio Cortázar's *Bestiario* (Bestiary), *Final del juego* (End of the game), *Las armas secretas* (Secret weapons) and *Todos los fuegos el fuego* (All fires the fire).

The fictional work of Borges not only is a prominent representative of fantastic literature but stands on its own as a towering contribution to philosophical literature. Besides his also philosophically relevant work in books of poetry like *El hacedor* (The maker) or *El oro de los tigres* (The gold of the tigers), or in essays such as *Historia de la eternidad* (History of eternity) and *Otras inquisiciones* (Other inquisitions), Borges wrote a series of short stories that are considered amongst the most fertile sources of philosophical intuitions concerning topics such as the nature of time and space, the boundaries of reason and language, the problem of personal identity, the existence of alternative universes, the ontology of literary objects, and free will.

Although Borges was not a professional philosopher and did not try to articulate anything resembling a systematic philosophical theory, it is possible to find in his work recurrent philosophical positions, for instance, a steadfast skepticism concerning our understanding of reality and a constant suggestion that perhaps the only way to make sense of reality would be to treat it as a sort of metaphysical fiction. But perhaps the most significant philosophical contribution by Borges resides in his masterful capacity to articulate through his short stories compelling philosophical puzzles, namely, fundamental questions to which every conceivable answer seems inadequate and that often take the form of conceptually possible scenarios. The following is just one example of Borges' contribution to philosophy through the articulation of a puzzle by the use of a thought experiment, in this case dealing with the ontology of literary artworks.

In what is in fact his first published short story, entitled "Pierre Menard, autor del Quijote" (Pierre Menard, author of Don Quixote), Borges invites us to imagine a French writer of the late nineteenth century who intends and succeeds in writing a novel which has exactly the same text as the classic Don Quijote written centuries earlier by Miguel de Cervantes. Menard accomplishes this incredible feat not by copying or remembering the text of Cervantes's famous novel, but by undergoing an otherwise normal process of creation. In order to establish the incredible claim that in fact we are dealing with two different novels that share a single text, one authored by Cervantes and another by Menard, the narrator of the story proposes the existence of properties that separate the two novels. Among the properties that distinguish them are, first, Menard's choice for the setting of his novel, namely, the land of Carmen during the century of the battle of Lepanto and Lope de Vega, and, second, Menard's use of a Spanish infused with an archaic style that suffers from a certain affectation, in contrast to Cervantes's style, completely normal for an early seventeenth-century author. If indeed these and other features are sufficient to distinguish two different works that nevertheless share a common text, then Borges has managed to show that the ontological distinction between literary artworks and their texts is a principled one. Thus, in the hands of Borges a philosophical puzzle like the one arising from the ontological reality of literary artworks finds not only a wonderful articulation in the form of a short story but a potential philosophical solution in the form of a compelling thought experiment.

Another way in which philosophical considerations appear in literary artworks has to do with general conceptual frameworks like the one that establishes a metaphysical distinction between the human and the natural spheres. According to this distinction, there is a sphere corresponding to human reality in which objects are conceived as belonging to a comprehensible order governed by artificial and purposeful rules. There is also a sphere that corresponds to the natural world in which objects are seen as belonging to a system governed by laws that are indifferent to human goals and desires. Very often such a metaphysical separation of the human and natural worlds is also conceived as staging an ongoing clash between the two in which the natural world typically overcomes the human world. A geographical region where nature acquires the enormous proportions of the Amazon jungle or the Andean cordillera is bound to produce an impression on the people who live there who consequently are inclined to accept a version of such a metaphysical picture.

The clash between the human and the natural spheres is particularly noticeable in the literature produced by the first Europeans who arrived to the Americas. Whether these authors were conquistadores, friars, or searchers for mythical riches, they struggled with an American continent's challenge in the form of its overwhelming size and

387

unknown natural reality. Their perceived struggle against a radically different reality sometimes led to a serious attempt to try to understand it by an effort to chart the territory and its inhabitants with all the epistemic and ethical challenges associated with such an enterprise. Some representative examples of this type of literature are accounts of the new land emphasizing the novel fauna and flora of the region, as in Gonzalo Fernández de Oviedo's *Sumario de la natural historia de las Indias* (A summary of the natural history of the Indies) and *Historia natural y general de las Indias* (The natural and general history of the Indies), or personal chronicles of expeditions that took their narrators to strange and dangerous regions, as in Alvar Núñez Cabeza de Vaca's *Naufragios* (Shipwrecks) account of his wonderings for nine years in the deserts of North America.

However, it is during the twentieth century that a type of literature that captures the opposition between the human and natural spheres emerges in the form of a string of literary masterpieces. For instance, the Uruguayan Horacio Quiroga in a book of short stories entitled *Cuentos de amor de locura y de muerte* (Stories of love, madness, and death) described the delirious desolation of characters surrounded by an inscrutable and maddening jungle. This was a profound expression of the perils of confronting nature. Later, in *Los pasos perdidos* (The lost steps) the Cuban Alejo Carpentier used the intractable Amazon jungle as the background for an individual's search for his identity under the excuse of searching for the origin of music, leading to his helpless metaphysical dissolution in the form of losing both his most important musical composition and his most significant human relationship. And in such works as *La hojarasca* (Leaf storm) and particularly *Cien años de soledad* (One hundred years of solitude), the Colombian Gabriel García Marquez played the role of an implacable demiurge who seals the fate of the Buendía family and the whole town of Macondo by placing them in the midst of an unforgiving and ultimately invincible jungle that swallows up everything recognizably human.

Perhaps the most radical of these types of literary works in which nature acquires such a metaphysical standing is found in what is often considered the greatest Brazilian novel of the twentieth century, namely, João Guimarães Rosa's *Grande sertão: veredas* (The devil pay in the backlands) (1956). In this extremely complex novel Rosa presents the vast and desolate land of the Brazilian region known as the "sertão" not just as an external world defiant to the human will but rather as an immense theater of consciousness. Here, nature's imposing and unlimited reality becomes assimilated into the consciousness of the novel's main character in such a way that the metaphysical opposition between the human and natural spheres is resolved in the most sweeping form: the sertão becomes an indistinguishable extension of the main character's inner life.

Ethics and Politics

The fact that the American territories conquered by the Europeans were considered a New World led to the inevitable question concerning the type of society that was desirable in this new land. The answer came from the secular and religious powers in terms of appealing to their respective worldly and otherworldly domains of influence as

388

sources of inspiration and legitimacy in order to promote the adoption of particular social models. What is fascinating about this inventive process of conceptualizing and sometimes putting into practice new societal models is the diversity and creativity that went into it. For it is possible to find among the different political and social models not only the strictly hierarchical structures that mirrored those in place in the European conquering societies, but also new visions proposing alternative ways of governing and structuring the newly founded societies. In the case of Latin America, its literature reflected this social and political thought in works that contain philosophical contributions to the ethical and political dimensions of a still ongoing social and political process.

Some of the earliest literary works having a significant ethical and political dimension were those that dealt with the question concerning the social status of the inhabitants of the Americas. They are found in the attempts by the European conquerors to make sense of the indigenous American population's moral and political rights. The debate was especially acute during the first years after the conquest in which the very status of the local inhabitants as humans and then subjects of the Spanish empire was publicly examined by some of the leading thinkers of this period. Among them was Bartolomé de las Casas whose *Brevísima historia de la destrucción de las Indias* (1552) was particularly influential in establishing the profoundly unethical conduct of the people who carried out the conquest and its disastrous consequences for the indigenous cultures of the Americas. The debate concerning the moral and political rights of the conquered indigenous population was related to a broader effort begun earlier in Europe by humanist authors like Desiderius Erasmus and Thomas More who tried to put forth alternative social models in order to realize the ideals of a renewed Christianity based on a far more equitable distribution of wealth and resources. In fact, people such as the bishop of Michoacán Vasco de Quiroga used works like More's *Utopia* as models to structure some newly founded towns in the viceroyalty of New Spain that were under his direct influence.

Notwithstanding the efforts of people like las Casas and Quiroga to ameliorate the conditions of the local indigenous population, for all purposes the general political and social reality was one of destitution and practical slavery. It did not take long before such grim social conditions appeared in literary works produced most often by anonymous indigenous authors. Sometimes these literary expressions took the form of explicit and quite graphic works like the *Códice Osuna* (Codex Osuna) that portrays the terrible social and legal situation of the indigenous population living in Mexico City in the middle of the sixteenth century. Other times these works were more indirect in their critical stance toward the colonial status quo, as in the play *Ollantay* based on a pre-Columbian legend and written in the Quechua language. In this work an alternative utopian idyllic Amerindian state is presented in contrast not just to the oppressing political establishment under Spanish colonial rule but also to the European type of utopian state that essentially prolonged foreign social values.

Despite the existence of indigenous literary expressions that reflected their social conditions, the fact remains that during the colonial period the voice of the powerless sectors of society were in general silenced by a very effective control exercised by the central political and religious authorities. However, even within such closed societies important non-indigenous voices were heard in the form of a literature that by using subtle means of expression presented their critical take on the prevalent situation.

389

Amongst these voices one stands out for combining a sophisticated ethically conscious stance with the highest artistic creativity. This voice belongs to the Mexican nun Sor Juana Inés de la Cruz, one of the greatest authors of the Spanish language. She was a prolific author who published poems, plays, and essays often dealing with philosophically relevant issues. Her contribution to the emergent cultural and national identity of the people of the Americas during the colonial period, and, perhaps more significantly, to the ethical and political consciousness of marginalized sectors of the colonial society is found in two sets of literary artworks, one dealing with issues about cultural identity and the other with issues about gender.

The first set of Sor Juana's works (1952) with a significant contribution to ethical and political issues includes a collection of *villancicos* or carols that were sung in religious festivals and a *loa* or a short introductory allegorical play to her theatrical work *El divino Narciso* (The Divine Narcissus). In the *villancicos* Sor Juana is capable of capturing the unique but subdued perspectives of several subcultures of the viceroyalty such as Indians, Mestizos, Africans, and Creoles. In her *loa*, Sor Juana goes a step further by assimilating the ancient culture of the Aztecs to the new concert of Christian nations through an exercise of cultural and religious syncretism whose goal is to legitimize an emerging Mexican identity rooted in a glorious pre-Hispanic past. For the *loa* reinterprets ancient Aztec religious beliefs as sharing a recognizable world view compatible with Christianity, thereby making the case for their possessing a legitimate though distinct cultural identity.

The second set of relevant works containing ethical and political thoughts authored by Sor Juana includes those dealing with ideas about the oppressive situation for women living in a sexist society like colonial Spanish America. They include her famous poem, the *redondilla* "Hombres necios que acusáis a la mujer" (Foolish and unreasoning men who blame woman), and her essay-letter *Respuesta a Sor Filotea de la Cruz* (Answer to Sor Filotea de la Cruz). In the *redondilla* Sor Juana exposes the hypocrisy of the gendered roles of the viceregal society which not only operated under the assumption of the inferiority and submissiveness of women but covered up such unfair reality under the pretence of defending the values of purity and decorum. In her *Respuesta* Sor Juana's own personal experience of a sexist world takes a further and dramatic turn insofar as this is her defense against the intolerant and crushing force of the male establishment that ultimately silenced her. The essay-letter was written by Sor Juana as a response to the accusation leveled against her for criticizing the Portuguese theologian Antonio de Vieyra. But the *Respuesta* shows how the essential reason behind her critics' accusation was their objection to a woman's use of her natural capacity to exercise thought and artistic creativity. Since these capacities were seen by Sor Juana and her accusers as essentially coming from God, she turned the tables on them by arguing that their reasons against a woman's use of her natural intelligence and creativity were not only morally ungrounded but against God's design. In this way, the *Respuesta* comes across as a rebellious document that can be seen as an affirmation of intelligence and critical reason when confronted with dogmatism and prejudice, an incredible feat if one also remembers that it is a document coming from a nun living inside the closed world of the colonial Spanish Counter-Reformation.

A direct move toward the need for political emancipation from the European colonial powers took place in Latin America during the eighteen and nineteenth centuries.

390

With this move came the need to provide a justification for such radical social change and just as importantly for the type of society that was proposed as the substitute for the old one. Literature was an ideal vehicle to articulate such justification and it became a central component of the thrust into independence in the form of lyrical works, narratives, and essays conveying the relevant political ideas.

A good example of how lyrical works expressed the emergent sense of a separate cultural and national identity that occurred during the late eighteenth and early nineteenth centuries is the romantic and civic poetry produced by José Joaquín de Olmedo, Andrés Bello, and José María Heredia. For instance, Olmedo (1825) in his poem "La victoria de Junín" (The victory of Junin), while offering a eulogy to the movement for independence of the emerging nations of Latin America, struggles with the fact that the emerging identity of these nations sits awkwardly between the original European and the Amerindian cultures. Around the same time, Bello (1979) produces his poems "Alocución a la poesía" (Address to poetry) and "Oda a la agricultura de la zona tórrida" (Ode to the agriculture of the Torrid Zone) where the issue of identity also emerges and is resolved by the recurrent strategy of grounding such identity on the distinctive natural reality of this region of the world. If Bello looks in the direction of nature as the touchstone for legitimizing the call for political and cultural autonomy, Heredia's poem "En el teocalli de Cholula" (At Cholula's teocalli) alludes to the ancient indigenous cultures of Latin America to give weight to similar considerations concerning the right of independence. However, in a more somber note Heredia also looks toward the ancient civilizations of the Americas as examples of the disasters of warfare and internal divisions, prefiguring what was going happen to the new nations of Latin America for the next two centuries – constantly plagued by wars and internal divisions.

Although the Latin American narrative of the nineteenth century continued the process of nationalistic and romantic justification for the then emerging identities of many countries, it is in the form of essays like Simón Bolívar's (1815) *Carta de Jamaica* (Jamaica Letter) and Domingo Faustino Sarmiento's (1845) *Facundo o civilización y barbarie* (Facundo: civilization and barbarism) that such process finds its most influential expression. In his *Carta de Jamaica* Bolívar is essentially concerned to lay the path for the autonomy of the emerging Latin American nations in terms of strategic moves that will lead to independence, for instance, by trying to establish the bankruptcy of the Spanish colonial model of governing and the readiness of the local peoples to take into their hands their own destinies. However, Bolívar was suspicious of the political view much in vogue during the eighteenth century that held the universal application of the same political model across world societies. For even though he accepted some universal principles that justify the call for national independence, he also suggested that the way in which each nation should implement its own path toward liberation and political success was directly dependent on their particular cultural, historical, and geographical reality.

Sarmiento shared with Bolívar the assumption that countries in Latin America had reached a point in their political development that called for independence from the original colonial powers. He also agreed that the actual execution of the political project called for taking into account the particular realities of the future nations in terms of their distinctive culture, history, and geography. However, while Bolívar was prepared to move in the direction of recognizing the open-endedness of the historical

391

process that could lead Latin American nations to a successful articulation of their autonomy, Sarmiento was far more inclined to believe that the forces of historical change were determined by such factors as geographical location, level of education, and even ethnic composition. Moreover, Sarmiento famously embraced a sociocultural dualism in which civilization was opposed by the forces of barbarism embodied in the rough social milieu of non-urban communities. Echoing the metaphysical clash between the human and the natural spheres, Sarmiento saw a similar clash between civilization and barbarism, the first identified with the sophisticated Western urbanite of a city like Buenos Aires and the second with the wild cunning gaucho of the Argentinean pampas. Because of his own political experience, Sarmiento also associated the possibility of a liberal democracy with the forces of civilization and the constant menace of dictatorships with the forces of barbarism. Hence, he believed that in countries like Argentina the only real hope that they could reach their full potential was in a sort of planned social engineering involving the introduction of social groups that had with them the promise of true civilization and the gradual elimination of those other groups that were unfit for such transformation.

Facundo o civilización y barbarie also contains as one of its core elements a meditation about power and the role of powerful figures, a subject that became an obsessive focus of attention for future Latin American writers. Both Bolívar and Sarmiento were themselves historical figures who, besides meditating about the nature of political power, also were in a direct position to exercise it, in Bolívar's case as a leading caudillo for the independence of South American nations and president of several of them, and in Sarmiento's case as president of Argentina. The irony is that despite their personal and intellectual challenges to the established autocracies they were powerless to avoid what became a scourge of most Latin American nations for the next two centuries, namely, the constant presence of authoritarian strong men in the form of chieftains, dictators, and revolutionary leaders. Nonetheless, it was with the work especially of Sarmiento that a very important subject of meditation and ultimately inspiration for Latin American literature began. That is, a meditation about the nature of power and its extreme exercise by such sinister figures as the Latin American dictators Juan Manuel de Rosas, José Gaspar Rodríguez de Francia, Manuel José Estrada Cabrera, and Rafael Leónidas Trujillo. Some of the most distinguished narrative works of this type are Miguel Angel Asturias's *El señor Presidente* (The President), Alejo Carpentier's *El reino de este mundo* (The kingdom of this world), Augusto Roa Bastos's *Yo, el Supremo* (The Supreme) (1974), Gabriel García Marquez's *El otoño del patriarca* (The autumn of the patriarch), and Mario Vargas Llosa's *La fiesta del chivo* (The feast of the goat).

Sarmiento's inclination toward the implementation of a social engineering project was not an isolated case but rather a pervasive frame of mind that took hold of the imagination of many Latin Americans politicians and authors during the second half of the nineteenth century. A new century was required for these ideas to find their criticism inside and outside the world of Latin American literature. The change had one of its fundamental roots in the slow but definitive recognition of the mixed racial heritage of most Latin American countries and the suggestion by many authors that such reality, far from being a disadvantage, was full of promise. In literature the transition occurs with the "costumbrista" literature of the end of the nineteenth century, and with essays like the very influential *Ariel* by José Enrique Rodó published in 1900. In these works and, above all, in Rodó's essay a new strategy to ground a Latin American identity is born, alluding not just to the local historical and geographical circumstances but to a critical opposition to alternative versions of Western civilization in terms of the emergence of a different type of Latin American identity.

A significant development of the new sense of identity was the proposed existence of epistemic perspectives associated with the emerging majorities in many Latin American countries often based on a mixture of races and ethnicities. Initially literature captured such epistemic perspectives by the use of a sophisticated and highly educated form of expression as in José Vasconcelos's philosophical essays *La raza cósmica* (The cosmic race) and *Indología* (Indology) where he praises in particular the *mestizo*. Later the literature that tried to make sense of such epistemic perspectives took the form of an excursion into the real lives and particular language of this social group's members. Two notable examples are the novels *Los ríos profundos* (Deep rivers) by the Peruvian José María Arguedas who explores the *mestizo* perspective of the Andean region, and *Changó, el gran putas* (Shango, the baddest SOB) by the Colombian Manuel Zapata Olivella who offers a similar exploration this time of the Afro-Latin American reality.

In this form a considerable amount of Latin American literature produced during the past two centuries, when change and revolution permeated the region, ended up exhibiting political and moral content dealing with issues such as the possibility of a less unjust society, the nature of human rights, the recognition of diversity and pluralism, and the appropriation of marginal traditions. Indeed, the literary works that contained these ideas became key elements in many of the Latin American political movements of liberation and empowerment. Whether it is with the revolutionary emancipating agendas contained in the works of such figures as José Martí and José Carlos Mariátegui, or the ideological novels and poetry of José Revueltas, Nicanor Parra, and Mario Bennedetti, or more recently with the works of Latino-women, Chicano, gay, or "testimonio" literature by authors such as Cherríe Moraga, Rolando Hinojosa, Manuel Puig, Reinaldo Arenas, Miguel Barnet, or Rigoberta Menchú, a fundamentally political conception and use of literature became a central feature of Latin American literature.

Aesthetic Worldviews

A prime example within the Latin American literary tradition of a general aesthetic outlook that amounts to a worldview is found in the baroque, above all during the colonial period. Although the baroque begun as an artistic style introduced with the aim of satisfying an aesthetic sensibility linked to the European movement of Counter-Reformation, it took on a life of its own when it reached the Spanish and Portuguese American colonies. Here the dynamic inclusiveness of baroque aesthetics was used to capture the reality of a society that saw itself as being in a process of constant transformation involving the fusion of significantly different cultural and ethnic traditions. Furthermore, the inclusiveness of baroque aesthetics was very well placed to deal with the extraordinary richness and diversity of the land by absorbing it into its exuberant artistic products. In this way, the Latin American version of baroque aesthetics not only abandoned something like the Renaissance aesthetic model inspired by the doctrine of *imitatio* and classical proportion but reacted against such models by stressing aesthetic features like the new, the unexpected, the marvelous, the motley, and the disproportionate. In the case of literature the baroque expressed such aesthetic features by employing creative strategies like substitution, proliferation, condensation, permutation, intertextuality, intratextuality, and parody.

The most significant literary aesthetic manifestations of the Latin American colonial baroque outlook are found in the seventeenth century with such works as Bernardo de Balbuena's *Grandeza mexicana* (Mexican greatness) and again in the extraordinary work of Sor Juana Inés de la Cruz (1952), whose philosophical poem "Primero sueño" (First I dream) captures much of what is philosophically relevant from this aesthetic worldview. In her long epistemological poem Sor Juana presents an intellectual voyage by means of poetry that begins and ends inside a dream but that actually reveals an effort by the intellect to comprehend reality. By using an eclectic mixture of ideas coming from among other sources the Hermetic and Neo-Platonist traditions, Sor Juana not only places the quest for knowledge at the core of human endeavors but suggests the ultimate mysterious character of reality. Poetry then becomes also a sort of intellectual revelation about the limits of our understanding. In this sense, Sor Juana's philosophical poem sits uneasily between the skeptically infused thinking of modern philosophers like Descartes and Pascal and later romantic views that consider the quest for knowledge as the highest exercise of individual autonomy. Furthermore, given the enormity of the epistemic challenge posed by an essentially incomprehensible reality, the insistence to carry on with the effort to understand it mirrors the analogous rebellious stance that Sor Juana displayed in her musings about gender and identity.

In the twentieth century the work of Sor Juana and other baroque writers was recognized as a profound and still enormously fertile aesthetic worldview amenable to further exploration in the form of poetry, narrative, and literary criticism. Inspired by the work of the colonial baroque artists in literature, a whole movement identified as neo-baroque sprang up particularly amongst Cuban authors. Some neo-baroque outstanding literary products coming from Cuba are the novels *El siglo de las luces* (The Age of Enlightenment) by Alejo Carpentier, *Paradiso* by José Lezama Lima, and *Tres tristes tigres* (Three trapped tigers) by Guillermo Cabrera Infante. However, it is also possible to amplify the notion of a Latin American contemporary baroque aesthetic worldview to include among its representatives the work of one of the greatest literary figures of the twentieth century, namely, the work of the Mexican poet and essayist Octavio Paz. For instance, if there is a general feature that permeates Paz's essays, it is his synthetic capacity to assimilate in a coherent whole an enormously rich set of cultural and artistic traditions that mirrors nicely the baroque capacity to incorporate a diversity of sources in ways that other aesthetic approaches would find impossible.

Of Paz's fecund essayistic production two works can be singled out as capturing key stages in his intellectual and philosophical development. The first is perhaps his most famous essay, *El laberinto de la soledad* (1950) (The labyrinth of solitude). This essay constitutes Paz's effort to understand Mexican culture by recognizing its idiosyncratic perspective about universal issues such as human solitude. For Paz, cultures in general deal with this fundamental human trait by creating symbolic spaces whose main goal is to redeem human solitude in the form of meaningful practices. In the case of

Mexicans these symbolic spaces are found in ritualistic practices like the sacred ceremonies associated with the Day of the Dead and the more profane celebratory explosions related to traditional fiestas. The second essay, *El arco y la lira* (1956) (The bow and the lyre), is one that continued Paz's self-reflective attitude, but this time his focus is his own artistic activity as a poet. In this work Paz offers an account of literature in the form of a poetics. The question about the exact nature of whatever is communicated through a poem leads him to an extensive investigation into the possibility of reducing poetic utterances to other forms of expression and ultimately the general reducibility of artistic properties. Paz answers the latter by stressing the irreducibility of poetic experience, the function of poetry as a privileged tool for knowledge, and the identification of artistic properties with such poetic experience. In this way, poetry is understood as a sort of revelation capable of being universal and public at the same time that it is profoundly personal. The echoes of Sor Juana Inés de la Cruz's approach to art and poetry are unmistakable. It should not come as a surprise that the best essay about her work, *Sor Juana Inés de la Cruz o las trampas de la fe* (1982) (Sor Juana or, the traps of faith), was also penned by Paz who, with this work, closes a baroque circle by using his study of Sor Juana to indirectly shed light on his own practice as an outstanding poet and thinker.

In conclusion, Latin American literature contains a wealth of ideas that are not just recognizably philosophical but original in their way of dealing with fundamental issues related to metaphysics and epistemology, ethics and politics, and aesthetic worldviews. Furthermore, the Latin American literary works that articulate such philosophically relevant content are exceptional in their artistic and cultural merits providing an additional reason to explore and appreciate them.

Related chapters: 1 Pre-Columbian Philosophies; 3 Colonial Thought; 16 Language and Colonization; 18 Identity and Philosophy; 30 Cultural Studies.

References

Assis, J. M. (1881). *Memórias póstumas de Brás Cubas*. Rio de Janeiro: Typographia Nacional.
Bello, A. (1979). *Obra literaria*. Selección y prólogo, Pedro Grases & Cronología Oscar Samoano Urdaneta. Caracas: Biblioteca Ayacucho.
Bolívar, S. (1815). Carta de Jamaica. In V. Lecuna (Ed.). *Obras completas*. La Habana: Lexis.
Borges, J. L. (1944). *Ficciones*. Buenos Aires: Sur.
Borges, J. L. (1949). *El aleph*. Buenos Aires: Losada.
de la Cruz, Sor Juana Inés. (1952). *Obras completas de Sor Juana Inés de la Cruz*. (Alfonso Méndez Plancarte, Ed.). Mexico and Buenos Aires: Fondo de Cultura Económica.
de las Casas, B. (1987). *Brevísima relación de la destrucción de las Indias*. (A. Saint-Lu, Ed.). Madrid: Cátedra.
Gorostiza, J. (1939). *Muerte sin fin*. Mexico: Fondo de Cultura Económica.
León-Portilla, M. (1992). *Fifteen poets of the Aztec world*. Norman: University of Oklahoma Press.
Olmedo, J. J. (1825). "La victoria de Junín." In *Poesías completas*. (Aurelio Espinosa Pólit, Ed.). Mexico: Fondo de Cultura Económica, 1947.
Onetti, J. C. (1950). *La vida breve*. Buenos Aires: Sudamericana.
Paz, Octavio. (1950). *El laberinto de la soledad*. Mexico: Cuadernos Americanos, 1962.

Paz, O. (1956). *El arco y la lira.* Mexico: Fondo de Cultura Económica.

Paz, O. (1988). *Sor Juana or, the traps of faith.* (M. Sayers Peden, Trans.). Cambridge, MA: Harvard University Press (Original work published 1982).

Popol Vuh: The Mayan book of the dawn of life. (1985). (D. Tedlock, Trans.). New York: Simon & Schuster.

Roa Bastos, A. (1974). *Yo, el Supremo.* Buenos Aires: Siglo Vintiuno Editores.

Rosa, J. G. (1956). *Grande sertão: veredas.* Rio de Janeiro: Livraria José Olympio Editora.

Sábato, E. (1961). *Sobre héroes y tumbas.* Buenos Aires: Fabril.

Sarmiento, D. F. (1845). *Facundo o civilización y barbarie.* In *Obras de D. F. Sarmiento.* Paris: Belen Hermanos, 1885.

Villaurrutia, X. (1938). *Nostalgia de la muerte.* Buenos Aires: Sur.

Further Reading

González Echevarría, R., & Pupo-Walker, E. (Eds). (1996). *The Cambridge history of Latin American literature* (3 vols.). Cambridge: Cambridge University Press.

Smith, V. (Ed.). (1997). *Encyclopedia of Latin American literature.* London: Fitzroy Dearborn.

de la Cruz, Sor Juana Inés. (1988). *A Sor Juana anthology* (Alan S. Trueblood, Trans. and Intro.). Cambridge, MA: Harvard University Press.

León-Portilla, M. (1963). *Aztec thought and culture: a study of the ancient Nahuatl mind.* Norman: University of Oklahoma Press.

Nuccetelli, S. (2002). *Latin American thought: philosophical problems and arguments.* Boulder, CO: Westview Press.

Fernández Moreno, C. (Ed.). (1980). *Latin America in its literature.* (M. G. Berg, Trans.). London: Holmes & Meier Publishers (Original work published 1972).

28

Feminist Philosophy

OFELIA SCHUTTE AND MARÍA LUISA FEMENÍAS

This chapter focuses primarily on contemporary feminist philosophy in Latin America. By "contemporary" we mean feminist philosophy since the 1980s. It is during this period – and particularly since the 1990s – that feminist philosophy has become a recognized academic field in Latin America. Following an introduction situating its rise in a historical context, we examine methodological questions regarding feminist perspectives on activism, the use of gender as a category of analysis, the analysis of ethnicity/race and multiculturalism, and the uses and appropriations of Michel Foucault's discourse theory and Judith Butler's deconstruction. Attention to these methodological issues is crucial if we are to chart the emergence of this field and understand what it is about historical and cultural conditions in Latin America that fuels and energizes feminist debates. The key methodological issues we discuss are specifically linked to assessing the connections, broadly construed, between feminist theory and practice. Our overall analysis links up the achievements of feminist philosophy to the democratization processes in Latin America.

Feminist Philosophy in a Historical Context

Feminist philosophy does not function as an isolated field of knowledge. To a greater or lesser degree, it is interactive in dynamic dialogue or tension with feminist activism in the larger society as well as with interdisciplinary currents in feminist theory. To these extra-philosophical points of reference in the particular case of Latin America we must add the intra-philosophical transnational or international influences of U.S. and Western European feminisms which are filtered into academic feminist philosophy in Latin America through a variety of channels. These channels include the academic and personal experiences of Latin American feminists who have studied or received graduate degrees in philosophy in the United States or Western Europe (later returning to their countries of origin); the availability of books, journals, e-mail lists, and other transnational contacts through the internet and more traditional means; professional contacts generated at various international congresses; the seminars and colloquia offered at Latin American universities by Anglophone and Western European feminist philosophers; and so on. In other words, there is an overabundance of sources influencing the production of feminist philosophy in Latin America, a significant portion of which has extra-philosophical and/or extra-continental influences. And yet, we can also identify a strong tradition of feminist and women's movements in Latin America, whose debates and agenda energize and invigorate the feminist philosophical scene.

Like its U.S. counterparts, Latin American feminisms are often distinguished broadly according to a "first-wave" and "second-wave" periodization. The historical and political assessments of feminisms' achievements in Latin America, however, should not be modeled on the chronologies and criteria established outside the region. In the past, such a tendency has led to the distortion and devaluation of Latin American women's achievements and to the failure to understand the complexity of local practices (Femenías, 2006, p. 112). While avoiding a linear and Anglo-Eurocentric sense of periodization, it may still be useful to speak of "waves" in a qualified sense in order to mark the differences of emphasis and peaks of mobilization inevitably resulting from the historical and cultural orientations of feminist philosophy and the feminist movement. Given the uneven paths taken by academic feminisms in different countries and regions, it may be premature to speak of a "third wave," although we will suggest such an option in our analysis.

We could say in general – keeping in mind that generalizations regarding Latin American intellectual and cultural characteristics are subject to exception and contestation – that questions and movements regarding women's suffrage and the first print defenses of a libertarian female sexuality constitute the first wave. Historically, the first wave occurs in the last decades of the nineteenth century and up to the 1930s and '40s. This period coincides politically with the mobilization of women on behalf of liberal and socialist political movements, although the impact of anarchism at various stages of political mobilization can also be felt. Women's right to an education up to the superior levels – a vindication already voiced in the colonial seventeenth century by the acclaimed Sor Juana Inés de la Cruz (known retroactively as the first Hispanic American feminist) – was a matter of agreement among the early feminist activists, along with the right to vote. Together with the suffragist goals, the majoritarian feminist agenda of those decades was marked by the right to the administration of inherited and acquired property, the legal recognition of children born out of wedlock, and the strengthening of women's labor rights and rights within the family, including the right to divorce. More controversial among the early feminists were the demands to break down the "double" morality with regard to sexuality, which allowed men sexual freedom but constrained at least middle-class women, if not others, to a code of pre-marital virginity, normative if not compulsory heterosexuality, and monogamy within marriage. The demands for sexual freedom divided women who identified with the rhetorically conservative "moral" approach to attain political suffrage and with some civil (education, labor) rights and responsibilities, and those who embraced more egalitarian views on social and political change. At the 1910 International Feminist Congress held in Buenos Aires, the first to be held in Latin America, the former identified themselves as "feminine" and the latter as "feminist." The first group relied on such essentialist notions as women being the "soul" of the nation, thereby deserving full representation in the nation's political and economic life. Such an argument, which called on women's incorporation into the public sphere as a way of "elevating" the conscience of the nation, reifies the view (usually applied in a paternalistic and sexist manner) that women are somehow purer or more virtuous than men. In contrast to this ideologically conservative strategy, the feminist sexual libertarians tried to push forward a more democratic, egalitarian agenda, but they did not find enough national support to obtain consensus on the latter.

A relatively dormant period of feminist activism occurs around the middle of the twentieth century once the vote and a great number of civil, economic, and political rights were obtained. The "second wave" emerges in the 1960s partly as a collateral side-effect of the progressive social and political changes of this historical period, including the egalitarian agenda of the 1959 Cuban revolution. But, as was the case in the United States, feminist women challenged the masculine-dominant politics of the period, so that the autonomous women's/feminist movement in various parts of continental Latin America attains visibility in the course of the 1970s. This period, however, coincides with a surge of widespread anti-communist political repression. In 1973 the constitutional governments of Bolivia and Uruguay were overturned; this was followed in the same year by a military coup against the constitutional government of socialist Salvador Allende in Chile. Others fell in chain-like effect, including the government of María Estela Martínez de Perón in 1976 in Argentina. The military dictatorships in the Southern Cone and the various dictatorships in Central America left hundreds of thousands of dead or "disappeared" throughout Latin America in the repression and civil wars that took place during this period. This means that the emerging second-wave feminist organizing and activism as well as the academic freedom needed to support critical philosophy at universities were either formally suspended or driven underground in countries marked by these national political conflicts. Paradoxically for feminists caught in such circumstances, the United Nations organized the "Year of the Woman" (1975) followed by the "Decade on Women" (1975–85). This process placed women's issues at the forefront of an international agenda concerned with fostering global peace and development. Whether impelled to join this global project or to contest it on far more radical and autonomous local grounds, as happened in the case of some radical feminist groups in Mexico (where the 1975 UN conference was held), the invocation of "la causa de las mujeres" (women's cause) became linked to grassroots as well as high-end proposals for the democratization of Latin American societies and governments. In Chile the famous slogan "democracia en el país y en la casa" (democracy in the country and at home) energized feminists and pro-democracy advocates against the regime of Augusto Pinochet. In Argentina the famous protests of the Mothers of the Plaza de Mayo on behalf of their maternal and human rights to locate the disappeared broke down the legitimation of state violence and the dictatorship's "pro-family" façade. Out of these painful and traumatic political and everyday life situations it is clear to see how Latin American women and feminists gradually elaborated the important conception of women's rights as human rights and of human rights as inclusive of women's rights. By the time partial or full transitions to democracy took place in the 1980s in the countries moving out of the dictatorships, a network of Latin American women and feminist activists had been built whose rallying points were the Encuentros (meetings) held every couple of years throughout the region, beginning in 1981 (Alvarez et al., 2002a).

It was also in the 1980s (moving into the 1990s) that Women's Studies programs and centers were organized in many Latin American universities, as was the teaching of feminist philosophy in university curricula. With rare exceptions, among which we can cite the case of the Mexican feminist philosopher Graciela Hierro (1928–2003), who introduced academic discussions of feminist philosophy in Mexico in the 1970s, the conditions for teaching feminist philosophy in Latin American universities did not exist until the 1990s. These conditions are still restrictive due to the combination of past political problems, current economic constraints, and the generally androcentric orientation of philosophy as an academic discipline. Nonetheless, the great advances women have made in civil society and politics both regionally and worldwide since the 1980s put great pressure on universities to support academic women's studies, gender studies, and feminist studies – trends that in the short and long term lead to a greater recognition and support for feminist philosophy.

We could speak of a third wave of feminism in Latin America linked to the impact and response to the accelerated globalization processes of neoliberal capitalism. While these effects began to be felt in the 1980s, theoretical responses to them took a while to get organized, given the sometimes chaotic circumstances of the previous political period. Moreover, a priority of the "democratic transitions" was to stabilize the restored constitutional governments. By the mid- or late 1990s and the first decade of the twenty-first century, we find a critical reexamination of the concept of democracy, with more attention paid to the differences among women, not just in terms of class and religious affiliation, but of ethnicity, race, age, and sexual orientation. At the same time, the influence of postmodern theory is more visible in Latin American feminist philosophy, not in the sense of the direct importation of European or North American philosophers as such, but in the transformative sense, for example, of using and reappropriating elements of Foucauldian discourse theory or of queer theory as developed by Judith Butler as the objects of analysis may warrant it. Likewise, although Latin American feminist philosophers and theorists generally do not view themselves as "postcolonial," there are feminist appropriations of "translation" theory (inspired by the postcolonial theorist Edward Said) and of race/ethnicity (a topic of major interest to postcolonial critics). These recent directions, which could be identified as "third wave" or at a minimum as new orientations in contemporary feminist theory and philosophy, attend to approaches and issues exceeding the previous normative paradigms conceived since the 1960s. At the same time, the second and third feminist "waves" in terms of theoretical orientation coexist synchronically (so much so that this third moment, or turn, is often collapsed into the second). Some theorists simply use the term "neofeminism" to refer to feminisms since the 1960s, at which time issues of sexual violence against women and reproductive rights were brought more forcefully to the forefront than in the earlier suffragist period (Bartra, 2006, p. 1). The slippage in identifying the more recently emerging conceptual frameworks and directions, such as those taken by postmodern and postcolonial feminisms and queer theory, is understandable given the uneven development of feminist philosophy and theory across the continent and often in the same city. We will return to this issue in the section on feminist methodologies, below. The tension between these perspectives results in contested "identity" terrains and undoubtedly in misunderstandings, regrettable but not unusual, among some feminists.

Feminist Perspectives in Philosophy

Within the vast network of feminist perspectives it is possible to delineate some highlights in the last three decades. The late 1980s brought together the first international congresses of feminist philosophy held in Mexico City (1988) and Buenos Aires (1989) (Schutte, 1994, 1993, p. 212). Prior to this, Graciela Hierro is credited with organizing the first panel on feminism at a national philosophy congress in 1979. Throughout the 1980s and 1990s Hierro developed a feminist ethics of pleasure, for which she is best remembered (Hierro, 2007). In the late 1980s, the Argentine Association for Women in Philosophy was formed. This group produced the journal *Hiparquia* (1988–99), so far the only journal of feminist philosophy published in Latin America. The journal's founding members were Ana María Bach, María Luisa Femenías, Alicia Gianella, Clara Kushnir, Diana Maffía, Margarita Roulet, María Spadaro, and María Isabel Santa Cruz. In addition to the above and to those whose contributions we mention in our extended discussion of methodology, a list of feminist philosophers in Latin America includes, among others: María Pía Lara and María Herrera (Mexico; critical theory); Margarita Valdés (Mexico; applied ethics); Gloria Comesaña-Santalices (Venezuela; French existentialism, Beauvoir); Laura Gioscia (Uruguay; sexual minorities and women's rights). In feminist theology Virginia Azcuy and Marta Palacio (Argentina) are recognized in phenomenology. The question of the nature of feminist philosophy in Latin America does not arise for most feminist philosophers unless they are specifically dealing with the connection between theory and practice in the region (or closely related topics). By exploring key issues in feminist methodology as a historically situated debate arising from a Latin American context, however, we are poised to conceptualize some of the salient parameters distinguishing contemporary feminist philosophy in this region from its counterparts elsewhere.

Feminist Methodologies: Key Issues

Our goal here is to map a comprehensive conception of "feminist philosophy" born out of its own practices and debates in Latin America as theorists reflect on the meanings and challenges of feminism in their own societies and local contexts. Our conceptual map is not expected to coincide necessarily with traditional areas of expertise in philosophy as this discipline is currently subdivided. The thematic frameworks we identify and develop are based on "on site" discussions of key issues in feminist methodology. Among these we note (1) the dichotomy between academic feminism and feminist activism, and ways to mediate them; (2) the use and abuse of "gender" as a category of analysis; (3) the incorporation of ethnicity/race in Latin American feminist studies; (4) the uses and appropriations of Foucauldian discourse theory and Butlerian deconstruction.

The activist/academic dichotomy, and ways to mediate them

No less than in the United States, feminist philosophy in Latin America is challenged by the tension between feminist activism and academic feminism. The demands of

401

academic feminism and the professionalization of philosophy can place academic feminists at a distance from the battle for women's rights and for social change in the larger social and political arena. The tension between the academy and activism can be mediated by feminist philosophers in several ways, however. Among these are: the positing of feminist theory as a form of expertise whose object of knowledge is feminist activism; understanding feminist theory in terms of its ongoing, dynamic relationship between theory and praxis; and formulating feminist theory as the outcome of women's critical reflections on their lived experiences and on how the sense of a self, even a militant self, emerges specifically in interaction with and among women struggling for change. These three approaches to combining theory and action (or activism) need not be exhaustive of all possible approaches to the tension between academic and activist feminism, nor are they necessarily exclusionary, in the sense that taking one of these approaches necessarily rules out another. What is at stake here is more often a style of doing theory, given a researcher's feminist commitments, her field of specialization and, within those fields, the issues that take on primary attention on account of their special interest or urgency.

The first approach mentioned above takes feminist theory as a form of expertise whose object of analysis is feminist activism – and more broadly, the women's movement in particular and women's role in social movements in general. Social science research as the theoretical analysis of social movements has contributed significantly to Latin American feminist theory. For example, the Argentine social theorist Elizabeth Jelin (1996, 1990) has written extensively on the role of the "new" social movements in the transitions to democracy in the 1980s as well as on the issue of women's rights as human rights. One important characteristic of social movements is their grassroots origin beyond the traditional structures of political parties. Feminist scholarship in the social sciences has been able to target the study of women's movements and of women's participation in various other social movements, thereby highlighting new forms of women's agency as citizens, women's contributions to democratic processes in Latin America, and women's capacity to organize on behalf of issues such as the need for safe drinking water, adequate housing, reproductive health, indigenous people's rights, and human rights. In addition to these larger social or community oriented issues, as the feminist movement grew, research has been applied to the analysis of the feminist movement as such and its impact on society. For example, the Cuban-born political scientist Sonia Alvarez, both singly and in collaboration with other researchers, has provided numerous theoretical analyses of the feminist movement in Latin America (Alvarez et al., 2002a; Alvarez, 1990, 2002b).

A second way of relating academic theory to activism is to focus on the dynamics of the relationship between feminist theory and political practice. The Mexican feminist philosopher Griselda Gutiérrez, for example, argues for a pluralistic approach *within feminist theory* to the analysis and interpretation of social movements. She stresses, too, that it is also the plurality of different currents in the feminist movement which historically can be said to give birth to the use of gender as an analytic category in feminist theory (Gutiérrez, 2002, p. 9). Her non-reductionistic approach to feminist theory and practice allows for dialogue and debate within each category (theory, practice) as well as for the actualization of an ongoing dynamism and contestation across them. This pluralistic approach contrasts with reductionistic approaches to what it means to be a feminist or, for that matter, what it means to be a woman, whose effect is to narrow down the "permissible" or "legitimate" rationale for feminist methodology.

A third way of relating theory and practice/activism is through the politicization of human subjectivity and through the use of the personal narrative, combined with analysis, regarding the critical understanding of feminism and of the feminist movement in terms of one's lived experience. While some variations of this approach are based on local adaptations of the transnational radical feminist maxim "the personal is political," others more broadly correlate the recent history of the feminist movement in Latin America with reflections gathered from one's personal experience. A good example of a feminist philosophical analysis born out of this perspective is the work of the Panamanian philosopher Urania Ungo. She bases her approach on the view that the goal of the feminist movement in Latin America was not just to change the institutions, but to change life itself (*cambiar la vida misma*) (Ungo, 2002, p. 97). This perspective was reached by Latin American women who met at the first Encuentro Feminista Latinoamericano y del Caribe held in 1981. Ungo traces the history of the Latin American feminist movement in the last two decades of the twentieth century, along with the challenges and conflicts women have faced and still face, in terms of this radical existential and transformational goal, which is at once both personal and political (Ungo, 2000).

The use and abuse of "gender" as a category of analysis

Another methodological debate centers on the legitimacy of using the category of "gender" as a foundational category of feminist analysis. This debate is too quickly over-simplified if it is seen simply as one between "pro-gender" feminists and their opponents (however the latter identify themselves). There are both conceptual and circumstantial reasons why the so-called "gender perspective" has been criticized and at times repudiated. Let us point to the circumstantial factors first before addressing the conceptual.

Early second-wave theory in Latin America often relied on a conceptual framework in which "patriarchy" was the dominant target of analysis and sociopolitical change. While the term "androcentrism" was also used in feminist discourse, the foundational critique of "patriarchy" (loosely understood as the socioeconomic and ideological conditions legitimating the power of men and of male-dominant institutions over women) served as the glue that bound many feminists. When "patriarchy" was posited as the unitary cause of women's oppression, the category "woman" (or the plural "women") functioned to designate the subject(s) of liberation. On one hand, the axis patriarchy–woman served to identify the subordination, exclusion, or marginality that women suffered in a patriarchal society. On the other, it served to mobilize female subjects toward their own emancipation and the transformation of a patriarchal and masculine-dominant world. In addition to the unitary account of oppression linked to the category of "patriarchy," a second focus of analysis, "capitalism," was often adopted, whether as part of, or alongside, that of "patriarchy." In this second case, feminism called for economic justice in addition to, or alongside, the end to masculine dominance. For many women who became radicalized during this period, either "patriarchy" or "capitalist patriarchy" became the object of militant protest and political transformation. Some found it politically unacceptable when feminist theory evolved, shedding these older

403

conceptual frameworks. The new terminology focused on "gender" as a foundational category of analysis, replacing "woman" and the corresponding notion of her exclusion / subordination in "patriarchy." A new way of speaking and theorizing about women's issues became dominant. In Latin America, it became known as "la perspectiva de género" (the gender perspective) or "el enfoque de género" (the gender focus). This category became so user-friendly that anyone could use it in politics to refer to women's issues, whether or not the intent was feminist. In many cases, the "focus on gender" was used as an alternative to feminist analysis or as a way of softening the more radical and militant critiques of patriarchy.

Moreover, the "focus on gender" came to Latin America from abroad. In the Spanish language, as a Romance language, "sex" and "sexual difference" were the usual ways of distinguishing women from men, as well as "feminine" from "masculine." Until given its prominent role in feminist theory, "género" in Spanish usually meant "species" or "kind" (as in "el género humano," humankind) or, if referring to masculine/feminine differences, its domain was grammar (gendered nouns, pronouns, and adjectives) (Schutte, 1998b). In view of these circumstantial factors, some reject not just the user-friendly "gender focus" (abused by non-feminists) but the whole category of gender as a critical category of analysis in feminist theory (Gargallo, 2007, pp. 83–5). Unfortunately, this wholesale rejection of feminist gender theory creates a great deal of misunderstandings since the uses of "gender" perspective and "gender" theory in Latin American feminist studies also include the radical questioning of gender and sexual normativity, a point that appears to be lost to its critics.

One helpful approach in this regard is offered by Urania Ungo. She notes that while the origins of the category "gender" in feminist theory (her example is Gayle Rubin's analysis of the "sex/gender system") are clearly marked within a feminist framework, nowadays the concept of gender in Central America rules over discussions far removed from the concept's original political and theoretical context (Ungo, 2002, p. 22). Ungo distinguishes the category of gender used in academic feminist theory and even among social "planners" intent on changing the subordination of women from the use of the phrases "gender focus" or "gender perspective" by women organizers who use the latter to replace a feminist vision of society (2002, pp. 23–4). The "gender focus," Ungo explains, is separated or cut off from "the body of theory not only found at its origin but which [actually] gives it its meaning" (2002, p. 24, our trans.). In this displacement of meaning, the "gender focus" becomes synonymous with "women's problems" as identified within the parameters of current masculine-dominant ideologies, whether of Left, Right, or Center. But it also erases the history of the 1960s feminisms which, from the Left, challenged the practices of masculine dominance within its ranks, placing gender alongside class in the debates over revolution and social transformation (2002, p. 25).

Intense debates as to whether to use the terminology of "women's studies" or "gender studies" have also taken place in the United States, and especially in academic programs and departments. These are complex issues and each orientation offers various advantages and limitations. It is important not to promote vilifications of one approach or another. If feminist theory is to evolve over time, we need to be able to re-signify our concerns. We need to use new categories and transformative perspectives if needed as paradigm shifts take place. Latin American feminists' translation,

404

adaptation, and re-signification of concepts and theories coming from abroad show the resilience of the Latin American feminist movement and of Latin American philosophy in the course of globalization processes (de Lima Costa, 2007). We emphasize that cultural *mestizaje* (mixture) and hybridity have been features of Latin American philosophy in general (Schutte, 1993) and feminist theory in particular (Montesino, 2002, pp. 275–7; Femenías, 2006, pp. 97–125). In other words, in Latin America knowledge does not respond to a homogeneous cultural, intellectual, or existential lived experience, nor should such homogeneity be held up as a normative ideal. The task is to maintain a high level of critical analysis and reflection on the ways in which various categories and terms, old and new, continue to be used.

Theorizing ethnicity/race and cultural diversity as an inherent aspect of feminist methodology

Despite the importance of categories such as gender or sexual difference in feminist critical analysis, these are insufficient to capture the complexities of women's concrete lives and vulnerabilities to discrimination and oppression. Even if we add the variable of "class" or economic sector, feminist theory in Latin America requires the consideration of race and/or ethnicity as categories aimed at articulating the obstacles and challenges to inclusiveness and participation – indeed, to having fair access to social justice – affecting members of marginalized and oppressed social groups within these categories. In Latin America, notions of race (and to some extent, ethnicity) diverge quite strongly from those traditionally operating in the United States. Given the vast majority of mixed-race people throughout the continent, so-called white privilege often extends to part of the mixed-race population, especially if they have become assimilated into the middle and upper class lifestyles and values. But race and ethnicity, or ethno-race, are not only heterodesignated; they are self-ascribed. It is important to understand the ways in which feminist theory is transformed by the practices and cognitive contributions of women who identify as members of marginalized or oppressed ethno-racial groups, identifications that motivate them in their collective protests for social justice.

From different regions (Brazil and the Caribbean, the Andean countries, the Southern Cone, and others) there emerge at least two relatively delimited lines of investigation: one concerning mulata/o and black populations; the other concerning original peoples. The situation of women within and across these groups should be conceptualized as heterogeneous. For example, in addition to intra-group gender differences, there are differences in the degree to which people adapt to or resist interaction and contact with outsiders. One underlying feature affecting members of these ethno-racial groups, nonetheless, is the historical weight of oppression embedded in state policies of racism and internal colonialism directed at their populations. It is to these conditions that feminist theoreticians of ethnicity and race turn their attention.

The Bolivian anthropologist Silvia Rivera Cusicanqui and her collaborator Rosana Barragán (1997) published one of the first anthologies in South America on subaltern and postcolonial studies. According to Rivera Cusicanqui and Barragán the debates initiated in India in subaltern studies offer useful theoretical tools to examine the specific situation of women in Latin America and of the great popular indigenous movements whose fundamental demand is centered on the recognition of their ethnic identities.

405

They note, however, that unfortunately such texts from points in the global South usually reach Latin America via the influence of academics in the global North. The entry of Latin American theorists into this type of South–South discussion, they maintain, must be from their own standpoint, not one which is already mediated or heavily determined by the conceptual frameworks derived from the North. Specifically, they argue that embracing a subaltern studies criticism of colonialism and its aftermath does not mean the rejection of Western thought if only because, as postcolonial theorists have shown, one of the features of colonial education was to form subjects according to the norms and values of the colonial enterprise (Rivera Cusicanqui & Barragán, 1997, p. 13). Postcolonial critique therefore means reengaging and contesting Western thought in light of the historically given experiences of those marked by colonialism and its legacies.

In an earlier work focusing on the lives of indigenous and mestiza women in Bolivia, Rivera Cusicanqui and her research team emphasize the importance of reaching an understanding of diversity allowing for points of convergence between, on one hand, the concepts of freedom, equality, and development found in "modernizing projects" and, on the other, the cultures of peoples whose deep belief systems are extraneous to such projects (Rivera Cusicanqui, 1996, pp. 13–14). These methodological observations lead to a nuanced and highly contextualized notion of negotiating and recognizing identities and differences within a critical, dialogical, and postcolonial concept of democratic pluralism, with the goal of "accelerating the construction of a completely just society" (1996, p. 13, our trans.).

Rivera Cusicanqui denounces the conditions of "internal colonialism" in which indigenous peoples in Bolivia (and, by extension, in other parts of the Andean region) have lived up until even the last decades of the twentieth century. Despite Bolivia's formal political independence from Spain in the nineteenth century, colonialism subsisted for indigenous peoples due to the ethno-racially stratified nature of society (socioeconomic and political internal colonialism) and to the subjective, psychological "internalizing" among members of such colonized groups of a sense of social inferiority (the psychological complement of the socioeconomic and political oppression). Rivera Cusicanqui argues, methodologically, that using the separate variables of gender and ethnicity is inadequate for understanding the situation of indigenous and economically underprivileged mestiza women. "The only foundation on which to sustain a politics that overcomes gender and cultural discrimination is a good understanding and full representation of the reality of indigenous women" (Rivera Cusicanqui, 1996, p. 14, our trans.). She further explains that in addition to working with women in fully indigenous communities, such an understanding must not rule out attending to the experiences of underprivileged chola (mestiza) women in contexts exposed to modern, integrated, or mixed sociocultural settings because if they are poor, they, too, need to be considered for equitable treatment within the parameters of the larger society (1996, pp. 14–15). In other words, there must be innovative research methods aimed at understanding the heterogeneous conditions affecting the inequities faced by indigenous and mestiza women whether they are migrants or reside in their communities of origin and whether their communities are fairly traditional in ethnic terms or have been moderately or largely impacted by modernizing projects.

406

Rivera Cusicanqui's analysis shows that as a result of colonialism and the imposition of modern socioeconomic structures, indigenous women were doubly displaced from their traditional roles in society. In their resistance to such displacement, they tend to prioritize struggles on behalf of their ethnic and class (not necessarily gender) identities. Their struggles expose ways in which the dominant (white or white-identified) culture has declared itself "universal," thereby ethnicizing and racializing indigenous cultures as inferior. In popular movements that include some organizations led by women, the more urgent priority has been a demand for ethno-racial recognition as a necessary step for the fair distribution of resources. Correlatively, we note that feminist theory in the global North and programs of aid to women in the global South patterned on the former (whether managed by Northern or Southern elites) need to step down from their presumed universal platforms so as to allow for the transformational input of women from subaltern social and global sectors whose voices and perspectives are fundamental to an inclusive sense of feminism and democracy (Schutte, 1998a; Femenías, 2007).

Afro-descendant women in Latin America constitute another sector demanding visibility in the Latin American women's movement and in the various struggles for economic and social justice. In Latin America and the Caribbean, the social constructionist analysis of race can be very useful. The notion of race can be seen to arise out of the history of colonialism and its two-prong subordination of indigenous and African/Afro-descendant peoples: economically, through the enslavement or exploitation of these populations; culturally, through the imposition of a socio-symbolic order tied to the foundational authority and reproduction of white privilege. The intersection of dominant racialized, class, and gender norms shows how gender is racialized and race engendered, as well as the economic impact of class, which has the effect of "whitening" the more successful Afro-descendants unless they reject such identifications. But critics of the concept of "race" often see it as an illegitimate way (that is, a racist way) of classifying people into superior or inferior types. It therefore makes sense that feminists appealing constructively to the notion of Afro-descendant identity generally do so through the category of "ethno-race" or, alternatively, by incorporating "race" into the category of "ethnicity." This methodological approach denounces and rejects racism at the same time that it acknowledges the value of cultural heritages embraced by Afro-descendant peoples and the importance of empowering the members of these communities in the attainment of social justice.

Moreover, the analysis of ethno-race, researchers warn, needs to be flexible, attentive to internal differences, and capable of articulating political goals with local contexts and historical circumstances. For example, the Dominican feminist Ochy Curiel points out that although the concept of Negritude has been a starting point for political action, its essentializing capacity has led to a "largely homogenized . . . subject": the "black woman" (Curiel, 2007, p. 190, our trans.). She emphasizes that the point of Afro-descendant women's feminism, though, is to combat racism, heterosexism, and class exploitation, and not to overlook the forms of oppression experienced by Afro-descendant lesbians (2007, pp. 189–90). Another non-heteronormative feminist approach to Afro-descendant cultural practices is offered by the anthropologist Rita Segato, who has studied the religious beliefs of the Umbanda in Brazil. These beliefs often break with the concept of the "family" found in "white culture" or they may construe sex and gender identities in ways that symbolic identifications (masculine, feminine) do not

407

necessarily match biological sex (Segato, 2003, pp. 181–223). Curiel's and Segato's approaches show that, methodologically, the attention to concrete as opposed to abstract universals and the influence of deconstruction and postmodern feminisms have allowed more flexibility in subverting the multiple racist, heterosexist constructs of "the black woman" and "the mulata" that find their ways into the symbolic order and cultural imaginaries of Latin American and Caribbean peoples.

In a recent work, María Luisa Femenías (2007) has argued that feminist theory in Latin America needs to become self-aware with regard to its ethnic (or multi-ethnic) speaking position. This means that "white" feminists must not ethnicize the perspectives of Afro-descendants and of indigenous women, as if they (the white theorists) were not speaking from an ethnic location themselves. Femenías's argument on behalf of inclusiveness and cross-cultural dialogue is important because all too often feminist theory has focused on issues of sex and gender (or class) without paying sufficient attention to ethno-race. It is important to recognize that the social reproduction of ethno-racial forms of subordination can affect relations within women's groups as much as it does the population at large. If the goal of feminism is to overcome those structures that both produce and reproduce the subordination of women, an inclusive multi-ethnic/racial approach, open to the voices of the less privileged and critical of ethno-racial and class privilege within feminist theory and activism, is necessary.

The uses and appropriations of Foucauldian discourse theory and Butlerian deconstruction

Foucault's analysis of discourse as power-knowledge has been highly influential in opening up previously marginal areas of knowledge, such as those of Afro-descendant cultures, but more importantly, those dealing with non-normative sexualities, as we shall see next. Thus, the project of inclusion is not premised on the concept of assimilation but on a critique of the *episteme* (that is, the undisputed conceptual framework of a given historical period) that supports the practices of racism and other forms of discrimination while pretending to uphold the universal citizenship of all. Despite the fact that the critique of racism and other forms of domination can be undertaken within the general framework of a broadly "enlightened" perspective grounded in universal norms and values, when it comes to analyzing and focusing on specific exclusionary practices, some scholars have adopted the postmodern perspectives of Foucault and Judith Butler. In particular, the Chilean Olga Grau (2004) and the Brazilian Guacira Lopes Louro anchor their projects in the use of destabilizing methodological approaches including, as Lopes Louro notes, queer theory (2004, p. 57). These scholars propose an approach critical not only of exclusionary practices concerning women, but of the multiple ways in which the mechanisms of inclusion/exclusion affect numerous other aspects of individuals' lives and social relations. The use of destabilizing approaches is not intended to resolve conflicts or tensions. The goal is to put into play the constant dynamic resulting from individuals' resistance to social structures and institutions whose normalizing force continually affects the construction of their social identities, as with the case of sexual and gender identities.

One important consequence of this theoretical approach is the attention paid to discursive practices insofar as these become the sites of exclusionary practices and norms. For example, while feminists of various methodological approaches tend to be concerned with how bodies – especially women's bodies – are represented and spoken about, whether medically, in popular culture, or other contexts, the methodological focus on exclusionary aspects of discursive practices adds a highly critical and nuanced approach to understanding violence and discrimination. When discursive practices are analyzed in terms of the normalizing and/or destabilizing aspects of power relationships, as happens in the approaches taken by Foucault and Butler, the ways in which gender and sexual identities are codified for mass distribution, regulation, and consumption can be critically assessed and demystified in a relatively straightforward, effective manner. For example, Olga Grau has shown that in Chile in the 1990s the term "family" functioned as a sign of stability, normalization, and reproduction of values across generations, whether the discourses in which the term "family" appeared came from the modern state in its post-dictatorial transition, the Chilean Catholic church, or an international body such as the United Nations. Grau calls this confluence and intensification of discursive effects "el fenómeno de la hiper-representación" (the phenomenon of hyper-representation) by which the family (as sign) comes to represent hyperbolically the value of stability, continuity, and unification in a world marked by historical processes of globalization and neoliberalism that brought about significant dislocation, fragmentation, and change (Grau, 2004, pp. 128–9). Looking at the psychological, social, and legal effects of this confluence of discursive effects from the side of those suffering its exclusionary consequences alerts us to the patterns of discrimination and violence experienced by those whose sexual identities do not conform to the heteronormative model of gender and sexuality on which the discursive practices rest and which they reiterate. In other words, Grau notes the cumulative effects of presumably independent discursive practices (church, modern state, international agencies) as these connect and intersect, pushing out through their normalizing force those very elements that call in question both the adequacy and fairness of the normalizing representations and practices.

New Orientations

The introduction of methodological perspectives associated especially with the third and fourth topics discussed above (race/ethnicity, discourse analysis) has vast consequences for a broadly understood "postcolonial" – or, as some prefer to call it, a "decolonizing" – approach to feminist philosophy in Latin America. Significant epistemic shifts are required when feminist philosophy adopts a self-critical approach to the discursive practices in which it itself engages and when part of this self-critical approach involves taking a de-hierarchized glance at the roles ethno-racial, not just class and sexual, differences may play in the cognitive models and claims undertaken. A mark of our times is no longer to focus only on the political goals of justice and equity for women (and more generally, for the marginalized and oppressed) but to pay special attention as well to the ways in which such goals are conceptualized and represented discursively for and by intellectuals and scholars, institutional agents, activists, the media, or individuals in every capacity acting by themselves or with others in efforts to bring about change. The professional training philosophers have acquired in their traditional

409

areas of expertise plays an important role in lending clarity, insight, and strength to feminist inquiry. Yet professional philosophy has all too often depended on a Euro-centric or an Anglocentric – not just an androcentric and heteronormative – discourse to make its case heard. The ethical (dialogic) and political (democratizing) principles engaging feminist philosophy therefore lead to a decolonizing force in its methodo-logical orientation which, on one hand, continues to put in question the blind spots of sexism and androcentrism while, on the other, opens up space for those marginal and oppressed voices that our colonial legacies to date have silenced or kept from being fully heard.

Related chapters: 13 Liberation Philosophy; 22 Philosophy, Postcoloniality, and Post-modernity; 25 Contemporary Ethics and Political Philosophy; 30 Cultural Studies.

References

Alvarez, S. (1990). *Engendering democracy in Brazil: women's movements in politics*. Princeton: Princeton University Press.

Alvarez, S. (2002b). Latin American feminisms go "global": trends of the 1990s and challenges for the new millennium. In S. Alvarez, E. Dagnino, & A. Escobar (Eds). *Cultures of politics / politics of cultures* (pp. 293–324). Boulder, CO: Westview Press,

Alvarez, S. et al. (2002a). Encountering Latin American and Caribbean feminisms. *Signs*, 28:2, 537–79.

Bartra, E. (2006). *Neofeminism in Mexico*. Working Paper #33. Durham: Duke-UNC Program in Latin American Studies.

Curiel, O. (2007). Los aportes de las afrodescendientes a la teoría y la práctica feminista: desuni-versalizando el sujeto *mujeres*. In M. L. Femenías (Ed.). *Perfiles del feminismo Iberoamericano*, vol. 3 (pp. 163–90). Buenos Aires: Catálogos.

Femenías, M. L. (2006). Afirmación identitaria, localización y feminismo mestizo. In M. L. Femenías (Ed.). *Feminismos de París a La Plata* (pp. 97–125). Buenos Aires: Catálogos.

Femenías, M. L. (2007). *El género del multiculturalismo*. Bernal: Universidad Nacional de Quilmes.

Gargallo, F. (2007). Multiple feminisms: feminist ideas and practices in Latin America. In M. L. Femenías & A. Oliver (Eds). *Feminist philosophy in Latin America and Spain* (pp. 73–86). New York: Rodopi.

Grau, O. (2004). Familia: un grito de fin de siglo. In O. Grau, R. Delsing, E. Brito, & A. Farías. *Discurso, género y poder (Chile 1978–1993)* (pp. 127–47). Santiago de Chile: Universidad Arcis-La Morada.

Gutiérrez Castañeda, G. (2002). Prólogo. In G. Gutiérrez Castañeda (Ed.). *Feminismo en México: revisión histórico-crítica del siglo que termina* (pp. 9–23). Mexico City: UNAM – PUEG.

Hierro, G. (2007). The ethics of pleasure. In M. L. Femenías & A. Oliver (Eds). *Feminist philo-sophy in Latin America and Spain* (pp. 197–207). New York: Rodopi.

Jelin, E. (Ed.). (1990). *Women and social change in Latin America*. Atlantic Highlands, NJ: Zed.

Jelin, E. (1996). Women, gender, and human rights. In E. Jelin & E. Herschberg (Eds). *Constructing democracy: human rights, citizenship, and society in Latin America* (pp. 177–96). Boulder, CO: Westview Press.

de Lima Costa, C. (2007). Unthinking gender: the traffic in theory in the Americas. In M. L. Femenías & A. Oliver (Eds). *Feminist philosophy in Latin America and Spain* (pp. 167–86). New York: Rodopi.

Lopes Louro, G. (2004). *Um corpo estranho*. Belo Horizonte, Brazil: Autentica.

Montesino, S. (2002). Understanding gender in Latin America. (D. Cohen & L. J. Frazier, Trans.). In R. Montoya, L. J. Frazier, & J. Hurtig (Eds). *Gender's place: feminist anthropologies of Latin America* (pp. 273–80). New York: Palgrave Macmillan.

Rivera Cusicanqui, S. (1996). Los desafíos para una democracia étnica y genérica en los albores del tercer milenio. In S. Rivera Cusicanqui (Ed.). *Ser mujer indígena, chola o birlocha en la Bolivia postcolonial de los años 90* (pp. 17–84). La Paz: Ministerio de Desarrollo Humano.

Rivera Cusicanqui, S., & Barragán, R. (Eds). (1997). *Debates post coloniales: una introducción a los estudios de la subalternidad*. La Paz and Rotterdam: Editorial Historias, SEPHIS & Taller de Historia Oral Andina.

Schutte, O. (1993). *Cultural identity and social liberation in Latin American thought*. Albany: State University of New York Press.

Schutte, O. (Ed.). (1994). Special cluster on Spanish and Latin American feminist philosophy. *Hypatia*, 9:1, 147–94.

Schutte, O. (1998a). Cultural alterity: cross-cultural communication and feminist thought in North–South dialogue. *Hypatia*, 13:2, 53–72.

Schutte, O. (1998b). Latin America. In A. M. Jaggar & I. M. Young (Eds). *A companion to feminist philosophy* (pp. 87–95). Malden, MA: Blackwell.

Segato, R. L. (2003). *Las estructuras elementales de la violencia*. Buenos Aires: Prometeo and Universidad Nacional de Quilmes.

Ungo, U. A. (2002). *Conocimiento, libertad y poder: claves críticas en la teoría feminista*. Panama: IMUP & UNICEF.

Ungo, U. A. (2000). *Para cambiar la vida: política y pensamiento del feminismo en América Latina*. Panama: IMUP.

Further Reading

Femenías, M. L., & Oliver, A. (Eds). (2007). *Feminist philosophy in Latin America and Spain*. New York: Rodopi.

29

Teaching Philosophy

MARÍA CRISTINA GONZÁLEZ AND NORA STIGOL

1. Teaching Philosophy as an Academic Field

Teaching philosophy is now considered an academic field in its own right. This is suggested not only by the existence of academic journals on the topic but also by the inclusion of this field among other more traditional ones in national and international events. Teaching philosophy involves a number of problems. The standard problems consist of teaching philosophy to children, in secondary or high schools, and to college students pursuing different careers at tertiary, university and non-university levels. The latter may involve several specific courses, such as theory of knowledge, philosophy of science, and bioethics, and requires selection of appropriate materials, which may include films, videos, drama, television, or multimedia.

Yet philosophers interested in teaching philosophy have scarcely analyzed practices, methodologies, and related matters at the college level. Those are perhaps the most important aspects of teaching philosophy because those who have graduated in philosophy will reach teaching positions at all academic levels, as well as produce philosophy and do research – they are philosophy's professionals.

The significance of these was emphasized at the Ninth Inter-American Congress of Philosophy in Caracas (1979), when a large group of Latin American philosophers discussed the issue of teaching philosophy in Latin America. Furthermore, the recent increase in the number of Ph.D.s awarded in philosophy in Latin America, and their influence at all levels of university teaching positions, contributes to the relevance of this topic.

Teaching philosophy is thus a philosophical field that is, as such, related to other fields. In particular, it is not possible to detach it from the way philosophy itself is conceived. Therefore, to philosophically reflect on teaching philosophy at Latin American universities for professional training in this field it is necessary to refer not only to the ways of doing philosophy in Latin America, but also to the ways of conceiving philosophy itself, since these have consequences for the methods of teaching. The attitude assumed toward philosophy and philosophizing will definitely have an impact on both the teaching goals and the selected content and methodologies applied.

But when compared to the teaching of other disciplines, such as physics or geography, in the teaching of philosophy there is no general consensus about what exactly is the subject matter. Risieri Frondizi has noted that "there is no agreement about what

412

philosophy is, and this fact is reflected in its teaching methods." He adds, "[d]isagree-ments are not accidental or temporary, they are related to the nature of philosophizing" (1979, p. 13; here and henceforth translations are ours). We believe that Frondizi's contribution at the Ninth Inter-American Congress of Philosophy (1979) is fundamental to any reflection on the topic at hand, since it raises three important questions that are intimately related: (1) *why* teach philosophy, i.e., what do we want to achieve through its teaching; (2) *what* to teach, i.e., what content should be taught, taking into account the goals to be achieved; (3) *how* to teach, i.e., what type of methodology should be applied, considering goals and content.

In this chapter we examine some significant contributions by Latin American philo-sophers to the teaching of philosophy at Latin American universities. The interest of Latin American philosophers in this topic is especially important because the institu-tionalization of philosophical studies as an autonomous area is quite recent: in the past, philosophical studies in Latin America were included in humanistic studies in general; these were part of the humanistic educational profile.

In Latin America, departments of philosophy offer a *cursus honorum* (course require-ment) that leads to a major in philosophy or in teaching philosophy. This *cursus honorum* takes four or five years and includes a small number of general courses: literature, anthropology, sociology, linguistics, history, and a considerable number of philosophical subjects – most of them compulsory. Students who have graduated from high school, who are usually seventeen or eighteen years old, attend these courses.

It is in this precise context of syllabi with twenty to twenty-five named philo-sophical courses (logics, metaphysics, ethics, and so on) that a diagnosis has been done and problems and solutions pointed out by some contemporary Latin American philosophers. Here we will focus on the teaching of philosophy at Argentinean universities, excluding postgraduate studies that usually consist of a set of seminars and a Ph.D. thesis – students undertaking the latter already have previous philosophical training. We will look closely at Rabossi's ideas on the models of teaching philosophy, their rela-tions with certain philosophical views, and the consequences of applying them.

2.   Conceptions of philosophy

Let us first consider, however, the work of other contemporary Latin American philo-sophers. The Mexican philosopher Fernando Salmerón has explored the issue of teach-ing philosophy. In the course of his analysis of the subject matter of philosophy of education, he notes the ambiguity of the term "philosophy" and introduces a distinction of special interest for our topic (1991, p. 13). In his view, that term has two meanings: one broad, the other strict. According to its broad meaning, "philosophy" refers to certain representations or doctrines which try to express the structure of the world through a more or less coherent connection of concepts or simply images. "Doing this, the philosopher attempts to understand his own destiny and the rationale of the world at the same time; that is why he presents his intertwined ideas about the ultimate struc-ture of reality with value principles and moral ideals that explain the behavior of an individual or of a whole community" (1991, p. 14). In the strict interpretation, the term "philosophy" refers to "an activity, an analytic, theoretical, intellectual enterprise that, with a proper scientific energy, faces different kinds of problems – logical, semantic, epistemological problems – using certain methods . . ." (1991, p. 14). In our view, the common feature of those who have worked on the topic of teaching is that they rely on the strict rather than on the broad meaning of philosophy.

Jorge Gracia has made a distinction that proves useful in connection with his general overview of the developments in philosophy in Latin America between 1940 and 1980. Gracia (1983, p. 162 ff.) first distinguishes two different attitudes adopted toward the aim of philosophy and the methodology applied with reference to that goal. There are what he calls "committed philosophies," which aim at liberation and ideological independence along with social changes, utilizing rhetorical persuasion as the road to liberation. In addition, there are "academic philosophies," whose purpose is knowledge and not action as in the case of the philosophies of liberation, although Gracia recognizes that knowledge and action have strong bonds.

But Gracia makes a further distinction within the academic philosophies. On the one hand, there are those who essentially use an expository method. Those who apply this method express and describe their conceptions and points of view in some detail, but do not provide or use arguments to support them or convince their opponents of the "truth" of these points of view. In any case, rhetoric is their best instrument for sharing their own beliefs or intuitions. On the other hand, we have the philosophical trends that are fundamentally argumentative, which conceive of argumentation as an inherent task of philosophical activity. For them, this activity does not consist of expressing ideas, theses, beliefs, or intuitions, no matter how interesting they might be; on the contrary, it consists of sound argumentation in favor of beliefs, ideas, intuitions, and theses.

3.   Teaching Philosophy as Teaching a "Know How"

Eduardo Rabossi often discussed the issue of teaching philosophy. He also led a research group devoted to it, financed by the University of Buenos Aires. The team was composed of professors and researchers from that university as well as the National University of La Plata. María Cristina González, Nora Stigol, Ana Claudia Couló, Margarita Costa, María Isabel Santa Cruz, Martha Frasinetti, Guillermo Obiols, Francisco Olivieri, and Laura Agratti, among others, took part in the enterprise. Some of them – particularly Obiols and Frasinetti – were interested in teaching philosophy at non-university levels. Obiols and Frasinetti both provided outstanding contributions to the topic.

Rabossi's starting point is the Kantian *dictum* that philosophy cannot be taught, only philosophizing can (see, for example, *Kritik der reinen Vernunft*, A 858, B 863/66, and *Logik*, Introduction. On Kant's idea about philosophy and its teaching, see Eduardo García Belsunce, 2007, chapter 4). Rabossi then introduced some distinctions which made possible the design of the teaching techniques that were put into practice at the Faculty of Philosophy and Letters of the University of Buenos Aires (Rabossi, 1986, 1987, 1993, 1994, 2000a, 2000b; Rabossi et al., 1986, 1993; González & Stigol, 1993) in the courses he taught there.

The proposal put forward by Rabossi, and others who identify with the argumentative way of doing philosophy, assumes the Wittgensteinian idea of philosophy as being

414

essentially a practice, i.e., an activity which implicates a set of critical and argu-mentative abilities and capacities, as Salmerón also recognizes. This methodology for teaching philosophy turns on a well-known distinction between "knowing that" and "knowing how" coined by Gilbert Ryle (1949): teaching philosophy is understood as teaching a "know how." For Ryle, "knowing that" amounts to propositional know-ledge, i.e., the clause "that" is followed by a statement expressing that something is or is not the case. But knowing how is followed by an expression that denotes operations, actions, activities. "I know that the solar system has nine planets" and "I know how to ride a bicycle" are typical examples of the two types of knowledge.

Bearing this distinction in mind, the philosopher is someone who masters a class of abilities and skills of a certain type, in principle associated with critical thinking and the management of concepts and arguments, not someone who knows a certain theory or a group of philosophical theories, even though his or her knowledge is as precise and thorough as possible. This way of conceiving of the philosopher and his or her activity qua philosopher will have consequences when applying a methodology for teaching philosophy. However, this does not mean ignoring the value of knowing the theoretical corpus which has been organized throughout the history of philosophy. Rather, it just implies the defense of philosophy as an activity in the same vein as Salmerón, Gracia, and also José Gaos conceive of it.

Thus, when suggesting techniques or methodologies for teaching philosophy at the university level, two issues will have to be taken into consideration: (1) what is the aim or goal to be achieved (e.g., the adequate profile of a graduate in philosophy), and (2) the conception of the philosophy involved in this goal.

To deal with both issues, it is first necessary to identify a philosophical development in context, which in the case of concern here is the particular situation of philosophy in Latin America, the features that characterize it and, in a way, that have determined its development and evolution.

4.   The Status of the Profession in Latin America

Different philosophers have pointed out many difficulties that have affected the devel-opment and evolution of philosophy in Latin America. Though there are differences among countries, certain general features are present in all of them. Some originate from situations external to philosophy itself, some are linked to a philosophical style which has prevailed, others to the organization of universities, and yet others to the relationship among colleagues within the philosophical community.

We will now consider some of these features. The first is related to what Rabossi (1994) called "to philosophize in the periphery." For him, the fact that Latin Americans are importers of philosophy, which was received and adopted without elaboration, is a con-stituent of philosophizing in this region. Europe and the United States – where many of our philosophers were educated – are certainly the suppliers. However, as Rabossi says, importing philosophy is not something negative as such. In central countries, import and export of philosophical ideas is a constant and enriching fact. It is bad if we turn ourselves into passive receivers, unable to elaborate on the imported ideas within our own perspective. This way of philosophizing, according to some authors, led to a lack

415

of original and foundational proposals with the ability to break down traditions and start new ones. There has not been an autochthonous philosophical tradition emerging from our own specific problems. It is often said that we have just repeated, rephrased, defended, elucidated, at most rethought and criticized points of view that do not belong to us and whose roots are found in European or American philosophical schools or philosophers.

This situation would explain the intensity and frequency of debates, among Latin American philosophers, about the existence of a Latin American philosophy. The Peruvian philosopher Francisco Miró Quesada (1979, p. 167) draws our attention to this fact and points out that "to think about the ideal of having an authentic philosophy means that the Latin American thinkers have doubts about their capacity of doing it [. . .] This awareness means two things at the same time: we feel the necessity of doing authentic philosophy and we feel the distress of not having enough capacity to do it." However, it must be mentioned that in Latin American philosophy it is also possible to find original, creative, and significant contributions (see Nuccetelli, 2003).

A second feature that should be mentioned, which has proved to be one of the most serious difficulties in the development of academic and cultural life, especially in philosophical activity within Latin America, is related to factors external to philosophy itself and is therefore an obstacle to its progress. These factors are the different political, social, and economic factors, sometimes of great seriousness, that have marked the history of Latin American countries. Philosophical activity – inside and outside the universities – could not be detached from these factors and has been inevitably contingent upon such political turbulence. The unfortunate consequences resulting from these factors include massive resignations of professors, exile, arbitrary manipulation of institutions not only in teaching but also in research, and the lack of intellectual freedom and resources. No doubt, all this denotes an unfavorable environment for the development of intellectual practices. In general, the political and social situations in the countries of this region have been an unsuitable context for university activity. In addition, there is something pointed out by Rabossi (1994, 1996) that was in fact quite common in the first decades of the twentieth century: the Faculty of Philosophy and Letters of the University of Buenos Aires was founded not to train professionals (as was the case with the faculties of Law, Medicine, and Sciences that existed at the time), but to create an environment where values of a "spiritual nature" were a priority and where students and professors could focus on the study of sciences and humanities in an altruistic way. Its motto was "culture for the sake of culture." "This initial mistake about the role of the Faculty and particularly about a career in philosophy," Rabossi says, "has determined its subsequent history" (1996, p. 4) and has possibly been one of the factors which has most hindered the route to legitimate professionalism of philosophical practice, forcing teachers and researchers – over many years – to share their time with extra university jobs, such as having a lawyer's or a doctor's consulting office (see Romero, 1952, p. 18). In fact, full-time teaching at universities is a relatively recent achievement.

The idea that philosophy is not a professional activity, but rather a general cultural discipline which gives a certain cultural splendor to amateurs, has been common in Latin America (perhaps this is one of the reasons why, for a long time, the majority of students at the Faculties of Philosophy were women). Gracia (1983, 1987) mentions three other common features in our Latin American idiosyncrasy – very much rooted in it – which are obstacles to the development of philosophy in this part of the world: personalism, euphuism (*preciosismo*), and elitism. He considers them as "problems that have to do with a general attitude Latin Americans have regarding the discipline" (1987, p. 219).

Personalism refers to the idea that philosophy is the expression of a personal intuition, whose truth can only be judged by the subject of the experience. Philosophy differs from science because it is not an academic enterprise that implies mutual exchange and cooperation. On the contrary, its personal characteristic hinders dialogue, debate, and criticism. Given this feature, Latin American philosophers ignore each other.

In the same vein of thinking, Francisco Romero (1952, p. 18) writes, "First of all, our countries live in an isolated way, and the philosophical nucleus of each of them, always an unconnected minority, ignore each other; philosophers therefore lack the necessary stimulus of communication. Only during these last years has a determined action of interchange and mutual knowledge begun . . ." Isolation is frequently followed by an ignorance of the philosophical work produced by Latin American colleagues. As noted before, Latin American philosophers often prefer to read the work of philosophers from central countries rather than each other's works. One of the consequences of this situation is the absence of a Latin American philosophical community where discussion and philosophical dialogue could develop, creating a rich interchange of ideas. Rabossi used to say that if we examined Latin American philosophical journals, we would notice the lack of articles that produce deep discussions. However, this situation has changed recently in an incredible way.

These changes are related to the phenomenon of "philosophical panamericanism," named by Gracia (1983, p. 147 ff.). According to him, an attitude of dialogue among philosophers of the different countries of the American continent started during the 1940s and may be summarized as follows: Philosophical panamericanism contributed greatly to the development of philosophy in our region. It was, in short, the beginning of interchange and dialogue amongst philosophers from various countries of the continent. In the twenty-first century, it amounts to one of the remarkable features of philosophical activity in Latin America. It is characterized by the existence of international agreements among institutions, societies of philosophers of the same or different orientations, and the exchange of publishing projects and professors.

Philosophical personalism is linked to the idea of philosophizing as a unique, subjective experience that can only be expressed in a literary, rhetorical, and grandiloquent style in which form is more important than the value and coherence of the ideas to be explained. This is what Gracia calls "euphuism."

Finally, Gracia mentions elitism. By this he means the attitude frequently found among Latin American thinkers who consider philosophy as an activity independent from other intellectual activities and superior to all of them, meant only for an elite group of thinkers living in an exclusive ivory tower. This attitude, which was not always shared by the European philosophical tradition, obviously leads to isolation which is harmful for the elaboration of a mature philosophy.

Gracia points out other problems related to practical aspects of teaching philosophy, which are mainly the consequence of the features previously mentioned. According to him, traditional teaching – called the "Prevalent Model" (Rabossi et al., 1986, 1993) – has favored learning by heart and repetition over argumentative and critical thought,

417

as well as the use of secondary sources, particularly manuals and class notes, at the expense of work on original sources. In the third article of the resolution approved at the Ninth Inter-American Congress of Philosophy (1979, p. 20) previously mentioned, the necessity of basing teaching on authentic works is emphasized. These practices came about mainly because of lack of knowledge of other languages and also, sometimes, the difficulty in obtaining genuine material. The lack of training on elaborating and writing a philosophical work is another shortcoming of traditional teaching noted by Gracia.

5.   Some Models for Teaching Philosophy

5.1.   The Prevalent Model

Let's now consider the Prevalent Model in two of its versions (Rabossi et al., 1986). This model has long predominated in Latin American universities. According to Gracia, it is associated with the expositive point of view of academic philosophy, and is based on the conception that philosophy is, above all, a "know that." This conception clearly determines the goal of the model, which is not to train philosophers so that they can produce and elaborate their own philosophies, participate in the international philosophical community, and discuss and exchange ideas with their peers argumentatively and critically. On the contrary, its purpose is to make the student know, in a deep and serious way, the different philosophical positions and theories produced in the course of history. This model rests on the assumption that learning philosophy consists in the acquisition of information about the most outstanding philosophers. The philosophical past is recalled and repeated as a substitute for one's own creative philosophical thinking. In this way, there is a confusion of some sort between doing philosophy and recording philosophical ideas. From this point of view, philosophy *is* the history of philosophy. Teaching philosophy in Latin America "has been the victim of exaggerations of this type of conception. Any subject was transformed into the study of its historical evolution," Frondizi states (1979, p. 14). It is important to underline that when favoring this model, not only is the importance of transmitting erudite information about the eminent philosophical works produced throughout history emphasized, with its subsequent increase in number of courses or class hours, but also the topics at hand are presented and developed historically. In fact, it is frequently found in our philosophy departments that the so-called "systematic subjects" (metaphysics, ethics, theory of knowledge, etc.) are still historical: what is dealt with is the history of a certain philosophical discipline, such as history of ethics or history of a certain issue (see González & Stigol, 2008).

According to the Prevalent Model, students are trained to acquire some skills and capacities, such as knowing by heart, absorbing, summarizing, outlining, commenting, paraphrasing, etc., and the importance of the history of philosophy is emphasized at the expense of the teaching of philosophical problems and their solutions as well as the arguments.

The evaluation resources used in this model are consistent with its goals and the skills in which the students are trained; in this way, the evaluation tools are exams (mid-term or finals, oral or written) which consist of presentations by students on a certain topic or aspect, briefly developed, or short papers based on paraphrases, commentaries, and quotations with little or no elaboration at all. The expectations of students' performance are based on their capacity to memorize, reproduce literally, and summarize the material. Giving personal opinions, doubting, assuming positions of their own regarding a certain topic, and any other critical attitude are excluded. Accordingly, professors appear as intermediaries between famous philosophers and the students. Their class format is of course the magisterial lecture, where to be good is to be a reliable source of information. Students are supposed to be receptive and passive, do detailed note-taking, and raise questions only when the information is not clear. They are neither allowed nor willing to criticize or discuss the content of lectures. Clearly, this model mainly emphasizes the informative aspects of teaching rather than the formative ones.

By contrast, Gaos, when asked by the authorities of the University of Mexico to change curricula and syllabi in 1953, argued that what had to be modified was the methodology of teaching philosophy rather than the curricula and syllabi. Later, his recommendations were included in a book, *La Filosofía en la Universidad*, together with other works about teaching philosophy, published in 1956. In the first pages, Gaos (p. 13) says: "At the Faculty, lecturing is the method that prevails in teaching philosophy [. . .] But no lectures, including those that could augment knowledge, can give what undoubtedly defines university teaching – which cannot be the providing of more or less serious *information* about the areas that make up philosophy. University teaching has to *educate* (*formar*) in these disciplines."

Gaos takes education to fall under the Kantian dictum without mentioning the German philosopher. He writes, "education (*formación*), the highest imperative of the university setting, requires not only teaching philosophy but also philosophizing" (p. 14). Accordingly, he recommends that students and teachers work together in seminars, which are as important for philosophy as laboratories are for science. The issue about the importance of seminars in university teaching will be discussed further later.

The legitimacy and importance of transmission of information in the teaching/ learning process of philosophy is of course beyond any doubt. Rather, Gaos, Frondizi, Rabossi, Salmerón, and others question that such a process can consist merely of the transmission of information. But what exactly is the information referred to here? Salmerón (1991, p. 113 ff.) argues that it is of three types: (1) information about general historical, political, and social events related to a philosophical product; (2) more specific historical information related to the personal reasons or context which prompted, for example, Plato or Descartes to elaborate the philosophical theories they did; (3) information about philosophy itself that is not historical. It is the essential information for the philosopher's work that deals with rules, techniques, and logical procedures that must be acquired by the student, particularly in courses of logic and methodology. Laura Benítez (1987) has added the need for teaching formative subjects, such as propaedeutic or instrumental courses, noting the careless way in which they are currently treated in some Latin American institutions.

As described by Rabossi (1987, 1993, 2000), the Prevalent Model in Argentina and Latin America generally has assumed two modalities that, according to him, are not the correct ones if the intention is to train philosophers who can develop a critical, creative, and original philosophical activity. Rabossi called these two modalities the "Dogmatic Model" and the "Eclectic Model." A model comprises various ways of conceiving the teaching/learning of philosophy; at the same time, these models are formalized or institutionalized in the curricula (more on this later).

The first of these models – the Dogmatic Model – rests on the idea of the existence of "a philosophical system (or at least an articulate group of philosophical theses) which is true, and thus, as a consequence, ranks as genuine knowledge" (Rabossi, 1993, p. 15). This system is capable of being transmitted in the teaching/learning process as such, leaving no space for other philosophical proposals, but only for "guardians in charge of repairs, diffusion and compliments." The only thing a philosopher can possibly do when faced with this system is to try to understand it and defend it from possible attack. The reasons used for its defense cannot be really philosophical; generally they are political, religious, or personal preferences which are absolutely unjustified. This approach does not deny philosophical creation, but contends that it manifests itself only when a "true" philosophical system is elaborated. Clearly, this model was prevalent during colonial times, when submission to the conqueror and the Catholic Church was part of everyday life.

The Eclectic approach, for Rabossi, is the one that prevails in Latin American universities, mainly in public universities. Private universities, especially religious ones, have preferred the Dogmatic approach. Unlike the latter, the Eclectic Model denies the existence of a unique or true philosophical system, which makes it seem more acceptable, but on the other hand it admits that many or maybe all philosophical systems have part of "the truth"; this model "advocates a curious distribution of philosophical truth in some, many or all philosophical theories" (Rabossi, 2000, p. 104); a distribution that, by the way, the model cannot explain.

The Prevalent Model in its two versions has been frequently linked to the sort of curricula that González and Stigol (1995) call "closed curricula." Briefly, these curricula are characterized by their lack of flexibility and freedom to choose a philosophical and thematic orientation for the students. The Critical Model is related to the "open curricula" (see Gaos, 1956, p. 25 ff.). Again, another recommendation of the resolution of the Ninth Inter-American Congress was to give flexibility to the curricula (1979, p. 21).

5.2. The profile of graduate students

Before presenting the Critical Model, let us have a look at the profile of graduate students in philosophy in Latin America. Laura Benítez writes (1987, p. 228): "In spite of the reiterative attempts at establishing a proper profile of a graduate in philosophy, we do not know precisely what to expect from one. The profile has been determined outside the University and depends on educational politics, the pressure of the demographic explosion, the economic crisis and even on preferences or interests of coordinators and counselors." In Rabossi's view (1993, p. 17), there are serious disagreements about the matter. Some adopt a "vocational perspective" that takes graduates to be educated men and women who have been in touch with remarkable thinkers and have developed into people who are able to repeat and paraphrase what those thinkers have

420

said. On this perspective, culture is confronted with the idea of a future occupation or profession. Philosophy is studied without any economic interest and without expecting an economic reward for being trained in it.

A second perspective defends an "ideological vision" according to which graduates must endorse a certain political, religious, or social ideology. Their mission has to be the defense of an allegedly desirable and just cause. So the philosopher is to be an activist related to that cause (recall here Gracia's "committed philosophies").

Finally, again following Rabossi, there are those who defend a "professional vision." Graduates must be able to develop a profession, after specific training, with an economic remuneration. They must develop certain conceptual skills and abilities that will enable them not only to propose, defend, and discuss philosophical theses in the traditional sense, but also to argue for or against them. Rabossi (1994, p. 83) maintains:

> The phenomenon (of professionalism) implies two closely related aspects. The first is the practice of a paid occupation which has social relevance, demands special knowledge and abilities and requires a training period which ends when getting a degree legally recognized by the state. The second is linked to the existence of a recognized set of rules of art, the adequate handling of contents considered relevant, the recognition of shared criteria of excellence, the existence of an institutional operative sub-structure, the establishment of a basic *cursus honorum*, the existence of specialized journals and the use of minimum patterns of professional behavior.

Of course, Rabossi advocates this vision of graduates, which is based on the Critical Model of teaching, while the other two are related to the Dogmatic and Eclectic Models. For him, "only the critical method is useful for the professional demands of the philosopher" (1993, p. 18).

We saw above that this is not the goal of the Prevalent Model. The professional status of philosophers in this sense is a recent phenomenon in Latin America. The vocational vision was undoubtedly the one that had primacy when teaching philosophy began in our countries. The ideological vision coexists with the professional one; there is no confrontation between them. Moreover, they sometimes complement each other. In fact, when a career in philosophy was created at national and private universities, the process of structuring its professional status began. Its creation implied the acknowledgement of philosophy as an autonomous discipline, like other disciplines taught at different colleges. However, the foundation of colleges (or "faculties") of humanities in the subcontinent did not mean the automatic recognition of its professionalism. Bear in mind Rabossi's comment concerning the foundation of the Faculty at the University of Buenos Aires. Time and effort have been necessary to recognize its graduates as professionals in philosophy. The group called "the Founders" by Romero had a main role in this process.

5.3. *The Critical Model*

If philosophy is conceived in terms of knowing how, this is as an activity that involves mainly an argumentative, rational, and creative practice. Furthermore, if the main aim

421

of philosophical education at universities is the training of professional philosophers, and not – or at least not only – transmitters of philosophy or historians of philosophical ideas, then the Eclectic and Dogmatic Models of teaching/learning philosophy are not the most appropriate ones. Rabossi (1987, 1993, 2000; Rabossi et al., 1986; González & Stigol, 1993, 1995) has proposed the implementation of another teaching/learning model, whose name, "Critical Model," alludes to the Kantian dictum mentioned above. Recall that this model is related also to Salmerón's strict philosophy and to the philosophical argumentative style mentioned by Gracia. According to this model, the process of teaching/learning intends to train future philosophers by acquiring certain abilities and skills which are characteristic of philosophy, aiming at the production of philosophical theses and argumentation. The modalities and roles of teachers and students are very different from the ones of the Prevalent Model. Expositive classes where the professor transmits information and the students have a receptive role are replaced by active ones. Seminars are therefore the best alternative, since they are devoted to a certain topic and/or work in philosophy, and gather together a small number of students, thus allowing for active participation.

Among others, Gaos (1956) has argued for the need to include seminars in the education of a philosopher. Their mission is to initiate students into philosophizing as such, to introduce them to the art of doing philosophy. He distinguishes two kinds of seminars: "seminars about texts" and "seminars about theses." The first ones center round the greatest philosophical works of all time. They help sharpen competences in reading and analysis. In his view, the study of one of these works should extend over several academic years and if possible under the same professor. Gaos emphasizes the idea of personal work with a single professor as something essential for the educational development of philosophers, because for him the only way of teaching and learning is to work together, the one who knows how with the one who wants to know. However, we do not think this is central, insofar as this methodology is institutionally adopted, because contact with different professors allows students to become familiar with different personal styles, which is also something that is valuable in their training. Thesis seminars in Gaos's proposal are something like the final stage of philosophical education; that is, the student's capacity to elaborate his or her first personal work. But seminars of all these kinds play an important role in the training of graduates by, for example, reducing the number of mandatory courses and thus allowing students to choose according to their preferences, specializations, and needs.

There are two other features which distinguish the Critical Model from the Prevalent one. One is about evaluation resources. Exams and monographs are replaced by reading guides, sessions of presentation and debate of a critical short paper, elaborated by students and discussed by peers, stimulated and monitored by the professor. The other distinguishing feature concerns the relationship between philosophy and history of philosophy, since the difference between doing philosophy and doing history of philosophy is emphasized. Knowledge of the history of philosophy as well as notable philosophical works is considered and valued as a tool. It allows students to examine and find out how the great philosophers performed their own job, their own "know-how" to reach their theses or theories. It also allows them to recognize their good ideas and mistakes. It offers possible solutions and suggestions; it hints at useful ways of undertaking personal research.

422

6. Consequences of the Defense of the Critical Model

The analyzed topics bring forth some consequences that arise from the methodo-logical proposal of the Critical Model. It is clear that in conceiving philosophy and its teaching in this way, the space for debate fortunately has no limits. Also, some of the authors that have worried about the issue of teaching philosophy in Latin America have also dealt with the controversies concerning the identity of Latin American philo-sophy, intimately connected to the first issue, in an explicit and formal way (others have done it implicitly and informally). The profundity and development of these controversies, as well as other philosophical polemics which have led to new disciplinary areas, are only possible in a context of the enunciation of theses and elaboration of arguments, so as to give an account of the legitimacy of the debate and its possible solution.

Undoubtedly, the destiny of the philosophy of a country and a region, as Salmerón would say (1991, p. 72), is linked to the quality of its teaching. Improving the teach-ing of our discipline at our universities will possibly allow the elaboration of a genuine Latin American philosophy capable of expressing creative and new positions of its own and connected to other areas of culture, art, and science.

Related chapters: 14 Analytic Philosophy; 18 Identity and Philosophy; 24 Latin American Philosophy; 25 Contemporary Ethics and Political Philosophy.

References

Benítez, L. (1987). El problema de las materias propedéuticas en la enseñanza actual de la filosofía. In L. Valdivia & E. Villanueva (Eds). *Filosofía del lenguaje, de la ciencia, de los derechos humanos y problemas de su enseñanza* (pp. 227–32). México: UNAM.

Frondizi, R. (1979). La enseñanza de la filosofía en América Latina. In *La Filosofía en América*. Proceedings of the IX Congreso Interamericano de Filosofía (pp. 13–21). Venezuela: Sociedad Venezolana de Filosofía.

Gaos, J. (1956). *La filosofía en la universidad*. México: Imprenta Universitaria.

Garcia Belsunce, E. (2007). *Cuestiones Kantianas*. Buenos Aires: Prometeo Editorial.

González, M. C., & Stigol, N. (1993). La enseñanza de la filosofía como la enseñanza de una técnica: el problema de los instrumentos de evaluación. In E. Rabossi & G. Obiols (Eds). *La filosofía y el filosofar: problemas en su enseñanza* (pp. 47–57). Buenos Aires: Centro Editor de América Latina.

González, M. C., & Stigol, N. (1995). Notas sobre los planes de estudio de las carreras de filosofía en el nivel universitario. Communication in "Segundas jornadas para el mejoramiento de la enseñanza de la filosofía." UBA. Universidad Nacional de Río Cuarto. Argentina.

González, M. C., & Stigol, N. (2008). La enseñanza de la filosofía y el canon filosófico: algunas reflexiones. In D. Pérez & L. Fernández Moreno (Eds). *Cuestiones filosóficas. Ensayos en honor a Eduardo Rabossi*. Buenos Aires: Catálogos Editorial (Forthcoming).

Gracia, J. (1983). Panorama general de la filosofía latinoamericana actual. In K. Cramer, J. Gracia et al. *La filosofía hoy en Alemania y América Latina* (pp. 142–95). Córdoba: Círculo de Amigos del Instituto Goethe.

Gracia, J. (1987). Problemas en la enseñanza de la filosofía en Ibero América. In L. Valdivia & E. Villanueva (Eds). *Filosofía del lenguaje, de la ciencia, de los derechos humanos y problemas de su enseñanza* (pp. 219–25). México: UNAM.

423

Miró Quesada, F. (1979). Posibilidad y límites de una filosofía latinoamericana. In *La filosofía en América*. Proceedings of the IX Congreso Interamericano de Filosofía (pp. 167–87). Venezuela: Sociedad Venezolana de Filosofía.

Nuccetelli, S. (2003). Is Latin American thought philosophy? *Metaphilosophy*, 4, 524–37.

Rabossi, E. (1987). Enseñar filosofía y aprender a filosofar. In L. Valdivia & E. Villanueva (Eds). *Filosofía del lenguaje, de la ciencia, de los derechos humanos y problemas de su enseñanza* (pp. 201–8). México: UNAM.

Rabossi, E. (1993). Enseñar filosofía y aprender a filosofar: Nuevas reflexiones. In E. Rabossi & G. Obiols (Eds). *La filosofía y el filosofar: problemas en su enseñanza* (pp. 13–23). Buenos Aires: Centro Editor de América Latina.

Rabossi, E. (1994). Filosofar: profesionalismo, profesionalidad, tics y modales. *Cuadernos de Filosofía*, 40, 81–7.

Rabossi, E. (1996). Clase alusiva del 16 de agosto de 1996. *Espacios de Crítica y Producción. 100 años*. Buenos Aires, Facultad de Filosofía y Letras, 19–20, 2–5.

Rabossi, E. (2000). Sobre planes de estudio, enfoques de la filosofía y perfiles profesionales. In E. Rabossi & G. Obiols (Eds). *La enseñanza de la filosofía en debate* (pp. 99–108). Buenos Aires and México: Novedades Educativas.

Rabossi, E., González, M. C., & Stigol, N. (1986). Un modelo de enseñanza-aprendizaje para un enfoque crítico de la filosofía. *Revista de Filosofía y Teoría Política*, 27:7, 158–63. La Plata: Universidad Nacional de La Plata.

Rabossi, E., González, M. C., & Stigol, N. (1993). Los seminarios en la enseñanza de la filosofía. In E. Rabossi & G. Obiols (Eds). *La filosofía y el filosofar: problemas en su enseñanza* (pp. 41–56). Buenos Aires: Centro Editor de América Latina.

Romero, F. (1952). *Sobre la filosofía en América*. Buenos Aires: Raigal.

Ryle, G. (1949). *The concept of mind*. London: Hutchinson.

Salmerón, F. (1991). *Enseñanza y filosofía*. México: Fondo de Cultura Económica.

Further Reading

Alberini, C. (1953). Génesis y evolución del pensamiento argentino. *Cuadernos de Filosofía*, Buenos Aires, Facultad de Filosofía y Letras, UBA. Año V–VI, 10–11–12, 7–18.

Cramer, K., Gracia, J., et al. (1984). *La filosofía hoy en Alemania y América Latina*. Córdoba, Argentina: Círculo de Amigos del Instituto Goethe.

Gracia, J. (1987). La filosofía y su historia. *Revista Latinoamericana de Filosofía*, XIII:3, 259–78.

Pucciarelli, E., Fatone, V., et al. (1975). *Cuadernos de filosofía*. Buenos Aires, Facultad de Filosofía y Letras, UBA. Año XV, 22–3.

Rabossi, E. (1985). El análisis filosófico en la Argentina. In M. Dascal, J. Gracia, E. Rabossi, & E. Villanueva (Eds). *El análisis filosófico en América Latina* (pp. 25–32). México: Fondo de Cultura Económico.

Roig, A., Palau, G., et al. (1994). *Cuadernos de filosofía. Dossier 45 años de filosofía en Argentina*. Buenos Aires, Facultad de Filosofía y Letras, UBA, 40.

Romero, F. (1952). *Sobre la filosofía en América*. Buenos Aires: Editorial Raigal.

Salles, A., & Millan-Zaibert, E. (Eds). (2005). *The role of history in Latin American philosophy. Contemporary perspectives*. Albany, State University of New York Press.

UNESCO. Organización de las Naciones Unidas para la Educación, la Ciencia y la Cultura. (1990). *La enseñanza, la reflexión y la investigación filosóficas en América Latina y el Caribe*. Madrid: Tecnos.

30

Cultural Studies

ARTURO ARIAS

It has become common to state that Latin American cultural studies "entered the academic scene" in the 1980s, elaborating a critique of the symbolic production and everyday living experiences of social reality in the continent. I would argue this is not entirely a new phenomenon in Latin America. On the contrary, the ideologues of Latin American independence, heavily influenced by French Enlightenment thinking, worked along these lines by default. In their attempt to elaborate a new epistemology from the perspective of the new countries then being configured, they seldom made distinctions between "philosophy," "literature," "political tracts," and other forms of written knowledge; nonetheless, given the heritage of "the lettered city," they exercised quasi total intellectual hegemony, and enjoyed enormous political respect, benefiting from the explicatory power of what Avelar calls "the traditional aura of the *letrado*" (1999, p. 12). The phrase "lettered city" was originally conceived by Uruguay critic Angel Rama (1984), of whom more is said later. *Letrados* (men of letters) were not competing with ideologues because they were the ideologues themselves, the producers of symbolic capital. Their autonomy enabled them to feel equally at home in all kinds of genres, and they covered the terrain presently circumscribed by traditional disciplines.

Letrados were for the most part *criollos*, full-blooded Spaniards born in the Latin American colonies. They were the early protagonists of national public spheres in the hemisphere. Described by Román de la Campa as intellectuals whose "lust for power" cohabited with "isolated acts of literary transgression" (1999, p. 74), they intervened to legitimize exemplary narratives of national formation and integration in the process of constructing the nation itself as a symbolic entity, constituting its national imaginaries through discourses, symbols, images, and rites. Letrados imagined themselves at the vanguard of progress, often playing a role integrating those of military leader, prophet, priest, judge, and man of letters. All of these were linked to an active political career and to political considerations. Nineteenth-century literary production, then, established an ideological hegemony that interpellated individuals and transformed them into subjects who identified with the discursive formation named by the letrado.

Following this logic, we can rightfully claim that, since the 1800s, Latin American thinkers have produced a certain kind of knowledge that articulates the collective imaginaries and symbolic codes framed in variously written cultural manifestations with their political, historical, and social context. This is the generally recognized definition

425

of cultural studies as we know them today. They were likewise involved in an intuitive search for a socio-semiotic reorientation of their understanding of their own selves and of their national place in the world, while also attempting to define what modernity meant for their young nations. We could argue that this process began with the struggle for independence from Spain, and cite Mexico's first novelist José Joaquín Fernández de Lizardi, Venezuelan poet Andrés Bello and Central American philosophe José Cecilio del Valle as examples of its earliest exponents. They do not yet serve our purpose of identifying a Latin American cultural genealogy because, during most of the nineteenth century, *letrados* wrote primarily about national, not hemispheric or Latin American, issues. Indeed, the name "Latin America" was not even coined until the second half of the nineteenth century . . . by the French. *Amérique latine* first appeared in French emperor Napoleon III's *Lettres sur l'Amèrique du Nord*, as a goal for expansion during his reign. Therefore, we often begin with the publications of both Cuban poet José Martí's essay *Nuestra América* (1891), which appeared first in New York and then in Mexico City, and with Uruguayan essayist José Enrique Rodó's *Ariel* (1900). It is in these texts, both aiming toward political and ethical transformations, that the question of what it means to be a modern Latin American subject, qua Latin American subject, first emerges in a perspective that we could presently define as "interdisciplinary," with the caveat that it made its presence felt before traditional disciplines had been configured in the continent. The problematics and methodologies of Latin American cultural studies thus predate the generally recognized field of cultural studies. Still, they are centered on issues of colonialism and postcolonialism, although in relation to Latin American identity, and they intuitively configure a new thinking, an event, an encounter and a response long before the Birmingham model – traditionally credited with the invention of the concept of "cultural studies" in the 1950s, primarily through the efforts of Stuart Hall and Raymond Williams – or the French school of cultural studies that emerged in the 1960s – Barthes, Benjamin, Althusser, Rancière, Fanon, and Bourdieu, whose work emphasized the role of practice and embodiment in social dynamics – came into being. Roberto Rivera (2004) has suggested that one of the predicaments of neo-colonial intellectuals is to have to borrow theories that were not designed to address the problems they are most anxious to resolve. One of the unexpected consequences is that Latin Americans have often invented cultural products that greatly resemble those that Europe would only "discover" later. Rivera cites Sor Juana Inés de la Cruz's conception of Neo-Platonism and Juan José Arévalo's design of a disciplinary panopticon.

Latin American intellectuals undoubtedly began to focus on continental issues rather than national ones in response to the U.S. expansion into the Caribbean basin as a result of the Spanish-American War (1898). This crucial event took place 50 years after Mexico was forced to cede the present-day states of California, Nevada, Utah, and parts of Colorado, Arizona, New Mexico, and Wyoming – losing more than 500,000 square miles, or about 40 percent of its territory – in the Mexican–American war (1848), an event soon followed by the 1857 occupation of Nicaragua by confederate William Walker, who invaded that country and proclaimed himself president. The more aggressive entrance of the United States into the Latin American sphere in 1898 initiated a new era of difficult North–South relations, as the United States attempted to control the politics and economies of most countries of the Caribbean Basin, and later began constructing an inter-oceanic canal. President Theodore Roosevelt justified this intervention with the "Roosevelt Corollary" to the Monroe Doctrine, which implied that the United States could step into Latin America at will, supposedly to prevent intervention by Europe. When Nicaragua threatened to build a competing canal, the United States occupied the country (1909), overthrowing president José Santos Zelaya and imposing a dictator in his place. The United States landed Marines in Nicaragua, who would stay until 1933, just as it had previously done in Cuba, the Dominican Republic, Puerto Rico, and Panama.

This foreign policy poisoned U.S.–Latin America relations during most of the twentieth century. If Martí had anticipated this move in *Nuestra América* by signaling the danger of appropriating knowledges not created to solve the problems of Latin American postcolonial societies as explicatory power for thinking about turn-of-the-century postcoloniality and about the problematics of postcolonial nation-states, it was in the wake of the Spanish American War that *Ariel* (1900) emerged as an attempt to explain the cultural and metaphysical differences between North American and Latin American cultures by associating the former with the materialist and utilitarian elements embodied in Shakespeare's Prospero, from *The Tempest*, and the latter with a utopian ideal of spiritual and intellectual unity of Latin America with Spain and Europe, figured by Ariel, from the same play, a character capable of sacrificing material gain for spiritual concerns. Rodó's influence on young intellectuals up to the 1940s was enormous, and the principle of Latin uniqueness in its struggle with the United States had great resonance throughout the twentieth century. Rodó's critique, flaws notwithstanding, described an articulation of postcoloniality wherein the residues of colonial domination had seeped into the post-independence state. This also created a reclamation of anticolonial resistance, which would frame the grand narrative of Latin American cultural studies' self-constituting genealogy.

Building on this legacy of signifiers as markers of "meaning," Alfonso Reyes attempted in *Visión de Anáhuac* (1956) to reconfigure a fractured post-revolutionary Mexican identity by reconciling and blending pre-Columbian and modern-day Mexican cultures. With the Dominican critic Pedro Henríquez Ureña, and fellow Mexicans Antonio Caso and José Vasconcelos, he founded the Ateneo de la Juventud. This joint effort would pave the way both for the emerging notion of *mestizaje* ("mixed," implying mixed Spanish and indigenous ancestry) and for the elaboration of a cultural aesthetics. The first, originally articulated in *Visión de Anáhuac*, would find its highest expression in Vasconcelos's *La raza cósmica* (1925), where the idealized image of *mestizaje* as an end-of-history "cosmic race" inaugurates a contentious site of nation-building and racial politics. The second, prefigured in Reyes's *Cuestiones estéticas* (1955a), would be achieved by Henríquez Ureña's systematization of cultural production in *Seis ensayos en busca de nuestra expresión* (1928), *Literary Currents in Hispanic America* (1945), and *Historia de la cultura en la América Hispánica* (1947). In these works, Henríquez Ureña conceives of Latin American literary production, organized for the first time into a coherent whole, in terms of what Walter Mignolo (2000) has more recently labeled the history of the modern/colonial world, in an attempt to understand the historical formation and ethno-racial conformation of the continent. Thus, despite appearances, Henríquez Ureña's vast oeuvre is not strictly literary criticism, but a mapping of the "frame" of Latin American cultural production and a history of how literature becomes the primary means for the conformation of an epistemological subjectivity within the various nations of the continent. Like many contemporary practitioners of cultural studies, Henríquez Ureña worked, in Julio Ramos's words, "in the interstitial site of the essay, with transdisciplinary devices and ways of knowledge" (Ramos, 1998, p. 39).

In *Notas sobre la inteligencia Americana* (1955b) and *Posición de América* (1982) Reyes would return to issues of *mestizo* subjectivity by rearticulating another variable of cultural fusion of Western and indigenous values. He did not escape the "ethnocentric and reverse-ethnocentric benevolent double bind" (Spivak, 1999, p. 118) that effectively denies indigenous peoples their own "worlding," as Vasconcelos had not either, though he avoids the latter's missteps. Vasconcelos ultimately re-wove the threads of colonialism into his national narrative, whereas Reyes remained critical of European positionality and argued for an American identity constructed in opposition to what we would presently label as "Eurocentrism."

Fernando Ortiz attempted to grasp the complex transformation of cultures brought together by the power of colonialism and by imperial history. He coined the critical category of "transculturation" in 1940, in his now classic *Contrapunteo cubano del tabaco y del azúcar*. The term also represents a way of going around the problematical concept of acculturation, which represented an ethnocentric bias, a one-way street for non-Western cultures, whose only alternative was the assimilation of the imposed Western model. Transculturation, in contrast, became a two-way alternative, by which two cultures could influence each other despite confrontation and struggle. Important as this concept is, it did not enter mainstream debate until Angel Rama rearticulated it in the 1970s. From that time forward, it would prove to be one of the most important, durable, and most quoted categories in the continent's cultural debate.

A mention should also be made of Edmundo O'Gorman's historiographic questioning in the 1950s. In *La invención de América* (1958), O'Gorman opposed the traditional concept of the discovery of the Americas, an innovative reading of the primary sources from original perspectives. O'Gorman is often singled out as one of the pioneers of postcolonial studies in Latin America. In his best-known work, he argued – predating some of Said's latter conclusions about "Orientalism" – that America was "invented," not "discovered," as it was the result of a phantasmatic projection of Western thinking more than a chance discovery. In 2005, Mignolo would add, in *The Idea of Latin America*, to O'Gorman's conception that America was an "invention" saturated with "coloniality," that is, conceived at the intersection of the expansion of Europe over the New World.

According to the narrative memorialized by Stuart Hall, the Birmingham School emerged in the late 1950s from literature and the humanities. What is traditionally recognized as Latin American cultural studies, however, emerged primarily from the social sciences in the 1960s, when the cultural essays produced by the intellectuals I have discussed, and others, became fused with sociological and anthropological research in an attempt to account for the events then taking place in the continent. These systems of thought included dependency theory, internal colonialism, and theology of liberation, as well as the pedagogy of the oppressed, and an emerging reflection on popular cultures and on the legacy of Western thinking in a heterogeneous and contradictory continent. All these lines of thought were combined with the innovative production of literary and popular culture in the 1960s, including *boom* literature, street theater, the new cinema, or the *nueva canción* movement in popular music, to deliver a new understanding of both symbolic production and social imaginaries on the continent, thus systematizing an original way of understanding cultural reality that would continue in the 1990s.

One of the most visible of these approaches was dependency theory in economics, which began in the late 1950s under the guidance of the Director of the United Nations Economic Commission for Latin America (CEPAL, in Spanish), Raúl Prebisch. Prebisch and his colleagues were troubled by the fact that economic growth in the advanced industrialized countries did not necessarily lead to growth in the poorer countries. On the contrary, their research suggested that economic activity in the richer countries often generated serious economic problems in poorer nations. That possibility had not been predicted by classical economic theory, which assumed that economic growth would benefit all countries even if the wealth was not always equally shared. Thus, dependency was defined by Theotonio Dos Santos as ". . . a certain structure of the world economy . . . that . . . favors some countries to the detriment of others and limits the development possibilities of the subordinate economics . . ." (Dos Santos, 1970, p. 226).

Three common assumptions were associated with most dependency theories. First, dependency theory characterized the international system as comprised of two sets of states, variously described as dominant/dependent, center/periphery, or metropolitan/satellite. The dominant states were the advanced industrial nations. The dependent states were those Latin American nations with low per capita gross national products (GNPs), relying heavily on the export of a single commodity for foreign exchange earnings. Second, they maintained that external forces were of singular importance to the economic activities within dependent states. These external forces included multinational corporations, international commodity markets, foreign assistance, communications, and any other means by which the advanced industrialized countries could represent their economic interests abroad. Thirdly, the definitions of dependency indicated that the relations between dominant and dependent states were dynamic because their interactions not only reinforced but also intensified the continual growth of unequal patterns. By repudiating the central distributive mechanism of the classical model, discounting aggregate measures of economic growth, and encouraging nation-states to pursue policies of self-reliance, dependency theory represented a uniquely original approach. The Marxist and post-Marxist view of international relations would constitute the economic, social, and political backbone of interdisciplinary cultural studies, as they congealed in the late 1970s and 1980s.

The same could be said for the concept of internal colonialism. Close to dependency theories, internal colonialism is a concept whose origins can be traced to the mid-1960s, in the work of Mexican social scientists Rodolfo Stavenhagen and Pablo González Casanova, who wanted to explore links between class and ethnicity (Stavenhagen, 1965; González Casanova, 1969, p. 33). Internal colonialism took a step away from the idea of *mestizaje* and "social integration" as vehicles of social mobility. Instead, it addressed the political inequalities between regions within a single society. The category added an indigenous dimension to the description of the uneven effects of state development on a regional basis, and to the exploitation of subalternized groups, who constituted a colonized people within the nation-state. An internal colony typically produced wealth for the benefit of those closely associated with the power apparatus of the state,

429

usually located in the capital city. Thus, members of the internal colonies were distinguished by cultural variables such as ethnicity, language, or religion, and excluded from
prestigious social and political positions, which were hegemonized by members of the
metropolis displaying Eurocentric traits. The main difference between the neocolonialism
implicit in dependency theory and internal colonialism was the source of exploitation.
In the former, the control came from outside the nation-state; in the latter, it came from
within it. This new approach addressed the gradual racialization process with a
significant non-European population.

In 1968, the so-called radical group of anthropologists of Mexico's National School
of Anthropology and History, nicknamed *los siete magníficos* (the Magnificent Seven)
developed a more radical take on the concept of internal colonialism that not only exposed
its limits, but also conceptually buried the classical Mexican anthropological notions
of *mestizaje* and *indigenismo* as originally developed by Gonzalo Aguirre Beltrán, thus
breaking the close relationship between Mexican anthropology and official nationalism. Led by Arturo Warman and Guillermo Bonfil Batalla, they published *De eso que
llaman antropología mexicana* (Warman et al., 1970; Bonfil, 1970). The group also included
Margarita Nolasco, Mercedes Olivera, and Enrique Valencia as its major figures. They
complained that Mexican *indigenismo* had attempted to incorporate indigenous peoples
into a dominant "national" and "modern" system because Mexican anthropology
had placed itself at the service of the state, thus abandoning the scientific and critical
potential of the discipline. Warman unfortunately reversed himself in the 1980s. He
became Director of the Procuraduría Agraria (Ministry of Agriculture) in the Salinas
de Gortari government (1988–94), and provided the rationale for privatizing the *ejidos*
(communal lands distributed by the Cárdenas government to landless peasants from
1934 to 1940 as a land reform program) in accordance with neoliberal restructuring
in 1991. He subsequently published in praise of the North American Free Trade
Agreement (NAFTA), at a time when the Mexican people, intellectuals, and indigenous
groups opposed it. Indeed, the way NAFTA was approved by the Mexican government,
without any public inquiries or popular consent, marked the emergence of the indigenous Zapatista movement in Chiapas, and the beginning of the end for the Partido
Institucional Revolucionario (PRI), which ruled Mexico since 1920, and lost power
in 2000.

Despite Warman's latter positioning, the debates ensuing from the *siete magníficos*
in 1968, furthered by other members of the group such as Mercedes Olivera, who lived
with Maya refugees during the 1980s and helped create Maya feminist organizations
in the 1990s, would impact ethnic and indigenous theory in Central America in the
1980s, as well as Chiapas and South America a decade later. These political experiences and the scholarship that evolved from them ultimately enabled Mignolo to
develop the concept of post-Occidentalism in the 1990s. The latter concept, originally
named in passing in 1974 by Fernández Retamar in "Nuestra América y Occidente,"
which will be explained further in this same chapter, questions and critiques Western
paradigms (including global paradigms) at work in the interpretation of Latin
American societies and cultures, including scholarship.

Liberation theory embraced the premises of both dependency theory and internal
colonialism, and put a moral spin on them. Liberation theology was a sequel to the
Second Vatican Council (ending in late 1965), which turned the church upside down

by stating that, instead of saving people for the afterlife, the Catholic Church's role should be to improve the life of the poor on this earth. This idea led to a questioning of traditional models of pastoral work by many priests and nuns in Latin America. In August 1968 the Second General Conference of CELAM (Latin American Episcopal Council), known as the Medellín Conference, used a structure of reality/reflection/pastoral consequences to "apply" Vatican II to Latin America (Berryman, 1984, chapter two). Out of this meeting emerged the beginnings of liberation theology, with an emphasis on *concientización* (conscientization, or raising awareness), which implied an acceptance of Paulo Freire's methodology, as I will explain below. The premises of this movement, however, were not systematically theorized until the publication of Gustavo Gutiérrez's *Theology of Liberation* (1971) and Hugo Assmann's *Theology for a Nomad Church* (1971). The main methodological innovation of liberation theology is to approach theology (i.e., to speak of God) from the viewpoint of the economically poor and oppressed because they are a privileged channel of God's grace. Its main lines included the rejection of the notion of a "separation of planes" (spiritual and temporal) in favor of a single history of humankind; an ideological critique of the orthodox church; the assertion that while the definitive kingdom of God was beyond history, it needed to be built by partial realizations within history; and, finally, that conflict, even class struggle, was part of history. What was most radical was not the writing of highly educated priests and scholars, but the social organization of church practice through the model of Christian base communities. Theologian Leonardo Boff and others strove to create a bottom-up movement in practice, with biblical interpretation and liturgical practice designed by lay practitioners themselves, rather than by the orthodox church hierarchy. Leonardo Boff and his brother Clodovis state in their book that "it is *only* this effective connection with liberating practice that can give theologians a 'new spirit,' a new style, or a new way of doing theology" (Boff and Boff, 2000, p. 22). Furthermore, with its emphasis on the "preferential option for the poor," the practice (or *praxis* to use Gramsci and Freire's concept) was as important as the belief, if not more so; the movement was said to emphasize *orthopraxis* over *orthodoxy*. Base communities met in small gatherings where the Bible could be discussed and grassroots political organization could take place. Liberation theorists placed a high value on lay participation, an approach that influenced the Latin American Subaltern Studies Group, formed in 1992 and dissolved in 2000, which defined itself as a "small interdisciplinary academic 'affinity group' . . ." (Rodríguez, 2001, pp. 29–30).

Along the same line, Paulo Freire points to what he labeled a "culture of silence" in *Pedagogy of the Oppressed*, by which he understands that dominated individuals lose their ability to critically respond to a culture that is forced upon them by a dominant social sector. A long-time Brazilian adult educator, Freire worked to help subaltern peoples find a voice. In 1968, he published *Pedagogy of the Oppressed*, an English translation of which appeared in 1970, in which he claimed that the subject's ontological vocation was to act upon and transform his/her world, and in so doing move toward ever new possibilities of fuller and richer life, individually and collectively. He added that every human being, no matter how "ignorant" or submerged in the culture of silence he or she might be, is capable of looking critically at the world in a dialogical encounter with others. His pedagogy was aimed at providing the proper tools for this encounter, so that the subaltern individual could gradually perceive his/her personal and social reality as well as the contradictions in it, become conscious of his/her own perception of that reality, and deal critically with it. Freire's pedagogy became closely associated with the efforts of liberation theology because his emphasis on dialogue struck a strong chord with Catholic missionaries concerned with popular and informal education. His concern with *praxis*, however contradictory that might be, also led to Latin American concerns for subaltern subjectivity, and eventually allowed for a reevaluation of *testimonio* (testimony) as an anti-literary literary genre.

The list of individuals who, emerging in the wake of 1960s upheavals, made fundamental contributions to what became cultural studies in the 1980s includes Darcy Ribeiro. Ribeiro was a Brazilian anthropologist who brought indigenous peoples to the forefront of his country's history. Of his many books, the one about the mythology and art of the Kadiweu is considered the most important. However, he enters the genealogy of Latin American cultural studies mainly through his *O processo civilizatório* (1987), where he analyzes the emergence of sociocultural formations with the goal of understanding the causes of unequal socioeconomic development and exploring the perspectives for so-called "backward peoples." Ribeiro is convinced that theories of history do not account for these societies, given modernity's tendency to homogenize national origins. He outlines a massive amount of anthropological data about social, cultural, and economic facts regarding the formative period of hemispheric ethnic groups that points towards a new theory of culture and an alternative gaze on indigenous populations in the Americas. His insights would transform future perceptions of the indigenous subject.

The incorporation of popular cultures into cultural analysis was introduced by Mexican Carlos Monsiváis. Monsiváis's often satirical writings celebrate the marginalized popular cultures of Mexico City that, in his understanding, unconsciously decolonize themselves, as a way to criticize Mexico's high-brow cultural space and its culture/power relations. This counterpoint enables Monsiváis to analyze historical obstacles contriving to prevent Mexico's passage into modernity along the lines of high-brow/low-brow cultural tension. The majority of his chronicles were published between 1970 and 1995, though they are still ongoing, and he is best known for *Amor perdido* (1977). In them, he celebrates the beleaguered inhabitants of super-crowded Mexico City, popular energy and its transmogrification into mass-mediatic iconography, turning "the negative into sources of a compensatory pride" (Egan, 2001, introduction). His writing becomes a ritual performance allowing the reader to observe a culture of poverty that brings forth redemptive signs of emergent change.

We see another trend in Cuba, where, writing from that nation's Marxist perspective, Roberto Fernández Retamar attempted in *Calibán* (1971) to refute Rodó's idealization of a Europeanist "Ariel" by presenting the "cannibal" figure in *The Tempest* as a "proletarian" alternative. Despite its Cuban-Marxist orientation and its insistence on placing Martí at the foundation of an essentialist *mestizo* identity in Latin America, Fernández Retamar's text paved the way toward opening a discussion on the possibilities of elaborating a post-Western ideology, an issue mentioned in his subsequent essay "Nuestra América y Occidente" (1974) in *Para el perfil definitivo del hombre* (Fernández Retamar, 1981). Still, the substitution of Ariel by Caliban seems to underscore the influence of Europe, since they are both Shakespearean characters, thereby, as Spivak has pointed out, enforcing a "foreclosure" of indigenous presence in the debate on Latin

American identity (Spivak, 1999, p. 118). What Spivak did not note, as Ofelia Schutte has pointed out, is that in Latin America the indigenous subject is indeed the privileged interlocutor of the West, whereas the African descendant is not. Retamar introduced a reading that linked Caliban primarily to the African presence in the Caribbean, by way of Fanon's deconstruction of former Eurocentric readings of this Shakespearean character.

Julio Ramos has been cited for arguing that the difference between traditional Latin Americanist thinking up to around the publication of Fernández Retamar's article, and Latin American cultural studies as it evolved in the 1980s, was rooted in the fact that the former evinced a belief in the integrative capacity of national literatures and art, whereas the latter criticized the concept of a national culture as an apparatus of power (Ramos, 1998; Trigo, 2004a, p. 6). Perhaps it would be better to say that earlier essays, however heterogeneous and irreducible to the autonomous principles they might have been, were framed by a set of epistemological and metaphysical principles aimed at nation-building, a phenomenon that presupposed economic modernization, cultural modernism, and democratization, whereas Latin American cultural studies, as we know them now, emerged from the fissures, cracks, and fault lines of the failed process of nation-building and its nadir in the late 1980s. Therefore, the seminal role of Ribeiro, Freire, Fernández Retamar, or Monsiváis, among others, working on the interstices of the essay with transdisciplinary methodologies, justifies their recognition in the genealogy of Latin American cultural studies.

During the late 1970s, it was Angel Rama's reformulation of the category of transculturation in *Transculturación narrativa en América latina* that provided the groundwork for Latin American cultural theory as it evolved in the 1980s, even if Rama's theorization remains within the realm of literature. As Miller states, Rama focused on the possibilities implied by transculturation as a form of narrative transitivity between cultures, even when those cultures stood in asymmetrical relations of power (Miller, 2004). However, neither the model devised by Ortiz, nor Rama's modifications, created a general theory of transculturation, thus leaving the category open to further debate and modifications by cultural studies practitioners of the 1980s and 1990s. Ultimately, the concept of "transculturation" was either replaced or fused in the 1980s by/with newer conceptual categories, such as "hybridity" (García Canclini) and "heterogeneity" (Cornejo Polar).

By the end of the 1980s most academics agreed that the macro-narratives of the 1960s were no longer adequate for explaining the fast changes introduced by emergent globalization (Del Sarto, 2004, p. 156). One of its consequences was the idea that literature and all forms of "high culture" had lost their position as the cornerstones of national cultures; that traditional intellectuals had in turn lost their ground as *letrados* guiding national communities, and that the very idea of nation-states as the only (or at least privileged) political and cultural synthesis faced serious, perhaps insurmountable challenges. This complex set of ideas led to a revision of the theoretical models of the 1960s. The reformulation of methodologies resulted in the conformation of what would come to be labeled "Latin American cultural studies." Nevertheless, Del Sarto takes pains to underline that these creative revisions, even when they ventured into new epistemological paths, were done in dialogue with the continent's tradition of critical thinking: in her own words, they were "not the product of epistemological

433

ruptures but instead of concrete historical continuities" (2004, p. 157). Needless to say, what some people consider a new epistemological path, others consider a rupture.

Hybridity was popularized by cultural anthropologist Néstor García Canclini in *Culturas híbridas* (1989), shortly before an analogous concept was introduced to the English-speaking world by Homi Bhabha. Both conceptualizations were problematized together in U.S. academic institutions. Mixing anthropological analysis with art criticism and references to Bourdieu's symbolic relations, García Canclini's book became, as has been pointed out by many critics, a turning point in the emergence of a field of Latin American cultural studies. García Canclini argues that tradition and modernity became articulated through mutually dependent needs. Within his logic, there is interplay whereby modern symbolic representations are woven in the fabric of traditional cultural production and vice versa, rendering new identities through cultural difference. Hybridity thus focuses on the ambivalence of cultural authority. It shifts away from ontological authenticity – that is, away from the idea that there is a stable, coherent, knowable self that is conscious, rational, autonomous, and universal, so that no physical conditions or differences substantially affect how this self operates – as a political articulation of contradictory identities struggling for hegemony within nation-states as well as in transnational spaces. We are done here with the Enlightenment notion that the self knows itself and the world through reason, or rationality, posited as the highest form of mental functioning. García Canclini's definition of culture as a field of production, circulation, and consumption of symbolic goods and signs has framed the concept of culture as a necessary and inevitable transformational practice that precludes all essentialisms. As Del Sarto stated, hybridity became a central paradigm during the 1990s as a descriptive category, forcing most theorizations on the field to allude to it (2004, p. 181).

In this same period, Antonio Cornejo Polar's concepts of heterogeneity and contradictory totality, as framed in *Escribir en el aire* (1994), also had significant theoretical impact, relocating theoretical debate within the problematic of ethnic issues. Derived from his understanding of Peruvian ethnic conflicts and his re-reading of Peruvian political philosopher José Carlos Mariátegui's (1894–1930) *Seven Interpretive Essays on Peruvian Reality* (1928), Cornejo's conceptualization implies the existence of conflictive historical processes that cannot be solved within a diversity of homogeneous ethnic cultures. He argues that multiple inter-crossings do not lead toward syncretism, but instead emphasize "aporetic conflicts" (that is, conflicts that represent a final impasse) and alterities. His theory of culture thus refuses synthesis and fusion. He urges recognition of the complexity and difficulties of this process as a colonially-produced space of extreme ambiguity and contradictory meanings, thus pointing toward the emergence of the notion of the "coloniality of power," which entered the lexicon of Latin American theorists in 1991 through Aníbal Quijano's seminal article "Colonialidad y modernidad/ racionalidad" published in *Perú Indígena*.

In the early 1990s, the recently constituted Latin American Subaltern Studies Group called into question the role of the academy in reading and representing the subaltern. For these scholars, academic work should have focused on making subaltern voices heard in academia (Rodríguez, 2001, p. 9). The popularity of Rigoberta Menchú's *testimonio* provided them with an anti-literary literary genre with which to make their case. However, as Trigo has pointed out in "Why do I do cultural studies?" (2000,

434

p. 78), they failed to realize the epistemological fetishization of the text as the ground of unmediated truth and the consequent political fetishization of the poetics of solidarity that enabled the critic's identification with the testimonial subject. The ongoing debate that subalternism generated put into question the very nature of "cultural studies." Nevertheless, by understanding the latter category as a mechanism for problematizing cultural and cross-cultural practices, scholars could work across linguistic, national, ethnic, and cultural borders, not to mention differences in social class. In this transition, the object of study shifted from the formal aspects of given cultural genres, usually within specific national frameworks, to the portrayal of everyday cultural detail, non-traditional or alternative knowledge producers, and the conditions and effects of sedimented linguistic turns. In this sense, Latin American cultural studies allowed for the exploration of imaginary, ex-centric representations of otherness, underlining both the creative energy of subaltern events and their attempts to create more just and egalitarian societies in the face of globalization.

After peaking in the first half of the 1990s with subaltern studies and its debates on *testimonio*, Latin American cultural studies seemed to enter an epistemological and institutional crisis by the end of the century. Some critics believe that a hyper-deconstructive dynamic and a theoretical saturation led scholars to lose sight of the object of study. A will on the part of critics to identify with the subject also contributed to a reification of abstract categories. Nonetheless, Walter Mignolo and Aníbal Quijano's concept of the "coloniality of power," conjoined with their corollaries, colonial semiosis, border gnosis, geopolitics of knowledge, and post-Occidentalism, operating sometimes as epistemic metaphors deployed to move thinking beyond Western and Eurocentric conceptualizations, provided a new way of framing the issues of cultural production and agency. Mignolo framed these issues, while recognizing Quijano's contribution, in his book *Local Histories/Global Designs* (2000). The popularity of those concepts can be attributed in part to the reemergence of indigenous issues in the Americas, as exemplified by the Nobel peace prize awarded to Menchú in 1992, the emergence of the Zapatista movement in 1994, and the election of Evo Morales as Bolivia's president in 2004 after years of grassroots agitation in the Andes.

In the first decade of the twenty-first century, the effects of globalization have further modified the concept of culture. Besides its economic impact, globalization produces symbolic goods generated by a libidinal economy, in Trigo's understanding, which enables the circulation and consumption of many other material goods (Trigo, 2003/2004, p. 269). Thus, to understand the role of culture, and the role of transculturation, one has to understand the interrelationships between political economy and libidinal economy, between the exchange value of merchandise and the exchange value of cultural signs, between work and desire, and between producers and consumers. Along similar lines, George Yúdice has theorized how diverse social groups, whether hegemonic or subaltern, have come to see culture as a resource to be negotiated within powerful transnational, globalized contexts, shaping the meaning of contemporary cultural phenomena and transforming both identity politics and cultural agency "relating to the international pacts, interpretive frameworks, and institutional conditionings of comportment and knowledge production" (Yúdice, 2003, p. 4).

The divergent lines chosen by Mignolo and Yúdice illustrate the broad, heterogeneous space covered by contemporary Latin American cultural studies. Both point to

435

alternative paths that lead to a similar end: that of transformation, of changing the terms of Latin America's present conundrum. A "Washington consensus" coined in reference to the neoliberal economic reforms championed by U.S. experts in the 1980s – reforms that generated a U.S.-centric perspective and style of governance – have recently been subjected to deepening dissent and outright refusal in Latin America. We could very well conclude that cultural studies and cultural approaches in general are presently elaborating a critique of the web of signs that might make it possible to break away from the subordinate, neocolonial role assigned to the continent under the present system. In this sense, we seem to have come full circle, back to the concerns that launched cultural critique at the beginning of the twentieth century in the first place.

Related chapters: 12 Marxism; 13 Liberation Philosophy; 20 *Mestizaje* and Hispanic Identity; 21 Liberation in Theology, Philosophy, and Pedagogy; 22 Philosophy, Postcoloniality, and Postmodernity; 23 Globalization and Latin American Thought.

References

Assmann, H. (1975). *Theology for a nomad church*. Maryknoll, NY: Orbis (Originally published 1971).

Avelar, I. (1999). *The untimely present: postdictatorial Latin American fiction and the task of mourning*. Durham: Duke University Press.

Berryman, P. (1984). *The religious roots of rebellion*. Maryknoll, NY: Orbis.

Boff, L., & Boff, C. (2000). *Introducing liberation theory*. Maryknoll, NY: Orbis.

Bonfil, G. (1970). Del indigenismo de la revolución a la antropología crítica. In A. Warman, G. Bonfil et al. (Eds). *De eso que llaman antropología mexicana*. Mexico: Editorial Nuestro Tiempo.

Cornejo Polar, A. (2003). *Escribir en el aire: ensayo sobre la heterogeneidad socio-cultural en las literaturas andinas*. Lima: Latinoamericana Editores (Original work published 1994).

De la Campa, R. (1999). *Latin Americanism*. Minneapolis: University of Minnesota Press.

Del Sarto, A. (2004). Introduction: part II: foundations. In A. del Sarto, A. Ríos, & A. Trigo (Eds). *The Latin American cultural studies reader* (pp. 153–81). Durham: Duke University Press.

Dos Santos, T. (May 1970). The structure of dependence. *American Economic Review*, 60, 231–36.

Egan, L. (2001). *Culture and chronicle in contemporary Mexico*. Tucson: University of Arizona Press.

Fernández Retamar, R. (1981). Nuestra América y Occidente. In *Para el perfil definitivo del hombre* (pp. 520–38). Havana: Letras Cubanas (Original work published 1974).

Fernández Retamar, R. (1989). *Caliban and other essays*. (E. Baker, Trans.). Minneapolis: University of Minnesota Press (*Calibán* originally published 1971).

Franco, J. (2002). *The decline and fall of the lettered city: Latin America in the Cold War*. Cambridge: Harvard University Press.

Freire, P. (1970). *Pedagogy of the oppressed*. (M. B. Ramos, Trans.). New York: Continuum (Original work published 1968).

García Canclini, N. (1989). *Culturas híbridas: estrategias para entrar y salir de la modernidad*. Mexico: Grijalbo.

González Casanova, P. (1969). Internal colonialism and national development. In L. Horowitz, J. De Castro, & J. Gerassi (Eds). *Latin American radicalism*. New York: Random House.

Gutiérrez, G. (2002). *A theology of liberation: history, politics, and salvation*. 15th Anniversary edn. Maryknoll, NY: Orbis (Original work published 1971).

Hall, S. (1996). Cultural studies and its theoretical legacies. In D. Morley & K-H. Chen (Eds). *Stuart Hall: critical dialogues in cultural studies* (pp. 262–75). London: Routledge.

Henríquez Ureña, P. (1945). *Literary currents in Hispanic America.* Cambridge, MA: Harvard University Press.

Henríquez Ureña, P. (1947). *Historia de la cultura en la América Hispánica.* Mexico: Fondo de Cultura Económica.

Henríquez Ureña, P. (1960). *Seis ensayos en busca de nuestra expresión. Obra crítica.* E. S. Speratti Piñero (Ed.). Mexico: Fondo de Cultura Económica (Original work published 1928).

Lomnitz, C. (July–Dec., 2000). Bordering on anthropology: the dialectics of a national tradition in Mexico. *Revue de synthèse,* 4e S. 3–4, 345–80.

Mariátegui, J. C. (1971). *Seven interpretive essays on Peruvian reality.* (M. Urguidi, Trans.). Austin: University of Texas Press (Original work published 1928).

Martí, J. (1977). *Obras completas.* Vol. 15: *Nuestra América.* Caracas: Biblioteca Ayacucho (Original work published 1891).

Mignolo, W. D. (2000). *Local histories/global designs: coloniality, subaltern knowledges, and border thinking.* Princeton: Princeton University Press.

Mignolo, W. D. (2005). *The idea of Latin America.* Malden, MA: Blackwell.

Miller, M. G. (2004). *Rise and fall of the cosmic race: the cult of mestizaje in Latin America.* Austin: University of Texas Press.

Monsiváis, C. (1977). *Amor perdido.* Mexico: ERA.

O'Gorman, E. (1977). *La invención de América.* Mexico: Fondo de Cultura Económica (Original work published 1958).

Ortiz, F. (2002). *Contrapunteo cubano del tabaco y del azúcar. Edición crítica.* E. M. Santí (Ed.). Madrid: Cátedra (Original work published 1940).

Quijano, A. (1991). Colonialidad y modernidad/racionalidad. *Perú Indígena* (Lima), 13:29, 11–20.

Rama, A. (1984). *La ciudad letrada.* Hanover, NH: Ediciones del Norte.

Ramos, J. (1998). The trial of Alberto Mendoza: paradoxes of subjectification. *Journal of Latin American Cultural Studies,* 7:1, 39–54.

Reyes, A. (1955a). *Cuestiones estéticas.* Mexico: Fondo de Cultura Económica.

Reyes, A. (1955b). *Notas sobre la inteligencia Americana.* Mexico, Fondo de Cultura Económica.

Reyes, A. (1956). *Visión de Anáhuac.* Mexico: Fondo de Cultura Económica.

Reyes, A. (1982). *Posición de América.* Mexico: Nueva Imagen.

Ribeiro, D. (1987). *O processo civilizatório: etapas da evolução sócio-cultural.* 10th edn. Petrópolis: Vozes.

Rivera, R. (2004). *A study of liberation discourse: the semantics of opposition in Freire and Gutierrez.* New York: Peter Lang.

Rodó, J. E. (1988). *Ariel.* (M. S. Peden, Trans.). Austin: University of Texas Press (Original work published 1900).

Rodríguez, I. (2001). Reading subalterns across texts, disciplines, and theories: from representation to recognition. In I. Rodríguez (Ed.). *The Latin American subaltern studies reader* (pp. 1–32). Durham: Duke University Press.

Spivak, G. (1999). *A critique of postcolonial reason: toward a history of the vanishing present.* Cambridge, MA: Harvard University Press.

Stavenhagen, R. (1965). Classes, colonialism, and acculturation. Essay on a system of inter-ethnic relations in Mesoamerica. *Studies in Comparative International Development,* 1:6, 53–77.

Trigo, A. (2000). Why do I do cultural studies? *Journal of Latin American Cultural Studies,* 9:1, 73–93.

Trigo, A. (2003/2004). Apuntes para una crítica de la economía política de la cultura en la globalización. *Revista Estudios. Revista de Investigaciones Literarias y Culturales,* 22/23, 269–302.

Trigo, A. (2004). General introduction. In A. del Sarto, A. Ríos, & A. Trigo (Eds). *The Latin American cultural studies reader* (pp. 1–14). Durham: Duke University Press.

Vasconcelos, J. (1958). *La raza cósmica. Obras completas*, t. II (pp. 903–42). Mexico: Libreros Mexicanos (Original work published 1925).

Warman, A., Bonfil, G., Nolasco, M., Olivera, M., & Valencia, E. (1970). *De eso que llaman antropología mexicana*. Mexico: Editorial Nuestro Tiempo.

Yúdice, G. (2003). *The expediency of culture: uses of culture in the global era*. Durham: Duke University Press.

31

Deontic Logic and Legal Philosophy

PABLO NAVARRO

I. Introduction

Legal philosophy in Latin America does not differ significantly from philosophical studies of the law in the United States, Germany, the UK, or Sweden. The main doctrines and problems that define the conceptual agenda of legal philosophy have not remained unnoticed in Latin America. Many contributions of Latin American legal philosophers are analysis of the most important contemporary legal theories such as Kelsen's pure theory of law, Hart's practice theory, or Dworkin's law as integrity, even if legal philosophy in Latin America is much more than an exegesis of doctrines developed in other regions of the world. In general, these received theories have been used not only as targets for critical studies but also as starting points for original developments. Latin American legal philosophers have made valuable contributions in deontic logic, the theory of legal systems, the dynamical nature of law, the legitimacy of law, the philosophical basis of liberalism, etc. I cannot review all of these contributions in this chapter. Rather, I shall attempt to provide a general picture of legal philosophy in Latin America by focusing on certain authors and problems according to the following criteria:

(a) I shall focus on contemporary deontic logic and philosophy of law. My objective is to review contributions that are still regarded as influential in the international context of legal philosophy. According to this restriction, a very original theory like the so-called 'egological theory of law' developed by Carlos Cossio (Argentina) or the ideas on deontic logic advanced by Eduardo García Máynez (Mexico) will not be analyzed here since they are no longer debated in contemporary legal philosophy.

(b) I shall use the expression '*Latin American* legal philosophy' as shorthand for 'Legal philosophy developed *in* Latin America.' As a result I shall only deal with legal philosophy developed *in* Latin America by philosophers who have substantially contributed to this discipline. It is worth noticing that for political, economical, or academic reasons, Latin America has suffered from a dramatic exodus. Many brilliant jurists and philosophers like Mario Bunge (Argentina), Héctor Neri-Castañeda (Guatemala), Ernesto Garzón Valdés (Argentina), and Roberto

Mangabeira Unger (Brazil) have developed outstanding academic careers *outside* Latin America. Although I shall mention them incidentally, their contributions to legal theory must not be overlooked.

(c) No clear boundaries define the conceptual content of legal philosophy. Although a significant part of this discipline refers to normative theories about law and society, digging into these philosophical domains requires taking into account questions about moral and political philosophy which lie outside the scope of this essay. For this reason, I shall only consider contributions on the nature of law and legal theories, the connections between rights and principles, the structure of legal systems, and the foundations of deontic logic. Even more, I shall only comment on works that belong to the *analytic* tradition and other philosophical approaches will only be mentioned here incidentally.

II.   On Law and Morality

In Latin America, the old dispute between legal positivism and natural law theories has not referred to the definition of law or the duty to obey unjust legal system but rather these classical problems have been displaced by more sophisticated philosophical controversies. In this respect, four contemporary contributions about the conceptual connections between law and morality are worth mentioning, i.e., the doctrines advanced by Carlos Nino (Argentina), Cristina Redondo (Argentina), Fernando Atria (Chile) and Jorge L. Rodríguez (Argentina). Although all these contributions refer, by and large, to the justification of judicial decisions, for the sake of simplicity they can be grouped into two subclasses: the normativity of law (Nino and Redondo) and the nature of legal reasoning (Atria and Rodríguez).

1.   Concepts of law and justificatory legal reasoning

Carlos Nino was an analytical legal philosopher who made an outstanding contribution to ethics, legal philosophy, criminal law, and constitutional theory (Nino, 1985, 1991, 1994, 1996). His conception of legal theory is firmly anchored in his rejection of conceptual essentialism, that is, the idea that the analysis of *the* concept of law is the proper task of legal philosophy. Our legal practices are too complex to be captured by a single concept which could explain all our relevant intuitions about this social and normative phenomenon. According to this conception, legal philosophy must take into account several concepts of law and the selection of a particular one will depend on objectives and attitudes that guide our philosophical enquiry; that is, we can adopt different concepts of law according to our theoretical objectives.

Nino claims that *the* concept of law assumed by legal officials, e.g., judges when they justify decisions on legal rights and duties, is morally tainted. Nino rejects a traditional view on legal justification, which reconstructs this process as a complex of legal norms and facts proved in court. Even more, Nino emphasizes that it would be a *logical* fallacy to conclude that judicial decisions are justified only by legal norms. His arguments can be briefly sketched in the following way: the justification of legal decisions could be analyzed in two different forms. On the one hand, a judge uses a *legal* norm because he believes that it offers the right *moral* answer to a certain controversy. In this case, the fact that the norm is a legal one is irrelevant because its moral content determined its acceptance. Thus, if judges apply a norm because they believe that this offers a right moral solution, their justificatory reasoning cannot be distinguished from an ordinary moral one. On the other hand, judges apply legal norms because they have been enacted by legal authorities. In this case, judges accept legal norms only in virtue of their specific social origin and as a consequence they are committed to apply these norms even if they do not regard them as a right moral solution. However, the *fact* that a norm has been enacted by a certain authority does not posses practical relevance. *Social* facts – like other facts – are inert as sources of normative claims, and we cannot legitimately draw normative conclusions from factual premises. The social origin of a legal norm could be relevant only to the extent that another nonlegal norm confers on the first one a practical value. This nonlegal norm is no longer accepted by its origin but in virtue of its content. Therefore, this ultimate normative premise is accepted as a moral norm.

2. Law and reasons for action

Nino's argument on the conceptual connection between law and morality points out that the normativity of law actually depends on moral reasons. The explanation of the normativity of law is regarded as one of the most important problems in contemporary legal philosophy. There are many different issues entangled here, but two questions seem to be the main ones: What types of reasons for action are legal norms? And to what extent can legal reasons justify actions and decisions against our ordinary moral reasons? Latin American legal philosophers have not overlooked these questions, and a detailed analysis of the problem of legal normativity can be found in Cristina Redondo's book, *Reasons for Action and the Law* (1999).

In her book, Redondo realizes that critics of legal positivism like Nino claim that positivism is not able to explain why legal norms can provide genuine reasons for action. Redondo defends legal positivism and rejects the notion that the practical relevance of law depends on moral norms. On the contrary, she claims that valid legal norms could genuinely make a practical difference. In order to defend her thesis, she deals with a highly debated topic: the fragmentation of practical reasoning. Her conclusion is that we can have true legal answers as well as right, but different, moral answers to the same practical problem.

According to Redondo, the debate on the relation between law and morality makes sense only when morality refers to a specific set of reasons that can be at odds with legal norms. If, by definition, moral norms occupy a higher hierarchical position in our practical reasoning, then no practical conflict could stem from the intersection between law and morality. Therefore, we cannot classify reasons as moral or legal in accordance with the position that they occupy in practical reasoning. In particular, we cannot accept that morality is the ultimate premise in non-fragmentary practical reasoning. Other-wise, moral norms are no longer regarded as substantive reasons that compete with other reasons but as a set of norms that actually provides the definitive solution to a practical problem. This shift in our reconstruction of moral reasons (i.e., from right and competing reasons to ultimate reasons) hides the fact that the statement 'moral norms are the ultimate ones in our practical reasoning' is not a description of the structure of our moral world. Rather, it is an analytical statement that depends only on the new meaning attributed to the expression 'moral norms'. In other words, the argument over-looks the fact that even if moral reasons were good candidates to be ultimate reasons, it would be wrong to conclude that our ultimate reasons are by their own nature also moral ones. This new concept of moral norms deprives them of any substantive value and refers only to formal attitudes. As a consequence, this argument on the moral nature of ultimate premises of justificatory reasons cuts no ice with legal positivism.

3. The limits of law and legal reasoning

Legal reasoning is unfortunately a neglected topic in Latin American legal philosophy. Although there are interesting contributions on legal argumentation, coherence of law, and other related topics, there is no set of relevant works that analyzes the nature and function of legal reasoning in a systematic way. A remarkable exception is the book *On Law and Legal Reasoning*, by Fernando Atria (2002). According to Atria, theories of law and legal reasoning are conceptually intertwined since a theory of legal reason-ing both presupposes and applies a theory of law. To the extent that the application of norms is grounded on a specific conception of law, our legal theories must cohere with our legal reasoning. For this reason, it is not sensible to endorse a positivistic approach to law and, at the same time, to defend an anti-positivistic theory of legal reasoning.

Atria's basic strategy is to distinguish between autonomous and non-autonomous institutions. The autonomy of an institution is basically shown by the formal nature of its rules. For example, even if it were true that in a chess game my king is in a dram-atic situation, I could not invoke this fact as a reason for moving twice. In this respect, legal norms are not like the rules of chess. Law is not an autonomous institution since in legal reasoning we can always mention other substantive reasons that defeat legal rules in particular cases.

Legal reasoning is formal as well as substantive and this means that legal norms are not autonomous reasons that preempt moral norms. In other words, legal reasoning is guided by rules but does not depend on them. Even if the main function of legal norms were to make difference in our practical reasoning, these norms would not exclude other moral reasons that are relevant in a particular case. Thus, the identification of the scope and force of legal norms does not depend exclusively on the decisions of legal author-ity, for substantive moral reasons also contribute to the justification of a legal decision (On the difference between the scope and force of legal norms, see Moreso & Navarro 1997; Navarro et al., 2004.)

In his analysis of legal theories, Atria deals with the most important positivist doctrines (e.g., those of Hart, Raz, Schauer, Alchourrón and Bulygin, and so on) and offers a careful analysis of some relations between the limits of law and judicial discretion. In particular, as a conclusion of his discussion of the problem of legal gaps, he claims that even if it were admitted that legal indeterminacy stems from the 'silence of law', it would not be necessarily true that there is no right answer in these cases of normative gaps. For example, if a couple disagrees on where to spend their holidays, the husband is not entitled to ask a judge in order to force his wife to fly to a place chosen by him. Atria's arguments emphasize that law is silent on this specific issue, e.g., the place where the holidays are to be spent, but we can still find a right answer to this controversy. According to him, a judge must reject the husband's claim. There-fore, the thesis of judicial discretion does not follow from the thesis about the limits of law. This conclusion undermines positivistic approaches and requires exploring the nature of our legal practices without the constraint imposed by legal positivism.

4. *Judicial decision and defeasibility of legal norms*

According to a traditional view, legal reasoning is formal by its very nature. In order to justify their decisions judges subsume particular facts into the scope of a general norm, and a legal solution is derived as a logical consequence of both valid general norms and facts that have been proved in court. One of the main problems of this reconstruction stems from the unavoidable conceptual gap between the limited number of circumstances mentioned by a general norm and the richer set of facts that defines a particular controversy. The question is: To what extent are those circumstances that legislators have not considered in the formulation of general norms relevant for justifying a judicial decision? A well-known answer to this question points out that general norms cannot provide a right solution to particular cases and that a justified legal decision must also take into account other normative resources, e.g., legal principles, moral norms, etc. Unexpected events can always make a practical difference and defeat the solution provided by a general norm. Thus, the problem of the defeasible nature of law is that legal norms cannot provide conclusive reasons, and deductive reasoning must be sub-stituted by more substantive arguments which incorporate evaluative elements in the identification and application of law. For this reason, it is claimed that defeasibility is a serious challenge to legal positivism since a complete identification of legal norms would always depend on moral evaluation (Alchourrón, 1993).

One of the best reconstructions of the defeasibility of legal rules can be found in Jorge Rodríguez's *Lógica de los sistemas normativos* (Rodríguez, 2002; see also Rodríguez, 2000). In his book, he analyzes the relations among legal systems, logically derived norms, legal principles, and the defeasibility of legal norms. Although 'defeasibility' is connected to a wide range of different problems, it mainly refers to a logical problem about the rules that define the notion of logical consequence (i.e., non-monotonic logical con-sequences) as well as to an epistemic challenge about the revision of our beliefs (i.e., revision theories).

Rodriguez's arguments are built on a set of analytical distinctions which are neces-sary in order to make a clear separation between description and evaluation of law: legal texts and legal norms, norms and normative propositions, identification and revi-sion of legal systems, normative contradiction and legal defeasibility, etc. As Rodriguez shows, defeasible norms cannot guide behavior because no normative solution can be detached from them in particular controversies. Deontic detachment, like factual detachment, is possible only if the circumstances mentioned in the antecedent of conditional general norms are regarded as a sufficient condition of normative conse-quences. For this reason, the defeasible nature of law would be at odds with our other central intuitions about law, for example, its motivational role. Legal norms guide our behavior only to the extent that we can use them in order to find a legal answer to specific or particular situations. However, if we accept that legal norms are defeasible, then we should also accept that we always need to revise their scope and force in particular contexts. In other words, legal norms do not provide the solution to our practical problems.

Rodriguez rejects the anti-positivistic idea hidden in the argument of legal defeasibility. He concludes that nothing compels us to accept an evaluative guided process of interpretation of legal norms as the only path that we can follow in order to identify legal norms. In particular, he stresses that the admission of implicit exceptions can be explained in terms of hierarchical orderings and revisions of the conceptual content of legal norms.

III.   Legal Rights and Legal Principles

Dworkin's criticism of legal positivism is one of the most important episodes in contemporary legal philosophy. In his famous attack against legal positivism, Dworkin claims that (a) principles and individual rights are intrinsically connected, (b) legal principles, unlike norms, have a dimension of weight, and (c) the weight determines the right solution to a conflict between legal principles. There are many interesting essays on these ideas in Latin America (see, for example, Carrio, 1971), but here I discuss only the important contributions made by Carlos Bernal (Colombia) and Juan Antonio Cruz Parcero (México).

1.   Carlos Bernal: Rights, principles and the principle of proportionality

In 2005, Carlos Bernal published one of the best philosophical studies about rational criteria for applying legal principles. His book *El principio de proporcionalidad y los derechos fundamentales* offers in its more than 900 printed pages a detailed analysis of the principle of proportionality which guides the balance between competing fundamental rights protected by constitutional principles and ordinary legislation. Not even a brief summary of this book could be attempted here and only a very general perspective of its main ideas can be offered in this chapter.

The abstract nature of principles (i.e., the fact that their normative relevance does not depend on the occurrence of a specific set of circumstances) explains why there is almost always more than one principle applicable to a certain case. Thus, even if it were true that a certain principle P is relevant for protecting an individual's rights, it would not follow that P is the right answer to a particular controversy. In spite of Dworkin's insistence on the existence of right answers, he has not offered a precise reconstruction of the criteria needed in order to provide a rational ordering of conflicting legal principles. In the Continental tradition, the principle of proportionality has been regarded as both a normative and conceptual tool for dealing with this problem. This principle establishes that a law could affect fundamental rights only if (a) it is strictly necessary and effective in order to protect another constitutional right and (b) the sacrifice of a constitutional right is not disproportionate or unreasonable relative to the protection of another fundamental right.

Fundamental rights are often mentioned by highly abstract constitutional clauses. Thus, to a great extent the problem of the application of fundamental rights is that their main function is to protect people against unconstitutional decisions but at the same time their content is developed by ordinary legislation. For this reason, Bernal says that the idea of proportionality plays a very important role in two different dimensions. On the one hand, it captures that rights are not absolute claims but rather they can be genuinely affected by political decisions. On the other hand, it provides a normative standard which justifies judicial decisions against the validity of ordinary legislation.

Bernal rejects both objectivism and skepticism about right answers and the justification of judicial decision. His reconstruction is built on the background of different philosophical perspectives, e.g., analytic philosophy, discourse theory, etc., and these conceptual resources allow him to defend two main theses: the principle of proportionality is necessary in order to determine the content of fundamental rights and, at the same time, it plays a decisive role as a limit to discretionary decisions made by the highest courts.

2. Cruz Parcero: Individual rights and social goals

One of the classical problems of legal philosophy is the nature of *legal* rights and its conceptual and normative connections with other types of rights and normative standards. Juan Antonio Cruz Parcero (Mexico) has published two important books on this problem: *El concepto de derecho subjetivo* (1999) and *El lenguaje de los derechos* (2007). In the first book, Cruz Parcero revises the analytical grounds which are actually needed in our theories of fundamental rights. He focuses mainly on the reconstruction and evaluation of the work of important contemporary philosophers such as Kelsen, Hart, and Dworkin. He vindicates Hohfeldian distinctions as a basic tool in order to understand the relations between rights and other normative positions, e.g., obligations. After examining different traditions, Parcero claims that it makes no sense to speak of legal rights as radically different and unconnected to moral and political rights. The domain of rights is something like a multicultural country where we can express the same ideas in different languages. Thus, in order to identify the conceptual content of our legal rights we often need to build a moral or political argument that justifies a particular legal solution. In particular, concepts like human or fundamental rights cannot be properly analyzed without moral arguments.

In his second book, Cruz Parcero emphasizes the relevance of our language of rights and the types of arguments that is generated by such discourse. He deals with the most important consequences of a theory of rights: the problems of social rights, collective rights, the connection between rights and persons, and the ideological commitments which stem from a theory of rights. In the background of his analysis lies the tension between individual rights and social goals. He defends the idea of right against its critics, e.g., radical feminism, communitarianism, etc., but he also stresses that no reconstruction of our rights could absolutely detach this normative position from other ideals like the welfare of our neighbors and political communities.

IV. Law and Legal Systems

Analytical studies on legal systems have received a decisive impulse from two books: *Normative Systems* (1971), written by the Argentine professors Carlos Alchourrón and

445

Eugenio Bulygin, and *The Concept of a Legal System* (1970) by Joseph Raz. These studies develop different models that are deeply entrenched in our legal culture and both models can be sketched as follows.

According to Raz, the dynamical nature of law makes it necessary to distinguish between momentary and non-momentary legal systems. Whereas momentary legal systems are sets of norms which meet the criteria of legal validity in a particular moment non-momentary legal systems are sequences of momentary legal systems. The normative chain formed by a norm N1 and another higher norm N2, which authorizes the creation of N1, is a relation of legal validity. This relation determines the *genetic structure* of a non-momentary legal system. On the contrary, punitive and regulative relations between norms determine the *operative structure* of momentary legal systems. A genetic criterion would be a test for deciding if a certain momentary legal system is part of a non-momentary legal system, but operative relations provide criteria of membership of a norm in momentary legal systems.

On the contrary, Alchourrón and Bulygin interpret law as a deductive momentary system. Following this view, the structure of legal systems is not completely captured by genetic or operative relations: Law is much more than a set of explicitly enacted norms in different times, since it includes *implicit* norms that can be logically derived from a specific normative basis. The conceptual content of such a basis cannot be fully grasped without deriving its logical consequences. Focusing on the logical consequences of legal norms, a 'rationalization' of the content prescribed by legal authorities at a particular time would be possible.

Alchourrón and Bulygin recognize that one of the great merits of Raz's book was to make explicit the distinction between momentary and non-momentary legal systems, but they also claim that his analysis was not altogether successful. In particular, Raz fails to separate different logical relations (e.g., membership from inclusion) in his analysis of both concepts of legal systems (see Bulygin, 1982). According to Alchourrón and Bulygin, a set is defined by its elements, and no changes in the *extension* of a certain set can be made without affecting its identity. So, the addition of a norm N1 to a normative set S changes the identity of this set, i.e., it is replaced by another set S1. As a result of the act of promulgation, a new set of norms S1 is added to the sequence of systems belonging to a certain non-momentary legal system. This set S1 is formed by the explicitly enacted norm plus the logical sum of its logical consequences and the consequences of the other valid norms of the system. This set of norms added by the promulgation of a norm is a *defined* set in the sense that we can determine by the application of logical rules if a norm belongs or not to this set.

A very important discovery made by Alchourrón and Bulygin was the logical asymmetry between the process of introduction and derogation of legal norms (Alchourrón & Bulygin, 1979, 1981). The traditional view on legal derogation assumed that the elimination of norms – like the promulgation of norms – results in a well defined set of norms, but in the case of the elimination of logically implicit norms that are entailed by more than one explicitly formulated norms, we have no logical criterion for identifying which explicit norm should be dropped in order to eliminate the derived norm. The philosophical significance of this discovery lies in the analogy between derogation and changes in scientific theories. Indeed, this analogy was the starting point in the development of the well-known AGM model (developed by Alchourrón, Gärdenfors, and

446

Makinson) which explains rational belief changes. This model has a deep impact on different fields like epistemology and artificial intelligence and it is still highly influential in contemporary logic and analytic philosophy.

The controversy about the systematic nature of law often overlooks a clear distinction between the law as a normative system and the system of legal science. A noteworthy exemption can be found in several works published by Professor Ricardo Caracciolo (Universidad de Córdoba, Argentina) on the relation between the structure of law and legal knowledge (Caracciolo, 1988). According to Caracciolo, the systematic nature of law must be clearly separated from the systematic nature of legal theories. In the first case, we deal with the elements of a particular normative set, e.g., *norms* of Argentinean law, but in the second case we take into account *propositions* about the norms of a particular community. Systems are more than a haphazard collection of elements. Indeed, systems require specific relations among the elements of a particular set. So, which relations can guarantee that law is a system of norms? It must be realized that a sound answer to this question cannot be inferred from the systematic nature of legal theories. Insofar as legal theories are similar to other scientific models, it seems intuitive to claim that legal science must build its information in a systematic way, i.e., it must be structured as a deductive set of legal *propositions*. However, nothing follows from this fact in relation to the systematic nature of the set of legal *norms*. Moreover, if norms are understood as social facts, it is not altogether clear that these *facts*, like other events of nature, can be related by systematic relations, e.g., logical consequences. Thus, a legal system would not be a natural event but rather a conceptual scheme built by legal science in order to determine the legal status of certain actions and state of affairs.

V.   Deontic Logic and Legal Philosophy

Deontic logic contains the most important and original contribution to contemporary philosophy made by Latin American legal philosophers. Although many studies are valuable in this field, Carlos Alchourrón and Eugenio Bulygin's works are the most internationally recognized contributions. Their most important ideas are discussed below (see Alchourrón & Bulygin, 1971, 1979, 1981).

1.   Norms and normative propositions

A major philosophical problem is the application of logic to normative discourse. Traditionally, logic is confined to true or false statements, but norms – in particular, legal norms – are prescriptive and they cannot be analyzed in terms of their truth-values. This problem was to a large extent ignored by deontic logicians because philosophers used to assume an analogy between descriptive statements about norms and the prescriptive discourse of norms. This analogy stems from an ambiguity of ordinary language since we can use the same expressions (e.g., 'you must not park here') as a prescription of behavior or as a description of some regulation. A great merit of Alchourrón and Bulygin's work was to demonstrate the difference between a logic of norms and a logic of propositions about norms (i.e., normative propositions). From this

447

distinction between norms and normative propositions follows some important consequences. In particular, concepts like completeness and coherence of legal systems
can be properly characterized only in a logic of normative propositions. Even more, as
Alchourrón and Bulygin show, the existence of both normative gaps and incoherence
in legal systems make the distinction between these two logics interesting because
both overlap when we refer to complete and coherent systems of norms (e.g., critical
morality).

2. The principle of normative closure

Lawyers often assume that law is a complete (gapless) normative system. As an argument for defending the completeness of legal system, they sometimes invoke the principle of normative closure, 'If p is a nonprohibited action in S, then p is permitted in
S.' Moreover, they regard this principle as an analytical one, and claim that it cannot
be rejected in a logical reconstruction of normative discourse (see Raz, 1979; see also
Moreso, Navarro, & Redondo, 2002; Bulygin, 2004). Alchourrón and Bulygin provided
a complete refutation of this classical point of view. Their argument is built on the already
mentioned distinction between norms and normative propositions.

At a descriptive level, a certain action can be obligatory in a system S and prohibited by the norms of another system S1. This means that it makes no sense to dispute
the deontic status of a certain action without a previous identification of the system
of reference. In this respect, the normative proposition 'The action p is obligatory' is
true in relation to a system S if and only if the norm 'Op' belongs to the consequences
of S.

This idea can be represented by the following symbols (see Alchourrón & Bulygin,
1984):

$$Ops = \text{'Op'} \in CnS$$

The normative proposition Ops *describes* the fact that the norm 'Op' belongs to the
logical consequences of the system S. By the same token, the prohibition of an action
p according to a system S can be represented as follows:

$$Vps = \text{'Vp'} \in CnS$$

However, the expression 'legally permitted' is ambiguous and refers to two very
different situations, i.e., two different facts make propositions about a legal permission
true. On the one hand, we use the expression 'legally permitted p' in order to describe
that no norm in a system S actually prohibits *p*. On the other hand, 'legally permited
p' also means that an explicit or implicit norm in a System S authorizes p. In order to
avoid confusion, I will distinguish between 'weak permission' and 'strong permission'
respectively.

Weak permission: an action *p* is legally weakly permitted if and only if p is not prohibited in a legal system S. In symbols:

$$P_w p = \text{'Vp'} \notin CnS$$

Strong permission: an action p is strongly permitted if and only if p has been explicitly or implicitly authorized by a legal authority, i.e., a norm that permits p belongs to the legal system. In symbols:

$P_s p =$ 'Pp' $\in$ CnS

Therefore, the principle of closure 'Nonprohibited actions are permitted' (henceforth PC) admits two interpretations according to the two meanings of 'permitted'. The weak version says that an action p is weakly permitted in S if and only if no norm that prohibits p belongs to S, that is:

PC(w): 'If p is a nonprohibited action in S, then p is *weakly* permitted in S.'

In symbols, this interpretation looks like 'Vp' $\notin$ CnS $\rightarrow P_w p$. However, given that, by definition, 'weakly permitted p' only means that p has not been prohibited, such interpretation expresses a tautology, and this analytical character is evident after the substitution of equivalent expressions:

PC(w'): 'If p is a nonprohibited action in S, then p is a nonprohibited action in S.'

In symbols, 'Vp' $\notin$ CnS $\rightarrow$ 'Vp' $\notin$ CnS. As any other tautology, this analytical truth cannot be denied, but it does not guarantee that a legal system is complete. This true expression says only that nonprohibited actions are not prohibited in a legal system, and this is precisely what happens in cases of legal gaps because no normative consequences can be derived.

A more promising interpretation of the principle PC arises from the strong meaning of 'permitted'. By definition, 'strongly permitted p' means that p has been explicitly or implicitly authorized in S, i.e., $P_s p =$ 'Pp' $\in$ CnS. In this respect, PC says:

PC(s): 'If p is a nonprohibited action in S, then p is *strongly* permitted in S.'

In symbols, this strong interpretation is: 'Vp' $\notin$ CnS $\rightarrow P_s p$. After substitution of the equivalent expression, it follows that 'Vp' $\notin$ CnS $\rightarrow$ 'Pp' $\in$ CnS. Unlike the weak interpretation, the truth of the strong interpretation is not a matter of its meaning, but it actually depends on the fact that legal authorities have explicitly or implicitly permitted actions that are not prohibited. For example, suppose that a legislator decides that fishing is prohibited on Monday and Friday, but permitted the rest of the week. In this case, our authority explicitly allows a certain action and, according to this norm, it is true that fishing is permitted in these days. There is a contingent legislative fact (i.e., the enactment of a norm) that guarantees the truth of our statement about the permission of fishing.

Some important differences between the strong and weak interpretation of PC are captured by Table 31.1.

Finally, two special cases must be mentioned. On the one hand, a legal authority could decide in advance the permission of all nonprohibited actions. For example, the legislator could enact a *norm* of closure according to which actions that have not been

Table 31.1

Weak interpretation	Strong interpretation
It is analytically true.	Its truth depends on facts.
Its negation is necessarily false.	Its negation could be true.
Its truth is compatible with the existence of legal gaps.	Its truth is not compatible with the existence of legal gaps.
No normative contradiction stems from the prohibition of a weakly permitted action.	The prohibition of a strongly permitted action results in a normative contradiction.

prohibited are permitted. This norm closes the system, that is, it eliminates normative gaps, but such a norm is contingent, and like any other fact, its existence cannot be proved by logic. The existence of a norm of closure in a legal system sheds light on the truth conditions of the strong version of PC. This principle says that nonprohibited actions are strongly permitted in a certain legal system S. If a *norm* of closure actually belongs to the system S, then it is also true that there are no normative gaps in this system.

On the other hand, one can wonder about the conceptual relations between strong and weak permissions in relation to the coherence and completeness of legal systems. Three possibilities are worth mentioning. First, in an incoherent system S, a certain action p could be strongly permitted, but from this fact it does not follow that p is also weakly permitted in S. Therefore, in a logic of propositions about norms the formula $(P_s p \rightarrow P_w p)$ must be rejected. Second, the formula $(P_w p \rightarrow P_s p)$ is not valid in a logic of propositions about norms because its antecedent is true and its consequence is false in cases of legal gaps. Third, only if the normative system is a complete and a coherent one can both concepts of permission overlap. That is, the formula $(P_s p \leftrightarrow P_w p)$ is true only if it refers to a complete and coherent normative system.

VI.   Philosophical Doctrines in Latin America

Many valuable analytical contributions have not even been discussed here, e.g., Rolando Tamayo (Mexico) on dogmatics and legal science, Daniel Mendonca (Paraguay) on the theory of legal systems and legal presumptions, Claudio Michelon (Brazil) on the role of reason and the authority of law, Juliano Maranhão (Brazil) on refinement of legal norms, Juan Pablo Alonso (Argentina) on legal coherence. Even if analytic philosophy is the mainstream in Latin American philosophy of law, there is a vast horizon of other philosophical conceptions. For example, in Latin America, we can find hermeneutic theories of law, law and economics, etc. In order to take them into account we need only a small change in our focus of analysis. I have no doubt that this expansion in our universe of analysis would be justified, but unfortunately this task cannot be undertaken in this essay. Only two examples of non-analytical legal theories will be briefly considered here:

(a) *Critical theory of law.* Critical theories of law have grown in different Latin American countries, e.g., Argentina and Brazil, but the most well-known critical community is placed in the University of Los Andes (Bogotá, Colombia). Unlike other critical schools which show a huge influence of psychoanalysis, French Marxism, or German critical theory, this Colombian group uses conceptual categories and strategies similar to those developed by critical legal studies in the United States. A good example is the book *La teoría impura del derecho* by Diego López Medina, with a preface by Duncan Kennedy (López Medina, 2004). This book underlines the differences between the contexts of production and reception of theories and shows the transformations in both theories and legal practices provoked by the implantation of a foreign philosophical doctrine. This study offers a careful analysis of the evolution of Latin American legal culture (and the Colombian culture in particular) and it is a required reference for those philosophers who seek to understand the richness of different conceptual movements in Latin America.

(b) *The rhetoric of law.* In spite of its long tradition, studies on legal rhetoric still offer in Latin America very original and challenging contributions to legal philosophy. The so-called 'school of Recife', and their most internationally well-known scholars J. M. Adeodato (Recife) and Torquato Castro Jr. (Pernambuco), have developed a very fine analysis of law as rhetoric, understanding rhetoric as a form of discourse. Both Adeodato and Castro have studied under the supervision of Tercio Sampaio Jr., perhaps the best well-known contemporary Brazilian legal philosopher who contributed to the diffusion in his country of some fundamental works (e.g., Viewheg's *Topic*) of Continental legal philosophy.

The rhetorical approach of the School of Recife helps us to rediscover classical problems and authors in a new light. For example, in these contributions we can find important insights on the rhetorical enthymeme and Aristotle's views on argumentation, the influence of Ihering in the development of Brazilian legal dogmatics, relations between ethics and science in Hartmann's work, the role of metaphors in the analysis of law, the concept of *proairesis*, etc. Indeed, a very important task developed by Adeodato and Castro is to show the pervasive importance of a rhetorical perspective on law from classic texts to modern dogmatics and its influence in different discourses, e.g., theology, social science, jurisprudence, etc. (see Adeodato 1989, 2002, and Castro Jr., 2003, 2005).

The book, *Ética e retórica*, by J. M. Adeodato (2002) is a good example of the fine work of the school of Recife. In this book, Adeodato analyzes the main topics of jurisprudence: the nature of law, positivism and anti-positivism, the dogmatic perspective, the relation between truth and law, and so on. One of Adeodato's main ideas, and also a basic assumption of the school of Recife, is the following: We can leave aside substantive disagreements about truth in law and provide an analysis of how our legal discourse influences our forms of life and theoretical attitudes. As a natural consequence of this rhetorical perspective, the school of Recife is skeptical about the ultimate grounds of our moral and political discourse, but this skepticism does not result in indifference toward ethics and political problems. On the contrary, the belief that there are no ultimate truths leads them to very distinctive positions where political tolerance, the recognition of moral plurality, and acceptance of social differences are emphasized.

451

VII.   Conclusion

In this chapter, I have argued that the relevance of contemporary Latin American legal philosophy is shown by its contribution to a common (e.g., international) conceptual environment. However, it must be pointed out that Latin American legal philosophers have received the same insufficient attention in the United States and the UK as many other important works produced in Scandinavia, Italy, Spain, Poland, etc. As an example of this disconnect between Anglo-American legal philosophy and legal philosophy developed in other regions of the world, let me mention two of the most important handbooks of legal philosophy published in the last decade: Patterson (1996) and Coleman and Shapiro (2002). They contain more than 1,500 pages, and there are plenty of references to the work of leading figures as well as to the secondary literature. However, it is very hard to find in such references any mention of the works of Latin American (or Spanish, Italian, Finnish, etc.) legal philosophers. It must be pointed out that these contributions have not been published in journals that are hard to find nor have they been written in exotic languages. On the contrary, Latin American as well as Italian or Spanish scholars often write in English and their books and papers have been published by the most prestigious journals and publishers.

Related chapters: 14 Analytic Philosophy; 15 Paraconsistent Logic; 24 Latin American Philosophy; 26 Philosophy of Science; 32 Metaphysics; 34 Formal Epistemology and Logic.

References

Adeodato, J. M. (1989). *O problema da legitimidade*. São Paulo: Forense.
Adeodato, J. M. (2002). *Ética e retórica*. São Paulo: Saraiva.
Alchourrón, C. (1993). Philosophical foundations of deontic logic and the logic of defeasible conditionals. In J. J. Meyer et al. (Eds). *Deontic logic in computer science: normative systems specifications* (pp. 43–84). New York: Wiley & Sons.
Alchourrón, C., & Bulygin, E. (1971). *Normative systems*. New York: Springer.
Alchourrón, C., & Bulygin, E. (1979). *Sobre la existencia de las normas jurídicas*. Venezuela: Universidad de Carabobo.
Alchourrón, C., & Bulygin, E. (1981). The expressive conception of norms. In Hilpinen, R. (Ed.). *New studies in deontic logic* (pp. 95–124). Dordrecht: Reidel.
Alchourrón, C., & Bulygin, E. (1984). Permissions and permissive norms. In W. Krawietz et al. (Eds). *Theorie der Normen* (pp. 349–71). Berlin: Duncker & Humblot.
Atria, F. (2002). *On law and legal reasoning*. Oxford: Hart Publishing.
Bernal, C. (2005). *El principio de proporcionalidad y los derechos fundamentales*. Madrid: Centro de Estudios Constitucionales.
Bulygin, E. (1982). Time and validity. In A. Martino (Ed.). *Deontic logic, computational linguistics and legal information systems* (pp. 65–81). Amsterdam: North Holland.
Bulygin, E. (2004). On legal gaps. In P. Comanducci & R. Guastini (Eds). *Analisi e Diritto 2002–2003* (pp. 21–8). Torino: Giappichelli (Original work published 1982).
Caracciolo, R. (1988). *El sistema jurídico. Problemas actuales*. Madrid: Centro de Estudios Constitucionales.

Carrio, G. (1971). *Legal positivism and legal principles*. Buenos Aires: Abeledo Perrot.

Castro Jr., T. (2003). *A pragmática das nulidades e a teoria do ato jurídico inexistente* (Unpublished Ph.D. dissertation). São Paulo.

Castro Jr., T. (2005). Interpretação e metáfora no direito. In P. Carvalho et al. (Eds). *Segurança jurídica na tributação e estado de direito* (pp. 663–72). São Paulo: Noeses.

Coleman, J., & Shapiro, S. (Eds). (2002). *The Oxford handbook of jurisprudence and philosophy of law*. Oxford: Oxford University Press.

Cruz Parcero, J. A. (1999). *El concepto de derecho subjetivo*. Mexico: Fontamara.

Cruz Parcero, J. A. (2007). *El lenguaje de los derechos*. Madrid: Trotta.

López Medina, D. (2004). *La teoría impura del derecho. La transformación de la cultura jurídica en America Latina*. Bogotá: Legis.

Moreso, J. J., & Navarro, P. E. (1997). Applicability and effectiveness of legal norms, *Law and Philosophy, 16*, 201–19.

Moreso, J. J., Navarro, P. E., & Redondo, M. C. (2002). Legal gaps and conclusive reasons. *Theoria. A Swedish journal of philosophy, 68*, 51–65.

Navarro, P., Rodríguez, J., Sucar, G., & Orunesu, C. (2004). Applicability of legal norms. *Canadian Journal of Law and Jurisprudence, 17*, 337–60.

Nino, C. S. (1985). *La validez del derecho*. Buenos Aires: Astrea.

Nino, C. S. (1991). *The ethics of human rights*. Oxford: Oxford University Press.

Nino, C. S. (1994). *Derecho, moral y política*. Barcelona: Ariel.

Nino, C. S. (1996). *The constitution of deliberative democracy*. New Haven: Yale University Press.

Patterson, D. (Ed.). (1996). *A companion to philosophy of law and legal theory*. Oxford: Blackwell.

Raz, J. (1970). *The concept of a legal system*. Oxford: Oxford University Press.

Raz, J. (1979). Legal reasons, sources and gaps. In J. Raz (Ed.). *The authority of law* (pp. 53–77). Oxford: Oxford University Press.

Redondo, M. C. (1999). *Reasons for action and the law*. Dordrecht: Kluwer.

Rodríguez, J. L. (2000). Normative relevance and axiological gaps. *Archiv. für Rechts und Sozialphilosophie, 86*, 151–67.

Rodríguez, J. L. (2002). *Lógica de los sistemas normativos*. Madrid: Centro de Estudios Constitucionales.

32

Metaphysics

LIZA SKIDELSKY

Metaphysics in Latin America includes at least three main perspectives. One consists in the exegesis of metaphysical theories of both classic philosophers such as Plato, Aristotle, and Kant, and of the Anglo-American and continental traditions. Most contemporary academic work at Latin American universities is devoted to the exegetical inquiry of the main figures of the history of metaphysics such as Nietzsche, Heidegger, and Derrida on the continental side, and Quine, Strawson, and Wittgenstein on the analytical side. This chapter, however, does not address that type of historical perspective.

The second line attempts to develop original metaphysical approaches or systems based on the main continental philosophers but oriented to the particular characteristics of Latin America's historical, economic, and sociological conditions. This trend is thus based on two metaphilosophical assumptions. One holds that metaphysics is about constructing systems of ideas, or it should at least offer a whole perspective of human nature; the other, that philosophy in Latin America should advance its own points of view and develop its own proposals based on the particular context in which Latin American philosophers are situated – thus, moving away from the main philosophical concerns of European and North American philosophy. This perspective captures one of the senses of "Latin American philosophy," namely, the sense in which this is a philosophy *about* Latin America.

The third perspective focuses on metaphysical questions, trying to develop suitable solutions to problems posed by philosophers from different traditions such as rationalism, empiricism, pragmatism, etc. The metaphilosophical assumptions here are that what matters are the universal metaphysical problems such as time and space, causation, identity, freedom and determination, mind and body, and so on, on one hand, and that philosophical practice consists in solving problems, on the other. This, of course, does not mean that such practice cannot yield systematic theories. However, these theories do not intend to offer a comprehensive and definitive system on a certain subject. This point of view has been mostly developed by Latin American philosophers in the analytical tradition. In this sense, "Latin American philosophy" means philosophy done by philosophers that were born and/or educated in Latin America.

My aim in this chapter is to review some of the main accounts by Latin American philosophers working on both metaphysical approaches and problems. Although I will not be able to cover all of the significant work being done in each perspective,

I will try to provide an indicative overview of some representative topics. I have distinguished between two perspectives for the purposes of presentation, but it is important to bear in mind that the divide between philosophical ideas is never as sharp as represented in theoretical taxonomies. Thus, the chapter is divided in two sections. In the first section, I will focus on metaphysical approaches or systems on the nature of the self, and on Latin American identity. In the second section, I will address some accounts that aim to propose a solution to the metaphysical problems of causality, universals, mind and body, and ontological issues in logic.

Metaphysical Approaches

Nature of human being/person/self

The nature of the human being is one of the main subjects addressed by Latin American philosophers. Some of the prominent contemporary philosophers that have developed theories of the self or human nature are Antonio Caso (Mexico, 1883–1964), Risieri Frondizi (Argentina, 1910–85), Mauricio Beuchot (Mexico, b. 1950), Carlos Astrada (Argentina, 1894–1970), and Luis Oyarzún (Chile, 1920–72).

Caso

Influenced by Bergson's metaphysical spiritualism, Antonio Caso conceives the human as a spiritual reality beyond nature that adopts different facets through its existence: as an individual, person, spiritual being, social being, etc. (Caso, 1975; Hernández Uría, 2004). Any living being is an individual in comparison to physical things. Physical things can be divided and still continue being things – unlike individuals, which are indivisible, and they have meaning as long as humans are in constant relation with them through their actions. Among individuals, there is a hierarchy of vital power: The highest and most perfect form of individuality is the animal organism, and among them, the human being. This superiority is owed to human's intellectual and moral powers. These qualities make individuals persons.

Persons play a social role. Only persons can conceive the ideals and moral values that govern social relationships. Unlike things that are passive-receptive aggregates, persons are active-spontaneous wholes with purposes and values. Values are patterns of behavior that govern our social relationships, the most important of which – following Aristotle's axiology – is personal realization. This realization can only be achieved in a social-historical context. Thus, each person is an individual in the sense that she is herself (i.e., a sui generis essence) and can only be so (i.e., fulfill her essence) in interaction with other persons. This creates a second nature – besides the first biological nature directed to survival – which consists of culture. Culture is the synthesis of values.

The social facet based on the creation of values is only possible because humans are spiritual beings. This spirituality goes above and beyond physical nature, and it allows humans to achieve their comprehensive formation through education. This formation includes the shaping of both intellectual qualities and the will. It cannot be based exclusively on intellectual qualities since they make humans selfish, and given that a

455

person's realization takes place in society, she needs to develop – mainly through the will – the capacity to sacrifice herself in favor of others. Freedom plays a fundamental role in this process of personal formation. Without education there is no culture, and without freedom there is no education. This approach underlies Caso's defense of native people's rights. Native people have the right to receive a humanistic education in order to achieve a civilized organization and be included in a united society that respects differences. In this project, the state should be the guarantor and should be careful not to infringe the rights of the individual; otherwise, it becomes a totalitarian state.

Frondizi

According to Miró Quesada (1980), Risieri Frondizi is the first philosopher from the third generation of Latin American philosophers to develop a philosophical system about the self. Frondizi holds a theory of the self in which the continental and analytical influences that marked his education can be seen (Frondizi, 1953, 1970). The analytical side is present in his elucidation of the concepts that are used to refer to ourselves, such as *experience*. The self is constituted by its activities in relation to the objects of experience or consciousness. Thus, unlike Casos's spiritual conception of the human, he held an "authentic empiricism" in the sense that our knowledge begins with experiences about the world and ourselves. This experience is not restricted to unilateral perceptual experiences, but to the "whole experience," that is, the experience that includes every dimension of life (Gracia & Millan-Zaibert, 2004).

From Köhler and his *Gestalt* theory, Frondizi took the idea that the self is a structure that has properties that are not present in the constituents of the whole. Thus, unlike both the Cartesian substance, which is something above and beyond our experiences, and the Humean atomism, which reduces the whole self into its parts, Frondizi posits that the self is the empirical structural unity of consciousness. Hence, the self as a structure depends on its constitutive elements (that is, the experiences), but it is not reduced to them; even though the experiences that constitute the self are mutable, complex, and dependent, the self is unique and permanent. The self is the "unity of its multiple states" (Frondizi, 1970, p. 131).

This ontological approach comes with an axiology that conceives of humans as creative beings. Since the self is a dynamic structure that develops historically in relation to its objects, its essence is a creative one. Opposed to subjectivism and objectivism in axiology, Frondizi holds a situational ethics (i.e., to choose the higher value in a value hierarchy for every situation) that does not imply an ethical relativism, but increases the moral sentiment and creative activity. This is because the quality of the creative activity and its outcome is measured by the values that they embodied (Frondizi, 1977).

Beuchot

Influenced by medieval philosophy, Mauricio Beuchot (1997) has developed Analogical Hermeneutics in which reference to the being is possible. In this reference to the being, the logos is the main instrument because it creates sense and reflects our understanding of the world. Thus, language has an active and practical dimension; through language we commit ourselves in practical or ethical ways. This practical dimension of language is what has been forgotten and has led to forms of nihilism and relativism. In contrast to the univocal hermeneutics of modernism, whose searching for a perfect language has led to nihilism, or the equivocal hermeneutics of postmodernism, which has led to relativism, Beuchot puts forward Analogical Hermeneutics. This proposal aims to extend the margins of text interpretation without losing the possibility of getting closer to a delimited truth or sense.

The task of recovering the confidence in language or judgment – after Cartesian doubt – lies in the acknowledgment of the limits of the human condition. Although there is always the possibility of error, of incorrect judgments, there is still the possibility of correct assertions that allow humans to reach the truth or the being. Thus, in spite of its limits, human nature can attain knowledge of the being through analogical speech – i.e., metaphorical expressions, analogical reasoning, etc. – at the heart of which lies the tension between similarity and difference. This kind of speech allows us to produce the multiplicity of senses while getting in touch with the being and expressing truths. In his later writings, Beuchot (2005) applied his Analogical Hermeneutics to the specific problem of the relationship between human rights and multiculturalism. Again, in contrast to the perspectives that favor the individual or communitarian rights, Analogical Hermeneutics – which is based on the tension between similarity and difference – allows the similarity without rejecting the differences.

Astrada

Carlos Astrada attended courses in Germany given by Hartmann, Scheler, Husserl, and Heidegger, among others. Influenced by Heidegger's *Being and Time*, Astrada developed, between 1930 and 1950, an existential humanism anchored in the concrete temporal existence of the finite human being (for example, Astrada, 1942). In his dialectical period (1950–70), Astrada incorporated Marx's dialectical approach, developing a humanism that takes into account the social and historical nature of humans. On his view, taking on human's finiteness opens up the possibility of freeing us from alienation and attaining self-realization through a transforming and dialectical praxis. This process culminates in a socialist society.

El mito gaucho (The gaucho myth, 1948) is an example of how existential and dialectical concepts are applied to the Argentinean essence. This monograph goes from ontology to politics in an effort to recover the mythical origin of the gaucho (the nineteenth-century nomad cowboy of the Pampas) with an eye to developing an authentic popular nationalism during a turbulent historical period of Argentina. For Astrada, two factors intervene in the origin of the gaucho: blood (which consists of vital predispositions) and environment (weather, landscape, etc.). On the blood factor, the gaucho is mainly a Spanish/Arabic-Indian hybrid. Nevertheless, the environmental factor: La Pampa, a vast plain in Argentina, is the most crucial one. This solitary region is used by Astrada to describe what it means to be Argentine, what is his origin and his forgotten destiny of freedom.

Oyarzún

While Astrada took the *gaucho* as Argentinean essence, Luis Oyarzún (1967) – who was concerned with recovering the subject matters typical of Chilean culture – identified

457

two stereotypes of the Chilean: the *huaso*, a conservative and prejudiced farmer, and the wanderer, an adventurer portrayed by his passion and imagination. According to Oyarzún, Chilean social and cultural history can be characterized by the permanent ideological conflict between these conservative and liberal types. Thus, the Chilean roots are found in this dual national identity.

Latin American identity

Leopoldo Zea (Mexico, 1912–2004), Augusto Salazar Bondy (Peru, 1925–74), Luis Villoro (Spain/Mexico, b. 1922), and Francisco Miró Quesada (Peru, b. 1918) are among the most influential philosophers that have been concerned with the question of Latin American cultural identity. Starting from Zea's proposal regarding the need to develop an "authentic" philosophy made in and about Latin America, I will present the main ideas of the thinkers who have debated with him. Of course, this polemic – as well as the work of these authors – does not exhaust the subject of Latin American identity. There are prominent figures, such as José Vasconcelos, included in this volume, and others, such as Rodolfo Kusch (Argentina, 1922–79) and Emilio Uranga (Mexico, 1921–88) whom I will not be able to address here.

Influenced by the historicism of Dilthey, Scheler, and Ortega y Gasset – the latter through José Gaos, Leopoldo Zea considers that the history of ideas is the best methodology for recovering the Ibero-American intellectual past. As a result of the collapse of European values in World War II (values which didn't represent Ibero-America), a question arose as what the Ibero-American consisted of. To address this question, Zea – along with many others Latin American philosophers such as Miró Quesada, José Luis Romero (Argentina, 1909–77), Arturo Ardao (Uruguay, 1912–2003), João Cruz Costa (Brazil, 1904–78), Ernesto Mayz Vallenilla (Venezuela, b. 1925), Roberto Fernández Retamar (Cuba, b. 1930) – began working to recover Ibero-American thought from the nineteenth and twentieth centuries by publishing national histories of thought. The outcome of this research was the discovery that Latin American philosophers have gone far beyond assimilating an imported philosophy; instead, they have developed an original and authentic thought that reflect the reality of Latin America.

As for his own approach, against the extreme European and Indo-American positions – the first rejected the pre-Colombian elements in Ibero-American culture, and the second rejected everything that was European, Zea expressed the need for a permanent dialogue. Since European culture is part of Latin American culture, the subject matters of reflection are also those of the European culture, but since the concrete development of those subjects depends on the particular contexts in which they are anchored, the outcome is Ibero-American thought with its own solutions to its own situational problems. In contrast to the European political, social, and cultural order that put the Latin American on the side of barbarism, the mission of the Ibero-American thinker is to question and deconstruct this occidental thinking while denouncing the multiple forms of dependence (Zea, 1953). Since the 1960s, this has been known as the discourse of liberation (Gómez-Martínez, 1997).

The Zea–Salazar Bondy debate occupies a prominent place in the search for an Ibero-American philosophy. Both philosophers assume that philosophy is the consequence of an "authentic" reflection to which the question of Ibero-Americanism can make a contribution, but they disagree on how to attain authentic Ibero-American philosophy. Zea starts from the concrete human being in his situational context – i.e., the Mexican – to arrive to the more universal problems related to the essence of the Ibero-American human being. Thus, he reaches the conclusion that the Ibero-American debate began with the las Casas–Sepúlveda polemic about whether the Ibero-American had a soul. Later on, this problematic took other forms; for example, through the rejection of expressions of Ibero-American humanity, such as Ibero-American philosophy, which was labeled the "philosophy of underdevelopment" (Zea, 1969).

Augusto Salazar Bondy works in the opposite direction. He concluded his search for the universal human being by identifying it with the European-American. This identification has the consequence of importing not only the problems and solutions already posed within those centers, but also the methodology that characterized professional, scientific, and rigorous philosophy. The diagnosis is that Ibero-American philosophy has not yet reached the level of rigorous authentic philosophy because of historical underdevelopment and domination. Once this historical condition is overcome, it will be possible to develop an original philosophy (Salazar Bondy, 1968). Thus, although both philosophers search for an authentic philosophy and believe that the mission involves replacing the European-American vertical domination with a dialogical horizontal interaction, their treatment of the relationship between liberation and authentic philosophy is the opposite. While Zea considers that original Ibero-American philosophy already exists and will lead to liberation, Salazar Bondy believes that liberation is necessary for the region to achieve an authentic philosophy.

According to Luis Villoro (1972, 1987) – who was born in Spain but developed his philosophical career in Mexico – Latin American philosophy should aim to universal problems through a rigorous methodology. Latin American philosophy should attempt to address a pure conceptual task through the exercise of an autonomous reason without any dogmatic ideological component, that is, without a set of unjustified beliefs whose sole function is to legitimize political power. This does not mean that philosophy should not be a socially committed and liberating practice. A rigorous philosophy tries to examine the existing doctrines and beliefs, through the use of reason, in order to develop clear and precise reflections that question these doctrines. Thus, a liberating philosophy consists in the practice of rational critical thinking – using the tools provided by analytic philosophy – rather than in a dogmatic political ideology.

Villoro believes that the expansion of mainstream philosophy is unavoidable and since it will be linked to the development of science and technology, the role of philosophy – although different from that of science – should be oriented toward science. Latin American philosophy should collaborate in the conceptual clarification of science and the establishment of relationships among different scientific disciplines with the help of logic and philosophy of science. Like Salazar Bondy, Villoro considers that the way to attain the cultural independence of a professional philosophy in an industrialized world depends on certain minimal conditions related to economic and technological development. Once globalization is achieved, there will be no center–periphery distinction and cultural equality will be attained through a universal professional philosophy.

Francisco Miró Quesada (1981) has also participated in this debate regarding "authentic" philosophy and the cultural identity of Latin America. According to this author,

459

there are two ways of understanding the philosophical practice of his generation. For the minority, philosophy consists in reflecting on one's own reality, that is, the Latin America reality; for the majority, it consists in the contributions to the universal philosophical problems that are relevant to contemporary reflection, thus assuming the European legacy and trying to be on the same level. Like Villoro, Miró Quesada considers that Latin American philosophy should attain the rigorousness that characterizes analytic philosophy, thus making Latin American cultural progress possible. Again, he concurs with Villoro in the belief that occidental expansion carried a positive value, namely, the ideal of rational life. In accordance with this, he has introduced logic and philosophy of science in Peru.

Miró Quesada (1974) has also proposed one of the most influential configurations of the philosophical periods in Latin America. He distinguishes among four generations of "philosophical practice." The patriarchs are the first generation. They were the non-professional philosophers-founders, including Antonio Caso, Carlos Vaz Ferreira (Uruguay, 1872–1958) and Enrique Molina Garmendia (Chile, 1871–1964). The second is that of the "Forjadores" ("Forgers"). In this period, Francisco Romero (Argentina, 1891–1962) plays a central role owing to his efforts to integrate Latin American philosophers. The technical generation is the third group, which is divided into regionalists – those who think that philosophy is about the Latin American reality, and universalists – those who believe that philosophy involves reflecting on universal problems. The last generation is composed of the third generation's disciples, who followed different philosophical trends.

Metaphysical Problems

Most of the work within the metaphysical problems perspective in Latin America has been done as an inquiry into ontological issues in fields such as philosophy of science, logic, philosophy of language, and philosophy of mind. In addition, the majority of the philosophers working within this perspective have been (partially) educated in Latin America; they have completed their doctoral studies abroad, and are teaching at British and American universities. In this section, I will review some of the proposals concerning the problems of causality, universals, the nature of the mind, and ontological issues in logic. Of course, there are other metaphysical problems that have been addressed by Latin American philosophers, such as possible worlds, and space and time – the work of José Alvarado Marambio (Chile) deserves mention regarding the first topic, while contributions by Juan Rodríguez Larreta (Argentina) and philosophers of science such as Laura Benitez and José Antonio Robles in Mexico, and Marcelo Levinas in Argentina have being important to the second.

Causality

What is causality? What kind of ontological entities are involved in this relationship? Is causality in the world or is it merely a human construct? Does causality imply determinism? Are causes and reasons to be identified? This and other similar questions regarding causality have been mostly developed, in Latin America, by philosophers of

460

science. Mario Bunge (Argentina, b. 1919) was the first Latin American philosopher to offer an extensive analysis of the status of this notion in science. I will focus on his work, though many other Latin American philosophers of science after Bunge have been concerned with this subject – for instance, Wilfredo Quezada Pulido in Chile and Hernán Miguel in Argentina.

Mario Bunge is a well-known philosopher of science who has played an important role in introducing analytic philosophy in Latin America, especially in Argentina in the 1950s and 1960s, though most of his academic work has been done abroad. In 1959 he published *Causality. The Place of the Causal Principle in Modern Science*, a work that was translated into Spanish in 1961 by EUDEBA (the University of Buenos Aires publishing house). In this book, Bunge defends the notion of causality against the idea suggested by quantum physics that determinism has no role in modern science. Bunge defines causal determinism, distinguishing it from other forms of determinism. In Bunge (1999) the notion of causality is applied to social sciences.

Countering Humean empiricism, Bunge endorses the well-known thesis that causality cannot be equated with constant conjunction since the latter can exist without the former. Countering the understanding of causality as a mathematical function, Bunge holds that functional relations do not express causality, only constant conjunction; moreover, as mathematical formulas they are ontologically neutral. According to Bunge (1959, 1999), causality is a real phenomenon, an internal relation among events. It is a way of generating events by two types of causal mechanisms: the transfer of energy, and a triggering signal – for instance, by giving an order. The second type of causality is particularly important because it is characteristic of unstable systems such as biological and social systems. The causal relationship in these latter systems is nonlinear in the sense that the amount of the effect exceeds the amount of the cause.

Causality is a mode of determination – not the other way around – as well as spontaneity, chance, and purpose. These modes of determination are frequently intertwined. Thus, determination should not be understood in a narrow sense as causal determinism – i.e., the thesis that every event has a cause – since there are types of determination that are not causal. Scientific determinism in a wide sense claims that everything is subsumed under laws, assuming in this way that there are no magical events or miracles. In this picture, there is room for different degrees of freedom in human action: freedom of will among options, freedom to create new conditions, and the acknowledgment of the legality in the word and the use of this knowledge to modify the environment and ourselves. Thus, "Freedom, far from being the negation of determinism, is a form of it: it is the victory of lawful self-determination over the external compulsions and constraints fitting, in turn, other laws" (Bunge, 1959, p. 107).

Finally, Bunge claims, against the rationalist tradition, that causes and reason should be conceptually distinguished although they are inseparable in thought and action. Whereas causes are real events that can produce changes, reasons are constructs that may or may not be valid. The first notion pertains to the realm of ontology while the second corresponds to the realm of justification. Thus, reasons appear in philosophical descriptions while only scientific explanations can appeal to causes. Despite this conceptual distinction, reason is powerless without causality, as action probably is ineffective without reason (Bunge, 1999, p. 59).

461

Universals

In addition to particular objects (e.g., apples), the world appears to contain properties of these objects (e.g., color), and relations between them (e.g., bigger/smaller than). The nature of these universals, and the relationship between them and the particulars, have been subjects of inquiry since the birth of philosophy. This topic has received extensive treatment by Gonzalo Rodriguez-Pereyra (Argentina, b. 1969), who studied philosophy as an undergraduate and taught in Latin American universities, and is currently teaching abroad. His main contribution to metaphysics has been the development of a view, resemblance nominalism, as a solution to the problem of universals. According to Rodriguez-Pereyra (2002), this problem should be understood not as the "One over Many" – that is, how can two particulars be identical in nature?, but as what he calls "Many over One" – that is, how can a particular be in some sense multiple (e.g., red, square, and hot) given that it is numerically one? This means that to solve the problem of universals one has to give the truthmakers for sentences of the form "*a* is F," where "*a*" stands for a particular and "F" is a predicate that, according to those who believe in properties, picks up a *natural* or *sparse* property.

For those who believe in universals or tropes, such truthmakers would include universals or tropes. But the resemblance nominalist eschews universals or tropes. According to him, what makes *a* F is that *a* resembles all other F-particulars. This resemblance, of course, is not based on sharing universals or having resembling tropes. Instead this resemblance between *a* and the other F-particulars is an ultimate and brute fact. This theory has several important features. Among them are: the relevant F-particulars are the F-particulars in any possible world, not just those in the actual one, and the relation of resemblance holds not only between concrete particulars like houses and people, but also between pairs (two-membered classes).

The first feature, which commits resemblance nominalism to a controversial version of realism about possible worlds, is introduced to solve a resemblance nominalist version of the so-called problem of coextensive properties. The second feature is introduced to solve Goodman's difficulty of the so-called imperfect community. One of the strengths of Rodriguez-Pereyra's resemblance nominalism is that it meets Goodman's difficulties and, also, a new difficulty that he calls the *mere intersections difficulty*. That the relation of resemblance is let to link classes shows that resemblance nominalism is nominalism in the traditional sense of the word, i.e., in the sense of rejecting universals, not in the more modern sense of rejecting abstract objects. Rodriguez-Pereyra argues that resemblance nominalism is superior to theories that postulate universals or tropes because it avoids ad hoc entities.

Rodriguez-Pereyra (1997) has also argued for metaphysical nihilism – the thesis that there could have been no concrete objects – through a version of the so-called subtraction argument. Rodriguez-Pereyra (2005) has given arguments for the thesis that an important class of synthetic propositions (including negative propositions) must have truthmakers. In addition, he has argued against the entailment principle according to which the truthmaker of a proposition is also a truthmaker of the propositions entailed by the proposition in question, and has argued that the bundle theory, when correctly understood, need not be incompatible with the possibility of distinct but indiscernible particulars.

Mind

The metaphysical problems I will address in this section concern the field of philosophy of mind. Some of the topics covered by this field include the nature of the mind (e.g., its ontology and architectural organization), its relationship to the body (e.g., ontological mind–body relationships such as supervenience, realization, causality, and mind–body theories such as the psycho-physical identity theory, functionalism), and the relationship between commonsense psychology and scientific psychology. Since one of the most prominent Latin American philosophers of mind was Eduardo Rabossi (Argentina, 1930–2005), I will devote this section mainly to his work. Nonetheless, I will also briefly present the work being done by other representative Latin American philosophers.

Eduardo Rabossi not only introduced philosophy of mind in Latin America: he played a leading role in the development of analytic philosophy in Latin America around the 1960s together with other philosophers such as Bunge and Moro Simpson. While he devoted most of his academic life to the teaching of philosophy of language and metaphysics at the University of Buenos Aires, he also worked to strengthen of philosophical institutions in Argentina (he was a cofounder and president of the Argentine Society for Analytic Philosophy and cofounder of the Philosophical Association of the Argentine Republic) and to consolidate the bonds between Latin American countries. In a sense, he played a political-philosophical role similar to that of Francisco Romero at the time. Besides, he also contributed to the study of ethics and human rights.

His work concerning philosophy of mind focused on philosophical subjects such as the status of commonsense psychology, the psycho-physical identity theory, the multiple realizability thesis, supervenience, and causation, on the one hand, and on metaphilosophical matters such as naturalism in philosophy of mind, and the relationship among cognitive psychology, philosophy and common sense, on the other. Regarding the former problems, he devoted extensive publications to the status of commonsense or folk psychology. Rabossi (1979, 2008) claims that folk psychology is not a theory, but a craft. It is composed of the immutable "basic convictions" of common sense that are related to people (their existence and identity), the normality of the behavior of people and objects, and "subsidiary convictions" concerning our behavior as human agents. Examples of basic convictions include: the existence of objects, persons and acts of consciousness, and regularity in nature.

On the metaphilosophical problems concerning mind, Rabossi (2002) opposes the traditional canon of philosophy that considers that the task of philosophy (of mind) is utterly different to that of (cognitive) science in its domain, problems, methods, and outcomes. He holds a metaphilosophical naturalism which instead advocates "interface relationships" between these areas. Thus, instead of conceiving a categorical division in which the task of philosophy of mind consists in the a priori elucidation of mental concepts while the task of cognitive psychology involves the development of empirical theories about mental phenomena, Rabossi claims that there are various interactive roles that a naturalist philosopher can adopt. These roles range from creating intellectual tools and offering a conceptual foundation for science to formulating empirical hypotheses or utilizing scientific outcomes to confirm or refute philosophical theses. Within this degree of "interface relationships" Rabossi chooses a mixture of Wittgensteinian elucidations plus a Dennettian work routine and a plurality of disciplines plus a strategy

463

that allows suitable links to be made between commonsense psychology and scientific psychology while respecting the peculiarities of each one.

Other topics addressed by Latin-American philosophers of mind include questions related to the philosophy of cognitive science, such as the architecture and evolution of the mind, and issues concerning perception and consciousness. Since there are currently several Latin American philosophers working on these subjects, I will introduce each set of problems through the work of one of the representative philosophers from only three countries: Mexico, Chile, and Brazil. Thus, Maite Ezcurdia's (Mexico, b. 1966) work is related to both topics, while that of Francisco Pereira's (Chile, b. 1974) and Paulo Coelho Abrantes's (Brazil, b. 1951) concern the first and the second set of problems, respectively.

Maite Ezcurdia has made contributions to two areas within the metaphysics of mind: the first concerns linguistic competence and the defense of the Chomskyan innateness of the language faculty (Ezcurdia, 2008); the second concerns consciousness, specifically, qualia, the nature of perceptual content and self-consciousness. On the latter, she has defended a representationalist account similar to Michael Tye's. However, her most significant contribution has been on issues concerning self-consciousness. She holds that self-thoughts, that is, thoughts reported in public language by 'I', require a self-representation whose role is to hook up with certain informational, volitional, and dispositional states of the subject in a way that allows actions (in certain conditions) to be the result of coordination between these states (Ezcurdia, 2001).

Francisco Pereira has made contributions to the philosophy of perception, particularly on issues concerning disjunctivism, introspective discrimination, and nonconceptual content. He has argued that visual experiences are indeed better understood intentionally as contentful experiences whose proper function is to carry information about objects and properties in the subject's immediate environment, as long as we accept that perceptual and non-perceptual (hallucinatory) visual experiences are essentially different (Pereira, 2006). In addition, he claims that some of these experiences may carry a different kind of content, which is not necessarily structured by Neo-Fregean concepts (Pereira, 2007).

Paulo Coelho Abrantes was one of the first philosophers to teach philosophy of mind in Brazil, starting in the mid-1990s. He came to this area as a result of his concerns with cognitive science, especially analogical reasoning and its bearing on scientific activity. He adopts an overall naturalistic orientation in his research which is focused on foundational problems in different approaches to the evolution of the mind in the hominid lineage, especially in the so-called dual inheritance theory, that is, the view that humans are products of the interaction between biological evolution and cultural evolution. Abrantes (2006) defends the significance of commonsense psychology's role – understood as representational and interpretational skills – in the evolution of the mind, advocating for a perspective on humans as agents constructed by social and cultural environment.

Ontological issues in logic

Some of the main ontological problems in logic include ontological commitment (i.e., the entities whose existence we are committed to, given a set of beliefs or theories of the world), formal ontology (i.e., mathematical theories, based on logical systems, about properties and relations of certain entities), and the nature of abstract entities (such as propositions and mathematical entities). Latin American philosophers that have been concerned with ontological questions in logic include Tomás Moro Simpson (Argentina, b. 1939), Oswaldo Chateaubriand Filho (Brazil b. 1940), Raúl Orayen (Argentina/Mexico 1942–2003), Guillermo Hurtado (Mexico, b. 1962), and Max Freund (Costa Rica, b. 1954). Of course, there are other representative Latin American philosophers concerned with this subject, but here I will focus on the contributions of the authors mentioned above.

Formas lógicas, realidad y significado (Logical forms, reality and meaning, 1964) by Tomás Moro Simpson was the first book written about philosophy of logic in Spanish by a Latin American philosopher. In this book, Moro Simpson discusses the theses of Russel, Frege, Church, Quine, and Strawson on semantics, as well as ontological commitment. A sign of the book's value is that it is still used across Latin America for graduate and undergraduate courses. Oswaldo Chateaubriand Filho is a founder member of the Sociedade Brasileira de Lógica. Some of his main lines of research are Platonism in mathematics, the foundations of intuitionism, logical form, and language and ontology. His recent publications include Chateaubriand Filho (2003, 2007), in which he claims that Quine's proposals for solutions to the problems of ontological commitment, ontological reduction, and criteria of identity cannot be sustained. In Chateaubriand Filho's view, the technical notion of ontological commitment does not have a satisfactory formulation; Quine's technical model-theoretic formulation of ontological reduction is an ad hoc device and Quine's idea that an ontology of pure sets can satisfy his well-known criterion of "no entity without identity" is illusory.

Raúl Orayen was born in Argentina and taught at various Argentinean universities until he joined the Instituto de Investigaciones Filosóficas, Mexico, in 1982, where he worked until his final days. His work is concerned with ontological issues such as ontological relativity, and ontology in Meinong and Frege. *Lógica, significado y ontología* (Logic, meaning and ontology, 1989) brings together his views on these and other problems related to logical form and validity, defending an intensional approach against Quine's extensionalism. On the other hand, he raised a problem for set theory that it is known as "Orayen's paradox." His contribution has been acknowledged by compilations of articles on his work, such as Moretti and Hurtado (2003) and Ezcurdia (2007).

In his 1998 *Proposiciones russellianas* (Russellian propositions), Guillermo Hurtado offers an ontological theory of first-order quantificational logic. This theory gives an account of the ontological nature of propositions, propositional functions, logical form, and quantification which differs from both Frege's and Russell's accounts in several aspects, but adopts some of their basic ideas in a different way. According to Hurtado, the link of predication is not a constituent of a proposition, but of a relation mode of it. This proposal avoids Bradley's regression, for the link of predication has a relational nature but is not, in itself, a relation. He also proposes an account of the ontological nature of logical form and quantification. In his 2004 essay, "What is a change?", he expands the ontological theory of *Proposiciones russellianas* in order to give an onto-logical account of change according to which a change is a kind of conjunction of states of affairs and times.

Max Freund has developed logical and philosophical theories that assume an extended form of conceptualism as a metaphysical theory of universals. Conceptualism postulates concepts as the ontological grounds for predication. Presupposing this philosophical view as the ontological background theory, Freund (1994, 2007) has constructed logics that capture the logical conditions for the predication of sortals, identity under a sortal, and relative (sortal) quantification. He has also developed second-order logics that constitute formal ontologies of conceptualism, that is, formal theories on the conditions of existence and predication of universals. Freund has also devised conceptualist philosophical theories on the nature of computability and on the ontological nature of possible worlds.

Related chapters: 14 Analytic Philosophy; 18 Identity and Philosophy; 26 Philosophy of Science; 33 Epistemology; 34 Formal Epistemology and Logic.

References

Abrantes, P. (2006). A psicologia de senso comum em cenários para a evolução da mente humana. *Manuscrito*, 2:1, 185–257.

Astrada, C. (1942). *El juego metafísico: para una filosofía de la finitud*. Buenos Aires: El Ateneo.

Astrada, C. (1948). *El mito gaucho*. Buenos Aires: Cruz del Sur.

Beuchot, M. (1997). *Tratado de hermenéutica analógica*. Mexico: UNAM.

Beuchot, M. (2005). *Interculturalidad y derechos humanos*. Mexico: Siglo XXI/UNAM.

Bunge, M. (1959). *Causality. The place of the causal principle in modern science*. Cambridge, MA: Harvard University Press. Reissued in 1979 as *Causality in modern science*. New York: Dover Publications.

Bunge, M. (1999). *Buscar la filosofía en las ciencias sociales*. Madrid: Siglo XXI.

Caso, A. (1975). *La persona humana y el estado totalitario. Obras completas*. Mexico: UNAM.

Chateaubriand Filho, O. (2003). Quine and ontology. *Principia*, 7:1–2, 41–74.

Chateaubriand Filho, O. (2007). Logic and ontology. In A. Bobenrieth Miserda (Ed.). *Ciencias formales y filosofía* (pp. 23–46). Valparaiso: Edeval.

Ezcurdia, M. (2001). Thinking About Myself. In A. Brook & R. Devidi (Eds). *Self-reference and self-awareness* (pp. 179–203). Amsterdam: John Benjamins.

Ezcurdia, M. (Ed.). (2007). *Orayen: de la forma lógica al significado*. Mexico: UNAM.

Ezcurdia, M. (2008). Conocimiento del lenguaje. In C. Cornejo & E. Kronmuller (Eds). *Ciencias de la mente: aproximaciones desde Latinoamérica* (pp. 325–53). Santiago de Chile: JC Sáez Editor.

Freund, M. A. (1994). A minimal logical system for computable concepts and effective knowability. *Logique et Analyse*, 34:4, 339–66.

Freund, M. A. (2007). A two-dimensional tense-modal sortal logic. *Journal of Philosophical Logic*, 36:5, 571–98.

Frondizi, R. (1953). *The nature of the self: a functional interpretation*. New Haven: Yale University Press. Reprinted: Carbondale: Southern Illinois University Press, 1971.

Frondizi, R. (1970). *El yo como estructura dinámica*. Buenos Aires: Paidós.

Frondizi, R. (1977). *Introducción a los problemas fundamentales del hombre*. Mexico: FCE.

Gracia, J., & Millan-Zaibert, E. (2004). Rizieri Frondizi ante la condición humana. Availablae from: http://www.ensayistas.org/critica/generales/C-H/argentina/risieri.htm.

Gómez-Martínez, J. L. (1997). *Leopoldo Zea*. Madrid: Ediciones del Orto.

Hernández Uría, V. M. (2004). Antonio Caso y su concepto del hombre. In A. Saladino García (Ed.). *Humanismo mexicano del siglo XX* (Vol. I, pp. 19–32), Toluca: Universidad Autónoma del Estado de México.

Hurtado, G. (1998). *Proposiciones russellianas*. Mexico: UNAM.

Hurtado, G. (2004). What is a change? In M. Ezcurdia, R. Stainton, & C. Viger (Eds). New essays in the philosophy of language and mind. *Canadian Journal of Philosophy*, 30(Suppl.), 81–96.

Miró Quesada, F. (1974). *Despertar y proyecto del filosofar latinoamericano*. Mexico: FCE.

Miró Quesada, F. (1980). La filosofía de Risieri Frondizi. In J. Gracia (Ed.). *El hombre y su conducta: ensayos filosóficos en honor de Risieri Frondizi*. Río Piedras: Universidad de Puerto Rico, Editorial Universitaria.

Miró Quesada, F. (1981). *Proyecto y realización del filosofar latinoamericano*. Mexico: FCE.

Moretti, A., & Hurtado, G. (Eds). (2003). La paradoja de Orayen. Buenos Aires: EUDEBA.

Moro Simpson, T. (1964). *Formas lógicas, realidad y significado*. Buenos Aires: EUDEBA.

Orayen, R. (1989). *Lógica, significado y ontología*. Mexico: UNAM.

Oyarzún, L. (1967). *Temas de la cultura chilena*. Santiago: Universitaria.

Pereira, F. (2006). Metaphysical disjunctivism and the intentional theory of perception. In E. Di Nucci & C. McHugh (Eds). *Content, consciousness, and perception: essays in contemporary philosophy of mind*. London: Cambridge Scholars Press.

Pereira, F. (2007). Contenido perceptual y la insuficiencia de la tesis conceptualista. *Analítica*, 1, 43–69.

Rabossi, E. (1979). ¿Porqué el sentido común importa a la filosofía? *Manuscrito*, 3:1, 43–55.

Rabossi, E. (2002). Filosofía de la mente y filosofía de la psicología: la agenda, la práctica, el dominio. *Azafea*, 4, 21–43.

Rabossi, E. (2008). Acerca del sentido común, la filosofía y la psicología de sentido común. In A. Gianella, M. C. González, & N. Stigol (Eds). *Pensamiento, representaciones, conciencia. Nuevas reflexiones* (pp. 17–47). Buenos Aires: Alianza.

Rodriguez-Pereyra, G. (1997). There might be nothing: the subtraction argument improved, *Analysis*, 57:3, 159–66.

Rodriguez-Pereyra, G. (2002). *Resemblance nominalism. A solution to the problem of universals*. Oxford: Oxford University Press.

Rodriguez-Pereyra, G. (2005). Why truthmakers. In H. Beebee & J. Dodd (Eds). *Truthmakers: the contemporary debate* (pp. 17–31). Oxford: Oxford University Press.

Salazar Bondy, A. (1968). *¿Existe una filosofía de nuestra América?* Mexico: Siglo XXI.

Villoro, L. (1972). Perspectivas de la filosofía en México para 1980. In VVAA, *El perfil de México en 1980* (pp. 607–17). Mexico: Siglo XXI.

Villoro, L. (1987). Sobre el problema de la filosofía latinoamericana. *Cuadernos Americanos*, 1:3, 86–104.

Zea, L. (1953). *América como conciencia*. Mexico: Ediciones Cuadernos Americanos.

Zea, L. (1969). *La filosofía americana como filosofía sin más*. Mexico: Siglo XXI.

33

Epistemology

ELEONORA CRESTO

I. Introduction

This chapter examines the development of a number of areas in theory of knowledge in Latin America during the past fifty years, with special emphasis on analytic epistemology, broadly understood.

The overall picture of Latin American epistemology can be organized to reflect a few major research traditions, while also acknowledging the existence of substantial overlap among them. First, there is a tradition of phenomenological studies, in the sense of Husserl, Heidegger, Merleau-Ponty, and their ensuing schools; exegetic scholarship on such authors has usually been combined with more systematic approaches to philosophy, within a phenomenological framework; cf. for instance the work of Eugenio Pucciarelli (1907–95) and more recently, of Roberto Walton (b. 1942) in Argentina, and of José Gaos (1900–69) and Antonio Zirión (b. 1950) in Mexico, to mention a few authors. But there is also a robust line of work on the philosophy of the seventeenth and eighteenth centuries, which, by its very nature, has a concomitant epistemological component; consider, by way of illustration, the influential work on Kant by Chilean philosopher of science Roberto Torretti (b. 1930), and the Argentine Kant scholar Mario Caimi (b. 1947), among many others. Third, there is a lively line of research on both ancient and modern skepticism; in many cases, this approach has naturally led to reflections on skepticism of a more systematic vein. Finally, there is a full-fledged analytic theory of knowledge, which includes both the type of discussions the Anglo-Saxon world would refer to as "mainstream epistemology" and the type of theoretical elaborations that arise out of programs with a pragmatist or Wittgensteinian bent, in a broad sense. In general, analytic-style epistemology in Latin America is younger than the historically and phenomenologically oriented approaches; in most cases, its development was originally encouraged by the work of philosophers who were deeply knowledgeable about the history of philosophy, and possessed a deep understanding of the history of skepticism.

A few further comments on the third and fourth research traditions mentioned above are in order. A leading figure in studies of skepticism in Latin America is, without doubt, the Brazilian philosopher Oswaldo Porchat Pereira (b. 1933), founder of the so-called *Neo-Pyrrhonian School*. We can also place in this tradition the Argentine philosopher

468

Ezequiel de Olaso (1932–96), a well-known specialist in modern skepticism, and, more generally, in seventeenth-century philosophy, particularly in the work of Leibniz. Olaso's later work, moreover, builds bridges with contemporary discussions of mainstream epistemology. He was one of the first philosophers to introduce the discussion of typical problems of analytic epistemology in Argentina – particularly in connection with contemporary responses to skepticism – and was eager to motivate his students to pursue that path. In any case, the first book wholly devoted to analytic epistemology written originally in Spanish was due to the Mexican philosopher Luis Villoro (b. 1922); Villoro's seminal book (*Creer, saber, conocer*, Mexico: Siglo XXI Editores) appeared originally in 1982, and was translated into English in 1998; it was actually preceded (and succeeded) by years of philosophical discussions that resulted in many motivating papers and lectures, particularly at the Instituto de Investigaciones Filosóficas of the Universidad Nacional Autónoma de México (UNAM).

This overview would not be complete without making explicit reference to Ernest Sosa, one of the most important representatives of mainstream analytic epistemology. His perspectivist conception of knowledge and his view on epistemic virtues are well known and appreciated. Sosa was born in Cuba, but educated in the United States, where he developed his entire academic career. Notwithstanding, Sosa has kept a close relation with Latin American philosophical communities. He has been a regular visitor to Argentina and Mexico, where he has participated in congresses and other academic events on a regular basis. Spanish versions of his best-known articles appeared in Latin American journals (such as *Análisis Flosófico* and *Revista Latinoamericana de Filosofía*, both edited in Buenos Aires) even earlier than their English counterparts; throughout these writings, he has greatly influenced the local scene. Many of these papers have been collected in Sosa (1992).

We should also mention here a further group of people composed of young philosophers who, although they were born and sometimes graduated in Latin America, are at present pursuing their professional life somewhere else (such as Sosa's former student Juan Comesaña, currently at the University of Wisconsin, Madison); in many cases, they still maintain links with the Latin American community.

Let's make clear from the outset that my interest in this chapter is restricted to works in epistemology written in Spanish or Portuguese, which have therefore not always been accessible to an English-speaking audience. Furthermore, the chapter examines neither phenomenology (and other continental approaches) nor works on the history of philosophy (as opposed to works in which historical research is linked to the elaboration of novel positions, or to the analysis of contemporary discussions). That is, this chapter is devoted exclusively to (some aspects of) the third and fourth research traditions mentioned above. And although it is clear that the boundaries between different areas of philosophy are vague, I have made efforts to restrain the discussion both to what most writers would agree to call "core epistemological problems," and to authors who have conceived of themselves as mainly engaged in epistemological research – as opposed to research on closely related topics in the philosophy of language, metaphysics, philosophy of science, or philosophy of mind, to mention a few possibilities. In certain cases, I mention some lines of research at the margins of core epistemological reflections, but without entering into details. It should be borne in mind, however, that such work at the interface plays an important role at the time of shaping the atmosphere in which contemporary Latin American epistemology is developed. The topics in the four sections below include the neo-Pyrrhonian tradition in Brazil, Olaso's reflections on knowledge and skepticism, Villoro's main contribution to analytic epistemology, and the pioneer work of epistemologist Wonfilio Trejo in Mexico. The final section offers an overview of current analytic epistemology in Latin America.

II. Porchat Pereira and the Neo-Pyrrhonian School

Porchat Pereira (professor emeritus at the Universidade de São Paulo, and founder of the Center for Logic and Epistemology at the Universidade Estadual de Campinas) has developed a distinctive position he has called *neo-Pyrrhonism*, based on the legacy of Ancient Pyrrhonism. In a prior stage he had proposed a particular vindication of common life (which in his view should be carefully distinguished from common sense – the later being full of prejudices, false beliefs, and superstitions), and even earlier he had embraced a type of existential abandonment of philosophy, which does not conflate with skepticism. Here I will mainly focus on his mature writings. Many of his articles appeared in journals such as *Manuscrito* (Brazil) and *Revista Latinoamericana de Filosofía* (Argentina), among others; his most important papers have been collected in his 1993 and 2007 volumes.

Porchat Pereira attempts to vindicate the importance of a skeptical view (correctly formulated) for present-day philosophy. Philosophy – so we are told – promises to explain the world, to dissipate contradictions; soon we discover, however, that the discordance (*diaphonia*) we find pre-theoretically in everyday experience gets even stronger within philosophy. If we keep the demands of critical rationality alive we should withdraw assent, and thus end up in *epokhé* (suspension of judgment). Notice that *epokhé* also concerns non-philosophical discourse: it concerns any human belief that proposes itself as genuine knowledge.

But what happens after achieving a state of *epokhé*? In a certain sense, nothing has changed. We are left with what the skeptic calls the phenomenon, what appears. What appears to be is not, qua appearance, the object of research, precisely because it cannot be the object of doubt. Even though the phenomenon is essentially relative to those to whom it appears, this should not lead to mentalism or subjectivism, which would represent a form of opinion. We experience ourselves as human beings living a common life among other humans. Thus we should not identify phenomenicity with the "internal" world: actually, the (neo-)Pyrrhonian – as well as her ancient counterpart – suspends judgment on the very notion of representation, and its intelligibility. The problem of modern skepticism and the reality of the external world is then alien to Pyrrhonism. Related to this, Porchat Pereira points out that Hume's attempt to mitigate Pyrrhonian skepticism with the aid of the intervention of the irresistible force of nature is actually the result of a mistake: Pyrrhonism, well understood, *is* a type of naturalism (cf. his 1991 paper "Sobre o que aparece"; reprinted in 1993).

Can modern and contemporary science rebut Pyrrhonism? According to Porchat Pereira, the situation is just the opposite: well understood, contemporary science is (neo-)Pyrrhonian. The ancient Pyrrhonian has traditionally been an apologist of empirical science; Pyrrhonians are sensitive to similarities and differences, to observed regularities, which appear to us as essentially contingent and revisable. Thus Pyrrhonism defends the legitimacy of *techné*, which, as opposed to *episteme*, can be perfectly structured within the phenomenic world. Indeed, current philosophy of science no longer gives importance to the old notion of *episteme*. Of course, the current scientific scenario is much more complex than that of the ancient skeptic, so we need a re-elaboration of crucial Pyrrhonic concepts; this Porchat Pereira sees as an urgent task for neo-Pyrrhonism.

As a particular instance of his vindication of phenomenism, Porchat Pereira also analyses the role of skeptical argumentation (cf. his "Ceticismo e argumentação," reprinted in 1993). Dogmatic argumentation advertises itself as providing an absolute form of persuasion. Against this, the Pyrrhonian exposes the relative character of such arguments; within Pyrrhonism, dialectic is turned into an instrument of demystification. But not just that: the skeptic uses ordinary language and arguments in everyday life. Thus, argumentation is subordinated to the practical needs of life, and has the aim of establishing relative consensus, within a framework of shared concepts and standpoints. As neo-Pyrrhonians – Porchat Pereira tells us – we should seek to vindicate argumentative discourse as such, and dissociate it from dogmatic goals.

In later works Porchat Pereira extends phenomenism to the concept of truth and reality (cf., "Verdade, realismo, ceticismo," reprinted in 2007). As we have seen, once he suspends judgment on dogmatic claims, the contemporary Pyrrhonian guides his life according to pre-theoretical common notions: in this way he delineates something close to "objectivity-to-us," in Putnam's sense (without, however, formulating this as part of a defense of a philosophical view). But even though so-called normal perceptions are not given any epistemological privilege over anomalous ones, the skeptic still takes the later as *anomalous*, and hence as inadequate from the point of view of the general economy of the phenomenical world; the skeptic distinguishes, like any human being, between normal and abnormal, adequate and inadequate, the right, the correct, and the wrong. Moreover, the meaningfulness of words in relation to things is just a particular case of meaningful associations between parts of the phenomenical world, mediated by human intervention. Under this phenomenical conception of language, we can talk of a correspondence between words and objects, between sentences and events of the world. This correspondence is internal to the phenomenical world. Within this world, to think is to think "correspondentially"; to say something is to talk "correspondentially": such a correspondence appears as condition of intelligibility of our own discourse. What the skeptic rejects is just the *philosophical* theory of truth.

We can hence redefine truth, introducing a notion of phenomenic truth, by analogy to the way Sextus Empiricus dealt with the notions of doctrine, dogma, or criterion. Perhaps – Porchat Pereira suggests – the prestige of classic *aletheia* had restrained Sextus from extending his strategy to "truth" as well, but it need not restrain us. Such a theory is meant to do full justice to commonsense intuitions, and to preserve them; Porchat Pereira takes it to be close to Quine's understanding of Tarski's theory as disquotational, as well as to Austin's theory of truth. The phenomenal notion of truth is philosophically neutral: it is actually pre-philosophical. Related to this, Porchat

471

Pereira contends that our tendency to read common sense, and its discourse, so as to make it a sort of antecedent of the philosophical doctrine of metaphysical realism is incorrect. Rather, we project onto common sense our philosophical habits, thus reading the former under a distorting light. Hence, by analogy with the operation on truth, Porchat Pereira also suggests the construction of a skeptical (phenomenical) realism, which is equally neutral concerning metaphysical interpretations.

Porchat Pereira's work has been highly influential in the Brazilian philosophical milieu. Among his students, Plínio Junqueira Smith (currently Professor at Universidade São Judas Tadeu) has followed the neo-Pyrrhonian thread into new developments. In a number of early papers he defends the argument of *diaphonia*: philosophical questions are actually compelling, but it is not possible to rationally find true answers to them. Later he suggests that we redirect our efforts to examine the very problems that made *diaphonia* possible in the first place; by rejecting the assumptions of the questions we would attain the best opportunity to avoid the unsolvable conflicts of philosophy. Related to this point, he favors the use of Wittgenstein's insights to spot false philosophical riddles; this – Smith contends – seems to be the best way to remain faithful to Wittgenstein's own legacy – rather than engaging in the business of providing new interpretations *of* Wittgenstein's writings.

In later papers, however, Smith modifies this position, and contends that advocating the rejection of assumptions was as dogmatic as defending the theories that depended on such assumptions. Thus he arrives at a different formulation of his skepticism. (Many of these papers have been collected in Smith, 2005.) Philosophical questions arise out of peculiar interpretations of ordinary language, but no philosophical solution could be deemed acceptable for all philosophers. As it happens, then, when one examines particular philosophical controversies one perceives that philosophy, at least regarding its more basic problems, makes little progress and does not get closer to the truth. A correct understanding of this situation becomes consequential at the time of adopting a right stance on many issues discussed in contemporary epistemology. Thus, for example, far from seeing internalism as the source of skepticism and externalism as the solution to skeptical difficulties, Smith believes that the very debate is a dogmatic debate, in which one should suspend judgment (cf., 2006). In short, his general strategy in epistemology (as well as in other areas, such as philosophy of mind and language) has been to place doubts and put into question the very presuppositions of the problems under scrutiny, thus showing that the theoretical equilibrium between the competing theories does not permit us to choose rationally.

Other philosophers influenced by the neo-Pyrrhonian tradition at São Paulo (broadly considered) include Roberto Bolzani Filho (at Universidade de São Paulo), and Luiz Antonio Alves Eva (now professor at the Universidade Federal do Paraná). Bolzani Filho has embraced a critical stance on neo-Pyrrhonism, and has developed a line of work on Academic Skepticism. Alve Eva's research is also mostly oriented to skepticism in the history of philosophy; he has proposed novel interpretations and considerations on Descartes' dream argument as well as on Montaigne and modern skeptics. Also in connection with this tradition, Otávio Bueno (at the University of Miami) has developed a view in which he exploits the relation between neo-Pyrrhonism and current issues in the philosophy of science, particularly from the perspective of Bas van Fraassen's constructive empiricism.

III.   Knowledge and Skepticism: The Legacy of Ezequiel de Olaso

A researcher at Argentina's National Council for Scientific and Technical Research (CONICET) since the early 1960s, Olaso taught at various Argentinean universities, including Universidad de Buenos Aires and Universidad Nacional de La Plata. As a Leibniz scholar, a large portion of his work deals with the study of the influence of ancient skepticism on early modern philosophers – topics that I cannot address here. Let me focus instead on some of his most characteristic epistemological theses. Many of them concerned the identification of correct interpretations of ancient skepticism, and the morals we can draw from such considerations for present-day discussions on skepticism and the concept of knowledge.

In a series of papers, Olaso examines the nature of skeptical inquiry, or *zetesis*; if we interpret skeptical research as a search for the truth, as the moderns did ever since Montaigne's writings, then we make the skeptic procedure irrational. But skeptic search is not aimed at truth; in this respect Olaso analyzes interesting similarities and differences between this attitude and that of Dewey's and Peirce's pragmatism. Research is the activity that enables skeptics to distinguish between that which is an object of inquiry and that which is not (*azetetos*): this distinction replaces the criterion of truth, which the skeptic cannot have. Thus the skeptic searches in order to attain suspension of judgment, and, ultimately, imperturbability. It is worth mentioning here that in earlier works Olaso had elaborated on the distinction between *doubt* and *epokhé*, and relied on this distinction to claim the inadequacy of several reconstructions of the skeptical theses, such as Moore's. A truly Pyrrhonian skeptic cannot doubt: the man who is sometimes assaulted by doubts with respect to his own opinions, or which can be induced to doubt by others, has not yet ceased to be a dogmatic.

Olaso's arguments to the effect that appearances are *azetetos* – and hence that they have a non-cognitive nature – enable him to examine contemporary phenomenism and contend that it should not be assimilated to skepticism (Olaso, 1977); within this background he undertakes a criticism of some of Chisholm's ideas. He further suggests that we use the Spanish word *saber* (as opposed to *conocer*) to refer to the activity that delivers the particular kind of information we obtain from appearances [both *saber* and *conocer* are translated as "to know" in English]. We should rest content with the *pragmatic function* of such information, without trying to turn it into bona fide knowledge.

In further articles (see especially Olaso, 1988) Olaso shows that the word *zetesis* figures at the very core of the description of the Pyrrhonian methodology by Sextus; once again, well understood, this fact should not be problematic. Actually, we can trace the use of this word back to two very different situations. (i) One of them refers to the "normal" refutatory practice of the skeptic aimed at *epokhé*. (ii) For a second, very different use of *zetesis*, Olaso shows how the skeptic applies the well-known paradox of research (as presented in Plato's *Meno*) against the dogmatics, in a pincer movement: The skeptic starts by conceding dogmatic principles for the sake of argument without actually accepting them, and then, via the paradox of research, concludes that he, the skeptic, indeed does not know – but then dogmatics do not know either. We have to conclude that Pyrrhonians do not practice *zetesis* "with an open spirit," even though they strongly suggest that they do: according to Olaso, this implicit tension is indeed the source of the many misunderstandings we find among commentators.

Olaso's reserve concerning the attractiveness of Pyrrhonian skepticism as a whole – and hence his reserve on the attractiveness of developing a contemporary position that seeks to rescue the Pyrrhonian spirit – was to become more explicit in his later work. In his (1992) work he argues that the best reconstruction of the skeptical strategy should assume that skeptic attacks go piecemeal. If the skeptic postulated the existence of overarching equipollence, then he would behave just as a dogmatic: this would be a non-self-limited assertion, with respect to something that is not self-evident. Unfortunately, at times this is exactly what Sextus does. How shall we interpret the more bothersome passages? To answer this question, Olaso first engages in an interesting and detailed discussion regarding different possible formulations of a "principle of charity" that might be assumed to hold at the time of understanding others; the scope of his discussion here is very broad, and not limited to the interpretation of historical texts. He then applies the result of his analysis to the problem at hand, and argues that the most we can do in this case is provide charitable interpretations of strong versions of partial aspects of Pyrrhonism that are methodologically correct. By contrast, those who aspire to offer a strong version of Pyrrhonism itself are methodologically faulty – and, ultimately, doubtfully charitable. The inescapable conclusion is that Pyrrhonism as a whole can hardly be maintained. No attempts to give global interpretations succeed: we should better focus on scrutinizing brilliant partial aspects of skeptical objections.

Olaso develops further consequences of these ideas in a polemic with Villoro, and later in Olaso (1996), where he adopts a critical stance on contemporary strategies against skepticism in mainstream analytic philosophy. Pyrrhonian skepticism is stylistically peculiar in that it unfolds in multiple arguments, which are meant to target different people and doctrines: the skeptic proceeds ad hominem. Thus, the skeptic does not assert a particular norm of perfect knowledge; rather, he uses the one that the dogmatic provides to him. If this is so, arguments that purport to show the self-refutation of skepticism (on the grounds that skeptics presuppose a particular conception of knowledge) are non-starters. In general, overall strategies against Pyrrhonian-style skepticism are hardly likely to succeed. However, by proceeding piecemeal, just as the skeptic does, we will often have a neat, simpler way of meeting many skeptical challenges. The reason is that, even though many skeptical arguments are very solid, their force derives from the dogmatic theses they are meant to attack; given that in many cases we are not really prone to endorsing such thesis, their scope is actually more limited than what we might have thought.

IV.   Luis Villoro and the Beginnings of
Systematic Studies in Analytic Epistemology

In his (1998) work, Villoro (now emeritus professor at UNAM) offers an attractive, original picture of knowledge, belief, and justification, which at the same time does not disregard broader topics that have usually fallen beyond the realm of analytic epistemology, such as a discussion of what humans should take to be the ultimate values for a meaningful life. As we shall see, Villoro conceives of the study of knowledge as intimately tied to practical and ethical reflections; as with other authors, here we shall

474

not be concerned with those aspects of his rich work that are not directly related to epistemological issues.

Villoro starts by recalling the classical analysis of knowledge in terms of necessary and sufficient conditions, which he will later criticize as inadequate; he also draws an interesting parallel between the task of conceptual analysis and the "method of variations" as understood by the phenomenological school. He then focuses on the concept of belief. He rejects the characterization of beliefs as mental states, and favors the dispositional view, where dispositions, in turn, are to be understood as acquired internal states. It should be noted that "belief" here is understood indistinctly either as an all-or-none affair or as a gradable concept. He dubs the former "belief in a strong sense," or *certainty*, and the latter "belief in a weak sense," or *presumption*. Somewhat controversially, however, he also contends that in the last case the correct situation should be rendered as our fully believing (or failing to believe) a more or less probable proposition – rather than as our believing in a higher or lower degree an exact proposition.

How can belief be knowledge? From the first person point of view, belief in the strong sense equals knowledge. From the third person point of view, by contrast, certainty and knowledge part ways, because reasons can be judged to be insufficient. Villoro then argues that to know is to believe something for reasons that are objectively sufficient. This leaves us with the task of explicating objectivity, in Villoro's sense. To do so, he relies on the concept of "epistemic community," or a community composed of all possible subjects that have access to the same reasons. Thus he proposes two basic conditions for the existence of objective reasons: intersubjectivity and irrevocability. On the one hand, we speak of intersubjectivity when there is coincidence among all possible subjects of the community. This does not entail the existence of *consensus* within the community, which would amount to *effective* coincidence. Progress is possible precisely because the two ideas do not collapse. On the other hand, when should we say that there are reasons that can revoke a given justification? Given Villoro's framework, reasons are limited to those that can arise within a given epistemic community. Hence, supplementary reasons are historically determined. The historicity of knowledge (the relativization of the notion of objectivity to historical and social conditions) is the only valid alternative to skepticism.

Based on these considerations, Villoro proposes to replace the traditional definition of knowledge by a new one, according to which S knows that p if and only if: (1) S believes that p; and (2) S has objectively sufficient reasons to believe that p. Notice that the traditional truth condition is absent from Villoro's analysis. "Objectively sufficient reasons" acts as a criterion of truth, in the sense that such reasons are enough for S to assert that her belief is true: they *guarantee* the truth, but they do not imply it with necessity (unless p is itself a necessary proposition). This is as it should be – Villoro claims – given that we want empirical knowledge to be fallible.

Villoro argues in detail that the proposed definition is superior to the traditional one, in many different senses. To begin with, in the traditional analysis, if the truth condition is independent of the justification condition, then it is not applicable to any proposition or to any subject; if it is applicable, then it is not independent. Villoro also shows that Gettier cases are not a problem for his definition, whereas other attempts to fix the traditional account fail. His definition also enables him to offer solutions to

475

various well-known paradoxes of the literature, such as the so-called Harman–Kripke paradox.

The book also addresses an interesting reflection on the distinction between the Spanish verbs *conocer* and *saber* (similar distinctions are found in other romance languages, such as French or Italian, but not in English, as we have already pointed out). As opposed to *saber* (which refers to propositional knowledge), *conocer* amounts to having direct experience of something; Villoro promptly points out that the phenomenological school has offered a yet unmatched analysis of this concept. Among other things, it requires the integration within one unity of the various partial experiences of an object. In order to know in this sense we need beliefs as well: we aim to state how the object is, not only how it appears – and certainly we aim to say much more than just *that it is*. Moreover, in order to assert that I know in this sense I can only take into account one particular type of reasons: those that constitute personal experiences. By contrast, to justify to others the claim that we have personal knowledge (*conocimiento*) we have to justify our having propositional knowledge (*saber*) of our personal knowledge. The resulting picture is that of a net, where each instance of propositional knowledge refers to other instances of both personal and propositional knowledge, and vice versa. The entire net finally rests on the direct experience of various people (including ourselves – but also other fellow beings whose testimony we have indirectly acquired).

The discussion of personal knowledge leads Villoro to compare *science* and *wisdom*. Whereas science attempts to subsume particular events under general laws, wisdom focuses on concrete occurrences in all their complexity. Its aim is not to explain by objective reasons, but to search for meaning, and to gain personal understanding of the meaning of things in relation to humans. The highest forms of wisdom seek to understand the world in relation to supreme values, where supreme values are in turn defined as those that could direct the life of any human being as a member of the human species.

These reflections ultimately lead Villoro to address explicitly the relation between knowledge and practice. Villoro argues that practical success shows that the belief that guided the action was true, and hence systematic success can act as a sufficient reason to talk about both propositional and personal knowledge (here Villoro appeals implicitly to a sort of inference to the best explanation, though he does not put it in these terms). Not all criteria of truth are practical, though (against, e.g., Althusser): logical relations, or coherence with other beliefs, to mention a few examples, can also work as adequate criteria. But, in any case, our motives to know can always be reduced to our interest in attaining both practical efficacy in our actions and meaning in our life; we do not seek knowledge for its own sake.

Insofar as our beliefs play a fundamental role in concrete life, we would do well to pay attention to a theory of the precepts that regulate our intentional actions – i.e., an ethics of belief. To this effect Villoro proposes a number of norms, such as the duty to search for the truth, and to tolerate other people's beliefs; such rules can at the same time be conceived of as conditions of rational thought. Knowledge is seen as the product of a struggle: reason has to discover and fight the influence of personal motives that try to accommodate the truth to our needs and desires; we can also discover a struggle between our personal interest and that of the species. Within this framework, dogmatism and skepticism are depicted as two opposite forms of intolerance, which seek to affect collective beliefs so as to fit the interests of particular people or groups. An ethic of beliefs aims to state rules to liberate us from these various forms of domination, including the domination by any form of ideology.

Also at the UNAM, at about the same period, we find the work of Wonfilio Trejo (1927–87). His main ideas on phenomenism, realism, and perception were finally published in his 1987 work. The book begins by examining the paradox of phenomenism: if phenomenism is right, then either skepticism about the external world is right, or we should conclude that what is real depends on what is possible to affect us; either case, phenomenism is self-refuted. He carefully reviews Moore and Ayer's attempts to solve the paradox, and finds them wanting. Trejo then proposes his own solution to the problem of how can sense data play a role in the knowledge of physical objects. His answer is that sense data only have a relational role, and one can only describe what they are in terms of relational predicates. In this respect he discusses Chisholm's approach to the subject extensively, and offers several lines of criticism. He proposes, like Chisholm, a causal theory of perception, but without Chisholm's adverbial interpretation. His theory also leads him to examine the nature of causal, or dispositional, properties of physical objects. They are not essential properties – he contends – and are not reducible to their observable effects either. He addresses carefully Carnap's work, and finally favors an intensionalist interpretation, in Chisholm style – though, again, he departs from Chisholm in several respects. He then uses all these resources to discuss the meaning and epistemic status of theoretical terms. Trejo ends his work by offering further clarifications on the relation between the agent and its own sensations. The relevant relation is finally described as a relation of *transparency*, or "perceptual consciousness." It is found to be a theoretical relation, akin to the relation between a magnetic field and the movements of a needle.

V.   Current Analytic Epistemology in Latin America

For the most part, current production in analytic epistemology in Latin America appears in specialized journals. At present there are many philosophical journals edited in Latin America, and some of them have high international standards, with blind peer review and strict requirements for acceptance – the most important ones are *Revista Latinoamericana de Filosofía* (Argentina), *Análisis Filosófico* (Argentina), *Crítica* (Mexico), *Diánoia* (México), and *Manuscrito* and *Principia* (Brazil). In this section I will give priority to those philosophers who have adopted a systematic view, particularly through one or more representative books; the interested reader is advised to turn to the aforementioned journals for further information on the complex scenario of current Latin American epistemology, particularly for the work of younger authors.

At present, the main Latin American philosophical communities that produce analytic epistemology are in Mexico (especially at the Instituto de Investigaciones Filosóficas, UNAM), in Argentina (particularly through – though not limited to – the work done by the Grupo de Acción Filosófica, which meets regularly at the Universidad de Buenos Aires), and in Brazil, at various universities. Let me address the main lines of research developed by these communities.

477

(i)   In addition to Villoro, several other people at the UNAM have influenced younger generations of Mexican epistemologists; among these we should include Margarita Valdés, and the Uruguayan-born philosopher Carlos Pereda, even though epistemology has not been at the center stage of their reflections. Pereda's work has been mainly concerned with the nature of argumentation; he characterizes disputation not only as a matter of reason but also as an activity that implies moral responsibility, in the light of which an ethic of argumentation is required; see his (1994) work, in which he also makes various remarks on epistemological problems. In addition, and working at the interface with philosophy of science, León Olivé has written on sociology of knowledge – mainly scientific knowledge; very critical of relativism, he has sought to defend objectivity over relativistic epistemological accounts; cf. for instance his (1988) work.

A lively line of research on Wittgensteininan epistemology deserves attention. Alejandro Tomasini Bassols has written extensively on many aspects of Wittgenstein's philosophy. In his (2001) work he addresses in detail the traditional analysis of the concept of knowledge, the array of Gettier-type problems, the general problem of skepticism, and various topics on perception, memory, self-knowledge, and truth. He offers a Wittgensteinian treatment of each of these questions and compares it with what he calls the "classical" approach to theory of knowledge. Following Wittgenstein, Tomasini argues that the classical theory of knowledge is basically the result of many conceptual misunderstandings. After Wittgenstein, the efforts to find foundations for knowledge should be dismantled, which should lead us to a new class of epistemology.

From a different perspective, Guillermo Hurtado develops in a series of essays a line of research centered on the notion of belief. Hurtado considers that the philosophical study of belief should precede the study of knowledge, for which we should take into account the way the vocabulary of belief is displayed in social practices and social institutions. In his 2000 work he argues against the "dogma" that any of our beliefs can be false; fallibilism is, like skepticism, a revisionary doctrine and as such it carries the burden of proof. In later works Hurtado proposes new distinctions to tackle the epistemological task with richer resources, drawn from an analysis of ordinary language. To this effect he distinguishes between two uses of the notion of "doubt," and connects them with the notion of "suspicion" (*sospecha*), which, according to Hurtado, has not received the attention it deserves in analytic philosophy.

Other researchers at UNAM include Claudia Lorena García and Ángeles Eraña, with work on naturalized epistemology. Outside UNAM, Juan González, (at the Universidad Autónoma del Estado de Morelos) also pursues research at the interface between cognitive sciences and epistemology, whereas Pedro Stepanenko (at the Centro Peninsular en Humanidades y Ciencias Sociales, UNAM at Mérida, Yucatán) has written on skepticism, as well as on the first person point of view and its perceptions – this time related to Kant's studies.

(ii) In Argentina, Samuel Cabanchik has contended, in a Wittgensteinian spirit, that the traditional epistemological enterprise was an impossible project, as it already contained the elements that led to its own destruction (Cabanchick, 1993). One important feature of old-style epistemology was the conception of language as a medium in which we could reconcile objective and subjective certainty, and the assumption that philosophy was aimed at an objective truth; Wittgenstein has given us the tools to make this situation explicit. Once we abandon a perspective on philosophy that denies the peculiar power that language has over its users, the destructive task of skepticism becomes idle.

There is also a research tradition on pragmatist theory of knowledge, broadly conceived. In a recent book, Daniel Kalpokas (currently at Universidad Nacional de Córdoba) makes a general assessment of Richard Rorty's criticism of modern epistemology and of his attempt to transcend it by means of his conception of pragmatism (Kalpokas, 2005). His criticism leads Kalpokas to present a theoretical alternative to reconstruct epistemology on anti-Cartesian bases, without relying on foundationalism or representationalism. The main theses of Kalpokas's book are thus that Rortian pragmatism does not constitute a genuine departure from the past (it is rather an *aporetic* attempt to separate itself from the Cartesian–Kantian standpoint) and that, well understood, a universalist conception of justification and truth constitutes a philosophical alternative that avoids the problems of the Rortian position, while also offering a path to keep the philosophical reflection about knowledge alive. Other researchers enrolled in this tradition at the Universidad de Buenos Aires include Federico Penelas, who has defended the Rortian conversationalist concept of justification against its critics; Penelas takes justification to be basically a social fact, and attempts to dismantle the counter-intuitive consequences that supposedly follow from giving up the idea that truth is the goal of inquiry (cf., Penelas, 2005). On a somewhat different line, Eleonora Cresto works on formal epistemology, within which she has sought to build a Peircean-based epistemological picture that could take both voluntary and involuntary aspects of our epistemic life into account (cf., for instance, Cresto, 2002). In addition, at the Universidad Nacional de La Plata María Cristina di Gregori has done research on pragmatism and relativism, whereas recent graduates from the Universidad de Buenos Aires, such as Federico Pailas, have pursued work on knowledge attribution. It should be mentioned here that several other Latin American philosophers have engaged either in Wittgensteinian or pragmatist-based reflections on philosophy, although the emphasis has not always been epistemological.

(iii) In Brazil, Paulo Francisco Estrella Faria, at the Universidade Federal do Rio Grande do Sul, concentrates on the epistemology of self-knowledge (cf., for example, Faria, 2001). His general approach to epistemological topics combines a qualified reliabilism about epistemic entitlement and an uncompromising externalism about intentional content. As a reliabilist, Faria holds that epistemic entitlement is largely a matter of suitable placement and proper employment of information systems (perception, memory, testimony, reasoning) whose trustworthiness is, in the normal case, taken for granted rather than reflectively assessed; hence, knowing does not entail knowing that one knows. Yet, entitlement is nevertheless a matter of epistemic responsibility, a point which reliabilism has often been accused of bypassing. Faria's approach to the issue, backed by his externalism about content, aims at dissociating responsibility from control: cognition is a matter of circumstances which may well evade the subject's epistemic access, let alone her control. In his recent work, Faria has accordingly started to articulate a notion

479

of cognitive luck which parallels that of moral luck as discussed in ethics by Bernard Williams and others.

The work of Roberto Horácio de Sá Pereira at the Universidade Federal do Rio de Janeiro, devoted to skepticism, neo-Pyrrhonism, and Wittgenstein's theory of knowledge, deserves to be mentioned. Other Brazilian analytic philosophers who have engaged in epistemological reflection include Ernesto Perini dos Santos, currently a professor at the Universidade Federal de Minas Gerais, with work on Ockham-style answers to skepticism, and Danilo Marcondes de Souza Filho, at the Pontifícia Universidade Católica do Rio de Janeiro, who has also pursued research on skepticism, though with a greater emphasis on linguistic problems – and hence beyond the limits of this chapter.

Finally, note that analytic philosophy arrived late in Latin America, and even after establishing itself as an important philosophical force, it was slow to influence epistemological thought. Even now, the theory of knowledge occupies a small place compared to other areas of analytic research, such as philosophy of language or philosophy of science. Still, these days analytic epistemology is clearly gaining new impulse, and it is reasonable to expect new developments on the subject by new generations of philosophers.

Acknowledgments

Thanks are due to Alejandro Cassini, Alejandro Miroli, Gustavo Ortiz-Millan, Plínio Junqueira Smith, and Ezequiel Zerbudis for useful information and suggestions.

Related chapters: 14 Analytic Philosophy; 15 Paraconsistent Logic; 26 Philosophy of Science; 32 Metaphysics; 34 Formal Epistemology and Logic.

References

Cabanchick, S. (1993). *El revés de la filosofía. Lenguaje y escepticismo*. Buenos Aires: Biblos.

Cresto, E. (2002). Creer, inferir, aceptar: una defensa de la inferencia a la mejor explicación apta para incrédulos. *Revista Latinoamericana de Filosofía*, 28, 227–55.

Faria, P. (2001). Discriminação e conhecimento direto. In G. Hurtado (Ed.). *Subjetividad, representación y realidad* (pp. 9–29). Puebla: Universidad Autónoma de Puebla.

Hurtado, G. (2000). Por qué no soy falibilista. *Crítica*, 32, 59–97.

Kalpokas, D. (2005). *Richard Rorty y la superación pragmatista de la epistemología*. Buenos Aires: Ediciones del Signo.

Olaso, E. de (1977). Saber sin conocer. *Manuscrito*, 1, 65–82.

Olaso, E. de (1988). Zetesis. *Manuscrito*, 11, 7–32.

Olaso, E. de (1992). El escepticismo y los límites de la caridad. *Revista Latinoamericana de Filosofía*, 18, 219–40.

Olaso, E. de (1996). Racionalidad y escepticismo. In O. Nudler (Ed.) (1996). *La racionalidad: su poder y sus límites* (pp. 143–52). Buenos Aires, Barcelona, and Mexico: Paidós.

Olivé, L. (1988). *Conocimiento, sociedad y realidad. Problemas del análisis social del conocimiento y del realismo científico*. Mexico: Fondo de Cultura Económica.

Penelas, F. (2005). Una defensa del conversacionalismo epistémico. *Análisis Filosófico*, 25, 5–20.

Pereda, C. (1994). *Vértigos argumentales*. Barcelona: Anthropos-Universidad Autónoma Metropolitana.

Porchat Pereira, O. (1991). Sobre o que aparece. *Revista Latinoamerica de Filosofia*, XVII:2, 195–229. Buenos Aires. Reprinted in Porchat Pereira (1993a), pp. 166–212.

Porchat Pereira, O. (1993a). *Vida comun e ceticismo*. São Paulo: Editora Brasiliense.

Porchat Pereira, O. (1993b). Ceticismo e argumentação. *Revista Latinoamericana de Filosofia*, XIX:2, 213–44. Buenos Aires.

Porchat Pereira, O. (1995). Verdade, realismo, ceticismo. *Discurso*, 25. São Paulo. Reprinted in Porchat Pereira (2007).

Porchat Pereira, O. (2007). *Rumo ao ceticismo*. São Paulo: EDUNESP.

Smith, P. J. (2005). *Do começo da filosofía e outros ensaios*. São Paulo: Discurso Editoral.

Smith, P. J. (2006). Conhecimento, justificação e verdade. *Dissertatio*, 14, 1–17.

Sosa, E. (1992). *Conocimiento y virtud intelectual*. Mexico: Fondo de Cultura Económica.

Tomasini Bassols, A. (2001). *Teoría del conocimiento clásica y epistemología wittgensteiniana*. Mexico: Plaza y Valdés.

Trejo, W. (1987). *Fenomenalismo y realismo*. Mexico: UNAM.

Villoro, L. (1998). *Belief, personal, and propositional knowledge*. (D. Sosa & D. McDermid, Trans.). Amsterdam and Atlanta: Rodopi Editions (Original work published 1982).

Further Reading

Garzón Valdés, E., & Salmerón, F. (1993). *Epistemología y cultura. En torno a la obra de Luis Villoro*. Mexico: UNAM.

Prado, Jr., B., Porchat Pereira, O., & Ferraz, T. S. (1981). *A filosofia e a visão comun do mundo*. São Paulo: Editora Brasiliense.

Wrigley, M. B., & Smith, P. J. (Eds). (2003). *O filósofo e sua história: uma homenagem a Oswaldo Porchat*. Campinas: Coleção CLE.

34

Formal Epistemology and Logic

HORACIO ARLÓ-COSTA AND EDUARDO FERMÉ

Formal epistemology utilizes formal tools in order to deal with traditional epistemological problems. Bayesian epistemology is an important sub-area of formal epistemology where degrees of belief are represented by probability functions and belief change is modeled via conditionalization (or via alternative methods depending on the application). Bayesian confirmation theory has been, in turn, a very influential part of Bayesian epistemology (especially in areas like philosophy of science). At least this has been the case in the United States and Europe, but not in Latin America where the influence of Popperian philosophy of science has dominated the scene.

In the mid-1980s there was a small revolution in formal epistemology, when various philosophers proposed exact but non-probabilistic theories of belief change and induction. The theories were formal in their presentation but they eschew the various forms of probabilism prevalent in Bayesian epistemology. Various important scholars in Latin America were part of this endeavor.

The main formal tools in Bayesian epistemology are the theory of probability and statistics. The central formal tools in this new wave of non-probabilistic theories of fixation of belief were logical (especially tools developed by philosophical logicians).

Before we elaborate more on this, let us motivate in a preliminary way the notion that is central to the new theories developed in the 1980s: the notion of belief revision.

Suppose that you believe that Peter finished his paper this evening (p); and that you also believe that if Peter finished his paper this evening he will be in the local bar having a beer with his friends (if p, then q). Now you learn that Peter is not in the local bar this evening (not q). What should you believe next? It seems that logic alone is not enough to determine your epistemic state after you learned not q. Apparently you have to *choose* between some options to determine how to change view. For example, you might think that the conditional saying that Peter should be in the local bar if he has finished his work for the day is very reliable. In this case, presumably you will give up the belief that Peter finished his paper this evening. Or you might be quite sure that Peter finished his paper this evening (perhaps he sent you a copy of the finished paper). In this case you might decide to give up the conditional. To use a technical term, it seems that you have to compare how well *entrenched* is p with respect to the conditional 'if p then q.' This presupposes that the information in our belief set is ordered according to an *entrenchment relation*.

Even the relatively simpler act of ceasing to believe one piece of information cannot be straightforwardly described by using logic alone. Say that you believe that Mary is a musician (m). Then you cease to believe so. To contract m from your view it is not enough to just delete it from your epistemic state. For in order to give up m successfully one should give up as well sentences that entail it, like: 'Mary plays the cello in the local symphony orchestra.'

The first type of example is an example of a *revision*. In this case one introduces a new piece of information into the current epistemic state and readjust the background information in such a way that the new result is consistent. In the second case one eliminates a piece of information from a given epistemic state. This type of change can be called *contraction*.

What can be said in general about revisions and contractions? Are there general axioms that regulate these changes? Are there reasonable ways of constructing these operations? Philosophers considered these questions in the early 1980s and late 1970s. Perhaps the first to consider the problem carefully was Isaac Levi (Levi, 1967) and, a few years later, William Harper. But these approaches were constructive, rather than axiomatic, and still utilized a Bayesian machinery to construct the change operations.

The Argentine philosopher Carlos Alchourrón and his collaborators Peter Gärdenfors and David Makinson published a seminal paper on contraction and revision in 1985 (Alchourrón et al., 1985). The paper was published in a logic journal (*The Journal of Symbolic Logic*) and it adopted an axiomatic approach. As expected, the main techniques used in the paper were of a logical and algebraic type. The approach taken in the paper is usually known as the AGM theory of belief change.

Alchourrón continued his work in this field until his death in 1996. The purely logical work in this field has had numerous consequences in various other fields inside and outside philosophy. For example, it has had an important impact in contemporary epistemology, philosophical logic, and jurisprudence. But also during the 1980s and 1990s this work made a fruitful contact with research done in AI (Artificial Intelligence). Alchourrón had positions both in Law and Philosophy in Buenos Aires, but he also maintained an important relation with the department of Computer Science of UBA (Universidad de Buenos Aires) and before that with ESLAI (Escuela Superior Latinoamericana de Informática). The two authors of this chapter were students of Alchourrón in the 1980s and 1990s: one of them (Arló-Costa) coming from philosophy (UBA) and the other (Fermé) from computer science (UBA).

In the following section we will present a brief overview of the work of the main students of Alchourrón (and some more recent work in this area in Latin America). This can give the reader an idea of how this field has evolved in Latin America since the mid-1980s. The following sections introduce some of the main features of the AGM theory as well as more recent developments.

Our chapter will cover only the application of logical techniques to the solution of the problem of how to represent belief change (which, we will argue below, can be seen today as one of the central problems of contemporary epistemology). Much of this work is related to formal work in the area of rational choice (especially the use of choice functions as used by Amartya Sen and others). This work is also intimately connected with work in other areas of philosophical logic (deontic logics, logics of time and action, conditional logics, epistemic logic, etc.), but we will not have the space here to cover these

483

interactions. By the same token we cannot refer to work in other areas of logic that might be relevant to this issue (like recursion theory and theories of formal learning, for example). We will limit our contribution to review the creation of logically oriented theories of belief change since the mid-1980s in Latin America.

Belief Revision in Latin America: The Legacy of Carlos Alchourrón

Argentina was one of the places where the AGM theory was born. It was there that Alchourrón and Makinson met for the first time, in the late 1960s. They started to collaborate in the formalization of the dynamics of legal codes, in particular the problem of how to derogate a law from a code. It is in this area that they define for the first time functions based on maximal subsets of a legal set that fails to imply the derogated law (meet functions). Gärdenfors, on the other hand, was mainly interested in developing a semantic for counterfactual conditionals. His approach was axiomatic rather than semantic. He wanted to develop a purely epistemic semantics for these conditionals, without the heavy ontological commitments of possible-worlds semantics. As an editor of the Swedish journal *Theoria*, he received the article by Alchourrón and Makinson and realized that they had all been looking at the same formal problem from different points of view. So they decided to join forces and this resulted in the AGM seminal paper (Alchourrón et al., 1985). This paper shows that the functions proposed by Alchourrón and Makinson satisfy the postulates proposed by Gärdenfors. Moreover, the paper offers a complete characterization of these postulates. For an overview of other historical details about this paper see Carnota and Rodriguez (2009).

A few years after the meeting of Alchourrón and Makinson, Alchourrón founded a Logic group, in the Philosophy Department of the University of Buenos Aires. There he worked with his students and colleagues in a wide spectrum of topics: modal and deontic logic, conditional logic, and finally, logic of theory change. Initially the group included two logicians from the department of philosophy (UBA): Gladys Palau and Carlos Oller, and two students: Sandra Lazzer (directed by Gregorio Klimovsky) and Horacio Arló-Costa (directed by Alchourrón).

After the publication of the paper by Alchourrón et al. (1985), Alchourrón and Makinson continued their collaboration regarding formal aspects of the theory of theory change. Together they proposed, for example, contraction functions based on eliminating from the current theory a selection of the sentences that effectively contribute to implying the contracted sentence. The theory that thus arises is usually called *safe contraction* (Alchourrón & Makinson, 1985). Although this theory is as important as the one offered in Alchourrón et al. (1985), it has been somewhat neglected in recent years.

At the end of the 1980s, Alchourrón became Professor of the ESLAI (Escuela Superior Latinoamericana de Informática) where he maintained a close collaboration with Adolfo Kvitca and Raul Carnota, AI researchers from the Computer Science Department of UBA. As a result, the Logic group was extended to encompass the AI group. This type of interdisciplinary collaboration was common in other parts of the world (AI was particularly influenced by philosophy at this point – this continues to be the

:ase to some extent, although statistics is today more influential). AI researchers were nterested in explaining how to update databases and looked for general theories of :evision produced by philosophers (see Carnota & Rodriguez, 2009). It was from this unified group that the first Latin American works in belief revision emerged.

In the last years of his life, Alchourrón developed a formal system capturing the essentials of the notion of defeasible conditionalization. His definition of the defeasible conditional is given in terms of a strict implication operator and a modal operator f which can be interpreted as a revision function at the language level (see Alchourrón, 1995, and references to later work in Fermé & Rodriguez, 2006). Alchourrón's theory of conditionals is quite peculiar. It differs both from the theories of conditionals offered by philosophers and the theories of *non-monotonic inference* proposed by computer scientists. Probably his proposals are not completely understood yet (see, nevertheless, Fermé & Rodriguez, 2006, for a recent analysis of Alchourrón's theory).

Besides the work of Alchourrón, several students and researchers of the group started working on different extensions and applications of the AGM model. Among them we can mention the following scholars (in alphabetical order).

Horacio Arló-Costa joined the group, as a student, when it was founded. In 1990 he traveled to the United States in order to continue his (doctoral) studies under the direction of Isaac Levi (Columbia University, NYC). His Ph.D. thesis continued to focus on some of the topics that he studied under Alchourrón: belief revision semantics for epistemic conditionals and non-monotonic notions of consequence (Arló-Costa, 1999). His most recent work has focused on finding a complete axiomatization for the decision-theoretic models of belief change that Isaac Levi presented in (Levi, 2004). Surprisingly perhaps, the notion of contraction that thus arises diverges in many important points from the AGM notion of contraction (Arló-Costa & Levi, 2006). He has also studied models where the notion of epistemic value used in decision-theoretic models is indeterminate and accounts of contraction where the underlying notion of rationality is *bounded* (in the sense of Simon or Gigerenzer, that is, a notion that is sensitive to cognitive and computational limitations of the agents in question), as well as probability-based notions of belief change (Arló-Costa & Parikh, 2005).

Verónica Becher joined the group as a student in 1988 and after a short period went to British Columbia to work under the advice of Craig Boutilier. She returned to the group in 1993. She worked in two main areas: First, she proposed a model of abduction based on the revision of the epistemic state of an agent (Boutilier & Becher, 1995). Second, she analyzed the simplest way to define AGM functions with iterations based on the ideas proposed by Alchourrón and Makinson's work on safe contraction (Areces & Becher, 2001). Gladys Palau, one of the founding members of the Logic group, directed Becher's doctoral dissertation.

Raúl Carnota is a mathematician who specializes in Artificial Intelligence, but is interested in logic and non-monotonic reasoning. He was one of the founders of the interdisciplinary group. His work focused on the use of belief revision as a foundation for rational update in knowledge bases and its relation with non-monotonic reasoning. Recently he has written about the history of AGM (Carnota & Rodriguez, 2009).

Eduardo Fermé joined the group as an MS student in 1988. His work consisted in developing extensions for AGM functions. He analyzed the controversial contraction postulate of recovery and proposed alternative contraction functions that do

485

not obey the postulate (Fermé, 2001). He worked on revision functions where the new information is not always accepted, developing models in two different ways: fixing a "limit" of credibility for a belief in order to be accepted (Hansson et al., 2001) and models of partial acceptance of the new belief (Fermé & Hansson, 1999). More recently his work has focused on studying the AGM model for belief bases.

Ricardo Rodriguez also joined the group when taking his first steps as a researcher in 1988. On the one hand, his initial work focused on characterizing revision functions that do not satisfy the recovery postulate. He also studied ways of circumventing well-known impossibilities in order to give semantics to conditional sentences via change operations (Becher et al., 1999; Fermé & Rodriguez, 2006). On the other hand, his main contribution centered on studying notions of belief revision with a different underlining semantics based on ideas used in approximate reasoning (similarity, possibility, and other). In particular, taking seriously Gärdenfors' idea that non-monotonic reasoning and belief revision are two sides of the same coin, he proposes a very original notion called *pessimistic reasoning*.

A second wave of researchers in belief revision also was directly influenced by Alchourrón. In 1992 Alchourrón went to Bahía Blanca (Universidad Nacional del Sur, Argentina) where he taught a seminar in belief revision. The audience was the AI group guided by Guillermo Simari. The group focused its work on the problematic of argumentative systems, in particular on the model proposed by Simari and Loui (1992). The group was favorably impressed, and two years later, during the Argentine Symposium on Theoretical Aspects of Artificial Intelligence (ATIA94), they presented several ongoing works relating argumentative systems and belief revision. The Simari group is still working today. Two of the most salient researchers in the group working on belief revision have been Marcelo Falappa and Simari. Falappa worked on models of non-prioritized revision with a "limit" of credibility (Hansson et al., 2001), on mapping different presentations for belief bases, and finally, with Simari and Gabrielle Kern Isberner on establishing the relation between belief revision and argumentative systems (Falappa et al., 2002).

Independently of Alchourrón's group, we can find in Brazil two different groups that have worked on belief revision in recent years. On the one hand we have the group located in the Universidade Federal do Rio de Janeiro. In this group Mario Benevides, Sheila Veloso, and some students such as Odinaldo Rodrigues started working on belief revision in 1991. In particular, they focused on adapting the AGM axiomatic for its use in pseudo-definite sets (i.e., they assume that a knowledge base is a definite clause set and a rule is a literal). The first paper on belief revision produced by this group was published in the Brazilian Symposium of Artificial Intelligence in 1994. In January 1994 Rodrigues left the group and went to England. He currently lives and works in England (he teaches at King's College, London). His work focuses on the applicability of belief revision principles to non-classical logics, software engineering, and areas dealing with conflict resolution (such as social choice theory).

The second group is the "Logics, Artificial Intelligence and Formal Methods Group" from the IME at the University of São Paulo. In the area of belief revision the main researcher of the group is Renata Wassermann, whose works originally focused on change functions for resources-bounded agents (Wassermann, 1999; Wassermann & Hansson, 2002). Wassermann joined the group as a student in the early 1990s and

486

then went to the ILLC (Amsterdam) in order to obtain her Ph.D. There she contacted important belief revision researchers (Hansson & Rott, for example) and continued to work on belief revision. She returned to São Paulo in 2000, where she guided the area of belief revision, in particular in applying belief revision to ontologies. Today, the group constitutes one of the most important groups that still work on belief revision in Latin America.

As we see, the seeds sown by AGM grew in Latin America, mainly due to the work of Carlos Alchourrón. However, we can mention another Latin American researcher who made a big contribution in this area: the Argentine Alberto Mendelzon. Mendelzon worked in the area of databases and during the 1980s he was interested (as was a significant portion of the AI community) in characterizing rules for updating knowledge bases. During these years, a lot of papers were published tackling this problematic and proposing models for updating. Mendelzon (with Hirofumi Katsuno) took these models and constructed a unified approach with them. This work was the origin of the influential model of "Updating," proposed by these authors in Katsuno and Mendelzon (1992). Updating is a kind of belief change closely related to belief revision but starting with a very different point of view: In AGM the world is assumed static and the agent must revise his belief when acquiring new information; in Updating the world changes and the agent must adapt his knowledge to external changes. Update was also intimately related to the work of the philosopher David Lewis on conditionals (update is the qualitative counterpart of a probabilistic model for updating that Lewis called imaging). The original paper on updating is one of the most influential papers in the belief revision literature. Alberto Mendelzon died in June 2005.

In recent years the study of models of belief revision has returned to the philosophical community. The foundational work on belief change has continued and various philosophical applications have been discussed. For example, some of the recent philosophical work on belief revision has focused on applications in the area of philosophy of science. An Argentine scholar who has worked in these areas is Eleonora Cresto. She completed a Ph.D. at Columbia University in 2006 under the direction of Isaac Levi (*Inferring to the Best Explanation: A Decision Theoretic Approach*, Columbia University, 2006) and since then she has worked on extending the AGM model to structural changes (Cresto, 2008). Her most recent work on belief and contextual acceptance has been pre-published in FEW (Formal Epistemology Workshop). Cresto is currently a researcher in CONICET (Consejo Nacional de Investigaciones Científicas y Técnicas, Argentina).

The AGM Approach

In the AGM account a *theory* is represented by a set of K, which is a set of propositions in a (at least propositional) language L closed under logical consequence Cn, where Cn is an operator that satisfies the basic Tarskian properties: inclusion ($X \subseteq Cn(X)$), idempotence ($Cn(Cn(X)) \subseteq Cn(X)$), and monotony ($Cn(X) \subseteq Cn(Y)$) if $X \subseteq Y$), as well as supraclassicality, deduction, and compactness. Consequently for every theory K we have that: $Cn(K) = K$.

As we explained above AGM recognizes three types of theory change: *expansion, contraction*, and *revision*. Expansion is the process of introducing a proposition α in the

487

theory K and taking the logical consequences; contraction is the process of eliminating a proposition α from the theory K; and revision consists also in introducing a proposition α in the theory K but under the requirement that the revised theory be consistent.

Expansion is a very simple operation and consists in adding set-theoretically the new proposition a to the theory and then closing the set under logical consequence. We use the notation '$K + \alpha$' to refer to the expansion of the theory K with the sentence a, and we define the operation as follows: $K + \alpha = Cn(K \cup \{\alpha\})$.

Contraction and revision are more complex operations and it is not possible to define them univocally by a formula. The AGM trio appealed in this case to the axiomatic approach. Some basic axioms that characterize the operations have been proposed. We use the notation '$K - \alpha$' to refer to the contraction of a theory K by a proposition α. The AGM postulates for contraction are:

Closure	$K - \alpha$ is a theory, whenever K is a theory.
Inclusion	$K - \alpha \subseteq K$.
Success	If $\alpha \notin Cn(\emptyset)$, then $\alpha \notin K - \alpha$.
Vacuity	If $\alpha \notin K$, then $K - \alpha = K$.
Extensionality	If $\alpha \leftrightarrow \beta \in Cn(\emptyset)$, then $K - \alpha = K - \beta$.
Recovery	$K = (K - \alpha) + \alpha$.

Closure says that the outcome of a change performed in a theory must be a theory. *Inclusion* says that when we contract K by α we always obtain a subset of K, i.e., no proposition is added. *Success* says that a contraction of K to exclude α does in fact give up α, unless α is a tautology (due to closure, $K - \alpha$ includes all the tautologies). In the limiting case that $\alpha \notin K$, *vacuity* says that nothing needs to be done to eliminate α from K. The postulate of *recovery* says that when we contract a theory to get rid of α, and then add α back again to the result of the contraction, we recover the initial theory. *Extensionality* says that contracting with logically equivalent sentences must yield the same result.

The postulates listed above are called the *basic* AGM (or Gärdenfors) postulates. In addition to them, the AGM trio provided postulates for contraction by a conjunction. In order to contract a conjunction $\alpha \wedge \beta$ from a theory K, we must either give up α or give up β. Now, if α is suppressed upon contracting by $\alpha \wedge \beta$, we expect that if a proposition δ has to be removed in order to remove α, then it will also be removed when $\alpha \wedge \beta$ is removed:

Conjunctive inclusion   If $\alpha \notin K - (\alpha \wedge \beta)$, then $K - (\alpha \wedge \beta) \subseteq K - \alpha$.

On the other hand, if a proposition δ in K is not suppressed either in the contraction of K by α or in the contraction of K by β, then δ must not be suppressed in the contraction of K by $\alpha \wedge \beta$:

Conjunctive overlap $K - \alpha \cap K - \beta \subseteq K - (\alpha \wedge \beta)$.

The last two postulates are called the supplementary AGM (or Gärdenfors) postulates. In the presence of the basic postulates, the supplementary postulates are equivalent to saying that either $K - (\alpha \wedge \beta) = K - \alpha$ or $K - (\alpha \wedge \beta) = K - \beta$ or

$K - (\alpha \wedge \beta) = K - \alpha \cap K - \beta$. Perhaps this condition is more transparent than the two conditions we just presented. It shows the possible ways in which a conjunction can be removed from a theory.

AGM revision functions are also characterized by a set of postulates (where $K_\perp$ denotes the inconsistent theory – the set of all sentences of the underlying language):

Closure $K * \alpha$ is a theory, whenever K is a theory.
Success $\alpha \in K * \alpha$
Inclusion $K * \alpha \subseteq K + \alpha$.
Vacuity   If $\neg\alpha \notin K$, then $K + \alpha \subseteq K * \alpha$
Consistency   If $\neg\alpha \notin Cn(\varnothing)$, then $K * \alpha \neq K_\perp$.
Extensionality   If $\alpha \leftrightarrow \beta \in Cn(\varnothing)$, then $K * \alpha = K * \beta$.

where *closure* and *extensionality* are similar to the corresponding postulates in the theory of contraction. *Success* gives a tacit priority to the incoming information by saying that the new proposition must be part of the transformed theory. *Inclusion* and *vacuity* say that when the new input does not contradict the background theory, revision should go by expansion. *Consistency* guarantees that the new theory $K * \alpha$ must be consistent (unless in the case where α is itself inconsistent).

As in contraction, supplementary postulates are also proposed. Let us now analyze the revision of a theory K by a conjunction $\alpha \wedge \beta$. The central idea is that, if K is to be changed minimally so as to include two sentences, α and β, such a change should be possible by first revising K with respect to α and then expanding $K * \alpha$ by β, provided that β does not contradict the beliefs in $K * \alpha$.

Superexpansion $K * (\alpha \wedge \beta) \subseteq (K * \alpha) + \beta$.
Subexpansion   If $\neg\beta \notin K * \alpha$, then $(K * \alpha) + \beta \subseteq K * (\alpha \wedge \beta)$.

Rott proposes alternative supplementary postulates, which, in presence of the basic revision postulates, are equivalent to *superexpansion* and *subexpansion*. The postulates proposed are for revising by a disjunction:

Disjunctive overlap $(K * \alpha) \cap (K * \beta) \subseteq K * (\alpha \vee \beta)$.
Disjunctive inclusion   If $\neg\alpha \notin K * (\alpha \vee \beta)$, then $K * (\alpha \vee \beta) \subseteq K * \alpha$.

As in contraction, in the presence of the basic postulates, the last two postulates are equivalent to saying that $K * (\alpha \vee \beta) = K * \alpha$ or $K * (\alpha \vee \beta) = K * \beta$ or $K * (\alpha \vee \beta) = K * \alpha \cap K * \beta$.

We have seen that contraction and revision are characterized by two different sets of postulates. These postulates are independent in the sense that the postulates of revision do not refer to contraction, and vice versa. However, it is possible to define revision functions in terms of contraction functions, and vice versa, by means of the following identities:

    Levi identity: $K * \alpha = (K - \neg\alpha) + \alpha$
    Harper identity: $K - \alpha = K \cap K * \neg\alpha$

The AGM trio proves that if a function satisfies the AGM contraction postulates, then the revision function defined via the Levi identity satisfies the AGM revision postulates. In the same way, given an AGM revision function the contraction function defined via the Harper identity is an AGM contraction function.

The postulates define the behavior of a change function. However, they do not indicate how to construct revisions and contractions. One way to construct contraction functions is by means of selection among the maximal subsets of K that do not entail the sentence to be contracted, called *remainders*. If we denote by $K \perp \alpha$ the remainder set of K with α (where α is not a tautology), the idea is to select a subset of elements of $K \perp \alpha$ and take the intersection of them:

$$K - \alpha = \cap \gamma(K \perp \alpha)$$

This construction was introduced by Alchourrón and Makinson in 1982 and was called *partial meet contraction*. One of the major achievements of the AGM paper is to show that *partial meet contraction* not only provides a method to construct contraction functions that satisfy the basic Gärdenfors postulates, but also provides a characterization of them; i.e., all functions that satisfy the Gärdenfors postulates can be constructed via a selection function on the remainder sets. The AGM paper also provides an extension of this basic procedure to cover the supplementary postulates presented above.

So far nothing has been assumed about the selection function γ. The central idea of AGM is to focus on a subset of selection functions that are 'rationalizable' via a relation. In fact, the idea of γ picking out the 'best' elements of $K \perp \alpha$ can be made more precise by assuming that there is an *ordering* of the maximal subsets in $K \perp \alpha$ that can be used to pick out the top elements.

Technically, if M(K) denotes the *union* of the family of all the sets $K \perp \alpha$, where α is any proposition in K that is not logically valid, then it is assumed that there exists a *transitive* and *reflexive* ordering relation $\leq$ on M(K). Now, when $K \perp \alpha$ is nonempty, we can define a selection function that picks up the maximal elements by requiring:

(Def γ) $\gamma(K \perp \alpha) = \{K' \in K \perp \phi \colon K'' \leq K'$, for all $K'' \in K \perp \alpha\}$.

A contraction function that is determined from $\leq$ via the selection function γ given by (Def γ) will be called a *transitively relational partial meet contraction function*. Then we have the nice result (the main result in the AGM paper) that the eight postulates for contraction (including the two supplementary postulates) completely characterize the transitively relational partial meet contraction functions.

The Logic of Theory Change and Epistemology

Why the logic of theory change is relevant to epistemology? The standard answer to this question is that (a) the logic of theory change has some relevance for the understanding of the process of belief change, and that (b) the justification of belief change is a central topic in contemporary epistemology.

Let's start with the second issue. Traditional epistemology is centrally interested in elaborating responses to skepticism. Therefore it is centrally concerned with the justification of belief. Nevertheless, during the 1980s, various philosophers questioned this emphasis on justifying static bodies of belief. Perhaps the first to mount this attack was Isaac Levi (Levi, 1980). Levi was influenced by the writings of C. S. Peirce and other doctrines of pragmatist pedigree. Bayesian epistemologists continued this criticism during the 1980s. Perhaps Bas van Fraassen managed to express at the end of the decade the common sentiment of many of these epistemologists when he spoke of a *new epistemology*:

> The old we might call *defensive epistemology*, for it concentrates on justification, warrant for, and defense of one's beliefs. The whole burden of rationality has shifted from justification of our opinion to the rationality of change of opinion. (1989, p. 170)

But even if the justification of change of opinion is the central concern of this new epistemology, why is it that the logic of theory change has anything interesting to say about the business of justifying belief change?

Peter Gärdenfors (1988) presented various arguments linking the work of AGM with the new epistemology of the sort that van Fraassen sketched in his book. The central idea is that theories (understood in the logical sense we gave them in the previous section) could be used to represent the *epistemic commitments* of rational agents. Levi presented the central philosophical idea in Levi (1980). Obviously the explicit beliefs of an agent are finite and can be represented via *a set* of sentences S. But we can say that the logical closure of S (*Cn*(S)) encodes the rational commitments of the agent. The implicit idea is that the object of change is constituted by the epistemic commitments of the agent. Theories represent these commitments. Now the logic of theory change has been connected with an epistemological theme via the notion of epistemic commitment.

Gärdenfors presents a more radical idealization according to which "a rational state of belief is one that is in equilibrium under all forces of internal criticism." Belief revision occurs in response to "epistemic inputs," which "can be thought of as the deliverances of experience or as linguistic (or other symbolic) information provided by other individuals (or machines)" (Gärdenfors, 1988, pp. 9–10).

What Is an Epistemic State?

AGM remains one of the most influential theories of belief change available in the literature. But in recent years some of the central assumptions of the theory have been questioned and various alternatives to and extensions of AGM have been proposed. We cannot provide a complete survey of these theories here. We mentioned above the work of some of the main students of Alchourrón, paying special attention to the work of authors from Latin America. We will now consider some of the main philosophical reasons adduced to modify or extend AGM.

One common philosophical argument insists that the objects of change cannot be theories. Theories contain an infinite number of sentences (if the underlying language

491

is infinite) and many of them might seem irrelevant. If one believes α, a belief set over a language that contains β will also contain sentences like $\alpha \vee \beta$, or $\alpha \vee \neg\beta$, even if one has never heard of β. It might seem more reasonable to represent the epistemic state of an agent via a limited number of sentences that correspond (roughly) to explicit beliefs. This goes in the direction of representing epistemic states by sets of sentences that are *not* closed under logical consequence. In the literature these sets are usually called *belief bases*. Sven Ove Hansson has defended this view in a number of writings (see Hansson, 1999, for a textbook presentation of his ideas).

The central idea is that changes are always performed on the belief base. One might be committed to the logical consequences of a base. If a *derived* belief loses support it will be automatically discarded. The following example, due to Hansson, makes this explicit.

> Example (Hansson): I believe that Paris is the capital of France (α). I also believe that there is milk in the fridge (β). Therefore, I believe that Paris is the capital of France if and only if there is milk in the fridge ($\alpha \leftrightarrow \beta$). I open the fridge and find it necessary to replace my belief in β with belief in $\neg\beta$. I cannot then, on pain of inconsistency, retain both my belief in α and my belief in $\alpha \leftrightarrow \beta$.

If one represents the current epistemic state by a theory then both α and $\alpha \leftrightarrow \beta$ are elements of the belief set. When one opens the fridge and finds no milk one has to choose between retaining α and retaining $\alpha \leftrightarrow \beta$. The retraction of $\alpha \leftrightarrow \beta$ is not automatic. But in the belief base approach the option of retaining $\alpha \leftrightarrow \beta$ does not even arise. Since β is a basic belief, while $\alpha \leftrightarrow \beta$ is a derived belief, when β is removed, the bi-conditional is immediately removed.

Although Hansson's example is quite convincing, the situation can be reversed. Consider the following example:

> Example: On March 12, 2008 I believe that governor Spitzer will resign effective March 17, 2008 (α). I also believe that David Paterson will become governor of New York on March 17, 2008 (β). Therefore, I believe that governor Spitzer will resign effective March 17, 2008 if and only if David Paterson becomes governor on March 17, 2008 ($\alpha \leftrightarrow \beta$). Now (say on March 13) I learn that governor Spitzer has not resigned ($\neg\alpha$). I cannot then, on pain of inconsistency, retain both my belief in β and my belief in $\alpha \leftrightarrow \beta$.

Structurally the examples are similar. However, in spite of the fact that β is a basic belief and $\alpha \leftrightarrow \beta$ is a derived belief, it seems more reasonable to retain $\alpha \leftrightarrow \beta$ and to reject β. At least this seems a permissible epistemic strategy. Notice, nevertheless, that if one uses bases to represent this example, this strategy is impossible. The rejection of $\alpha \leftrightarrow \beta$ would be automatic.

This example seems to show that the representation of epistemic states via bases can be too rigid, limiting the epistemic options of the agent in an unreasonable manner. In spite of this and other problems there is an important literature on bases. Many applications, for example in computer science, depend on representing epistemic states via bases.

Departures from AGM

Some of the postulates of AGM contraction, like recovery, are quite controversial. The following example gives an idea of the doubts about recovery:

Example (Levi): A coin has been tossed and it landed heads. Now you give up the belief that the coin has been tossed. Presumably this requires withdrawing the belief that it landed heads. Now you regain the belief that the coin has been tossed. Should you believe that it landed heads?

It seems that the answer to the question in the previous example is no. But recovery requires a positive answer. Many think that this is a convincing counterexample to recovery. So, something has to go in the usual constructions of contraction.

Let's go back to the partial meet contraction construction; $K - \alpha = \cap\gamma(K\perp\alpha)$. The basic idea is to make a selection from a feasible set given by the remainder set $K\perp\alpha$. Levi has nevertheless proposed that the remainder set is not the right feasible set in contraction. He proposed instead to focus on the *saturatable* contractions $S(K, \alpha)$. A set belongs to $S(K, \alpha)$ if and only if it is a closed subset of K whose expansion with the negation of α yields a maximal and consistent set. It is easy to see that $K\perp\alpha$ is a subset of $S(K, \alpha)$. Then one can focus on the operation obtained by defining: $K - \alpha = \cap\gamma(S(K, \alpha))$. This is enough to knock down *recovery*.

The second important insight that Levi introduces in the literature of belief revision is to appeal to a notion of *epistemic value*. This leads to a sophisticated model of belief change, which is grounded on decision-theoretical ideas. Let V be a real value function whose range is the set of propositions. The notion of value is supposed to obey some basic structural axioms. For example:

(Weak Monotony) If $X \subset Y$ then $V(X) \leq V(Y)$.

So, even if X is a strict subset of Y, the informational value of X and Y might be equal (perhaps because the extra information in Y is useless).

Now we can define the selection over a saturatable set as follows:

(V) $\gamma(S(K, \alpha)) = \{Y \in S(K, \alpha): V(Y) \geq V(X), \text{ for all } X \in S(K, \alpha)\}]$

Hansson and Olsson (see the references in Hansson, 1999) characterized the contraction function based on saturatable sets in terms of the following postulates: *Closure, Inclusion, Success, Vacuity, Extensionality* and

Failure   If $\alpha \in Cn(\emptyset)$, then $K - \alpha = K$.

Hansson and Olsson proved also that if the selection function on the saturatable sets is defined via V, then the contraction obtained also satisfies the Gärdenfors supplementary postulates. But, as we explained above, the theory that thus arises does not obey recovery. The recent work of Levi extends the aforementioned ideas and develops models of expansion and contraction by appealing to decision-theoretical insights

(Levi, 2004). The model of contraction that thus arises (see Arló-Costa & Levi, 2006) diverges even more markedly from AGM contractions (and coincides axiomatically with the model presented on the basis of completely different motivation in Rott & Pagnucco, 1999). This type of work merges logical techniques with applications of decision theory. In some way this makes a connection with the Bayesian theories prevalent in Bayesian epistemology before the introduction of AGM.

Even although some of the basic and extended AGM postulates have been recently questioned, the axiomatic approach utilized by AGM has transformed the work in this area. The use of the axiomatic approach made possible the use of logical methods in addition to the decision-theoretical approaches utilized by philosophers in the 1970s and '80s. At least two generations of philosophical logicians have extended the original AGM approach in recent years, creating in the process an entirely new branch of philosophical logic. As a result, today we have a more unified understanding of the area of epistemic logic (first introduced by the seminal work of Jaakko Hintikka in the 1960s).

Moreover, the use of the axiomatic method made possible a clear and exact discussion of the various relevant issues related to rational changes of view. Much of the work in contemporary *formal epistemology* is in one way or another related to this type of discussion.

Related chapters: 14 Analytic Philosophy; 15 Paraconsistent Logic; 26 Philosophy of Science; 31 Deontic Logic and Legal Philosophy; 33 Epistemology.

References

Alchourrón, C. (1995). Defeasible logic: demarcation and affinities. In L. Fariñas del Cerro, G. Crocco, & A. Herzig (Eds). *Conditionals: from philosophy to computer science* (pp. 67–102). Oxford: Oxford University Press.

Alchourrón, C., Gärdenfors, P., & Makinson, D. (1985). On the logic of theory change: partial meet contraction and revision functions. *Journal of Symbolic Logic*, 50, 510–30.

Alchourrón, C., & Makinson, D. (1985). On the logic of theory change: safe contraction. *Studia Logica*, 44, 405–22.

Areces, C., & Becher, V. (2001). Iterable AGM functions. In H. Rott & M. Williams (Eds). *Frontiers of belief revision* (pp. 261–77). Dordrecht: Kluwer.

Arló-Costa, H. (1999). Belief revision conditionals: basic iterated systems. *Annals of Pure and Applied Logic*, 96, 3–28.

Arló-Costa, H., & Levi, I. (2006). Contraction: on the decision-theoretic origins of minimal change and entrenchment. *Synthese*, 152, 129–54.

Arló-Costa, H., & Parikh, R. (2005). Conditional probability and defeasible inference. *Journal of Philosophical Logic*, 34, 97–119.

Becher, V., Fermé, E., Lazzer, S., Oller, C., Palau, G., & Rodriguez, R. (1999). Some observations on C. Alchourrón's theory of defeasible conditional. In P. McNamara & H. Prakken (Eds). *Norms, logics and information systems* (pp. 219–30). Amsterdam: IOS Press.

Boutilier, C., & Becher, V. (1995). Abduction as belief revision. *Journal of Artificial Intelligence*, 77, 43–94.

Carnota, R., & Rodriguez, R. (2009). AGM theory and artificial intelligence. Forthcoming in Erik Olsson (Ed.). *Science in flux*. Dordrecht: Springer.

Cresto, E. (2008). A model for structural changes of belief. *Studia Logica*, 88, 431–51.

Falappa, M., Kern-Isberner, G., & Simari, G. (2002). Explanations, belief revision and defeasible reasoning. *Artificial Intelligence*, 141, 1–28.

Fermé, E. (2001). Five faces of recovery. In H. Rott & M. Williams (Eds). *Frontiers in belief revision* (pp. 247–59). Dordrecht: Kluwer.

Fermé, E., & Hansson, S. O. (1999). Selective revision. *Studia Logica*, 63, 331–42.

Fermé, E., & Rodriguez, R. (2006). DFT and belief revision. *Análisis Filosófico*, 27, 373–93.

Gärdenfors, P. (1988). *Knowledge in flux: modeling the dynamics of epistemic states*. Cambridge, MA: MIT Press.

Hansson, S. O. (1999). *A textbook of belief dynamics: theory change and database updating*. Dordrecht: Kluwer.

Hansson, S. O., Fermé, E., Cantwell, J., & Falappa, M. (2001). Credibility-limited revision. *Journal of Symbolic Logic*, 66, 1581–96.

Katsuno, H., & Mendelzon, A. (1992). On the difference between updating a knowledge database and revising it. In P. Gärdenfors (Ed.). *Belief revision* (pp. 183–203). Cambridge: Cambridge University Press.

Levi, I. (1967). *Gambling with truth: an essay on induction and the aims of science*. New York: Knopf.

Levi, I. (1980). *The enterprise of knowledge: an essay on knowledge, credal probability and chance*. Cambridge, MA: MIT Press.

Levi, I. (2004). *Mild contraction: evaluating loss of information due to loss of belief*. Oxford: Oxford University Press.

Rott, H., & Pagnucco, M. (1999). Severe withdrawal (and recovery). *Journal of Philosophical Logic*, 28, 501–47.

Simari, G., & Loui, R. (1992). A mathematical treatment of defeasible reasoning and its implementation. *Artificial Intelligence*, 53, 125–57.

van Fraassen, B. (1989). *Laws and symmetry*. Oxford: Clarendon Press.

Wassermann, R. (1999). Resource bounded belief revision. *Erkenntnis*, 50, 429–46.

Wassermann, R., & Hansson, S. O. (2002). Local change. *Studia Logica*, 70, 49–76.

Part IV

Biographical Sketches

35

Some Great Figures

GREGORY D. GILSON AND GREGORY FERNANDO PAPPAS

Acosta, José de (1539–1600)

José de Acosta was a Spanish-born Jesuit theologian, naturalist, and missionary. He entered the Society of Jesus at a young age and eventually became a lecturer in theology. In 1570, Acosta was sent to Lima, Peru, as a missionary, theological scholar, and academic administrator. During his sixteen years in Latin America, he traveled extensively in present-day Peru, Chile, Bolivia, and Mexico, carefully observing and recording the physical geography and the indigenous cultures of those regions. He founded several colleges in Latin America and occupied various important academic and political positions. Acosta returned to Spain in 1587. He died in Salamanca, where he was the rector of the Jesuit College of Salamanca.

Acosta is best known for two works: *Historia natural y moral de las Indias* (*Natural and Moral History of the Indies*, 1590) and *De Procuranda Indorum Salute* (On the necessity of attending to the well being of the Indians, 1588). The *Historia* is a wide-ranging empirically based description of the physical geography and natural history of the indigenous cultures of the New World, including the Aztecs and the Incas. *De Procuranda Indorum Salute* is dedicated to the problems associated with "civilizing" and Christianizing the indigenous peoples of Latin America. Acosta's philosophic significance lies largely in his criticism of Iberian Neo-Scholasticism and as arguably the founder of the Critical Tradition of Latin American philosophy. In the *Historia*, Acosta is not content with merely describing natural phenomena such as earthquakes, volcanoes, tidal activity, the shape of the earth, the trade winds, and the origins of the indigenous peoples of America, but rather seeks systematic explanations of their causes. Further, Acosta is consistently dissatisfied with authoritative Scholastic and biblical explanations of such phenomena, often pointing out their inaccuracy and insufficiency. Rather, Acosta pursues a scientific and empiricist approach to explaining such geophysical phenomena. Acosta often rejects dogmatic Scholastic demonstration in favor of explanation based on experience and hypothesis.

Alberdi, Juan Bautista (1810–84)

Juan Bautista Alberdi was born in Tucuman, Argentina. He attended the University of Buenos Aires and received a law degree from the University of Cordoba. He was a member of the Asociación De Mayo (Association of May) which eventually became the Salón literario. While a member of this group, he wrote *Fragmento preliminar al estudio del derecho* (Preliminary fragment of the study of law, 1837). The essay explains and defends the *caudillo* (or chieftains) system of government in general and the dictator Juan Manuel de Rosas in particular. The group was nevertheless broken up by Rosas and in 1838 Alberdi was forced to flee first to Montevideo and then to Chile. With the fall of Rosas in 1851, Alberdi returned to Argentina as part of the Generation of 1837. In 1852, Alberdi produced his famous *Bases y puntos de partida para la organización política de la República Argentina* (Bases and starting points for political organization of the Argentine Republic). The *Bases* follows Bolívar's call for a strong, almost king-like executive, but also emphasizes liberal reforms. In contrast to Bolívar and Sarmiento, Alberdi did not think that Latin America ought to promote and understand its unique racial, cultural, and geographic identity, but rather ought to look back to Europe for the basis of its laws, language, religion, educational system, and government. He saw the revolution itself as merely a division of Spain into two halves, Spanish Europe and Spanish America. Alberdi believed that Europe represented civilization both culturally and economically whereas everything in America that is not European is barbaric and savage. To promote the goal of cultural and economic civilization, Alberdi advocated an ambitious immigration and foreign investment policy. This policy is summed up in his famous phrase, "to govern is to populate."

The ideas expressed in the *Bases* significantly influenced construction of the Argentinean constitution of 1853. The constitution instituted a number of liberal reforms, including an extensive bill of rights. It established a democratic federal government with a strong executive, but still significantly decentralized political power in favor of the provinces. Alberdi traveled to Europe the following year in an effort to attain international recognition of independent Argentina. He remained in Europe for most of the remainder of his life, returning to Argentina for only three years to serve as senator from Tucuman.

Bello, Andrés (1781–1865)

Andrés Bello was born and educated in Caracas, Venezuela. He studied and taught a wide variety of subjects including philosophy, law, medicine, and classics at the University of Caracas. Bolívar sent him to London in 1810 to establish international recognition of the revolutionary government of the newly independent Venezuela. Bello remained in Great Britain for nineteen years where he worked as a teacher, journalist, translator, and poet. While in London, he published several poems including *Silva a la agricultura de la zona tórrida* (Agriculture in the Torrid Zone, 1826). The work celebrates rural life in Latin America and decries the vices of urban life. Bello also studied Roman and Spanish medieval law and became interested in the ideas of early Utilitarians such as James Mill and Jeremy Bentham. In 1829, he moved to Chile to become the undersecretary of foreign affairs. Remaining in Chile for the rest of his life, Bello became a leading literary figure, legal theorist, and statesman. He founded the University of Chile in 1842 and served as its first rector until 1865.

Bello's *Principios de derecho de gentes* (Principles of people's law, 1832) is perhaps his greatest legal work. The treatise deals with the recognition of new states, the definition of war, and the principles of international interventionalism. Bello's approach to international law combines natural law theory with aspects of Utilitarian-based practical law. In an astounding feat, Bello almost single-handedly wrote the Chilean Civil Code of 1855. The code is strongly influenced by the Napoleonic Code but also reflects his knowledge of Roman and medieval Spanish law. The Chilean Civil Code was soon adopted by nearly all newly independent Latin American countries in civil matters relating to persons, property, inheritance, and contacts. Bello's most important purely philosophic text, *Filosofía del entendimiento* (Philosophy of understanding, 1881) is an empiricist text, which Gaos described as the greatest expression of Spanish American philosophy.

Bilbao, Francisco (1823–65)

Francisco Bilbao was a radical Chilean political theorist and romantic idealist. At an early age, he had association with José Lastarria, who invited him to join the influential *Literary Society of Santiago*. Lastarria also published Bilbao's first major work, *Sociabilidad chilena* (Chilean sociability, 1844). *Sociabilidad* is a scathing critique of the Spanish, and especially Catholic influence on Latin America. The work was publicly burned and Bilbao was exiled to Europe. He returned to Chile briefly in 1850 but was soon exiled again to Peru, France, and finally Argentina, where he remained until his death. In 1858, Bilbao wrote *La ley de la historia* (The laws of history) which emphasizes the normative as opposed to the merely descriptive quality of history. The work compares the English-influenced, Protestant United States with the Spanish-influenced, Catholic "Disunited States." He calls for a new synthesis of philosophy, politics, and history to replace the old synthesis of feudalism and Catholicism. Like Bolívar, Bilbao calls for an international federation of Latin American states based on liberty and equality. The argument is carried further in *La América en peligro* (America in danger, 1862) and *El evangelio americano* (American gospel, 1864) where he warns that Latin America must reject Catholicism and Spanish influence in favor of a federation of humanity, guided by reason.

Bolívar, Simón (1783–1830)

Simón Bolívar was born into a wealthy Creole family in colonial Venezuela. As a military leader he went on to liberate much of northern Latin America from Spanish rule and founded five independent republics. As a political philosopher and statesman he would rule countries, write constitutions, and establish the basic conceptual framework (Bolivarism) for generations of Latin American political thinkers. Bolívar was educated primarily in Europe. His famous teacher Simón Rodríguez emphasized Empiricist

501

thinkers such as Locke, Hobbes, Buffon, Montesquieu, and Rousseau. Bolívar famously vowed to liberate South America during a trip to Rome that immediately preceded his return to Venezuela in 1807. He became involved in revolutionary activities precipitated by Napoleon's invasion of Spain in 1808. He was a member of the Caracas junta that in produced a formal declaration of Venezuela's independence in 1811. The Spanish military aided by colonial royalists soon forced him to flee to New Granada and eventually to Jamaica. While in Jamaica, he wrote his famous *Carta de Jamaica* (Jamaica letter, 1815). The letter appeals for Britain's assistance in the war for independence. It also calls for a united Latin America, an idea that has become an essential component of Bolivarism. Over the next six years, Bolívar liberated La Gran Colombia (contemporary Venezuela, Colombia, Panama, and Ecuador) and became its dictatorial constitutional president. In 1825, Bolívar and Antonio José de Sucre defeated the last Spanish resistance in Peru and the newly formed country of Bolivia. The following year, he wrote the Bolivian Constitution which was later also adopted by Peru.

In the broadest sense, Bolívar rejected monarchy and believed in the democratic social contract approach to political philosophy established by Locke and Rousseau. However, unlike these thinkers, Bolívar did not accept the idea that liberal democracy is the natural result for all societies. According to Bolívar, there is no single political system that is universally appropriate for all nations. Bolivarism maintains that the national character, history, and geographic circumstances should help determine the social and political arrangement that is best for a nation at a particular moment in history. Bolívar was one of the first Latin American thinkers to contemplate the special circumstances created by the *mestizo* character of the peoples of Latin America. According to Bolívar, the unique diversity of ethnic, racial, and cultural backgrounds of the people of Latin America required new and different forms of political organization from those of North America and Europe.

Casas, Bartolomé de las (1484–1566)

Bartolomé de las Casas was a Spanish colonist, Dominican priest, Bishop of Chiapas, and tireless supporter of the basic human rights of Amerindians. Born in Seville, las Casas first traveled to Hispaniola in 1502 to take care of his father's property. As a result, he ended up initially participating in the institution of *encomienda*, which was an economic and social arrangement whereby the Spanish Crown formally granted the labor of Amerindians to Spanish colonists. In return, the Colonists were to defend the colony as well as civilize and Christianize the Amerindians. A basic assumption of the *encomienda* system was that Amerindians were less than fully human and therefore natural slaves, not vested with human or property rights.

In 1514, las Casas is said to have had a religious revelation. He gave up his *encomienda* and spent the rest of his life engaged in various political and literary activities designed to protect the basic human rights of Amerindians. In the early 1540s las Casas presented the Spanish court with his *Brevísima relación de la destrucción de las Indias* (Very brief account of the destruction of the Indies). The work describes, and some say greatly exaggerates, the mistreatment of Amerindians by the Spanish colonists. In 1551, las Casas engaged Juan Ginés de Sepúlveda in the famous public debate at Valladolid over the justice of the Spanish conquest. In the debate, Sepúlveda and las Casas assume the same basic Aristotelian and Thomistic principles. Sepúlveda argued that Amerindians are barbarians and therefore natural slaves that need to be subdued before they can be civilized and Christianized. In contrast, las Casas argued that the Amerindian's cultural practices were compatible with being fully rational. Even though their beliefs were false, their reasoning was good and therefore justified their conclusions. There are four meanings of "barbarian" according to Aristotle. The category "barbarian in the strict sense" does not apply to the Amerindians. Amerindians are not "barbarians" by "nature," i.e., it is not part of their "essence" but a result of accident and circumstances. Las Casas also argued that war can only be justified to prevent the death of innocents, whereas the war against Amerindians was primarily a war of greed.

Las Casas believed his most important work to be *Historia de las Indias* (History of the Indies). The work is both a chronicle of events in Latin America during his lifetime and a damning indictment of Iberian colonialism. For political reasons he did not allow it to be published until after his death. Las Casas did, however, publish the introduction, *Historia apologética* (Apologetic history, ca. 1529) in his lifetime.

Caso, Antonio (1883–1946)

Antonio Caso was the first professor of philosophy at the National University of Mexico after its reorganization following the revolution of 1910. As an active member of the anti-positivist group, Ateneo de la Juventud, he severely criticized the Científicos, who were influential in the later government of Porifirio Díaz. Caso had an extensive knowledge of both historical and contemporary philosophy. He was most influenced by the intuitionism of Henri Bergson, the pragmaticism and emphasis on religious experience of William James, and the biological vitalism of Nietzsche and Schopenhauer. His criticism of positivism stemmed from his belief that the exclusively rationalistic and scientific approach to philosophy ignores important parts of human experience, specifically experiences involving the senses, Christian charity, the unconscious will, and religious experience. Caso also believed that the positivists themselves lacked traits of character essential to philosophy, such as heroism and disinterestedness.

Caso's writing are voluminous, but he is probably best known for his *Problemas filosóficos* (Philosophic problems, 1915), *La existencia como economía como desinterés y como caridad* (Existence as economy, as disinterestedness, and as charity, 1919), and *Discursos a la Nación Mexicana* (Discourses to the Mexican nation, 1922). Caso saw the human being as essentially dualistic. On the one hand, humans are egoistic and utilitarian, and on the other they are heroic and possess a disinterested impulse that can give rise to aesthetic creation and Christian charity. *Problemas* is devoted to explicating the heroic and disinterested aspect of the human being, a project Caso believed was neglected by the positivists. *La existencia* pragmatically relates the disinterested and heroic individual to society and culture. *Discursos* is a nationalistic plea to Mexican officials to develop the innate heroic impulse that might give rise to a virtuous Mexican culture.

503

Cruz, Sor Juana Inés de la (1651–95)

Sor Juana Inés de la Cruz was a prolific Mexican poet, dramatist, essayist, and scholar. She is best known as a literary figure and also for her feminist philosophy, depicted in both her writing and lifestyle. Cruz is said to have been an intellectual prodigy, reading and writing in Latin at a very young age. As a young woman, she was popular at the Mexican viceregal court. She became a nun in the Convent of Santa Paula at age 16 and for the next two decades she wrote poetry, essays, plays, and pieces for religious services and events of State. Cruz enjoyed the patronage and support of many in the Mexican viceregal court, which afforded her great intellectual freedom and scholarly resources. Several of her works deal with freedom, women's capacities and rights, and existing power relations between men and women. "Hombres necios" ("Foolish Men," ca. 1680) criticizes the sexism of her time and accuses men of the irrationality they claim to find in women. Juana's most famous feminist piece is *Respuesta a Sor Filotea* (Reply to Sor Philothea, 1691). The essay is a reply to a letter written by the Bishop of Puebla. In the letter the Bishop suggested that women ought to limit their study to the topic of theology and not concern themselves with secular themes. Cruz's *Respuesta* is autobiographical in nature and defends the capacity and right of women to education and secular knowledge. The *Respuesta* also defends an empirical, early-Enlightenment approach to knowledge and investigation of the world.

da Costa, Newton Carneiro Affonso (b. 1929)

Newton Carneiro Affonso da Costa is an internationally renowned Brazilian mathematician, logician, and philosopher. He has published more than two hundred articles and several books, which have collected more than a thousand citations. He is best known for his work in mathematical logic, the foundations of mathematics, the foundations of physics, and the application of logic and mathematics to the philosophy of science and artificial intelligence. Da Costa is one of the creators of paraconsistent logic, formulated in *Sistemas formais inconsistentes* (Inconsistent formal systems, 1963). Classical logical systems have the feature that any theory that entails contradictory propositions is trivial in the sense that any proposition follows from it. Da Costa showed that, by using paraconsistent logic, it is possible to formulate inconsistent but non-trivial theories. In paraconsistent logical systems inconsistencies are isolated inferentially, and do not imply everything. This is useful because mathematicians and scientists often continue to work in theoretical and logical systems even after inconsistencies have been discovered in them. Paraconsistent logics have also been extremely useful in computer science and artificial intelligence. See, for example, the article by da Costa and V. S. Subrahmanian, "Paraconsistent Logic as a Formalism for Reasoning about Inconsistent Knowledge Bases" (1989).

Closely related to his work in paraconsistent logic is da Costa's development of the notion of partial truth or quasi-truth. The classical notion of truth is typically understood in terms of some sort of correspondence with reality. Roughly speaking, the proposition "snow is white" is true if and only if it corresponds to the fact that snow is white. Alfred Tarski's formulation of truth in formalized languages can

504

be interpreted as offering a characterization of the notion of truth as correspondence. Partial or quasi-truth provides a generalization of Tarski's account of truth for contexts that include partial information. The approach also allows for the possibility that both a proposition and its negation are quasi-true. This approach explains various aspects of scientific practice, including the possibility of reconciling otherwise incompatible scientific theories. These issues are examined in detail in da Costa and Steven French's *Science and Partial Truth: A Unitary Approach to Models and Scientific Reasoning* (2003).

Dussel, Enrique (b. 1934)

Enrique Dussel was born in Argentina. He is a philosopher and historian of the Latin American church who has lived in Mexico City since he was forced to flee Argentina in 1975. He has been a professor at Universidad Autónoma Metropolitana in Mexico City since 1976. Dussel is one of the earliest proponents of the philosophy of the liberation, an important version of which he has developed throughout his career. He has consistently been opposed to modernity and modern philosophy, and he has always advocated an ethics articulated around the suffering and liberation of the poor. His more recent work develops a Latin American philosophy that critically responds to modernity and globalization, known as transmodernity. He is the author of over forty books that critically examine liberation theology, Marxism, feminism, Western philosophy, ethics, aesthetics, and ontology. Dussel's best-known works include *Filosofía de la liberación* (The philosophy of liberation, 1980), *Ethics and Community* (1988), *El encubrimiento del Indio* (The invention of the Americas, 1995), and *The Underside of Modernity* (1996). The *Philosophy of Liberation* attempts to establish a general philosophic framework in which the voices of Hispanic America and the Third World ("the other as the other") can be expressed. *Ethics and Community* develops a social ethics from the perspective of liberation philosophy. The work hinges on the need for ethics to overcome morality. Morality is any practical system of totalitarian order. Ethics is the future order of liberation that will seek justice for the poor and oppressed. *The Invention of the Americas* attacks the "myth of modernity," first articulated by Hegel, which privileges European culture and morality by disguising it as universal and the necessary product of civilization. *The Underside of Modernity* is a collection of essays designed to begin "a dialogue with the hegemonic European–North American philosophical community." The essays continue to develop the philosophic and ethical thesis that Eurocentrism prevents the economic development of the poor and oppressed. Some of the essays in the book directly address prominent European–North American philosophers, including Richard Rorty and Charles Taylor.

Frondizi, Risieri (1910–83)

Risieri Frondizi was an Argentine prolific writer, philosopher, and educator. Although Frondizi studied with Francisco Romero in Argentina, his relation with North American philosophers was also key to his philosophical development. He entered Harvard

505

and studied with pragmatist philosophers such as C. I. Lewis, R. B. Perry, W. Kohler, and especially A. N. Whitehead. Throughout his life, Frondizi remained in a constant dialogue with philosophers from all the Americas. Frondizi taught in Michigan, Venezuela, Pennsylvania, Puerto Rico, Texas, Illinois, and Argentina. In his 1945 book, *El punto de partida del filosofar* (The starting point of philosophy), he defended the thesis that experience is the necessary point of departure and permanent reference of all genuine philosophizing. Experience is a process constituted by my self, my activity, and the objects that this activity is concerned with. A general philosophy of experience must proceed to study each of these elements without making the mistake of forgetting that they are given as part of an indivisible totality. Frondizi embarked upon this project, which culminated in a book about the self, *Substancia y función en el problema del yo* (The nature of the self, 1952), and one about value, *¿Qué son los valores?* (What is value?, 1957). For Frondizi, the self is an organic unity that is dynamic and structural. The relation between the self and the elements that constitute it is a "gestalt" one. In regard to values, Frondizi offered a way to overcome the antithesis between objectivism and subjectivism. They both start with an abstraction and not with value as it is experienced. Value is better conceived as a "gestalt" quality. This means that it is a quality that depends on but cannot be reduced to empirical qualities. A value is a synthesis of objective and subjective contributions that emerges and has meaning in concrete human situations. Frondizi played an important role in establishing the first journals, classes, and organizations dedicated exclusively to philosophical inquiry in many places in Latin America.

Gaos, José (1900–69)

José Gaos was a Spanish-born phenomenonologist and existentialist philosopher who permanently emigrated to Mexico in 1938 as a result of the Spanish Civil War. He was most influenced by Edmund Husserl, Martin Heidegger, and Ortega y Gasset. He was influential in establishing professional philosophical institutions in Mexico, including, in 1945, the formation of the first professional philosophy journal *Minerva: Revista Continental de Filosofía*. In the broadest sense, Gaos embraced the importance of modern logic and the analytic method of philosophy in the project of phenomenology. In his 1941 review of Antonio Caso's *Positivismo, neopositivismo y fenomenología* (Positivism, neo-positivism and phenomenology, 1941), he followed Caso's rejection of the logical positivist and scientificist approach to philosophy emanating from the Vienna Circle, while emphasizing the importance of modern logic and the analytic method of conceptual analysis to accurately represent the essential systematic nature of philosophy. Nevertheless, he held that that philosophy must ultimately be subjective because it can only be authentically accepted and understood by the individual.

Throughout his career, Gaos remained committed to existential or anthropological phenomenology. In the late 1940s and early 1950s he was committed to Heidegger's project of combining Husserl's phenomenology and hermeneutics with Kant's transcendental method to form a new, comprehensive idealist metaphysics developed by an analysis of consciousness rather than by using scientific methods. Starting in the 1950s, Gaos began to abandon this comprehensive idealist project and instead began to develop a series of separate phenomenologies dedicated to describing the content, origin, and significance of various areas of human reality, including a phenomenology of reason, a phenomenology of pride, a phenomenology of categories, and a phenomenology of human nature. Somewhat paradoxically, Gaos maintained that all these phenomenologies were related and represented a new comprehensive philosophy, without being an idealist metaphysics. Gaos' work is developed in numerous articles and lectures, including *Filosofía de la filosofía* (Philosophy of philosophy, 1947), *Discurso de filosofía* (Discourse on philosophy, 1959), and *Filosofía contemporánea* (Contemporary philosophy, 1962). Throughout his career, Gaos translated numerous German and English philosophic texts into the Spanish language, including his well-known translation of Heidegger's *Being and Time*.

González Prada, Manuel (1848–1918)

Manuel González Prada was Peru's most influential voice of reform following the War of the Pacific, in which Chile defeated and occupied Peru. He became a radical critic of the institutions that governed Peru and a founding symbol of Peru's new national identity. González Prada's call for radical reform is summed up in his famous dictum, "Old men to the tomb, young men to work." He was very influential on future Peruvian revolutionaries and is generally considered to be the founder of postcolonial *indigenismo* (the project of incorporating Amerindians into civil society while preserving their unique culture and individuality). After Peru lost the War of the Pacific to Chile, González Prada undertook a prescriptive analysis of Peruvian history that roundly condemned the conquest and Spanish colonialism. He criticized nearly every institution in aristocratic, postcolonial Peru. The Catholic Church, the military, and the aristocratic government of Peru were corrupted and diseased beyond redemption. The only answer to the country's problems was for the youth to reorganize the country, taking into account the long exploited and neglected Amerindians. Much of his thought during this time period was utilitarian and positivist. Following a long trip to Europe (1892–8), his ideas became increasingly radical, anarchistic, and nihilistic. His criticisms of the superstition and oppression of the Church and of the state of Peruvian democracy increase in their ferocity. His support of the Amerindian cause in Peru continued, but arguably with a more Marxist tone. His essays and speeches are collected in *Páginas libres* (Free pages, 1894) and *Horas de lucha* (Hours of struggle, 1908).

Gracia, Jorge J. E. (b. 1942)

Jorge J. E. Gracia was educated in Cuba, the United States, Canada, and Spain. Gracia is the author of fourteen books about metaphysics, philosophical historiography, philosophy of language/hermeneutics, medieval and Latin American philosophy. His first works are on metaphysical issues related to individuality and individuation in Francisco Suarez and the early Middle Ages. This research culminated in a systematic treatment of the subject in *Individuality: An Essay on the Foundations of Metaphysics* (1988).

507

This led to an interest in the metaphysics of philosophical and religious texts. He wrote four books related to textuality and interpretation: *Ontological Status, Identity, Author, Audience* (1996), *A Theory of Textuality: The Logic and Epistemology* (1995), *Philosophy and Its History: Issues in Philosophical Historiography* (1992), *How Can We Know What God Means? The Interpretation of Revelation* (2001). In these books the ontological nature of texts, their identity conditions, as well as their relation to authors and audiences are fully explored. For Gracia metaphysics, in particular categories, inform all our thought and therefore need to be taken seriously. Since 2000 his work has focused on showing how discussion of ethnicity, race, and nationality needs to be grounded on adequate metaphysical categorizations. In *Hispanic/Latino Identity: A Philosophical Perspective* (2000) Gracia makes the case for a non-essentialist view of Hispanic identity. Hispanic identity is to be understood in familial historical terms and not in terms of shared common traits. Hispanics are the people of Iberia, Latin America, and some segments of the population in the United States after 1492 – and descendants of these people anywhere in the world as long as they preserve close ties to them. In *Surviving Race, Ethnicity, and Nationality: A Challenge for the Twenty-First Century* (2005) Gracia explores race, ethnicity, and nationality together and attempts to present a systematic and unified theory about them with particular emphasis on the metaphysical and epistemological issues that these phenomena raise. More recently, Gracia has published *Identity, Memory, and Diaspora: Voices of Cuban-American Artists, Writers, and Philosophers* (2008) and *Latinos in America* (2008).

Haya de la Torre, Victor Raúl (1895–1979)

Victor Raúl Haya de la Torre is best known for founding the Alianza Popular Revolucionaria Americana (APRA) in 1924, while exiled in Mexico The APRA was a Marxist-inspired populist social reform movement designed to fight imperialism, nationalize and internationalize land and industry, and unify Latin America both with itself and with the rest of the exploited and oppressed people of the world. The movement came into existence when Haya was able to form a student–worker alliance between Peruvian university students and textile workers in San Marcos. Haya used the APRA as a political platform to run for the presidency of Peru in 1930. Though Haya lost the election and never gained power, he remained the head of APRA, which continued to be a significant political party in Peru for the next 40 years.

In his *El antiimperialismo y el APRA* (Anti-imperialism and the APRA, 1936), Haya analyses the events in Latin America during the first decades after independence and argues for the necessity of the APRA. Haya criticizes both the increased foreign investment and the growth of monopolistic enterprises and proletarianization of Amerindians and the middle class in Peru. The APRA would unite the exploited Amerindians, middle class, and workers to produce a nationalist, anti-imperialistic society. Haya contributes to the *indigenismo* movement with his *¿Adónde va Indoamérica?* (Where is IndoAmerica going?, 1936) and "Aprismo, Marxismo y espacio-tiempo historico" (Aprismo, Marxism and historical time-space). These essays argue that the notion of Indo-America ought to replace Latin America as the historical basis that underlies America's evolutionary progression toward socialism.

Hostos, Eugenio María de (1839–1903)

Eugenio María de Hostos was a Puerto Rican-born social philosopher, educator, and political activist for the cause of Antillean independence. After receiving his primary and secondary education in Spain, Hostos became involved in the Cuban revolutionary movement in New York in 1869. Following a trip around South America, he settled in the Dominican Republic and dedicated himself to improving the educational system in Latin America. From 1889 to 1898 he was a professor at the University of Chile. After Cuban liberation and the transfer of Puerto Rico from Spain to the United States, Hostos returned to New York in a failed attempt to gain autonomy for Puerto Rico. Hostos returned to the Dominican Republic in 1899 and remained there for the rest of his life.

Hostos was a positivist in the sense that he looked to history to determine the rational and moral principles that society and the individual ought to adopt. He also believed in an essentially utilitarian analysis of societal and individual need and improvement. Nevertheless, his belief in free will, idealism, and existentialism sharply distinguished him from both Marxist material determinist and social Darwinist versions of positivism. Hostos's two most famous works are *Tratado de moral* (Treatise on morals, 1888) and *Tratado de sociología* (Treatise on sociology, 1904). The former is a meditation on the duty of an individual in civilized society. The latter uses history to diagnose the pathological conditions that exist in Latin American society and prescribes a program designed to repair the state and its organs to health.

Ingenieros, José (1877–1925)

José Ingenieros was a Spencerian positivist, psychologist, and a founding member of the Socialist Party of Argentina. His most famous work, *El hombre mediocre* (The mediocre man, 1920), influenced a whole generation of Argentine thinkers. Ingenieros studied law and medicine at the University of Buenos Aires. His doctoral thesis concerned abnormal psychology and criminology. From 1904 to 1912 he held the positions of Professor of Experimental Psychology at the University of Buenos Aires and Director of Psychiatric Observation for the police. During this period, Ingenieros wrote *Principios de Psicología* (Principles of psychology, 1911). The book expands the biological process of evolution to include the individual in his social environment. The thinking individual is depicted as adopting customs and morality as a means to struggle for existence in terms of profession, class, race, and sex.

In *The Mediocre Man*, Ingenieros attacks modern men who live without the spiritual idealism required for evolutionary progress. These men lack an original character and merely seek to cope with societal relations as they currently exist. Ingenieros analyzes and diagnoses the current societal and educational conditions that produce mediocre men. Ingenieros advocates a new ethics of aristocracy of merit, where superior men of talent, virtue, and personality take control of society. These men must openly resist organized mediocrity and vulgarity in contemporary society. Ingenieros was a positivist and therefore did not believe in a reality that transcends human experience. Nevertheless, he believed in a naturalistic conception of ideals and that metaphysics was

509

not only possible but necessary to promote the ideals whereby mediocrity might be overcome. In *Hacia una moral sin dogmas* (Towards a morality without dogmas, 1953), Ingenieros, inspired by Emerson, argues for a conception of morality based in experience and nature and not on dogma or anything transcendent. In his *Proposiciones relativas al porvenir de la filosofía* (Propositions regarding the future of philosophy, 1918) Ingenieros explains that the role of metaphysics is to form hypotheses that cannot be tested by experiment. These hypotheses are not, however, to be a priori speculations. Rather they are to be probabilistic conjectures based on the latest empirical data. The legitimacy of these synthetic propositions will be determined by their analytic compatibility with the results of science.

Korn, Alejandro (1860–1936)

Alejandro Korn was an Argentinean intellectual who spent the first half of his life practicing medicine as the director of a hospital for the insane, and the last thirty years of his life as a professor of philosophy and dean at the University of Buenos Aries. Korn was a late member of the generation of 1880 but eventually outgrew the strictly scientific and positivistic doctrines of that group. It was his reading of Schopenhauer, Bergson, and especially Kant that caused him to see the limitations of materialism, scientific determinism, and social Darwinism. Korn maintained that a proper explanation of human personality, value, and freedom are beyond the reach of positivistic philosophy. Science, which is entirely quantitative, is capable of describing all phenomena that take place in space. Science provides the raw empirical data required for inductive inferences regarding the objective outer world. However, the conclusions and truths expressed by science, he argues, are always probabilistic and relative to particular pragmatic circumstances. Science can never explain, Korn maintains, the conscious subject who interprets objective reality and possesses freedom and dignity.

According to Korn, the scope of philosophy is the inner subject and in particular how the subject freely reacts to and values objective facts. Korn explains his conception of human freedom in *La libertad creadora* (Creative freedom, 1930). Humans are free and autonomous, not subject to biological or physical determination, and yet nevertheless, they must struggle to negate obstacles in both the external and inner worlds. Triumph over external obstacles emancipates one from material servitude and leads to economic freedom. Inner obstacles to ethical freedom include misguided impulses and emotions. Taken together, external economic freedom and inner ethical freedom provide complete human freedom. Korn's *Axiología* (Axiology, 1938) explains that human values are a combination of individual subjectivity combined with the collective life of a culture. Ethical norms, such as justice and tolerance, are the result of the collective desire for individuals to minimize conflict, live in harmony, and protest against the excess of the industrial age. Korn criticizes the positivist faith in science and indifference to religion, and recognizes the importance of spiritual values. Korn's *Influencias filosóficas en la evolución nacional* (Philosophic influences in the evolution of a nation, 1912) explains the emergence of positivism in Argentina as a result of the history of conflict between philosophy and science that can be traced back to colonialism.

510

Lastarria, José Victorino (1817–88)

José Victorino Lastarria was a leading liberal Chilean intellectual and the most famous student of Andrés Bello. He was a prolific writer, active editor of journals, and a general literary advocate. His most famous work, *Investigaciones sobre la influencia social de la conquista y del sistema colonial de los españoles en Chile* (Investigations on the social influence of the conquest and the colonial system of the Spanish in Chile, 1844) was delivered on the occasion of the first anniversary of the University of Chile. The *Investigaciones* condemns and rejects the Spanish heritage of Chile. He accuses the Spanish of exploiting natural resources and setting up governmental and educational systems explicitly designed to produce "three centuries of gloomy existence without movement." Lastarria saw the mixture of races that produced the mestizo to be a tragedy and condemned the class system whereby the Spanish refused to engage in any mechanical art or useful profession. The *Investigations* is one of the earliest manifestations of Latin American positivism. Following Comte, Lastarria asserts that Chile must adopt systems of government and education based on laws of progress that will enable its citizens to evolve into a new kind of human existence and freedom. Lastarria argues for a complete separation of the church from both state and education.

Lastarria was briefly exiled to Peru for his radical views but was soon allowed to return to Chile. He continued to argue and work for liberal reforms. In his major work, *América*, Lastarria criticizes Europe for not sufficiently recognizing and appreciating the profound transformation in human existence that democratic America embodied. He supported European immigration to Latin America but only if the immigrants brought civilization, capital, and mechanical skills. They also needed to be willing to become part of the new American society, and abandon European allegiances and interests.

Lemos, Miguel (1854–1917)

Miguel Lemos was a leading Brazilian positivist in the tradition of Auguste Comte. In 1871, Lemos joined Benjamin Constant Botelho de Magalhães, Antônio Carlos de Oliveira Guimarães, and Raimundo Texeira Mendes to organize the Sociedade Positivista or the Positivist Association of Brazil. The Sociedade Positivista played a significant role in the reform of Brazilian education and politics, including the ultimate conversion of Brazil from a monarchy into a republic in 1889. After the conversion, the group attempted to set up a Comtean sociocratic utopia or dictatorship of positivist intellectuals in Brazil. The goal was never achieved but the group was nonetheless very influential in the early republican government, as is illustrated by the Brazilian flag which bears the positivist slogan, "Order and Progress."

While in Paris in 1880, Lemos wrote *Luis de Camões*. The work, based on Comte's doctrines, encouraged the descendants of Iberian colonialists to abandon hatreds and renew bonds of love and gratitude with their mother country after independence. In 1881, Lemos returned from Paris, took control of the Sociedade Positivista, and along with Texeira Mendes founded the Templo da Humanidadade or the Temple of Humanity. This positivist church was founded to undermine the power of the Catholic

511

Church in Brazil by promoting the secular religion of humanity advocated by Comte. The Templo was a significant advocate for the abolition of slavery. Texeira Mendes published his plan for abolition in *Apontamentos para a Solução do Problema Social no Brasil* (Annotations on the solution of Brazil's social problems, 1880). The Temple also opposed the immigration of Chinese in a plan to replace African slave labor with Asian "semi-slave" labor.

Mariátegui, José Carlos (1895–1930)

José Carlos Mariátegui was a Peruvian political philosopher and Marxist activist. His ideas have been profoundly influential on subsequent political thinkers and socialist revolutionary movements in Peru. As a youth Mariátegui founded, edited, and wrote for several socialist newspapers, including *La Razón* and *Nuestra Época*. He was a journalist in Europe from 1920 to 1922, where he was steeped in the European Marxist milieu that existed immediately following World War I. He returned to Peru in 1923 and spent the rest of his short life applying Marxist thought to the political and economic situation in Peru.

Mariátegui worked with Victor Raúl Haya de le Torre to found the Marxist Alianza Popular Revolucionaria Americana (APRA) movement and the socialist literary magazine *Amauta*. In 1925, Mariátegui published *La escena contemporánea* (The contemporary scene). This book consisted of a collection of essays that analyzed contemporary events within a Marxist context. Some of the events analyzed included the rise of fascism, the state of democracy, the imperialism of the United States, and the state of Amerindians. Mariátegui's most famous work is *Siete ensayos de interpretación de la realidad peruana* (Seven essays on the interpretation of Peruvian reality, 1928). The seven essays apply Marxist theory to the historical development of religion, economics, education, regionalism, and literature in Peru. The work reflects Mariátegui's belief that European Marxism cannot be blindly applied to Peru. If a socialist revolution is to occur there, it must be based on and take into account the unique historical and material conditions in Latin America. Specifically, Mariátegui claims that for Marxism to succeed in Peru, the revolution must seek to incorporate indigenous peoples into civil society and respect the spirit of pre-colonial beliefs and practices regarding land and agriculture. Mariátegui believed that the conquest interrupted a natural evolution that was occurring among the Incas toward an agrarian communist socioeconomic system and that the way to help the natives is through a change in their socioeconomic conditions. Disagreements with Haya and the direction of the APRA caused Mariátegui to found the Partido Socialista del Perú (Socialist Party of Peru) in 1928.

Martí, José (1853–95)

José Martí was a Cuban revolutionary leader, poet, and essayist. Martí vigorously opposed both Spanish and U.S. domination of Cuba. He spent most of his life in exile, but actively engaged in activities designed to liberate Cuba from Spanish control. Martí was exiled to Spain when he was just seventeen, where he earned degrees in philosophy and law from the University of Zaragoza. He also published in support of Cuban independence, including *El presidio político en Cuba* (Political prison in Cuba, 1871). This essay severely criticized the Spanish-run prisons in Cuba. He was forced to leave Spain in 1875. After living in Mexico and Guatemala, he briefly returned to Cuba before again being exiled to Spain. He spent most of the rest of his life in New York. While living in New York he wrote many essays explaining and analyzing the political, social, and economic conditions in the United States, including his famous *Escenas norteamericanas*. In 1892 he founded the Cuban Revolutionary Party to achieve the independence of Cuba and assist in that of Puerto Rico. He returned to Cuba in 1895 with a group of revolutionaries and was killed in combat before Cuba was ultimately liberated from Spanish rule in 1898.

Martí was an early critic of Spencerian positivism, despite his recognition of its utility in disengaging with prior belief systems. Martí opposed the claim that there is one universal ideal political organization for all societies. Rather political organization ought to be determined by the particular history and nature of the society as well as the geographic and physical realities of their environment. He advocated for the education of both Amerindians and newly emancipated African Americans. For Martí, the art of self-government in Latin America requires knowledge, self-criticism, avoiding imported methods and models, and an affirmation of unity in diversity as an ideal. Martí's ideas have been influential in a wide range of political ideologies including materialist-socialism and individualist liberal democracy. Martí's literary works were primarily published in newspapers and journals, but have been collected in his *Obras completas*.

Méndez Sierra, Justo (1848–1912)

Justo Méndez Sierra was a liberal Mexican positivist in the tradition of Herbert Spencer. Sierra became well known as a journalist, poet, and novelist at a young age, but his most significant work was in history and education. He was a prominent member of the group of positivist activists known as the Científicos, a group which was influential in the later government of Porifirio Díaz. As their name suggests, this group sought to modernize Mexico by replacing traditional religious and indigenously based beliefs, practices, and customs with scientific and utilitarian-based institutions. They believed that the path of social evolution would eliminate the Spanish, Amerindian, and even *mestizo* elements of Mexican society. While the group is blamed for many of the repressive policies of the Díaz regime, Sierra seems to have viewed this social evolution as a naturally unfolding Darwinian process working toward perfection and not something that ought to be promoted by repressive governmental policy. Sierra's most important literary work is *Evolución política del pueblo mexicano* (The political evolution of the Mexican people, 1910). This work describes Mexican society as a living and evolving being. He criticizes Spanish colonialism and its superstitious Christian legacy but sees the emergence of the *mestizo* as a positive dynamic stage in Mexican evolution. He advocates the passage of Mexico from an agricultural and military power to an industrial power. Sierra believed that industrialization was not merely an end in itself, but also required to protect Mexico from the domination of the United States.

513

Mora, José María Luis (1794–1850)

José María Luis Mora was born to a wealthy Creole family in Guanajuato, Mexico. He received a degree in theology in 1819 from Colegio de San Ildefonso where he remained as a professor and priest. Mora was perhaps Mexico's greatest political theorist during the first two decades following its official independence in 1821. He aspired to produce a progressive, independent, and above all liberal nation that nevertheless remained Catholic and Spanish. Mora was an important influence on Mexico's constitution of 1824 which promoted democracy, federalism, property rights, an independent judiciary, and Catholicism as the national religion. Mora saw federalism as a means to promote economic and political liberalism. He believed that a strong central government was necessary to provide law and order and to prevent regional and special interests from interfering with individual liberties. He also thought that a strong central government was required to restrain and transform Mexico's large Amerindian population. He explicitly rejected Bolívar's call for a united Spanish America.

In 1831, Mora wrote *Catecismo político de la Federación Mexicana* (Political catechism of the Mexican federation), an essay whose central thesis is that church activity and wealth should be controlled by the state. The *Catecismo* also advocated limiting the size and influence of the army. The essay was enormously influential and was used as a guiding document for the reform administration of Gómez Farías, 1833–4. After a revolt from the military and clergy, Farías was removed from office by General Santa Ana, and Mora was forced to flee to Paris where he remained until his death. While living in Paris, he published *Méjico y sus revoluciones* (Mexico and its revolutions, 1836) and *Obras sueltas* (Unrelated collected works, 1837).

Miró Quesada, Francisco (b. 1918)

Francisco Miró Quesada is a Peruvian analytic philosopher and logician. He has also concurrently worked in the area of political philosophy and ethics, developing a humanism based on ethical principles that proposes concrete socialist solutions to the problems facing Peru. Miró's early philosophic education was primarily in Continental philosophy, but the bulk of his work is in the area of logic, mathematical philosophy, and formal language. Both Continental and analytic elements are evident in his political philosophy. In 1941, he published *Sentido del movimiento fenomenológico* (Meaning of the Phenomenological Movement), which is an exegetical account of phenomenology as developed by Husserl and Heidegger.

Miró is credited with coining the term 'paraconsistent logic' in 1976, a term which he thinks has direct application to human reason. Miró claims that reason is best but imperfectly investigated by logico-mathematical techniques. In *Apuntes para una teoría de la razón* (Notes for a theory of reason, 1963), he develops a definition of historical reason that can investigate ideological and ethical issues within a valid formal logical and mathematical framework. *Las estructuras sociales* (Social structures, 1961) and *El Perú como doctrina* (Peru as doctrine, 1966) are direct applications of this definition of historical reason to political philosophy. His best-known formal work is *Filosofía de las Matemáticas* (Philosophy of Mathematics, 1980).

Rabossi, Eduardo (1930–2005)

Eduardo Rabossi was an Argentine analytic philosopher, philosophic organizer, teacher, and human rights activist. He published in many areas of philosophy including ethics, political philosophy, the philosophy of language, philosophy of mind, and metaphysics. In addition to his original work and publications, Rabossi translated many contemporary analytic works into Spanish. His involvement with Argentina and international philosophic and human rights associations includes being the founding president of Sociedad Argentina de Análisis Filosófico (SADAF), a founding member of Asociación Filosófica Argentina (AFRA), and an active member of Comisión Nacional de Desaparición de Personas (CONADEP).

Rabossi was an ethical naturalist, arguing that the propositions involving basic or vital human needs can bridge the is/ought gap because they are both objectively true or false, and at the same time, normative. Contingent, natural facts surrounding human nature, biological and psychological make-up, scarcity of resources, etc., determine basic human needs. In turn, these objectively and contingently determined human needs give rise to non-contingent norms involving basic human rights. Examples of basic or vital human needs that automatically give rise to moral rights include adequate nourishment and self-realization. Rabossi's ethical naturalism is presented in many publications including his 1983 articles, "Necesidades humanas y moralidad" (Human necessities and morality) and "Acerca de la fundamentación de la ética" (About the foundation of ethics). Naturalism also animates Rabossi's philosophy of mind, language, and metaphysics. His *La tesis de la identidad mente-cuerpo* (The thesis of the mind and body identity, 1995) rejects dualism in favor of monism and functionalism. Rabossi dismisses the idea that consciousness and its phenomenal properties pose a special problem for metaphysical and scientific analysis. He spells out his version of metaphysical naturalism in *Filosofía de la mente y filosofía de la psicología: La agenda, la práctica, el dominio* (Philosophy of mind and philosophy of psychology, 2002).

Ramos, Samuel (1897–1959)

Samuel Ramos was a student and eventual colleague of Antonio Caso at the National University of Mexico. He was most significantly influenced by the perspectivism and rational vitalism of José Ortega y Gasset of Spain. More specifically, Ramos uses these tools along with the psychological theories of Freud, Jung, and Adler in an attempt to construct a national philosophy of Mexico. In *Perfil del hombre y la cultura en México* (Profile of the person and culture in Mexico, 1934), Ramos psychoanalyzes Mexican culture. He asserts that the Mexican soul has been suffering from an inferiority complex ever since colonialism. As a result, all Mexican philosophy up to this point had been mere imitation of European philosophy. In *Historia de la filosofía en Mexico* (History of philosophy in México, 1943), Ramos expresses the dissatisfaction of the younger generation of Mexican philosophers with the romantic, biological vitalism of Caso and Vasconcelos, which he takes to be largely a reaction against rationalistic positivism. Instead, Mexican philosophy ought to begin with the historicized and psychologized reason unconsciously and vitally fused into the Mexican consciousness.

Only then could generic and universal concepts concerning the universe, society, and humanity be investigated to construct a Mexican national philosophy.

Rodó, José Enrique (1872–1917)

José Enrique Rodó was a Uruguayan philosopher, cultural leader, and politician. He is best known for his enormously influential short narrative essay, *Ariel* (1900). Though *Ariel* embodies some positivist elements, such as Spencerian social evolution, the work came to be seen as an inspirational anti-positivist manifesto by the younger generation in early twentieth-century Latin America. The narrative of *Ariel* is delivered to young students by a teacher named Prospero after the Duke in Shakespeare's *The Tempest*. *Ariel* advocates uniting Latin America into a Christian and Hellenistic meritocracy of virtue and value by instilling in its citizens a sense of aesthetic appreciation and high culture. In an introductory section of *Ariel*, Rodó praises the democratic, utilitarian, and economically powerful United States. He then proceeds to straightforwardly criticize the country that defeated Spain as an empire but also annexed territories and arrogantly intervenes in the internal affairs of Latin America. The cornerstone of North America's success is its strict faithfulness to a positivist, democratic, and utilitarianism conception of life. But the same elements that make North America economically successful cause its citizens to become spiritually mediocre and lacking in aesthetic, moral, and social values. Rodó tells Latin Americans to reengage the values of their ancient Greek and Roman Christian ancestry. He believed in democracy in the sense that everybody should have individual liberty and opportunity, but a proper democracy will also include a spiritual elite who wield significant influence and power within society. This spiritual elite should use Greek and Christian ideals to cultivate a harmonious society based on virtues such as charity, spiritual value, and aesthetic sense.

In *Los motivos de Proteo* (Motives of Proteus, 1909), Rodó advocates that each individual should discover and pursue their vocation, and fight to retain their own essential personality. Like *Ariel*, the principles expressed in *Los motivos de Proteo* are to apply both to the individual in society as well as to Latin American society in relation to the international arena and especially in relation to the United States. Rodó also published *El mirador de Próspero* (The mirror of Prospero, 1913), a collection of articles, speeches, and critical essays.

Romero, Francisco (1891–1962)

Francisco Romero continued the neo-Kantian, anti-positivist work of his teacher, mentor, and fellow Argentine, Alejandro Korn. Romero's work was also influenced by German idealists and existentialists such as Max Scheler, Wilhelm Dilthey, and Edmund Husserl. Like Korn, Romero held that there are aspects of human existence that cannot be explained within a positivistic philosophic framework. Romero called the aspect of a person that gives rise to freedom, *spirit*. Spirit enables human beings to transcend their subjective valuations which are based on empirical needs and desires, and value objects objectively. In *Filosofía Contemporánea* (Contemporary philosophy, 1941),

Romero tracks two thousand years of philosophers attempting to explain the concept of spirit. Romero identifies Kant, Hegel, and then Scheler as the most astute analysts of the human capacity to objectively value objects independently of their empirical value.

His primary contribution to philosophy is his work on the nature of the human being, a project sometimes called philosophic anthropology. *Papeles para una filosofía* (Notes for a philosophy, 1944) and *Filosofía de la persona* (Philosophy of the person, 1944) are early works in philosophic anthropology. The most systematic and comprehensive presentation of his dualistic conception of the human being occupies his classic book *Teoría del hombre* (Theory of man, 1952). On the one hand, the human being is an immanent, psychic individual, while on the other hand he is a transcendent, spiritual person. The difference between the individual and the person is best illustrated in the different nature and objects of their intentionality. The immanent individual is egoistic and utilitarian and is best described in positivistic (i.e., naturalistic and scientific) terms. The transcendent person looks beyond her individualistic interests toward objective universal value and is best described in idealist and existentialist terms. Romero's philosophy is largely devoted to describing the process of transcendence whereby the immanent individual might become a spiritual person. The importance of this process is illustrated in his thesis: "to be is to transcend."

Sahagún, Fray Bernardino de (1499–1590)

Fray Bernardino de Sahagún was a Spanish Franciscan missionary, and perhaps the first Western Aztec scholar. He studied at Salamanca before traveling to New Spain in 1529. He spent the next sixty years converting, teaching, and studying the Amerindians living in the Aztec cities of Tlaltelolco and Tepepolco, near Mexico City. Sahagún dedicated his life to understanding and documenting the Aztec view of their language, culture, history, philosophy, and religion. Sahagún, himself fluent in the Aztec language of Nahuatl, worked with native trilingual (Nahuatl, Spanish, and Latin) scholars to interview the elders of Tlaltelolco and Tepepolco. He documented all this information in his *Historia general de las cosas de Nueva España* (General history of the things of New Spain), better known as the *Florentine Codex*. This twelve-book collection was written primarily in Nahuatl, but was also translated into Latin and Spanish. The original work also contains more than 1,800 illustrations. The collection of books constitutes the most complete account of Aztec life before the Conquest.

The *Florentine Codex* was so controversial that the full Nahuatl version wasn't published until the nineteenth century. During the colonial period, only heavily censored Spanish and Latin versions were available. There appear to be two, arguably contradictory, reasons for this censorship. First, the Spanish and Christian authorities were afraid that the existence of such material might perpetuate idolatry, immorality, and barbarism among Amerindians and thereby interfere with the process of civilization and Christianization of the New World. Second, the rich cultural and religious heritage depicted in the text directly contradicts the claim that Amerindians are barbaric and subhuman, which was the primary justification for denying Amerindians basic human rights. Sahagún himself explicitly argues that the epistemic practices of the priests and wise men in Aztec culture were similar to those of Western philosophers and astrologers.

517

He also translated into Nahuatl numerous biblical materials such as sermons, Gospels, Psalms, and catechism.

Salazar Bondy, Augusto (1925–74)

Augusto Salazar Bondy was a Peruvian philosopher known for his earlier work in phenomenology and his later work in analytic philosophy and Marxist thought. He was primarily concerned with the topics of Latin American identity and liberation. After studying under José Gaos and Leopoldo Zea in Mexico, he enrolled in the École Normale Supérieure in Paris, where he became interested in the phenomenology and existentialism of Heidegger, Hartmann, Sartre, and Camus. In 1953, he received his Ph.D. in philosophy and became a professor at the National University of San Marcos. His first two books, *La filosofía en el Perú* (Philosophy in Peru, 1954) and *Irrealidad e idealidad* (Irreality and idealism, 1958) illustrate his dual and interconnected interests in the history of philosophic ideas in Peru and the phenomenological and ontological analysis of abstract objects (ideas). To be useful, philosophic ideas cannot be another person's interpretation of human events, but rather must be a direct expression of one's own concrete human existence. Only then can philosophy provide a guide for individual action and be used to solve the serious problems confronting Peruvian society. According to Salazar, the history of philosophy in Latin America shows that its ideas have been the product of European interests and European interpretations of Latin American events, having no originality or direct connection to the problems of Peru or wider Latin America. His philosophic project is to meditate on the problems of Latin America and attempt to use philosophical reflection to find solutions that provide real solutions for Peruvian society. Near the end of his life, Salazar takes a more analytic approach to the philosophy of value, as evidenced in *Sentido y problema del pensamiento filosófico hispanoamericano* (Hispano-American thought's sense and problem, 1969) and *Para una filosofía del valor* (For a philosophy of value, 1971).

Sarmiento, Domingo Faustino (1811–88)

Domingo Faustino Sarmiento was known as the Educator President of Argentina. Beginning in 1829, Sarmiento fought in the civil war in favor of the Unitarists and against the forces allied with *caudillo* Juan Manuel de Rosas. Except for a trip abroad to study the education systems of Europe and the United States, Sarmiento remained in exile in Chile from 1831 until the fall of Rosas in 1852. Despite his lack of formal education, he had literary and political associations with intellectual luminaries such as Echeverría, Alberdi, and Bello, while in Chile. His journalistic activity focused on attacking the *caudillo* (or chieftain) system of government, and in particular the use of that system by Rosas. In 1845, the newspaper *El Progresso* published his most famous work, *Facundo: civilización y barbarie* (Facundo: civilization and barbarism, 1845).

　　Sarmiento's masterpiece, *Facundo*, is ostensibly a criticism of *caudillos* such as Facundo Quiroga and Rosas, but it is also an explanation of why their rule is accepted. The book continues the colonial theme of civilization versus barbarism in the new world. However, instead of race serving as the fundamental fault line, Sarmiento stresses the difference between the civilized cities and the barbaric countryside. Though Sarmiento still identifies civilization with European culture and barbarism with indigenous culture, he alters the debate by maintaining that a person of any race will become a barbarian in the countryside and any race of person will become civilized in the city. Sarmiento identifies barbarism with the Amerindians, gauchos, and *criollos* that inhabit the vast pampas of Argentina. He thinks the unavoidable isolation and deprivation caused by the geographic conditions that exist in the pampas in the nineteenth century necessarily produce barbarism, despotism, and tyranny. The gaucho seeks the dissolution of civilized society because of the uselessness of moral and intellectual skills in his rural context. Only brute force and the rule of the strongest are respected. In contrast, the physical environment of the city promotes the rationalism and moral order required for education, culture, economic progress, and civilization. According to Sarmiento, the rule of *caudillos* such as Facundo and Rosas represent the conquest of the civilized city by the barbaric countryside.

Ofelia Schutte (b. 1945)

Ofelia Schutte was born in Cuba and received her Ph.D. in philosophy from Yale University. Originally trained as a scholar in Nietzsche and post-Kantian European Continental philosophy, she developed courses in Latin American philosophy and social thought at the University of Florida, Gainesville, beginning in 1980. In the early 1980s Schutte attended several international congresses where she met a number of philosophers from Latin America, further developing her interests in the philosophy of history, feminism, and liberation theory. In 1985 she was a Fulbright Senior Research Fellow at UNAM in Mexico City. Subsequently she has published extensively in Latin American philosophy and feminism, served as President of the Society for Iberian and Latin American Thought, traveled and lectured widely throughout the region, and held numerous editorial appointments in feminist and Latin American journals. In 1999 she moved to the University of South Florida in Tampa, expanding her research to postcolonial feminist theory, the work of José Martí, and recent Cuban women's narrative.

Schutte's first book, *Beyond Nihilism: Nietzsche without Masks* (1984), is a feminist critique of Nietzsche, but also elucidates the possibility of a liberation philosophy based on the rejection of metaphysical and moral dualisms. In particular, the dualism of inferior/superior (people) and good/evil reinforce authoritarian mentalities and prevent us from becoming healthy individuals. Schutte's *Cultural Identity and Social Liberation in Latin American Thought* (1993) addresses the history of Latin American intellectual and social movements from about the 1920s to the 1980s with special attention given to Mariátegui, Zea, the early liberation philosophers, and feminism. Schutte was one of the first U.S. philosophers to explicate and use ideas in Latin American philosophy in the study of feminism, ethics, and aesthetics. She has also been one of the most influential figures in promoting this research program within the U.S. academic community.

Sepúlveda, Juan Ginés de (ca. 1494–1573)

Juan Ginés de Sepúlveda is best known for his participation with las Casas in a public debate in 1551 in Valladolid concerning the justice of the Spanish conquest. The debate occurred shortly after the repeal of several provisions of the New Laws (1542) designed to phase out the economic system of exploitation known as *encomienda*. Sepúlveda used Thomistic and Aristotelian principles to argue that Amerindians were irrational barbarians and therefore natural slaves without basic natural rights, including property rights. He also supplies utilitarian justifications for "subduing" Amerindians so that subsequent generations might be more easily Christianized and civilized. With the publication of *Demócrates Segundo o De las justas causas de la guerra contra los indios* (A second Democritus: on the just causes of the war with the Indians) Sepúlveda cemented his reputation as one of the most influential defenders of the justice of the Spanish conquest. Other scholars point out that Sepúlveda's views were never very popular among the Spanish court or Spanish intellectuals in the sixteenth century.

Torretti, Roberto (b. 1930)

Roberto Torretti, born in Chile, is best known for his work in the history and the philosophy of physics and in particular the relation between geometry and space-time physics. Torretti's work is influenced by Immanuel Kant, as illustrated by his first book *Manuel Kant: estudio sobre los fundamentos de la filosofía crítica* (Immanuel Kant. A study on the foundations of critical philosophy, 1967). His work on the relation between geometry and physics continues in *Philosophy of Geometry from Riemann to Poincaré* (1978), and *Relativity and Geometry* (1983). In *Creative Understanding: Philosophical Reflections on Physics* (1990) Torretti expands his analysis to include how physical theories, in general, represent the world. His best-known book is *The Philosophy of Physics* (1999). This book is groundbreaking and original in that it explicates the philosophy of physics by examining the major seminal conceptual developments in physics itself, rather than merely tracing the history of the philosophy of physics. The final chapter is a comprehensive proposal of how to proceed in the investigation of currently outstanding issues in the philosophy of physics, including the reconciliation between physics and common sense, the proper understanding of laws of nature, the continuity of experience and the results of contemporary physics, and the relation between general concepts and particular facts.

Vasconcelos, José (1882–1959)

José Vasconcelos was a Mexican philosopher, historian, and sociologist. He criticized the positivists' reliance on empirical philosophy and utilitarian ethics, and was most influenced by Kant, Hegel, and Argentine socialist leader, Alfredo Palacios. Despite his rejection of positivism, Vasconcelos views human history in terms of three evolutionary stages: viz., the material or warlike, the intellectual or political, and the spiritual or aesthetic. These stages represent the progressive liberation of humanity from

520

material determination to an existence involving free choice based on the good and the beautiful. He believed that humanity is nearing the end of the second stage and is on the verge of entering the third.

Vasconcelos's prophetic book, *La raza cósmica* (The cosmic race, 1925) argues that the previous two stages of human evolution have given rise to four races of humanity: African, Asian, Amerindian, and Indo-European. The European, Vasconcelos holds, has been most successful in the second stage of evolution based on reason but is doomed to fall as humanity enters the third stage. Like Rodó, Vasconcelos was concerned about the possibility that North America would dominate Latin America, and he believed that the civilization of Latin America could flourish and even reign supreme if political and national ideals were replaced with identity based on the synthesis of race, a process he believed was already under way as humanity enters the third stage of evolution. The final stage of human evolution, which will be based on free spiritual and aesthetic choice, will give rise to a fifth, superior race: the cosmic race. While in previous stages of human evolution, racial superiority was defined in terms of racial purity, in the new and final stage, racial superiority will depend on a synthesis of heterogeneous elements. Vasconcelos also believed that the racially and ethnically diverse *mestizo* was the first manifestation of, or at least had a distinct advantage in becoming, the cosmic race.

Vaz Ferreira, Carlos (1872–1958)

Carlos Vaz Ferreira was a Uruguayan philosopher, writer, lawyer, and academic who introduced liberal, pluralistic values and pragmatic philosophical concepts to South America. In 1913, his university gave him the position and title of "maestro de conferencias" in recognition of his success as a lecturer and teacher. Between 1929 and 1941, he was president of the University of the Republic and put into practice some of his ideas on education. During this period, he was well known for his outspoken defense of academic autonomy against the dictatorship of Gabriel Terra. His first philosophical orientation was positivistic, but influenced more by John Stuart Mill than Comte or Spencer. Ferreira's mature thought was influenced by William James and Henri Bergson, and emphasized freedom and flexibility. Ferreira was against systems and dogmatism. For him, philosophy should start with lived experience and avoid rigid doctrines. In 1907, he published *Conocimiento y acción* (Knowledge and action) and *Moral para intelectuales* (Morals for intellectuals), followed by *El pragmatismo* (Pragmatism, 1909) and *Lógica viva* (Living logic, 1910) in. In all of his works, Ferreira attacked the narrow, purely rational concept of knowledge that excludes the dynamic vitality of reality and concrete human situations. In *Lógica viva*, he shows the negative consequences of thought and action from intellectual or logical fallacies. *Sobre el feminismo* (On feminism, 1933) is one of the earliest treatments of feminism in Latin American academia. *Fermentario* (Fermentative) appeared in 1938. For Ferreira, there was a disparity between reality and the intellectual tools used to simplify and reduce it into manageable terms. For him, our (useful) systems and classifications must not be confused with the complexity of situations. He advocated a morality that acknowledged the unique problems of each person and place, and sought to solve them accordingly.

Villoro, Luis (b. 1922)

Luis Villoro was born in Spain, but has spent most of his life in Mexico. He was influenced by the José Gaos's thesis that philosophy ought to proceed by thinking about one's own world, understood historically and contextually. In the 1940s, along with Leopoldo Zea and Emilio Uranga, he founded the Grupo Hiperión (Hyperion Group), dedicated to studying *"filosofía de lo mexicano"* (philosophy of that which is Mexican). *Hyperion* pursued an existentialist and phenomenological investigation of the nature of Mexican Being and ethos. The group later extended their investigation to include Third World identity, paving the way for later identity and liberation theorists such as Enrique Dussel. Villoro's *Los grandes momentos del indigenismo* (The great moments of indigenism, 1950) examines the historical development of Amerindian consciousness and the concept of indigenousness. Villoro's *Creer, saber, conocer* (Belief, knowledge, learning, 1982) is a more broadly analytic work in epistemology. The work denies skepticism and defends knowledge as objectively justified albeit historically and culturally situated belief. The work also severely criticizes scientism and especially its use as justification for colonial expansion and cultural conquest. Two more significant works by Villoro are *El proceso ideológico de la revolución de independencia* (The ideological process of the revolution of independence n, 1983) and *El concepto de la ideología y otros ensayos* (The concept of ideology and other essays, 1985). In both of these works, Villoro tries to diagnose what went wrong with the Mexican revolution of 1821. According to Villoro, the revolution's intellectual leaders lost touch with the Mexican people and instituted a codified scientific and liberation ideology that became a new instrument of domination. Villoro wants to abandon ideology and scientism to make room for historically rooted existential and phenomenological philosophy.

Vitoria, Francisco de (ca. 1483–1546)

Francisco de Vitoria was born in the Basque province of Alava and educated at University of Paris. He spent most of his career occupying a chair of theology at the University of Salamanca in Spain. Although he never set foot in Latin America, he may be considered a Latin American philosopher because of his work on the morality of the Spanish conquest and the natural rights of Amerindians. Vitoria is responsible for reviving Thomism at the University of Salamanca and is even credited with developing his own unique version, which came to be known as Vitorian Thomism. Emperor Charles V was significantly influenced by Vitoria's assertions that Amerindians possessed natural rights and by Vitoria's skepticism regarding the justice of the Spanish conquest.

Following Aquinas, Vitoria held that war was only justified against overt aggression and should be exercised only as a last resort. This view contradicted the widespread view that waging war and enslaving Amerindians was justified because they were pagans. Nor did Vitoria believe that being pagan made one essentially irrational or barbaric. According to Vitoria, the Amerindians' cultural practices were compatible with being fully rational. Vitoria held that the Spanish had the right to travel freely in Latin America in order to preach the Gospel and engage in trade. So long as Amerindians did not interfere with these activities, the Spanish had no right to cause harm to them or take their and. Vitoria also held that Spaniards were justified in interfering with Amerindians in order to prevent excessively brutal and oppressive acts toward innocents.

Zea Aguilar, Leopoldo (1912–2004)

Leopoldo Zea Aguilar was Mexico's greatest historian and critic of positivism in Latin America. Zea's original work involves founding contributions to the phenomenonological understanding of Mexican reality, and liberation and identity theory. The greatest philosophical influences on Zea include his teachers Antonio Caso and Samuel Ramos and especially the Spanish philosopher José Gaos.

Zea's two-part classic *El Positivismo en México* (Positivism in Mexico, 1943) and *El apogeo y decadencia del positivismo en México* (The apogee and fall of positivism in Mexico, 1945) diagnose how and why positivism was adopted and adapted to become the dominant philosophy of Mexico in the late nineteenth and early twentieth centuries. According to Zea, positivism was introduced to Mexico by Gabino Barreda in an attempt to establish order in the political and educational spheres after the disruption caused by the liberal reform movement of Benito Juarez, in which the military and the clergy lost their special privileges. The order established, however, merely resulted in a new form of neocolonial exploitations where the Mexican bourgeoisie served as a pawn mediating the exploitation of various social groups by foreign interests. Zea extended his analysis of positivism to include all of Latin America in *Dos etapas del pensamiento en Hispanoamérica* (The Latin American mind, 1949).

In the early 1950s Zea founded the Grupo Hiperión (Hyperion Group) devoted to the phenomenonological analysis of Mexican historical reality and identity, a project Zea believed must precede any authentic liberation theory. Zea maintained that authentic liberation requires people to assimilate or assume their particular historical situation to create a concrete but nevertheless universal philosophy of liberation and identity. This requires recognizing and selectively appropriating Western institutions and ideas as well as respecting and promoting the diversity and plurality of the Latin American reality. Zea calls this the "assumptive project" and characterizes it as a kind of Hegelian synthesis, the product of which to be transcended and selectively negated in a dialectical fashion. Some of Zea's greatest works on identity and authentic liberation include: *En torno a una filosofía americana* (About an American philosophy, 1945), *La filosofía como compromiso y otros ensayos* (Philosophy as compromise and other essays, 1952), and *Discurso desde la marginación y la barbarie* (Discourse on marginalization and barbarism, 1988).

Acknowledgment

We would like to thank Dr. Caroline Miles and Oscar Berrio for help with editing earlier versions of this chapter.

Further Reading

Crawford, W. R. (1961). *A century of Latin-American thought*. Cambridge, MA: Harvard University Press.

Davis, H. E. (1972). *Latin American thought: a historical introduction*. Baton Rouge, LA: Louisiana State University Press.

Lipp, S. (1969). *Three Argentine thinkers*. New York: Philosophical Library.

Nuccetelli, S. (2002). *Latin American thought: philosophical problems and arguments*. Boulder, CO: Westview Press.

Nuccetelli, S., & Seay, G. (Ed.). (2004). *Latin American philosophy*. Upper Saddle River, NJ: Pearson Education.

Gracia, J. J. E., & Millián-Zaibert, E. (2004). (Eds). *Latin American philosophy for the 21st century*. Amherst, NY: Prometheus.

Gracia, J. J. E., & Camurati, M. (1989). (Ed.). *Philosophy and literature in Latin America: a critical assessment of the current situation*. Albany: State University of New York Press.

Woodward, R. L. Jr. (Ed.). (1971). *Problems in Latin American civilization: positivism in Latin America, 1850–1900*. Massachusetts: D. C. Heath and Company.

Sanchez Reulet, A. (1949). *La filosofia latinoamericana contemporanea*. Mexico City: Union Panamericana.

Dussel, E. (2003). Philosophy in Latin America in the 20th century. In G. Fløistad (Ed.). *Contemporary philosophy*, Vol. 8: *Philosophy of Latin America* (pp. 15–59). Norwell, MA: Kluwer Academic Publishers.

Gianella, A. E. (2006). Eduardo Rabossi: professor and researcher. *APA Newsletter on Hispanic Issues in Philosophy*, 6:1, 6–8.

Hale, C. A. (1965). Jose Maria Luis Mora and the structure of Mexican liberalism *The Hispanic American Historical Review*, 45, 196–227.

Olivé, L. (2003). Philosophy in Latin America in the 20th century. In G. Fløistad (Ed.). *Contemporary philosophy*. Vol. 8: *Philosophy of Latin America* (pp. 229–242). Norwell, MA: Kluwer Academic Publishers.

Pappas, G. F. (2005). Frondizi, Risieri. In J. Shook (Ed.). *Dictionary of modern American philosophers*. Bristol, UK: Thoemmes Press.

Rivera-López, E. (2006). Rabossi on human needs and ethical naturalism. *APA Newsletter on Hispanic Issues in Philosophy*, 6:1, 3–6.

Romanell, P. (1975). Samuel Ramos on the philosophy of Mexican culture: Ortega and Unamuno in Mexico. *Latin American Research Review*, 10, 81–101.

Salmerón, F. (2003). Philosophy in Latin America in the 20th century. In G. Fløistad (Ed.). *Contemporary philosophy*. Vol. 8: *Philosophy of Latin America* (pp. 15–59). Norwell, MA: Kluwer Academic Publishers.

Zirión, A. Q. (2000). Phenomenology in Mexico: a historical profile. *Continental Philosophy Review*, 33, 75–92.

36

From Philosophy to Physics, and Back

MARIO BUNGE

1. Milieu

This is a report on my philosophical development and what I believe to be some of my contributions to philosophy. To understand both, it should help to know that I was born in Buenos Aires in 1919 during my country's golden age (1880–1930). At that time Argentina, which had fought for its independence from Spain starting in 1810, ranked fifth in gross domestic product (GDP) in the world, had a rather numerous middle class, a combative labor movement, a Radical (centrist) government, a growing Socialist Party, a vibrant civil society – and more indoor toilets than Canada. However, its economy was largely dominated by ranchers and British companies, and it lacked the welfare state that the Uruguayans enjoyed.

The Argentine intellectuals and professionals of that period read at least one foreign language, usually French, and tried to keep up with the latest European cultural fads. Nearly all of them were liberal, and many regarded themselves as positivists just because they admired science and, in particular, what was then called Darwinism but was actually Spencerianism – an evolutionary ontology only distantly related to evolutionary biology. The few philosophy books available sold quite well, not only in bookstores but also in newsstands.

The modernizing president Domingo F. Sarmiento, a freemason like most of his political friends, had been a teacher and science popularizer. He fought successfully for the secularization of public education, founded the first astronomical observatory in the southern hemisphere, as well as the Academy of Sciences; and weeks after Charles Darwin's death he organized a public homage to him at the grand Teatro Colón. Though still an agrarian country subjected to a strong British economic and political influence, as well as a strong French cultural impact, Argentina was generally regarded as the most advanced Latin American nation, and Buenos Aires as the Paris of the region.

My father, Augusto Bunge, was the black sheep of what was regarded as a patrician family. His father, Octavio, had a doctorate in law, was a judge, and became the Chief Justice of the country. My paternal grandfather was the only one of eight siblings to decline to buy a large tract of cheap fertile land in installments, for he held that "a judge must not owe money." As a consequence our branch of the family was the least affluent. He had eight children, six of whom distinguished themselves in different fields.

Augusto attended the Jesuit school, where he raked in all the prizes; but he claimed that the study of theology turned him into an atheist at age fourteen. He graduated in 1900 as a physician, with a doctoral thesis on tuberculosis (TB) as a social disease that earned him the gold medal. He was the first medical sociologist in Latin America, a member of the Socialist Party since his student days, and a congressman for twenty years. In 1936, the last year of his mandate, he presented a heavily documented bill on universal health insurance – which of course did not pass.

At home and in his wide circle of friends of nearly all political stripes, the main subjects of conversation were politics, literature, medicine, and the welfare state. I heard much about TB and its exploitation by private sanatoria, universal health insurance, the Versailles treaty, Goethe (whose *Faust* my father had translated), the leftist and pacifist American, French, and German novelists, the latest villainies of the incumbent government, the rise of Nazism, and the first Soviet five-year plan. Only science and philosophy were never touched on, although my father was an enthusiastic Darwinist, and taught me the ABC of evolutionary biology when I was about five. He was also awed by some of the recent cosmological discoveries and speculations, and kept a copy of Marcus Aurelius's *Thoughts* on his night table.

At that time only a few astronomers and biologists were doing scientific research in Latin America. The most famous Argentine scientists were the brothers Florentino and Carlos Ameghino, who had discovered and described thousands of fossils, and Eduardo Holmberg, a neontologist of the classical school (descriptive and systematic). José Ingenieros, the psychiatrist, polymath, popular essayist, and classmate, friend and political comrade of my father's, had published in French a big tome on physiological psychology; but it was not an original work, and left no mark on the country. My father's library, reasonably well stocked in classical literature and Socialist doctrine, contained a single scientific work – an eighteenth-century chemistry treatise. But there was a shelf of philosophical books.

2.   Philosophy or Physics?

The few philosophical books in my father's library drew my attention when I woke up intellectually, at sixteen. I was particularly intrigued by dialectics, which sounded profound and all-encompassing. When I asked my father what he thought about it, he replied: "According to Master Justo, it's just hocus-pocus." (Juan B. Justo, a neurosurgeon, had translated Marx's *Das Kapital*, founded the Argentine Socialist Party and its daily, *La Vanguardia*, and published in 1907 an interesting book on the theory and practice of history.)

Undeterred, I decided to find out by myself, and started reading Hegel and his materialist followers. For instance, I read some of Hegel (in French translation), some of Engels, Sydney Hook's *Hegel and Marx*, and Lenin's *Materialism and Empirio-Criticism*. Obviously, I had swallowed far more than I could digest. Thus, much of that stuff got stuck in my system until 1952, when my first exposure to mathematical logic made me throw it up. Before this epiphany I saw examples of dialectics in all the physics I read – but of course never bothered to look for any counterexamples, and never worried about the pre-Socratic vagueness of all that.

Another important source of philosophical information was the standard course on Logic and Scientific Method in my senior high-school year. Logic consisted in classical syllogistics, and scientific method in a discussion of some of problems and doctrines fashionable in France two decades earlier. The dominant philosophies at the Universidad de Buenos Aires were Bergson's intuitionism and the neo-Hegelianism of Croce and Gentile; in La Plata, Dilthey was influential through the teachings of Francisco Romero and his brother José Luis, the social historian and philosopher of history. Anglo-Saxon philosophy was known only at the new and distant university of Tucumán, mainly through the brothers Risieri and Silvio Frondizi.

My third philosophical source was the numerous secondhand bookstores. They were better stocked in philosophy than even the present-day Manhattan ones, for they were the resting places of the private libraries of many European *émigré* intellectuals. Unfortunately for us, none came from English-speaking countries, so that British and American books had to be ordered at great cost. Only Bertrand Russell's *Problems of Philosophy* circulated widely, and was a decisive influence on me. The university libraries subscribed to scientific journals but not to philosophical ones, because the philosophy professors did not read them.

Around 1930 psychoanalysis arrived in Buenos Aires, eclipsed the little scientific psychology there had been, and is still ruling there after having died everywhere else, even in New York. At that time Freud's books were available for a few cents at newsstands. I read some of them as well as two of Wilhelm Reich's, and made friends with a brilliant but crazy analyst who invited me to attend one of his sessions with patients of his. I was fascinated at first, but reading Russell's account of Pavlov's work cured me for good: I realized that psychoanalysis is a pseudoscience. In the summer of 1938, shortly before entering university, I wrote a book-length criticism of Reuben Osborn's *Freud and Marx*. I held that psychoanalysis was neither scientific nor compatible with Marxism. Fortunately this typescript, together with two novels, a drama in verse on Spartacus, and other adolescent rubbish, got lost.

Shortly before, physics had emerged on my intellectual horizon thanks to the popular books by two distinguished astrophysicists: Sir Arthur Eddington and Sir James Jeans. Both were very clear and eloquent defenders of idealism. Both scientists made cosmology fashionable, and persuaded many philosophers that modern physics had refuted realism and materialism. I wished to refute this view. But of course this necessitated acquiring some advanced knowledge of the very physical theories at stake, namely quantum mechanics, the two relativities, and theoretical astrophysics. This is why I decided to study physics at a university, and to continue reading philosophy on my own.

3. Apprenticeship

In 1938 I started my physics studies at the Universidad Nacional de La Plata. This was the only Latin American university with a physics research laboratory, where some work in spectroscopy had been done before my time. The two courses on general physics had been organized by two German physicists, Emil Bose and Richard Gans, in imitation of the famous "Pohl circus" in Göttingen, which had been attended by our professor,

Ramón G. Loyarte, a graduate of that university. His lectures in general physics were brilliant, clear, and packed with spectacular experimental demonstrations carried out by his German lab assistants. By contrast, Loyarte's lectures in theoretical physics were dull and somewhat outdated. He was utterly unaware of the philosophical load of the new physics – which was just as well since, except for Einstein's and Planck's writings, most of the literature on this subject at that time was rather confused.

Better courses in theoretical physics were offered at the Universidad de Buenos Aires. They were taught by Dr. Teófilo Isnardi, a graduate of the University of Berlin, who as early as 1927 had published an excellent philosophical criticism of the subjectivist or Copenhagen interpretation of quantum mechanics, in the *Revista de Filosofía*, founded by José Ingenieros and continued by his disciple, Aníbal Ponce. I "discovered" this article only a few years ago, and arranged for its reproduction in *Enseñanza de la Física*, the Latin American counterpart of the *American Journal of Physics*. I wish I had encountered Isnardi's paper when I worked as his first TA in theoretical physics. Or perhaps not, because I might have found out too soon that publishing philosophy in my country is like sowing in the sea.

I got the most intense intellectual stimulation at the weekly seminars that the physics students held at the two universities, with the occasional participation of a professor. There we reported on recent papers we had read in some of the main physics journals (not read by our professors), or on our own first crude scientific endeavors, such as a particle accelerator built in a garage, and my own stillborn theory of the electron. Nothing of the sort went on at the philosophy schools, where only books were read, idealism ruled, and debate was unknown. However, my information about the philosophy schools is secondhand: I got it from the two philosophy students that attended my seminar on the causality problem at the workers' school that I had founded in 1939.

That same year of 1939 I had the cheek to give two public lectures on "introduction to the great thinkers." The lectures, well attended and duly reported on in a fascist magazine by a police officer in plain clothes, were given at the seat of AIAPE, the association of anti-fascist intellectuals and artists founded at the beginning of the Spanish Civil War.

Those lectures were published immediately in two issues of *Conferencias*, a monthly that contained only the texts of lectures given at cultural NGOs. A similar publication was *Cursos y Conferencias*, of the Colegio Libre de Estudios Superiores, a sort of unofficial Collège de France that offered crash courses on subjects glossed over by the public universities. There, for a few pesos, one could learn something about genetics, Pavlov's psychology, Marxist philosophy, history of science, and other esoterica. That is where I first encountered the mind–body problem, in a course taught by Dr. Emilio Troise, a distinguished clinician.

That is also where I first met Francisco Romero, who had organized the Alejandro Korn Chair at that College. At the end of one of his lectures I approached him, and he asked me what I thought about the Heisenberg inequalities. I gave him a silly answer: "They constitute a pseudoproblem." He immediately replied: "Ah, that's what the neopositivists claim!" The truth is that at that time I had no opinion of my own: I had uncritically swallowed the Bohr–Heisenberg interpretation, which had been endorsed by the logical positivists. I have written elsewhere on Romero and my disagreements with his philosophy (Bunge, 2001). Here I only wish to emphasize that, although he was a retired army captain, Romero was a cultured, liberal, and generous man. He was not an original philosopher, but a popularizer of late German idealism. But Romero was the greatest philosophy promoter any nation can wish for. He encouraged all the Latin Americans seriously interested in our field, facilitated contacts, edited an uneven philosophical library published by the courageous Spanish Republican publisher Losada, and he also recommended books – not only in philosophy but also in litera-ture. (Someone stated maliciously that he had built his fame by corresponding with "toda esa negrada del continente" [all that pile of niggers around the continent].)

At the Colegio Libre, I also heard Rodolfo Mondolfo, the eminent historian of ancient Greek philosophy and an unorthodox Marxist in his youth. He had just been forced to leave Italy under the new race laws, and was appointed a professor of ancient Greek – not of philosophy! – at the Universidad Nacional de Córdoba, the oldest and most conservative in the country.

I did not take philosophy courses, but read voraciously in philosophy and its history, in several languages, on trains and in between physics classes. In 1942 José Babini, a mathematician and historian of science, invited me to visit the Institute of History of Science, in the provincial capital Santa Fe. This institute consisted of Aldo Mieli, his assistant, and Mieli's huge library. Mieli was a distinguished Italian specialist in this field, and another victim of the Italian race laws. The idea was to train me as a histor-ian of science, so that I would eventually teach the subject. I visited the Institute several times, gave a lecture at the university, and wrote two historico-philosophical booklets, one on Newton and the other on Maxwell, that were favorably reviewed in *Nature*. I also drew a list of problems that interested me, but Mieli complained rightly that they were all problems in the philosophy, not the history, of science. The military dictator-ship installed in June, 1943, solved the problem: it appointed a new rector, the fascist existentialist Jordán B. Genta, who sacked Mieli, Babini, and other anti-fascist academics. The other prominent fascist existentialist, Carlos Astrada, was made a professor at the Buenos Aires University. Astrada, who had studied in Freiburg under Heidegger, was the more open-minded and the less politicized of the two. He conducted a seminar on philosophical anthropology, which I attended a couple of times a decade later.

4. Starting Research and *Minerva*

Guido Beck, an Austrian physicist who had been Heisenberg's assistant at Leipzig, arrived in Buenos Aires in May, 1943, after having been a prisoner of the Vichy and Salazar regimes. I was his first, albeit not his best, Argentine student. We met a few days after he disembarked, and without further ado he gave me a problem on nuclear forces, which eventually resulted in two papers published in 1944, a long one in Spanish, and a short one in *Physical Review*.

Beck expected me to work full time in physics, as was the custom in Europe and in the United States. But the expression 'full time' was unknown in Latin America at that time: all intellectuals did many things at the same time, and this for several reasons. The first was that, with very few exceptions, they were all half-baked amateurs. The second was that there were more tasks than jobs: nearly everything remained to be done in an underdeveloped nation. The third reason was that, because there were so few specialists, there was no serious competition, so that it was not hard to stand out in any field. The fourth reason for seeking multiple jobs was that university salaries were insufficient to support a family. And the fifth reason was political instability, which made it advisable to hold several jobs in case some of them disappeared. (For example, Francisco Romero kept his Chair at the teachers' college after having been deprived of his university Chair.)

When Beck took me under his wing I resigned my honorary but time-consuming job at the workers' school, but kept reading philosophy. Moreover, the collusion of existentialism with fascism gave me the idea of organizing a review that would present a sort of united rationalist front against the onslaught of irrationalism. I hoped that such a coalition would include Thomists and open-minded phenomenologists and dialectical materialists. I sounded out Frondizi, Romero, Mondolfo, the mathematician Julio Rey Pastor, León Dujovne (the Spinoza expert), and a few others. Everyone agreed to collaborate except Dujovne, who apparently had adopted his beloved Spinoza's motto – *Caute*.

Minerva was born in 1944, with a combative editorial where I held that the war against fascism involved the philosophical fight against irrationalism, in particular the *astradas* and *gentas* (in lower case) in our milieu. Two thousand copies of the first issue were printed, and 1,000 of the subsequent issues. They were distributed throughout the continent, but I never received a cent from the bookstores and newsstands that sold it. *Minerva* was the only unofficial philosophical review in Latin America. It contained interesting articles by Frondizi, Mondolfo, Rey Pastor, Romero, and others, as well as short notes and many book reviews. But it lasted only six issues, and I have no evidence that it had any impact.

As I said before, in Latin America only scientists were in the habit of reading journals: philosophers read only books, and most of them suffered under a teaching overload anyway. Besides, most philosophers were caged in schools, and as such uninterested in what went on in other cages. People were not used to meeting in public, reading papers, and discussing them; so much so that the first philosophical association was organized only a year after Perón's fall. This was the Sociedad Argentina de Filosofía. At its first meeting (to which I was not invited) Francisco Romero spoke on science. When the moderator asked for comments, a high school teacher stood up and stated angrily that the speaker's view of science was outdated, even with regard to geography. Romero turned increasingly red in the face, and did not reply. After a long embarrassing silence, the moderator stated that the newborn Society was a society of friends, and as such shunned discussion.

Last, but not least, under authoritarian regimes university professors, particularly in the humanities, were expected to toe the party line. In Argentina this meant teaching either irrationalist pseudophilosophy or dogmatic Thomism.

In *Minerva* I published "¿Qué es la epistemología?" which was often quoted as being possibly the first general discussion in Spanish of philosophy of science. Some of the theses in that paper were: (a) philosophy is identical to the theory of science; (b) philosophy is unique among all the disciplines in that its own study is philosophical; and (c) these ideas can be elucidated with the help of certain algebraic notions. I still subscribe to (b) and (c) but reject (a) most emphatically. My second article in *Minerva* was a criticism of the philosophy of nature holding that, whereas the pre-Socratic and Renaissance philosophies of nature paved the way for ancient and modern philosophy, the romantic *Naturphilosophie* of Goethe, Schelling, and Hegel was a reaction against science. Its utter failure exemplifies the impotence of apriorism to grasp reality. I took Bergson's vitalism and Husserl's "positivism of intemporal essences" to task for claiming to have direct access to reality and thus circumventing and even opposing science. Today I stand by this thesis and add that the many-worlds metaphysics stemming from Saul Kripke's work has the same fatal flaw, apriorism, and is equally barren.

The fourth issue of *Minerva* was devoted to Nietzsche. It contained two high-level papers: one by Mondolfo on Nietzsche's vitalism, and another by Rey Pastor on fictionism, the philosophy proposed by Nietzsche's follower Hans Vaihinger. My own paper, on Nietzsche and science, analyzed his vitalist and pragmatist opinions on the search for knowledge, and criticized his praise of error and the "noble lie."

Between 1945 and 1952, I concentrated my efforts in physics, although I went on reading philosophy. I also organized a private seminar with half a dozen other amateur philosophers; we met monthly to discuss our essays as well as our readings, and we subscribed to several foreign philosophical journals, which we circulated among ourselves.

During that period I worked hard on my dissertation, which I finished at the end of 1952, and published four papers in physics and three in philosophy. One of these papers was "La fenomenología y la ciencia" (1951), where I attempted to confute Husserl's assertion, that phenomenology is a rigorous science – yet at the same time the exact opposite of science as commonly understood. The second was "Mach y la teoría atómica," a criticism of the great physicist's opposition to atomism. The third paper was my first publication in English: "What is chance?" (1951).

The two main theses of this paper were that chance is objective, and that randomness on one level may result in causation on the adjacent level or conversely, as in the case of Brownian motion. The first thesis was of course the realist or objectivist interpretation of probability that Popper popularized a few years later under the misleading name "propensity theory." (It is not a theory but a semantic assumption, and it does not apply to classical propensities such as a glass's propensity to shatter when dropped.) This second thesis attracted the attention of David Bohm, who in 1953 offered me a postdoctoral fellowship at the Institute of Theoretical Physics in São Paulo, Brazil. (At that time Bohm was doubly excommunicated: from the United States by McCarthyism, and from the Copenhagen church for having proposed what he wrongly called a causal interpretation of quantum mechanics.) Subsequently Bohm expanded considerably my conjecture in a book that he completed while staying at my house; he even included in it almost verbatim a text of mine on self-determination, as exemplified by inertia.

5. From Physics to Philosophy

Bohm's invitation came at the right time, for I was then down and out. Indeed, I had just been sacked from my university job – which I loved although it paid just enough to subscribe to two physics journals – and was thinking of emigrating. During the six

531

months I spent in São Paulo interacting with Bohm and other members of the Institute, I conceived the plans of two books. Back in Buenos Aires I kept thinking about the foundations of quantum mechanics and started work on the two planned books. At that time I wrote "Strife about complementarity," my first paper in the *British Journal for the Philosophy of Science* (1955). It was a rejoinder to the paper with the same title by Leo Rosenfeld. This was Bohr's coworker and spokesperson, one of the heavyweights mobilized by Bohm's revolt. In that paper, I criticized the standard interpretation of quantum theory, which I traced back to Berkeley's and Duhem's phenomenalism. (Popper and Ernest H. Hutten told me years later that they had been the referees who had recommended the publication of my paper.)

Ten years later, I met Rosenfeld at a relativity congress in London, and told him that I had recently realized that criticism was insufficient: that what was required was a realist alternative to the Copenhagen interpretation, and that I was currently working on this project. He misunderstood me as having recanted: he found it hard to believe that anyone could detach the mathematical formalism of quantum mechanics from its interpretation.

The year before, I had attempted to refute Berkeley's subjectivism in my "New dialogues between Hylas and Philonous." My main argument was not the usual one – the astonishing successes of science in accounting for reality – but, to the contrary, the frequent discrepancies between theory and reality. Such errors would not even be detected if the external world did not exist independently. This argument might also be used against the social constructivists who derailed the sociology of science some three decades ago.

Another paper of mine published at that time was "The philosophy of the space-time approach to the quantum theory," a criticism of the literal interpretation of Feynman's diagrams, which I regarded as mere mnemonic props rather than pictures of reality, if only because they conceive of positrons as electrons moving into the past. I also criticized Feynman's pragmatist conflation of laws with rules, and his claim that physics was basically completed the moment that all physical processes were shown, as he claimed, to be scattering processes. I understand that this paper provoked Feynman's notorious hostility to philosophy.

In 1954, I wrote "A critique of the frequentist theory of probability," which appeared two years later. In it I criticized Richard von Mises' frequency definition and interpretation of probability, which was used by most physicists as well as by Reichenbach, the young Popper, Church, and Suppes, none of whom knew of Jean Ville's (1939) devastating critique. Curiously, most philosophers and statisticians still believe that the frequency interpretation is the only alternative to the subjectivist view of probability as credence or strength of belief. Few of them have heard about the realist or objectivist interpretation suggested by Poincaré, Einstein, Smoluchovski, Fréchet, and others.

Frequentists regard probability as relative frequency, and as a property of collections of empirical data: they do not seem to know that physicists and biologists compute probabilities of single facts (states or events), and check them against empirical frequencies. And the subjectivists (or Bayesians) ignore the fact that scientists distinguish the objective facts they study from their more or less justified beliefs about them. For example, atomic physicists calculate and measure the probability that an individual atom in an excited state will decay to a lower-energy state within the next minute. There is no question of a von Mises "collective" here, nor of the theorist's (or experimentalist's) credence about such an event: The most accurate of all scientific theories treats chance as objective.

Characteristically, probability philosophers do not analyze such calculations. In particular, Carnap did not engage in such an exercise in any of the 500 pages of his book on the subject. Nor did Popper in his many papers on probability and indeterminism. Worse, after having defended von Mises's frequency theory, he adopted unwittingly the operationist belief that probabilities are properties of experimental set-ups. Like most physicists, he ignored the fact that the vast majority of quantum-theoretical calculations refer to free entities, that is, things that are not subjected to experimental perturbations. These considerations are central to the realist interpretation of quantum mechanics that I proposed a decade later.

Another paper dating from the same period was "Do computers think?" which challenged Alan Turing's affirmative answer. My main thesis was that computers are not creative, since they only do what their programmers order them. (In particular, not computers by themselves but computer-assisted programmers solve mathematical problems and play chess.) An additional thesis was that computers cannot conceive of either actual infinity or continuity, two central concepts of modern mathematics. Two decades later, I used these ideas to criticize the computer model of the mind, particularly as developed by Hilary Putnam. This and other papers dating from that time were collected in my *Metascientific Queries* (1959). Two selections of papers that appeared in the following decade were published in 1973 under the titles *Method, Model, and Matter* and *Philosophy of Physics*. The latter appeared also in French, Italian, Portuguese, Russian, and Spanish translations.

One of the theses of the latter book was that, contrary to what most textbooks teach, thermodynamics had not been reduced to classical mechanics, because the concept of chance is alien to the latter: in fact, the randomness condition (Boltzmann's *Ansatz*) has to be postulated separately. I also showed that, as a matter of fact, there were only a couple of full successful reductions: those of statics to dynamics, and of optics to electromagnetic theory. All the other alleged reductions were only partial. So, the reductionist project had failed even in physics: levels of analysis match real levels.

6. Causality and Levels

The one-year research fellowship gave me the leisure I needed to think not only of quantum mechanics but also of the two ambitious projects I had planned in São Paulo: determination and levels. I started the former with a long chapter on self-determination that did not satisfy me because it was mainly historical and based on secondary literature. I turned then to the causal problem, which most scholars thought had been killed by the quantum theory, as a consequence of which there were very few recent publications on it.

I started *Causality* by redefining causation in a non-Humean fashion. I claimed that modern science retained the Aristotelian notion of efficient cause along with those of final cause, chance, and self-determination. In particular, I saw in quantum mechanics the concept of the probability that a cause will produce a given effect – for example, the probability that an incident particle will be scattered by a target within a given solid angle. I also claimed that there are hardly any purely causal laws: rather, most laws have a causal range but are non-causal outside that interval. The net result was that determinism had been expanded rather than eliminated: we now had a set of determination categories and laws that intersected partially. Events and processes are subject to only two constraints: lawfulness and Lucretius's principle, *ex nihilo nihil*. I called this view *neodeterminism*. It is an ontological doctrine that includes classical determinism à la Laplace as a particular case.

My first opportunity to discuss these views came in an unexpected and roundabout fashion. In mid-1955, the Laboratory of Cosmic Physics in Bolivia invited me to attend a course on modern physics backed by UNESCO. The instructors were well-known specialists in cosmic rays, then a hot topic. But because one of the speakers failed to come. I was promoted from student to professor, and gave one of my lectures at a theater in La Paz. Back home, the Chilean participants invited me to give a course of lectures in physics and philosophy at their school, the prestigious Instituto Pedagógico. There I gave a couple of seminars in physics, and a crash course on causality, where I tried out the first draft of my book on the subject. The most active participant was Félix Schwartzmann, a learned professor with a keen interest in the philosophy of science. Another interesting Chilean experience was my public debate with the leading Marxist philosopher in Chile, a respected blind scholar. I also came in contact with some of the best Chilean anthropologists, which in turn motivated me, three years later, to propose and obtain the creation of the department of anthropology at the Universidad de Buenos Aires. So, yes, human life is largely a sequence of coincidences.

Back in Buenos Aires I completed the *Causality* manuscript and submitted it sequentially to six British and American publishers. All of them rejected it promptly without giving any reasons: obviously, the subject was dead, and the author a Third World physics professor. (I am not complaining: Their guillotine was quick, whereas nowadays it takes most publishers at least three months to send rejection slips.) Then, in mid-1956, I met Quine in Chile at the Latin American Congress of Philosophy, showed him my typescript, and asked for his advice. He suggested that I submit it to Harvard University Press, which I did. I signed the contract in mid-1957, but the book appeared only two years later. It was generally well received, reviewed at length in *Scientific American*, and reprinted thrice, the last time by Dover in 1979. The book was translated into seven foreign languages. However, my definition of causation was rightly criticized as being somewhat vague. I have since redefined it using the exact concepts of the state space approach.

The second project I imagined, a book on levels of organization, was written but, fortunately, never published. I say "fortunately" because in 1958 I discovered that I had conflated at least half a dozen different concepts designated by the same word, 'level.' I unfused these concepts in an article in the *Review of Metaphysics* (1960).

The concept I used in later work is this: A level is a set of concrete things that share some laws. One may distinguish the following levels: physical, chemical, biological, social, and artifactual (or technical). Every level may be subdivided into sublevels. For example, atoms and molecules constitute physical sublevels; and texts, musical scores, and engineering diagrams are included in the semiotic sublevel of the artifactual level. The set of levels is ordered by a relation of precedence defined by the part–whole relation:

L_n precedes L_{n+1} if every member of L_{n+1} is composed of one or more members of L_n. For example, the social level is constituted by social systems, such as families, whose parts are individual humans.

This concept occurs in discussions of the concept of emergence, known to scientists and familiar to philosophers under the name of supervenience. For instance, one says that molecules emerge from atomic collisions, and that cells emerged from the fusion of prebiotic precursors. The concept carries over from things to their properties and changes thereof (events and processes). For example, one says that temperature is a property of systems of atoms or molecules, not of the latter; likewise, that perception and decision are processes occurring in systems composed of zillions of neurons.

The ontological concept of a level occurs in some discussions of the epistemological concept of reduction – for example, in considering whether chemistry is reducible to physics, biology to chemistry, and sociology to biology. One may hold at once that the levels in question are quite distinct, and that the higher is unintelligible in depth if ignoring that its members emerged from lower-level entities. Thus, although sociology is irreducible to biology (contrary to the sociobiological thesis), it is impossible to understand social processes if one forgets that the protagonists of social facts are things with biological features such as metabolism and sex.

Emergence and levels have been recurrent themes in my work, most recently in my *Emergence and Convergence* (2003). In this book I also propose the thesis that increasing specialization, or branching-off, is accompanied by the parallel fusion or convergence of disciplines, as exemplified by biochemistry, neurolinguistics, cognitive neuroscience, and socioeconomics. The only necessary condition for performing such syntheses of two or more research fields is the existence of (bridge) laws containing key concepts of the precursor disciplines.

7. Teaching

During the Peronist governments the universities had been packed with party faithful, most of them incompetent, dishonest, or both. As a consequence hundreds of academics emigrated, and others took up jobs in the private sector. Shortly after Perón's fall in 1955, the universities were put into a sort of receivership: all university chairs were declared vacant, and public competitions were announced for all of them. The juries were usually composed of academics belonging to different universities, in some cases foreign ones. The net result of this process was that thousands of professors who had been appointed because of their political loyalty rather than for their competence were flushed out and replaced by people with reasonable curricula vitae who had been forced out of academia. As a consequence, in the space of a couple of years the universities started to flourish – until they sank again following the 1966 military coup.

The two private seminars I had been attending ceased to exist overnight. But our philosophy seminar was replaced with a much more numerous civil association that held well-attended meetings: the Agrupación Ríoplatense de Lógica y Filosofía Científica. The governing board of this association was composed of the logicians Gregorio Klimovsky and Jorge Bosch, the meteorologist and university administrator Rolando García, the eminent sociologist Gino Germani, and myself. And our modest private physics

535

seminar was advantageously replaced with the regular seminar at the renewed Department of Physics, which in the space of five years grew from no to nearly fifty persons who published in international journals.

One of the university chairs to be renewed was that of philosophy of science at the Universidad de Buenos Aires. Under the previous regime it had been held by a *protégé* of the military who taught a seminar on demonology. Ten individuals, among them myself, applied for the job. I learned only recently that my jury was composed of three academics I had contacted many years earlier, two of whom had published in *Minerva*: the philosophers Rodolfo Mondolfo and José Juan Bruera, and the mathematician Beppo Levi. Mondolfo and Levi had earned an international reputation before emigrating from Italy, and none of them belonged to the philosophical establishment. (Levi, though primarily an analyst, had been the first to state the famous axiom of choice and to discover that it had been tacitly used in many proofs. He used to attend our physics meetings and to berate us for our sloppy mathematics. I had consulted with him on certain integrals.) I won the competition.

Shortly thereafter, on April 1957, I started teaching my first philosophy course. I introduced a didactic innovation: Instead of holding formal lectures, I assigned a number of problems that we discussed in class. The students were expected to write a short essay on every problem, and they were graded on these essays in lieu of the final oral examination, which became a formality.

I believe I was the first philosophy professor in Argentina to bring journals to the classroom, and to organize the translation and distribution of journal articles, which I collected in the *Cuadernos de Epistemología*, of which more than fifty issues were published, but which were never used by my successors. I was also the first to discuss Popper in class, and to write a long review of his *Logic of Scientific Discovery* for *Ciencia e Investigación* in 1959, the organ of the Argentine counterpart of the AAAS. I praised the book but said that refutationism is no alternative to confirmationism, since falsifying *A* amounts to confirming not-*A*. Moreover, I held that it is simply not true that scientists are eager to have their pet conjectures refuted. And, although I had become a friend of Popper's in 1955, I did not join the Popper gang; moreover, I criticized the Vienna Circle while recognizing its merits – the cult of exactness and the (failed) attempt to keep close to science. My friendship with Popper ended abruptly in 1978, when I criticized in print his trialism and, in particular, his endorsement of psychoneural dualism.

Later in 1957 I also won the theoretical physics chair at the Universidad Nacional de La Plata, which I had held de facto since the year before. The chairman of the jury was Enrique Gaviola, the first Argentine astrophysicist, a strict adherent of operationism, with whom I had had many philosophical discussions, and the first Argentine to publish in *Philosophy of Science*. That same year I taught quantum mechanics at two different universities, and philosophy at one of them, for a total of US$170/month. Finally I was able to support my family teaching subjects I loved instead of tutoring, translating, writing encyclopedia articles, or engaging in uncertain business ventures.

I spent the 1960–1 academic year as a visiting professor of Philosophy at the University of Pennsylvania. That was the first time I could use a well-stocked library. I also gave talks at various universities and meetings. One of them was at a special session on simplicity of the American Association for the Advancement of Science. I attacked simplism, which I regarded as a myth, and noted that Nelson Goodman was among the instrumentalists who regarded simplicity as the seal of truth. Goodman, who at the time chaired the department I was visiting, and who was on the stage sitting next to me, vehemently denied the charge. Luckily, I had brought along a reprint of the paper in *Science* where he had made that assertion not so long ago, and I read out the relevant passage. Our relations since then have been rather frosty. *Simplex non est sygillum veri, sed veritas fuit casus belli!*

Back in Buenos Aires, full of enthusiasm, I wrote *Intuition and Science* (1962) and *The Myth of Simplicity* (1963). Gino Germani, the well-known sociologist and a colleague, asked me several times to fill in for him in one of his courses. Eduardo de Robertis, the famous histologist, asked me every year to address his advanced students. The eminent evolutionary biologist, my colleague Osvaldo A. Reig, whom I befriended, invited me to conduct a seminar on the philosophy of biology. Shortly thereafter both of us went to Montevideo and joined with the Uruguayan philosopher Mario H. Otero to organize the Grupo Uruguayo de Lógica y Epistemología. On the morning of our arrival we held a meeting on the concept of truth in mathematics at the Instituto de Matemática, and in the evening we met with the members of the departments of botany and zoology, and urged them to fuse them into a single department of biology – which they did.

I was happy working at a university that advanced rapidly, and where I felt useful. But at the end of 1962 there was a bloody confrontation between two army factions. Moreover, President Frondizi, my erstwhile friend, was deposed – reportedly because he had refused to condemn the Castro regime – and replaced with a yes-man. These events led me to take the decision to leave my country for good. Three years later the military took up arms and beat up professors and students. Around 1,000 former colleagues were dismissed or resigned, and those who could emigrated.

I accepted the first invitation that came: to teach the first semester of 1963 at the University of Texas. After that I taught physics and philosophy, first at Temple University (Philadelphia), and then at the University of Delaware. These jobs gave me the opportunity to improve my knowledge of logic, quantum mechanics, and the two relativities. While teaching relativistic thermodynamics, I discovered that the accepted formula for the Lorentz transformation of temperature was wrong, and got my student Bill Sutcliffe to write a paper on this problem, which was duly published.

I was invited to stay on at Delaware and later on to go to Yale. But I objected to the American intervention in Vietnam and the invasion of the Dominican Republic. (The antiwar movement started only one year later, when students began to be drafted.) So, I sought and obtained an Alexander von Humboldt fellowship, which I spent at the Institute for Theoretical Physics at the University of Freiburg (1965–6). This gave me the leisure I needed to write *Foundations of Physics*. In 1966 I immigrated to Canada for good.

Teaching philosophy of science led me to writing my *Scientific Research*, a task that took me nearly a decade to complete. I had to write it because none of the existing textbooks on the subject satisfied me. I found them remote from living science, and they missed subjects, such as the nature of problems, the logical analysis of theories, the interpretation of mathematical symbols, the nature and role of indicators, and the analysis of measurement, that I regarded as essential.

537

Worse, I was shocked by the confusions that plagued the methodology of science. One of them was the confusion between measurement and measure. A well-known philosopher of science, and subsequently some of his disciples, had held that the problem of measurement had been solved by Hölder's axioms for measure. He had mixed up the German words *Messung* (the empirical operation) and *Mass* (measure, such as length and area), hence a methodological problem with an application of point set theory. Since then I have written books for nearly all the courses I have taught, and lectured mostly from my own books. All of these have been monographs heavily indebted to the recent scientific literature on the subject. As a consequence all my lectures over the past four decades have been seminar sessions rather than lectures proper. That is, we discuss in every class a fragment of a book of mine or some scientific papers related to it.

In conclusion, I count myself very lucky to have been able to work in the two fields, philosophy and science, that I fell in love with when I woke up intellectually. I might not have done so if I had followed a normal academic career in either of them. As it is, I have been able to combine the advantage of professionalism (rigor) with that of dilettantism – freedom of choice of problems, reading material, academic partners, and even country.

Acknowledgment

I thank Professor Nuccetelli for having compressed the original text without loss of continuity.

Related chapters: 14 Analytic Philosophy; 15 Paraconsistent Logic; 26 Philosophy of Science; 29 Teaching Philosophy; 32 Metaphysics; 33 Epistemology; Formal Epistemology and Logic.

Books by Mario Bunge

(1959). *Causality: the place of the causal principle in modern science.* Cambridge, MA: Harvard University Press, 1959; Dover, 1979.

(1959). *Metascientific queries.* Springfield, IL: Charles C. Thomas.

(1962). *Intuition and science.* Englewood Cliffs, NJ: Prentice-Hall.

(1963). *The myth of simplicity.* Englewood Cliffs, NJ: Prentice-Hall.

(1967). *Scientific research I: the search for system.* Berlin, Heidelberg, and New York: Springer-Verlag, 1967 (Reprinted as *Philosophy of Science*, vol. 1. Transaction, 1988).

(1967). *Scientific research II: the search for truth.* Berlin, Heidelberg, and New York: Springer-Verlag, 1967 (Reprinted as *Philosophy of Science*, vol. 2. Transaction, 1988).

(1967). *Foundations of physics.* Berlin, Heidelberg, and New York: Springer-Verlag.

(1973). *Philosophy of physics.* Dordrecht: Reidel.

(1973). *Method, model and matter.* Dordrecht: Reidel.

(1974). *Treatise on basic philosophy.* Vol. 1: *Sense and reference.* Dordrecht: Reidel.

(1974). *Treatise on basic philosophy.* Vol. 2: *Interpretation and truth.* Dordrecht: Reidel.

(1974). *Treatise on basic philosophy.* Vol. 3: *The furniture of the world.* Dordrecht: Reidel.

(1979). *Treatise on basic philosophy.* Vol. 4: *A world of systems.* Dordrecht: Reidel.

(1980). *The mind-body problem*. Oxford and New York: Pergamon Press.

(1981). *Scientific materialism*. Dordrecht and Boston: Reidel.

(1983). *Treatise on basic philosophy*. Vol. 5: *Exploring the world*. Dordrecht and Boston: Reidel.

(1983). *Treatise on basic philosophy*. Vol. 6: *Understanding the world*. Dordrecht: Reidel.

(1985). *Treatise on basic philosophy*. Vol. 7: *Philosophy of science and technology, part I: formal and physical sciences*. Dordrecht and Boston: Reidel.

(1985). *Treatise on basic philosophy*. Vol. 7: *Philosophy of science and technology, part II: life science, social science, and technology*. Dordrecht and Boston: Reidel.

(1987). *Philosophy of psychology* (with Rubén Ardila). New York: Springer-Verlag.

(1989). *Treatise on basic philosophy*. Vol. 8: *The good and the right*. Dordrecht and Boston: Reidel.

(1996). *Finding philosophy in social science*. New Haven: Yale University Press.

(1997). *Foundations of biophilosophy* (with Martin Mahner). Berlin, Heidelberg, and New York: Springer-Verlag.

(1998). *Social science under debate*. Toronto: University of Toronto Press.

(1999). *The sociology–philosophy connection*. New Brunswick, NJ: Transaction.

(2001). *Philosophy in crisis: the need for reconstruction*. Amherst, NY: Prometheus.

(2003). *Philosophical dictionary*. Amherst NY: Prometheus.

(2003). *Emergence and convergence*. Toronto: University of Toronto Press.

(2004). *Ueber die Natur der Dinge* (with Martin Mahner). Stuttgart: S. Hirzel.

(2006). *Chasing reality: the strife over realism*. Toronto: University of Toronto Press.

(2008). *Political philosophy: fact, fiction, and vision*. New Brunswick, NJ: Transaction.

Index

This index lists only references to concepts, persons, and terms significantly discussed in this volume or relevant to cross-references in the chapters.

540

544